Leonard Lewisohn is Senior Lecturer in Persian an
Fellow in Classical Persian and Sufi Literature at the University of Exeter, UK. His previous books include *The Angels Knocking on the Tavern Door: Thirty Poems of Hafez* (2008, translated with Robert Bly), *Attar and the Persian Sufi Tradition: The Art of Spiritual Flight* (I.B.Tauris, 2006, edited with Christopher Shackle), *The Heritage of Sufism*, vols 1–3 (1999) and *Beyond Faith and Infidelity: The Sufi Poetry and Teachings of Mahmud Shabistari* (1995).

‘This volume is an utter delight to read. Edited with excellent intellectual rigour by Leonard Lewisohn, the essays written by a number of distinguished Iranian scholars and other specialists in Persian studies provide a literary, historical and philosophical overview and analysis of the *leitmotif* of Hafiz’s poetry, which is love.’

Bahā al-Dīn Khurramshāhī, author of *Ḥāfiẓ-nāma*, a two-volume Persian commentary on Hafiz’s poetry

‘Leonard Lewisohn brings together perhaps for the first time in *Hafiz and the Religion of Love in Classical Persian Poetry* a rich and diverse set of essays in a single volume written by renowned specialists on Hafiz. Few people have his lifelong devotion to Hafiz and profound knowledge of classical Persian poetry to be capable of producing such a work, which is indispensable to students and scholars of Hafiz and Persian literature.’

Mehdi Aminrazavi, Professor of Philosophy & Religion, University of Mary Washington, Virginia

‘With contributions by a number of prominent scholars, *Hafiz and the Religion of Love in Classical Persian Poetry* provides a highly focused, original, and engaging edited volume on one of the most cherished Persian poets and some of the most stimulating topics of classical Persian poetry.’

Kamran Talattof, Professor of Persian Language and Literature, University of Arizona

Hafiz and the Religion of Love in Classical Persian Poetry

edited by Leonard Lewisohn

Iran and the Persianate World

I.B. TAURIS
LONDON · NEW YORK

Published by I.B.Tauris & Co. Ltd in association with
Iran Heritage Foundation

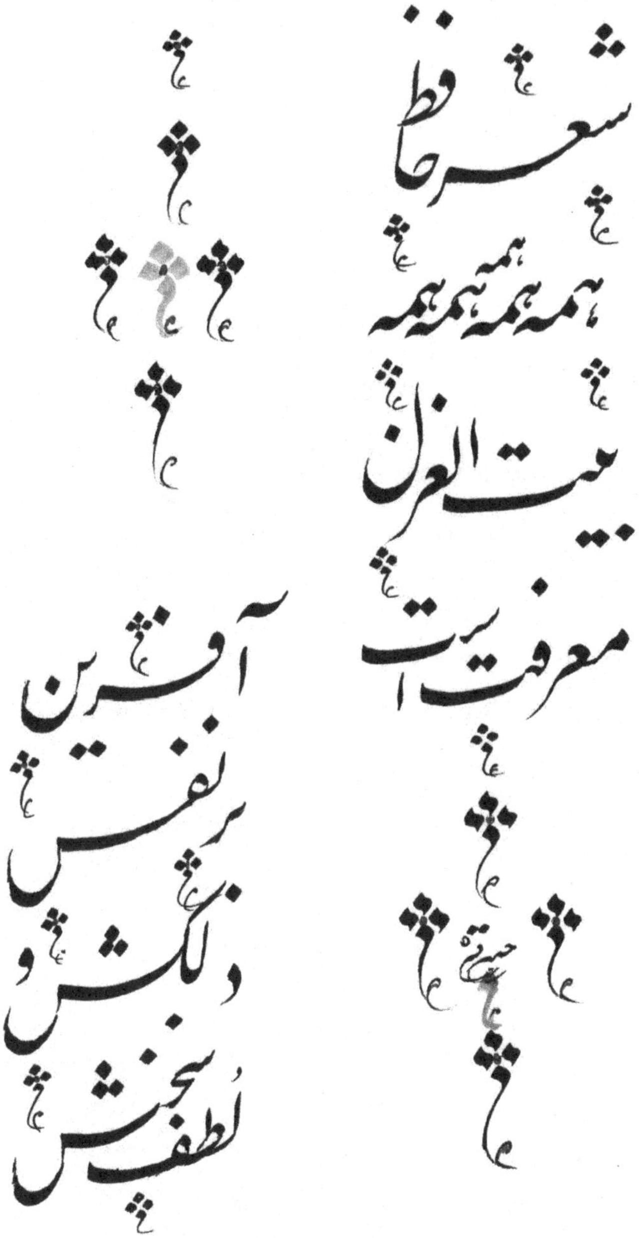
شعر حافظ همه بیت الغزل معرفت است
آفرین بر نفس دلکش و لطف سخنش

Each verse that Ḥāfiẓ pens is a masterpiece
of gnostic lore and sapience.
Let's praise his fetching turn of phrase
and his stunning power of speech.

Ḥāfiẓ, *Dīvān*, *ghazal* 275: 9

New paperback edition published in 2015 by
I.B.Tauris & Co. Ltd
London • New York
www.ibtauris.com

First published in hardback in 2010 by I.B.Tauris & Co. Ltd

Frontispiece calligraphy by Husayn Ilahi-Ghomshei

Iran and the Persianate World

ISBN: 978 1 78453 212 3
eISBN: 978 0 85773 660 4

A full CIP record for this book is available from the British Library
A full CIP record is available from the Library of Congress

Library of Congress Catalog Card Number: available

Designed and Typeset by 4word Ltd, Bristol, UK
Printed and bound by CPI Group (UK) Ltd, Croydon, CR0 4YY

The Assistance of the Iran Heritage Foundation is gratefully acknowledged.

MIX
Paper from
responsible sources
FSC® C013604
FSC
www.fsc.org

Contents

List of Contributors ix

List of Plates x

Foreword: Ḥāfiẓ of Shīrāz *PETER AVERY* xi

Editor's Introduction and Acknowledgements xxi

PART I
ḤĀFIẒ IN THE SOCIO-HISTORICAL, LITERARY AND MYSTICAL MILIEU OF MEDIEVAL PERSIA

Prolegomenon to the Study of Ḥāfiẓ 3
1 – Socio-historical and Literary Contexts: Ḥāfiẓ in Shīrāz
2 – The Mystical Milieu: Ḥāfiẓ's Erotic Spirituality
LEONARD LEWISOHN

PART II
ḤĀFIẒ AND THE SCHOOL OF LOVE IN CLASSICAL PERSIAN POETRY

The Principles of the Religion of Love in Classical Persian Poetry 77
HUSAYN ILAHI-GHOMSHEI

The Erotic Spirit: Love, Man and Satan in Ḥāfiẓ's Poetry 107
ALI ASGHAR SEYED-GOHRAB

The Radiance of Epiphany: The Vision of Beauty and Love in Ḥāfiẓ's Poem of Pre-Eternity *LEILI ANVAR* 123

PART III
ḤĀFIẒ AND THE PERSIAN SUFI TRADITION

Ḥāfiẓ and the Sufi *CHARLES-HENRI DE FOUCHÉCOUR* 143

The Religion of Love and the Puritans of Islam: Sufi Sources of Ḥāfiẓ's Anti-clericalism *LEONARD LEWISOHN* 159

Jalāl al-Dīn Davānī's Interpretation of Ḥāfiẓ *CARL W. ERNST* 197

Part IV
Ḥāfiẓ's Romantic Imagery and Language of Love

The Allegory of Drunkenness and the Theophany of the Beloved in Sixteenth-Century Illustrations of Ḥāfiẓ *Michael Barry* 213

Transfiguring Love: Perspective Shifts and the Contextualization of Experience in the *Ghazals* of Ḥāfiẓ *James Morris* 227

The Semiotic Horizons of Dawn in the Poetry of Ḥāfiẓ *Franklin Lewis* 251

Ḥāfiẓ and the Language of Love in Nineteenth-Century English and American Poetry *Parvin Loloi* 279

Bibliography 295

Index of Proper Names, Places, Works and Themes 319

Index of Persian and Arabic Technical Terms 327

Contributors

LEILI ANVAR is Lecturer at the Institut National des Langues et Civilisations Orientales in Paris and Head of the Department of Iranian Studies there.

PETER AVERY lived in Iran for many years before serving as Lecturer in Persian Studies at the University of Cambridge (1958–90). Author of many books and articles, his final work before his death in 2008 was an English translation of *The Collected Lyrics of Ḥāfiẓ of Shīrāz* (London: Archetype 2007).

MICHAEL BARRY is Lecturer in Persian and Islamic Studies at the Department of Near Eastern Studies, Princeton University. He was Consultative Chairman, Department of Islamic Art, at the Metropolitan Museum of Art in New York between 2005–9. He is the author of *Figurative Painting in Medieval Islam and the Riddle of Behzad of Herat (1465–1535)* (New York and Paris: Éditions Flammarion 2004).

CARL W. ERNST has been on the faculty of the Department of Religious Studies at the University of North Carolina at Chapel Hill since 1992, where he has served as department chair (1995–2000) and Zachary Smith Professor (2000–5). He is now William R. Kenan, Jr, Distinguished Professor and Director of the Carolina Center for the Study of the Middle East and Muslim Civilizations.

CHARLES-HENRI DE FOUCHÉCOUR held the Chair of Persian at the Institut National des Langues et Civilisations Orientales in Paris (1972–85), was Professor at the Universite de la Sorbonne Nouvelle (Paris III), as well as Director of the Institut d'Etudes Iraniennes in that University (1985–93). From 1993, he has been Professor Emeritus at the Universite de la Sorbonne Nouvelle. His annotated translation of the entire collected poetical works of Ḥāfiẓ: *Le Divān Œuvre lyrique d'un spirituel en Perse au XIVe siècle*, introduction, traduction du persan et commentaries, was published by Editions Verdier in Paris in 2006.

HUSAYN ILAHI-GHOMSHEI received his PhD in Islamic Theology and Philosophy in 1965 from Tehran University. A former Director of the National Library of Iran (1981–2), he is a lecturer and author on Islamic philosophy and Persian literature, who has (among his many other works) edited the collected poems of Ḥāfiẓ in Persian.

FRANKLIN LEWIS is Associate Professor of Persian in the Department of Near Eastern Languages and Civilizations at the University of Chicago.

LEONARD LEWISOHN is Senior Lecturer in Persian and Iran Heritage Foundation Fellow in Classical Persian and Sufi Literature at the University of Exeter, UK.

PARVIN LOLOI is a freelance scholar and writer who wrote her PhD thesis (University of Wales, Swansea) on English translations of Ḥāfiẓ and their influence on English poetry. She is author of *Hafiz, Master of Persian Poetry: A Critical Bibliography - English Translations since the Eighteenth Century* (London 2004).

JAMES MORRIS held (1999–2006) the Sharjah Chair of Islamic Studies at the University of Exeter, and has taught Islamic and comparative religious studies at Princeton, Temple University, the Sorbonne, and the Institute of Ismaili Studies in Paris and London. He is currently Professor of Islamic Studies at Boston College.

ALI ASGHAR SEYED-GOHRAB is Lecturer in Persian Language, Literature and Culture at Leiden University.

List of Plates

Heavenly and Earthly Drunkenness. By Sulṭān-Muḥammad, probably painted in Herāt, AD 1526 or 1527. Page from a *Dīvān* of *Ḥāfiẓ*. Harvard Art Museum, Arthur M. Sackler Museum, Promised Gift of Mr. and Mrs. Stuart Cary Welch, Jr. Partially owned by the Metropolitan Museum of Art and the Arthur M. Sackler Museum, Harvard University, 1988. In honour of the students of Harvard University and Radcliffe College, 1988.460.3. Photo: Allan Macintyre © President and Fellows of Harvard College.

Incident in a Mosque. By Shaykh-Zāda, probably painted in Herāt, AD 1526 or 1527. Painting (recto, text; verso, folio 77r) from a *Dīvān* of *Ḥāfiẓ*, left-hand side of a bifolio. Harvard Art Museum, Arthur M. Sackler Museum, Gift of Stuart Cary Welch, Jr., 1999.300.2. Photo: Allan Macintyre © President and Fellows of Harvard College.

Lady Belovéd within the Prayer-Niche, Holding A Sprig of Narcissi. By Muḥammadī of Herāt, ca. AD 1565. Detached album leaf. Soudavar collection, on loan to the Sackler Gallery of Art, Washington, D.C.

Majnūn First Sees Laylī in the Mosque-School within the Prayer-Niche. By Bihzād or his fellow-painter Qāsim ʻAlī. Herāt, AD 1494. Illustration to a *Khamsa* of Niẓāmī; British Library, Or. 68100, folio 106 verso.

Foreword: Ḥāfiẓ of Shīrāz

Peter Avery

Ḥāfiẓ of Shīrāz was born about 1315 and died in 1389 AD. Thinking of my experience of him, four incidents come to mind. The first is what happened one morning when, on the advice of my mentor, *Pīr*, I listened for several hours to a commentary on the poetry of Ḥāfiẓ delivered to me by a mullah. I was taken to a small mosque in Shīrāz with the injunction that, since I was a student of Ḥāfiẓ, it was necessary for me to listen to what a mullah had to say about him. Thus I spent the morning being told how every reference to wine, the rose, the nightingale and so forth could be, and should be, seen in a spiritual light: Ḥāfiẓ was reduced to a dealer in metaphors, all of which had a meaning justified by sanctity. I refrained, of course, from referring my interlocutor to the *Gulshan-i rāz* of Shabistarī, who died after 1340. In addition to its being a comprehensive key to Sufi imagery, it seems not to be doubted that it influenced Ḥāfiẓ; but this is not the place in which to go into the question of whether or not Ḥāfiẓ's, or for that matter Shabistarī's, thought was coloured by Ismailism. What should, however, be added in any discussion of the mystical significance of wine and intoxication is the fact that Abū Hāmid al-Ghazālī, one of the greatest Islamic and for that matter world thinkers, saw intoxication as the 'intoxication of love'. As Margaret Smith puts it: 'For His lovers, God pours out a draught from the cup of His love, and by that draught they are intoxicated, rapt away from themselves.'[1] Since Shīrāz has always been famous for its wines, in spite of these caveats it might be supposed that Ḥāfiẓ had, among other considerations, real wine in mind; there is evidence for this in one or two of his allusions to wine.

Of course, Ḥāfiẓ dealt in metaphor. The poet, especially, has to express the otherwise inexpressible. A possible criticism of the mullah's comments is that it might not be correct to attribute one particular set of meanings, based on one particular strand of belief or prejudice, to the metaphors the poet used. There is, however, no doubt that wine was a common metaphor for the spirit; to be remembered is Surah XII of the Koran, verse 36, where one of the prisoners in a dream saw himself pressing wine, and wine here stands for service to God, spiritual devotion. Take, for example, the fragment of Ḥāfiẓ, which may be translated as follows:

> Again the time has a head for discord:
> I and drunkenness and the incitement of the friend's eye!

I am continually astonished at the wheeling of fortune;
I don't know whom it'll take down next into the dust.

And if the Magian Elder were to spread a fire,
I don't know whose lamp would be kindled.

The deceit of the world is a well-known tale.
What will the dawn bring? The night is pregnant!

In this bloodletting on Doomsday's plain,
Pour you the blood of the beaker into the goblet.[2]

In the last couplet, 'blood' (*khūn*), might be said clearly to mean 'Spirit'. Garcin de Tassy, in his *Rhetorique et prosodie des langues de l'Orient musulman*,[3] lists nine examples of metaphor (*majāz*) in Persian poetry.

The second incident was a chance exchange with the elderly maidservant in an Iranian household, whom I met as she was leaving the room in which a group of us – including Dr Khānlarī – were talking about Ḥāfiẓ, with quotations from his *ghazal*s. As she came out I met her in the hall and while she was putting her feet back into her slippers, after delivering tea to the assembled company, I asked her what she thought of what was going on in the sitting room. She replied, 'I don't understand it but the words have been banging on my ears all my life and I love their sound.' Her life, incidentally, had been a very long one: she was old enough to remember the days in her native Khurāsān when the Turkamen raiders came down from the north and 'took away our sheep, and sometimes people, while we stayed in the refuge of the *burj* [the tower]'. Of course, these raids persisted well into the reign of Nāṣir al-Dīn Shāh, who died in 1896.

The third episode – and, for me, the most moving – was when I was travelling across country and my chauffeur and I chanced upon, as one often did on the highways of Iran, a large Mac-lorry parked with all its machinery taken out and strewn on the road around it, as the driver, with the wonderful mechanical *savoir-faire* of the Iranian, sorted out the fault prior to putting the pieces back and driving off. Next to this scene I spotted the driver's apprentice, sitting on the verge with a small book in his hand in which, as semiliterate people do, he was painstakingly reading with his finger, guiding his eyes along the lines of the text. I looked over his shoulder and saw that the book was the *Dīvān-i Ḥāfiẓ*. I asked him what he was doing. He said he was trying to learn how to read. I saw him several times subsequently and helped him in his studies, which he had begun with the poems of Iran's greatest and one of the world's greatest poets.

On a fourth occasion, I asked a slightly, if at all, literate youth whence he came. When he replied, 'Shīrāz', I immediately recited the famous verse 'If that Shīrāzī Turk were to get hold of my heart…', whereupon he proceeded to recite the rest of the poem. Literate or not, he knew his Ḥāfiẓ. Imagine giving a London cab driver the first line of a Shakespeare sonnet. It is unlikely that he would reply with the rest of the poem. The last three of these episodes speak of the universal feeling for and acquaintance with the works of Ḥāfiẓ throughout Iran and all levels of its people.

Thus it is that Ḥāfiẓ is a living entity in Iran today. A fact which brings us to the use of his text for bibliomancy: taking a *fāl*, omen, from the verses where the *Dīvān* falls open; *sortes Hafizianae*. But so all embracing are his verses, and on so many levels can they be read, that of course the augury to be derived from them is generally what the seeker expects or wants. Such is apt to be the case with scriptural writings in general; it is to be recalled that the works of Ḥāfiẓ, or he himself, have been known since his own time as the *Lisān al-ghayb*, 'The Tongue of the Unseen'.[4] And here touched upon is one of the most discussed aspects of Ḥāfiẓ's compositions and a major problem in attempts to translate them into another language: the subtle ambiguities, the marvellous wordplay, the several levels on which he can be interpreted.

Samuel Johnson said that while science books might be translated exactly, in translating history books precision is possible except where oratorical passages are concerned, because they are 'poetical'. He goes on to say that poetry cannot be translated, a consequence of which is that poets 'preserve languages; for we would not be at the trouble to learn a language, if we could have all that is written in it just as well in a translation. But as the beauties of poetry cannot be preserved in any language except that in which it was originally written, we learn the language.'[5] But in Johnson's time another genre was cultivated, by poets such as Dryden and Pope and himself: poets did not translate but composed what were known as 'imitations'. Edward Fitzgerald, who, incidentally, was a lover of Dryden's poetry, did not set out to translate the quatrains of Omar Khayyam. In a letter he remarks 'God Forbid' that he should be thought to be translating. He was, in fact, working in the now almost forgotten tradition of the Imitation.[6] Since he was possessed of the genius of a poet, his imitation is one of the most successful poems in the English language, but it is not intended to be a translation. Of it Fitzgerald used the coinage 'transmogrification'.

If the translator is not a poet but is anxious to convey in his own language what the poet said in his, then prose is the best choice. Sometimes, as in the instance of the Authorized Version of the Psalms, the prose translation takes on a specially exalted quality from the power of the original. Gertrude Bell's verse renderings of Ḥāfiẓ are a pleasure to read, and Sir William Jones' *A Persian Song* amused Byron. It goes:

> Sweet maid, if thou wouldst charm my sight
> And bid these arms thy neck infold;
> That rosy cheek, that lily hand
> Would give thy poet more delight
> Than all Bocara's vaunted gold,
> Than all the gems of Samarcand.[7]

Byron's coarse parody of it was not published in his complete poetical works until 1980. Dr Loloi describes it as 'a witty exercise in burlesque which merits detailed comparison with "A Persian Song"'.[8] It is known, however, that Byron admired Jones' display of skill in poetic technique in this particular translation. Jones' version is all very well (Byron's of course has really nothing to do with examination of the Persian original), but Jones is a long way from:

> If that Shīrāzī Turk captures our heart,
> For his Hindu dark mole I would forgive Samarqand and Bukhārā.[9]

with its connotation of the allure of cruelty in the Turk.

There is no need to go further in listing translations of Ḥāfiẓ. In his *Classical Persian Literature*, Chapter XIII,[10] Professor Arberry gives a most useful summary of various Ḥāfiẓ translations; and, more particularly, translations into several tongues are covered in detail in the *Encyclopaedia Iranica* article on Ḥāfiẓ. To this article our colleagues Franklin Lewis and Parvin Loloi, whose essays grace this volume, made valuable contributions. But above all the debt is great that we owe to the latter's *Ḥāfiẓ, Master of Persian Poetry: A Critical Bibliography*, with the subtitle *English Translations Since the Eighteenth Century*.[11] In conclusion here, it should be noted that when the aim is to convey what the poet really said, not what the translator thinks he might or ought to have been saying, versions in a kind of jingle, and even the better verse translations, do erect an extra curtain between a reader who does not know Persian and the original.

It is not only the charm of Ḥāfiẓ's verses that makes him such an important world poet, and the universality of his appeal to many different kinds of people and the whole gamut of their emotions. It is the way in which his poetry, although it grew out of a great tradition already established by his time, rides above all that preceded it, while it addresses itself to the hearts of everyone. It is as if, in our state of imprisonment beneath the Ptolemaic dome – as the cosmos was seen in Ḥāfiẓ's time – his purpose was to pierce that dome and reach the clear light of the Empyrean beyond it in a process propelled by love.

Here it is appropriate to mention the problem of fatalism in Persian literature. The fatalism which haunts the *Shāhnāma* of Firdawsī (died *circa* 1020 or 1025 AD) is not the kind reflected in the poetry of Ḥāfiẓ. As Dr Annabel Keeler, in her recently published *Sufi Hermeneutics: the Qur'an Commentary of Rashīd al-Dīn Maybudī*, makes clear,[12] Sufi 'fatalism' or concept of predestination should not be related to the idea of predestination as derived from a Zurvanite or pre-Islamic Iranian ethos.[13]

Sufism is totally hinged on Islam: for the Sufi, Man's life was pre-legislated for when God asked Adam, *Alastu birabbikum?* (Am I not your Lord?), and Adam replied 'Yes',[14] this was the Covenant between God and Man. It is to this Covenant that Ḥāfiẓ refers when he speaks of, for example, the inevitability of his being a drunkard. It is interesting to see him using the same formula of Firdawsī, on the immutability of the Written Decree, but in a different context. For Ḥāfiẓ says, 'The Written Decree cannot be erased', but he begins his couplet with, 'For me, from the beginning of Eternity, love was written'. Firdawsī has no reference to love. He begins his couplet with the formula, 'The Written Decree cannot be erased', but concludes with, 'For divine business is no light matter'.

The Sufi concept of predestination in no way militates against the idea of achievement of the ultimate bliss of being with God in the Empyrean beyond the malignant influence of the planets. But the whole question of predestination in Islam has been the subject of much debate and discourse, as – when we remember Jansen, Calvin or, for that matter, James Hogg, the 'Ettrick Shepherd', he of the *Private Memoirs and Confessions of a Justified Sinner*, to say nothing of St Augustine – has Christianity. My contention is that, so far as Sufi poetry is concerned, there is no need for us further to flounder in ambiguity or argument.

As for the universality of Ḥāfiẓ's appeal for over six centuries, it should be noted that his diction is, in fact, ordinary colloquial Persian, with words and phrases that can be translated into such colloquialisms as the English 'sure' and 'OK';[15] but in Ḥāfiẓ it is colloquial Persian raised to the level of high literary diction. Yet, how far his usage consists of ordinary conversational Persian, as common today as it ever was, must not be forgotten. The Persian language has changed less since the death of the poet Rūdakī in 940–1 AD than has English since that of Chaucer in 1400; Chaucer, of course, was Ḥāfiẓ's contemporary.

As for sectarianism, the divisions which can ruin civilizations, Ḥāfiẓ lifts his verses above any such conflicting positions. Whether or not he was a Sufi has been much discussed. His refusal to be identified with any particular sect, one might even say religion, is not at all alien to genuine Sufism. It is probable that he was a Sufi, but of a special kind; of his contempt for false Sufis his verses bear ample testimony. Some years ago it was interestingly suggested by the late 'Alī 'Aṣghār Ḥikmat that Ḥāfiẓ was in fact an Uwaysī Sufi. An Uwaysī Sufi acknowledges no living *Pīr* or easily recognizable ancestral guide, those guides to whose guidance exponents of Sufism attach such very great importance. He follows a spiritual guide of a more ethereal kind. In the case of the Uwaysī, this guide was Uways al-Qaranī, he who in legend is said to have inspired the Prophet Muḥammad. Hence Ḥāfiẓ's references to the sacred breath that emanates from the Yemen; that is to say, from the region where Uways al-Qaranī is supposed to have lived. In this context, and in that of Ḥāfiẓ's being above sectarian divisions – or for that matter any divisions at all,[16] including social and sexual – it is to be noted that the *Pīr* (not necessarily a personal *Pīr*) of whom he frequently speaks is the *Pīr-i Mughān*, the *Magian* Elder; that is to say, a Guide outside the Muslim fold, and who figures dramatically in the five-*bait Masnavī* cited above:[17]

> And if the Magian Elder were to spread a fire,
> I don't know whose lamp would be kindled.

with its obvious Magian or Zoroastrian associations. In Dr Khānlarī's version there is no reference to the 'Magian Elder', while in a manuscript dated 846/1442–3, a copy of which is in the author's possession, the verse does not occur at all. Khānlarī has for his verse 4:

And if the kindling stick spreads fiery sparks
I do not know whose lamp it will light,

with no reference to the 'Magian Elder'. Given that the 846/1442–3 manuscript does not include this verse at all, the Magian Elder might be a later addition, but it is more likely that it was in the original and later, with a mind to religious prejudices, deleted.

That his, so to speak, love-based free-ranging outlook aroused suspicion may be considered attested by, among other sources, Khwāndamīr.[18] He mentions the objection of Jalāl al-Dīn Shāh Shujā', the ruler of Shīrāz from 1357 to 1384, to a line of Ḥāfiẓ's to the effect that:

If Muslimism be of that which Ḥāfiẓ has,
Woe if today be followed by a tomorrow!

Shāh Shujā' saw this verse as a denial of the Day of Resurrection. Members of the religious classes who were jealous of Ḥāfiẓ seized the opportunity to propagate this indication of Ḥāfiẓ's heresy. Ḥāfiẓ was forced to apply to a great religious authority who happened to be passing through Shīrāz and who advised the poet to add another line, putting the offensive words into the mouths of Christian revellers outside a tavern door early in the morning, accompanied by 'drum and fife'.

The late Professor Minorsky, on meeting me in my first year at the School of Oriental and African Studies, asked me why I was studying Persian. When I answered, 'To read Ḥāfiẓ in the original', he replied, 'Don't forget, Mr Avery, that Ḥāfiẓ too was a political animal'. I have not forgotten and have appreciated Qāsim Ghanī's *Bahth dar athār u afkār u ahvāl-i Ḥāfiẓ*, with its details of Ḥāfiẓ's possible or probable political relations with, chiefly, rulers of Shīrāz in his time, and how these relations are reflected in his poetry.[19] A salient factor, where his verses are politically coloured, is that they generally take the shape of warnings. Thus they speak to us of tyranny accompanied by that not uncommon feature of oppressive regimes, secret police. On one occasion he says that, 'the wise bird does not go to the assembly tonight'.[20] Guarded against were to be the *muḥtasib*'s men, the secret agents of the censor of morals and policeman of the city wards. The obverse of this situation is that Ḥāfiẓ belonged to a special coterie; the *dowra* ('circle'), has always been and still is a feature of Iranian social and intellectual life, a feature characteristic of societies in which freedom of expression is restrained. Thus like-minded people may meet in the security of privacy, and exchange views. Ḥāfiẓ's is very much what might be called coterie poetry, taking the form of a code addressed to intimates who would understand allusions – to many of which, alas, we must remain largely blind and deaf.

In so far as there is any element of non-violence in Ḥāfiẓ's verses,[21] his message might be considered especially appealing in the times in which we are now living. Comparison of his works with those of the troubadours is not only justified by the fact that he too, though in a very different manner, deals with courtly love, but also, and more importantly, because with the flame of his poetry he succeeded in keeping alive a delicate cultural entity and true spirituality in times of cruelty and brutality, as did the troubadours during the European Dark Ages. As for courtly love, in the case of the troubadours it comes across to us as distinctly related to specific human situations: the peasant lass is perfectly real, and the cold and aloof great lady perfectly conceivable. Ḥāfiẓ, on the other hand, is free from the Occidental preoccupation with the *human* self. His lover and beloved are not represented by identifiable human beings. They appear in symbolic figures: the nightingale and the rose, for example. For him the problem of love is lifted above the mundane, tangible level: the *beloved* can be spelt with a small or a capital 'b'.

Achieved is a sense of exquisite beauty quite outside the everyday human sphere. It is the still loveliness of the miniature, translated into the movement and rhythms of poetry. It is the recollection of a beauty that presents the challenge of what is not to be obtained without the cultivation of a virtue excluding all that is carnal. We are transported from earth to heaven, and, as one or two nineteenth-century European travellers observed, in Iran earth and heaven often seem very close to each other. Iran is a plateau some 4,000 feet above sea level; it is a country where it is possible at four o'clock in the morning to read, during the darkness of night, by the light of the stars alone. The function of poetry as the preserver of cultural refinement in times of cultural degradation is never more evident than it is in the troubadours' and Ḥāfiẓ's poetry. They both established – or, in the case of Ḥāfiẓ, continued – a poetical tradition.

It should be emphasized that Ḥāfiẓ was heir to a great poetic tradition. Many tropes, such as for instance the Shīrāzī Turk, were inherited from predecessors. Sa'dī, it will be remembered, has a *ghazal* in which he says:

> At the hands of the Cathayan Turk nobody's endured
> Such cruelty as I have at the hands of the Shīrāzī Turk.

This is one of the more obvious quarryings in the mines of poetic conventions.

Niẓāmī-i 'Arūḍī Samarqandī's statement in the *Chahār Maqāla* ('Four Discourses'), where he is speaking about a poet's training, may be recalled. He says that a poet cannot attain any rank 'unless in the prime of his life and the season of his youth he commits to memory 20,000 couplets of the poetry of the Ancients, keeps in view (as models) 10,000 verses of the works of the Moderns, and continually reads and remembers the *diwans* [sic] of the masters of his art, observing how they have acquitted themselves of the straight passes and delicate places of song, in order that thus the different styles and varieties of verse may become engrained in his nature ...'.[22]

It can be said that poets are therefore constantly producing variations on themes suggested by their forerunners. Sa'dī gives us to infer that the Shīrāzī Turk's cruelty was far in excess of that experienced from the Cathayan Turk. As if to echo this theme, Ḥāfiẓ gives us to infer that his Shīrāzī Turk might also be crueller than those of Central Asia, the region of the Shīrāzī Turk's forebears, in the cities of Bukhārā and Samarqand, the metropolises of Tīmūr where his Turkish soldiers would be concentrated. Tīmūr threatened Shīrāz with those Turks in 1382 and invaded it in 1387, while he completely liquidated the ruling dynasty of Shīrāz in 1393, some three years after Ḥāfiẓ's demise. There seems to be no doubt that the spectre of Timur (and his Turks) hung over Shīrāz throughout much of Ḥāfiẓ's later life, but ironically among enlightened people his rigorous regime might have seemed at times to be preferred to the ever-warring Muzaffarid princes whom he eventually eliminated. In comparison with the torment of the Shīrāzī Turk's attractiveness, those fresh from Bukhārā and Samarqand are to be pardoned.

As for the various levels of meaning which confront the translator, it should be pointed out that the second hemistich of the Shīrāzī Turk poem is translatable in terms of readiness to barter Bukhārā and Samarqand for the mole on the Shīrāzī Turk's cheek. This interpretation has given rise to the legend that Tīmūr was vexed by Ḥāfiẓ's apparent contempt for that ruler's Central Asian capital cities. Another possibility is that, in the Shīrāzī Turk, Ḥāfiẓ might be alluding to his patron Shāh Shujā', of whose maternal Turkish ancestry he frequently speaks.

The variation might be wide, a long way from the theme that is being played upon, but the fixed point is that of retention of a balance. If Sa'dī has his Cathayan Turk to some extent exonerated, so Ḥāfiẓ must have the Turks of Bukhārā and Samarqand made less blameworthy than the Turk of Shīrāz. In Persian art, balance is a cardinal principal, between positive and negative, between the ins and outs of arabesque patterns. One of my old teachers of Arabic used to say, 'It's all algebra'. He was, in fact, thinking of the Arabic broken plurals, but in poetry it can be said that it is all geometry as well.

As if to prove the truth of Dryden's comment that 'it takes a poet to read a poet's mind', my collaborator, John Heath-Stubbs, in some translations of Ḥāfiẓ we produced when I was still a student, pointed out that there was observable in Ḥāfiẓ's poems a pattern of continuing referral to a dominant theme or themes. As so many have done since Ḥāfiẓ's time, with comments such as 'orient pearls at random strung',[23] Shāh Shujā' criticized Ḥāfiẓ, saying that 'each of your *ghazal*s fails from beginning to end to stay on one topic. Rather in each lyric three or four verses are in praise of wine and two or three concerning Sufism and one or two describing a beloved. Such a variability in a single lyric is contrary to the rules of rhetoric.'[24] Shāh Shujā' was wrong: 'orient pearls' were never strung less 'at random'. There was a pattern. It was an arabesque, going in and coming out, dependent on repetitions, both obvious but also suppressed, in alternate verses. We did an analysis on these lines in the introduction to the little book which we published. This book has been reissued both in the USA and the UK.[25]

This arabesque patterning brings to mind the discovery now being worked on by Mr Jason Elliot, and discussed in his book *Mirrors of the Unseen*.[26] The theory is that behind the intricate plaster-work and mosaics in Iran's ancient mosques, there is a series of persistent geometric designs. The arabesque pattern behind the imagery of the poetry seems to emanate from the same obsession with geometric symbols. This is an obsession that can be related to the constant longing on the part of Iranians – and indeed other Middle Easterners, if not all human beings – for order in place of chaos; in the case of the Iranians, for the trim pathways, canals and flowerbeds of gardens in place of the harshness, emptiness and tumbled rocks of the deserts beyond the garden walls.

Recognition of arabesque thematic patterns in poetry is of course germane to the problems facing those who would endeavour to reconstruct the texts of Persian poetry of former times, correcting the inadvertences of omission or inclusion of false verses, and other errors attributable to the scribes who have copied the poems through the centuries. The order and genuineness of verses might be more easily established if attention is paid to the thematic recurrence of associated images such as John Heath-Stubbs noticed and other colleagues have subsequently studied in detail.

But I must venture no further into the intricacies of textual criticism. Instead, I would just like to conclude with a plea that it should be remembered that Sir William Jones was at least right in calling his version of a famous Ḥāfiẓ poem *A Persian Song.* We must not, in dissecting and analysing the poetry of Ḥāfiẓ, forget that, whatever else he was, he was a singer. In his role as a poet he belonged to the class of minstrels: to use that word which is so difficult to translate, *rind*, in his guise as a poet, Ḥāfiẓ was of the type of rogues or scallywags. We are grateful to him, and to the troubadours, for it is through the power of song, of music, that great liberator of the soul from the body, that they preserved grace in an ever darkening world; grace, and a sense of humour, with fifes and drums.

Cambridge, July 2007

Notes

1 Margaret Smith, *Al-Ghazālī: The Mystic*, p. 109.

2 See A.J. Arberry's admirable *Fifty Poems of Hāfiz*, Poem XLVIII, but also *Dīvān-i Ḥāfiẓ*, ed. Khānlarī, II, p. 1057, Poem IV, where he gives a different reading in a quintuplet, *mukhammas*.

3 Paris 1873, pp. 66–70.

4 It has been argued that the title *Lisān al-ghayb* alludes not to Ḥāfiẓ in person, but to his words. However this may be, it is interesting that the historian Khwāndamīr also accords Ḥāfiẓ the title *Tarjumān al-asrār* ('The Interpreter of the Secrets') in his *Habīb al-siyar*, IV, pp. 314–15.

5 Boswell, *The Life of Samuel Johnson*, pp. 36–7.

6 Dryden has the comment, 'Mr. Cowley's Praise of a Country Life is excellent, but is rather an imitation of Vergil than a version.' In W.P. Ker (ed.), *Essays of John Dryden*, II, p. 244. It will be noted that here Dryden draws a distinction between 'imitation' and 'version' or 'translation'.

7 *A Grammar of the Persian Language*, p. 168.

8 *Hāfiz, Master of Persian Poetry: A Critical Bibliography – English Translations Since the Eighteenth Century*, pp. 60–4.

9 Peter Avery (trans.), *The Collected Lyrics of Háfiz of Shíráz*, Poem III, p. 21.

10 London: Allen & Unwin 1958; reprinted Surrey: Curzon Press 1994.

11 See note 8 above.

12 Oxford: Oxford University Press 2006. See particularly pp. 61ff. and the Index under 'Preordination' and 'Covenant'.

13 See Zaehner, *Zurvan: A Zoroastrian Dilemma* for an exposition of the connection in Firdausī's concept of predestination with what was in fact a Zoroastrian heresy, the belief that the cosmos is ruled by Time.

14 Qur'ān, VII, p. 172.

15 For example, in the dialogue poem (*Dīvān-i Ḥāfiẓ*, ed. Khānlarī, *ghazal* 194: 1) where the person addressed replies *Gufta bih chashm harchih tū gū'ī chunān kunand*, where the phrase beginning with *bih chashm* can be translated as: 'Sure, whatever you say, so they will act.'

16 Cf. R. Shafaq, *Tārīkh-i adabīyāt-i Īrān*, p. 333, and Arberry, *Fifty Poems*, p. 16.

17 Arberry, *Fifty Poems*; *Dīvān-i Ḥāfiẓ*, ed. Khānlarī, cf. pp. ix–x above.

18 *Habīb as-Sīyar*, III, p. 315.

19 *Baḥth dar āthār u afkār u aḥwāl-i Ḥāfiẓ*, vol. 1: *Tārīkh-i 'aṣr-i Ḥāfiẓ yā tārīkh-i fārs va maḍāfāt va iyālāt-i mujāvarih dar qarn-i hashtum.*

20 *Dīvān-i Ḥāfiẓ*, ed. Khānlarī, *ghazal* 458: 4.

21 See J. Christoph Bürgel's article 'Ambiguity: A Study in the Use of Religious Terminology in the Poems of Hafiz', in Glünz and Bürgel (eds), *Intoxication, Earthly and Heavenly: Seven Studies on the Poet Hafiz of Shīrāz.*

22 Translation by E.G. Browne, *Chahār Maqāla*, pp. 49–50.

23 See A.J. Arberry, 'Orient Pearls At Random Strung', pp. 699–712.

24 Khwāndamīr, *Habīb al-siyar.*

25 Peter Avery and John Heath-Stubbs (trans.), *Hafiz of Shīrāz: Thirty Poems.*

26 *Mirrors of the Unseen: Journeys in Iran.*

Editor's Introduction and Acknowledgements

Tempus omnia revelat, Ḥāfiẓ's verse preserves its immortality through contemporaneity. Ḥāfiẓ has street-touch. Comparing Ḥāfiẓ with the Bard, Peter Avery recalls in his Foreword above how much easier it is for the native – even an illiterate – Iranian to interpret the complicated theological, mystical and social references in Ḥāfiẓ's poetry, to revel in the nuances of his allusions, understanding and reciting his verses by heart with refinement and depth of feeling than it is for the modern educated English person to appreciate even the most basic literary allusions of Shakespeare's sonnets. Two external factors – literary and socio-linguistic – partially account for this. On the one hand, Persianate societies today remain bardic civilizations in which bricklayers sing the *ghazal*s of Sa'dī and Rūmī as they work, and discussion of the verse of Ḥāfiẓ and 'Irāqī regularly enriches the common man's hours of leisure. On the other, Iranians and Afghans and the natives of the other Persianate lands of Central Asia, such as Tajikistan, by and large speak exactly the same Persian tongue spoken in fourteenth-century Shīrāz by Ḥāfiẓ.

The world of religious wars, theological controversies and embattled fanaticisms that choked and filled Ḥāfiẓ's soul with the smoke and fumes of anti-clerical parodies and biting religious satire still prevails today – which is why his verse can accurately articulate and redress the same political passions that hold sway throughout the contemporary Persianate world. Whereas the fanaticisms and tribal sectarian quarrels over religion heard during Ḥāfiẓ's day are still audible on an hourly basis in Iran today from pulpit, radio and television, only a tiny minority of trained historians can imaginatively relocate themselves within a Protestant police state of England during Queen Elizabeth I's reign. Linguistically as well, the language of Shakespeare's plays appears to us as a quaint, archaic dialect at best, a dead language at the worst. Hence Ḥāfiẓ's *Sententiae* – unlike many of Shakespeare's – never grow out of date, today remaining as *à propos* to the modern context of political argument and social debate as they did in 1387 when, outside the ramparts of the city of Iṣfahān, Tamerlane erected minarets out of the severed sconces of its inhabitants.

Albeit immanent in popular consciousness, most of Ḥāfiẓ's mythopoesis – his language of analogy and capacity for thinking in symbols – is no longer part of the mental furniture of modern man. The aesthetic premises of his poetry are incomprehensible within the conceptual framework of modern anti-art movements such as surrealism, minimalism, abstract expressionism or 'pop' art, for the principles of his spiritual vision, being heart-based and focused on presential knowledge (*'ilm-i ḥudhūrī*), are completely alien to the presuppositions of the modern materialist society of the West. If we are to gain access to Ḥāfiẓ's 'visionary topography', as Daryoush Shayegan called it, recourse must be made to the first principles of the Islamic neo-Platonic tradition and to the traditional doctrines underlying the verse of all the Sufi poets who were intoxicated on the same bacchanalian metaphors and inspired by the same erotic images that fill his *Dīvān*.

The central aim of the chapters in this volume is to enable contemporary Western students of classical Persian poetry to reconnect with that lost symbolic universe and hopefully re-initiate themselves into the *mundus imaginalis* of Ḥāfiẓ and the entire galaxy of Persian poets who spoke his 'language of the invisible'. Even many modern educated Persians, afflicted by the anti-imaginative climate of the West, today find much of his symbolism incomprehensible. They delight in the great beauty of his poems but often view them as utterly meaningless. University-educated rationalists in Iran and Pakistan have deplored the metaphysical system behind Ḥāfiẓ's poems and the religious and sacred aspect of his symbolism as a kind of superstitious absurdity that is no longer within the range of intellectually respectable ideas. The Pakistani philosopher Muḥammad Iqbāl (d. 1938) and the radical Iranian modernist Aḥmad Kasravī (d. 1946) thus both castigated Ḥāfiẓ's poetry as socially 'decadent' and intellectually 'backward'. Sensible men who wish to raise the material and technological level of society, or who equate progress in education exclusively with the study of the social or physical sciences today, can no longer relate to the Sufi ideals of spiritual 'holy poverty' (*faqr*) which were sustained by the all-enveloping culture of *malāmatī* spirituality and ethics that underpin radically unconventional statements by Ḥāfiẓ like these:

> Why speak of 'shame' when my good name
> Is itself made of shame and blame?
> Why do you ask of 'name' – you know I am
> Ashamed of all you'd call good name?[1]

Unfortunately, just as Ḥāfiẓ's Religion of Love celebrated by this volume is anathema to the turbaned puritans regnant in Iran's 'Islamic' Republic, mention of his spiritual and metaphysical teachings remain largely taboo in the Academe, particularly in modern Persian Language and Literature departments in universities both East and West. Again, a strange similarity of bias between contemporary Ḥāfiẓology and academic Shakespeare studies exists. Since Frances Yates,[2] it is an open secret among Shakespeare scholars that the Hermetic Rosicrucianism and neo-Platonic Occultism of Elizabethean thinkers such as John Dee (d. 1609) and Giordano Bruno (d. 1600)[3] – along with the Christian Platonism of Marsilio Ficino (d. 1499)[4] – comprise the central philosophical sources of Shakespeare's teachings on love, yet the writings of these thinkers generally remain a body of 'excluded knowledge' which students are instructed not to investigate; mention Dee, Ficino or Bruno to the learned doctor of Shakespeare studies whose sere voice held his lecture hall spellbound – thereafter you talk to a box turtle. Ḥafiẓ studies today suffer from a similar conspiracy of silence. In modern literary studies and critical theory, especially in the contemporary West, the vertical purport and spiritual import of his symbolic imagery by and large are deliberately neglected, and the esoteric doctrines and metaphysical teachings inspiring his verse are treated as irrelevancies. Most interpretations of his poetry treat him simply as a brilliant court poet of an entirely secular and worldly bent. It is hoped that the chapters in the present volume, penned by the world's leading experts in classical Persian poetry, will serve in some minor degree to redress the calumny of decades of collective critical neglect of the spiritual sources and metaphysical bases underlying Ḥāfiẓ's teachings on love.

Part I of the volume, which places 'Ḥāfiẓ in the Socio-historical, Literary and Mystical Milieu of Medieval Persia', comprises two sections. In the first prolegomenon, Ḥafiẓ's oeuvre is contextualized within the medieval society of Shīrāz and in classical and modern Persian *belles lettres*. An overview of the little we know of Ḥafiẓ's life and times is then presented, followed by a lengthy review and re-evaluation of the courtly milieu of his poems and an examination of his relationship – and lack thereof – to various princes and patrons mentioned in his poetry. Here, I underline the fact that *Ḥafiẓ was not a court poet*, or at least not a professional panegyrist in the traditional sense of the word. An assessment of some of the causes of his supreme position in classical Persian lyrical poetry is also offered.

The second prolegomenon aims to summarize the key teachings of Ḥafiẓ's erotic spirituality. In particular, I explore the social, literary and metaphysical dimensions of the poet's most important symbol: the Inspired Libertine (*rind*). A survey of the erotic ethic of his romantic philosophy of *rindī* is offered, along with an outline of the two related contemplative disciplines practised by its *fedeli d'amore:* the Art of Erotic Contemplation (*shāhid-bāzī*) and the Art of the Erotic Gaze: Contemplation of Human Beauty (*naẓar-bāzī*). This section concludes with a study of Ḥāfiẓ's *malāmatī* ethic and his praise of the rite of the spiritual vagabonds (*qalandarī*).

Part II comprises three chapters devoted to the subject of 'Ḥāfiẓ and the School of Love in Classical Persian Poetry'.

In the volume's keynote chapter on 'The Principles of the Religion of Love in Classical Persian Poetry', one of Iran's most popular contemporary thinkers, Husayn Ilahi-Ghomshei, surveys the main themes and principles of the transcendental Religion of Love, *madhhab-i 'ishq*, in Persian and Arabic Sufi literature, as well as in classical Persian poetry. He shows how the sources of this mystical erotic doctrine appear both in the writings of the two great Sufi martyrs – Manṣūr al-Ḥallāj (executed 304/922) and 'Ayn al-Quḍāt Hamadhānī (executed 526/1132) – as well as in the earliest Persian court poets such as Rūdākī Samarqandī (d. 329/940) and Sanā'ī of Ghazna (d. 525/1131). Likewise, he points out how manifestations of the doctrines of that same School of Love can be found in the writings of Arab mystical poet–philosophers such as Muḥyī al-Dīn ibn al-'Arabī (d. 638/1240) and 'Umar ibn Fāriḍ (d. 633/1235), and in the Persian poetry of Niẓāmī of Ganja (d. 598/1202),

'Aṭṭār of Nishapur (d. 618/1221 or 627/1229), Sa'dī (d. circa 691/1292) and Jalāl al-Dīn Rūmī (d. 672/1273). The spiritual traditions that sustained this *madhhab-i 'ishq* and the terms in classical Persian literature which referred to antinomian mystics – *qalandars* (vagabonds, wild men), *rind* (inspired libertine), *qallāsh* (knave), *mubāḥī* (libertine), *dīvāna* (lunatic) and *lā-ubālī* (daredevil, desperado) – are analysed by the author, with appropriate verses by Sa'dī and Ḥāfiẓ praising both the daredevil *lā-ubālī* and the wildman *qalandar* attitude, cited to contextualize their doctrines. In Ḥāfiẓ's erotic spirituality, with his penchant for terms such as 'Love's creed' (*madhhab-i 'ishq*), the 'Magian master's faith' (*madhhab-i pīr-i mughān*) and the 'creed of inspired libertines' (*madhhab-i rindān*), those same doctrines again appear.

In the following chapter on 'The Erotic Spirit: Love, Man and Satan in Ḥāfiẓ's Poetry', Ali Asghar Seyed-Gohrab demonstrates how a mystical theory of love can be reconstructed from Ḥāfiẓ's *Dīvān*. Ḥāfiẓ's reliance on the Islamic creation myth as developed by the Persian Sufi mystics such as Najm ad-Dīn Rāzī over the preceding centuries, and his combination of bacchanalian imagery of wine and erotic love poetry with familiar Qur'ānic traditions and Persian Sufi doctrines, enabled him to succeed 'in interweaving the mystical version of the creation myth with a philosophy of earthly love'. Ḥāfiẓ's use of the term love corresponds entirely with his predecessors such as Sanā'ī, 'Aṭṭār and Niẓāmī, who were all influenced by Aḥmad Ghazālī's (d. 520/1126) seminal treatise *Savāniḥ*, the founding text of the School of Love in Sufism and the tradition of love poetry in Persian. Knowledge of the background of Sufi thought, argues Seyed-Gohrab – and, in particular, the ascetic (*zuhdiyyāt*), bacchic (*khamriyyāt*) and antinomian (*qalandariyyāt*) themes in his poetry – enriches our experience of reading Ḥāfiẓ's poetry.

Leili Anvar, in her lovely chapter on 'The Radiance of Epiphany: The Vision of Beauty and Love in Ḥāfiẓ's Poem of Pre-Eternity', also emphasizes Ḥāfiẓ's debt to the allusive poetic eroticism of Aḥmad Ghazālī's *Savāniḥ*. The trans-rational nature of the experience of love and the impossibility of expressing erotic experiences prosaically, emphasized by Ghazālī, made Ḥāfiẓ's choice of poetry as the language of love the perfect vehicle of expression, but one which necessarily – paradoxically – remains elusive to rational analysis. Exploring Ḥāfiẓ's conception of the Qur'ānic theme (VII: 172) of the 'Day of Pre-Eternity' or 'Day of the Covenant' (*rūz-i alast*) in pre-eternity, in what she calls his *ghazal* of pre-eternity, her chapter explores a number of Ḥāfiẓ's key themes – Love, Beauty, Grief (the paradox of joy in pain) and Longing – demonstrating how his erotic poeticization of these ideas have their literary sources in the topos of the religion of love in classical Persian poetry.

Sufism is the dominant tradition of Islamic spirituality that influenced Ḥāfiẓ and the most significant source of the imagery and symbolism in his *Dīvān*. For this reason a separate section of this volume (the three chapters in Part III) is devoted to 'Ḥāfiẓ and the Persian Sufi Tradition'.

After a lifetime of study of Ḥāfiẓ and the translation of his entire poetic oeuvre into French, Charles Henri de Fouchécour in his opening chapter on 'Ḥāfiẓ and the Sufi' underlines the importance of the fourteenth century as an epoch in Islamic civilization which saw the establishment of the great Sufi Orders throughout the Middle East, Central Asia and India. The author examines Ḥāfiẓ's wine symbolism and bacchanalian expressions, viewing them as comprising 'a language of mystery' alluding 'to something experienced', and yet indefinable and 'unthinkable rationally'. In this respect, he states that Ḥāfiẓ's *Dīvān* follows precisely the same bacchanalian Sufi hermeneutic proposed by Maḥmūd Shabistarī in his *Garden of Mystery*, who had demonstrated how profane poetic imagery could be used to vividly convey ideas of a spiritual order. Professor Fouchécour also gives a rough sketch of the Sufi world in which Ḥāfiẓ was situated, revealing the role played in it by key Sufi poets such as 'Imād al-Dīn Faqīh Kirmānī (d. 773/1372), one of Ḥāfiẓ's famous contemporaries. Surveying the mystical–intellectual terrain of the age, he analyses Ḥāfiẓ's very strong criticisms of the Sufis and examines the poet's Sufi terminology. He concludes that 'despite these strictures, Ḥāfiẓ declares the path of Sufism to be a good one, on one condition, however – that it lead beyond itself. As a way composed of rules, the Sufi Path should lead to where no rule exists save the Rule of Love ... [where] the entire hierarchy of perfection is abolished.'

My chapter on 'The Religion of Love and the Puritans of Islam: Sufi Sources of Ḥāfiẓ's Anti-clericalism' illustrates Ḥāfiẓ's role as Islam's supreme anti-clerical and anti-puritan poet. The desiccated Muslim piety of the ascetic (*zāhid*) is contrasted to the higher religion of *Eros* held by the poet's inspired libertine (*rind*); the dichotomy and difference in spiritual attitudes between the two – the latter's focus on outer rituals versus the former's inner contemplative 'intention' – is shown to be derived from the teachings of early Persian Sufis such as Kalābadhī and Junayd. The Sufi ethical and metaphysical doctrines sustaining his opposition to religious hypocrisy and sanctimony are analysed in detail. Ḥāfiẓ's predominant social attitude is shown to be *anti-hypocritical*, and his condemnation of hypocrisy as the 'supreme sin' traced back to its antecedents in Sufi thought: Anṣārī and Ghazālī in particular. Lastly, the Sufi sources of Ḥāfiẓ's counter-ethic of *malāmatī* bacchanalian piety, which redresses counterfeit religiosity and remedies the vice of hypocrisy, are explored. His theology of sin (counterbalancing the vice of pride, sin functions as an adjunct of humility), with its roots in the Sufi doctrine of Najm al-Dīn Rāzī and Rashīd al-Dīn Maybudī, is subjected to detailed analysis. The chapter concludes that the emphasis on God's mercy and forgiveness (*'afw*) of sin is the fundamental keynote theme of Ḥāfiẓ's moral theology.

Carl Ernst concludes this part of the volume with a study of 'Jalāl al-Dīn Davānī's Interpretation of Ḥāfiẓ'. Davānī (d. 908/1502) was a famous late classical Iranian mystical philosopher who lived a little less than a century after Ḥāfiẓ's death in Shīrāz. He wrote one of the earliest, if not the very first, separate commentary on his poetry, approaching the poet's verses from three perspectives: those of the philosophical mystics, the Sufis, and the Peripatetic and Illuminationist sages (*ḥukamā*). Davānī's hermeneutic involved a reading of individual words and coded symbols as metaphorically representative of unstated realities, an approach that was similar to 'the way of reading symbols in Persian literature from a Sufi perspective [found in] the *Gulshan-i rāz* of Maḥmūd Shabistarī (d. after 740/1340), a work doubtless known to Ḥāfiẓ as well as Davānī'. Sufi authorities such as 'Ayn al-Quḍāt, Ḥallāj, Ibn Khafīf and Rūzbihān are invoked in the Sufi section of Davānī's commentary. Throughout his commentary on Ḥāfiẓ, Ernst demonstrates that 'Davānī maintains ... a consistent hermeneutic that assumes a deep structure of concealing and revealing the divine mysteries as the operative principle behind all serious literature. ... It was just as natural and inevitable to employ a Sufi hermeneutic for the poetry of Ḥāfiẓ as it was for Sa'īd al-Dīn Farghānī (d. 701/1301), Ṣadr al-Dīn Qunawī (d. 752/1351), or 'Abd al-Ghanī al-Nābulusī (d. 1143/1751) to write detailed mystical commentaries on the Arabic poems of Ibn al-Farid.'

Part IV features four chapters on the topic of 'Ḥāfiẓ's Romantic Imagery and Language of Love'.

In the first chapter on 'The Allegory of Drunkenness and the Theophany of the Beloved in Sixteenth-Century Illustrations of Ḥāfiẓ', eminent art-historian Michael Barry decodes the mystical symbolism underlying Ḥāfiẓ's romantic imagery, as depicted in two famous Timurid-period illustrations of the *Dīvān* – featured respectively on the front and back cover of this volume. 'Such paintings', Barry reveals, 'underscore how much traditional readers in the Iranian and Indo-Muslim worlds perceived Ḥāfiẓ's *Dīvān* to be a pre-eminent allegory of Sufi love and mystical frenzy'. The artist's visual exegesis of Ḥāfiẓ's bacchanalian imagery – his depiction of the symbol of the tavern (*kharābāt*) – portrays the metaphysical drunkenness pervading all levels of Being, wine being a symbol for radiation of the Divine light and beauty – theophany – radiant within every atom of Existence. The Persian painter's depiction of wine becomes 'a metaphor for the all-connecting and all-pervading emanation of the divine creative clarity, from its most rarefied and immaterial heavenly configurations, to its densest and most visible embodiments on earth', namely 'the Divine Light's descent (*nuzūl*) from the higher planes of Being to the lower: in the careful hierarchy of Islamicized neo-Platonic thought and imagery upon which Ḥāfiẓ so much plays in verse'. Lastly, the theme of the Sophianic Feminine in Persian miniature painting, with its many correspondences in Ḥāfiẓian love mysticism, is analysed, with Barry adducing convincing arguments that, just as with the Persian visual art of painting, 'the mystical imagery of classical Persian Sufi epic – and lyrical – poetry thus can most definitely configure the Divine Belovéd as a female'.

In the second of these chapters, entitled 'Transfiguring Love: Perspective Shifts and the Contextualization of Experience in the *Ghazals* of Ḥāfiẓ', James Morris attempts to recreate, and thus remind us, of the poet's spiritual world view based on a perspective at once metaphysical, religious, aesthetic and ethical, where the entire creation is viewed as a theophany of the One divine Source. He focuses on the scriptural–symbolic correlates that are necessary to grasp the most essential spiritual realities in Ḥāfiẓ's poetry, which in turn reveal some of the basic rhetorical structures and presuppositions in his poetry. In order to illustrate these subjective shifts in perspective, Professor Morris analyses two *ghazals*, showing how the poet shifts line by line from the abstract to the particular, and from the general narrative to intimately personal voices in each verse, divine allusions (to Heart, Spirit and God) complementing the humanly individual work of understanding, a mental leap which the aesthetic of the *ghazal* demands of the reader.

The last two chapters in the volume discuss Ḥāfiẓ's poetry in relation to comparative literature: medieval European and Romantic English poetics respectively.

Franklin Lewis' study of 'The Semiotic Horizons of Dawn in the Poetry of Ḥāfiẓ' addresses the particular literary topos of dawn, the 'Alba', in Persian poetry in general, and in Ḥāfiẓ's poems in particular. The chapter opens with a survey of this topos in the medieval Provençal lyric in southern France and northern Italy, showing how the theme of the parting of two lovers at dawn was ingrained into European literary traditions and suffused medieval European and renaissance literature. Lewis then reveals how a certain kind of *Alba* topos in early Arabic Andalusian poetry existed, which was similar but not identical to its Provençal prototype. In Persian, a kind of *Alba* theme is shown to appear in Sanā'ī's *ghazals*. In the second half of his chapter, he examines Ḥāfiẓ's *ghazals*, to see if any of the criteria for the *Alba* genre can be found in them, but concludes to the negative: that the poet found the topos uninteresting or too clichéd to use. Nevertheless, making an inventory of Ḥāfiẓ's lexicon of dawn, he underlines that nearly one-fifth of the *ghazals* of Ḥāfiẓ explicitly refer to dawn or early morning, so that the topos of dawn is integral to his mythopoetic vocabulary.

In her chapter on 'Ḥāfiẓ and the Language of Love in Nineteenth-Century English and American Poetry', Parvin Loloi surveys the reception history of Ḥāfiẓ's poetry in English from the first translations into English verse by Sir William Jones in 1771 down to today. She summarizes the highlights, while underlining the drawbacks, in the versions done by nineteenth-century English and American translators, and some of the later renditions into English free-verse by the twentieth-century translators. As Loloi reveals, Von Hammer-Purgstall's German translation (1812) of Ḥāfiẓ's *Dīvān* had a huge impact on Goethe, Emerson and Tennyson in Europe and the USA, and played an important role, along with Orientalism, in revitalizing and renewing the literature and poetry of the Romantics. Likewise, through their readings of Sir William Jones, most of the English Romantics (Shelley, Keats, Byron, and Tennyson in particular) had a fairly advanced understanding of the love theory of classical Sufism; examples are adduced from their own works showing how the erotic content of their poetry is redolent of 'the Ḥāfiẓian garden of love'. Other examples adduced by Loloi show how Shelley's philosophy of Love, though steeped in neo-Platonism, also reflects his immersion in Jones' translations of Ḥāfiẓ and writings on Persian mysticism, and his cognizance and versification of the doctrines of Sufism in his own work. It was in Tennyson's poetry, however, that Ḥāfiẓ's influence can be seen most forcefully among all the Romantics; the Sufi imagery frequent in Ḥāfiẓ appears prominently in Tennyson's own poetry as well. In sum, we discover how widespread 'the Ḥāfiẓian language of love' has been in the work of both British and American poets throughout the nineteenth and twentieth centuries in the West.

Acknowledgements

The contents of the present volume are based on a conference on *Hafiz and the School of Love in Classical Persian Poetry*, convened in 2007 by the editor and James Morris at the Institute of Arab and Islamic Studies (IAIS) of the University of Exeter, UK. Largely funded by the Iran Heritage Foundation (IHF), the conference was also supported by the University of Exeter and the British Academy. I am very grateful to Mr Farhad Hakimzadeh, former Director of the IHF, for his support of every aspect of this volume – from the conference's initial conception to the book's final publication. I would like to thank Professors Tim Niblock and Rashid El-Enany, both former directors of the IAIS, for their help in conference organization. I am also grateful to the excellent support staff at Exeter – Laura Scrivens, Catherine Bell and Jane Clark – for their organizational assistance during the convening of the conference. I am much obliged to Terry Graham's kind hand in editing earlier drafts of my prose and to Jason Elliot's eye in critically scanning my translations of Ḥāfiẓ's verse in this volume.

A Note on Transliteration

Transliteration of Persian and Arabic words in this book follows the transliteration table of the *International Journal of Middle Eastern Studies*, except for the letter 'ż' (*zad*) which is rendered as 'ḍ' (as in Arabic). Persian words of Arabic origin, such as *Dīwān*, generally, but not exclusively, use 'w' instead of 'v' for the Arabic letter *wa*. The diphthongs are consistently rendered as 'aw' and 'ay'.

Leonard Lewisohn, 13 August 2009

Notes

1 *Dīvān-i Ḥāfiẓ*, ed. Khānlarī, *ghazal* 47: 8.

2 See, in particular, her *The Occult Philosophy in the Elizabethan Age*. Also, cf. J. Vyvyan, *Shakespeare and the Rose of Love: A Study of the Early Plays in Relation to the Medieval Philosophy of Love*.

3 See Ted Hughes, *Shakespeare and the Goddess of Complete Being*, pp. 18–61.

4 The best study of Ficino and Shakespeare remains Jill Line, *Shakespeare and the Fire of Love*.

Part I

Ḥāfiẓ in the Socio-historical, Literary and Mystical Milieu of Medieval Persia

Prolegomenon to the Study of Ḥāfiẓ 1 – Socio-historical and Literary Contexts: Ḥāfiẓ in Shīrāz

Leonard Lewisohn

Cité de l'amour

When Ḥāfiẓ was born in the city of Shīrāz some time between 710/1310 and 720/1320,[1] the cultural epoch into which our poet stepped was one of the richest in all human history. As the second leading cultural capital (after Tabriz) of medieval Persia, the artistic, intellectual and literary brilliance of fourteenth-century Shīrāz under Muẓaffarid rule is perhaps best comparable to fifteenth-century Florence under Cosimo and Lorenzo de Medici. The poets and philosophers who thrived in this intellectual centre of south-western Fars easily rival the likes of Marsilio Ficino, Botticelli, Michelangelo and Pico de Mirandelo, who were to fill the capital city of Italian Tuscany a century later. For several centuries, throughout all the domains of the Islamic world, Shīrāz had been renowned as House of Knowledge (*dār al-'ilm*),[2] the city vaunting its learned theologians, eloquent preachers, pious ascetics, ecstatic Sufis, erudite scholars, specialist theologians, great calligraphers, famous scientists and adept *hommes de lettres.* Many of the natives of the city still figure as the central pillars of classical Islamic civilization. Shaykh Rūzbihān Baqlī (d. 606/1210), one of the greatest exponents of paradoxical expression and certainly the most original author of works on Sufi erotic theology, had flourished there a century before Ḥāfiẓ. Sa'dī of Shīrāz, the greatest romantic and humanist poet in the Persian language, had died in 691/1292, less than a generation before Ḥāfiẓ's birth, while the Illuminationist (*Ishrāqī*) philosopher Quṭb al-Dīn Shīrāzī (d. 710/1311), author of the encyclopaediac work *Durrat al-tāj li-ghurrat al-Dubāj*, had walked its streets a few years before he was born.

This city of 'Saints and Poets', as Arthur Arberry called it,[3] was especially famous for its colleges and seminaries, its Sufi centres (*khānaqāhs*) and mosques, many of which had large accompanying gardens and possessed properties attached by charitable bequest to their grounds. The presence of these institutions, even if their administrators were often than not corrupt,[4] lent the town a peculiar sacred ambience in the popular imagination. In Shīrāz – claimed the fourteenth-century Morrocan world traveller Ibn Baṭṭūṭa, who visited the city during Ḥāfiẓ's life – the

Qur'ān is chanted more beautifully than anywhere else in the Muslim world. The city was also like Florence in being both hotly decadent and a hotbed of religious fervour,[5] with prayer assemblies, Qur'ān study classes, Sufi séances for *samā'*, lecture halls full of preachers calling the populace to repent their sins, recluses and ascetics (*zuhhād*) down every corner and alley,[6] vignettes of which appear everywhere in Ḥāfiẓ's verse.

The city also prided itself on vast cemeteries with mausoleums of its saints. 'In Shīrāz one thousand Sufi masters and saints or more are found', boasted Sa'dī in a poem describing the city in the thirteenth century, 'around whose head the Ka'ba continuously circumambulates'.[7] The most interesting work on Shīrāz's necropolis was a work penned by Junayd-i Shīrāzī in Ḥāfiẓ's lifetime called *The Thousand Mausoleums*, a guidebook landmarking all the important tombs as sites of visitation for travellers, adding in as an extra feature a backdrop account of the city's famous quarters.[8] This work provided a veritable tourist guide to the sacred sites and shrines of Shīrāz,[9] and for visitors who flocked there from all over Islamdom gave 'the impression that the whole of Shīrāz consisted of pious Sunnis'.[10] Among these holy sites, the tomb of the Sufi master Ibn Khafīf of Shīrāz (d. 371/982), renowned for his ascetic prowess, was the most popular spot of weekend visitation for the populace of the city, second only to Shāh Chirāgh, the tomb of Aḥmad ibn Mūsā, brother of the Shi'ite Imām 'Alī al-Riḍā, slain in 220/835.[11] Ibn Baṭṭūṭa describes how Tāsh Khātun, the mother of Sulṭān Abū Isḥāq Īnjū (reg. 743/1343–753/1353: the ruler of Shīrāz when Ḥāfiẓ was a youth), paid homage to 'the Imām, the Pole, the Saint, Abū 'Abdu'llāh Ibn Khafīf, known to them as the Shaikh, ensampler of the whole land of Fars and much reverenced by them, so that they come to his tomb morning and evening to seek a blessing. The Khātun visits the mosque every Thursday night; there is an oratory and a *madrasa*, where the judges and scholars gather as they do at the shrine of Aḥmad ibn Mūsā.'[12] The abundance of Sufi shrines and centres (*khānaqāhs*) in thirteenth- and fourteenth-century Shīrāz made the city renowned as the 'Citadel of Saints' (*burj al-awliyā'*).[13]

Ibn Baṭṭūṭa also recounted 'the strange custom' of seeing thousands of women fanning themselves cool in the sultry summer heat, who crowded on Monday, Thursday and Friday afternoons onto the balconies of the Ancient Mosque listening to famous preachers discourse.[14] 'I have never seen in any land so great an assembly of women',[15] he exclaimed, stunned by their sight. Aside from the beauties of the fair sex in Shīrāz (with vignettes of whom Ḥāfiẓ's verse abounds), the city was fabled for its vast bazaar (Ibn Baṭṭūṭa thought it more sumptuous than that in Damascus),[16] divided into sections by guild (an alleyway for fruit sellers, another corridor for goldsmiths, for cloth merchants, etc.). Shīrāz's gardens were full of fountains, their rills lined by fragrant orange trees and elegant cypresses: gardens so beautiful that they retained their reputation as a byword for lovely pleasances down to the nineteenth-century when the Romantic poets – Goethe and Schiller in Germany; Shelley, Keats and Tennyson in England; and later in the early twentieth century the modernist poet Rilke – indued their verse with the scent of the roses and sound of the songs of nightingales echoing through Shīrāz's meadows and gardens. Its large parks, fountains and gardens, imposing palaces, pleasances and promenades, gracious brothels (*bayt al-luṭf*) and many taverns (*kharābāt*) were all celebrated by all its great Persian poets. Ḥāfiẓ sang:

> What delight Shīrāz is! How peerless
> Her site and circumstance. Do not let her,
> O God, decline and fall from grace.
>
> ... Come to Shīrāz, entreat for grace
> Of the *Spiritus Dei* from her men
> Of letters there, versed in the sciences.[17]

And yet, while Ḥāfiẓ did mention the city of Shīrāz and its human and natural beauties frequently in his poetry, the poet's 'real' world lay elsewhere: this terrestrial topography was but a pretext to celebrate and an allegory to catechize his reader about the wonders of Love's metropolis. Ḥāfiẓ's real habitation was the *Cité de l'amour*, of which he claimed to be an eternal denizen, his beloved Shīrāz but its temporal place and local habitation on earth.[18] Ḥāfiẓ's eleven references to the city of Shīrāz in his *Dīvān*, far from being literal descriptions of its local place and habitation, as much depict the topography of the *mundus imaginalis* of this cosmopolis of *Eros* as figure as actual references to the city's bordellos, pleasances, gardens and taverns. These references are not simply to a fun-loving 'city full of love and erotic pleasures', as certain historians' imaginations fancifully project,[19] for in nearly all these references words such as 'love' (*'ishq*) or beauty (*ḥusn*) hover amid the surrounding lines, encasing, in some cases replacing, the city's physical geography with Love's supra-terrestrial utopia and ambience.[20] This romanticization of urban centres was an integral aesthetic dimension of the Persian love-lyric – *ghazal* – itself, found in many major classical Persian poets.[21] Thus, Khāqānī vaunted 'Here and in Damascus is the scale of Love [*dimashq-i 'āshiqī*]. Of Damascus cease to boast for love's a scale without need of gold',[22] and Rūmī celebrated the 'Damascus of Love' (*dimashq-i 'ishq*),[23] and Kamāl Khujandī boasted that Tabrīz is 'but half a league' away from Paradise,[24] just as 'Ubayd Zākānī, praising Shīrāz during the 1340s, extolled how 'By the fortune of the justice of the king [Abu Isḥāq Īnjū, reg. 743/1342–753/ 1353] who cares for the poor, the environs of Shīrāz are paradise on earth'.[25] Similarly, in Ḥāfiẓ's lyrics his physical birthplace melded into a metaphysical paradise of love:

> Shīrāz is a treasury of ruby lips, a quarry of beauty.
> Bankrupt jeweller that I am, it all makes me uneasy.
> So many drunken eyes I've seen, by God, in this town,
> I'm so filled with cheer that I've abandoned wine.
> The town abounds with coy coquettes in each of the six
> Directions – I'm broke, else I'd buy all six.[26]

Shīrāz inspires love in him; love inspires him to praise Shīrāz. 'The woes of Love are all but one single tale, yet how strange it is that everyone who tells it makes it sound so novel!', he says in one verse, before immediately in the next vaunting the beauty of Shīrāz, reminding the reader: 'Do not fault Shīrāz nor its delicious Rukhni waters and sweet breeze – This city is the beauty-spot of all the seven climes.'[27] In this fashion, the earthly metaphor of the heavenly city of Shīrāz, the temporal cynosure on the earth's surface of eternal Paradise, for Ḥāfiẓ came to illustrate the timeless story of his love:

> Our towns are copied fragments from our breast;
> And all man's Babylons strive but to impart
> The grandeurs of his Babylonian heart.

Shīrāz and the Galaxy of Fourteenth-Century Persian Poetry

To enter imaginatively into Ḥāfiẓ's times, we must examine in brief some of the literary figures and historical factors that gave shape and reality to this grand vision of *Eros*. The literary and philosophical thought of Ḥāfiẓ cannot be understood without comprehending something of the high culture of Persia, its monumental intellectual achievements, literary, theological and philosophical, as well as the local society of Shīrāz and contemporary politics of the province of Fars.

The poetic cosmos of fourteenth-century Persia blazed with some of the brightest luminaries in Persian poetic history, whose ideas Ḥāfiẓ absorbed and emulated, and whose verse he followed and imitated. As a poet, Ḥāfiẓ was a genius of transformative appropriation, supreme connoisseur of verse-aphorisms and epigrams, who specialized in selecting the choicest verses from the past masters of Persian and Arabic poetry, transcreating their imagery, improvising and improving on their ideas in his own original manner. Hardly a verse of Ḥāfiẓ can be found whose sound, form, colour or sense does not hark back to similar lines in the works of 'Umar Khayyām (d. 526/1131), Sanā'ī (d. c. 535/1140), Khāqānī (d. 595/1198), Niẓāmī (d. 598/1202), Ẓahīr Faryābī (d. 598/1202), 'Aṭṭār of Nīshāpūr (d. 618/1221), Kamāl al-Dīn Ismā'īl Iṣfahānī (d. 635/1237), Sa'dī (d. c. 691/1292), Jalāl al-Dīn Rūmī (d. 672/1273), Fakhr al-Dīn 'Irāqī (d. 688/1289), Nizārī Quhistānī (d. 721/1321), Awḥadī Marāghī (d. 738/1338), or other of the grand master poets of classical Persia.[28] His verse is also steeped in the poetry of Ibn Fāriḍ (d. 632/1235), the greatest Arab Sufi poet.[29]

Foremost among the poets of his own day whom Ḥāfiẓ respected, knew intimately and emulated was Khwājū Kirmānī (d. after 753/1352), a Sufi poet who lived in Shīrāz during much of his lifetime where he was a disciple of Amīn al-Dīn Kāzarūnī Balyānī, a Sufi master distinguished enough to be praised by Ḥāfiẓ in his poetry.[30] The spiritualized eroticism of Ḥāfiẓ, who 'is perhaps the first poet in the Persian-speaking world who perfectly realized the unity of the mundane and the spiritual sphere',[31] was largely indebted to Khwājū's ideas. In the erotic *mathnawī* verse of Khwājū, one finds explicit imagery of sexual union, intimate descriptions of carnal intercourse of the female beloved with her male lover. In Khwājū's *Mathnawī-yi Gul va Nawrūz*, for instance, the love-making of Nawrūz with Gul is described in meticulous detail. The lover and his mistress are likened to a single heart (*dil*), one of them composed of the first letter of the word (*Dal*) and the other its second letter (*Lam*), the two letters which make up the word for heart in Persian. One is described as wine, and the other as honey, so that 'before them lay the wine and honey. In their palms were dates and in their mouths sugar. Night and day they were transported beyond this realm of dust, unaware of the whirling spheres of heaven.'[32] In such verse, the erotic becomes the metaphysical, the sentient sexual made equivalent to the transcendental suprasensual. An identical sublimation of the Erotic into the Sacred and sacralization of sexual pleasure is also found in Ḥāfiẓ's verse. In Khwājū, as in Ḥāfiẓ, one finds the Dantesque, and later Petrachean, notion that there is more religion in the throes of earthly passion, though misdirected, than in the platitudes of holy beautitudes hymned by rote for heaven's sake, as Shelley expressed it so perfectly in his poem *Amor Aeternus*:

Wealth and dominion fade into the mass
  Of the great sea of human right and wrong,
When once from our possession they must pass;
  But love, though misdirected, is among
The things which are immortal, and surpass
  All that frail stuff, which will be or – which was.

Ḥāfiẓ apparently followed Khwājū's poetic style and views closely.[33] During the years Khwājū spent in Shīrāz they were close friends[34] and we find numerous *ghazals* in which Ḥāfiẓ responded to the Kirmānī poet's verse, and there is even a famous verse attesting to his fondness for Khwājū:

All agree that Sa'dī is the master of ghazal
But Ḥāfiẓ follows Khwājū's genre for style.[35]

As we see, there existed an all-pervasive tradition of eroticism, both metaphysical and physical, in the verse of at least one contemporary poet whom Ḥāfiẓ explicitly admired. Ḥāfiẓ not only voices his admiration of Khwājū's rhetorical prowess in the art of verse, but pays homage to the Kirmānī poet's iconoclastic spiritual vision: his lauding of infidelity as being superior to public displays of pharisaic ascetical piety, his declaration that lovers do not follow the conventional ways of orthodox religious piety and abstinence, his pursuit of notoriety and glorification of blame in the *malāmatī* tradition, and praise of selflessness as constituting the essence of the spiritual path – Sufi doctrines that are also of central significance in Ḥāfiẓ's anti-clerical erotic spirituality.[36]

The most important contemporary master lyrical poet was Salmān Sāvajī (d. 778/1376), who resided in Tabriz, the other major cultural capital city of Persia during this period. Salmān was 'the most frequently imitated poet of his own age'.[37] The great Kubrāwī Sufi Shaykh 'Alā' al-Dawla Simnānī (659/1261–736/1326) uttered no hyperbole at all when he asserted that 'the like of Simnām's pomegranates and Salmān's poems cannot be found anywhere'.[38] Even today, scholars judge Salmān to be 'one of the supreme Persian poets of his period: his *ghazal*s, after those of Sa'dī, Rūmī, and Ḥāfiẓ, fall into the first-class category'.[39] Salmān's *ghazal*s sometimes parallel those of Ḥāfiẓ so closely that it is clear that they both imitated and copied each other's poetry,[40] and in one line, where Ḥāfiẓ boasts that his own poetic abilities excel both Salmān and Khwājū, it is clear that Salmān was one of his touchstones of poetic excellence.[41]

Beside these superficial commonalities of rhetoric and image, rhyme and metre shared between them, and aside from – and even more important than – this respectful literary rivalry, Salmān and Ḥāfiẓ were both inspired by the same radical Religion of Love. *Eros* is the main concern of their verse, as Salmān boldly declares:

> I have no job but love. To play the lover's part to me
> Is creed and faith. Each man follows some sect and faith
> Which is his own. Of what concern to you is Salman's faith?[42]

Eschewing the pedestrian conventions of 'Muslim' exoteric piety just like Ḥāfiẓ, Salmān vaunts being a heretic on the Path of Love, glorifying his pursuit of 'blame' and 'ill-fame' in *ghazal* after *ghazal*:

> If being a Muslim lies in not adoring mortal beauty
> And renouncing wine, well I for one declare myself
> A lifetime heretic – if ever once I was a Muslim!
> The best path in love is blackening one's name, Salmān
> Take it from me: my life is spent in pursuit of ill-fame.[43]

The Religion of Love only obtains probity and righteousness through ill-fame. Piety on the Path of Love is realized by being tainted with reproach and affliction with the stigma of public rebuke. In respect to this world's wiles and ways the lover is always unwise – he is a fool. The lover's pursuit of shame and notoriety is poles apart from the ascetic's reasonable piety and calculated self-serving unctuous moral rectitude, for as Ḥilālī says in a verse:

> Abandon all shame and good name in the lane
> Where love's game is played, for the inspired
> Libertine's art does not sit well with holy piety.[44]

Another first-class Persian *ghazal* poet, the Sufi Kamāl Khujandī (d. 803/1400), was like Salmān also based in Tabriz and shared his ethos of love. All three were well acquainted with one another's poetry and belonged 'to a common literary culture, despite never meeting face to face'.[45] Kamāl wrote about twice as many *ghazal*s as Ḥāfiẓ, about a fifth of which, in my opinion, rank equal in accomplishment with the Shīrāzī master. Kamāl's many parallelisms in verse to Ḥāfiẓ's poems[46] are as important to Persian literary history as those of Salmān. He had lambasted Ḥāfiẓ in a *ghazal* written in reply (*javāb*) as a parallel poem (*naẓīra*) in the same metre and rhyme as one by Ḥāfiẓ, boasting: 'Although Ḥāfiẓ might be a rakish courtier serving Sulṭān Abū'l-Favāris,[47] in the stylistics of the *ghazal* he never matched the genius of Kamāl.'[48] Despite such literary rivalry, relations between the two poets was characterized overall by cordial and fraternal exchanges.[49]

As with Salmān, the unconventional Religion of Love in 'which repute and good name are not allowed', as Kamāl says (echoing Ḥāfiẓ's many similar statements to this effect[50]), is the most oft-repeated refrain throughout his poetry. The glorification of ill-fame and the vaunting of notoriety was in fact one of the central topoi of the anti-clerical repertoire and literary counter-culture that both poets shared in common:

> Neither of shame am I worried, nor of name take heed:
> For in my creed, repute and good name are not allowed.[51]

Kamāl also extols the 'Canon-Law of Love' (*sharī'at-i 'ishq*), praising and preaching the contemplation of beautiful faces as an act of religious devotion:

> Do not cover your face from those who'd gaze on it
> For in the Canon Law of *Amor*, judges say it is
> Allowed to contemplate the faces of the fair.[52]

Exactly the same erotic doctrine, which grants the lover permission to gaze upon his beloved's face,[53] runs through Sa'dī's poems[54] and fills all of Ḥāfiẓ's *ghazal*s as well.

Another major Persian poet contemporary with Ḥāfiẓ was 'Imād al-Dīn Faqīh Kirmānī (d. 773/1371), one of the most eminent Sufis of his age, whose *ghazal*s were mostly composed during Sufi séances in the *khānaqāh* that he directed in Kirmān.[55] Later Persian hagiographers have seasoned 'Imād's biography with various legends about Ḥāfiẓ's rivalry with him, which have recently been contested and shown to be spurious.[56] The parallelisms between the two poets' *ghazal*s are in fact so numerous that it's clear that his younger contemporary Ḥāfiẓ admired his verse and imitated him frequently.[57]

All in all, Ḥāfiẓ, Khwājū, Salmān, Kamāl Khujandī and 'Imād al-Dīn Faqīh are stars sparkling within a single literary galaxy of geniuses in fourteenth-century Persia. Their penchant for Sufi symbolism, sharing of the same poetic rhymes, metres, images and ideas (especially their use of the same bacchanalian imagery), not to mention theoerotic sensibility, poetic vision, mystical persuasion and metaphysical thought, exhibit an overall concordance.[58]

Belonging to the next generation, but evidently well known to Ḥāfiẓ, was Shāh Ni'matullāh Walī (d. 835/1431), the greatest Sufi master of the Timurid period. Ḥāfiẓ apparently had scant personal regard for him, responding to one of his *ghazals* in such a manner as to expose his profound difference of opinion in respect to the former's spiritual claims. So while some 'correspondence' between the two poets did exist, it hardly transcended the superficial literary level.[59] While Shāh Ni'matullāh and Ḥāfiẓ were discordant in their spiritual sensibilities despite an occasional superficial concordance of poetic rhyme, Shāh Ni'matullāh's foremost disciple, the great Tabrīzī Sufi poet Shāh Qāsim Anvār (d. 838/1434), venerated the poetry of Ḥāfiẓ and professed in his verse the same universal Religion of Love found in the *Dīvāns* of Ḥāfiẓ, Khwājū, Salmān, 'Imād and Kamāl. These following oft-cited verse gives a taste of Shāh Qāsim's transcendental love mysticism:

In pagoda and mosque, in Ka'ba and tavern,
The God of Love is the sole aim
And all the rest are just moonshine.[60]

Qāsim's line was directly patterned on the following verse from a *ghazal* composed by Ḥāfiẓ in the same metre and rhyme:

All three are one: the boon-companion,
The musician and the Saki, and what's betwixt
Them – this earthen and watery veil – is just a pretext.[61]

The major – perhaps the most unusual – poet contemporary with Ḥāfiẓ in Shīrāz was the extraordinary social satirist and master parodist 'Ubayd-i Zākānī (d. 772/1371).[62] A serious court poet known for his mellifluous bachanalian *ghazals* in the style of Sa'dī, 'Ubayd was the author of *qaṣīdas* in praise of Abū Isḥāq Īnjū and Shāh Shujā' and other local rulers.[63] Times and tastes change. Today he is regaled as classical Persia's chief pornographer both in prose and verse. Due to its distinctly Adult XXX content, his bold and fantastical sexually explicit verse (and prose), which many traditional scholars continue to denigrate as 'worthless',[64] of course remains unprintable in Iran's would-be Islamic Republic.[65] Throughout 'Ubayd' prose and verse the same rabidly anti-clerical sentiments present in Ḥāfiẓ frequently appear – as when he declares himself the foe of 'preachers with chilly breath', and the enemy of 'hypocritical Sufi shaykhs'.[66] 'Ubayd's caustic, sarcastic style, his courting of notoriety and ill-fame (*bad-nāmī*)[67] – his parodying of hypocritical Muslim clerics, lampooning of fake Sufis and spoofs on proud ascetics – are replicated exactly in Ḥāfiẓ's poems.[68] Although these refined caricatures of religious hypocrites did have an influence on Ḥāfiẓ, who was his junior,[69] his bawdy satires on the society of medieval Shīrāz were not by any means, as some scholars assert,[70] the chief inspiration underlying Ḥāfiẓ's doctrine of inspired libertinism or *rindī* (see below: Prolegomenon II, p. 31–55). In 'Ubayd's lyrics, which largely follow Sa'dī's style, the perplexing ethical and profound theological depths, amazing spiritual transports and the bewilderingly complex mystical allusiveness that fill Ḥāfiẓ's verse are completely absent. Both poets were indeed ardent social reformists, but in his use of satire and parody the discourse and voice of Ḥāfiẓ never descends to the facetious and libellous level that 'Ubayd almost always inhabits.[71] The intellectual fraternity between the two Shīrāzī poets was a product of shared social not of common spiritual attitudes, and lay, as Mu'īn rightly states, 'in their mutual opposition to hypocrisy, the irrepressibility of their poetic natures, and their fully developed penchant for pleasantry and jesting'.[72]

A host of lesser-known poets also flourished alongside Ḥāfiẓ in Shīrāz, whose poetic voices, moods and images all find resonances of their own in his verse. These include the likes of Princess Jahān-Malik Khātūn (d. after 795/1393), the greatest female poet of medieval Iran, who composed 'the largest known *dīvān* to have survived from any woman poet of pre-modern Iran',[73] and Bushāq Aṭ'amah-i Shīrāzī (d. 827/1423 or 830/1427), the supreme comic (and only culinary) poet in Persian literature, whose entire oeuvre consisted of lyrical lampoons on other poets using exclusively the imagery of food and eating. Most of Bushāq's *ghazal*s were deliberate parodies (*taqīḍa*) of Ḥāfiẓ and other contemporary poets, such as Shāh Ni'matu'llāh.[74]

The above overview of some of the major and minor poets contemporary with Ḥāfiẓ in fourteenth-century Persia only gives a very superficial indication of the immense richness of the Persian poetic tradition in which he was steeped. Scholars have long known the fact that many of Ḥāfiẓ's lyrics were composed in imitation of the metrical and rhyming schemes of previous *ghazal* writers in a time-honoured tradition. The entire *Dīvān-i Ḥāfiẓ* constitutes an intratextual commentary on the lyrical tradition present in Persia since the eleventh century, which is why in many editions of Ḥāfiẓ's *Dīvān* several pages of introduction are devoted to tracing the verses that he appropriated from previous poets, then recast and reused in his own poetry, a phenomenon which has been the subject of a number of long scholarly essays.[75]

Connoisseurship of Poetry in the Age of Ḥāfiẓ

The audience who listened to the recitation of Ḥāfiẓ's *ghazal*s were some of the most formidably educated and exactingly cultured men that Persians have ever been. When he recited or sung his poems – and 'Ḥāfiẓ' today is still a term used for a singer and bard[76] – to this intellectual nobility, he knew quite well that they were all supreme connoisseurs of verse. Many of his listeners were poets themselves who would have known by heart many *ghazal*s by his famous forebears ('Aṭṭār, Rūmī, 'Irāqī, Sa'dī...) and illustrious contemporaries (Salmān, Khwājū, Kamāl Khujandī...). In catering to that elite, supersophisticated circle of specialists, Ḥāfiẓ's success lay in how skilfully he could paraphrase, imitate, reply to and so hopefully excel those poets by his original manipulation of the same raw materials – images, symbols, ideas, metres and rhymes – that they had employed. Most of the *ghazals* and *qaṣīdas* written in the Age of Ḥāfiẓ were composed within this grand intertextual tradition of classical Persian poetry, in which the 'modern' poets would attempt to outdo 'classical' poets by 'replying to' (*javāb-gū'ī*), or 'welcoming' (*istiqbāl*) or 'following' (*tatabbu'*) their poems.[77] Verse-collecting, memorization of classical poetry was, has been, and probably always will be the chief natural cultural obsession in Persianate societies.[78] This craze certainly characterized Timurid Iran.[79] No matter how provincial their courts, nearly all of the Timurid princes in Mongol and Timurid Iran composed *Dīvāns* of poetry. Those who did not themselves versify were good connoisseurs of verse, and the Timurid period 'was not only full of poets, artists and scholars, but should be accounted in some respects as one of the most glorious periods of science and art'.[80] In Ḥāfiẓ's day all the Timurid princes vyed with one another in attracting would-be poet-laureates to their courts.[81] Unless the pitch and splendour of Ḥāfiẓ's lines could transcend the fortissimo eloquence of the likes of Sa'dī and Kamāl, unless he could articulate with greater epigrammatic precision and express in ways more fierce and overreaching the esoteric vision and spiritual values of Sufi poets such as 'Aṭṭār and Khwājū, the faculties of eyes and ears of these expert connoisseurs would cease to be amazed and he would suffer loss of princely patronage. Of course, this never happened to Ḥāfiẓ. Quite the opposite in fact, as he boasts:

> Once Love became my tutor in the art
> Of fine speech, all my words became
> Key postulates of debate in every coterie.[82]

If by basking in the luminescence of this resplendent firmament of Persian poets, Ḥāfiẓ's verse was indeed indued with lustre, the scintilla of their starry rhyme and verse has since largely been eclipsed by the Venusian fireball of his own *Dīvān*. In fact, not only is Ḥāfiẓ today considered to be the fairest of stars, last in the train of night in that heavenly company, he inhabits a sphere of his own before whom all other poets – those who wrote in the *ghazal* genre at least – sit mantled like chandeliers drowned in floodlighting.[83] In Shīrāz's citadel of saints he ranks as the greatest poet – save perhaps Sa'dī.[84] Ḥāfiẓ is not only the supreme Persian poet of the fourteenth century, but above and beyond that, as one scholar recently put it, he has come to be considered as the veritable 'spokesman of the Collective Unconscious of the entire Persian race...'[85]:

> After Firdawsī and Rūmī, Ḥāfiẓ is our third national poet. Whereas our *national heroic poem* epitomizing the mythological history of the Persians can be found in Firdawsī's *Book of Kings*, and Rūmī's *Mathnawī* and *Dīvān-i Kabīr* [*Shams*] represent the *national poetic chronicle of the Persian Sufi tradition*, Ḥāfiẓ's *Dīvān*

constitutes Persia's *national lyrical epic*, expressive of the Persian people's refined wit, beauty, satire, joy and struggle for social reformation.[86]

Collation and Commentaries on the Dīvān *Beyond Persia's Borders*

It wasn't until a little over a century following his death that Ḥāfiẓ's *Dīvān* underwent a critical compilation[87] under the tutelage of Prince Farīdun, b. Ḥusayn Bayqarā (d. 915/1509), who collected over 500 manuscripts scattered across cities throughout Islamdom at his court and ordered the formal collation of the *Dīvān*, which has since been passed down in the alphabetical form (arranged by end-rhyme) known to us today.[88] In one of the manuscripts from this collection written by a scribe named Shihāb al-Dīn 'Abdu'llāh Murvārīd, we find the epithet 'Tongue of the Invisible' (*Lisān al-ghayb*) attached to the poet's name for the first time.[89]

The first compiler of the *Dīvān* was a friend of Ḥāfiẓ who lived in Shīrāz under the reign of Sulṭān Abū'l-Fatḥ Ibrāhīm (reg. 817–38/1414–34), named Muḥammad Gulandām.[90] In his short introduction to this compilation, in one of the few utterly authentic historical accounts of the poet, Gulandām informs that Ḥāfiẓ's verse was internationally celebrated during his lifetime:[91]

> It took but a very short time for the literary empire over which his *ghazals* reigned to stretch from the outermost borders of Khurāsān up into Turkistān and down into India. It took but a brief instant for the convoys of his enchanting speech to reach the outskirts of the lands of Iraq and Azerbayjan. The musical séances of the Sufis [*samā'-i ṣūfiyān*] without his passionate poems soon came to lack warmth; likewise, unless graced by his tasteful speech the convivial banquets of kings were devoid of all relish, savour and enjoyment.[92]

From Gulandām's assertion it is clear that there is as much truth as hyperbole in Ḥāfiẓ's boasts:

> This itinerant Persian verse
>   sent errant on Bengal ways
> is delicious and rich enough
>   for Indian parrots to crunch
>   its luscious, sugary chunks.[93]

Or:

> Those Samarqandī Turks
>   and black-eyed girls of Kashmir
> All dance and flaunt their charms
>   to Ḥāfiẓ of Shīrāz's verse.[94]

If his poetry was legendary during his own lifetime, after his death the interpretative tradition of the Ḥāfiẓian heritage expanded vastly, mostly preserved outside the lands of Greater Persia, particularly in Ottoman Turkey[95] and Mughal India, where the most important and largest amount of commentaries on his *Dīvān* were written. The best known of these are the mystical commentaries in Turkish by Surūrī (d. 969/1561) and Sham'ī (d. 1000/1591). There was also the sober literary and grammatical commentary by Sūdī of Bosnia (d. 1006/1597) that was composed in Istanbul,[96] which formed the basis for most European interpretation of the poet.[97] But it says a lot about the still underdeveloped state of Ḥāfiẓ Studies today that while far more commentaries on the *Dīvān* were written in India than in Iran, Central Asia or Turkey, not a single one of these Indian commentaries has to date been published.[98] An exception to this rule is 'the clearest, best and most revealing of all ancient and modern commentaries in solving the difficulties in Ḥāfiẓ's poetry';[99] that is, the commentary on Ḥāfiẓ's *Dīvān* written in India circa 1026/1617 by Abū'l-Ḥasan 'Abd al-Raḥmān Khatmī Lāhūrī, only first edited and published in 1995. For fathoming the theosophical background and mystical subtleties of Ḥāfiẓ's esoteric language and theory of love, Lāhūrī's monumental work (over 4,000 pages of small print) is comparable in its significance to Muḥammad Lāhījī's (d. 912/1507) inimitable Persian commentary on Shabistarī's *Gulshan-i rāz*[100] or Ismā'īl Anqaravī's (d. 1041/1631) grand Turkish exegesis of Rūmī's *Mathnawī*.[101]

While the oldest Ḥāfiẓ manuscripts were preserved in the fifteenth-century courts of Timurid Persia and Central Asia and amongst the Mughals in India, the earliest printed edition of Ḥāfiẓ's *Dīvān* appeared under the imprint of the East India Company in Calcutta in 1791. Over the course of the nineteenth century several more editions were published in India.[102] Lithograph editions of Ḥāfiẓ began to appear in Persia during the mid-nineteenth century, but it was not until 1941 that the first major critical edition of Ḥāfiẓ's *Dīvān* (compiled by Muḥammad Qazvīnī and Qāsim Ghanī) was published, followed by a plethora of other scholarly editions. Seven or eight quite reputable scholarly editions today can be bought.[103] One of the best of these, to which most of the contributors to this volume have referred, is that compiled by Parvīz Nātil Khānlarī, containing 486 *ghazals*. Despite certain shortcomings,[104] Khānlarī's work remains still one of the best critical editions in print,[105] and recently has been used as the basis for translations of the entire *Dīvān* into French (by Charles de Fouchécour) and English (by Peter Avery).

Not once during the past 600 years has Ḥāfiẓ's *Dīvān* been off the top-ten Persian 'best-seller' list. Today, no self-respecting Afghan or Persian's personal library shelf lacks a copy of Ḥāfiẓ's *Dīvān*.[106] Universities in Iran have recently inaugurated a separate subfield of Persian literary criticism, known as 'Ḥāfiẓology' (*Ḥāfiẓ-shināsī*).[107] Modernist intellectuals, progressive Sufis and philosophers foolhardy enough to attempt to criticize Ḥāfiẓ from the standpoint of his morality, or mysticism, or politics, or poetry, or religion, or philosophy, or whatever, always seem to end up wringing their hands in remorse as they watch their clever carping immediately result in the plummeting of their own reputations. Inevitably, before the undying cult of Ḥāfiẓ's popularity, all other poets' names crouch in the shadow.[108] It would seem that due to the exceptionally high calibre of his poetry, the wise in heart only confirm their own folly and mediocrity by daring to quibble with his pronouncements:[109]

> You writers who write such bad poems, why
> Do you envy Ḥāfiẓ so much? His grace of speech
> That people love comes entirely from God.[110]

Beyond this undisputable conquest of his readers' heart and minds, what is perhaps even remarkable is that even though Ḥāfiẓ belongs squarely within the classical tradition of medieval Persian literature, to date no 'modern' poet has managed to compose poetry more *avant-garde* than his verse, nor even faintly rival his popularity in the marketplace of *belles lettres*.[111] As Khurramshāhī so aptly put it:

> On the one hand, Ḥāfiẓ appropriated for himself the quintessence of previous classical Arabic and Persian poetry and, on the other hand, he laid the weightiest burden of obligation upon all later Persian poetry. Even though today we have come along and totally changed the style and form of poetry, our modernist Persian poetry still remains all deeply affected by and in debt to Ḥāfiẓ. For instance, the 'Indian Style' [*sabk-i hindī*] of writing poetry is clearly visible in modernist poetry but in a slightly less glaring manner, as can be seen in the poems of modernist masters such as Amīrī Fīrūzkūhī [d. 1363/1984] and Shahriyār [d. 1367/1988], Nūdhar Parang [d. 1385/2006] and Sīyih – and yet all of them write in the style of Ḥāfiẓ.[112] ... I sometimes think that the world of the poetry of modernist poets such as Suhrāb Sihpihrī [d. 1359/1980] and Furūkh Farrukhzād [d. 1345/1966] is not any more intimate and near to us than the world of Ḥāfiẓ. The reason for this is that Ḥāfiẓ is concerned with *supraliterary* issues of enduring relevance, which are neither exotic, hackneyed clichés, nor expressed in a language alien to the contemporary mind.[113]

While the amount of studies devoted to Ḥāfiẓ's *ghazal*s printed in Persian annually is only about a tenth of the amount of scholarship produced on Shakespeare's sonnets each year,[114] it is certainly blossoming. In the late 1990s a Centre for Ḥāfiẓ Studies in Shīrāz (*Markaz-i Ḥāfiẓ-shināsī*), currently publishing its own *Ḥāfiẓ Research Review* (*Ḥāfiẓ-pazūhishī*), was launched.[115] Ḥāfiẓ bibliographies,[116] dictionaries, treasuries of his poetic terminology, learned articles on him in Persian specialist literary journals, not to mention countless monographs on Ḥāfiẓ and music,[117] Ḥāfiẓ and astrology, Ḥāfiẓ and philosophy... appear in print on an annual basis in Persian-speaking lands. For the Shīrāzī sage, the season's difference and the penalty of man is never felt in any time or place. And the reason for this lies in the *Ḥāfiẓocentric* nature of classical Persianate civilization.

The Ḥāfiẓocentricism of Persianate Civilization, and the Qur'ān

Scholars such as Louis Massignon and Paul Nywia have demonstrated how the religious conscience of Islam as well as its two main liturgical languages – Arabic and Persian – has been nurtured and shaped by the Qur'ān.[118] Although it is well known that it was customary in all medieval Islamic societies for children first to memorize the Qur'ān before pursuing other studies, students of Islam must here be reminded of a lesser-known but equally important literary truth, namely that all the Persianate civilizations of Islamdom (Ottoman Turkey, Safavid and Qajar Persia, Timurid Central Asia and Mughal India...) have for the past five centuries been 'Ḥāfiẓocentric' as well.[119] Up to the 1950s, Muslim children in Iran and Afghanistan and India were taught first to memorize the Qur'ān, and secondly to commit the poetry of Ḥāfiẓ to heart, thus absorbing in their grammar-school curriculum the sacred and revealed book of Islam alongside the verses of the inspired 'Tongue of the Invisible'. From Istanbul to Lahore, from the Persian Gulf to thithermost Transoxiania, for some five centuries *the* 'Book' of Islam – the Qur'ān – has in this fashion shared pride of place beside Ḥāfiẓ's *Dīvān*, a situation comparable to that which prevailed between the Bible and the plays of Shakespeare during the early seventeenth to the late nineteenth centuries in England and the United States.[120] Perhaps for this reason it is that, after the Qur'ān, the *Dīvān* of Ḥāfiẓ has been canonized as chief among three books of poetry used in Persianate societies for the purposes of divination (*tafā'ul*).[121]

'Ḥāfiẓ', *nom de plume* of Shams al-Dīn Muḥammad of Shīrāz, literally denotes one who is a 'Memorizer of the Qur'ān'. To speak of 'Ḥāfiẓ' is necessarily to speak of the Qur'ān,[122] and that he knew the sacred scripture by heart is apparent from a number of verses, for example:

> I swear, Ḥāfiẓ, by that Qur'ān you have by heart,
> I've found no poetry that's as sweet as yours.[123]

This testimony that his own poetry was intricately connected with his own absorption and reading and recitation of the Holy Scripture[124] is borne out by several other verses, where it is apparent that Ḥāfiẓ engaged in the contemplative discipline[125] of recitation of the Qur'ān at night:

> Oh Ḥāfiẓ in the darkness of poverty and in
> The solitude of the night, as long as you can sing
> And study the Qur'ān, do not sink into sadness.[126]

Ḥāfiẓ's teacher Qiwām al-Dīn 'Abdu'llāh,[127] who excelled in all fields of Islamic knowledge that were current in the age, typically would hold his classes in theology during the last third of the night, and at dawntide begin his lessons in the Qur'ān.[128] Ḥāfiẓ speaks of these midnight-to-dawn sessions of study in many verses:

To rise at dawn and seek what's sound
And wholesome as Ḥāfiẓ has done –
All I've done has come from the grace
And *embras de richesse* of the Qur'ān.[129]

Other verses of the *Dīvān* testify to Ḥāfiẓ's breadth of erudition in a variety of interpretations of Qur'ānic passages, particularly his understanding of the science of esoteric commentary on the Qur'ān.[130] Writing about a century after his death, Dawlatshāh claimed that 'Ḥāfiẓ had no peer in Qur'ānology. In both the esoteric and exoteric sciences he was a treasury of spiritual truths and mysteries.'[131] Perhaps the most famous of Ḥāfiẓ's statements about the Qur'ān, which contrasts his inspired breviary of mystical *Eros* with the formulary litany of Islam's sacred scripture, is this verse:

Eros come to your rescue, even if you,
Like Ḥāfiẓ, can chant the Qur'ān by heart
In all its fourteen different lections.[132]

Taking a cue from this verse, a contemporary Ḥāfiẓ scholar entitled a collection of his essays on the poet 'The Fourteen Lections'.[133] The term 'fourteen different lections' encompasses some 1,100 or so instances, whether minor or major, in the Qur'ān, which can generate different readings of particular verses.[134] These variant lections (called *Qirā'a* in Arabic) were based on textual variants promulgated by the seven earliest recognized 'readers' of the second/eighth century, above and beyond the recension of the Qur'ān made by the Caliph 'Uthmān in 30/650, which was the first codified 'orthodox' text of the Muslim scripture; to these were later added seven other 'readers', from whence the expression the 'fourteen lections' arose.[135] By placing a vowel sign or a dot over or under an Arabic letter in a different place, significant variations in the reading and understanding of such passages occur. In this verse, Ḥāfiẓ thus announces his erudition in being able to recite by heart all the textual variants – both in sense and recitation, fourteen in all – and the different possible readings which the consonantal Arabic text of the Qur'ān in diverse instances affords. His extraordinary powers of memorization, even rare among skilled theologians specializing in Qur'ān studies, no doubt would have caused his contemporaries to marvel.[136]

His absorption in Islam's holy scripture is also repeated in the preface to the *Dīvān* composed by his friend Muḥammad Gulandām, who tells us that the poet devoted much of his free time to 'diligent study of the Qur'ān' and 'annotation of the *Kashshāf*'[137] – a fact to which Ḥāfiẓ attests in another verse:

No reciter of scripture who stands in the *miḥrāb*
Of the Firmament has ever enjoyed such delight
As I have received from the wealth of the Qur'ān.[138]

Just as scholars have spoken of the 'Qur'ānization of the memory' in Islamic intellectual traditions, a similar phenomenon appeared in late classical Persianate civilization. In lands where Persian is spoken the *Dīvān* of Ḥāfiẓ has for centuries been canonized as a miraculous scripture; few critics today would probably disagree with Jāmī's view in the *Bahāristān* that 'some of his poems are downright miraculous'.[139] Ḥāfiẓ possesses a quality that only a handful of sacred texts and scriptures – the sayings of Lao Tzu or the *I Ching* in this respect come to mind – possess, which is that the intellectual veracity of his verse transcends the century of its composition. For Persian-speakers, his poems remain a sort of trans-sectarian, atemporal sacred text, a hallowed scripture venerated by Muslims, Christians and Jews in Iran, Tajikistan, Afghanistan and all throughout Central Asia, and by Hindus, Sikhs and Buddhists in India, not to mention admired by atheists and secular nationalists everywhere. 'Setting the matter of religion to the side', pronounced Mu'īn, 'to Persian-speakers the words of Ḥāfiẓ are considered to be as hallowed as any heavenly scripture of lofty spiritual rank. His *Dīvān* is one of the important pillars of Persian language, which till Doomsday will remain everlastingly immune from ruin and decline.'[140]

Ḥāfiẓ's Life and Times

Next to nothing is known about Ḥāfiẓ's adolescence, education and family.[141] We know that Ḥāfiẓ came from a well-to-do family, since the epithet *Khwāja* (Esquire) attached to his name (Khwāja Shams al-Dīn Muḥammad Ḥāfiẓ) was reserved for members of the nobility and gentility.[142] Nonetheless, we know nothing of his family, or their origins; even the name of his father is unknown.[143] Nearly everything we do know about the poet has been largely construed by later hagiographical accounts or by modern scholars reading political references into his *Dīvān* by hindsight. 'The attempt to write a conventional modern biography of a medieval poet like Hafez or Ferdowsi, in the form of a *bildungsroman* constructed out of ascertainable facts', Khurramshahī underlines, 'is itself an anachronistic venture. Modern biographies of modern poets, based on myriads of external sources and first-hand accounts, or even their own diaries and letters, may deepen our understanding of their poems. But to reverse the process and attempt to conjure up biographical details by over-literal interpretation of highly polished and traditional medieval poems is to pursue a chimera.'[144] Aside from a few poems which mention some of the famous figures who lived during his lifetime, which permit one to estimate approximately their date of composition, the *Dīvān* does not really provide enough material to formulate a biography of the poet.[145]

From the references that exist in his *Dīvān* (as pointed out above) and his penname, it is clear that in addition to having the text of the Qur'ān by heart, he excelled in the sciences of Qur'ān commentary (*tafsīr*) and recitation (*talawwut*). Dāryūsh Āshūrī's intertextual study demonstrated beyond all doubt that Ḥāfiẓ's *ghazals* are replete with the imagery, ideas, religious mythology and Sufi terminology taken directly from Maybudī's grand Qur'ān commentary.[146] From the numerous references to his 'forty' years of study[147] and 'the porch and arch of seminary college' (*madrasa*) and 'the numbing hum empty chatter of debate',[148] we know that he specialized in theology when he was a student. The theological texts that he studied in the beginning of the fourteenth century, some of which are mentioned by Gulandām, were the supreme classics of the period.[149] Being a member of the guild of the 'men of learning' (*ahl-i 'ilm*), throughout his adult life the poet evidently received a regular government stipend (*waẓīfa*) for his teaching and other professorial duties.[150] As can be seen in certain *ghazals*, he was also steeped in the teachings of the 'Greatest Master' Muḥyī al-Dīn ibn al-'Arabī (d. 638/1240),[151] and he both imitated the poetry[152] and versified the ideas of the Akbarian treatises of his latter-day followers such as Fakhr al-Dīn 'Irāqī (d. 1273).[153]

An extant manuscript penned by him proves him to have been a fine calligrapher.[154] Shīrāz was full of world-famous professors of theology and masters of Sufism, many of whom Ḥāfiẓ no doubt would have studied under in the first half of the fourteenth century.[155] One of these was his own teacher Qiwām al-Dīn 'Abdu'llāh, renowned for his austere piety and stern opposition to rationalist philosophy.[156]

All the fond fantasies and speculations about the women in Ḥāfiẓ's life – wives, mistresses, girlfriends, harlots – spun in later centuries by the writers of historical romances known as *tadhkiras* ('memoirs' [of poets, scholars, Sufis...]) cannot be verified by any contemporary chronicle. No historical records contemporary to him survive that would furnish any details about the women and loves of his life.[157] Anyway, as was noted so long ago, 'such domestic particulars [are not] to be expected from Persian biographers in view of their reticence on all matrimonial matters',[158] although some eminent scholars still persist in asserting, for example, that the following line alludes in fact to his wife's death:

> That friend whose presence made my house
> Seem a faery kingdom – of all faults she was free,
> Herself of faery substance head to toe.[159]

Yet 'there is nothing in the poem to show that his wife is the person referred to', as Browne points out.[160] There are other lines in his *Dīvān* where he alludes apparently to the death of a son; other *ghazals* seem to indicate that he had several children.[161]

We are fortunate in having a preface to the *Dīvān*, the authenticity of which is accepted by scholars today,[162] written by a close personal friend of the poet named Muḥammad Gulandām, who admired and collected his poems when Ḥāfiẓ could not be bothered to do so. The poet's preoccupation with theology, as well as the intellectual milieu and princely circles in which he moved, are there depicted vividly:

However, diligent study of the *Qur'ān*, constant attendance to the King's business, the annotation of the *Kashshāf*[163] and the *Miṣbāḥ*,[164] the perusal of the *Maṭālī*,[165] and the *Miftāḥ*,[166] the acquisition of canons of literary criticism and the appreciation of Arabic poems prevented him from collecting his verses and odes, or editing and arranging his poems. The writer of these lines, this least of men, Muḥammad Gulandām, when he was attending the lectures of our Master, that most eminent teacher Qiwāmu'd-Dīn 'Abdu'llāh, used constantly and repeatedly to urge, in the course of conversation, that he [Ḥāfiẓ] should gather together all these rare gems in one concatenation and assemble all these lustrous pearls on one string, so that they might become a necklace of great price for his contemporaries or a girdle for the brides of his time. With this request, however, he was unable to comply, alleging lack of appreciation on the part of his contemporaries as an excuse, until he bade farewell to this life ... in A.H. 791 (A.D. 1389).[167]

Ḥāfiẓ in the Courtly Milieu of Shīrāz

As a result of a number of studies over the course of the twentieth century by scholars such as Qāsim Ghanī, Muḥammad Mu'īn, Roger Lescot, Hellmut Ritter and 'Abd al-Ḥusayn Zarrīnkūb on Ḥāfiẓ's relationship to the political elite and princes of Shīrāz,[168] individual verses and sometimes entire *ghazals* have now been identified (with various degrees of certainty) as having been penned as occasional lyrics – sometimes panegryrics – to princes or noblemen, or directly prompted by political events. Since so many works already exist in both Persian or European languages with excellent accounts of the little we know of Ḥāfiẓ's mundane life, this prosaic socio-political context of his verse shall not be my focus here, so only a short summary will be offered.

Literary historians agree that many of Ḥāfiẓ's poems were occasional verse, the provenance of which can probably be traced back to the political vicissitudes and fluctuating fortunes of the last prince of the Īnjū dynasty and the succeeding Muẓaffarid rulers of Shīrāz, whose names and reigns are as follows:

Īnjū'id Dynasty

1. Abū Isḥāq Īnjū (reg. 743/1343–753/1353)

Muẓaffarid Dynasty

2. Amīr Mubariz al-Dīn Muḥammad Muẓaffarī (reg. 754/1353–759/1357)
3. Shāh Shujā' Muẓaffarī (reg. 759/1358–786/1384)
4. Zayn al-'Ābidīn (son of Shāh Shujā') (reg. 786/1384–789/1387). Tīmūr visits Shīrāz in 789/1387 just before Zayn al-'Ābidīn is deposed

5. Shāh Yaḥyā's short six-month reign (in 789/1387)
6. Shāh Manṣūr b. Shāh Muẓaffarī (cousin of Shāh Shujā') (reg. 791/1388–795/1392)[169]

Abū Isḥāq Īnjū was recognized as a 'tolerant and artistically minded prince'[170] and a 'generous patron of poetry'.[171] Religious tolerance and patronage of the arts were the hallmarks of his rule.[172] From all over Persia, poets thronged at his court, sowing the seeds of their panegyrical praise in the receptive earth of his adulation-loving ears.[173] A poetaster himself, he was a good connoisseur of the many poets who sought fame and fortune at his court. These included the sharpest poetic wits of the age, such as Khwājū Kirmānī, who dedicated two of his *mathnawī* poems (*Kamāl-nāma* and *Rawḍāt al-anwār*), several *qaṣīdas* and a strophe poem (*tarkīb-band*) to him,[174] and 'Ubayd Zākānī, who composed several panegyrics in his praise.[175] Abū Isḥāq was also 'one of the most beloved of princes whom Ḥāfiẓ praised', to whom quite a few of Ḥāfiẓ's *ghazals* (as panegyrics) are explicitly addressed.[176] Ḥāfiẓ wrote a *qaṣīda* of 44 couplets in praise of Abū Isḥāq.[177] Some scholars speculate, for instance, that some of the verses from the following *ghazal* were composed to bewail the passing of Abū Isḥāq's convivial and pleasure-loving court and reign:

> Friendship and camaraderie in men have fled
> And can't be found in anyone. O what's happened
> To kith and friends? When did comradeship
> And fellowship conclude? Where has gone friendship?
> The *aqua vitae*'s turned foul, overcast and dun;
> The man in green whose coming was so blissful, gone;
> What's happened to the vernal wind and Aries' fan?[178]

Whatever its political background, whether or not this *ghazal* was composed by Ḥāfiẓ as a memento of Abū Isḥāq's benevolent reign during the five-year police state of Mubāriz al-Dīn Muẓaffarī, who was 'orthodox, harsh, and not inclined to spare human life'[179] – as Ghanī insists on arguing[180] – by reducing its inspiration down to the lowest common temporal denominator, dating its provenance by decade or by year, the actual *meaning* of the poem is not thereby greatly elucidated. In any case, scholars are far from united in agreeing about the political circumstances that occasioned any of Ḥāfiẓ's poems.[181]

Prove if one could that Prince X was the poet's 'beloved', one can certainly more commonsensically extrapolate the *meaning* of Ḥāfiẓ's lament in the above poem to be a kind of contrapuntal analogue in verse cast in the same mould as the Duke's quip in prose to Escalus in Shakespeare's *Measure for Measure*, that 'there is so great a fever on goodness that the dissolution of it must cure it. Novelty is only in request, and it is dangerous to be aged in any kind of course as it is virtuous to be constant in any undertaking. There is scarce truth enough alive to make societies secure, but security enough to make fellowships accursed. Much upon this riddle runs the wisdom of the world. This news is old enough, yet it is every day's news.'[182] Furthermore, if conquests of provinces, bequests of patrons and boons of princes be all put to one side, Ḥāfiẓ's plaint in this poem is situated squarely within the Sufi literary genre dedicated to expounding the topos of the 'unhappy decay of true Piety and the Immoralities of the Age we live in',[183] identical to highly similar sentiments expressed two centuries earlier by 'Aṭṭār in his *Memoir of the Saints*, for instance.[184] The entire *ghazal* is thus best understood, I think, as a complaint against the general decadence of the times, in exactly the same vein as W.B. Yeats' stanza:

> All neighbourly content and easy talk are gone,
> But there is no good complaining, for money's rant is on.
> He that's mounting up must on his neighbour mount,
> And we and all the Muses are things of no account.[185]

One of the main patrons of Ḥāfiẓ was Abū Isḥāq's multimillionaire vizier 'Imād al-Dīn Ḥasan ('Ḥajjī') Qiwām al-Dīn (d. 754/1353), whose extravagant convivial gatherings and generosity the poet celebrated. 'The green sea of heaven and the ship of the crescent moon' are all 'drowned in the beneficence of Ḥajjī Qawām', sang Ḥāfiẓ in one verse.[186] Although the historian Mīrkhwand definitively confirms that Ḥajjī Qawām was 'the object of praise (*mamdūḥ*) of Ḥāfiẓ Shīrāzī',[187] a close examination of the main *qaṣīda* that he devoted to this vizier[188] reveals that the main purpose of the ode lies elsewhere. Out of its 40 verses, only 12 (vv. 11–21, 37, 40) concern the vizier; the rest upbraid the poet's ancient foe: the pharisetical ascetic (v. 8), or are dedicated to his usual bacchanalian, pastoral and erotic themes. One verse (30) features Ḥāfiẓ's personal interpretation of Ḥallāj's drunken apotheositic utterance: 'I am God' – *Anā'l-Ḥaqq*. Any discerning critic can thus view the vizier's person as merely a stained glass window through which Ḥāfiẓ's own poetico-mystical teachings irradiated. This seems to be the gist of his boast at the end of the poem (vv. 36–7):

> Many there are who are *Ḥāfiẓ*, who preserve the holy book
> But none like me the world through who can collect
> The minutiae of philosophy with the Qur'ān's text.
>
> With all this praise of mine bestowed on you
> I pray that life stretch out a thousand years for you,
> Though for the likes of you such rare wares do seem cheap.[189]

Although there is no doubt but that Ḥāfiẓ regarded Abū Isḥāq's reign fondly and mourned its passing with poigency,[190] other than a few stray allusions in his verse, there is no evidence that our poet was in any way formally 'attached' as a courtier to Abū Isḥāq's court.[191]

Following Abū Isḥāq, it was during the reign of the 'Holy Warrior for the Faith' – Mubāriz al-Dīn (754/1353–759/1358) – that so many of Ḥāfiẓ's *ghazal*s attacking religious fundamentalism and hypocrisy, and railing against town preachers, local ascetics and surly mystics masquerading as Sufis, were penned. After conquering Fars, as Ghanī informs us:

> Mubāriz al-Dīn began to show great respect and deference to the puritan ascetics [*zuhād*], jurisconsults and severe *Sharī'a*-oriented clerics. He focused popular attention on the sayings of the Prophet [*ḥadīth*], exegesis of the Qur'ān, and discussions pertaining to the religious law. All the taverns were closed down, their casks of wine emptied in the streets, and the town's dens of vice [*kharābāt*] boarded up. When the doors of the taverns are shut, what other shop will be left open except that of religious hypocrisy [*riyā*]?[192] He went to such excesses in prosecuting 'vice' and commanding people to pursue 'virtue', that the wits and the comics of the metropolis soon mocked him with the sobriquet 'the Policeman' [*muḥtasib*].[193]

Ḥāfiẓ often refers to this oppressive Islamicist dictator, the most celebrated verse in this context being:

> Although the breeze waft in the scent of roses,
> And the wine bring on good cheer, beware: don't drink
> To the tune of the harp – for sharp is the Policeman's ear.[194]

There are a number of other *ghazal*s in which Ḥāfiẓ complains about the 'Policeman's' ban on music, lamenting the 'cutting of the harp's lovely locks'[195] and 'boarding up the tavern doors'[196] in bowlderized Mubārizistān. In fact, it was partly as a foil to this religious dictatorship that Ḥāfiẓ elaborated his most famous symbol – the inspired libertine (*rind*) – as a representative of the spiritual and intellectual counter-culture of the city.

The religious inquisition instituted by this ruler has been compared (by 'Abd al-Ḥusayn Zarrīnkūb) with those that prevailed in Europe during the Middle Ages. During his reign certain books were banned as being 'useless texts' (*kutub maḥrūmat al-intifā'*), before being collected and their pages washed clean. Mubāriz al-Dīn at one point demanded that the poet Sa'dī's mausoleum be burnt down and recitation of his poems be forbidden in the city's Islamic Republic, since his hired mullahs had divined certain heretical sentiments in his verses. His son Shāh Shujā', however, intervened and persuaded him to change his mind, assuring him that he was personally confident of Sa'dī's penitent and pious nature.[197] Mubāriz al-Dīn's bloodthirsty and violent nature was notorious. It was said that he would sit in his chamber reciting the Qur'ān, and then would have criminals summoned before him, rise from his place and kill them with his own hands, before resuming his recitation.[198]

'I've heard rumours that you've executed 1,000 people by your own hand', Shāh Shujā' once asked his father.

'On the contrary, it was only 800 maximum'[199] came the reassuring riposte.

Having been cursed and threatened with death several times by his father,[200] Shāh Shujā' had foresight enough to blind and then depose him, snuffing out the nasty puritanical autocrat to the delight of the Shīrāzī intelligentsia.[201] Like everyone else, Ḥāfiẓ was ecstatic that the policeman was finally dead and gone. In a panegyrical *ghazal* addressed to Mubāriz al-Dīn's much beloved and admired vizier Abū Naṣr Abū'l-Ma'ālī in 759/1357,[202] he celebrated his demise:

> The cop is gone! How great the news! Oh heart, oh God,
> The world's full of wine and ale-drinking demigods.[203]

Ḥāfiẓ's delight in the newly liberated atmosphere of the city after the Shāh Shujā''s parricide of his puritanical father is evident from one of his *ghazals* that begins: 'At dawn, I heard a supernatural voice that conveyed good news to me: "It's the Age of Shujā' – drink wine and have no fear".'[204] During Shāh Shujā''s largely benevolent reign (761/1359–786/1384)[205] many of Ḥāfiẓ's greatest erotic and bacchanalian lyrics were composed, and scholars claim that over half the (quite few) references to Persian princes and patrons in Ḥāfiẓ's *Dīvān* were to Shāh Shujā'.[206] There seems to have been much personal affection between them,[207] for the poet and the monarch shared much in common in matters of taste and learning. Both had memorized the Qur'ān. Given the evident intimacy between the poet and the prince, some historians speculate he might have held a post in Shāh Shujā''s government.[208]

The monarch was a dilettante scholar with a powerful memory who was widely read in classical Arabic and Persian literature, Islamic law and theology.[209] He was also a fair poet with a minor *Dīvān*[210] to his name. The historian Mīrkhwand recorded that 'there are poems both in Arabic and Persian that he wrote that people still recite today'.[211]

Ḥāfiẓ addressed several panegyrical *ghazals* to Shāh Shujā' (in one, praising him as 'that epiphany of pre-eternal Grace, light to the eyes of Hope, that compendium of practice and knowledge, that *Anima Mundi* – Shāh Shujā''),[212] as well as one long ode (*qaṣīda*).[213] Using the poetic device of 'literary greeting' (*istiqbāl*), he also wrote *ghazals* which paid homage to the prince's own poems.[214] However, while reputable historical sources do indeed attest that Shāh Shujā' was an object of Ḥāfiẓ's praise (*mamdūḥ*),[215] he was also an object of his reproach and rebuke. Thus, in the same *ghazal*, referring to the ruler's Turkish family connection through his mother, Ḥāfiẓ indirectly reproaches the ruler for listening to slander by the poet's rivals.[216] Under Shāh Shujā''s reign, Ḥāfiẓ's fame reached its apogee, with him gaining renown and respect throughout the entire Persian-speaking world.[217]

During the final decade of the poet's life in Shīrāz, the instability of political circumstances increased as fortunes of the Muẓaffarid dynasty began to fluctuate and wane. Shāh Shujā''s son, Zayn al-'Ābidīn, succeeded him, but only held on to the reins of power for four years (786/1384–789/1387), before he was deposed. Mīrkhwānd[218] and 'Abd al-Razzāq Samarqandī,[219] contemporary Persian historians, tell us that Ḥāfiẓ composed the following *ghazal* for Zayn al-'Ābidīn on the occasion of the prince's returning from a battle and upon triumphal entry into Shīrāz:

> The firmament augured well for you;
> It gave you favour on that day you took
> Up arms – so as to test your gratitude
> And see how you'd give thanks and meet your dues.
> For kingship's pomp and glory are not worth
> A mite in Love's precinct. – Confess yourself
> A slave and acknowledge your servitude.
> Take heed of one who stumbled, yet God lent him
> A hand – and know from this that fallen men
> Must stir in you your pity and distress.
> And when you cross the threshold with the wine
> Cup-bearer! Bear good news, so your entrance cause
> These worldly griefs but once to leave my heart.
> The royal road of pomp and circumstance
> Has many perils. It is best you march atop
> That knoll with not much baggage on your back.
> The Sultan and his fighting men, in love
> With jewels and crowns – the dervish with his peace
> Of mind and nook fit for a vagabond.
> My eyes' very light! Allow me cite for you
> One Sufi *bon mot:* 'Peace excels resort
> To arms and is better than hostility.'
> To satisfy ambition, slake desire
> And gain one's ends depends upon one's thought
> And will: the king proposes his good deeds,
> Then God disposes His success and grace.
>
> Don't brush the dust and grime of poverty
> And contentment – Ḥāfiẓ – off your face.
> Those stains are better than the art of alchemy.

As can be seen from this poem, Ḥāfiẓ' gently subverts the brags of the prince's might such that the poem's text completely negates its political context. Admonishing the young prince, the poet extols the dusty vestiments of his dervish habit, and like Shakespeare's *Henry VI* ('my crown is call'ed content / A crown it is that seldom kings enjoy'[220]), vaunts the virtues of contentment and holy poverty, before upbraiding him:

> My eyes' very light! Allow me cite for you
> One Sufi *bon mot:* 'Peace excels resort
> To arms and is better than hostility.'[221]

In this profoundly Sufiesque *ghazal* devoted to the higher ethics of erotic theology and ideals of spiritual poverty, the poet spurns all material advantage, scorning aught but trust in God. Using exactly the same Sufi terms elsewhere,[222] he says: 'Tell the king, everyone's daily bread is already foreordained!' Thus, the poet scuppers the pretentions of rulers of all kingdoms who'd reign in any dominion other than the empire of the heart, turning his back on the boons of temporal lords. In fact, this so-called 'political poem' subverts the entire notion of what a panegryric is supposed to be.[223]

The Muẓaffarids ('Those who are Triumphant') were disintegrating both politically and dynastically. History soon let them reap the dragon's teeth – the traditions of parricide and fratricide that made the family socially so notorious in medieval Persia – they had sown. Less than two decades later, all members of the Muẓaffarid royal family were extirpated by that scourge of the late medieval Islamic world, Tamerlane.

Near Iṣfahān in 789/1387, during one of his military campaigns, Zayn al-'Ābidīn fell prisoner to Shāh Manṣūr, the cousin of Shāh Shujā', who imprisoned him and put him in chains.[224] Ḥāfiẓ, who by now had come to oppose Zayn al-'Ābidīn, a light-headed, proud and politically inept ruler,[225] was delighted at this turn of events, as can be seen from one *ghazal*.[226]

In the meantime, Tamerlane, having established his grip on Transoxiania, had been making incursions into Fars. Shāh Yaḥyā, a nephew of Shāh Shujā', took charge of Shīrāz at his bequest.[227] He managed to hold the citadel of saints for about half a year (late 789/1387), during which time Ḥāfiẓ, now in his late 60s or early 70s, wrote a famous *ghazal* for him.[228] Although, unusually enough, the poem does have very panegyical overtones – for its 'exaggerated magniloquence',[229] the poet was rebuked by a contemporary historian – yet deep theosophical meanings can be also found in some of its verses.[230]

In November, Tamerlane carefully collected and counted the heads of the population he had just massacred (historians still debate how many skulls there were: some say 70,000; some say 200,000) in Iṣfahān,[231] erecting 28 sconce minarets around the city which bore witness to the psychopathic nature of his brutality. At the head of his army of Turkic berserkers, he then marched on Shīrāz, where he arrived in December 789/1387.

Of Ḥāfiẓ's purported meeting with Tamerlane at the end of his life we know nothing, if indeed it ever took place, but evidence from the *Dīvān* suggests that he had even less sympathy for the limping conqueror than he did for Zayn al-'Ābidīn. In a famous verse penned a decade earlier,[232] Ḥāfiẓ had recorded his grief over Tamerlane's massacres and sacking of Transoxiania's cities. Dawlatshāh Samarqandī's legendary account, written a century later, of Tamerlane's upbraiding the aged poet during his visit for his prodigality – rebuking Ḥāfiẓ's readiness, in one of the earliest poems of the *Dīvān*, to bestow 'all the dominion of Bukhārā and Samarqand for the sake of a black mole of that Shīrāzī Turk'[233] – is probably but a fond biographer's romantic reverie. Yet the moral it inculcates is truer than all historical fact: that one erotic verse penned by Persia's greatest lyric poet – Shelley never more truly spoke when he said poets are 'the trumpets which sing to battle, and feel not what they inspire; the influence which is moved not, but moves. Poets are the unacknowledged legislators of the world'[234] – consigned to oblivion the imperial pretensions of the most fearsome state terrorist of the entire late Islamic Middle Ages.[235]

Remaining in Shīrāz for only two months, Tamerlane was called back to Samarqand on unfinished military business, at which point Shāh Manṣūr, b. Shāh Muẓaffarī, a cousin of Shāh Shujā', took the city from Shāh Yaḥyā in a bloodless coup. Manṣūr, who managed to hold on to the city for the next four years (791/1388–795/1392), was regarded highly by Ḥāfiẓ, who celebrated his rule in Shīrāz and the departure of Tamerlane with a *ghazal* dedicated to him.[236] Several other poems[237] in which verses are penned in praise of this prince appear in the *Dīvān*. Many of the years of Shāh Manṣūr's brief reign were preoccupied in fighting Zayn al-'Ābidīn, who, having escaped from prison and taken over the city Iṣfahān, tried numerous times to reconquer Shīrāz, although the incumbent prince proved a superior strategist in all their confrontations, on each occasion defeating Zayn al-'Ābidīn, before finally capturing and blinding him.[238] At the end of one of his most famous erotic *ghazal*s dedicated to the ruler, Ḥāfiẓ indirectly alludes to Shāh Manṣūr's success in one such intertribal battle, celebrating how 'Victory shone that day for Shāh Manṣūr, who single-handedly charged at the centre of a thousand of their troops and struck off heads of foes with his sword'.[239]

Shāh Manṣūr spent the last three years of his rule occupied in the conquest of towns and cities and military campaigns around Iran, until he finally died on the battlefield in 795/April 1393[240] bravely wielding his sword against Tamerlane, whom he nearly killed in combat, before the walls of the city.[241] Ḥāfiẓ had been fortunate enough to pass away three years earlier, in 792/1389, before the hated Tamerlane invaded his beloved city. A few weeks after the Samaraqandī Turk took the citadel of saints, he executed all the remaining representatives of the Muẓaffarid dynasty, save for only two family members (among them the blinded Zayn al-'Ābidīn), both of whom he exiled to Transoxiania.[242]

In the end, Abū Isḥāq Īnjū... Shāh Shujā'... Shāh Manṣūr, and their courts and the viziers who served them, figured as convenient and significant components of the poet's socio-political persona. But just as none save a handful of trained historians ever bring to mind the intrigues of the court of Queen Elizabeth when reading Spenser's *Faery Queen*, hardly a soul reading Ḥāfiẓ today recalls the exploits and escapades of Abū Isḥaq, Ḥajjī Qawām, Shāh Shujā', Zayn al-'Ābidīn or Shāh Manṣūr. The main reason that these princes and their ministers' names are not utterly forgotten today is because they have been stamped with the eternity of Ḥāfiẓ's genius.

Although a few panegyrical *ghazal*s to these rulers and patrons were penned by Ḥāfiẓ, his true addressee remains the beloved / Beloved *sui generis*, not his/her temporal incarnations. As Ghanī emphasizes, 'because of the fluctuations of political fortunes in fourteenth-century Persia – where cliques in power today were often replaced by parties opposing them tomorrow – Ḥāfiẓ usually extolled the person he aimed to praise [*mamdūḥ*] as a beloved [*ma'shūq*], using a lover's romantic language and the *ghazal*'s erotic lexicon for this purpose, which was one of peculiarities of the style of his *ghazal* composition'. This was not a personal idiosyncracy on his part, he reiterates, for during this period 'all writers and poets generally avoided all but indirect allusions to topical affairs, veiling their personal feelings in general statements'.[243]

So even when Ḥāfiẓ named names and praised princes by royal titles or patrons with their habitual laudatory sobriquets, the poet's key discourse remains unintelligible to those unfamiliar with the allusive language of *Eros*.[244] The praise he voiced of the personalities of patrons, princes or viziers does not concern any matter-of-fact history of their circumstances, but is to be taken symbolically, not literally.[245] Their personages figure more often than not as metaphors conveying a deeper message pertaining to his ethical teachings, general views on social reform, *malāmatī* spirituality or erotic-metaphysical vision.[246] In fact, *the least important idea* in any *ghazal* by Ḥāfiẓ that has panegyrical overtones is the physical person of the so-called object of praise (*mamdūḥ*). Ḥāfiẓ's sophisticated lyrics are love songs, paeans in praise of *Eros* both human and divine. Passion in love and dispassion vis-à-vis all worldly attachments are his two grand themes: 'The dervish has no need to bric-a-brac from the prince's court. All we own is a tattered cloak gone up in flames'[247]; 'The world and all its affairs is nought upon nought: I have verified this point a thousand times.'[248] While clearly proud of the fact that his poetry was widely admired and read in princely circles,[249] Ḥāfiẓ also vaunts his independence of kingly patronage and declares that he will not bother to return 'the greetings of any king who do not humbly abase themselves kiss the threshold of this door'.[250] Addressing the monarch, he declares: 'We shall not ruin the reputation of Sufi poverty nor forsake our contentment [*qanā'at*] with God. Go tell the King that everyone's daily bread has been preordained by Providence.'[251] Although Ḥāfiẓ was not by any means a republican, in the free-spirited avocation of his creed of love he was an independent spirit petulantly impatient of all political authority, boasting that 'the lover does not fear any judge, nor tremble before state police'.[252] Emerson, I think rightly, intuited that 'intellectual liberty, which is a certificate of profound thought'[253] is the central hallmark of Ḥāfiẓ's thought. Freedom – 'by grace of the bounty-of-*Amor* [*dawlat-i 'ishq*]'[254] – from palace and court, college and seminary, minister and mullah – expressed as a kind of *ekstasis*, an exit from self, an intoxication, is the source of all physical and spiritual pleasure for Ḥāfiẓ, as he exclaims:

> What bliss! – That instant of disassociation,
> When blessed by licence of intoxication,
> I exorcize my ties from both vizier and prince.[255]

In the introduction to his recent two-volume commentary on Ḥāfiẓ's poems, Muḥammad Isti'lāmī, a leading scholar of classical Persian Sufi literature and collator of the best critical edition of Rūmī's *Mathnawī*, underlines the fallacy of interpreting Ḥāfiẓ as if he were just another traditional Persian court poet. To illuminate *the essentially extra-courtly nature of Ḥāfiẓ's poetry*, the following passage bears citation:

> Ḥāfiẓ was not a professional panegyric poet who praised kings after the fashion of 'Unṣurī, Farrukhī and Amīr Mu'izzī. In many of the *ghazals* that he sent to kings and national ministers those verses where a said prince or vizier is the object of praise are set off from the rest of the *ghazal*. Compared to the rest of the lines in these *ghazals* (whose themes are largely erotic or mystical), those verses reveal an entirely different ambience. Nonetheless, some later authors who wrote historical works or memoirs of the poets – and following them modern scholars – have taken those few verses to imply that Ḥāfiẓ was a panegyric poet pure and simple. They believed him to have been affiliated, as were 'Unṣurī, Farrukhī and Amīr Mu'izzī, to a certain royal court. They have even taken great pains to establish that all the verses of a said *ghazal* constitute nothing but veiled praise for a certain king or vizier. For instance, wherever Ḥāfiẓ qualifies his beloved with the epithet of 'the royal rider' [*shahsavār*], they have laboured, even though the context absolutely dictates otherwise, to treat this term as synonymous with *Abū'l-favāris* ['lord of the riders'], one of the titles of Shāh Shujā'. They have not even bothered to notice that if such a phrase, for example, like 'the remedy for our weak heart lies in your lip'[256] is interpreted as being a species of panegyric praise, where will it all end up? Is this supposed to imply that Shāh Shujā' was asked to grant a kiss to Ḥāfiẓ by way of a royal boon from his blessed lip!? Such trite and superficial interpretations appear a dime a dozen in the works of many so-called 'Ḥāfiẓologists' today. But if we are to gain anything like a logical and rational understanding of Ḥāfiẓ's lexicon one basic point can't be stressed enough: *he was not a court poet.* The panegyric verses that he wrote in praise of kings and viziers in his *Dīvān* are quite few and far in between.[257]

Ultimately, while Shāh Shujā', Shāh Manṣūr and other rulers and statesmen featured in his *Dīvān* do have significance as personalities in the political theatre of horrors of medieval Persia, what Ḥāfiẓ lovers prize today is their conceptualization in Ḥāfiẓ's wider lyrical drama, not their historical role on the passing stage of time and place and circumstance. The bright parti-coloured robes of Ḥāfiẓ's immortal verse lay drapped over the shoulders of those patrons and princes indeed, but it was their honour and glory to serve 'as the temporary dress in which the poet's creations must be arrayed and which cover without concealing the eternal proportions of their beauty... for the alloy of costume, habit, etc., [is] necessary to temper this planetary music for mortal ears'.[258] The jottings of historians' gossip may occasionally lay bare the political *context* of this or that *ghazal* or line, but tell us nothing about the unvarying philosophical *subtext* of all Ḥāfiẓ's poems, which is love. *Eros* his polis, not Shīrāz; *Eros*, the object of his praise, not the court of any prince or vizier:

> You know I never did once peruse
> Those tales of Alexander or Darius,
> So don't ever ask me recite else
> But the words of faith and love.[259]

Prolegomenon to the Study of Ḥāfiẓ 2 – The Mystical Milieu: Ḥāfiẓ's Erotic Spirituality

Ḥāfiẓ and the Inspired Libertine (rind)

The philosophical significance and erotico-mystical connotations of the subversive piety of the 'inspired libertine', or *rind*, has preoccupied readers of Ḥāfiẓ's poetry for generations. The main reason for our fascination is that the whole notion of inspired libertinism (*rindī*) presents a major moral problem: as an ethical category disengaged from conventional piety (*taqwā*) and asceticism (*zuhd*), it leaves Ḥāfiẓ open to the accusation of simply being an advocate of hedonism and sybaritic debauchery. The virtually indefinable[260] and paradoxical ethic of the inspired libertine was summarized by the Iranian philosopher Dayyush Shayegan as follows:

> In this concept we find a sense of immoderacy, a behaviour out of the ordinary, shocking, scandalous, able to disorient the most composed spirits, a non-conformity which derives not so much from ostentation as from the explosive exhuberance of a vision so rich, so full, that it cannot manifest itself without doing violence to everyday banality and without breaking the limits defined by the normality of things. This term expresses, further, a predilection for the uncertain, for language that is veiled and masked, for hints and insinuations, which in the authentic *rend* are expressed in inspired paradoxes [*shaṭḥiyāt*] ... Finally, there is in this concept a boundless love of the divine such as we see in the great thinkers and mystics of Iranian spirituality; but detached from its mystical content, it is transformed into fanaticism and, steered by *hominess magni*, to the psychology of the mob.[261]

Although reconciling the differences between the unitive, ascetic and ecstatic tendencies of mystical traditions and the more mundane concerns of society has always been a fundamental problem in the history of religions, and is not particular to Islamic thought,[262] a number of other scholars – lacking any real nuanced insight into the psychology of religion, and unable to perceive any shades in the spectrum of religion and ethics beyond the conventional blackness of sin and whiteness of virtue – have in fact interpreted Ḥāfiẓ's doctrine of *rindī* literally as implying an advocacy of debauchery pure and simple.[263] Other students of the poet have equated Ḥāfiẓ's notion of the *rind* with a kind of Camusian immoralist existentialist *avant la lettre.* According to the latter interpretation, 'the free-thinking libertine [*rind*] is a enlightened mystic [*'ārif*] who will neither surrender himself to following the dictates of hypocritical spiritual leaders nor bend his knee to the brute power and dictatorial will of political authority. He rejects and regards them all with scornful indifference'.[264] Regarding these and other similar secular constructions put on the poet, Khurramshāhī judiciously comments:

> Although there is a type of *rind* who is an irreligious freethinker, the *rind* of Ḥāfiẓ is preoccupied and concerned with the obligations of religion. While he believes in and reflects upon the Life Hereafter, he does not fear it since he finds that divine Love and Grace are his real saviours. Nor does he rely on his own piety, knowledge, learning, or understanding. Contrary to the ascetic [*zāhid*] – even the true ascetic – the *rind* is not someone who goes to an extreme in giving priority to the Life Hereafter, neither does he consider the life of the world to be entirely insubstantial or without basis.[265]

The inspired libertine (*rind*) is the most manifest yet most camouflaged, the most publically promulgated yet most carefully disguised figure in Ḥāfiẓ's religion of love (*madhhab-i 'ishq*).[266] Ensconced and encoded within this key term can be found all the important theosophical notions in Ḥāfiẓ's thought. While the poetic terms *rind* and *rindī* occur frequently in earlier Persian theoerotic poets, especially in 'Aṭṭār,[267] these terms only take on a central role in the poetry of Ḥāfiẓ, who made them the key concept in his writing, using them to qualify his spiritual position and degree – and in this respect, he has no predecessor in Persian *belles lettres.*[268]

Although Ḥāfiẓ's conception of *rind* and *rindī* is multi-dimensional, there are basically three facets of his doctrine: social, literary and metaphysical, that will concern me here:

- the *rind* as a socio-political phenomenon
- the *rind* as a literary–allegorical trope belonging to the *qalandariyya* genre
- the *rind* as a symbol in Sufi erotic theology for a degree of advanced spiritual realization.

Each of these facets is examined individually below.

The Rindān: *Mafia of Medieval Persia*

Viewed from the social-historical perspective of fourteenth-century Shīrāzī society, the rogues and rakes (*rindān*) of Persia in Ḥāfiẓ's day were actually Mafioso thugs and hoodlums in charge of specific quarters of the city, exactly like Sicilian or

Italian gangsters who control large neighbourhoods of New York City, Chicago or Milan today. Although the *rindān* theoretically occupied the lowest rung in the social hierarchy, they were extremely powerful and feared for their ruthlessness, for most of the city's hired assassins, professional thugs and thieves belonged to their company. The princes who ruled the city were essentially in thrall to these gangs of thugs, for Ḥāfiẓ's Shīrāz, though famed abroad for its pious mystics and men of learning, was also a 'city of hoodlums' (*shahr-i rindān*).[269] As John Limbert explains: 'Few cities combined so much hedonism and so much spiritualism as Shīrāz. As far as the government was concerned, the dissipations of the *rendan* were preferable to the fasts of the *zahedan* or ascetics. For while the latter worked at the simplest jobs and paid few taxes, the former were steady customers of the *kharabat* (vice-dens) – the brothels (*beit al-lotf*), wine-shops (*sharabkhaneh*), opium-dens (*bangkhaneh*), and gambling houses (*qomarkhaneh*) – all of which paid *tamgha* to the treasury.'[270] The hoodlums were known for sensational adventurism (*mājarā-jū'ī*), contempt for conventional religious morality, along with a devil-may-care attitude (*lā-ubālīgarī*), and their deliberate courting of infamy and notoriety. In his chapter on the 'Ethics of Dervishes' in the *Rose Garden* (*Gulistān*), Sa'dī provides a good vignette of their typical conduct in Shīrāz a century earlier:

> A gang of hoodlums [*ṭāyifa-i rindān*] came across a dervish and spoke abusively to him, calling him bad names, striking him with blows, causing him sore offence and grievous bodily harm. He went to the Master of the Path (*pīr-i ṭarīqat*) to complain of their conduct. The latter replied, 'My son, this dervish mantle of yours is the garb of Contentment. Whoever wears the mantle yet cannot bear to have his desires thwarted is an impostor. Such are forbidden to wear dervish robes.'[271]

In only one *ghazal* does Ḥāfiẓ mention these lowlife hoodlums in the bars and brothels of Shīrāz, the *rind-i bazārī*, marketplace rakes[272] of the city's underbelly which fill the pages of other contemporary poets such as 'Ubayd Zākānī. The figure of the *rind* celebrated in his lyrics is not like these coarse and dissolute characters at all, but rather a nonconformist type of refined aesthetic and spiritual values.[273] In Ḥāfiẓ's inspired libertine appears a sophisticated aesthetic discernment and spiritual urbanity missing from the raffish hooligans who frequented Shīrāz's dens of vice. In this context, as Shayegan underlines, the word *rind* evokes:

> a lively lucidity, a *savoir faire*, a refinement of action, a tact that goes all the way to compliance, a discretion in speech, which are neither craft nor hypocrisy, nor an affectation of mystery; but can, outside their context, become those very things, being reduced to insidous shifts, not to say dissembling and imposture. Again, the term denotes an interior liberty, an authentic detachment from the things of this world, suggesting the deliverance, in however small a measure, of the man who, shaking off his tawdry finery, lays

himself open without sham, and naked to the mirror of the world; however, degenerated from its primitive context, this attitude can turn into one of exhibitionism, of posing and of mere libertinage.[274]

It is true that the word *rind* recalled to the majority of the poet's contemporary readers (and still does today) the spirit of the chivalrous ruffian; indeed, the reckless mystique and colourful character of these mobsters and desperados had influenced the development of the poetic and mystical image of the *rind* in medieval Sufi poetry.[275] That such connotations are an integral part of Ḥāfiẓ's poems cannot be argued away, but to posit a literal one-to-one equivalency between the two is absurd.[276] Arguments to this effect in a sophisticated form exhibit the debilitating effects of insisting that anything that is true must be exclusively true and that the presence of one implication necessarily diminishes the force of counter-implications that are also present.

What is clear is that the very ambivalence of the term enabled Ḥāfiẓ's inspired libertine to acquire a kind of *succès de scandale* through being coloured with association with the shady character of the infamous hoodlums of Shīrāz. Transforming their badge of infamy and dishonour and shame into acclaim and fame, the inspired libertine thus cut a dash through his poems as a kind of revolutionary religious intellectual in society, an iconoclastic rebel who adhered to the religion of *Eros* as a counter-faith to the prevailing hardline fundamentalist version of orthodoxy and the moribund Islamic puritanism of his day. In the conventional religiously oriented society of fourteenth-century Persia, the libertine of course had largely a negative social value. In the realm of spiritual truth, however – in respect to which many of the seminary-trained clerics, ascetics and Sufis of the period were in practice quite often impostors and fraudsters pretending piety – the rebellious social image of the libertine rake in all his dissolute and impious notoriety quite appropriately complemented, and in fact expressed in mirror image, the *real nature* of the ascetic Sufi or formalist Muslim cleric.[277] In one verse he even moans to his mistress that the 'inspired libertines' of her kingdom are in fact the true saints, but, alas, the cognoscenti of the spirit who might recognize these 'Friends of God' (*valī-shināsān*) have long ago departed:

For the pious rakes' thirsting lips nobody
Anymore can spare a cup, and those who could
Purview the saints seem all to have fled this land.[278]

As pointed out above, many of Ḥāfiẓ's most bitterly anti-clerical *ghazals* were composed under the fundamentalist dictatorship of Mubāriz al-Dīn (reg. 754/1353–759/1357) immediately following Abū Isḥāq Īnjū's tolerant reign (743/1342–754/1353). Comparing this king's 'religious Inquisition' with those that afflicted Europe a few centuries later, 'Abd al-Ḥusayn Zarrīnkūb highlights the dangerous political climate in which such *ghazals* were composed:

> During the 'born-again' king Mubāriz al-Dīn's reign of terror ... the struggle against this merciless hypocrite – who had been nicknamed the 'policeman' [*muḥtasib*] by the rogues of the city, being notorious for his excessively cruel and ruthless nature – was not the job of the ordinary thugs and rogues of the marketplace [*rindān-i bazārī*]. They were on the payroll of other strongmen and henchmen, since they attached themselves to whoever held power, and willy-nilly carried out the orders of the 'policeman'. No, the battle with this Mafioso 'policeman' prince was a job better left to those 'inspired libertines who were willing to hazard everything and risk wagering all away' [*rindān-i pākbāz*]. These men were the 'schoolman libertines', or 'rogues of the college' [*rindān-i madrasa*], who had insight into the reality of religion [*ḥaqīqat-i dīn*] and morality beyond such pretensions and falsehoods. It was they who realized that this sort of sanctimony and hypocritical display of piety was in fact the greatest threat to honest religion and morality.[279]

Hazardous as it was to express anti-prohibitionist sentiments in the Islamic Republic of Mubāriz's Shīrāz, these 'schoolmen libertines' struggled as best they could in the oppressive political climate. In the following verse in which he satirically refers to Mubāriz al-Dīn as 'the policeman',[280] Ḥāfiẓ even manages to draw a moral from his hypocritical religious behaviour, giving some mordant advice which will evoke sympathy in anyone who has ever lived under the strictures of a religious theocracy:

> Take your cue from the policeman and learn of him, oh heart
> The way of the libertines' inspired faith, for he is drunk
> Yet none of him suspects this true.[281]

If Ḥāfiẓ's *rind* were but an ordinary street thug and his notion of the inspired libertine's faith the literary equivalent of contemporary gangsta-rap, a lowlife hero so obvious and so material would be as blindly evident and boldly inarticulate as the Hollywood cowboy who preaches down the barrel of his smoking gun. Ḥāfiẓ, then, in elaborating the ethics and erotics of the inspired libertine, in declaring:

> I followed the path of the mad libertines for years –
> Long enough, until I was able with the consent
> Of intelligence to put my greediness into prison.[282]

or:

> Unbound romance and love and youth comprise
> The sum of our desires, for when the inner *sens*
> Of such ideas converge, the shuttlecock
> Of speech may then be struck.[283]

– certainly did not mean to glorify the dissolute lowlife of the *Kaffeehausliterat* or wax magniloquent over the nightlife pub-crawling through the bordellos and brothels of medieval Shīrāz, after the fashion of – say – Francois Villon's ballads or Arthur Rimbaud's (1854–91) revolt against Christianity in the name of a 'higher licentiousness' in *Une Saison en enfer*.[284] Ḥāfiẓ's *rind* is neither tricky politician, shameless opportunist, confidence man nor political crook. Such worldly con-men are in fact 'uninspired libertines', who lack the sacred dimension which is the soul of the *rind*; their fibbing and fabulation but expose the depths of their merely mundane deceit. The inspired libertine on the other hand reveals the world's deceit: 'wise-to-the-bait' of its charms, his actions serve to subvert and unmask the pretensions of the entire materialist mentality in both its religious and secular forms.[285]

The literary sources of Ḥāfiẓ's doctrine of the inspired libertine can be traced back to the sophisticated literary tradition of poetry written in praise of the rite of the spiritual vagabonds (*qalandariyya*) and the esoteric teachings of Islamic erotic spirituality grounded in *malāmatī* ethics, which will be explored below.

Ḥāfiẓ's Malāmatī *Ethic and the Rite of Spiritual Vagabonds (*Qalandariyya*)*

Shall I gulp wine? No, that is vulgarism,
A heresy and schism,
Foisted into the canon-law of love;–
No, – wine is only sweet to happy men.

– Keats[286]

The venerable Persian literary dictionary *Burhān al-Qāṭi'* (Decisive Argument) defines the *rindān* (sing. *rind*) as folk who are 'crafty, deceitful, clever, fearless, reprobate, desperados with a devil-may-care attitude about them [*lā-ubālī*]. They are called *rindān* because they repudiate all norms of society and reject the restraints of religious piety.' Following this literal definition, the dictionary then adds that 'they are people who outwardly behave in a blameworthy manner and although they incur blame [*malāmat*], inwardly they are of sound character [*salāmat*]'.[287] This latter connotation draws on the classic epigrammatic definition of the *malāmatī* way, that 'perseverance in endurance of blame is renunciation of security and safety [*al-malāmat tark al-salāmat*]'.[288]

Not only does the term *rind* thus by definition belong to the *malāmatī* lexicon, it was also an important word deriving from the Sufi literary genre known as 'Wildman poetry' (*qalandariyya*).[289] All Sufi poets and writers used the symbol of the *qalandar* to signify someone freed from the rites of hypocritical devotion in religion, liberated from the bonds and sanctions of socio-cultural convention,[290] and it is with this connotation that this figure appears as a popular poetic topos in the lyrics of Sanā'ī, 'Aṭṭār and Rūmī, in the hagiography and poetry of 'Irāqī, as well as in the

Dīvān of Ḥāfiẓ.[291] Centuries before Ḥāfiẓ, specifically in the Persian poetry of Sanā'ī and 'Aṭṭār, the *rindān*'s disreputable *malāmatī* character had been employed as a synecdoche to personify the mystic adept's pursuit of detachment from the ways of the world.[292] As 'Aṭṭār remarked:

> My work is turned all inside out
> With people. For the worst slur
> I think that ever I could incur
> Is commendation by the crowd.[293]

The Islamic counterpart of the Hindu *saddhu*, the *qalandar* was a religious mendicant, a holy vagabond or *faqīr* who attired himself in outlandish garb and often shaved all facial hair save the moustache, travelling from town to town occupied in devotional practices in order to mortify his soul and disengage himself from worldly concerns. The Sufi theoreticians of medieval Persia inform us that the difference between the *malāmatī* and *qalandar* mystics was that the former sought to conceal his acts of devotion and piety, whereas the latter endeavoured to overturn and destroy established customs.[294] In Ḥāfiẓ's poetry both tendencies are visible.

As an institution, the *qalandariyya* was closely connected with the early *malāmatī* tradition in tenth-/eleventh-century Nishapur in Khurāsān,[295] which later, under the leadership of Jamāl al-Dīn Sāwī (d. circa 630/1232), developed into separate orders with their own Khānaqāhs scattered all over Egypt, Libya, Turkey, Persia and India.[296] Historically speaking, the *qalandariyya* movement represented a sort of mass institutionalization of the high principles of the *malāmatī* moral philosophy. In Ḥāfiẓ's poetry the *qalandar* libertine (*rind-i qalandar*) stands at the summit of the spiritual hierarchy. The *qalandar* is the supreme mystical monarch before whom even the prince must bend his knee to receive his crown:

> Around the tavern door
>   The reprobates of God – *qalandar*s – swarm
> They withdraw and they bestow
>   The diadems of Empire.[297]

In this verse, Ḥāfiẓ's libertine wildmen (*rindān-i qalandar*) appear as 'opportunists' in the mystical realm. The term 'opportunist' is etymologically derived from the Latin *porta* (an entrance or passage through), an *opportunus* being that which offers an opening, or stands before an opening. Thus, for the Romans a *porta fenestella* was an opening through which Fortune could enter.[298] The wildman-libertine (*rind-i qalandar*) in this verse stands at the door of drunkenness, the same door, the same *opportunus* through which diadems, crowns and thrones have all issued forth, and through which they will pass away. Like Ahasureus, the mysterious Wandering Jew in Shelley's epic poem *Hellas*,[299] Ḥāfiẓ's *rind* is transported in ecstasy beyond time, space and place, gaining control by relinquishing control, acquiring power through detachment.[300] This spiritual ideal of detachment, represented by the inspired libertine and the *qalandar*, is praised by Ḥāfiẓ in another celebrated verse:

> I serve the will and *esprit* of that One
> Who commits to flames his own security,
> Who wears the rags of beggary, yet knows the lore of alchemy.
> A thousand enigmas subtler, finer spun than
> A strand of hair lie here. – Not everyone
> Who shaves his scalp can understand the *qalandar*.[301]

Throughout his *ghazals* (where two references to the *qalandarī* rite[302] and four to the *qalandar* himself[303] appear), Ḥāfiẓ flagrantly flaunts his fondness for this holy vagabond's anti-materialistic ideals.[304]

The poet also drew heavily on *malāmatī* doctrines,[305] at least ten of which he espoused, as Khurramshāhī has demonstrated *in extenso*. A summary of these doctrines is as follows:

- Submitting oneself to public censure and blame, while not fearing – indeed, not being offended at – the accusations and slander of religious fundamentalists.
- Renunciation of ambition for worldly rank, status, accompanied by indifference to being known for personal probity and goodness. Being reckless vis-à-vis political conciliations conventionally made to protect one's reputation, along with disregard for fame and name.
- Avoidance of any ostentatious display of ascetical piety and sanctimony, evading all public self-promotion of personal religiosity.
- Renunciation of hypocrisy (in order to cut off the root of hypocrisy, he even severely castigates himself to the point of calling himself a hypocrite so as to better censure hypocrisy).
- Having a critical outlook on all conventional social institutions: religious, academic, governmental, mystical (e.g. mosque, madrasa and *khānaqāh*).
- Renunciation of all claim to charismatic powers and visionary experiences.
- Concealing the shortcomings and covering up the faults and foibles of others.
- Repudiation of conceit, *amour propre*, egotism and self-satisfaction in the struggle against and mortification of the lower soul (*nafs*).
- Affecting shamelessness, feigning impiety, irreligiosity, perversity and blasphemy. The best example of this is Bāyazid's breaking of his fast during the day in public, although he was travelling, and hence by Canon Law was permitted to do this – so people would imagine him to be impious.
- Salvation through love.[306]

Although *malāmatī* conceptions are generally alien to Western philosophical ethics, in certain Gospel sayings such as 'Blessed are ye when men shall hate you, and when they shall separate you from their company, and shall reproach you, and cast out your name as evil...', a quasi-*malāmatī* sentiment – that one must live above the world and consider all worldy employments as things not to be desired but only endured and suffered, with the censure of the vulgar considered as an inevitable trial to be endured on the *via purgativa* – is proclaimed.[307] The anti-social attitudes, and the licence of affected shamelessness in Sufi *Malāmatī* teachings, have also often been compared to the school of Greek Cynics, Diogenes of Sinope's teachings in particular. However, *malāmatī* ethics are in this respect far more akin to the moral philosophy of Roman Stoicism. Seneca's saying, *Malis displicere laudari est* ('To displease the wicked is to be praised'), for instance, which distinguishes between the ignominy of a 'glory' that depends on the judgement of the illiterate masses and true 'renown' whose acclaim derives from the judgement of wise men, professes a Sufi sort of indifference to name and fame that expresses the *malāmatī* ethic perfectly. Paraphrased by Ben Jonson as 'To be dispraised is the most perfect praise',[308] Milton set Seneca's saying to verse in his *Paradise Regained*:

> For what is glory but the blaze of fame,
> The people's praise, if always praise unmixed?
> And what the people but a herd confused,
> A miscellaneous rabble, who extol
> Things vulgar and well weighed, scarce worth the praise,
> They praise and they admire they know not what;
> And know not whom, but as one leads the other;
> And what delight to be by such extolled,
> To live upon their tongues and be their talk,
> Of whom to be dispraised were no small praise?[309]

Following the English school of Radical Religious Dissent, William Blake, in stating in his Proverbs of Hell, 'Listen to the fool's reproach! It is a kingly title!' – seems to have been imparting a kind of *malāmatī* instruction – perhaps echoing Milton's views here.[310]

Sufis of all orders professed *malāmatī* doctrines in common. The dangers of hypocrisy, pride, unctuous self-righteousness and being wise in one's own conceit are constant themes in classical Sufi manuals.[311] The merging of *malāmatī* ethical doctrine into the repertoire of the Persian Sufi poetry is evidenced by the fact that figures such as the inspired libertine (*rind*), vagabond (*qalandar*) and brigand (*'ayyār*) all originally possessed negative social values, but reappeared with positive connotations accorded them by the Sufi poets. In the same spirit the Sufi poets celebrated infidelity and heresy, and extolled Buddhism, Zoroastrianism and Christianity as symbols for higher, esoteric modes of faith.[312] Ḥāfiẓ's *malāmatī* ethic is entirely based on this logopoetic Sufi symbolic language; his self-inculpation and penchant for incurring the blame and censure of the vulgar have, it must be stressed, *supra-aesthetic and meta-literary significance*. Rather than mere colourful metaphors limned with delightful erotic images, there are precise spiritual significances in verses such as these:

> People have aimed the arrow of guilt a hundred times
> In our direction. With the help of our Darling's eyebrow,
> Blame has been a blessing, and has opened all our work.[313]

As a purificatory experience, the self-abasement generated by being reviled publically turns the *malāmatī* unitarian away from creature to Creator, from the vulgar mob towards God. Blame thus strengthens faith, being much more efficacious than praise in directing the mystic's attention to the Supreme Cause and away from secondary causes. The mystical theology of the *malāmatī* doctrines in this verse can be traced back to a verse of the Qur'ān praising those whose love of God is so sincere that 'they do not fear to be censured by anyone who might censure them' (V: 54). 'To become an object of contempt and blame is marvellously efficacious in achieving sincerity in love', the early theoretician of Persian Sufism 'Alī Hujwīrī thus explained in his chapter on the *Malāmatī* School in the *Kashf al-maḥjūb*. 'The people of God have always been distinguished by being the butt of blame and censure of common people.'[314]

To put the above verse in its proper context now: by means of becoming a target of public vituperation (*malāmat*), the lover is blessed with the experience of an opening, the eyebrow here serving as a 'symbol *par excellence* to communicate Divine expressions and intimations, directing the wayfarer's attention towards Unity, just as the arching of the human beloved's eyebrow directs the lover's attention to his or her eye, face, and expressions.'[315]

In the same vein, one of the important principles of both profane love theory and the *malāmatī* theology of love is that the lover is always reviled and discredited.[316] A fundamental axiom of the Art of *Amor* in the Sufi tradition is that no romantic affair, human or divine, worldly or otherworldly, temporal or spiritual, is ever safe from public blame and slander.[317] In one verse, Ḥāfiẓ thus contrasts the dangers of a lover's intoxication to the 'security and safety' (*salāmat*) of the conventional life of the non-lover:

> In a nook safe from blame, how can we stay
> Secluded when your dark eye reminds us
> Always of the joy and mysteries of drunkenness?[318]

The lover's life is dangerous, the lover being by definition one who eschews what's safe and sound, for:

> Although consorting with what's safe and sound
> Seems, dear heart, to be a joy and a delight,

Love too has much grace and chic and charm,
And her side too must not be forsworn.[319]

The deliberate concealment of one's virtues and good deeds, and exposure of one's vice and faults – the invition of condemnation from the common herd by the *malāmatī* – is one of Ḥāfiẓ's perennial themes, as these two verses attest:

Don't expect obedience, promise-keeping, or rectitude
From me; I'm drunk. I've been famous for carrying
A wine pitcher around since the First Covenant with Adam.[320]

* * *

The name of Ḥāfiẓ has been well inscribed in the books,
But in our clan of disreputables, the difference
Between profit and loss is not all that great.[321]

Ḥāfiẓ's most famous poem in which he flaunts his bacchanalian ethics and erotic spirituality in the face of formalist Muslim clerics while celebrating the mystical theology of the Path of Blame, begins with these three key verses:

I'm well known throughout the whole city
For being a wild-haired lover; and I'm that man who has
Never darkened his vision by seeing evil.

Through my enthusiasm for wine, I have thrown the book
Of my good name into the water; but doing that insures that
The handwriting in my book of grandiosity will be blurred.

Let's be faithful to what we love; let's accept reproach
And keep our spirits high, because on our road, being easily
Hurt by the words of others is a form of infidelity.[322]

Hujwīrī's exegesis of *malāmatī* philosophy in his *Kashf al-maḥjūb* illuminates the theosophical teachings and meaning underlying Ḥāfiẓ's verses quite well:

> It has been decreed by God that whoever discourses about Him, He makes the butt of the world's abuse. Simultaneously, He preserves their consciousness from being preoccupied by that blame. This is a result of divine jealousy – for thus God protects His friends from paying attention to anyone save Him lest the non-initiates catch a glimpse of the beauty of their spiritual state. It also protects those devotees from self-regard and the hubris of self-consciousness. Hence, they don't become puffed up about themselves and succumb to

> self-righteous conceit [*'ujb*] and arrogance. Therefore, God has set the common herd over them to tongue-lash and blame them ... so that no matter what they do, they suffer blame and abuse ... For it is a fundamental axiom in the Way of God that there is no affliction or veil on the Way tougher than being wise in one's own conceit [*'ujb*].[323]

Ḥāfiẓ's defence of the erotics of the heart and the eye (the philosophy of *shāhid-bāzī*, discussed below, pp. 43ff.) against medieval Islamic Puritanism is manifest in the first verse above.

In the second verse, devoted to Sufi bacchanalian doctrine, Ḥāfiẓ basks in his *succès de scandale* at being blamed as a drinker of wine, in ruining his reputation – that 'good name' which is more culpable than any sin since it leads to self-righteous conceit (*'ujb*, as Hujwīrī observed). Whereas ascetic abstinence and religious piety often culminate in self-righteousness, the adoration of wine 'dissolves all the effects and traces of egocentric self-worship from the mystic's being. This verse thus exemplifies the poet's *malāmatī* tastes and disgust with the false reputation which ensue from fame and name and receiving public honours from people.'[324]

Lastly, in the third verse, the term *malāmat* is then explicitly invoked by the poet as he elucidates the metaphysical reason why the sage never feels aggrieved at the disapprobation and censure of the common horde of men.[325]

From this hasty overview of Ḥāfiẓ's views on the Sufi Path of Blame (which comprise but a tiny portion of these expressions), it is apparent how profoundly his radical spiritual nonconformism is indebted to the early *malāmatī* Sufi teachings.[326] As we can see, the ethic of the inspired libertine (*rind*) in his detachment from self and society, self-denigration and self-inculpation, anti-materialism and warm-hearted generosity, all have precise antecedents in Sufi *malāmatī* teachings. Ḥāfiẓ's imagery of the figure connected with the inspired libertine, who represents the highest degree of the lover, who repudiates the trammels of the ethical absolutes of conventional *Sharī'a*-oriented piety, who engages in the sport of gazing on beauty (*naẓar-bāz*) and is a lover of beautiful women/boys (*shāhid-bāz*), who drinks the dregs of love-passion (*durdī-yi dard*), who cares naught for fair name, ill-fame or shame (*nām u nang*), recking neither praise or blame, and who disdains preachers of ascetical piety (*zuhd u zāhid*), can be found exactly mirrored in verse after verse by Sanā'ī, 'Aṭṭār and Sa'dī in those *ghazal*s that belong to the literary genre of the *qalandariyya* which they composed.[327] As revealed above, the *qalandarī* imagery in medieval Persian Sufi poetry and the *qalandar* himself reflect *malāmatī* conceptions. With Ḥāfiẓ's highlighting of the romantic ideals of *rind* and *rindī* within this stock *qalandarī* poetic lexicon, a kind of semantic transformation took place, as Khurramshāhī observes:

> In accordance with his *malāmatī* perspective, Ḥāfiẓ came to view both the acceptable or 'good' characters and positions of society and the rejected or 'bad' figures and circumstances of society with a highly critical eye, subjecting

> them both to the harshest re-evaluation. Following the precedent set by Sanā'ī and 'Aṭṭār in this respect, he took the character of the inspired libertine (*rind*), which occupied a lowly, dishonourable social rank in the echelons and ranks of contemporary society, out from under the stairs, adopting it to be his own particular persuasion and rite of faith. From the antecedent mystical tradition Ḥāfiẓ took the theosophical outlook on the 'Perfect Man' [*insān-i kāmil*] or 'True Man', and with his own creative genius and mythological imagination attached this concept to the notion of the distracted and footloose *rind*, calling the thirsty *rind* a saint [*walī*].[328]

And in this fashion, the inspired libertine in Ḥāfiẓ's poetry became elevated to one of the most exalted spiritual ranks in his religion of love (*madhhab-i 'ishq*),[329] as will be seen from the ensuing discussion.

The Art of Erotic Contemplation (shāhid-bāzī)

> Lift up the tulip-cup: its eyes' drunken narcissus gaze,
> And set on me the label 'pervert'. With so many judges
> That are set over me, O Lord, who should I take to be my judge?[330]
>
> – Ḥāfiẓ

From the foregoing study, we see that the term *rind* in its simple outer, literal sense has two main connotations: (1) a clever, cunning and crafty person – an 'artful dodger' in Dickens' sense, or a 'rogue' in the Shakespearean sense; and (2) a person with a reckless, nonconformist, devil-may-care attitude unrestrained by any ties of conventional social morality.[331] However, the interior *symbolic* significance of the term, properly qualifying this rogue or libertine with the adjective 'inspired', is only revealed once we examine the metaphysical, erotic and ethical bases of the term.

The inspired libertine's antinomian ethic, or *rindī*, is described by Ḥāfiẓ as a kind of 'art'/'virtue' (*hunar*). The erotic ethic of *rindī* involves two contemplative disciplines practised by the *fedeli d'amore*, respectively called *shāhid-bāzī* and *naẓar-bāzī*.

The term *shāhid* means both 'seer' and 'witness', and as a technical term in Sufism, *shāhid-bāzī* (cavorting with she/he who is a Witness) is the art of contemplation of the divine in the mundane-human, beholding the divine in the mirror of human beauty, the latter bearing 'witness' to the former, the *shāhid* thus becoming an 'icon of beauty' or 'divine demonstration', one who bears 'witness' to the presence of divine. In this sense, *shāhid-bāzī* means 'sporting with beauty's icon' or 'cavorting with mortal forms of beauty that are demonstrative of divinity'. In the words of Henry Corbin: 'The *shāhid* denotes the being whose beauty bears witness to the divine beauty, by being the divine revelation itself, the theophany par excellence. As the place and form of the theophany, he bears witness to this beauty of the divine Subject Himself; because he is present to the divine Subject as His witness, it means that God is contemplating Himself in him, is contemplating the evidence of Himself.'[332]

Although the imagery of *shāhid-bāzī* is all-pervasive in Persian poetry, unfortunately there exists no adequate treatment of its erotic theology in any Western language.[333] Eve Feuillebois-Pierunek underlines the ambiguity of the practice in her definitive study of Fakhr al-Dīn 'Irāqī's (d. 688/1289) erotic theory:

> il désigne un jeune homme ou une jeune fille de toute beauté, pris comme miroirs ou 'témoins' de la Beauté divine. C'est aussi l'Image de Dieu dans le Coeur: témoin, contemplation et adorateur ne font alors plus qu'un. Certains soufis semblent avoir fait un usage régulier de supports humains de contemplation, et cette attitude est connue sous le nom de *shāhid-bāzī*, contemplation de la Beauté divine sous un forme humaine.[334]

In his chapter devoted to the meaning of the term in Ḥāfiẓ's poetry (which covers its usage by the important authorities of the Sufi Path who have written about *shāhid/shāhid-bāzī*, including 'Abdu'llāh Anṣārī [d. 482/1089], Qushayrī [d. 465/1074] and Rūzbihān Baqlī [d. 606/1210]), Aḥmad 'Alī Rajā'ī Bukhārā'ī reveals that 'in the Sufi lexicon, the Witness signifies both "the Absolute Good" and "Fair-faced" at once, with the connotation that the *shāhid* is one who bears "witness" to God's artifice'.[335] In this regard, Sufis often referred to the renowned saying of the Prophet: 'Indeed, God is beautiful and loves beauty.'[336] Alluding to this *ḥadīth*, while commenting on the Sufi poet Kamāl Khujandī's doctrine of *shāhid-bāzī* (Ḥāfiẓ's and Kamāl's erotic teachings are essentially identical), the Sufi hagiographer Ibn Karbalā'ī explains, 'Dhū'l-Nūn the Egyptian said: 'Whoever becomes an intimate of God becomes intimate with every beautiful thing [*shay' malīḥ*], every beautiful face [*wajh ṣabīḥ*], every beautiful form and every delectable fragrance [*rā'iḥa ṭayyiba*].'[337] The king of lovers and gnostics, Shaykh Abū Muḥammad Rūzbihān al-Baqlī pronounced: 'The inner aspect of the realm of divinity [*lāhūt*] is effortlessly incarnated in the realm of humanity [*nāsūt*], and the realm of humanity in turn reflects the beauty of the realm of divinity.'[338]

The reflection of divinity within humanity, described here by Rūzbihān, was based on the Sufi mystico-erotic doctrine that taught, similar to Aristophanes' speech in the *Symposium*,[339] that love always pursues wholeness and is essentially the desire of lover and beloved to merge into one. Under the sway of the divine theophany, the mystic's individual identity could virtually melt into that of his theophanic Witness, as 'Ayn al-Quḍāt Hamadānī (executed 526/1132: a disciple of Aḥmad Ghazālī) explains:

> The love of the contemplated Object/Witness [*shāhid*] becomes one with the divine contemplated Subject [*mashūd*], causing *shāhid* and *mashūd* to merge into one. You imagine this to be incarnationism [*ḥulūl*], yet it is not. It is the quintessence of mystical oneness [*ittiḥād*], and according to the religion of the

Verifiers [*madhhab-i muḥaqqiqān*], no other religion exists. Have you ever heard these verses?

> Anyone whose life does not rest
> upon that Idol, that Witness-of-Beauty,
> is no devotee, nor man of true austerity
> in the faith of infidelity.
> Infidelity is that you yourself
> become that Witness-of-Beauty.
> If infidelity is such as this
> No one else exists in unicity.[340]

If 'Ayn al-Quḍāt's statement gives a taste of the sophisticated antinomian theological doctrine sustaining this art of erotic contemplation, the following passage from a work by Quṭb al-Dīn al-'Abbād (d. 547/1152) contains the most revealing description of the spiritual psychology underlying its actual practice:

> It should be understood that in Sufi terminology there are many different sorts of (implications to the term) *shāhid*. The *shāhid* is that thing found to be acceptable to the eyes of the heart. It is an interior spiritual reality [*ma'nā*] that becomes attached to heart such that the heart beholds it in all its states, seeking deeper intimacy with it by envisioning it [*bi-dīdār-i ū uns talabad*], and the *shāhid* is one who 'bears witness'. Therefore, that which the spiritual wayfarer's heart becomes intimately attached to beholding, and which it contemplates in all its contemplative moments, such that that thing attests and bears witness to the soundness of its presential awareness-of-heart – that thing is the *shāhid.* As long at wayfarer languishes and longs for the sight of it, he is a spectator or observer [*mashāhid*], but as soon as by way of contemplative absorption and annihilation, he loses all personal qualification of self, drowning in the essence of the *shāhid*, he becomes a 'martyr' [*shahīd*: lit. 'one who has borne witness for his faith'].
>
> So whatever the wayfarer's heart hangs upon is his *shāhid*, whether this be a phenomenal form [*ṣūrat*], a song [*āwāz*], a verse, an idea, or a moment of meditation [*waqt*]. As for one who makes his *shāhid* out to be a beautiful face or a child, there is no warrant for this on the Sufi Path [*ni ḥukm-i ṭarīqatī-ast*]; rather, this belongs to the after-effects of the powers of concupiscence [*quwwa-yi shawat*]. In this fashion whenever the heart resolves to pursue its 'invisible Witness of Beauty' [*shāhid-i ghaybī*], and the base passional soul [*nafs-i ammara*] is unable to apprehend that Reality for itself, it attaches itself to a form in this visible phenomenal world, thus becoming bound and attached to a certain 'pretty face' which is an image of the divine workmanship, and that thing they call the *shāhid.*[341]

As this extraordinarily profound passage teaches, the Sufi's love of God is, psychologically speaking, *nolens volens*, couched in the terminology of human erotic relationships. Thus, while the *shāhid* is both 'an interior spiritual reality' through which the mystic experiences intimacy with the Divine, the reflection of that 'reality' can also become manifest in any mundane phenomenon, be it a person, song, verse of poetry or meditative mood. 'One is always in love with something or other', the Romantic poet Shelley admitted, 'the error, and I confess it is not easy for spirits encased in flesh and blood to avoid it, consists in seeking in a mortal image the likeness of what is perhaps eternal'.[342]

This refined amatory psychology obtained its most sophisticated elaboration in the *Sawāniḥ al-'ushshāq* ('The Lovers' Experiences'), written by Aḥmad al-Ghazālī (d. 520/1126), younger brother of Islam's great Sunni-Sufi theologian Abū Ḥāmid al-Ghazālī (d. 505/1111). In this short treatise, the first treatise on erotico-mystical love in the Persian language, Ghazālī describes the various erotic appearances of the beloved as constituting 'the physiognomy or intuitive discernment of love [*firāsat-i 'ishq*]'. The lover must have enough discernment and a sufficient understanding of physiognomy to recognize the physical appearances of the beloved in this world. 'Each of these [appearances]', states Ghazālī, 'lies upon the path of the lover's intuitive discernment through love; each of them is an expression of his spiritual or physical quest, or else some ill-aspect or deficiency in his quest. This is because love manifests certain signs beneath and behind the many veils that becurtain it, each of the spiritual realities [*ma'ānī*] is a sign of love that is displayed through the [semi-diaphanous] curtain of imagination [*parda-yi khiyāl*].'[343]

The true *shāhid*, says Ḥāfiẓ, is not simply a girl possessed of a 'slender waist and beautiful hair' – that is, some sexually attractive woman (or man) – but one whose beauty incarnates a certain ineffable *je ne sais quoi* that is described by Sufis as the metaphysical 'mystery-of-beauty' (*ān*):

> The beloved is not one with beautiful hair or a slender waist;
> Be the slave of that radiant face which has a *mystery-of-beauty*.[344]

By his elucidation of the metaphysics of the erotic theology sustaining the Sufi contemplative experience in the *Sawāniḥ*, Aḥmad Ghazālī established himself as a – if not *the* – founder of the literary topos and mystical persuasion that later came to be known as the 'religion of love' (*madhhab-i 'ishq*) in Islamic Sufism. In Ghazālī's *Sawāniḥ*, in 'Ayn al-Quḍāt's *Tamhīdāt* – and two centuries later, in the *Dīvāns* of Sa'dī, Awḥad al-Dīn Kirmānī, Ḥāfiẓ and Kamāl Khujandī – *shāhid-bāzī* became featured as one of the key contemplative disciplines of this new, challenging and radical Religion of Love. Following Ghazālī's lead, the erotic vocabulary of Sufi poetry came to be characterized by a parabolic quality, the result of a studied ambiguity which involved a reserve of meaning beyond the comprehension of the average intelligence. Exactly like the *trobar clus* poetry of the troubadours of Italy during this epoch, in classical Persian prose and poetry devoted to the art of erotic contemplation (*shāhid-bāzī*), it became virtually impossible to distinguish between the metaphysics of the spirit and the erotics of the flesh. The art historian A. Papadopoulo refers to this perspective as expressing an 'aesthetic of ambiguity',[345] a viewpoint suggesting, as John Renard points out, that 'the work does not coerce the viewer into attaching any one spiritual meaning to the form ... the viewer cannot always say for certain which painters, for example, intended their scenes of lovers in a paradisal garden to be taken as visions of heavenly reality, and which wanted the viewer to see merely an earthly picnic'.[346] Ghazālī's explicitly erotic vocabulary – couched in symbolic allusions (*ishārāt*) to describe the ambigious experience of love, whether sexual or sacral – was developed and enriched by his later Sufi followers, particularly Rūzbihān Baqlī of Shīrāz (d. 606/1210), whose views on 'beauty-worship' (*jamāl-parastī*)[347] were a key influence on Sa'dī's theoerotic verse.[348] Ḥāfiẓ was certainly familiar with Rūzbihān's views, and may have even been attached to his Sufi order.[349]

The most famous Persian Sufi teacher who made the erotic theology of *shāhid-bāzī* the foundation of his doctrine was Awḥad al-Dīn Kirmānī (d. 635/1238). In Kirmānī's Sufi tradition of erotic spirituality, a tradition to which Ḥāfiẓ's *Dīvān* directly belongs, human love forms a bridge across which every seeker necessarily must fare to reach the farther – divine – shore. This idea was encapsulated in an Arabic maxim: 'The phenomenal form is a bridge to the supra-formal Reality [*al-majāz qanṭarat al-ḥaqīqat*].'[350] Kirmānī's verses gives a good summary of the basic doctrine of *shāhid-bāzī*:

> Our soul's an infant on the Way;
> The Witness is its nurse. To sport
> And play with the Witness always is
> What gives the soul its sustenance.
> These fair forms that you contemplate
> Are not themselves that lovely Witness:
> They are just shadows cast from it.[351]

The practice of mystic-lovers such as 'Irāqī and Kirmānī, explains Jāmī apologetically in his biography of the latter, 'was that they always engaged in the scrutiny of the phenomenal forms of sensory beauty and by medium of those forms they contemplated the beauty of God Almighty'.[352] The contemplative discipline of *shāhid-bāzī*, as these verses and Jāmī's remarks about their author demonstrate, constitutes the main practice of the *rind*'s romantic religion, a practice of course completely at odds with conventional Muslim ethics confined within the boundaries of a priggish moral code based on the artificial and ultimately – the ontologically unreal – sacred/profane dichotomy.[353] The moral probity of the practice was left to depend entirely on the beholder's subjective *viewpoint*.[354] If he practised the discipline properly, the seer *shāhid-bāz* would be graced with a vision of the Sublime and divine through contemplation of fair faces (*rū-yi khubān*) which, though ostensibly ungodly and mundane, could be viewed as being a 'divine creation' (*sun'-i khudā-y*).[355] The human form beheld in selfless ecstasy becomes a 'theophanic witness' (gender is always ambiguous in Persian, but in Ḥāfiẓ's verse the Witness is nearly always female[356]). The inspired libertine's selfless gaze[357] on heavenly beauty in the mirror of earthly phenomenal forms invariably invites the condemnation of the prim, prudish guardians of the Muslim moral law. In the following verse, Ḥāfiẓ addresses the angry Sufi shaykh who reproached him for pursuit of romantic love, giving this formalist foe of his a robust riposte:

> I am not about to abandon love, nor the secret Witness,
> Nor the cup of wine. I have sworn off these things
> A hundred times, and I won't do it again.[358]

Unlike Christian theological doctrine, which distinguishes strictly between divine *agape* and human *eros*, holding the second to be a debased form of the first and only indulged at the expense of the former, in Ḥāfiẓ's metaphysics of love there is little or no differentiation between earthly human and heavenly divine love. In Ḥāfiẓ's erotic imagery, as Eric Schroeder observed, 'there is a changing relationship and a constant connection between the erotic and the metaphysical ... his erotic is not sentimental but charged with physical reality and an incipient metaphysical penetration which allows of a strange and wide-flung rhetoric in which the bodily and the cosmic lie together entangled'.[359] Indeed, as Ḥāfiẓ provocatively challenges: 'What will anyone who has not nibbled on the apple within the chin of the beautiful Witness understand of the fruits of Paradise?'[360] – romantic love forms a wonderful bridge to Divine *Eros*. The ambiguity of such erotic imagery could be fully exploited by the use of *double entendre* or amphibology (*īhām*) by Religion-of-Love poets – a poetic device of special significance in Ḥāfiẓ's poetics.[361] Erotic contemplation thus became a kind of religious injunction among the poets of this school such as Awḥad al-Dīn Kirmānī, Sa'dī,[362] Khwājū, Kamāl Khujandī, and particularly Ḥāfiẓ, who enjoined it with pontifical tones throughout his *Dīvān*:

> Don't kiss anything except the sweetheart's lip
> And the cup of wine, Ḥāfiẓ; friends, it's a grave mistake
> To kiss the hand held out to you by a puritan.[363]

According to the tenets of Ḥāfiẓ's erotic spirituality (I cite here Lāhūrī's marvellous exegesis of this verse):

> the adept should not seek the grace of anyone but the human figurative beloved [*ma'shūq-i majāzī*] and human love [*maḥabbat-i majāzī*] since she is a vehicle by means of which one attains union to the True Beloved [*ma'shūq-i ḥaqīqī*] and True Love [*maḥabbat-i ḥaqīqī*]; by the intermediary means of the

> figurative human beloved and human love one may unite oneself with the True Beloved and experience True Love – for (as the Arabic adage goes) 'the figurative is a bridge to the Real' ... It is a grave error to kiss the hand of and pledge oneself to those who sell their ascetic abstinence for the sake of riches, worldly rank and status.[364]

In this fashion, the *malāmatī* lover's adherence to the creed of romantic love and practice of the art of erotic contemplation served as an antidote to the blame and hatred that he invariably incurred from Muslim pharisees.

The Erotic Gaze: Contemplation of Human Beauty sub specie aeternitatis (naẓar-bāzī)

A complementary aspect of the erotic contemplation of the inspired libertine in Ḥāfiẓ's verse is the poetic genre of the theoerotics of the eye, in which the poet casts a playful regard on beauty (*naẓar-bāz*) and beholds the divine in the mirror of human beauty insofar as the latter bears 'witness' (*shāhid*) to the former. Ḥāfiẓ refers to this key-concept in various constructions[365] altogether ten times in the *Dīvān*. In the three out of four instances the term *naẓar-bāz* is associated with the word 'inspired libertine' (*rind*) and/or the word 'lover' (*'āshiq*),[366] and in all five instances where he refers to his infatuation with 'the sport of the visual regard' and boasts of playing the 'game of glances' (*naẓar-bāzī*), he characterizes the practice as being one of the lover's foremost accomplishments.[367] In one of these instances, when speaking about the ambiguous metaphysical gaze that contemplates physical human beauty, Ḥāfiẓ boasts:

> I am a lover and a libertine, a player of
>   The game of glances with eyes that gaze in love.
> Such myriad arts and skills are my ornament:
>   I say it plain – in fact, I show it off.[368]

His contemplative regard for human beauty (*naẓar-bāzī*) is 'an art of particular significance to Ḥāfiẓ, a key term in the poetry of which he boasts in many verses',[369] as Khurramshāhī informs us. Translated here as 'game of glances with eyes that gaze in love', *naẓar-bāzī* means literally 'playing with one's glance', 'to cast a flirtatious glance upon' or 'to capriciously regard mortal beauty'. It is the gaze of the mystic who engages in the 'Witness Game' (*shāhid-bāzī*). Ḥāfiẓian aesthetics dictates the sacrality of human love and beauty, for as Lāhūrī in his commentary pronounces: 'It is only through the forms of mortal beauty [*suwar-i husniyya*] that God-as-Absolute in reality can attract the hearts of lovers to Himself.'[370] Explaining the contemplative technique of his erotic gaze, Lāhūrī comments that 'the gnostic of Shīrāz [Ḥāfiẓ] spent most of his time absorbed in contemplation of the True Beauty [*jamāl-i Ḥaqīqī*]', and for this purpose resorted to regarding the appearances of figurative human beauty [*tawaṣṣul bih maẓāhir-i ḥusniyya-yi majāzī*] ... his eyes preoccupied in contemplation of the True Beauty [*jamāl-i ḥaqīqī*] through the veil of the appearances of these moon-faced ladies'.[371] Thus, *to be human is to 'regard' human beauty*, the measure of humanity lying in the capacity to love and to experience the erotic in all its degrees human and divine, according to the Religion-of-Love poets.[372]

With this brief introduction into the two key contemplative disciplines of Ḥāfiẓ's erotic spirituality, we are now in a better position to re-examine the amatory psychology of the wild romantic *rind* who incarnates their practice.

One of the key verses summarizing Ḥāfiẓ's erotic theology of inspired libertinism (*rindī*) is the following:

> *Zāhid ar rāh bi rindī nabarad ma'dhūr-ast /*
> *'Ishq kārī'st kay mawqūf-i hidāyat bāshad*
>
> If the zealous puritan never found the way
> To penetrate into Romance's universe, well,
> He's forgiven – since Love's a business that hinges
> On inculcation and tutelage.[373]

By pairing *rindī* in the first hemistich with Love (*'ishq*) in the second, the poet makes *rindī* homologous to love, while love, in turn, is affirmed to be the quintessence of *rindī*. Thus one may deduce that loverhood (*'āshiqī*) and inspired libertinage (*rindī*) are identical in essence, a teaching that Ḥāfiẓ professes in a number of other verses as well.[374] In Persian Sufi poetry of the *qalandariyya* genre, the pairing of lover (*'āshiq*) and libertine (*rind*) is very common, as we can see in this verse by Shāh Ni'matu'llāh:

> Since faith and creed of *qalandars* consists in taking lovers
> And libertines as examples, we too take *qalandar* ways.[375]

Exactly the same juxtaposition of these terms appears throughout Kamāl Khujandī's *Dīvān* as well, as in this verse:

> It's clear as day that I'm a lover and a libertine;
> In paying homage to your visage, I am true as dawn.[376]

This ubiquitous terminological cohabitation of loverhood and libertinism (*rindī va 'āshiqī*) in Ḥāfiẓ's *Dīvān*, and in the works of these two other major Sufi poets contemporary with him, reveals the *rind* to be a *fedeli d'amore* who adopts *Eros* and infatuation with Beauty-as-Beloved in all manifestations as his personal religious creed. Turning from Eternity towards the realm of space and time, this mystic lover, who is an *extreme romantic*, contemplates God's appearances as the Beautiful (*al-Jamīl*) through His theophanic human form (*shāhid*), founding a cult of love upon the adoration of beauty.[377] This is the meaning of so many of Ḥāfiẓ's plaints, such as the following verse:

> *Man Ādam-i bihishtī-am ammā darīn safar*
> *ḥālī asīr-i 'ishq-i javānān-i mahvasham*
>
> I am Adam come down from heaven
> Yet, here and now, in this journey, remain
> Bewitched – ensnared in love
> With youths with faces like the moon.[378]

In Ḥāfiẓ's erotic theology it is only through the romantic experience of becoming ensnared by earthly beauty through contemplation of the theophanic witness (*shāhid*) that the mystic paradoxically obtains release from the bonds of selfhood, which is why he says:

> I broadcast it out loud, and in this boast take delight:
> I am Love's bondslave, free of earth and heaven both.
> I was an angel and the supreme paradise my sanctuary;
> It is man who brought me to this deserted cloister.[379]

In the universe of Romance and the realm of *rindī*, liberation from the confines of mortality can only be obtained by the lover casting his glance (*naẓar-bāzī*) on the Sublime-in-mundane-disguise; that is, by practising the art of contemplation of the theophanic witness (*shāhid-bāzī*) whose presence gives him visual testimony of the existence of heavenly love and beauty. The Ishrāqī philosopher Muḥammad Dārābī, in his commentary on this verse, thus explains:

> How should Love's bondslave – who is not fettered by any attachment, nor subject to any of the degrees of being, nor bound by the chain of existent beings either in this world and the Next and so is king over the realms of Appearance and Reality – not be delighted and find gratification in knowing that the entire cosmos is subject to Him? For his 'slavery' is the source of all liberty ... Being detached from everything, he is free, and from that standpoint he realizes that all the appearances in the world are but diverse manifestations of that Beauty, and thus he is also *with* everything...[380]

'Inspired' by being 'enthralled' to Love, the 'libertine' is thus paradoxically 'free' through being fettered by the bonds of romantic attachment. Shāh Ni'matullāh provides a subtle summary of this romantic 'theology of liberation' through servitude to love preached by the inspired libertine in his essay on the *Spiritual Degrees of the Inspired Libertines* (*Marātib-i rindān*):

> In our creed the inspired libertine is subject to no veil whatsoever, whereas the hapless puritan ascetic (*zāhid*) is veiled by dint of his own abstinence and devotion ... Since the inspired libertine is not subject to anything, how should he be fettered by learning and books? ... The words of the inspired libertines [*qawl-i rindān*] reflect their cognizance of the fact that the entire world consists of God's Beauty [*jamāl Allāh*], since 'God is Beautiful and loves beauty'. Therefore, the lover who is fond of the world through the love he harbours for God, in reality loves God alone through God's own love, for the beauty of the product in reality returns back to the Producer Himself. What a subtle matter![381]

The inspired libertine, like the *qalandar*, is thus detached from the world, whence his castigation of all those concerned with its affairs, whether sanctimonious pharisaical puritans or princes enthralled by the sceptre and crown of rule. It is in this spirit that Ḥāfiẓ preaches:

> Why should the inspired rogue who sets the world on fire
> Bother himself with wise counsel and advice? This world's
> Labours it is that require reflection and deliberation.[382]

Unconcerned with the material realm and all its labours (*kār-i mulk*), the kingdom of the inspired libertine/rogue/lover is *not of this world*, his soul not enmeshed in the political woes and economic weal of his day and age.[383] This denigration of 'wise counsel and advice' (*maṣlaḥāt-andīshī*) by Ḥāfiẓ's libertine in this verse was modelled on the following verse by Sa'dī: 'The reasoner ['*āqil*] is a thinker and sere prudent deliberator over what's wise. Come, profess the Religion of Love [*madhhab-i 'ishq*], and free yourself from both thinking and deliberation.'[384] The inspired libertine's works are labours of love. He scorns the Sufi mantle (*khirqa*)[385] and spurns the king's crown[386] as well as the cleric's gown, resting his brow beside the drunkard's head on the tavern stoop.[387] He vaunts the beggar who glories in the kingdom of love and smashes the crown of worldly dominion.[388] He takes louts for personal confidantes.[389]

Ḥāfiẓ's exploitation of plebeian vocabulary,[390] which subverts the spiritual materialism of the exoteric religious and political authorities, is dictated by the higher standpoint of the *secta amoris* which he follows. The libertine–lover soon realizes that the dross of his being can only become refined in the alembic of blame (*malāmat*).[391] This is because (as Maybudī put it): 'Blame is the entire substance of the lover's soul. All his assets lie in enduring the reproach of the vulgar [*malāmat*]. What sort of lover is he who cannot take blame?'[392] Blame (*malāmat*) has a very positive effect on the spirit 'because there is safety in derision', as Yeats understood,[393] for unless the spirit endures the blame of all and sundry it can never sever its ties with this lower realm and approach the beloved.[394] Since blame focuses his attention away from himself towards divine Unity, *malāmat* becomes the first authentic spiritual degree of the inspired libertine/lover.

At this juncture, having suffered reproach and abuse, the lover now becomes bereft of all avarice and desire for the world. The barbs of criticism hurled by friend and foe alike catapult him onto the higher stage of spiritual isolation (*tajrīd*) and denudation of self (*tafrīd*); from this standpoint, blame (*malāmat*), now appears paradoxically as a kind of grace which emanates the beloved's zealous exclusiveness (*ghayrat*). 'You should understand that he who is accepted by us is rejected by people and whosoever is accepted by people is rejected by us', Hujwīrī states, explaining the thinking behind this erotic doctrine. 'To incur blame [*malāmat-i khalq*] from the vulgar is therefore the very sustenance of God's lovers. By receiving that blame, one finds proofs of God's acceptance. This is, in fact, the mystical persuasion of the saints [*mashrab-i awliyā*].'[395] It is exactly in this vein that Ḥāfiẓ counsels that blame is an integral aspect of any affair of Amor:

> Whoever deserts your pathway because of blame
> Will never prosper whatsoever he does, and in
> The end expiates his error with endless shame.[396]

Characterizing Ḥāfiẓ as a follower of the 'path of blame' (*mashrab-i malāmatī*) while interpreting this verse, Lāhūrī explains that because 'the lover of God is always subject to blame from people, the affairs of any lover who pays heed to such blame will never prosper. Since he has already given his heart up to the beloved, to all others he must be indifferent.'[397]

When the inspired libertine-lover succeeds in maintaining fidelity in *Amor* despite blame, at this level, his figurative human beloved (*ma'shūqa-i majāzī*) becomes his 'representative of supernatural beauty in the flesh [*shāhid*]' with whom he cavorts (*shāhid-bāzī*). The lover's playful engagement with the beloved (*shāhid-bāzī*) is thus the intermediate degree of *rindī*, generated from the stage of *malāmat*.[398] At this stage, the lover becomes identified with the higher religion of 'real infidelity' (*kufr-i ḥaqīqī*), an integral part of the Religion of Love (*madhhab-i 'ishq*) as well. In the Persian Sufi tradition the stock symbol of such successful endurance of blame in love is the legendary Shaykh Ṣan'ān, who converted to Christianity on falling in love with a Christian girl, his theophanic witness. We should take San'ān as a model of the perfect *malāmatī* lover, Ḥāfiẓ counsels:

> If you profess yourself a devotee of
> The highway of most noble Love
> Never give a second thought for name
> Or what men say is all 'ill-fame',
> Recall the cap and gown
> Of great Shaykh San'ān –
> For months in hock, set in
> The wine-seller's shop for pawn.[399]

However, only when he is utterly detached from his 'self' does he reach the second degree of Romance – that is, of *rindī* – which is the level of 'being a beloved' (*ma'shūqī*). It is from this level that the selfless discourse of the inspired libertines issue forth.[400]

At the third and highest degree, the lover attains divine Unity. There, he discovers Absolute Love itself, becoming detached from all created being, freed from selfhood, indifferent both to both praise and blame, and even detached from the beloved her/himself. In sum, there are three spiritual levels through which the inspired libertine gradually ascends: 'At the first stage of *rindī* is the degree of loverhood [*'āshiqī*], transcending the created material realm. The second stage is that of being a beloved [*ma'shūqī*], which transcends duality, and the third degree is that of Love [*'ishq*] and divine Unity [*tawḥīd*].'[401]

From this overview of the romantic vision of the inspired libertine, it is clear that from Ḥāfiẓ's erotocentric perspective, *rindī* denotes the lover's awareness of the 'Fine Arts' of *Amor*, which comprise his gnosis of the beloved/Beloved, his discernment of the aesthetics of erotic contemplation and the erotic gaze (*shāhid-/naẓar-bāzī*) on the physical plane, and finally his cognizance of Love's metaphysics. *Rindī* is thus the mystic romantic's personal conviction and creed during his progress and ascension towards the world of Absolute Love. This *via purgativa* and ascension of the lover into 'the height of Love's rare Universe'[402] is an experience quite different from the rough encounter with the Mafioso thugs and hoodlums in the back-alleys of medieval Shīrāz by Sa'dī's dervish. Instead of being robbed of one's material possessions by hoodlums in the material marketplace, the mystic *rind* undergoes a process of spiritual denudation, in which the landscape of his heart is cleared of all attachments and filled with God. For this reason, only the inspired libertine/rake (*rind*) who has endured blame, not the puritan ascetic who follows religious rites by rote, achieves salvation in love's religion, as Ḥāfiẓ states:

> The ascetic had too much pride so could never soundly
> Traverse the Path. But the rake by way of humble entreaty
> And beggary at last went down to the House of Peace.[403]

The term *rind*, it is useful to remember in this context, is derived from *randa*, the 'carpenter's plane'. In his commentary on Shabistarī's *Gulshan-i rāz* (*Garden of Mystery*), Muḥammad Lāhījī (d. 912/1507), drawing on this etymology, describes the inspired libertine (*rind*) as 'one who has cast away and shaved off all the forms of multiplicity and determined forms of being with the carpenter's plane of self-obliteration and self-annihilation [*randah-i maḥw va fanā'*]...'.[404] The habitation of the inspired libertine is the Tavern of Ruin (*kharābāt*), where he cannot be qualified by any spiritual or temporal description (*awṣāf*). He is free from the concrete properties (*aḥkām*) of being, having become emancipated from all ties of the world in all its confusing multiplicity.[405] Echoing Lāhījī's definitions, Lāhūrī likewise explains that:

> The *rind* according to the terminology of this noble company [the Sufis] signifies a person who has shaved off all the attachments of the realm of illusory multiplicity – whether these pertain to the Necessary or possible Being and their Divine Names, Attributes, pre-determined archetypal prototypes, characteristics and qualities along with all their various concrete aspects – with the carpenter's plane [*randa*] of annihilation and obliteration [*maḥw u fanā'*] from the reality of his self. In this manner he has freed himself of everything. Thus he becomes the crown of the world and mankind. No other creature attains the summit of his exalted degree.[406]

As we can see, in Ḥāfiẓ's lexicon terms such as *rind*, *zāhid*, *qalandar*, and so forth, have meanings quite contrary to what they seem to literally represent. They are symbolic references encoded in poetic language to express the realm of experience of the heart's initiates,[407] reflecting both the mystical themes of romantic experience (*rindī*) on the Sufi *via purgativa* (with the plane of spiritual practice shaving clean the psyche of the impurities of material existence), which are in turn derived from the literary tradition of the *malāmatiyya*, *qalandariyya* and the 'Religion of Love' topos in classical Persian poetry.

Notes

1 Zarrīnkūb, *Az kūcha-i rindān*, p. xii. For an extended discussion of his date of birth, see 'Alī Akbar Dihkhudā, 'Ḥāfiẓ Shīrāzī', *Lughat-nāma*, vol. 5, pp. 7490–1. Qazvīnī believed him to have been born in 715/1315 (see Mu'īn, *Ḥāfiẓ-i shīrīn-sukhan*, I, p. 139).

2 Limbert, *Shīrāz in the Age of Hafez*, pp. 108–18; Zarrīnkūb, *Az kūcha-i rindān*, pp. 9ff.

3 A.J. Arberry, *Shīrāz: Persian City of Saints and Poets.*

4 Ḥāfiẓ heaps scorn on these corrupt charitable endowments in one place in his *Dīvān* (ed. Khānlarī, *ghazal* 45: 4). Also, cf. Zarrīnkūb, *Az kūcha-i rindān*, p. 7, citing Qazwīnī's *Nuzhat al-qulūb*, p. 138.

5 As Zarrīnkūb observes: 'Judging by what can be seen from his *Dīvān*, Ḥāfiẓ's age was a time full of corruption and sin, hypocrisy and crime.' *Az kūcha-i rindān*, p. 38.

6 *Ibid.*, p. 8.

7 Sa'dī, *Kulliyāt-i Sa'dī*, Furūghī, p. 726; cited by Jahramī, 'Mākhaz-i andīshahā-yi Sa'dī: Rūzbihān Baqlī Shīrāzī', p. 101.

8 'Isā b. Junayd Shīrāzī, *Tadhkira-yi Hazār-mazār.*

9 A good overview of these sites is given by Betteridge, '*Ziārat:* Pilgrimmage to the Shrines of Shīrāz'.

10 Annemarie Schimmel, 'The Ornament of the Saints', p. 105.

11 On the tombs of Shīrāz, see Betteridge, '*Ziārat:* Pilgrimmage to the Shrines of Shīrāz'.

12 Cited by Arberry, *Shīrāz: Persian City*, p. 62.

13 Zarrīnkūb, *Justujū'ī dar taṣawwuf-i Irān*, p. 226.

14 Cited by Zarrīnkūb, *Az kūcha-i rindān*, p. 11.

15 Cited by Arberry, *Shīrāz: Persian City*, p. 52.

16 Cited by Zarrīnkūb, *Az kūcha-i rindān*, p. 10.

17 *Dīvān-i Ḥāfiẓ*, ed. Khānlarī, *ghazal* 274: 1, 4.

18 *Shahr-i 'ishq*, *Dīvān-i Ḥāfiẓ*, ed. Khānlarī, *ghazal* 261: 5.

19 Zarrīnkūb, *Az kūcha-i rindān*, pp. 11, 22.

20 'Ḥāfiẓ's entire vision is dominated and overshadowed by love. It happens exactly the same way that, for example, a history of real events becomes attenuated during the time of romance when one falls in love. Love is always present there and visible, flowing through his vocabulary. Even when a certain historical event appears to have been clearly the occasion of a certain poem, the [romantic] inspiration animating it immediately dissipates and dissolves that history. For Ḥāfiẓ, love is the underlying cause of the world.' Fouchécour, *Hafiz de Chiraz*, introduction, pp. 15–16.

21 Schimmel, *The Poet's Geography*, p. 9.

22 *Dīvān-i Khāqānī*, vol. 2, p. 791 (*ghazal* 31, v. 4).

23 *Kulliyyāt-i Shams ya Dīvān-i kabīr*, V, 2494/26367.

24 *Dīvān-i Kamāl al-Dīn Mas'ūd Khujandī*, ed. Dawlatābādī, introduction, p. 4. See also my 'The Life and Times of Kamāl Khujandī', pp. 164–5.

25 Cited by Zarrīnkūb, *Az kūcha-i rindān*, p. 205, n. 1.

26 *Dīvān-i Ḥāfiẓ*, ed. Khānlarī, *ghazal* 329: 5–6, *.

27 *Ibid.*, *ghazal* 40: 8–9.

28 Ṣafā, *Tārīkh-i Adabiyāt-i Īrān*, III, pp. 1072–3. For parallels between these poets and Ḥāfiẓ, see Khurramshāhī, *Ḥāfiẓ-nāma*, I, pp. 40–90.

29 Zarrīnkūb, *Az kūcha-i rindān*, p. 64.

30 See Mu'īn, *Ḥāfiẓ-i shīrīn-sukhan*, I, pp. 306–13; Browne, *Literary History of Persia*, III, pp. 293–5. On Ḥāfiẓ's praise of Amīn al-Dīn, see Arberry, *Shīrāz: Persian City*, p. 142; Ghanī, *Baḥth dar*, I, pp. 70–1, 124, 166–8. See also my essay in this volume, pp. 164–6.

31 Schimmel, 'Ḥāfiẓ and His Contemporaries', p. 943.

32 Cited by Jalāl Khāliqī-Muṭlaq, 'Tan-kāma-sarayī', p. 27.

33 On important verse-parallels between Ḥāfiẓ and Khwājū, see Manṣūr Rastigār-Fasā'ī, *Ḥāfiẓ: paydā'ī va pinhān-i zindigī*, pp. 20–1; Browne, *A Literary History of Persia*, III, pp. 294–5; *Dīwān-i Khwājū Kirmānī*, ed. Qāni'ī, *passim*; Khurramshāhī, *Ḥāfiẓ-nāma*, I, pp. 68–74; 'Alī Akbar Dihkhudā, *Lughat-nāma*, V, pp. 7497–8.

34 Ṣafā, *Tārīkh-i Adabiyāt-i Īrān*, III, p. 1073.

35 The *ghazal* from which this verse derives is featured in a number of good manuscripts, although it is found neither in Qazwīnī's or Khānlarī's editions; for a good overview of opposing scholarly opinions on this verse, see Mu'īn, *Ḥāfiẓ-i shīrīn-sukhan*, I, pp. 306–8.

36 See the various verses by Khwājū concerning these issues, cited by Ḥasan Anvarī in his introduction ('Ṭarz-i sukhan-i Khwājū') to *Dīwān-i Khwājū Kirmānī*, ed. Qāni'ī, pp. vi–viii. See also Yāsimī, 'Salmān va Ḥāfiẓ', pp. 599–602.

37 Yārshāṭir, *Shi'r-i fārsī dar 'ahd-i Shāhrukh*, p. 83.

38 Samarqandī, *Tadhkirat al-shu'arā'*, ed. 'Abbāsī, p. 286.

39 Yāsimī, *Sharḥ-i aḥwāl-i Salmān Sāvajī*, p. 105.

40 Mu'īn, *Ḥāfiẓ-i shīrīn-sukhan*, I, pp. 329–34, Browne, *Literary History of Persia*, III, pp. 296–8, and Taqī Tafaḍḍulī's introduction to *Dīvān-i Salmān Sāvajī*, ed. Mushfiq, pp. xxvii–xxxii, where the poetic parallels between them are presented. Ṣafā, *Tārīkh-i Adabiyāt-i Īrān*, III, p. 1013 points out 'the unity of metre, rhyme, and poetic imagery in some of the *ghazals* of Salmān and Ḥāfiẓ is so omnipresent as to make one imagine that these two masters were in correspondence with each other, consciously vying with one other in composing similar *ghazals*'. For further parallelisms, see Khurramshāhī, *Ḥāfiẓ-nāma*, I, pp. 79–85.

41 *Dīvān-i Ḥāfiẓ*, ed. Khānlarī, *ghazal* 251: 13.

42 *Dīvān-i Salmān Sāvajī*, ed. Mushfiq, p. 182.

43 *Ibid.*, p. 232.

44 *Dīvān-i Hilālī Chughatā'ī*. This verse is cited in the famous 1960s Iranian music programme: *Barg-i Sabz*, no. 293.

45 Losensky, 'Kamāl of Khojand'.

46 On which, see Khurramshāhī, *Ḥāfiẓ-nāma*, I, pp. 85–90; Mu'īn, *Ḥāfiẓ-i shīrīn-sukhan*, I, pp. 337–9; Ghanī, *Baḥth*, I, pp. 34–5.

47 Referring to the Shīrāzi ruler Abū'l-Favāris Jalāl al-Dīn Shāh Shujā' (reg. 760/1358–786/1384) to whom Ḥāfiẓ addressed several panegyrics.

48 *Dīvān-i Kamāl Khujandī*, ed. Shidfar, vol. 1, p. 451 (*ghazal* 428, in reply to Ḥāfiẓ's *ghazal* 163 [vv. 9–10], ed. Khānlarī). Ghanī (*Baḥth*, p. 34) believes the entire *ghazal* from which this verse was drawn was written as a welcoming response (*istiqbāl*) to Ḥāfiẓ's original. But Kamāl's comments about Ḥāfiẓ are indeed sometimes abusive (cf. Lewisohn, 'The Life and Times of Kamāl Khujandī').

49 Dawlatabādī, 'Kamāl Khujandī va Ḥāfiz Shīrāzī', in idem., *Tuḥfa-yi darvīsh*, pp. 529–35.

50 *Dīvān-i Ḥāfiẓ*, ed. Khānlarī, *ghazals* 8: 3; 47: 8; 444: 5, in which 'name and shame' (*nām u nang*) are repudiated.

51 *Dīwān-i Kamāl Khujandī*, ed. Shidfar, no. 233: 1.

52 *Ibid.*, no. 282: 5

53 For a discussion of this doctrine in classical Islamic love philosophy, see Griffen, *The Theory of Profane Love Among the Arabs*, pp. 118–37.

54 Sa'dī, *Kulliyāt-i Sa'dī*, ed. Muḥammad 'Alī Furūghī, *ghazal* 309, p. 524 (*maqṭa'*); *ghazal* 251: 7.

55 See J.T.P. De Bruijn, "Emād al-Dīn 'Alī Faqīh Kermānī', *EIr*, VIII, pp. 378–9.

56 See *Dīvān-i qaṣā'id va ghazaliyyāt-i Khwāja 'Imād al-Dīn 'Alī Faqīh Kirmānī*, ed. Rukn al-Dīn Humāyūn-Farrakh (who discusses the relationship between Ḥāfiẓ and 'Imād Faqīh), pp. lxv–lxviii. Mu'īn, *Ḥāfiẓ-i shīrīn-sukhan*, I, pp. 322–6, also discounts these legends.

57 See the examples given by Mu'īn, *Ḥāfiẓ-i shīrīn-sukhan*, I, pp. 324–6.

58 Cf. Mu'īn's remarks to this effect: *ibid.*, I, p. 324.

59 There is a large bulk of scholarship on the relationship (or lack thereof) between the Ḥāfiẓ and Shāh Ni'matu'llāh, of which Ḥamid Farzām, *Taḥqīq dar aḥwāl va naqd-i āthār va afkār-i Shāh Ni'matu'llāh Walī*, pp. 276–301, provides a learned overview. For discussions about the *ghazal* in question, see Mu'īn, *Ḥāfiẓ-i shīrīn-sukhan*, I, pp. 293–6, and 'Alī Aṣghar Maẓharī Kirmānī, 'Shāh Ni'matu'llāh Walī Kirmānī va Khvāja Ḥāfiẓ Shīrāzī', pp. 12–21.

60 *Kulliyāt-i Qāsim-i Anvār*, p. 281: 4621.

61 *Dīvān-i Ḥāfiẓ*, ed. Khānlarī, *ghazal* 418: 7. Parallel adduced by Mu'īn, *Ḥāfiẓ-i shīrīn-sukhan*, I, p. 298.

62 See Hasan Javadi, trans. *'Obeyd-e Zakani: the Ethics of Aristocrats and Other Satirical Works.*

63 See J.T.P. De Bruijn, "Ubayd-i Zakānī', *EI*², X, p. 764.

64 'Abbās Iqbāl's squeamish judgement about his 64 largely pornographic quatrains in his introduction to *Kulliyāt-i 'Ubayd Zākānī*, ed. Maḥjūb, p. xli.

65 His pornographic works have been fully published in the West in Persian (*Kulliyāt-i 'Ubayd Zākānī*) and a large selection translated in Paul Sprachman's *Suppressed Persian: An Anthology of Forbidden Literature*, pp. 44–75.

66 *Kulliyāt-i 'Ubayd Zākānī*, 'A. Iqbāl's introduction, p. xli.

67 Cf. the reference to *bad-nāmī* in *Kulliyāt-i 'Ubayd Zākānī*, *ghazal* 78, v. 575, replicated by Ḥāfiẓ's *ghazal* (ed. Khānlarī) 177: 5 (composed in the same metre and rhyme).

68 Mu'īn, *Ḥāfiẓ-i shīrīn-sukhan*, I, pp. 315–16 on this, and also pp. 320ff. for the literary parallels between the two poets.

69 *Ḥāfiẓ-i shīrīn-sukhan*, I, p. 315.

70 Riyāḥī, *Gulgasht*, p. 59; Zarrīnkūb, *Az kūcha-i rindān*, p. 48.

71 Ḥāfiẓ never used *hazl* or *hajv*, as Khurramshāhī ('Ḥāfiẓ dar farhang-i mā u farhang-i mā dar Ḥāfiẓ', p. 137) stresses.

72 Mu'īn, *Ḥāfiẓ-i shīrīn-sukhan*, I, p. 315, n. 28.

73 See Dominic Brookshaw, 'Odes of a poet-princess: the *ghazals* of Jahān-Malik Khātūn', p. 174, who also points out that there is a 'noticeable degree of overlap in the rhyme, meter and content ... between the *ghazals* of Ḥāfiẓ and Jahān-Malik' (p. 188, n. 60), with the implication that they influenced each other.

74 See Rastigār-Fasā'ī, ed., *Kulliyāt-i Bushāq Aṭ'amah*, introduction, pp. lxvii–lxxviii; and Mu'īn, *Ḥāfiẓ-i shīrīn-sukhan*, I, pp. 345–9, who provides a shortlist of these parodies of contemporary poets. See also Ghanī, *Baḥth*, I, pp. 35–8, for his parodies of Ḥāfiẓ.

75 For example, on the influence of Sa'dī on Ḥāfiẓ, see, e.g.: Adīb Ṭūsī, 'Muqāyisa bayn-i shi'r-i Sa'dī va Ḥāfiẓ', pp. 40–60. On Rūmī's influence on Ḥāfiẓ, see Khurramshāhī, 'Ḥāfiẓ va ghazaliyyāt-i Shams', in

his *Az sabza tā sitāra*, pp. 181–92. For further parallels between other poets and Ḥāfiẓ, see idem., *Ḥāfiẓ-nāma*, I, pp. 40–90.

76 'Azīz Dawlatabādī, 'Kamāl Khujandī va Ḥāfiz Shīrāzī', in his *Tuḥfa-yi darvīsh*, p. 534. See also Franklin Lewis' essay in this volume (p. 267, notes 33–5), where the same point is made.

77 For further discussion of this phenomenon, see my 'The Life and Poetry of Mashriqī Tabrīzī', pp. 115–17. On this grand tradition in Ḥāfiẓ's poetry, see Carl Ernst's judicious comments in his *The Shambhala Guide to Sufism*, pp. 163–4.

78 Although written in 892/1487 (nearly a century after Ḥāfiẓ's death), Dawlatshāh Samarqandī's remark about the over-abundance of poetry in late Timurid Iran easily holds true of the earlier literary milieu of fourteenth-century Shīrāz as well: 'Today everywhere you go, you find hordes of impostors laying claim to this profession [of poetry]. Wherever you listen is heard some poet muttering his doggerel verse, wherever you look appears some subtle wit, pleasant jester or critic (*laṭīfī u ẓarīfī u naẓīrī* [also names of Timurid poets]), yet they cannot tell the difference between verse and barley, between rhyme and an ass's rump. As the adage goes "the abundance of anything reduces its worth"' (*Tadhkirat al-shu'arā'*, ed. M. 'Abbāsī, p. 13).

79 See Yārshāṭir, *Shi'r-i fārsī*, pp. 57–71. The poetry fad was particularly widespread among the Sufis, who, as Ghanī (*Baḥth dar āthār*, II, p. 480) points out, from the eleventh century onwards had begun using poetry in their *samā'* ceremonies and preaching assemblies for contemplative and homiletic purposes.

80 Yārshāṭir, *Shi'r-i fārsī*, p. 54.

81 Browne, *A Literary History of Persia*, III, pp. 207–8.

82 *Dīvān-i Ḥāfiẓ*, ed. Khānlarī, *ghazal* 211: 7.

83 The two aspects of Ḥāfiẓ's superior genius and supremacy in being 'the greatest Persian poet', as 'Alī Muḥammad Ḥaqq-shinās ('Ma'nā va āzādī dar shi'r-i Ḥāfiẓ', pp. 157–8) observes, lies (a) in his intratextual appropriation of other poets' meanings and metaphors in such a manner that his transcreations invariably consitute an improvement on their lines, and (b) the inability of all later poets to improve on him by their own verse imitations.

84 As Ghanī points out, 'the impact of Ḥāfiẓ on the city of Shīrāz has been so tremendous that even the bare mention of the word Shīrāz often evokes the name of Ḥāfiẓ in the listener's mind, for which reason a contemporary poet in a verse speaks of Shīrāz as the "cradle of Ḥāfiẓ"'. *Baḥth*, II, p. 688.

85 Khurramshāhī, 'Ḥāfiẓ dar farhang-i mā u farhang-i mā dar Ḥāfiẓ', in idem., *Ḥāfiẓ Ḥāfiẓa-yi mā'st*, p. 128 – drawing heavily on the depth psychology of C.G. Jung. His statement is echoed by Zaryāb-khū'ī's (*Ā'yina-yi jām*, p. 24) view that 'Ḥāfiẓ is a compendium of our [Persian] culture and the symbol and archetype of the Persian spirit'.

86 Khurramshāhī, 'Ḥāfiẓ dar farhang-i mā', p. 132.

87 The earliest copy of his poems is an incomplete manuscript composed 20 years after his death; see Zarrīnkūb, *Az kūcha-i rindān*, p. xiii.

88 See *Dīvān-i Ḥāfiẓ*, ed. Khānlarī, II, pp. 1146–7; Fouchécour, *Hafiz de Chiraz*, introduction, p. 12. This manuscript is currently in the British Library: Or. 3247.

89 See *Dīvān-i Ḥāfiẓ*, ed. Khānlarī, II, p. 1148.

90 See *Ibid.*, II, pp. 1136–7, and his 'Darbāra-yi muqadama-yi jāma-yi *Dīvān*, pp. 1145–9.

91 Dihkhudā, *Lughat-nāma*, V, p. 7493.

92 Cited by Mu'īn, *Ḥāfiẓ-i shīrīn-sukhan*, II, p. 684.

93 *Dīvān-i Ḥāfiẓ*, ed. Khānlarī, *ghazal* 218: 3; Browne, *Literary History*, III, p. 283.

94 *Dīvān-i Ḥāfiẓ*, ed. Khānlarī, *ghazal* 431: 9; Browne, *Literary History*, III, p. 283.

95 Cf. J. Schimdt, 'Ḥāfiẓ and Other Persian Authors in Ottoman Bibliomancy: the Extraordinary Case of Kefevī Hüseyn Efendi's *Rāznāme* (Late Sixteenth Century)'.

96 See Sūdī Busnawī, *Sharḥ-i Sūdī bar Dīvān-i Ḥāfiẓ*, preface by S. Nafīsī, p. 6.

97 Schimmel, 'Ḥāfiẓ and His Contemporaries', p. 939.

98 Lāhūrī, *Sharḥ-i 'irfānī-yi ghazalhā-yi Ḥāfiẓ*, I, Khurramshāhī's introduction, p. ii. For a good overview of commentaries on his *Dīvān*, see Rādfar, *Ḥāfiẓ-pazhūhān va Ḥāfiẓ-pazhūhī*, pp. 271–97.

99 Lāhūrī, *Sharḥ-i 'irfānī-yi ghazalhā-yi Ḥāfiẓ*, I, Khurramshāhī's introduction, p. iv.

100 Lāhījī, *Mafātīḥ al-i'jāz fī sharḥ-i Gulshan-i rāz.*

101 Anqaravī, *Sharḥ-i kabīr-i Anqaravī bar Mathnawī-yi Mavlavī.*

102 Bahā al-Dīn Khurramshāhī, 'Printed Editions of the *Divān* of Hafez', *EIr*, XI, pp. 479–80.

103 For an excellent discussion of these editions, see *ibid.*, pp. 479–83.

104 Some of these shortcomings are detailed by Aḥmed, 'Naẓarī bar *Dīwān-i Ḥāfiẓ* Chāp-i Duktur Qāsim-i Ghanī va Qazwīnī va Chāp-i Duktur Khānlarī'; idem., 'Credibility of the Diwan of Ḥāfiẓ Published by the Late Mr. Qazwini and by Dr. Khānlarī', pp. 63–82. For other critical comments on Khānlarī's edition, see Ḥusayn Haravī, 'Sukhanī az taṣḥīḥ-i jadīdī az *Dīvān-i Ḥāfiẓ*', pp. 141–55; and idem., 'Nuktahā dar taṣḥīḥ-i *Dīvān-i Ḥāfiẓ*', pp. 177–202.

105 On this edition, see the bibliography, s.v. 'Ḥāfiẓ'.

106 Mu'īn, *Ḥāfiẓ-i shīrīn-sukhan*, II, p. 690.

107 See Bahā al-Dīn Khurramshāhī, 'Rawnaq-i bāzār-i Ḥāfiẓ-shināsī', in his *Chārdah ravāyat*, pp. 142–8, for a good account of Iranian scholarship on Ḥāfiẓ down to the late 1980s.

108 As Mu'īn observed: 'All the most articulate and persuasive writers in history have thrown up their hands, despairing of ever matching his eloquence, acknowledging their impotence to create anything equal to his verse'. *Ḥāfiẓ-i shīrīn-sukhan*, II, p. 686. For a good discussion of why Ḥāfiẓ always has the final say and ends up defeating the Iranian literary reformists and modernist critics who would accuse him of being 'out of step with the times', see Hamadānī, 'Chirā Ḥāfiẓ? Ta'ammulī dar ma'nā-yi tārīkhī-yi Ḥāfiẓ-shināsī-yi mā', pp. 2–10.

109 See, for instance, Lloyd Ridgeon's studious analysis of the controversy raised by Kasravī's diatribes against Ḥāfiẓ and the resultant rage they aroused in Iranian literary circles in the 1930s in his *Sufi Castigator: Ahmad Kasravi and the Iranian Mystical Tradition*, chapters 6, 7. Several decades earlier the modernizing Pakistani philosopher Muḥammad Iqbāl (1873–1938) had also penned a devastating tirade against Ḥāfiẓ in his Persian poem *Asrār al-khudā*, but in later editions of the poem, due to the vociferous protests by Indian literati, he immediately recanted his invective and excised the offending passage. There are also the largely forgotten controversies over Ḥāfiẓ's verse between Taqī Raf'at (who attacked the poet) and Malik al-Shu'arā Bahār (who defended him), not to mention Nimā's hollow quibbling with Ḥāfiẓ's views of love. On the latter, see Firoozeh Papan-Matin, 'Love: Nima's Dialogue with Hafez', pp. 173–92.

110 *Dīvān-i Ḥāfiẓ*, ed. Khānlarī, *ghazal* 37: 11. Trans. Bly and Lewisohn, *The Angels*, p. 30.

111 Hamadānī, 'Chirā Ḥāfiẓ?', p. 3.

112 Khurramshāhī, 'Ḥāfiẓ dar farhang-i mā', p. 151.

113 *Ibid.*, p. 144.

114 Hamadānī, 'Chirā Ḥāfiẓ?', p. 2.

115 See www.hafezstudies.ir for further details of this centre. *Ḥāfiẓ-pazūhishī* is a journal published in Shīrāz (inaugurated in 1996), edited by Jalīl Sāzigār-nizhād, currently (2009) in its thirteenth volume.

116 See the 662-page bibliography of Ḥāfiẓ studies in Nīknām, *Kitāb-shināsī-yi Ḥāfiẓ.*

117 Cf. Margaret L. Caton, *Hāfez: 'Erfān and Music as Interpreted by Ostād Mortezā Varzi.*

118 Massignon, *Essai*, trans. Clark, pp. 34–6; Nywia, *Exégèse coranique*, p. 22.

119 On this phenomenon, see Shafī'ī-Kadkanī, 'Ḥāfiẓ va Bīdil', p. 35, and Mu'īn, *Ḥāfiẓ-i shīrīn-sukhan*, II, pp. 683–6, who compares the place occupied by the Qur'ān in Arabic with Hāfiẓ's *Dīvān* in Persian – whence Zarrīnkūb's exclamation: 'Who's *not* obsessed with Ḥāfiẓ in Iran?' (*Az kūcha-i rindān*, p. xv). In his autobiography, Sadriddin Aini describes how illiterate peasants and farmers ploughing in the fields of Tajikistan sang Ḥāfiẓ's and Bīdil's poetry by heart (*Bukhara Reminiscences*, pp. 165–6), and how he was taught to memorize Ḥāfiẓ's poetry from age six (pp. 97f.). On Ḥāfiẓ's place in classical Tajik literature, see Yury Boboev, *Muqaddama-yi adabiyāt-shināsī*, pp. 171–2, 179 (with thanks to Dr Gurdofarid Miskinzoda for this reference).

120 On which, see Marx, *Shakespeare and the Bible*, p. 1.

121 Mu'īn, *Ḥāfiẓ-i shīrīn-sukhan*, II, p. 695. The other two most studied texts are the *Kulliyāt* of Sa'dī and the *Mathnawī* of Rūmī.

122 'On ne peut, en lisant – ou mieux, en écoutant – les *ghazal* de Hāfez, manquer de relever la presence constante, explicite ou non, de la Parole révélée dans le Coran'. Monteil and Tajvidi (trans.), *L'amour, l'amant, l'aimé: cente ballades du Divān (-i Ḥāfiẓ)*, introduction, p. 13. See also the essay by James Morris below, pp. 227–34.

123 *Dīvān-i Ḥāfiẓ*, ed. Khānlarī, *ghazal* 438: 7.

124 Many scholars have demonstrated the link between Ḥāfiẓ's artistic style and the Muslim missal: see Khurramshāhī, 'Uslūb-i hunarī-yi Ḥāfiẓ va Qur'ān', pp. 3–20; Partaw 'Alavī, 'Iqbabāsāt-i Khwāja Shīrāz az aȳāt-i Qur'ān-i majīd va ishārāt bi-āhādith va tafāsīr', in idem., *Bāng-i jaras*, pp. 37–86.

125 Enjoined in the Qur'ān itself; for a good account of which, see Waley, 'Contemplative Disciplines in Early Persian Sufism', pp. 497–548.

126 *Dīvān-i Ḥāfiẓ*, ed. Khānlarī, *ghazal* 250: 10. Trans. Bly and Lewisohn, *The Angels*, p. 14.

127 See Gulandām's introduction given in 'Ḥāfiẓ Shīrāzī', in Dihkhudā, *Lughat-nāma*, V, p. 7489.

128 Zarrīnkūb, *Az kūcha-i rindān*, p. 19.

129 This verse is found in five of the manuscripts used by Khānlarī in his edited *Dīvān*, *ghazal* 312.

130 *Dīwān-i Khwāja Ḥāfiẓ-i Shīrāzī*, ed. Anjawī-Shīrāzī, p. 228, l. 15. Also cf. Zarrīnkūb's discussion: *Az kūcha-i rindān*, pp. 58–60.

131 Cited by Ghanī, *Baḥth*, I, p. 50.

132 *Dīvān-i Ḥāfiẓ*, ed. Khānlarī, *ghazal* 93: 10. My translation here follows Khurramshāhī's (*pace* Sūdī's) reading of the second hemistich as *gar kh^{w}ud*, and not Khānlarī's *lectio* (= *var kh^{w}ud*). Further discussion of the meaning(s) of this verse is given in Khurramshāhī, *Chārdah ravāyat*, pp. 27–8.

133 Khurramshāhī, *Chārdah ravāyat.*

134 *Ibid.*, p. 23.

135 See R. Paret, 'Ḳirā'a', in *EI*², V, pp. 127–9.

136 Zarrīnkūb, *Az kūcha-i rindān*, p. 19.

137 E.G. Browne, *A Literary History of Persia*, III, p. 272.

138 *Dīvān-i Ḥāfiẓ*, ed. Khānlarī, *ghazal* 312: 9. Trans. Bly and Lewisohn, *The Angels*, p. 62.

139 Cited by Ghanī, *Baḥth*, I, p. 49.

140 Mu'īn, *Ḥāfiẓ-i shīrīn-sukhan*, II, p. 686.

141 Baha' al-Din Khorramshahi, 'ii. Hafez's Life and Times', *EIr*, XI, p. 465.

142 Zarrīnkūb, *Az kūcha-i rindān*, p. 15; Dihkhudā, *Lughat-nāma*, V, pp. 7490f.

143 Zarrīnkūb, *Az kūcha-i rindān*, p. 15. See also Taqī Pūrnāmdāriyān, 'Ḥāfiẓ, 1. Zindigī va rūzigār', in *Dāneshnāme-ye Zabān-o Adab-e Fārsī*, II, pp. 637–44.

144 Khurramshāhī, 'ii. Hafez's Life and Times', *EIr*, XI, p. 468.

145 Zarrīnkūb, *Az kūcha-i rindān*, pp. xii–xiii.

146 *'Irfān u rindī dar shi'r-i Ḥāfiẓ.*

147 *Dīvān-i Ḥāfiẓ*, ed. Khānlarī, *ghazal* 124: 6.

148 *Ibid.*, *ghazal* 357: 3.

149 Zarrīnkūb, *Az kūcha-i rindān*, pp. 18–20.

150 This is proven by a fragment (see *Dīvān-i Ḥāfiẓ*, ed. Khānlarī, II, p. 1085; and Ghanī's discussion in *Baḥth*, I, pp. 414–15) that he wrote under the rule of Shāh Manṣūr when a niggardly vizier inadvertently decreased this stipend. However, it should be stressed that Ḥāfiẓ studiously avoided taking charity from publically-funded endowments: 'Even though my Sufi robe be hocked in pawn at the tavern, come and look – you'll not find a single diram in the records of public endowments in my name!' *Dīvān-i Ḥāfiẓ*, ed. Khānlarī, *ghazal* 462: 3.

151 'It is a matter of extreme probability that Ḥāfiẓ was well versed in the school of Ibn 'Arabī and his commentators. Taking into account this deep influence and general popularity of the Akbarian school among the intelligentsia of Ḥāfiẓ's day, combined with the poet's fiery and sensitive nature and penchant to absorb philosophical, theological and mystical ideas and thoughts current in the culture contemporary to him, it would be absurd to maintain that he was entirely uninformed, uninfluenced by, lacked interest in, or held himself aloof from the Shaykh's teachings' (Khurramshāhī, *Ḥāfiẓ-nāma*, I, p. 600). Elsewhere, Khurramshāhī (*Dhihn va zabān-i Ḥāfiẓ* [2005; 3rd edn], p. 420) adjudicates even

more positively that 'the mystical philosophy of Ḥāfiẓ (*'irfān-i Ḥāfiẓ*) is the complicated speculative theosophy of Ibn 'Arabī and his followers. *It was not the simplistic Iranian mysticism of the 11-12th centuries*'. See also Zarrīnkūb's (*Az kūcha-i rindān*, pp. 188–90) extended analysis of Ḥāfiẓ's immersion in the intellectual milieu of fourteenth-century Shīrāz, where Akbarian teachings were very much the fashion.

152 Some of 'Irāqī's verses imitated by Ḥāfiẓ are given by Zarrīnkūb, *Az kūcha-i rindān*, pp. 220f., n. 52.

153 As Khurramshāhī shows, at least in one *ghazal* (no. 148, ed. Khānlarī), Ḥāfiẓ paraphrased the theosophy of 'Irāqī's *Lamā'at*, which is based on Akbarian teachings, see *Ḥāfiẓ-nāma*, I, 596–607, particularly his commentary on v. 3.

154 Zarrīnkūb, *Az kūcha-i rindān*, p. 206, n. 14.

155 *Ibid.*, p. 19.

156 *Ibid.*, p. 9.

157 Cf. Zarrīnkūb, *Az kūcha-i rindān*, p. 26. Mu'īn's observations (*Ḥāfiẓ-i shīrīn-sukhan*, I, pp. 138–42) about verses in the *Dīvān* alluding to his wife, children and family are entirely speculative and incapable of definitive historical demonstration.

158 Browne, *A Literary History of Persia*, III, pp. 287–8.

159 Such as Haravī, *Sharḥ-i ghazalhā-yi Ḥāfiẓ*, II, p. 910; the line comes from *Dīvān-i Ḥāfiẓ*, ed. Khānlarī, *ghazal* 210: 1.

160 Browne, *A Literary History of Persia*, III, p. 288. The theory that *ghazal* 210 by Ḥāfiẓ was written in praise of his wife is also accepted by Zarrīnkūb, *Bā kāravān-i hullih*, p. 239, though criticized by Mihdī Burhānī ('Mājarā-yi hamsar-i Ḥāfiẓ', pp. 123–37), who points out that in the history of classical Persian literature, aside from Nāṣir-i Khusraw, practically no poet ever made any reference to his wife or wife's name.

161 Ṣahbā, 'Sukhanī chand dar bāb-i aḥwāl va ash'ār-i Ḥāfiẓ', pp. 175–8. See also Zarrīnkūb (*Az kūcha-i rindān*, pp. 17–18) and Dihkhudā (*Lughat-nāma*, V, p. 7490) on his so-called brothers.

162 On which, see *Dīvān-i Ḥāfiẓ*, ed. Khānlarī, II, pp. 1147f.

163 The celebrated commentary of the *Qur'ān* by al-Zamakhsharī.

164 Of the many works by this name, that of al-Muṭarrizī (d. 610/1213) on Arabic grammar is probably intended.

165 The *Maṭāli'u'l-Anẓār* of al-Bayḍāwī (d. 683/1284) is probably intended.

166 The *Miftāḥu'l-'Ulūm* of as-Sakkakī (d. 626/1229) is probably intended.

167 This translation and the four accompanying notes to its text are cited directly from E.G. Browne, *A Literary History of Persia*, III, p. 272.

168 The classic studies of the political background and social environment of Ḥāfiẓ's poetry remains Ghanī's *Baḥth dar āthār*, vol. I, and Mu'īn, *Ḥāfiẓ-i shīrīn-sukhan*, vol. I, a ground revisited by Zarrīnkūb, *Az kūcha-i rindān*, pp. 1–126. In English, a good overview of political context of his poetry, his patrons and panegyrics, and the courtly circles and princes which favoured him, can be found in Browne, *A Literary History of Persia*, III, pp. 274–91 (an account based on the Indian critic Shiblī Nu'mānī); Arberry, *Shīrāz: Persian City of Saints and Poets*, pp. 139–60; Schimmel, 'Ḥāfiẓ and His Contemporaries', pp. 933–6; Jan Rypka, *A History of Iranian Literature*, pp. 264ff.; Khorramshahi, 'ii. Hafez's Life and Times', *EIr*, pp. 465–9. Limbert's excellent *Shīrāz in the Age of Hafez* may also be perused.

169 Fouchécour, intro.: *Hafiz de Chiraz*, pp. 49–69; P. Jackson, 'Muẓaffarids', *EIr*, VII, pp. 820–2; H. Roemer, 'The Jalayirids, Muzaffarids and Sarbadārs', pp. 1–41; Bosworth, *The New Islamic Dynasties*, pp. 264–5; Mu'īn, *Ḥāfiẓ-i shīrīn-sukhan*, I, pp. 264–70; Limbert, *Shīrāz in the Age of Hafez*, pp. 33–45.

170 Annemarie Schimmel, 'Ḥāfiẓ and His Contemporaries', p. 934.

171 H. Roemer, 'The Jalayirids, Muzaffarids and Sarbadārs', in P. Jackson et al. (eds), *Cambridge History of Iran*, VI, p. 13.

172 Zarrīnkūb, *Az kūcha-i rindān*, p. 45.

173 *Ibid.*, pp. 22–3.

174 See *Dīwān-i Khwājū Kirmānī*, ed. Qāni'ī, p. 549, 569–70, 584–7.

175 *Kulliyāt-i 'Ubayd Zākānī*, ed. Maḥjūb, Index, s.v. 'Shāh Shaykh Abū Isḥāq'.

176 See Khurramshāhī's discussion of the range of Ḥāfiẓ's poems composed during the reign of Shaykh Abū Isḥāq (*Ḥāfiẓ-nāma*, I, pp. 754–6), and the references given there.

177 *Dīvān-i Ḥāfiẓ*, ed. Khānlarī, II, pp. 1034–7.

178 Khurramshāhī, *Ḥāfiẓ-nāma*, I, p. 644. *Dīvān-i Ḥāfiẓ*, ed. Khānlarī, *ghazal* 164: 1–2.

179 Schimmel, 'Ḥāfiẓ and His Contemporaries', p. 934.

180 Cited by Khurramshāhī, *Ḥāfiẓ-nāma*, I, p. 644.

181 For instance, Ghanī (*Baḥth dar āthār*, I, p. 101–3) speculates that *ghazal* 162 (*Dīvān-i Ḥāfiẓ*, ed. Khānlarī) was written around 743/1343, right after the accession of Abū Isḥāq Īnjū, but Haravī (*Sharḥ-i ghazalhā-yi Ḥāfiẓ*, II, p. 713) thinks that the *ghazal* was inspired by the poet's fear of Tamerlane, while Khurramshāhī (*Ḥāfiẓ-nāma*, I, p. 638), momentarily kowtowing to Ghanī's theory, sees nothing political in it at all, writing, 'from head to toe this whole poem is surcharged with mystical gratitude and delight'.

182 *Measure for Measure*, III.ii.215–24. The Duke's quip to Escalus.

183 Cf. Cicero's frequently cited phrase, 'O tempora, O mores', which Shakepeare versified in his exclamation: 'it is a strange-disposèd time...' (*Julius Caesar*, I.iii.33).

184 'This day and age are an era when discourse [of Sufism] has become utterly masked behind the veil, when impostors pretend to be representatives of genuine spirituality and mimic the adepts of the heart'. *Tadhkirat al-awliyā'*, ed. Isti'lāmī, p. 8.

185 Yeats' poem, from 'The Curse of Cromwell'.

186 *Dīvān-i Ḥāfiẓ*, ed. Khānlarī, *ghazal* 11: 10. 'This verse by the Master of the Poets Khwāja Ḥāfiẓ', stated Samarqandī (*Maṭla'-i sa'dayn*, Part 1, p. 265), 'offers sufficient praise of Ḥajjī Qawām's stature'. For further discussion of Ḥāfiẓ and Ḥajjī Qawām, see Zarrīnkūb, *Az kūcha-i rindān*, pp. 24–5; Stockland, 'The *Kitab-i Samak 'Ayyar*', *Persica*, XV (1993–5), p. 161.

187 *Rawḍat al-ṣafā*, ed. Zaryāb, II, p. 749.

188 *Dīvān-i Ḥāfiẓ*, ed. Khānlarī, vol. II, pp. 1031–40.

189 *Ibid.*, vol. II, p. 1033, vv. 36–7.

190 Cf. *Ibid.*, *ghazal* 203: 7 (*Rāstī khātim-i fīrzūza-yi bū ishāqī / khʷush darakhshīd, valī dawlat-i mosta'jil būd*, on which see Khurramshāhī, *Ḥāfiẓ-nāma*, I, pp. 754–9; Zarrīnkūb, *Az kūcha-i rindān*, pp. 27–8).

191 Contrary to what Zarrīnkūb speculates, asserting that Ḥāfiẓ 'was like a courtier at his court' (*Az kūcha-i rindān*, pp. 27 and 31).

192 The author here paraphrases a verse by Ḥāfiẓ (*Dīvān-i Ḥāfiẓ*, ed. Khānlarī, *ghazal* 197: 6), composed during Mubāriz al-Dīn's reign: 'They have bolted up all the doors of the Taverns. Great God! Let them not leave open the House of Deceit and Hypocrisy!' This verse belongs to one of some 15 to 20 *ghazals* composed by Ḥāfiẓ in protest against the fundamentalist Islamist regime of Mubāriz al-Dīn, as Qāsim Ghanī (*Baḥth*, I, p. 216) points out. Zarrīnkūb's own turn of phrase was directly borrowed from Ghanī's, *ibid.*, p. 214.

193 Ghanī's *Baḥth*, I, p. 214. The *Muḥtasib* was a special vice-squad police officer concerned with controlling matters of public morality, particularly the prevention of wine-drinking. Ḥāfiẓ's ironic mockery of the sere and grave man who acts like 'a ruler in the gatherings of fair beauties by day and by night commands the vice squad (*muḥtasib*) in drinking wine' (Nāṣir-i Khusraw) is a stock topos in Persian poetry. See Dihkhudā, *Lughat-nāma*, XII, pp. 17978–9, s.v. *muḥtasib*.

194 *Dīvān-i Ḥāfiẓ*, ed. Khānlarī, *ghazal* 42: 1. This verse is cited by Mīrkhwand in his history of the period *Rawḍat al-ṣafā*, ed. Zaryāb, II, p. 744; and also mentioned by Samarqandī, *Maṭla'-i sa'dayn*, Part 1, pp. 269–70, as having been composed in protest by Ḥāfiẓ to this ruler.

195 Khurramshāhī, *Ḥāfiẓ-nāma*, I, pp. 735–6; Barzigar-Khāliqī, *Shakh-i nabāt-i Ḥāfiẓ*, p. 503.

196 *Dīvān-i Ḥāfiẓ*, ed. Qazwīnī and Ghanī, *ghazal* 202: 1. For other *ghazals* referring to this Islamist dictator, see Ghanī's *Baḥth*, I, pp. 215–17.

197 Zarrīnkūb, *Az kūcha-i rindān*, p. 51.

198 *Ibid.*, p. 51.

199 Ghanī's *Baḥth dar āthār*, I, p. 219.

200 *Rawḍat al-ṣafā*, II, p. 746.

201 Samarqandī (*Maṭla'-i sa'dayn*, Part 1, p. 304) uses the final verse of an entire philosophical 'fragmentary poem' (*qiṭa*) by Ḥāfiẓ (*Dīvān-i Ḥāfiẓ*, ed. Khānlarī, II, pp. 1071–2) to sardonically summarize the incident: 'He who was the delight of his eyes had a needle poked through his seeing eyes by him at last.'

202 Haravī, *Sharḥ-i ghazalhā-yi Ḥāfiẓ*, III, p. 1490, citing Ghanī, *Baḥth dar āthār*, I, pp. 128–9. This is one of two *ghazal*-panegyrics addressed to this vizier, the other being no. 453 in Khānlarī's edition.

203 *Dīvān-i Ḥāfiẓ*, ed. Khānlarī, *ghazal* 354: 4.

204 Punning on the monarch's name *shujā'* ('the Brave'): *ibid.*, *ghazal* 278: 1.

205 On which see Ghanī's *Baḥth dar āthār*, I, p. 336ff.

206 Khorramshahi, 'ii. Hafez's Life and Times', *EIr*, p. 467.

207 Zarrīnkūb, *Az kūcha-i rindān*, pp. 122–4.

208 *Ibid.*, pp. 112–13.

209 On the basis of a single verse in one of Ḥāfiẓ's *ghazals* (*Dīvān-i Ḥāfiẓ*, ed. Khānlarī, *ghazal* 163: 2), which was satirized by Kamāl Khujandī: 'My beloved, who never went to school and couldn't even write a line / By a single glance solved the tangled issues of a myriad professors', Ghanī asserts (*Baḥth*, I, p. 361) that the entire *ghazal* was a panegyric for Shāh Shujā'. But since Shāh Shujā' had actually gone to school and wrote excellent prose and poetry both in Persian and Arabic, it is improbable that the *ghazal* could have been a panegyric for the prince (as Haravī, *Sharḥ-i ghazalhā-yi Ḥāfiẓ*, II, p. 704, rightly argues). Many commentators (e.g. Lāhūrī, II, *Sharḥ-i 'irfānī*, pp. 1292–3; Haravī, *ibid.*) consider the verse to allude to the Prophet Muḥammad, who was illiterate (*ummī*). But the fifth line of the *ghazal* does mention Abū'l-Favāris, an epithet for Shāh Shujā' (as Isti'lāmī, *Dars-i Ḥāfiẓ*, I, pp. 470–1, points out).

210 Ghanī, *Baḥth*, I, pp. 344–61.

211 *Rawḍat al-ṣafā*, II, p. 760.

212 *Dīvān-i Ḥāfiẓ*, ed. Khānlarī, *ghazal* 288: 8. See also Ghanī, *Baḥth*, I, p. 365.

213 *Dīvān-i Ḥāfiẓ*, ed. Khānlarī, II, pp. 1027–30; and *Dīwān-i Ḥāfiẓ*, ed. Qazvīnī and Ghanī, pp. qiv–qka.

214 *Istiqbāl* is defined as when 'the later poet acknowledges the work of his predecessor openly and publically, but takes the initiative in receiving him and bringing him into the present literary environment' (Losensky, *Welcoming Fighani*, p. 12). On Ḥāfiẓ's 'welcoming' *ghazals* written 'after' Shāh Shujā', see Ghanī, *Baḥth*, I, pp. 353, 355, 358, 361; Zarrīnkūb, *Az kūcha-i rindān*, pp. 122f.

215 Ghanī, *Baḥth*, I, p. 39, 344 (referring to Sa'd al-Dīn Unsī, who compiled the prince's *Dīvān*).

216 'The King of the Turks gives heed to the speech of pretenders / He should feel shame at the blood of Siyavush, wrongly shed.' The word 'pretender' (*muda'ī*) means 'one who falsely lays claims', and here indicates 'the false lover' (comparable roughly to the topos of the *lauzengiers*, false flatterers, talebearers found in Italian troubadour poetry) who has no sense or taste for love's heights and depths, ecstasies and agonies (cf. Khānlarī's *ghazals* 78: 4; 426: 1). Haravī (*Sharḥ-i ghazalhā-yi Ḥāfiẓ*, I, p. 449) explains: 'In Firdawsī's *Shāhnāma*, Siyāvush was the husband of Farangīs, daughter of Afrāsiyāb, King of the Turānians (enemy of Iranians). Because of the malicious gossip conducted against Farangīs by Afrāsiyāb's brother Garsīvaz, she incurred her father Afrāsiyāb's wrath and was put to death. In order to avenge her murder, the Iranians waged many years of war against the Turānians. The reference to 'Siyāvush's blood, wrongly shed' is to the death that Siyāvush suffered as a consequence of his wife's murder and the ensuing long years of warfare between the two kingdoms. The 'King of the Turks' in this line refers to Afrasiyāb, who was willing to listen to and be influenced by envious tale-bearers and ultimately bloody his own hands with Siyāvush's blood because of this. The 'King of the Turks' is interpreted by Lāhūrī (*Sharḥ-i 'irfānī-yi Dīvān-i Ḥāfiẓ*, II, p. 1390) and Barzigar-Khāliqī (*Shākh-i nabāt-i Ḥāfiẓ*, p. 276) as a reference to Shāh Shujā'. The latter comments: 'The poet compares himself to Siyāvush and Shāh Shujā' to Afrāsiyāb, and in this line entreats him not to listen to the envious who criticise his poetry' (*ibid.*, p. 277).

217 Zarrīnkūb, *Az kūcha-i rindān*, pp. 125–6.

218 *Rawḍat al-ṣafā*, II, p. 761.

219 *Maṭla' al-sa'dayn*, cited by Haravī, *Sharḥ-i ghazalhā-yi Ḥāfiẓ*, III, p. 1834; Ghanī, *Baḥth*, I, pp. 373–4.

220 *King Henry VI*, Pt III, III.i.64–5.

221 *Dīvān-i Ḥāfiẓ*, ed. Khānlarī, *ghazal* 442. The political background of this *ghazal* in general and some of its moral teachings in various lines in particular is discussed by Niyāz-Kirmānī, *Dawlat-i pīr-i mughān*, pp. 179–86.

222 *Dīvān-i Ḥāfiẓ*, ed. Khānlarī, *ghazal* 40: 10 (repeating *faqr va qanā'at*).

223 Cf. Zarrīnkūb's discussion of Ḥāfiẓ's critical attitude to this prince: *Az kūcha-i rindān*, p. 159.

224 *Rawḍat al-ṣafā*, II, p. 764.

225 His arrogant behaviour was the probable cause of Tamerlane's invasion of Iran: see Ghanī, *Baḥth*, I, p. 383.

226 *Dīvān-i Ḥāfiẓ*, ed. Khānlarī, *ghazal* 298: 7 ('Drink wine and spare the world, for by your lasso's curl / The evil miscreant's neck is now captive in chains'); see Haravī, *Sharḥ-i ghazalhā-yi Ḥāfiẓ*, II, pp. 1271–2; Zarrīnkūb, *Az kūcha-i rindān*, pp. 160–1.

227 H.R. Roemer, 'The Jalarids, Muzaffarids and Sarbadārs', pp. 60–1.

228 *Dīvān-i Ḥāfiẓ*, ed. Khānlarī, *ghazal* 298. See Zarrīnkūb, *Az kūcha-i rindān*, p. 82 (and notes). Ghanī, *Baḥth*, I, pp. 376–80, cites five other *ghazals* that were also composed for Shāh Yaḥyā: nos. 12, 206, 384, 413, 425 in *Dīvān-i Ḥāfiẓ*, ed. Khānlarī.

229 *Al-Mu'jam*, cited and discussed by Zarrīnkūb, *Az kūcha-i rindān*, pp. 82–3; 228–9, n. 30.

230 As revealed by Muḥammad Dārābī, *Laṭīfa-yi ghaybī*, p. 24 and Lāhūrī, *Sharḥ-i 'irfānī*, III, pp. 2081–2.

231 Ghanī, *Baḥth*, I, pp. 383–9.

232 According to Samarqandī's *Maṭla' al-sa'dayn*, the verse: 'Do not devote your heart to the fair, Ḥāfiẓ: Look at what that Samarqandī Turk did to the folks of Khwārazm' (*Dīvān-i Ḥāfiẓ*, ed. Khānlarī, *ghazal* 431: 8) was penned in sympathy for the victims of Tamerlane's brutality; see Zarrīnkūb, *Az kūcha-i rindān*, p. 160; Ghanī, *Baḥth*, I, p. 374, n. 1.

233 *Tadhkirat al-shu'arā'*, ed. 'Abbāsī, p. 341, citing *Dīvān-i Ḥāfiẓ*, ed. Khānlarī, *ghazal* 3: 1; the dubious historicity of the quaint tale about this verse, which, though unconfirmed by any contemporary historians, is discussed in detail by Browne, *A Literary History of Persia*, III, pp. 188–9; Ghanī, *Baḥth*, I, pp. 393–5, and Zarrīnkūb, *Az kūcha-i rindān*, p. 159.

234 Shelley, 'A Defence of Poetry', in Kwasny (ed.), *Toward the Open Field*, p. 76.

235 See Zarrīnkūb's profoundly engrossing discussion of Ḥāfiẓ's attitude towards Tamerlane: *Az kūcha-i rindān*, pp. 159–62.

236 *Dīvān-i Ḥāfiẓ*, ed. Khānlarī, *ghazal* 237; see Ghanī, *Baḥth*, I, p. 401, and also Mumtaḥan, 'Sukhanī chand dar mājarā-yi zindigī-yi Shāh Manṣūr Muẓaffarī: mamdūḥ-i Khwāja Ḥāfiẓ Shīrāzī', pp. 431–64.

237 Ghanī, in *Baḥth*, I, pp. 403–6, lists and discusses four other *ghazals* composed for Shāh Manṣūr, as well as several verses found in later manuscripts of his *Sāqī-nāma* which praise the prince. In a very late manuscript of one of Ḥāfiẓ's key erotic *ghazals* (*Dīvān-i Ḥāfiẓ*, ed. Khānlarī, *ghazal* 338; cf. Ghanī's discussion, *Baḥth*, I, pp. 415–16 of the line), mention of Shāh Manṣūr also appears in one line (*Man ghulām-i Shāh Manṣūram...*); there also exists another panegryical *ghazal* (not in Khānlarī's edition) in praise of the ruler; mentioned by Ghanī, *Baḥth*, I, pp. 414–16, found in *Dīwān-i Khwāja Ḥāfiẓ*, ed. Qazvīnī and Ghanī, no. 329, pp. 224–6.

238 Ghanī, *Baḥth*, I, pp. 406–8.

239 *Dīvān-i Ḥāfiẓ*, ed. Khānlarī, *ghazal* 149: 12. Isti'lāmī (*Dars-i Ḥāfiẓ*, I, pp. 439–42), sees the *ghazal* as primarily devoted to love, and only panegyrical in its last four verses, but Fouchécour (*Hafiz de Chiraz: Le Divān*, p. 456) describes it as a wholly panegyrical poem: 'celui d'un courtisan dont l'expression court entièrement sur le register de l'amour'.

240 Manz, *The Rise and Rule of Tamerlane*, p. 72.

241 Ghanī, *Baḥth*, I, pp. 425–32.

242 *Ibid.*, I, pp. 436–8.

243 *Ibid.*, I, p. 101. See also Zarrīnkūb's (*Az kūcha-i rindān*, pp. 82–3) discussion of Ḥāfiẓ's small number of his panegyrical poems and his use of the indirect erotic language of the *ghazal*.

244 Discussing Ḥāfiẓ's panegyrical poems, Khurramshāhī (*Dhihn va zabān-i Ḥāfiẓ*, 3rd edn, p. 420) observes: 'Since Ḥāfiẓ's mind was mainly preoccupied by erotic lyricism and "the erotic" comprises the most

accessible aspect and common theme of his discourse, we need therefore to remember that he did not regard the "Object of praise" himself [*mamdūḥ*] very highly when he wrote in the panegyric genre, for he saw no need to act in a manner contrary to his own natural inclinations.'

245 As Fouchécour (*Hafiz de Chiraz*, introduction, p. 15) stresses, 'in Ḥāfiẓ's *Dīvān* the literal meaning is always subordinate to the metaphorical one. Metaphor is the realm in which the poet develops his thought.'

246 The main problem in using the *Dīvān* for sourcing biographical details is that such an approach often leads to deliberate neglect of theological, mystical, ethical and homiletic dimensions in those verses themselves, the *dicta* of which are moreover *exempla* not to be taken literally. Thus, Zarrīnkūb was honest enough to concede that his own historically oriented approach has serious drawbacks since: 'in some cases the expression of the poet appears to be so vague and arcane that one cannot ever interpret its meaning in a literal sense. It is true that there are a few verses that directly allude to the poet's patron and object of praise [*mamdūḥ*] whom he celebrates with the qualities of a beloved [*ma'shūq*] – and how many of his beloveds are in fact just a king or vizier! – but in many places his language is extremely vague and deceptively multifaceted [*rindāna*], because of which one cannot interpret his words ... in which simple references to historical circumstances are situated cheek by jowl with the most complex theosophical and mystical mysteries ... to mean simply what they literally profess.' *Az kūcha-i rindān*, p. xiv.

247 *Dīvān-i Ḥāfiẓ*, ed. Khānlarī, *ghazal* 150: 5.

248 *Ibid.*, *ghazal* 292: 2. In this context, Ḥāfiẓ's disdain of worldliness belongs squarely to the *contempti mundi* or *zuhdiyya* genre of the Sufi theoerotic lyric (*ghazal*) and has *absolutely* nothing to do with an espousal of 'the doctrine of unreason' or 'intellectual nihilism' (!) as Arberry weirdly speculated (*Fifty Poems of Ḥāfiẓ*, introduction, pp. 29, 31). On this genre (*dhamm al-dunyā*) in Sufism, see Ritter, *Ocean*, chap. 2 ('The World'); in Ḥāfiẓ (cf. the term *istighnā*), see Mu'īn, *Ḥāfiẓ-i shīrīn-sukhan*, I, pp. 473–4. Cf. John Donne: 'What fragmentary rubbidge this world is / Thou knowest, and that it is not worth a thought; / He honours it too much that thinkes it nought' ('The Second Anniversary', pp. 82–4).

249 *Dīvān-i Ḥāfiẓ*, ed. Khānlarī, *ghazal* 163: 10.

250 *Ibid.*, *ghazal* 110: 4.

251 *Ibid.*, *ghazal* 40: 10.

252 *Ibid.*, *ghazal* 355: 9.

253 R.W. Emerson, *Journals*, 1847; quoted in *Works*, VIII, p. 417. I am grateful to Farhang Jahanpour for providing this reference in his 'Hafiz and Ralph Waldo Emerson' (unpublished typescript), p. 6.

254 *Dīvān-i Ḥāfiẓ*, ed. Khānlarī, *ghazal* 324: 3.

255 *Ibid.*, *ghazal* 324: 11.

256 *Ibid.*, *ghazal* 35: 4; see Isti'lamī's refutation of the interpretation of this poem as a panegyric: *Dars-i Ḥāfiẓ*, I, p. 159 (*ghazal* 34).

257 Muḥammad Isti'lāmī, *Dars-i Ḥāfiẓ*, I, pp. 53–4.

258 Shelley, 'A Defence of Poetry', in Kwasny (ed.), *Toward the Open Field*, p. 56.

259 *Dīvān-i Ḥāfiẓ*, ed. Khānlarī, *ghazal* 264: 7. Also cf. *ghazal* 477: 4.

260 Mentioned more than 80 times in the *Dīvān*, 'perhaps no other word in the entire *Dīvān* of Ḥāfiẓ is more difficult to define', observed Khurramshāhī, 'and yet by far the most significant and constructive thesis advanced by Ḥāfiẓ lies embedded within the term *rind*' (*Ḥāfiẓ-nāma*, I, p. 403). Likewise, Pūrjavādī reflects: 'The primordial postern into the universe of Ḥāfiẓ's thought is *rindī*, which is the veritable key to the door of the philosophy of Persian spirituality' ('Rindī-yi Ḥāfiẓ', *Bū-yi jān*, p. 219).

261 'The Visionary Topography of Hafiz', pp. 224–5.

262 See the essays by M. Sells and R. Woods in Barnard and Kripal (eds), *Crossing Boundaries.*

263 I am referring to the fashionable view that conceptualizes the *rind* as merely a 'debauchee', and sees the *qalandar* as but a 'dissolute hoodlum', Ḥāfiẓ's praise of the *rind* being viewed as simply 'his championing of an anti-culture low-life', conceiving that 'to read anything other than social outcasts and men of ill-repute in Hafez's *rend* and *qalandar* is to miss the point ... by *rend* Hafez did not mean anything other than a derelict, an embodiment of sin and dissoluteness occupying the basest position

in society' (Ehsan Yarshuter, 'Hafez I. An Overview', *EIr*, XI, p. 463). Advocates of this viewpoint consequently refuse to acknowledge that the poet's usage of these terms can have any possible higher symbolic meaning, any refined mystical sense or, indeed, any esoteric significance at all. But assuming their views are correct leads to an extremely absurd conclusion. Namely, that – to take but a single instance – the demandingly complex and intricately argued 3,000-page commentary written by Abū'l-Ḥasan 'Abd al-Raḥmān Khatmī Lāhūrī on Ḥāfiẓ's *Dīvān* is complete balderdash. This seems to be exactly what the same scholar argues when he categorically asserts that 'reading Hafez as codified poetry implying an esoteric meaning' is 'not dissimilar to the explanations offered by addicts of "conspiracy theories" in political affairs' (*ibid.*, p. 464). In Iranian intellectual circles, reductionist views based on this sort of socio-political 'new criticism' unfortunately represent by no means a minority opinion today – even if such theories have been refuted by solid text-based research into the *Dīvān* by formidable and serious scholars such as Khurramshāhī, Fouchécour, Pūrnāmdāriyān and Isti'lāmī. One reason for these distortions is that the horizons of Ḥāfiẓ's poetic cosmology are so broad as to allow his admirers and enthusiasts to easily mould his verses to suit their own earthly or heavenly preconceptions, and so he has been labelled everything from free-thinker (*āzād-andīsh*), to Mazdean, to orthodox Shī'ite, to faithless agnostic (*ibāḥī*), to philosopher, to Ḥurūfī... For a survey of the wide divergence of scholarly opinion about the poet, see Qarāguzlū, 'Ḥāfiẓ dar miyān-i haftād u dū millat', pp. 61–74.

264 Zarrīnkūb, *Az kūcha-i rindān*, pp. 47–8.

265 *Ḥāfiẓ-nāma*, I, p. 408. Elsewhere Khurramshāhī writes: 'The tolerance, open-mindedness, liberality and humaneness which are visible for all to see in Ḥāfiẓ's crystalline verses, have caused those so-called "free-thinkers" without any particular religious commitment and without any interest in gnostic spirituality, to fall into the delusion and harbour the mistaken conception that he was such a free-thinker who was weak in his own faith.' *Ibid.*, I, p. 3. A similar observation is made by N. Pūrjavādī, 'Rindī-yi Ḥāfiẓ', *Bū-yi jān*, p. 330. On Ḥāfiẓ's personal religious views, particularly concerning eschatology, see Khurramshāhī, 'Ḥāfiẓ va inkār-i ma'ād?', in his *Dhihn u zabān-i Ḥāfiẓ*, pp. 93–123.

266 On which see Murtaḍawī, *Maktab-i Ḥāfiẓ*, p. 418.

267 Sārimī, *Muṣṭalahāt-i 'irfānī wa mafāhīm-i bar-jasta dar zabān-i 'Aṭṭār*, pp. 329–33.

268 Pūrjavādī, 'Rindī-yi Ḥāfiẓ', *Bū-yi jān*, p. 228.

269 The phrase is Zarrīnkūb's coinage, from the title of his study of Ḥāfiẓ: 'Down Rogues' Alley' (*Az kūcha-i rindān*, pp. 3–5, 7–8).

270 Limbert, *Shīrāz in the Age of Hafez*, pp. 104–5.

271 *Gulistān-i Sa'dī*, ed. Khaṭīb Rahbar, II: 40, p. 221.

272 For the one *ghazal* in which he uses this phrase, see *Dīvān-i Ḥāfiẓ*, ed. Khānlarī, *ghazal* 186: 6.

273 Murtaḍawī, *Maktab-i Ḥāfiẓ*, p. 145, n. 1; Pūrnāmdāriyān, *Gumshuda-yi lab-i daryā*, p. 24.

274 Shayegan, 'The Visionary Topography of Ḥāfiẓ', in *Temenos*, p. 224.

275 Zarrīnkūb rightly speculates that 'the careless desperado attitude and their notoriety-seeking of the hoodlums [*rindān*] may have been interpreted as a model for mystical detachment', *Az kūcha-i rindān*, p. 4.

276 Pūrnāmdāriyān underlines that 'The *rind* in Ḥāfiẓ's poetry is not the marketplace ruffian [*rind-i bazārī*] whose entire character personified avarice and hypocrisy, but, rather, the collegiate and intellectual libertine [*rind-i madrasī va rawshanfikrī*]', *Gumshuda-yi lab-i daryā*, p. 24.

277 Cf. 'Rindī-yi Ḥāfiẓ', in Pūrjavādī, *Bū-yi jān*, p. 286.

278 *Dīvān-i Ḥāfiẓ*, ed. Khānlarī, *ghazal* 93: 3. My translation is based on Isti'lāmī's interpretation (*Dars-i Ḥāfiẓ*, I, p. 303), but follows Khānlarī's text of the verse. On various interpretations of this verse, see Khurramshāhī, *Ḥāfiẓ-nāma*, I, pp. 407, 440 and Lāhūrī, *Sharḥ-i 'irfānī*, I, pp. 443–4.

279 Zarrīnkūb, *Az kūcha-i rindān*, p. 51.

280 As Ghanī relates (*Baḥth dar āthār*, I, p. 215), this nickname was given to him by his son and assassin-successor Shāh Shujā' in a distich which Ḥāfiẓ here paraphrases: 'The libertines [*rindān*] have forsworn their love for wine – all of them, that is, except the policeman who's drunk without wine.'

281 Cited by Ghanī, *Baḥth dar āthār*, I, p. 216, this verse is found in manuscript 'L' in *Dīvān-i Ḥāfiẓ*, ed. Khānlarī, *ghazal* 122.

282 *Dīvān-i Ḥāfiẓ*, ed. Khānlarī, *ghazal* 312: 1.

283 *Ibid.*, *ghazal* 150: 8. The original Persian is *'Ishq u shabāb u rindī majmū'a murād-ast/ chūn jam' shud ma'ānī, gū-y bayān tavān zad.* In the above translation, 'Unbound romance' renders the idea of *rindī*. The term *ma'ānī* by way of the poetic device of amphibology (*īhām*) alludes to the science of ideas and rhetoric (*'ilm-i ma'ānī va bayān*) in literary theory, whilst in grammar, *ma'ānī* denotes the underlying meanings of a poet's ideas, with *bayān* signifying 'the clarity of speech or expression, and the faculty by which clarity is attained'. Thus, *'ilm al-bayān* (the science of expression') is considered to be a subsection of the science of eloquence (*'ilm al-balāgha*), and *bayān* ('speech') itself is defined as 'whatever lifts the veil from a concealed idea (*ma'nā*)' (Abū Ṭāhir al-Baghdādī, *Qanūn al-balāgha*, cited by G.E. von Grunebaum, 'Bayān', *EI*², I, p. 1114). (Also cf. Khurramshāhī, *Ḥāfiẓ-nāma*, I, p. 611.) Although these grammatical and literary significations of *ma'ānī* and *bayān* in this verse are important (contrary to what Isti'lāmī, *Dars-i Ḥāfiẓ*, I, pp. 444–5, argues), conveying the idea that when ideas are rightly assembled one can speak finely, the meaning of the verse has little to do with such literary and rhetorical connotations. To understand Ḥāfiẓ's particular use of the term *ma'ānī* (plu. of *ma'nā*) in this verse, the philosophical meaning of the term *ma'nā* needs to be understood. I have translated *ma'ānī* as inner *sens* here because, as Julie Scott Meisami points out, 'The poetic use of the terms *ma'nā*, *ma'nawī*, suggests something similar to the *significatio* or *sen* referred to by the medieval European poets as the "deeper meaning" underlying the surface of the poem' ('Allegorical Gardens in the Persian Poetic Traditions', p. 259, n. 71). The *ma'ānī*, which the poet states need to be assembled in order to speak properly, are the *archetypal meanings*, or *ideal realities* or *spiritual meanings* underlying the phenomena of which they are mere shadows, as is elaborated by Shabistarī in the *Gulshan-i rāz* (in Muwaḥḥid, ed., *Majmu'a-i athar*, p. 97, vv. 721–4; this passage is discussed in detail in my *Beyond Faith and Infidelity*, pp. 181–3). Furthermore, Ḥāfiẓ's meaning is better comprehended once we realize that he was paraphrasing the following two verses from Rūmī's *Dīvān-i Shams*, which summarize the esoteric meaning of his verse perfectly (Ḥāfiẓ's poem is in the *Baḥr-i muḍāra'-i musaddas-i akhrab u sālim* metre, whereas Rūmī's poem is in the *Baḥr-i muḍāra'-i musaddas-i akhrab-i makfūf-i maḥzūf* metre: they are very similar): 'Love and loverhood and youth and things like these / Came together [to make the] Spring's delight and sat beside each other. // They had no form and then they came merrily into form. / That is to say: the imaginal entities have become cast into phenomenal forms. Just look!' (*Mastī u 'āshiqī u javāvī u jins-i īn / Āmad bahār-i khurram u gashtand hamnishīn // Ṣūrat nadāshtand, muṣawwar shudan khwush / Ya'nī mukhayyilāt muṣawwar shudeh bibīn*). In this sense, both poets' verses allude to the combination of what Avicenna called *intellecta* (Arabic: *ma'ānī ma'qūla:* intelligible notions or abstract ideas), which determine and cause – similar to Plato's Ideas (cf. Rūmī, *Mathnawī*, ed. Nicholson, VI: 3180) – the descent of all phenomena into this sentient realm and determine their 'formulation' into objects of sense (cf. Oliver Leaman, 'Ma'nā. 2. In Philosophy' *EI*², VI, p. 347). As Lāhūrī (*Sharḥ-i 'irfānī*, II, p. 1213) comments on the verse: 'in love and youth is manifest both the spiritual and physical powers of man in their [best] condition, and in unbound romance [*rindī*] is obtained detachment from worldly interests, and thus these three comprise the sum of the wayfarer's desires.' In sum, man's rational soul (*nafs-i nāṭiqa*) obtains the perfection of its powers in unbound romance (*rindī*) and love and youth, for these three are physical signs of the perfection of those supersensible realities (*ma'ānī*), signs that serve to 'actualize' all the possible objectives (*majmū'a-yi murād*) of the soul, and allow it to perfectly 'express' – itself that is, to become rational (= human).

284 But for an interesting reading of Rimbaud as a Sufi poet, however, see Adonis, *Sufism and Surrealism*, trans. J. Cumberbatch, pp. 193–211.

285 Cf. Lewis Hyde's study of *Trickster Makes the World: Mischief, Myth and Art*, p. 13.

286 'Lines to Fanny', in Keats, *Complete Poems*, p. 362.

287 Cited by Khurramshāhī, *Ḥāfiẓ-nāma*, I, p. 404. For further references and definitions of *rind*, see Dhū'l-Riyāsitayn, *Farhang-i vāzhahā-yi īhāmī dar ash'ār-i Ḥāfiẓ*, pp. 222–3; F. Lewis, 'Hafez and *Rendi*', pp. 483–91; Mazār'ī, *Mafhūm-i rindī dar shi'r-i Ḥāfiẓ*, pp. 104–51.

288 A saying ascribed to the *malāmatī* master Ḥamdūn Qaṣṣār (d. 271/884) by Hujwīrī, *Kashf al-maḥjūb*, ed. Zhukovskii, p. 74, line 2.

289 De Bruijn, 'Rind', *EI*[2], VIII, p. 531; *idem.*, 'The *Qalandariyyat* in Persian Mystical Poetry, from Sana'i Onwards', pp. 75–86; see also Skalmowski, 'Le *Qalandar* chez Ḥāfeẓ', pp. 275–86.

290 Javad Nurbakhsh, *Sufi Symbolism*, vol. 6, pp. 123f.

291 On Ḥāfiẓ and *qalandariyya* doctrine, see Bukhārā'ī, *Farhang-i ash'ār-i Ḥāfiẓ*, pp. 551–5; De Bruijn, 'Hafez's Poetic Art', pp. 473f.

292 Zarrīnkūb, *Az kūcha-i rindān*, p. 4; Mazār'ī, *Mafhūm-i rindī dar shi'r-i Ḥāfiẓ*, pp. 55ff.; Khurramshāhī, *Ḥāfiẓ-nāma*, I, pp. 404–6; Āshūrī, *'Irfān u rindī dar shi'r-i Ḥāfiẓ*, pp. 287–303.

293 *Dīvān-i 'Aṭṭār*, ed. Tafaḍḍulī, p. 64.

294 Trimingham, *The Sufi Orders in Islam*, pp. 266f., citing Suhrawardī's *'Awārif.*

295 Zarrīnkūb, *Justujū'ī dar taṣawwuf-i Irān*, pp. 336ff.

296 T. Yazizi, 'Ḳalandariyya', *EI*[2], IV, p. 473; on Sāvī and the *qalandars*, see Ahmet Karamustafa, *God's Unruly Friends*, pp. 40–4.

297 *Bar dar-i maykada rindān-i qalandar bāshand / kay satānand va dahand afsar-i shāhanshāhī.* In *Dīvān-i Ḥāfiẓ*, ed. Khānlarī, *ghazal* 479: 3.

298 See Richard Onians, *The Origins of European Thought*, pp. 343–8, cited by Hyde, *Trickster*, p. 43.

299 In Shelley, *Complete Poems*, p. 334; *Hellas*, II: 766–806.

300 Cf. George Herbert's memorable verse (from the poem 'Content'): 'Give me the pliant mind whose gentle measure / Complies and suits with all estates; / Which can let loose to a crown, and yet with pleasure / Take up within a cloister's gates.'

301 *Dīvān-i Ḥāfiẓ*, ed. Khānlarī, *ghazal* 174: 6–7.

302 *Ibid.*, *ghazals* 174: 7; 442: 6.

303 *Ibid.*, *ghazals* 79: 7; 366: 2; 389: 8; 479: 3.

304 On which, see Mu'īn, *Ḥāfiẓ-i shīrīn-sukhan*, I, pp. 436–7; Rajā'ī Bukhārā'ī, *Farhang-i ash'ār-i Ḥāfiẓ*, pp. 551–5. Cf. Ritter's discussion (*Ocean*, pp. 502–6) of Ḥāfiẓ's *qalandariyyāt.*

305 Murtaḍawī in his *Maktab-i Ḥāfiẓ*, pp. 113–47, devotes an entire chapter to his *malāmatī* thought and Mu'īn features an extensive discussion of the same in his *Ḥāfiẓ-i shīrīn-sukhan*, I, pp. 425–37. See also the following note.

306 Adapted from Khurramshāhī, 'Andīshahā-yi malāmatī-yi Ḥāfiẓ', in his *Chārdah ravāyat*, pp. 74–86; also reproduced in idem., *Ḥāfiẓ-nāma*, II, pp. 1090–7, where suitable verses from the *Dīvān* are given to illustrate each doctrine.

307 Bausani (*Religion in Iran*, p. 221) believes that the historical origins of Muslim *malāmatī* mysticism should be sought in Christianity. The probable connections between the Christian and Muslim *malāmatī* forms of spirituality have recently been highlighted by Sergey Ivanov, *Holy Fools in Byzantium and Beyond*, ch. 13.

308 *Cynthia's Revels* III: 3.15–16.

309 Milton, *Paradise Lost*, III, vv. 47–56 in *Milton: Complete Shorter Poems*, p. 472. Carey's erudite notes reference the citations from Seneca and Jonson given above.

310 William Blake, 'The Marriage of Heaven and Hell', in *Blake: Complete Writings*, p. 152.

311 Khurramshāhī, 'Andīshahā-yi malāmatī-yi Ḥāfiẓ', in his *Chārdah ravāyat*, p. 75.

312 See my 'The Esoteric Christianity of Islam: Interiorisation of Christian Imagery in Medieval Persian Sufi Poetry', pp. 127–56, and my 'Sufi Symbolism and the Persian Hermeneutic Tradition', pp. 255–308.

313 *Dīvān-i Ḥāfiẓ*, ed. Khānlarī, *ghazal* 356: 3. Lāhūrī (*Sharḥ-i 'irfānī*, IV, pp. 2434–5) offers a lengthy theosophical explanation of this line, the gist of which is that the technical term 'eyebrow' refers to 'the two bow's length' (*qāba qawsayn*) mentioned in Qur'ān, LIII: 9 in reference to Muḥammad's vision of God. This is 'the station of all-inclusive divine Unity [*waḥidiyyat*] which encompasses the two arcs of [Necessary] Being and Possibility, and is also the Muḥammadean Station'. 'Having one's work unclenched or opened up' indicates realization of this spiritual station in which 'one's own essence and attributes become transformed into God's Essence and Attributes'. Since this station pertains to Muḥammad in particular, anyone who realizes this station must have a character of similar stamina to the Prophet's capable of enduring blame and abuse 'since blame has a great effect in purifying love'. He concludes that this verse 'indicates the poet's realization of the station of the two bow's length' and having suffered so much blame, like the Prophet, 'his affairs were made to prosper ("be opened") through attaining that station'.

314 *Kashf al-maḥjūb*, ed. Zhukovskii, p. 68.

315 See Nurbakhsh, *Sufi Symbolism*, vol. 1, p. 4, s.v. *ābrū*.

316 See also Chebel, *Encyclopédie de l'amour en Islam*, II, pp. 266–7 (s.v. *Reproches*). Rūmī devotes an entire *ghazal* to this principle: see *Kulliyyāt-i Shams ya Dīvān-i kabīr*, II: 742/7790–4.

317 The theological origins of this doctrine in Islam, which is tracable back to the story of Joseph and Zulaykhā in the Qur'ān, is similar to the spirit of the topos of the 'test of love' (*assai*) among the Provençal troubadour poets, on which see Paz, *The Double Flame: Love and Eroticism*, pp. 107–8.

318 *Dīvān-i Ḥāfiẓ*, ed. Khānlarī, *ghazal* 426: 7.

319 *Dīwān-i Ḥāfiẓ*, ed. Qazvīnī and Ghanī, *ghazal* 272: 7.

320 *Dīvān-i Ḥāfiẓ*, ed. Khānlarī, *ghazal* 21: 1. Trans. Bly and Lewisohn, *The Angels*, p. 43.

321 *Dīvān-i Ḥāfiẓ*, ed. Khānlarī, *ghazal* 75: 9. Trans. Bly and Lewisohn, *The Angels*, p. 10.

322 *Dīvān-i Ḥāfiẓ*, ed. Khānlarī, *ghazal* 385: 1–3. Trans. Bly and Lewisohn, *The Angels*, p. 21.

323 *Kashf al-maḥjūb*, p. 69.

324 Haravī, *Sharḥ-i ghazalhā-yi Ḥāfiẓ*, III, p. 1606. Also cf. Khurramshāhī, *Ḥāfiẓ-nāma*, II, pp. 1091–3, who devotes several pages to commentary on this *ghazal*, discussing Ḥāfiẓ's relation to the *malāmatī* school.

325 The infinitive form *ranjīdan* of the verb used here connotes: 'to be hurt', 'take offence', 'to get offended', 'to be wounded', 'to suffer'. This line paraphrases a verse by Sa'dī with the same metre, rhyme and identical meaning (Khurramshāhī, *Ḥāfiẓ-nāma*, II, p. 1097). Explaining the subtle Sufi metaphysical doctrine underlying Ḥāfiẓ's verse, Lāhūrī (*Sharḥ-i 'irfānī-yi Dīvān-i Ḥāfiẓ*, IV, p. 2562) paraphrases the mystical theology of the poet as follows: 'Our theosophical persuasion [*mashrab*] consists in keeping faith with and preserving any true bonds of relationship that we have formed with everyone, cheerfully and gaily bearing the burdens of blame of all and sundry, and not becoming distressed and unhappy in any respect. The reason for this is that in our mystical way [*ṭarīqat*] and according to the tenets of our theosophical persuasion, getting offended and hurt by (attention to the illusion of) what's other [*ghayr*, than God] constitutes infidelity [*kāfarī*] and "hidden polytheism" [*shirk-i khafī*]. This is because those who have realized the spiritual station of pure divine Unity [*maqām-i tawḥīd-i ṣarf*] apprehend by direct vision that there is no other really existing being and active agent in existence except God Almighty, and that all other entities, qualities and actions are annihilated, null and void. They comprehend that every delight they experience is a radiance cast by the light of absolute divine Beauty [*jamāl-i muṭlaq*] and consider that every pain and grief that afflicts them to be a ray cast by the light of absolute divine Majesty [*jalāl-i muṭlaq*]. Thus, if they were to become offended by some irritation whilst being endowed with such traits of character, they would be allowing someone else to participate and share in the divine activity – which would constitute virtual heresy on the Sufi way [*kufr-i ṭarīqat*] and hidden polytheism.'

326 For a comprehensive overview of the *malāmatī* doctrines contained in Ḥāfiẓ's verse, see Mu'īn, *Ḥāfiẓ-i shīrīn-sukhan*, I, pp. 425–33.

327 Khurramshāhī, *Ḥāfiẓ-nāma*, I, pp. 404ff.; Murtaḍawī, *Maktab-i Ḥāfiẓ*, pp. 144–8.

328 Khurramshāhī, *Ḥāfiẓ-nāma*, I, p. 407; here citing Khānlarī *ghazal* 93: 3 translated above.

329 On which see Murtaḍawī, *Maktab-i Ḥāfiẓ*, p. 418.

330 *Dīvān-i Ḥāfiẓ*, ed. Khānlarī, *ghazal* 338: 4.

331 See also Mu'īn's study of the term in *Ḥāfiẓ-i shīrīn-sukhan*, I, pp. 369–71.

332 *The Man of Light in Iranian Sufism*, p. 92.

333 Perhaps the most thorough study of the Sufi theology the *shāhid* is given by H. Ritter in his *The Ocean of the Soul*, pp. 484–502. There are also a number of other orientalists, such as Schimmel (*Mystical Dimensions*, pp. 289–93), Fouchécour, de Bruijn (*Persian Sufi Poetry*, pp. 39, 67) and Eve Feuillebois-Pierunek (*A La Croisée des Voies Célestes*, index, s.v. *shāhedbāzī*), who have studied aspects of the erotic theory underlying *shāhid-bāzī*. Peter Wilson, 'The Witness Game: Imaginal Yoga & Sacred Pedophilia in Persian Sufism', gives a popular account of the practice. In Persian, there are an abundance of scholarly works on the subject, for an overview of which see Jalāl Sattārī, *'Ishq-i ṣūfiyāna*, chap. 10. Rajā'ī Bukhārā'ī's *Farhang-i ash'ār-i Ḥāfiẓ*, pp. 361–6, provides a basic analysis of the Sufi background of the concept in Ḥāfiẓ's poetry.

334 Feuillebois-Pierunek, *A La Croisée des Voies Célestes*, p. 70.

335 *Farhang-i ash'ār-i Ḥāfiẓ*, p. 361. *Shāhid* (witness) is also one of the divine Names found in the Qur'ān, denoting 'God-the-Universal-Witness' – that is, the divine Omniscience aware both of the Invisible (*ghayb*) and the Visible (*shāhada*) (IX: 94). The term has juridical significations as well, although these are seldom referred to in Persian poetry – on which see R. Peters, art. 'Shāhid', *EI*², IX, pp. 207–8.

336 Furūzānfar, *Aḥādīth-i Mathnawī*, p. 42.

337 Cited in al-Daylamī, *Kitāb 'aṭf al-alif*, trans. Vadet, *Le Traité d'Amour Mystique d'al-Daylami*, n. 244, p. 118. See also the discussion of this saying by Ernst, 'Rūzbihān Baqlī on Love', p. 184.

338 Karbalā'ī Tabrīzī, *Rawḍāt al-jinān*, I, pp. 506–7.

339 Symposium, 192e – drawing on White's (*Love's Philosophy*, p. 56) analysis.

340 'Ayn al-Quḍāt Hamadhānī, *Tamhīdāt*, p. 115, no. 162.

341 Bukhārā'ī, *Farhang-i ash'ār-i Ḥāfiẓ*, p. 364, citing al-'Abbādī's *Al-taṣfiya fī aḥwāl al-mutaṣawwifa*, pp. 211–12. This passage is largely based on the section on the 3rd *bāb* on the *shāhid* in Qushayrī's *Risāla:* see *Tarjama-i Risāla-yi Qushayrī*, edited by Furūzānfār, pp. 130–2. It is significant that Gīsū Dārāz, in his commentary on this passage in his *Sharḥ-i Risāla-yi Qushayrī*, pp. 375–6, links such views to 'the words of Rūzbihān, Shaykh Khwāja [Ḥāfiẓ] and Sa'dī, and their true masters who are Shaykh Aḥmad Ghazālī and Qāḍī 'Ayn al-Quḍāt – peace be upon all their spirits – and as for Muḥyī al-Dīn Ibn 'Arabī, don't ask me, because he professes the entire world to be God's witness!'. Cf. also Ritter's discussion in *The Ocean*, pp. 485–502.

342 From his introduction to his great romantic poem *Epipsychidion*.

343 *Sawāniḥ al-'ushshāq*, ed. Ritter, ch. 38, p. 58. For further discussion, see my 'Divine Love in Islam', in *Encyclopaedia of Love in World Religions*, I, pp. 163–5; and also my 'Sawanih', in *Encyclopaedia of Love*, II, pp. 535–8.

344 *Dīvān-i Ḥāfiẓ*, ed. Khānlarī, *ghazal* 121: 1. For an overview of the meaning of *ān*, see J. Nurbakhsh, *Sufi Symbolism*, I, pp. 32–3.

345 Papadopoulo, *Islam and Muslim Art*, pp. 144 ff., cited by Renard, *Seven Doors to Islam*, p. 127.

346 Renard, *Seven Doors*, p. 127.

347 On Ḥāfiẓ's practice of 'Beauty Worship', see Murtaḍawī, *Maktab-i Ḥāfiẓ*, pp. 775–94.

348 Jahramī, 'Mākhaz-i andīshahā-yi Sa'dī: Rūzbihān Baqlī Shīrāzī', pp. 95–112.

349 *Ḥāfiẓ-i shīrīn-sukhan*, I, pp. 420–4; and also Mu'īn's introduction to Rūzbihān's *Le Jasmin des fidèles*, pp. 54–63.

350 See my 'Romantic Love in Islam', in *Encyclopaedia of Love*, II, pp. 513–15. This adage was epitomized in Rūmī's verse in the *Mathnawī*: 'What is beloved is not a phenomenal form, whether it be the love of this world or love of the Next' (*Mathnawī*, II, ed. Nicholson, v. 703).

351 *Dīvān-i rubā'iyyāt-i Awḥad al-Dīn Kirmānī*, pp. 70–1; p. 233.

352 Jāmī, *Nafaḥāt al-uns*, p. 589.

353 See my *Beyond Faith and Infidelity*, chap. VI, for further discussion of this transcendental erotic theory in Persian poetry.

354 As Jāmī explains: 'If the spiritually realized mystic [*'ārif*] sees beauty, he contemplates the beauty he sees as something divine, as belonging to God, as a loveliness that has descended down through various degrees of existence. But the common man who is a non-mystic [*ghayr-i 'ārif*], doesn't possess such a regard [*naẓar*], it would be better if he refrained from contemplation of the fair lest he fall headlong into a chasm of perplexity', *Nafaḥāt*, p. 588. Describing the impoverishment of the common man's 'regard' for beauty, the American philosopher of aesthetics Elaine Scarry points out: 'It sometimes seems that a special problem arises for beauty once the realm of the sacred is no longer believed in or aspired to. If a beautiful young girl or a small bird, or a glass vase, or a poem, or a tree has the metaphysical in behind it, that realm verifies the weight and attention we confer on the girl, bird, vase, poem, tree. But if the metaphysical realm has vanished, one may feel bereft not only because of the giant deficit left by that vacant realm, but because the girl, the bird, the vase, the book now seem unable in their solitude to justify or account for the weight of their own beauty. If each

calls out for attention that has no destination beyond itself, each seems self-centered, too fragile to support the gravity of our immense regard' (*On Beauty and Being Just*, p. 47). This dichotomy between ordinary human vision and the refined mystically cognizant divine 'regard' for beauty is an oft-broached subject in Sufi erotic poetry. Sa'dī states: 'It's said glancing on the faces of the fair [*naẓar bi-rū-yi khubān*] is forbidden. Indeed – and yet, not the regard which I have. I contemplate the mystery of the ineffable Creator displayed in your countenence, witnessed there as if reflected in a mirror' (*Kulliyāt*, p. 427). Elsewhere, Sa'dī issues the supreme *fatwā* of the manifesto of the Sufi Romantics: 'Regarding a beautiful face [*rukh-i zībā*] is permissible in the Religion of Love (*madhhab-i 'ishq*), with this condition – that it be done constantly! (*ibid.*, p. 502; *ki guft*). Thus the determination of the meaning of Ḥāfiẓ's poetic images does not depend so much on the polarity of the sacred or profane, moral or immoral, but on the 'authenticity' of the heart – that is to say, an interior discrimination between what constitutes sincere or hypocritical conduct, a discernment between the erotic regard that is unitary, holistic and leads to an imaginal synthesis, and the analytical, ratiocinative perspective that is always divisive. That is one reason why, in Ḥāfiẓ's lexicon, images drawn from the repertoire of profane poetry ultimately have greater sacred import than the same imagery drawn from religious poetry.

355 As Ḥāfiẓ states: *Dīvān-i Ḥāfiẓ*, ed. Khānlarī, *ghazal* 91: 8.

356 My own three decades of study of Ḥāfiẓ's *Dīvān* convinces me of the truth of Isti'lāmī's judgement that 'the term *shāhid* in Ḥāfiẓ's writings simply has the meaning of a person with a fair face [*zībārū'ī*] and a beloved female mistress [*ma'shūq*], and if critics have said or written that it refers to pretty-faced boys, this is wrong' (*Dars-i Ḥāfiẓ* I, pp. 326–7). Elsewhere, he writes that 'there are more than 15 verses in Ḥāfiẓ's *Dīvān* where this term [*shāhid*] refers to a person with a fair face [*zībārū'ī*], and in most of these instances it cannot be said to refer to the face of a pretty *boy*' (*ibid.*, I, p. 98). He adds that: 'in most of the instances where Ḥāfiẓ employs the word *shāhid*, his regard is for a beautiful woman, or else it remains ambiguous – whether the reference is to a woman or a pretty boy, although it is far more reasonable to assume the former' (*ibid.*, I, p. 292). Isti'lāmī emphasizes that there is only *one* specific instance in the *Dīvān*, where *shāhid* can be definitively said to be male (*ibid.*, I, p. 345, referring to *Dīvān*, *ghazal* 170: *Dars-i Ḥāfiẓ*, I, p. 477 – *zāhid-i khalvat-nīshīn*, not in Khānlarī's ed.). I should also add that the prevalence of the mainly female *shāhids* in Shīrāz in 'Ubayd's poetry (*Kulliyāt-i 'Ubayd Zākānī*, pp. 45: *ghazal* 45, v. 4; 113; *ghazal* 114: v. 1, p. 323, lines 5–6) adds greater weight to Isti'lamī's opinion. This viewpoint of course is contested by some other scholars (cf. Ritter, *Ocean*, p. 481 *infra*; Sīrūs Shamīsā, *Shāhid-bāzī*, pp. 165–70) who largely consider his *shāhid* to be exclusively male, and *shāhid-bāzī* simply pederasty.

357 *Dīvān-i Ḥāfiẓ*, ed. Khānlarī, *ghazal* 484: 10: 'Thought of self and will of self have no place in the realm of the libertine: in our creed, self-will and self-conceit are sacrilege.'

358 *Ibid.*, *ghazal* 345: 1. Trans. Bly and Lewisohn, *The Angels*, p. 51.

359 Schroeder, 'Verse Translation and Hafiz', p. 215.

360 *Dīvān-i Ḥāfiẓ*, ed. Khānlarī, *ghazal* 224: 9. This follows Khwājū's erotic doctrine of the identity of human and divine love vis-à-vis divine Reality exactly: *'Ishq-i majāzī dar rah-i ma'nā ḥaqīqat-ast / 'ishq ār chi pīsh-i ahl-i ḥaqīqat majāz nīst* (Romantic Love on the Path of Reality is itself True and Divine / although for the truthful adepts there's no love at all that is not divine!' *Dīwān-i Khwājū Kirmānī*, p. 214, *ghazal* 76: 8.

361 For the major study of this device in his poetry, see Murtaḍawī's *Maktab-i Ḥāfiẓ*, pp. 455–515.

362 This is particularly clear in Sa'dī's *ghazals*. The following verses from three different *ghazals* celebrate his flagrant adoration of the female *shāhid:* (1) 'Sa'dī, what a disharmonious creature it is / who claims he's got a heart but not a sweetheart.' (2) 'If you are a man, do not censure Sa'dī / for no man did ever live not inclined to the beautiful fairy-faced nymphs [*parī-ruyān*].' (3) 'Sa'dī's name is everywhere associated with *shāhidbāzī* / but that is not a flaw; in my creed it is the highest praise / The Muslim with his ritual prayers, the infidel with his heresy, and me and love: / In secret everyone you see has their own form of faith.' *Kulliyāt-i Sa'dī*, ed. Furūghī, pp. 465, 468.

363 *Dīvān-i Ḥāfiẓ*, ed. Khānlarī, *ghazal* 385: 9. Trans. Bly and Lewisohn, *The Angels*, p. 22.

364 Lāhūrī, *Sharḥ-i 'irfānī*, IV, p. 2566. In confirmation of the rectitude of Ḥāfiẓ's abhorrence of sycophantic fawning over the hands of so-called holy men, Khurramshāhī (*Ḥāfiẓ-nāma*, II, p. 1097, in his commentary on this line) cites Imām 'Alī's dictum: 'Do not kiss the hand of anyone except the hand of a woman by way of sensual passion [*shahwat*] or a child by way of compassion [*raḥmat*].'

365 Once: *naẓarbāzān*; twice: *naẓarbāzī'yi*; thrice: *naẓarbāzī*; and four times: *naẓarbāz*.

366 Fouchécour, '*Naẓar-bāzī*: le jeux du regard selon un interprète de Hāfez', p. 5. See *ghazals* 31: 9; 47: 9; 305: 2, where both terms (*naẓar-bāz* and *rind*) are mentioned together; and 107: 11 (*ṣūfiyān* and *rind*).

367 Fouchécour, '*Naẓar-bāzī*', p. 6. See *ghazals* 188: 1; 206: 3; 268: 8; 271: 3; 349: 7.

368 *Dīvān-i Ḥāfiẓ*, ed. Khānlarī, *ghazal* 305: 2. *'Āshiq u rind u naẓar-bāzam u mīgūyam fāsh / Tā bidānī ki bi chandīn hunar ārasta'am!*

369 Khurramshāhī, *Ḥāfiẓ-nāma*, I, pp. 705–6. See also Āshūrī, '*Rindī va naẓar-bāzī*; Fouchécour, '*Naẓar-bāzī*', pp. 3–10.

370 *Sharḥ-i 'irfānī-yi Dīvān-i Ḥāfiẓ*, I, p. 428.

371 *Ibid.*, IV, p. 2562.

372 Cf. Sa'dī's lines in the *qāṣīda* beginning: *Har 'ādamī ki naẓar ba yikī nadārad u did / bi-ṣūratī nadahad ṣūratī'st lāya'qil* (*Kulliyāt*, p. 728), repeated in another *qāṣīda* (beginning: *Bi-hīch yār...*) in this form: *Har 'ādamī ki naẓar ba yikī nadārad u did / bi-ṣūratī nadahad ṣūratī'st bar dīvār* (*ibid.*, p. 720).

373 *Dīvān-i Ḥāfiẓ*, ed. Khānlarī, *ghazal* 154: 3.

374 Cf. Pūrjavādī's analysis of this verse, 'Rindī-yi Ḥāfiẓ', *Bū-yi jān*, pp. 234–5; 246. The other verses include: 'To be a lover is the wont and way of inspired libertines who suffer adversity...' (*Dīvān-i Ḥāfiẓ*, ed. Khānlarī, *ghazal* 155: 4); 'Initially it appeared an easy thing to learn the art of love and the inspired libertine, but how I've eaten out my heart and soul in pursuit of this lore!' (*ibid.*, *ghazal* 301: 2). Also, cf. *ghazal* 131: 7.

375 *Chūn madhhab-i qalandar rindī u 'āshiqī-ast / Rindāna mā ṭārīq-i qalandar girifta-īm.* In Shāh Ni'matullāh Walī, *Kulliyāt-i ash'ār-i Shāh Ni'matu'llāh Valī*, ed. Nurbakhsh, *ghazal* 1125: 3.

376 *Chūn rūz rawshan-ast ki mā rind u 'āshiqīm / chūn ṣubḥ dar parastash-i rū-yi tū ṣādiqīm.* In *Dīwān-i Kamāl Khujandī*, ed. Shidfar, II.1, *ghazal* 668: 1, p. 695.

377 Cf. *Dīvān-i Ḥāfiẓ*, ed. Khānlarī, *ghazal* 338: 1, 4.

378 *Ibid.*, *ghazal* 329: 3.

379 *Ibid.*, *ghazal* 310: 1, 3. Translation of v. 3 by Peter Russell.

380 Dārābī, *Laṭīfa-yi ghaybī*, p. 90.

381 *Risālahā-yi Shāh Ni'matu'llāh Valī*, I, pp. 231–2.

382 *Dīvān-i Ḥāfiẓ*, ed. Khānlarī, *ghazal* 271: 4.

383 'The Kingdom of this World flourishes through pious deeds, ascetical exercises and austerity, and preserving one's honour and fair name intact, while the *rind*'s work lies precisely in relinquishing and disregarding such actions, in destroying and disengaging himself from all material things. It is in this sense of the word that the inspired libertine, metaphorically speaking, "sets the world on fire'." Pūrjavādī, 'Rindī-yi Ḥāfiẓ', *Bū-yi jān*, p. 233.

384 *Kulliyāt*, ed. Furūghī, p. 606.

385 The term 'Sufi robe' (*khirqa*) is used 54 times in the *Dīvān*; in every instance his usage is derogatory, symbolizing insincerity, impurity and hypocrisy.

386 For example, more than half of the 16 references to the term 'royal crown' (*tāj*) in the *Dīvān* are derogatory.

387 *Dīvān-i Ḥāfiẓ*, ed. Khānlarī, *ghazal* 78: 4.

388 *Ibid.*, *ghazal* 403: 9.

389 *Ibid.*, *ghazal* 445: * (*jāhil* = lout).

390 See Ātashisawdā, 'Zabān-i 'āmmiyāna dar *ghazal*-i Ḥāfiẓ', pp. 85–112.

391 Speaking of Iblīs' experience of tribulation in love of God, 'Ayn al-Quḍāt Hamadhānī writes: 'Do you know what Love's touchstone is? One is affliction [*balā*] and wrath [*qahr*], and the other is blame [*malāmat*] and maltreatment [*madhillat*] ... One must suffer torment in love yet persevere in fidelity. In

this fashion, the lover becomes cooked by the beloved's mercy and wrath. Otherwise, he remains raw and nothing will ever come of him.' *Tamhīdāt*, p. 221, no. 283.

392 *Kashf al-asrār*, V, p. 60. Maybudī's doctrine here is directly derived from Anṣārī's teaching in the *Ṣad maydān*, where, in the fifteenth Field of Abstinence (*wara'*), the Master of Herat states that piety is increased by enduring public blame for one only ever learns to abstain from worldly excesses 'by being taunted by one's enemies [*shimātat-i ḥaṣmān*: i.e. who rejoice at one's misfortunes]' (*Majmu'a-yi Rasā'il-i fārsī-yi Khvāja 'Abdu'llāh Ansāri*, ed. Sarvar Mawlā'ī, I, p. 269).

393 The celebrated first verse of his poem 'The Apparition'.

394 Khurramshāhī, *Ḥāfiẓ-nāma*, II, pp. 1091, citing Hujwīrī, *Kashf*, p. 68.

395 *Kashf al-maḥjūb*, ed. Zhukovskii, p. 70. Cf. 'If the world hate you, ye know that it hated me before it hated you. If ye were of the world, the world would love his own; but because ye are not of the world, but I have chosen you out of the world, therefore the world hateth you' (John 15: 18–19).

396 *Dīvān-i Ḥāfiẓ*, ed. Khānlarī, *ghazal* 217: 4, reading *malāmat* for *malālat.*

397 *Sharḥ-i 'irfānī-yi Dīvān-i Ḥāfiẓ*, I, p. 730.

398 Pūrjavādī, 'Rindī-yi Ḥāfiẓ', *Bū-yi jān*, p. 243.

399 *Dīvān-i Ḥāfiẓ*, ed. Khānlarī, *ghazal* 79: 6.

400 '*Rindī* pertains to the realm of the 'Transcendental I' of the poet inspiring the exterior utterance of his personal 'I': the Self beyond the temporal self, the Oversoul above the human soul, the interior voice of genius. But to penetrate into the realm of *rindī*, one must accept the presence of this dichotomy and duality of – human versus divine – identities within one poetic voice, and realize that the proper universe of *rindī* is 'selflessness.' Pūrjavādī, 'Rindī-yi Ḥāfiẓ', *Bū-yi jān*, pp. 223–4.

401 *Ibid.*, p. 244.

402 Shelley, 'Epipsychidion', 589.

403 *Dīvān-i Ḥāfiẓ*, ed. Khānlarī, *ghazal* 84: 7.

404 Lāhījī, *Mafātīḥ al-i'jāz fī sharḥ-i Gulshan-i rāz*, p. 521.

405 *Ibid.*, p. 534.

406 Lāhūrī, *Sharḥ-i 'irfānī-yi Dīvān-i Ḥāfiẓ*, I, p. 202, commenting on *Dīvān-i Ḥāfiẓ*, ed. Khānlarī, *ghazal* 48: 3. The linking of the inspired libertine with transcendence and the highest degree of love is also the main theme of Shāh Ni'matullāh Walī's (1330–1431) treatise on the *Spiritual Degrees of the Inspired Libertines* (*Marātib-i rindān*) cited above.

407 As the poet says: 'Whoever became an initiate of the heart remained in the sanctum of the Friend, but those who did not comprehend this affair remained entangled in it.' *Dīvān-i Ḥāfiẓ*, ed. Khānlarī, *ghazal* 175: 1.

Part II

Ḥāfiẓ and the School of Love in Classical Persian Poetry

The Principles of the Religion of Love in Classical Persian Poetry

Husayn Ilahi-Ghomshei

translated by Leonard Lewisohn

It's a matter of creed for me: goblets of wine,
My love's lips just like rubies, this is my doctrine
I won't forsake. Puritans, I offer you apologies.

Ḥāfiẓ[1]

The Genealogy of the Religion of Love in Persian Poetry

From ancient times Persian literature has featured many references to the 'Religion of Love' (*dīn-i 'ishq* or *madhhab-i 'ishq*), represented as being the only true faith, the creed most acceptable in the eyes of God. In classical Persian poetry, the most famous verses where this concept seems to have first been vocalized are by Rūdākī Samarqandī (d. 329/940):

What use is it to serve one's turn to face
The Mihrab in your prayers, when all your heart
Is set upon the idols of Taraz and of Bukhara?
What God accepts from you are love's transports,
But prayers said by rote He won't admit.[2]

Rūdākī's younger contemporary, the Sufi martyr Manṣūr al-Ḥallāj (d. 304/922), when asked which religious creed he followed, in the same vein pronounced: 'I follow the religion of my Lord' (*Anā 'alā madhhabī rabbī*).[3] Ḥallāj's bold claim was embraced by many of the later Sufis, such as his follower 'Ayn al-Quḍāt Hamadhānī (executed 526/1132) who alluded directly to the 'Religion of Love' in this key passage in his *Tamhīdāt*:

> The lovers follow the religion and the community of God. They do not follow the religion and creed of Shāfi'ī or Abū Ḥanīfa or anyone else. They follow the Religion of Love and the Religion of God [*madhhab-i 'ishq wa madhhab-i khudā*].

> When they behold God, this visionary encounter of God [*liqā-yi khudā*] becomes their religion and creed; when they see Muḥammad, this visionary encounter with Muḥammad [*liqā-yi Muḥammad*] becomes their faith [*īmān*]. When they behold Iblis, that station's vision becomes to them [the meaning of] infidelity. Thus it is possible to understand what the faith and religion of this group consists in, and from whence derives their 'infidelity'.[4]

Underlining the scriptural basis for their radical theology of love, Sufis referred to the famous Qur'ānic verse affirming that God, notwithstanding recusants among mankind, will bring forth a people 'whom He loves and who love Him' (*yuhibbuhum wa yuhibbunahu*, V: 54). They interpreted this verse as referring to the saintly company who are lovers of God and who in turn are beloved by God. Similarly, one finds another Qur'ānic verse (II: 165) states: 'The believers are stauncher in their love of God.'

The earliest major Persian Sufi poet to make love an axiom of an individual mystical theology and personal religious creed was Sanā'ī of Ghazna (d. 525/1131). In one verse, Sanā'ī thus identifies both his Sufi path (*ṭarīqat*) and his sectarian creed (*kīsh*) as being 'Love' itself:

> Why do you ask about my creed and faith tradition?
> It's clear. My creed is *Eros. Amor* is my canon.[5]

Similarly, in another verse, Sanā'ī incites the reader to 'Rise up and show forth the high stature of Love, tor the Muezzin has said: "Rise up to pray!"' Here, the poet informs us, like Rūdakī before him, that true ritual prayer in practice is enacted by a lover and in reality sustained by love. 'The divine Muezzin', he declares, 'summons you to rise up and demonstrate in every action of your life the high stature of love, since life itself is nothing but one constant *adoratio amoris*' The same teaching, using a similar metaphor, we find enunciated a few generations later by Jalāl al-Dīn Rūmī (d. 1273):

> In *eros* lies transcendent heights which rise
> And summon us to music that's immortal.
> Save to seek those erotic highs
> One should never dance, never revel.[6]

Niẓāmī of Ganja (d. 598/1202), the leading author of epic romantic poetry in Persian literature, must also be counted among the chief prophets of the Religion of Love in Persian *belles lettres*. In his romantic epic poem *Khusraw and Shīrīn*, Niẓāmī teaches that the only role that man is fit to play in the entire theatre of Existence is that of the lover in the following verses, where Love is featured as a kind of *Anima Mundi*:

Naught else but love's my labour: that's my logo;
So long as I'm alive, don't offer me another motto.
All face towards love to supplicate in every
Temple under Heaven's eye. The galaxy
Itself wouldn't have an earth unless across
The surface *Eros*' water coursed to save its face.
Become a slave to love! All righteous thought consists
Of this, for that's the task of the heart's adepts.
The cosmos *is* love in sum and all the rest deceit;
Save *Amor*'s play, all else's an idle game and sport.[7]

Niẓāmī, long before Newton, had posited that the entire scale of creation and Nature was permeated by a reciprocally acting gravitational force that he named 'Love':

Attraction works on human temperament its lure
And that attraction sages predicate of love,
So when you ponder this in depth then you'll perceive
That *Eros* holds the cosmos up: all stands through love,
And if once Eros lose its grip on Heaven's wheel
The great globe itself would forfeit its bloom and weal.[8]

Niẓāmī continues to glorify love in the next verses and describes the fundamental message of his poetic composition as a summons to Love:

Devoid of *Eros*, life appeared to me soulless.
I sold my heart and in its place a soul purchased.
I've filled the rims and cornices of the globe
With *Amor*'s smoke. I've made the eyes of reason doze.[9]

After Niẓāmī, the next great prophet of the Religion of Love in Persian poetry was 'Aṭṭār of Nishapur (d. 618/1221 or 627/1229). Like the poets mentioned above, in line with the Qur'ānic doctrine of love (V: 54), 'Aṭṭār believed the only commendable and worthwhile connection between man and God to be a Lover–Beloved relationship. Like many other Muslim mystics before him, 'Aṭṭār emphasized that the superiority and pre-eminence of Adam over the other angels lay in Adam's/man's love-passion and agony.[10] In fact, in 'Aṭṭār spiritual teachings, the cure for all psychological and spiritual ailments lies in the transformative suffering and passion of love (*dard*).[11] That is why he asks for that passion to be increased:

Give me an ounce of pain, O you
Who cure all pain, for left without
Your pain, my soul will die.
To heretics let heresy apply,

And to the faithful – grant them faith;
But for the heart of 'Aṭṭār, let
One ounce of your pain remain.[12]

Muḥyī al-Dīn ibn al-'Arabī (d. 638/1240) of Andalusia in Spain, known as the *Shaykh al-akbar*, the 'Supreme Shaykh', was one of the first Sufis to describe the Religion of Love in a specifically ecumenical sense. In his theosophical works composed in Arabic, he gave explicit theological expression to a separate religious creed that he called the Religion of Love (*Dīn al-ḥubb*) – a faith which embraced all manifestations of reality – while encompassing yet transcending their divergent appearances. The following verses are among the most famous and admired lines ever composed in Islamic – if not world – civilization on the theme of this transcendental erotic religious creed:

Pasture between breastbones
and innards.
Marvel,
a garden among flames!

My heart can take on
any form:
for gazelles, a meadow
a cloister for monks,

For the idols, sacred ground,
Ka'ba for the circling pilgrim,
the tables of the Toráh,
the scrolls of the Qur'án.

I profess the religion of love;
wherever its caravan turns
along the way, that is the belief,
the faith I keep.[13]

The other great Arab mystical poet – a contemporary of Ibn 'Arabī who lived in Egypt – who belonged to this same School of Love was 'Umar ibn Fāriḍ (d. 633/1235). Ibn Fāriḍ's entire poetical oeuvre is one immense paean in praise of love's mysteries, a hymn composed in exposition of the subtleties, sublime degrees and mystical states of Islamic erotic spirituality. Although all his verse was composed in Arabic, many of the later literati of Persia honoured his genius by giving him the honorary title of 'Ḥāfiẓ of the West'. In his famous Wine-ode (*Qaṣīda-yi khamriyya*), Ibn Fāriḍ describes in great detail the quickening qualities and effects of wine upon the spirit – wine being used here as an allegory for the elixir of love and its intoxication. To relish the spirit and convey the taste of this wine and also to give a small glimmer of the grandeur of the sublime station of love in his verse, it must suffice here to cite the two opening and two concluding verses of this poem:

In memory of the beloved
  we drank a wine;
    we were drunk with it
  before the creation of the vine.

The full moon its glass, the wine
  a sun circled by a crescent;
    when it is mixed
  how many stars appear.

Its two final verses are:

For there is no life in this world
  for one who lives here sober;
    who does not die drunk on it,
  prudence has passed him by.

So let him weep for himself,
  one who wasted his life
    never having won a share
  or measure of this wine.[14]

Over the rest of this period of what might be called 'the Golden Age of Classical Persian Literature' – the thirteenth through fifteenth centuries – the 'Religion of Love' (*madhhab-i 'ishq*) became increasingly celebrated in verse by major poets such as Jalāl al-Dīn Rūmī (d. 672/1273), Sa'dī (d. circa 691/1292) and Ḥāfiẓ. Their contributions to this central current of Islamic erotic spirituality is discussed below.

The Religion of Love in Rūmī

It will be worthwhile to explore Rūmī's own understanding of this transcendental *madhhab-i 'ishq*, since he devotes so many verses of his ecstatic poetry to claiming that the religion of love transcends not only Islam, but every other religion as well. He thus begins one long *ghazal* announcing the supra-Islamic nature of Eros as follows:

In the summa of *Amor*
    where's the idiom of Islam?

Where's one master exegete
of *Eros* whose lore suffices
to crack the code of its complexities?[15]

In another *ghazal*, he delineates the above distinction between the esoteric creed of love and exoteric Islam in greater detail:

Get lost! The lover's *secta amoris* is the reverse
Of other faiths and creeds, for from the one you love
Untruth and perfidy beats kindness and sincerity,
Her fabrications inspirations, her sin all gratuity,
All ill from her is just, her taunts all right and meet,
Her temple is the Ka'ba, silk-soft her adamant.
The nettle's sting from her I think is better than
Rose petals and sweet basil. If scoffers then poke fun
And say: 'It's deviant – this crooked creed you've got!'
Reply: 'Her eyebrow is my creed. I bid for it
And laid down life for this – the "creed of crookedness"!
It's all I need, I'll waste no words. Go read the rest in silence.'[16]

We find him again extolling in a quatrain the superiority of love's 'crooked creed' over the so-called 'straight' way of formalistic Islam:

Her tresses' tip our fetish-cult
And eye that's drunk and impudent –
That is the creed which we adopt.
They say that healthy piety is something else,
Assert sound faith is different, aside from these,
But from their 'sound faith' and 'creed of wholesomeness',
We choose her deviant, uneven ways and crookedness.[17]

This same strict distinction and difference between the formal creed of Islam and the higher transcendental religion of love is reaffirmed by Rūmī in a number of other quatrains in his *Dīvān* as well. In the following two quatrains, he maintains that love's esoteric faith supersedes conventional religion and is something apart from the other world's traditional sects:

Erotomaniacs is what we are: lovesots;
The Muslims they're a different lot. We're spindly ants;
King Solomon's another sort. A burning, aching heart
And sallow faces seek of us: the abattoir's on a different street.[18]

Know it for certain that the lover's not a Muslim
For in the creed of love there's neither infidelity
Or faith – once you fall in love, you have no body,
No soul, no heart, no mind: who ain't like this, ain't nothin.[19]

In his mystical epic 'The Rhyming Spiritual Couplets' (*Mathnawī-yi ma'nawī*), Rūmī frequently celebrates the 'Religion of Love' as well. The following verse from his *Mathnawī* constitutes his most famous statement concerning the pre-eminence of this higher *secta amoris*:

Love's state is apart
  from religions and faith
God is the lover's creed –
  God is the lover's state.[20]

The Religion of Love in Ḥāfiẓ

Ḥāfiẓ is Persia's greatest erotic lyricist who remains the supreme – and in some senses the last – prophet of the Religion of Love in Persian literature. There are many verses in his *ghazal*s that appear as a manifesto of this transcendental creed:

Both human beings and spirits take their sustenance
From the existence of love. The practice of devotion
Is a good way to arrive at happiness in both worlds.[21]

Become a lover; if you don't, one day the affairs of the world
Will come to an end, and you'll never have had even
One glimpse of the purpose of the workings of space and time.[22]

In Persian literature, the Prophet Ḥāfiẓ's collected poems (*Dīvān*) constitute a sacred scripture which, just like the works of Sa'dī, is a faithful reflection of the divine Beloved's countenance. Both poets were prophets; both composed poetic Scriptures that remain miracles of beauty in Persian, their verses appearing as divine signs (*āyat*) of loveliness and grace. For Ḥāfiẓ, the entire world reflects the grace and loveliness of the divine countenance, for, insofar as 'Wheresoever you turn, there is the Face of God' (Qur'ān, II: 115), that Face reveals and casts a ray of the infinite divine beauty in the mirrors of man, cosmos, microcosm and macrocosm:[23]

Your beautiful face divulged to us
  the chapter and verse of divine grace,
    which is why nothing exists

save grace and comeliness
  in our scriptural exegesis.[24]

This same theophany of beauty also cast its ray upon Ḥāfiẓ's verse, gleams of which were reflected through various poetic images such as 'Idol' (*but*), 'Christian child' (*tarsā-bachchih*), 'Magian child' (*mugh-bachchih*), 'Cup-bearer' (*sāqī*) and 'Friend' (*yār*). When these images are apprehended by any reader attuned to Ḥāfiẓ's symbolic universe, they arouse intoxication and selflessness, freeing one from conceit, self-centredness and egotism. Thus, in the following verse in his *Dīvān*, we see how the 'Magian child' appears to rob the poet of his egocentric faith and initiate him into love's esoteric creed:

Just when the Magi's child strolled along (the thief
  of hearts and wrecker of belief)
At once the Muslim puritan was carried off,
  from all his friends divorced himself.[25]

Ḥāfiẓ's religion of love teaches devotion to that essential Beauty whose loveliness reappears time and time again in the guise of various symbols among other Sufi poets.[26] This is particularly evident in the lines from the following *ghazal*, which is one of the most famous erotic poems in all of Persian literature:

Her hair was still tangled, her mouth drunk
And laughing, her shoulders sweaty, the blouse
Torn open, singing love songs, her hand holding a wine cup.

Her eyes were looking for a drunken brawl, her mouth
Full of jibes. And this being sat down
Last night at midnight on my bed.

She put her lips close to my ear and said
In a mournful whisper these words: 'What is this?
Aren't you my old lover – Are you asleep?'

The friend of wisdom who receives
This wine that steals sleep is a traitor to love
If he doesn't worship that same wine.[27]

As the last stanza indicates, Ḥāfiẓ professes that anyone who does not revel in drinking the wine of love is a heretic and traitor to love's creed (*kāfar-i 'ishq*). This statement makes better sense if we decode the reference to wine as being metaphorical of the theophany of beauty in the raiment of mortal beings. In the most important mystical commentary on the *Dīvān* of Ḥāfiẓ, written by Sayf al-Dīn 'Abū'l-Ḥasan 'Abd al-Raḥmān Khatmī Lāhūrī (fl. seventeenth century in India), the commentator, when explaining this poem, alludes to the particular meaning given to the term 'infidel', or 'traitor' or 'heretic' *(kāfar)* in the philosophy of Ibn 'Arabī, as being 'someone who conceals the existence of God through manifestation of existing phenomena'.[28] Lāhūrī explains that the mystic versed in Sufi erotic theology should not allow phenomena to veil his vision of Noumena, and should realize that the transcendent beauty must - and can only - be contemplated through the translucent veil of human beauty. Paraphrasing Ḥāfiẓ, Lāhūrī states:

> That Transcendent Beloved Being then spoke, stating that any gnostic who is a confidant of the arcane mysteries, who recognizes the true face of such an affair, when given such a wine - that is, beauty and loveliness decked out in the garb of the veiled presentment of a figurative mortal sweetheart - will only end up veiling and concealing this display of God, this divine theophany, unless he does becomes a worshipper of beauty [*ḥusn-parast*]. This is because it is through the forms of mortal beauty [*suwar-i husniyya*] that God-as-Absolute in reality attracts the hearts of lovers to Himself.[29]

For Ḥāfiẓ, as for the other followers of the religion of love, this adoration of beauty (*jamāl-parastī*) reveals itself through the cult's opposition to the self-aggrandizing *Sharīʿa*-oriented Islam of the common mob of Muslims. To relish the taste of this erotic faith, say the Sufi poets, one must divorce old barren reason from bed (along with its religion pursued for selfish worldly ends) and take the daughter of the vine to spouse instead, just as Iran's greatest bacchanalian poet 'Umar Khayyām (d. circa 519/1125–527/1132) taught.[30] Edward Fitzgerald, in his classic translation of Khayyām, while slightly misrepresenting the letter, perfectly conveys the spirit of this idea in this quatrain:

> You know, my Friends, how long since in my House
> For a new Marriage I did make Carouse:
> Divorced old barren reason from my Bed,
> And took the Daughter of the Vine to Spouse.[31]

Ḥāfiẓ also uses exactly the same terminology to refer to his conversion to this transcendental nonconformist religion of love. He sprinkles his verse with a variety of terms to this end: 'Love's creed' (*madhhab-i 'ishq*),[32] the 'Magian master's faith' (*madhhab-i pīr-i mughān*),[33] the 'creed of inspired libertines' (*madhhab-i rindān*),[34] the 'faith of the Sufi Path' (*madhhab-i ahl-i ṭarīqat*)[35] and, occasionally, simply 'our creed' (*madhhab-i mā*).[36] Among these terms, each of which have a slightly different connotation in his erotic spirituality, the following verses comprise his key statements:

Don't allow the flirty side-glances of beauties
To teach you injustice. We know that in the religion of love
Each act returns with its own consequences.[37]

* * *

The only prayer apse
The heart of Ḥāfiẓ has
Is your eyebrow's arch
For in our faith
It's you alone, none else
Commands obeisance.[38]

* * *

Above homage and obeisance to lunatics
Do not seek more from us, for our sect's master
Professed all intellectualism to be wickedness.[39]

* * *

'To wear the dervish robe and then to drink wine,
That's not a rite of true doctrine.'
I said. 'Indeed,' she said, 'but in the Magian
Master's rite of faith, that's all holy doctrine.'[40]

* * *

I followed the path of the mad libertines for years
Long enough, until I was able, with the decree
Of intelligence, to put my greediness into prison.[41]

* * *

On the spiritual road, being uncooked and raw
Is a mark of unbelief; it's best to move along the path
Of fortune with nimbleness and springy knees.[42]

While much of the poetry of Rūmī, Sa'dī and Ḥāfiẓ has been penned by way of exposition of the Religion of Love, the abstruse spiritual principles of this faith remain virtually unknown to many students of Islamic thought, whether in the East or in the West. Below I will provide an overview of the basic principles of Islam's erotic theology as depicted by the classical Persian poets, illustrated by examples from the Qur'ān and Persian literature.

The Primordial Disposition of Man and the Religion of Love

According to the Qur'ān, man was created with an 'original disposition that God instilled within him' (*fiṭrat Allāh*) and formed with a 'fundamentally immutable God-given nature' (*lā-tabdīl li-khalqi'llāhi:* XXX: 30). Basing themselves on this evidence from their holy scripture, Persian poets drove this classical theological doctrine up several theosophical notches higher, maintaining that man's nature had been already moulded and framed to develop according to the nature of the divine attributes of Beauty, Truth and Goodness, and inclined to follow the 'Straight Path of Love and Mercy' (*'ishq, maḥabbat, raḥmat*) long before birth. As human beings, we thus enter the world with faith in the divine innately deposited within the depths of our selves, for, according to the Prophet's renowned saying: 'Every child is born according to his original disposition [*fiṭra*]; then his parents make him into a Jew, a Christian, or a Zoroastrian.'[43]

Therefore, in the narrow sectarian sense of the word, no one is 'born' a Muslim[44] – much less a Hindu, Buddhist, Christian, Jew or Zoroastrian – but rather every person is moulded into becoming a 'believer' subject to the influence of their parents, wider society and cultural environment. At the same time, it should be emphasized that all these faiths, setting aside the excrescences, excesses and superfluities to which each has been heir, is quintessentially moulded according to that same God-given 'original disposition' within humankind. Thus, all the world's religions may be viewed as divergent manifestations of that one primordial faith of man – that is, the religion of his original disposition (*fiṭra*).

Each of these faiths, having its own fair share of opportunistic power-seeking, theological deviance, sanctimonious cant, snobbish bias, hypocritical pretence, unctuous piety, priggish affectation and bigoted prejudice, along with a host of other vices, has become separated from and spurned its sister, considering its fellow travellers in the realms of Faith as damned – apostates, infidels or heretics, destined for Hades and Gehenna. Nonetheless, in every religion one can always find a small number of true adepts, saints and men of God, who are its spiritually realized gnostics and poets who are attuned to the Divine. Among this elect company one finds few divergences and disagreements save in respect to terminological expressions and modes of ritual practice pertaining to incidental forms of exoteric dogma, which are irrelevant to the quintessential reality of their faith. The true believers within every religion, as Rūmī puts it, are like rays of a single lamp:

If ten lamps are together in one place
  each one is different from the next in form.
You cannot tell apart the light of each
  when you are looking at them, there is no doubt.[45]

Whatever their exterior denomination, the soul and spirit of the faithful reflects their insight into God's comprehensive mercy which encompasses and embraces all men, good and ill alike:

Besides the soul and understanding in
the ass and cow, there's a sense and soul in man
that's different. Again, besides this human sense
and intellect, the saintly souls in bliss
have higher cognizance. The souls of brutes
possess no unity; from that *anima vitalis*
don't seek for oneness. If a single base
man eat some bread, another man who's base
will not be full, and if one brute bears weights
his neighbour's not distressed. No, he rejoices
to hear he's died, or dies of jealousy
when good accrues to him or profit sees
has come to him. Thus, souls of dogs and wolves
are set in castes apart: yet there're no halves,
but only wholes in lions' souls.[46]

Therefore, it is wrong to assert we enter into the world devoid of all faith and belief and only subsequently personally select a religion for ourselves. On the contrary, each person is born with love for the Good, Beautiful and True innately instilled within him. If he doesn't deviate from the 'straight path of his original disposition', this primordial love will mature and develop within him and direct him along his course in life. The sole purpose underlying the mission of the prophets in the various religions is to bring people back to that original disposition. The reason we need to hearken to their summons is that our original spiritual disposition, exactly like our physical metabolism, is constantly plagued by myriad diseases, afflicted with moral and/or metaphysical amnesia due to various hindrances which impede its healthy progress and block its natural advancement. The different heavenly scriptures of the world's faiths brought by their prophets are analogous to medicinal cures for these ailments. They are reminders to men, while their various legal codes – Canon Law (*sharīʿa*) – must be considered as different paths of development and maturation adapted to the diverse religious needs of various peoples. Insofar as the original disposition of man is one and the same, and all the prophets have been sent by the One God, it is unreasonable to assume that the religions of mankind should or can differ in their fundamental principles from each other. The mission of the prophets is thus precisely tailored to suit the original disposition of man, comprising a summons to contemplate the Good, Beautiful and True. In the words of Maḥmūd Shabistarī (d. after 740/1339):

That Day when Faith was written down
within the heart, the clay of man
was moulded in the human form,
The word of God was sent down then
and holy books revealed to men
so you'd recall your vow again.[47]

In several places in the Qur'ān, allusion is made to the triad of these transcendent qualities that bring delight to the heart and salvation to the soul. As Rūmī puts it:

> Since prophethood's the guide to liberty,
> Believers get their liberty from prophets free.[48]

In the pursuit of goodness, knowledge and beauty, we receive such a sense of joy and experience so much rapture and delight that we even forget personal sorrow and grief; we become, as Sa'dī says, steeped so deep in the delight of contemplation that 'all the world's woes have no effect'. In Islamic erotic spirituality, this is best illustrated in the famous Sūrah XII (Joseph) in the Qur'ān, where we read how Zulaykhā, the wife of the Pharoah of Egypt, summoned a group of her Egyptian women friends to her palace. She wanted them to see her favourite slave-boy Joseph, with whom she was madly infatuated, for themselves. As soon as he strutted in the room, the ladies, who had all previously found fault with Zulaykhā for her passion for him, immediately recanted their prudery, being smitten by the overwhelming loveliness of his 'human form divine'. Wildly besotted with him, they slit their wrists with the same knives she'd given them to peel fruit, exclaiming: 'This is not a human being, but some gracious angel!' (XII: 31). By preaching a religion of passionate love (*'ishq*), poets such as Ḥāfiẓ or Sa'dī similarly intend to advocate the idea that by falling in love and observing the courtesies of lover and beloved, men and women may realize transports of consciousness unbeknownst to normative conformist religious piety. In this fashion, we may attain felicity and salvation both in this world and the next, which is, by the way, precisely the sense intended by Ḥāfiẓ's well-known exhortation:

> Go strain your every nerve to gain the high degree of love;
> The benefits will be immense if only you could make that voyage.[49]

Such is also the purport underlying Sa'dī's celebrated description of the mystical 'stages of love' in these verses at the beginning of his *Būstān*:

> If you desire to chart your way across
> This ground, first hamstring all the horses
> You'd use to journey back. Then contemplate
> The mirror of your heart until the state
> Of purity you slowly find. If the perfume
> Of love befuddles you till you're drunken,
> You'll probe about to seek that timeless vow
> You made to God. Your quest's on foot till now,
> But once you're there, you'll fly on wings of love,
> Till certainty the veil of phantasy
> Rends aside and nothing but the Court
> Of Majesty remains to veil your heart.[50]

The Religion of Love and Antinomian Traditions in Islam

A thousand enigmas subtler, finer spun than
A strand of hair lie here, and thus not everyone
Who shaves his scalp can understand the rite of the Wildman.[51]

– Ḥāfiẓ

Like Christianity, Islam harbours many important antinomian traditions. By the eleventh century, antinomian mystics who considered that Islamic ritual practices and the sacred Law (*sharīʿa*) could be dispensed with, leaving them free to commit any transgressions and sins that they wanted to on the basis of their inspired mystical vision and enlightened understanding, had appeared among the Sufis.[52] One of these antinomian traditions that originally developed among early Shiʿite groups was the doctrine of *Ibāḥat* (libertinism).

A variety of terms in classical Persian literature soon became used to refer to these antinomian mystics: *qalandar*s (vagabonds, wildmen), *rind* (inspired libertine), *qallāsh* (knave), *mubāḥī* (libertine), *dīvāna* (lunatic) and *lā-ubālī* (daredevil, desperado). The latter term, literally meaning 'I couldn't care less', indicates a cavalier attitude that damns the consequences of all prodigal and immoral conduct. We find many verses by Saʿdī and Ḥāfiẓ praising both the daredevil *lā-ubālī* and the wildman *qalandar* attitude.[53] Saʿdī says:

For learned quartos what use has the reckless lover?
Why should the lunatic's moonstruck mind forbear
To hear the preacher's horatory admonitions?
Why should lovers give a twit about abuse
And calumny from friend or foe? There's not
Much choice in either case: they suffer on the rack
Of love or bear the weight of slurs and smears.[54]

In the following lines, Ḥāfiẓ celebrates the perfect antinomian lover in the person of the Sufi Shaykh Ṣanʿān, who fell in love with a Christian girl, abandoned Islam, and through his apostasy demonstrated his true faith to the Religion of Love:

If you profess yourself a devotee of
The highway of most noble Love
Never give a second thought for name
Or what men say is all 'ill-fame',
Recall the cap and gown
Of great Shaykh Ṣanʿān –
For months in hock, put in
The wine-seller's shop for pawn.[55]

In another verse, Ḥāfiẓ again celebrates the legend of the *qalandar*, referring indirectly to Shaykh Ṣan'ān, who found faith and piety in binding on Christian cincture at the bidding of the Christian girl:

> What rapturous, enchanting moments
> that holy roaming dervish has
> who fares through all the stations of
> the mystic way, who in the tangled knots
> of the Christian girdle that he wears
> still tills his rosary and hymns
> angelic litanies and prayers.[56]

In these verses, Persia's two most famous love lyricists, Sa'dī and Ḥāfiẓ, boldly announce their avocation of *Eros*' creed. Making full use of the antinomian vocabulary available in Persian, they declare themselves *Fedeli d'amore*, indifferent to the blame and reproach of those cold souls who are disbarred from the throes of erotic passion and thus banned from entry into the precincts of *Amor*. As faithful servants of Love's Path, they understood that 'nothing exists save grace and comeliness'[57] in the pursuit of love, and readily declared themselves ready to succumb to all its passions and temptations.

Although terms such as *lā-ubālī*, *qalandar*, *rind*, *qallāsh*, *mubāḥī* and *dīvāna* originally had exclusively profane meanings – referring to various types of thugs, hooligans, debauchees, lunatics, profligates, rakes and other ne'er-do-wells of society – they were soon taken over by the Sufis and integrated into the Persian Sufi poetic lexicon, where they were given positive connotations denoting higher degrees of mystical realization. Thus, the profligate became identified with a mystic of high degree, the debauchee with a pious man of prayer, the vagabond equated with a disengaged spirit liberated from sensual desires, the knave a member of the saintliest company, and the lunatic the truly Inspired Man attuned to the Voice of God. Of course, it is easy to see why today many literary critics in secular circles, who are more often than not utterly alienated from the traditional symbolic cosmos in which such emblems, symbols, tropes and types all functioned as part of a common 'hermetic' discourse familiar to all connoisseurs of verse, find themselves voicing doubts and disagreements about which sense precisely – profane or sacred, human or divine – such metaphors should convey. Unfortunately, most of the younger generation of Persian-speaking literati, being immersed in secular Western values, no longer recall the higher symbolic connotations of these terms. To their understanding, Ḥāfiẓ thus remains the supreme decadent and hedonist poet, leader of the world's grand debauchees. To complicate matters further, the poetic device of *īhām* (amphibology) allowed the Sufi poets to marry heaven and earth, and, so to speak, condone poetic ambivalence, so that the distinctive allegorical metonymy of terms in the Sufi symbolic lexicon lent a diversification to their usages, allowing them to broadly connote both the colourful, literal 'profane' connotations *as well as* the higher figurative senses pertaining to those transcendental symbolic meanings.

If we approach the transcendental significance of some of these symbols, how the process leading to the sublimation of these metaphors occurred – and thus the *raison d'être* sustaining them – is easy to discern. The phrase 'it is delightful to be mad', for example, poetically speaking conveys a self-evident sense. Understood spiritually, however, the phrase makes no sense whatsoever unless we understand it to imply a madness *above* and *beyond* reason, rather than *below* reason: the lower, irrational – psychotic – insanity.[58] Likewise, the expression 'the joys of intoxication' makes perfect sense to every secular sensibility attuned to wine's bacchanalian pleasures. But to the philosophical temperament focused on progress in the spiritual life, it makes sense only when it refers to the drunkenness that contemplation of the Beautiful inspires – or, as the Sufis say, the ecstatic rapture that the sight of the beauteous visage of the Cup-bearer (*sāqī*) arouses in the beholder – stimulating intoxication without any hangover. In the same vein, the joys of freedom extolled by the Sufi poets involve their liberation from the vices of greed, anger, pride and emancipation from the vanity of ambition for honours and high rank. Liberty is as much a spiritual virtue as licence is a moral vice. That wanton witness-of-beauty (*shāhid-i harjā'ī*) celebrated in Sufi mystical poetry is that icon of supreme loveliness, whose ravishingly attractive countenance is everywhere reflected, both in man and nature alike.[59] When Sufi mystics proudly announce that they 'revel in the delights of desire [*havas*]', their apparently sybarite sentiment takes as its transcendental reference point the 'grand desire' of the adept to realize freedom from selfhood, as Rūmī states:

> There lies in no man's head
>   Such desire as lies in mine;
> The desire I sense is such that
>   I'm bereft of all ken of self.[60]

Similarly, Sanā'ī boasts of his own 'desire' (*havas*) animating his poetic inspiration:

> The magic diablerie of conjurers
>   from Indian lands, graces
>   his breath of inspiration;
> The subtle Chinese portraitists
>   whose art all faces unmasks
>   lend his desires animation.[61]

In Ḥāfiẓ's verse as well, we find that the fulfilment of desire in love implies a freedom from self-interest and the renunciation of selfish desire:

My heart – disport
Your head: loveplay's
Not jesting business.
Nobody has yet struck
Eros's shuttlecock
With Desire's bat.[62]

Here Ḥāfiẓ contrasts the transcendental nature of 'true love' (*'ishq*) to the pursuit of idle erotic amusement, which in comparison seems but a kind of shallow 'sport' (*bāzī*) and selfish 'desire' (*havas*): this term here having no transcendent mystical implication. In this respect, Ḥāfiẓ often clarifies that the flames of his erotic longing and fire of his desire (*ātash-i havas*) were not inspired by any temporal passion, but that his passion was enkindled in pre-Eternity when the uncreated souls of men first professed divine love for their Lord:

Flushed and scorched in desire's sultry flames today
Ḥāfiẓ's heart not only now aches with woe,
A brand of grief sears him likes the anemone
For now, for always – and since pre-eternity.[63]

This type of holy antinomianism and pious libertinism is best described in a *ghazal* by Rūmī devoted to the 'lovers' and the 'gnostics', which describes them as a debauched company of profligates and libertines. In this poem he employs all the important technical terms used in Islamic theology to refer to antinomian debauchees – in particular, the *mubāḥī*, a wild libertine who is utterly outside the pale of all Islamic faith and piety, and the *ibāḥatī*, the pursuer of libertine ways. For those who believe that Sufism constitutes a basically heterodox anti-Islamic mystical ideology falsely masquerading under Muslim robes, Rūmī's poem brings unwelcome news, for he immediately subverts his own subversive rhetoric, clarifying that there is a higher mystical significance beneath his profane terms:

Today we've got songs and an amphora
  full of wine and the music of *Samā'*;
A Saki stone-drunk bears us the wine
  among this crowd of wayward libertines.
They're 'far-out' libertines, in fact, they've passed
  beyond existence – not decadent, demented
Dope-fiend types, high on hemp or hash:
  the blacked-out addicts of the lowlife.[64]

In the first line of this *ghazal*, the 'Saki stone-drunk' (*Sāqī-yi bad-mast*) is a symbol for Rūmī's spiritual master Shams-i Tabrīzī. He also clarifies that this 'crowd of wayward libertines' (*jam'-i mubāḥī*) are lovers – that is, spiritually advanced mystics who have 'passed beyond existence' into a realm where the limitations of the illusory Selfhood, with its 'me' and 'thee', are abolished. Such 'libertines' are not lowlife substance abusers giggling time away on hashish, nor common dope addicts huddling among the dregs of society, but transcendentalists who have not only transcended themselves, but have dismissed the Angel of Death from their dominion.[65]

In exactly the same manner as Rūmī, Ḥāfiẓ (supposedly a hedonist and founding father of libertine teachings in Persian poetry) also clarifies that he eschews self-indulgent antinomianism (*mubāḥāt*) in one important verse:

> Heart-friend, I guide you well along Salvation's way:
> Neither by sin vaunt iniquity nor hawk austerity.[66]

The Sin of Repentance in the Religion of Love

Although Repentance (*tawba*) is normally listed as the first stage of the Sufi path, in the religion of love, repentance came to be considered a reprehensible vice and terrible sin. In a *ghazal* whose rhyme phrase is 'I have repented' (*tawba kardam*), Rūmī thus quips:

> In the sacrament of penitence's sin
>   and in the exercise of penance's crime,
> Neck-deep I lay, but now of all that sin
>   I make amends: my penance was the crime.[67]

In his *Mathnawī*, Rūmī describes how the black slave Bilāl, one of the earliest converts to Islam, was tortured by his Jewish owners for his new faith. The Prophet's wealthy companion, Abū Bakr (who eventually emancipated Bilāl), advised him to conceal his beliefs from his cruel overlord. Bilāl, however, was unable to dissimulate and hide his fervour for God, despite being stretched out in the hot Arabian desert sun and beaten with clubs capped with thorns until he bled. In the following verses, we hear Abū Bakr advise Bilāl to 'repent' of his indiscretion, and how Bilāl rejects repentance:

> Again, he said, 'Repent!' Again, at once
>   he did, but *Eros* whisked away repentance.
> Repentance of this ilk he carried on,
>   till penance caused him detestation.
> He spoke his faith out loud, his flesh gave up
>   to Fortune's frowns, adversity, hardship.
> 'My penitential vows, Oh Prophet, you
>   oppose, yet every vein is full of you!

There is no room in me for *culpa mea,*
  for penance, penitence or penalty!
All sacraments of penance such as this
  I scorn. Who'd ever spurn eternal bliss?!
For *Eros* is a mighty force: I'm trounced
  by his imperious might; I'm crushed;
In *Eros*' bitter, vinegary furor
  I'm sweet and luscious – savoury as sugar.'
... To be a lover, yet act with patience,
  sangfroid to hold to vows of penitence,
This is, great soul though you indeed may be,
  a senseless, comical absurdity:
For patience's but a snail, *Eros* is a dragon;
  the latter all divine, the former only human.[68]

Here we see Love considered to be a 'sacred sin' that is paradoxically the source of all piety and religious belief. According to this erotic creed, the quintessence of Islam lies in committing the 'divine crime' of love, and to repent of love is sin and heresy. A good flavour of these wildly passionate sentiments that permeate all classical Persian poetry in general, and underpin Sufi erotics in particular, can be found in these three verses by, respectively, Rūmī, Saʿdī and Ḥāfiẓ:

Alas, what sin or crime is this, of which
Repentance of its but vile wickedness?
Behind, I'd dodge but cannot flee away;
Before, I'd come yet there's no place to stay.[69]

Go tell all men, go let the folk
Be told that I'm a lover and a drunk.
  This name and fame, I boast of it,
I'm proud to say all vows I've broke...[70]

The bedrock of our famous repentance seemed
To be tough as granite. Look, the delicate
Glass cup has split the repentance at the first blow.[71]

The most famous illustration of this critical attitude towards the ascetic ideals of 'repentance' in classical Persian poetry is found in 'Aṭṭār's story of the pious Sufi master Shaykh Ṣan'ān, mentioned above. Following the promptings of a dream, Ṣan'ān travelled with a large band of disciples from Mecca to Byzantium. There, seeing an unveiled Christian girl in a window, he was smitten by love. She disdained him at first, forcing him to spend sleepless nights on her doorstep. Eventually, however, she relented and accepted him as her lover, but to test the sincerity of his love, subjected him to several trials – demanding that he renounce Islam, burn the Qur'ān, drink wine and work for her as a swineherd. He acquiesced to all his beloved's commands, eventually becoming the model pious heretic of the Sufi religion of love. All of Ḥāfiẓ's poetry, as I have shown elsewhere, is saturated by this tale.[72] In the following lines from 'Aṭṭār's account, we hear the Shaykh's disciples urging him to recant and repent of his blasphemous passion. But to all their entreaties, he makes only flippantly sacrilegious replies:

> 'My sheikh,' urged one, 'forget this evil sight;
> Rise, cleanse yourself according to our rite.'
> 'In blood[73] I cleanse myself,' the sheikh replied;
> 'In blood, a hundred times, my life is dyed.'
> ... Another cried: 'Enough of this; you must
> Seek solitude and in repentant dust
> Bow down to God.' 'I will,' replied the sheikh,
> 'Bow down in dust, but for my idol's sake.'
> And one reproached him: 'Have you no regret
> For Islam and those rites you would forget?'
> He said: 'No man repents past folly more;
> Why is it I was not in love before?'[74]

Eventually, the love-spell cast by the girl was broken and the prayers of his distressed disciples, for months at their wits' end on how to win the shaykh back into the fold of Islam, were heard. The swineherd Sufi shaykh awoke from the dream of Christianity. However, soon after he cut off his Christian cincture and headed back with them to Mecca, she pursued him hotly, tragically dying – a Muslim, of course – in his arms.[75]

Ultimately, the shaykh did 'repent' of his love passion, but his repentance was not so much a formal 'turning back' as a passage out of exoteric into esoteric Islam – a casting-off of the phantasy of conventional faith for the reality of true devotion. Shaykh Ṣan'ān, having passed through the crucible of erotic romantic passion, experienced a fresh conversion to religion based upon the principles of love. He was no longer the desiccated ascetic Sufi of ere, but a fiery *Fedeli d'amore*.

The Worship of Wine in the Religion of Love

Classical Persian poems are normally filled with extravagant praise for the cupbearer (*sāqī*), goblet (*sāghar*), wine-vat (*khum*) and drunkenness (*mastī*), winehouse (*maykhāna*), tavern (*kharābāt*), tavern-master (*pīr-i kharābāt*), and so on. Indeed, many of the clichés and stock metaphors in Persian erotic poetry are bacchanalian,[76] with the lover (*'āshiq*) usually described as a witless wanderer (*parīshān*), a headless and footless vagabond (*bī-sar u pā*), a drunkard (*mast*), who is constantly intoxicated (*mast-i mudām*), transported in selfless rapture (*bīkhᵛīshī*), 'out of his mind' and bereft of self-consciousness (*bīhūshī*). Such bacchanalian terminology is not personally subjective vagaries that express the poet's melancholic moods, but actually cognitively precise descriptions that depict exactly the lover's intoxication during contemplation of the beloved's beauty, his excitement at imagination of her phantom (*khiyāl*) and his rapture at the recollection of her beauty previously witnessed in time-before-time on the Day of the pre-Eternal Covenant (*rūz-i alast*) between man and God.[77]

Since the reflection of the Beloved's beauteous countenance is everywhere cast down and reflected in the 'goblets of phenomena' throughout the Tavern of the Universe, the lover is always intoxicated and bereft of self in a drunken transport. Loving that absolute Intellectual Beauty, he attains the spiritual station of 'true idolatry' (*but-parastī-yi ḥaqīqī*),[78] which is the inner meaning of Ḥāfiẓ's verse:

> The Friend's reflection cast upon the goblet's surface
> – Her countenance there – in contemplation I've witnessed.
> Of such timeless drunken pleasure, you are, alas, oblivious.[79]

Ḥāfiẓ's 'timeless drunken pleasure' is not of the unessential or accidental kind, but rather substantial, since the intoxication it bestows – unlike the drink made from the vine or imbibed through the heady wine of ambition, pride and thoughtlessness is not followed by any hangover or morning-after headache. Hence, it can never be nullified by repentance or by a recovery of sobriety. Those drunk on this wine never commit the sin of becoming teetotallers; as Sa'dī says: 'no man drunk on that wine served up at the dawn of pre-Eternity becomes sober until vespers are said on the night of the Day of Resurrection.'

This pre-Eternal 'wine of the Covenant' (*sharāb-i alast*), mentioned so often by Sufi *fedeli d'amore*, refers to the recollection of the pledge that was sealed in pre-Eternity (*ahd-i Alast*) between the uncreated souls of Adam and their Lord. 'Am I not your Lord [*alastu bi-rabbikum*]?', God asked the yet uncreated souls of Adam's offspring. In this unconscious and uncreated state, they professed: 'Yes, we bear witness to it [*balā shahidnā*]'.[80] Humankind's troth plighted to God in that atemporal moment of Islam's metahistory comprises the Sufi Religion of Love's unwritten constitution. What is missing from this narration for the ordinary reader is the fact that the word *balā*, which means 'yes' in the above verse in Arabic, signifies 'calamity' as well. The Sufis took the implication of this Arabic linguistic pun very seriously, believing that the human soul in Eternity before its incarnation in time had actually committed itself in advance to undergo all life's trials and tribulations.

The 'wine of the Covenant' that the mystic imbibes thus tastes 'bitter', just like the fruit of the vine. Although this wine is quite capable of making a man pass out in a drunken stupor 'under the table', as Ḥāfiẓ says,[81] its 'bitterness' has always been interpreted by the Sufis as an allegory for the pains and troubles man must endure when he mobilizes himself in service to his fellow men. In fact, 'servitude to mankind' is both the best description of love's creed and the best indicator of one's love for God. All questions posed in Love's catechism can be answered with one single riposte: 'Service'.

This 'bitterness' was given an even more creative exegesis by the Persian *fedeli d'amore*, who compared it to relishing the sapiential 'taste' of drunken rapture (*dhawq-i mastī*) in contemplation of the beloved. The pleasure of that vision and their acquiescence to the Beloved's will cause its whole bitter taste to turn to sweetness, an experience which Sa'dī's memorable verse celebrates:

> For others, the wine of the torments of love
> Is gall, but for us, the liquor we imbibe
> We take from the hand of the Friend
> So it becomes sweet and delicious.[82]

A number of Ḥāfiẓ's verses underscore the same bittersweet sentiment:

> Although the thorn hurts your spirit, the rose asks pardon
> For this wound; the sourness of wine is more easily tolerated
> When one remembers the sweet flavour of drunkenness.[83]

Ḥāfiẓ also boasts of being famed as a drunkard from the very first day of the pre-Eternal Covenant (*rūz-i alast*),[84] and rails against the ascetic who cannot understand that his intoxication with human beauty is a necessary consequence of his vow in pre-Eternity to follow love's religion:

> Oh, ascetics, go away. Stop arguing with those
> Who drink the bitter stuff, because it was precisely
> This gift the divine ones gave us in Pre-Eternity.[85]

Elsewhere, he directs his attention beyond this temporal sphere and speaks of being drunk on the wine of the Covenant:

> How blessed is the man who, like Ḥāfiẓ,
> Has tasted in his heart the wine made before Adam.[86]

That wine is exactly the same whose cup-bearer Niẓāmī invokes in his *Sāqī-nāma* within his romantic epic *Sharaf-nāma*:

> Cast sleep away, O Saki, from your eyes
>   and pass to lovers who are pure that wine
> That is purest claret, which all the schools
>   of law accept and sanction as divine.
> Come, Saki, from the village-elder's cask
>   that honey-sweet wine pour into our flask;

Don't give us wine which legal schools have banned
 but wine through which Faith's principles are crowned.[87]

Similarly, Ibn Fāriḍ, in a key verse from his *Wine Ode*, celebrates the 'sin' of his drunken bacchanalian adoration of wine as follows:

But they said: 'You've drunk sin!'
 No, indeed, I drank only
  that whose abstention
is sin to me.[88]

The Immediate Present Moment (naqd-i waqt) *in the Religion of Love*

Since love transforms the stuff of the past or future into effects and assets consumed in the present and 'now', the devotee of the religion of love lives in the present moment. The lover is always the 'Child of the Moment' (*ibn al-waqt*), as Rūmī put it:

The Sufi is 'a son of the moment;'
The word *mañana* is unheard of on the Way.[89]

The Sufi is 'a son of the moment;'
In quest of purity he holds the moment close
Like a son clings to his father.[90]

In his *Discourses*, Rūmī explains the theosophical doctrine underlying this notion as follows:

> Some men look at the beginning, and some men look at the end. These who look at the end are formidable and powerful, for their gaze is fixed on the final issue of things and the world beyond.
>
> Then, there are those who look at the beginning, who are more elect. They say, 'What need is there for us to look at the end? If wheat is sown at the beginning, barley cannot be reaped in the end, or if barley is sown, wheat shall never be harvested.' So their gaze is set on the beginning.
>
> There are others who still more elect: they gaze neither upon the beginning nor do they contemplate the end. Being absorbed in God, neither beginning nor end ever enter their minds.[91]

Since the *fedeli d'amore* who pursue love's creed understand the preciousness of the present moment, they know that time must not be wasted in expectation of any future Resurrection. Anyway, for them the Resurrection shall never come since it has already occurred! That is why Ḥāfiẓ rebukes the ascetic for the emptiness of his promise of a future paradise:

> When Paradise is mine today as cash in hand,
> Why then should I be taken in and count upon
> The puritan's pledge of tomorrow's kingdom?[92]

Sa'dī enunciates this same doctrine in one verse:

> Eternal youth with its great fortune and felicity
> Belongs to he who's next to you; he's never had his day;
> He knows no age: his home's in highest heaven.[93]

Living in the here and now, the lover finds heaven and earth transfigured: he becomes a denizen of heaven. 'The Resurrection becomes your very *état d'âme* in the immediate present of Now [*naqd-i ḥāl*]',[94] as Rūmī puts it. Not only is the Resurrection an immediate experience (*naqd-i ḥāl*) for him, but all the great events of history – the myths, legends, and the tales of the heroes and saints of yore – are felt as living experiences apprehended in the present. They are not hoary tales of a bygone past. They represent the ready cash and coinage of the lover's soul, whose shillings and pence he spends here and now. For poets such as Sa'dī and Ḥāfiẓ, the references to the legends of Moses and his revelation on Mt Sana'i (Qur'ān, VII: 142–5), or the tales of Abraham and the tyrant Nimrud who cast him into the furnace,[95] are not simply colourful poetic devices – which the Arabic rhetoricians pedantically categorize as being a 'proverbial allusion' (*talmīḥ*)[96] – but actual occurrences within the poet's soul. This interiorization of religious mythology within the psyche of the poet is reflected in Ḥāfiẓ's verse about Moses' vision of God in the Burning Bush:

> Here's pitch black night, there lies the Valley of Peace
> Before my feet, so where's Moses' light,
> Mt. Sanai's Burning Bush and the promised sight?[97]

In reference to the story of Abraham being cast into the furnace, likewise Sa'dī says:

> Although I'm cast like Abraham into the furnace of
> Affliction, it would not matter: glowing with your love
> I'd bask among the basil shoots and tulips in your garden.[98]

All the tales of great lovers and the fables of the heroic champions of yore thus become part of the soul's psychohistory. They pertain the inner journey of the poet. That is why the epic tales of Firdawsī, the versified romances of Niẓāmī, and 'Aṭṭār's story of Shaykh Ṣan'ān's infatuation with the Christian girl comprise the stuff of their verse in the here and now. These are not legends, but living facts of the heart that appear constantly in their verse; they are, as Emily Dickinson says, 'Bulletins all Day from Immortality'. In a single verse, Sa'dī thus summarizes the entire epic romance of *Khusraw and Shīrīn* by Niẓāmī:

> I realized it then, that very first day when
> With Shīrīn my affair began: I knew that in
> The end, sweet life itself I would abandon.[99]

As Niẓāmī relates, a beautiful Armenian princess named Shīrīn ('Sweet one') was a concubine of the Sasanian monarch Khusraw Parvīz II (reg. 591–628 AD). A stone sculptor called Farhād,[100] renowned for his physical prowess, was a rival with the king for her affections. Recognizing the all-consuming nature of his rival's attachment to his concubine, Khusraw declines to murder him, thinking it more prudent to give his mighty sculptor rival the seemingly impossible task of carving a canal through a mountain to allow for the flow of milk from the pasture to her palace. Even more smugly, Khusraw promised Farhād his concubine as a reward for his efforts should they succeed. When, surprisingly, Farhād meets the challenge and carves out the canal, Khusraw dupes him by telling him that Shīrīn has died, leading Farhād to cast himself off the mountain in despair to his death.

Ḥāfiẓ, in a single verse, summarizes another romantic legend from Firdawsī's epic (*The Book of Kings, Shāh-nāma*) as follows:

> I have fallen into Patience's lowest pit
> Where, empassioned by the candle of Chigil[101]
> And, enkindled by love's flame, I have been burnt.
> The prince of Turks knows not my good or ill...
>   Where's Rustam the champion?[102]

Ḥāfiẓ here compares his condition with that of the Persian hero Bīzhan, son of Gīv and nephew of Rustam.[103] During an adventure in the lands of Turan (Central Asia), Bīzhan encounters Afrāsiyāb's daughter Manīzha, who falls in love with him. Afrāsiyāb,[104] referred to here by the poet as 'the prince of Turks', was the most prominent of the Turanian Turkish kings. When he discovers their illicit romance, Afrāsiyāb imprisons the hated Iranian hero Bīzhan in the well of Arzhang. Rustam, the renowned champion of the Iranian forces, eventually goes to Turan in disguise and rescues Bīzhan from the well, bringing Manīzha with him back to Iran.

Likewise, the Sufi poets consider the appearance of Jesus as an ever reoccurring event sustaining them in the present, using in this context the metaphor of the 'Messiah's breath of inspiration' (*dam-i masīḥ*). Ḥāfiẓ alludes to this in two verses:

> Love's physician is compassionate and endowed
> With the breath of Jesus,

But whom should he assuage
If you are without pain?[105]

To whom may I relate such a subtlety?
She killed me – my stony-hearted mistress,
Yet possessed the life-giving breath of Jesus.[106]

Since God's grace is vouchsafed to the lover immediately in the present moment, the supplications and prayers offered up in the Religion of Love are neither to obtain welfare in the present here and now nor salvation in the future life. From the great archangels, whether they be Gabriel or Michael, down to the inhabitants of the fairy kingdom, denizens of the demon empire and the kingdom of the beasts, and then up to Satan's disobedience and pride, followed by Adam's sin and later repentance, along with all the graces and calamities sent by Heaven which have been recorded in holy scriptures about past communities – in the Religion of Love such circumstances fill the mystic's *presential awareness*. These legends are tangible issues of the present moment that facilitate the lover's pursuit of *Eros*, food for his soul that he consumes *hoc tempore* in the pursuit of knowledge, goodness and beauty, which incite him to excel in the only serious sport: *Amor*. Thus, for example, referring to Noah's Ark cast upon the flood, Ḥāfiẓ says:

Don't desert your mates and quit the ark
Of Noah, Ḥāfiẓ, else this typhoon of
Vicissitudes shall blow your ship to bits.[107]

Conclusion

From the above review of the doctrine of the Religion of Love in classical Persian poetry, several conclusions may be drawn.

Firstly, it is clear that there is an actual religion – or faith – of love (*dīn yā madhhab-i 'ishq*) in Persian mystical literature. The proponents or prophets of this erotic faith comprise some of the greatest poets of the Persian language. They include the likes of Niẓāmī, Sa'dī, Rūmī and Ḥāfiẓ, who have been sent by God-as-*Eros*, charged with the mission of converting mankind to their philosophy of love.

In the second place, this religion of love is founded on principles of love innate within each human being, in accordance with the original disposition that God instilled within him that prompt him to pursue and love Beauty, Knowledge and Goodness.

Thirdly, this religion is not contrary to the tenets of any of the other divinely revealed religions of mankind. Anyone can become a votary of the religion of love regardless of previous socio-cultural conditioning, for conversion to love's creed lends new life to the faith which one already has.

Fourthly, this religion's essential message is one of friendship, affection, peace and living with mutual toleration of others. The tranquillity and peace generated by love's faith also inculcates such basic values as courtesy, kindness, compassion and mutual respect of others.

Fifthly, the principles of this erotic faith appear in all the world's advanced cultures whether in East or West. Its prophets feature as the greatest poets, sages and saints of all the oriental and occidental civilizations.

Sixthly and lastly, the religion of love is the universal faith of all existing beings. From a cosmological standpoint, all beings, from the tiniest atom up to the most complex of organisms, all things, whether animate or inanimate, are followers of the religion of love, and ultimately whatever they do is subservient to Love's command. As Niẓāmī says:

> Don't fall foul and get in trouble
>   over these living, breathing idols.
> They're demigods, yet worship not
>   themselves, so follow not their cult.
> Each wanders round caught up in a daze,
>   distracted and dizzy as a compass;
> They quest and probe throughout the east and west
>   to seek the One from whom they're manifest.[108]

Notes

1 *Man nakhvāham kard tark la'l-i yār u jām-i may / Zāhidān ma'dhūr dārīdam ki īnam madhhab-ast. Dīvān-i Ḥāfiẓ*, ed. Khānlarī, *ghazal* 30: 6. All renditions of the poetry in this essay, unless otherwise indicated, are by the translator.

2 Nafīsī (ed.), *Muḥīt-i zindigī va aḥwāl u ash'ār-i Rūdakī*, p. 503.

3 'Ayn al-Quḍāt Hamadhānī, *Tamhīdāt*, p. 22.

4 *Tamhīdāt*, pp. 114–15.

5 *Dīvān-i Ḥakīm Abū'l-Majd Majdūd b. Ādam Sanā'ī Ghaznavī*, ed. Mudarris Raḍavī, p. 913. *Az kīsh u ṭarīqatam chi pursī? 'Ishq-ast marā ṭarīqat u kīsh.*

6 Rūmī, *Kulliyāt-i Shams*, ed. Furūzānfar, IV, p. 225, *ghazal* 1992, v. 21067. I will revisit Rūmī's teachings on love later on.

7 From his *Khusraw u Shīrīn*, in Dastgirdī (ed.), *Kulliyāt-i Ḥakīm Niẓāmī Ganjavī*, p. 95 (12: 2–4).

8 *Khusraw u Shīrīn*, in *ibid.*, p. 96 (12: 23–5).

9 *Khusraw u Shīrīn*, in *ibid.*, p. 96 (12: 26–7).

10 See Qur'ān II: 33–4.

11 [For further discussion of *dard* in 'Aṭṭār, see Waley, 'Didactic Style and Self-Criticism in 'Aṭṭār', pp. 215–16. Ed./trans.]

12 *Manṭiq al-ṭayr*, ed. Gawharīn, p. 14, vv. 251–2. See also my introduction to my *Guzīda-yi Manṭiq al-ṭayr*.

13 The translation featured here is by Sells, *Stations of Desire: Love Elegies from Ibn 'Arabi*, pp. 72–3; for the original Arabic, see Ibn 'Arabī, *The Tarjumán al-Ashwáq*, ed. and trans. Nicholson, Ode XI, p. 19.

14 Translation by Homerin, *'Umar Ibn al-Fāriḍ: Sufi Verse, Saintly Life*, pp. 47, 51.

15 Rūmī, *Kulliyāt-i Shams*, ed. Furūzānfar, V, p. 58, *ghazal* 2207, v. 23405. *Dar khulāṣa-yi 'ishq ākhar shīva-yi Islām kū? Dar kushūf-i mushkilātash ṣāḥib-i i'lām kū?*

16 *Ibid.*, IV, pp. 150–1; 1869, vv. 19706–8, 197013–14. *Raw madhhab-i 'āshiq rā bar-'aks-i ravishhā dān, Kaz yār durūghīhā, az ṣidq bih u iḥsān. / Ḥāl-ast maḥāl-i ū, muzd-ast vabāl-i ū, 'Adl-ast hama-yi ẓulmash, dād-ast buhtān. / Narm-ast durūsht-i ū, Ka'ba-st kinisht-i ū, Khārī kay khalad dilbar, kwūshtar zih gul u rayḥān. / Gar ta'na zanī, gū'ī: 'Tu madhhab-i kazh dārī. Man madhhab-i abrūyash bikhrīdam va dādam jān. / Z'īn madhhab-i kazh mastam, bas kardam u lab bastam, Bar dār-i dil-i rawshan, bāqiyash furū mīkhwān.*

17 *Ibid.*, VIII, p. 221, Quatrain 1314. *Mā madhhab-i chishm-i shūkh-i mastash dārīm. Kīsh-i sar-i zulf-i but-parastash dārīm. / Gūyand: 'Juz īn har du buvad dīn-i durust.' Az 'dīn-i durust' mā shikastash dārīm.*

18 *Ibid.*, VIII, p. 38, Quatrain 225. *Mā 'āshiq-i 'ishqīm u musalmān digar-ast. Mā mūr-i ḍa'īfīm u Sulaymān digar-ast. / Az mā rukh-i zard u jigar-pārih ṭalab. Bāzārchih-i qaṣab-furūshān digar-ast.*

19 *Ibid.*, VIII, p. 130, Quatrain 767. *'Āshiq tu yaqīn dān kay Musalmān nabvad. Dar madhhab-i 'āshiq kufr u īmān nabvad. / Dar 'ishq, tan u 'aql u dil u jān nabvad. Har kas kay chinīn nagasht ū ān nabvad.*

20 *Mathnawī-yi ma'nawī*, ed. Nicholson, II: 1770.

21 *Dīvān-i Ḥāfiẓ*, ed. Khānlarī, *ghazal* 443: 1. Translation by Robert Bly and Leonard Lewisohn, *The Angels Knocking on the Tavern Door*, p. 53.

22 *Dīvān-i Ḥāfiẓ*, ed. Khānlarī, *ghazal* 426: 5. Trans. Bly and Lewisohn, *Angels*, p. 49.

23 [See also the essay by Leili Anvar in this volume. Ed./trans.]

24 *Dīvān-i Ḥāfiẓ*, ed. Khānlarī, *ghazal* 10: 8. *Rū-yi khūbat āyatī az luṭf bar mā kashf kard. Zān sabab juz luṭf u khūbī nīst dar tafsīr-i mā.*

25 *Ibid.*, *ghazal* 165: 4. *Mugh-bachchih-ī mīgudhasht, rahzan-i dīn u dil. Dar pay-i ān āshinā az hama bīgāna shud.*

26 As I have explained elsewhere: see my 'Of Scent and Sweetness: 'Aṭṭār and his Legacy in Rūmī, Shabistarī and Ḥāfiẓ', pp. 43–4.

27 *Dīvān-i Ḥāfiẓ*, ed. Khānlarī, *ghazal* 22: 1–4. Trans. Bly and Lewisohn, *Angels*, p. 78.

28 *Sharḥ-i 'irfānī ghazalhā-yi Ḥāfiẓ*, ed. Khurramshāhī *et al.*, I, p. 428.

29 *Ibid.*

30 *Imshab may-i Jām yik manī khᵛāham kard. Khᵛud rā bi-raṭl-i may ghanī khᵛāham kard. / Awwal si ṭalāq 'aql u dīn khᵛāham kard. Pas dukhtar-i raz rā bi-zanī khᵛāham kard.*

31 *Rubáiyát of Omar Khayyam*, trans. Fitzgerald, ed. Nicholson, Quatrain 40, p. 176.

32 *Dīvān-i Ḥāfiẓ*, ed. Khānlarī, *ghazal* 119: 7.

33 *Ibid.*, *ghazal* 193: 6.

34 *Ibid.*, *ghazal* 312: 1.

35 *Ibid.*, *ghazal* 213: 2; 426: 6 (*madhhab-i ṭarīqat*).

36 *Ibid.*, *ghazal* 133: 10.

37 *Ibid.*, *ghazal* 119: 7. Trans. Bly and Lewisohn, *Angels*, p. 48. *Sitam az ghamza miyāmūz ki dar madhhab-i 'ishq. Har 'amal ujrī va har karda jazā'ī dārad.*

38 *Dīvān-i Ḥāfiẓ*, ed. Khānlarī, *ghazal* 133: 10. *Bijuz abrū-yi tu miḥrāb-i dil-i Ḥāfiẓ nīst. Ṭā'at ghayr-i tu dar madhhab-i mā natavān kard.*

39 *Ibid.*, *ghazal* 48: 4. *Varā-yi ṭā'at-i dīvānagān zi mā maṭalab. Ki shaykh-i madhhab-i mā 'āqilī guna dānist.*

40 *Ibid.*, *ghazal* 193: 7. *Guftam sharāb u khirqa ni āyīn u madhhab-ast. Guft īn 'amal bi madhhab-i pīr-i mughān kunand.*

41 *Ibid.*, *ghazal* 312: 1. Trans. Bly and Lewisohn, *Angels*, p. 61. *Sālhā payravī madhhab-i rindān kardam, Tā bi-fatwā-yi khirad dīv bi-zindān kardam.*

42 *Dīvān-i Ḥāfiẓ*, ed. Khānlarī, *ghazal* 426: 6. *Dar madhhab-i ṭarīqat khāmī nishān-i kufr-ast. Ārī ṭarīq-i dawlat chālakī'st u chastī'st.*

43 [Cited by William Chittick, *The Vision of Islam*, p. 138. Ed./trans.]

44 [Other versions of this *ḥadīth* read: 'Every child is born a Muslim...' See Robinson, *The Sayings of Muḥammad*, p. 13. The wider theological ramifications of this *ḥadīth* are explored in D.B. Macdonald, 'Fiṭra', *EI*², II, pp. 931f. Ed./trans.]

45 *The Mathnawí of Jalálu'ddín Rúmí*, ed. Nicholson, I: 678–9. Translation by Alan Williams, *Rumi, Spiritual Verses: the First Book of the* Masnavi-ye Ma'navi, vv. 682–3, pp. 67–8.

46 *Mathnawī*, ed. Nicholson, IV: 409–14.

47 Shabistarī, *Gulshan-i rāz*, ed. Muwaḥḥid, vv. 418, 421, p. 84.

48 *Mathnawī*, VI: 4541.

49 *Dīvān-i Ḥāfiẓ*, ed. Khānlarī, *ghazal* 137: 4.

50 *Kulliyāt-i Sa'dī*, p. 203.

51 *Dīvān-i Ḥāfiẓ*, ed. Khānlarī, *ghazal* 174: 7 ['Wildman' has been used to render *qalandar* here. Ed./trans.]

52 [On which, see M.G.S. Hodgson, 'Ibāḥa (II)', *EI²*, III, pp. 662–3. Ed./trans.]

53 [There are six instances where Ḥāfiẓ praises the *qalandar* and *qalandarī*: see *Dīvān-i Ḥāfiẓ*, ed. Khānlarī, *ghazals* 79: 7; 366: 2; 389: 8; 479: 3; 174: 7; 442: 6. Ed./trans.]

54 *Lā-ubālī chi kunad daftar-i dānā'ī rā. Ṭāqat-i va'ẓ nabāshad sar-i sawdā'ī rā. / 'Ashiqān rā chi gham az sar-zanash-i dushman u dūst? Yā gham-i dūst khurad ya gham-i rusvā'ī rā.* In *Kulliyāt-i Sa'dī*, p. 417.

55 *Gar murīd-i rāh-i 'ishqī fikr-i badnāmī makan. Shaykh Ṣan'ān khirqa rahn-i khāna-yi khammar dāsht.* In *Dīvān-i Ḥāfiẓ*, ed. Khānlarī, *ghazal* 79: 6.

56 *Ibid.*, *ghazal* 79: 6–7. *Waqt-i ān shīrīn-qalandar khᵛush ki dar aṭvār-i sayr, Dhikr-i tasbīḥ-i malak dar khalqa-i zunnār dāsht.*

57 *Ibid.*, *ghazal* 10: 8.

58 [This idea is well expressed in Blake's anecdote: 'Cowper came to me and said: O that I were insane always. I will never rest. Can you not make me truly insane? I will never rest till I am so. O that in the bosom of God I was hid.' *Blake: Complete Writings*, p. 772. Ed./trans.]

59 This is the purport of Shakespeare's verses in sonnet 53: 'Describe Adonis, and the counterfeit / Is poorly imitated after you; / On Helen's cheek all art of beauty set / And you in Grecian tires are painted new / Speak of the spring, and the foison of the year: / The one doth shadow of your beauty show, / The other as your bounty doth appear, / And you in every blessed shape we know.'

60 Rūmī, *Kulliyāt-i Shams*, ed. Furūzānfar, vol. 4, p. 302, *ghazal* 1620, v. 16957. *Havasī-ast dar sar-i man ki sar-i bashar nadāram. Man az īn havas chunānam ki zi khʷud khabar nadāram.*

61 *Dīvān-i ... Sanā'ī*, ed. Raḍavī, p. 546. *Bā nafasash siḥr-namāyān-i Hind. Dar havasash chihra-gushāyān-i Chīn.*

62 *Dīvān-i Ḥāfiẓ*, ed. Khānlarī, *ghazal* 261: 6. *'Ishq-bāzī kār-i bāzī nīst ay dil sar bibāz / var na gūyi 'ishq natvan zad bi-chūgān-i havas.*

63 *Ibid.*, *ghazal* 57: 8. *Ni īn zamān dil-i Ḥāfiẓ dar ātash-i havas ast / ki dāghdār-i azal hamchū lālih-i khvud-ru'ast.*

64 Rūmī, *Kulliyāt-i Shams*, ed. Furūzānfar, vol. 6, pp. 15–16, *ghazal* 2637, vv. 27975–8. *Imrūz samā'ast u sharāb-ast u ṣurāḥī; yik Sāqī-yi bad-mast, yikī jam'-i mubāḥī. / Zān jins-i mubāḥī kay az ān sū-yi wujūd-ast; nay ibāḥatī-yi gīj, hashīsh muzhājī. / [Rūḥī'st mubāḥī kay az ān rūḥ chishīda-ast. / Kū rūḥ-i qadīmī u kujā rūḥ-i riyāḥī. / Dar pīsh-i chinīn fitna va dar dast-i chinīn may: Yā Rabb! chih shavad jān-i musalmān-i ṣalāḥī.]*

65 See the same *ghazal* 2637, v. 27986.

66 *Dīvān-i Ḥāfiẓ*, ed. Khānlarī, *ghazal* 278: 6. *Dilā dilālat-i khayrat kunam bi rāh-i najāt. Makan bi fisq mubāḥāt u zuhd ham mafarūsh.*

67 Rūmī, *Kulliyāt-i Shams*, ed. Furūzānfar, vol. 4, p. 36, *ghazal* 1685, v. 17660. *Dar jurm-i tawba kardan, būdīm tā bi gardan / Az tawbahā-yi karda, īn bār tawba kardam.*

68 *Mathnawī*, ed. Nicholson, VI: 897–902; VI: 969–70.

69 Rūmī, *Kulliyāt-i Shams*, ed. Furūzānfar, vol. 4, p. 66, *ghazal* 1735, v. 18199. *Zihī gunāh ki kufr-ast tawba kardan az ū / Ni pas, ṭarīq-i gurīz va ni pīsh jā-yi maqām.*

70 *Kulliyāt-i Sa'dī*, p. 546.

71 *Dīvān-i Ḥāfiẓ*, ed. Khānlarī, *ghazal* 20: 2. Trans. Bly and Lewisohn, *Angels*, p. 59.

72 See my 'Of Scent and Sweetness', pp. 49–51.

73 The original Persian reads *khūn-i jigar*, literally meaning 'the liver's blood', but by extension signifies bitterly wept tears that are 'bloody tears torn from the heart', or 'tears of blood drawn out of the gut'.

74 *Manṭiq al-ṭayr*, ed. Gawharīn, vv. 1269–70; 1277–80; translation by Davis and Darbandi, *The Conference of the Birds*, pp. 61–2.

75 See 'Attar, *The Conference of the Birds*, translation by Davis and Darbandi, 'The Story of Shaykh Sam'an', pp. 57–75.

76 [On which, see: Javad Nurbakhsh, *Sufi Symbolism*, I, see 'Part 2: Sufi Symbolism of Wine, Music, Mystical Audition (*Samāʿ*) and Convivial Gatherings', pp. 125–214. Ed./trans.]

77 [For a thorough discussion of this theme in Ḥāfiẓ's poetry, see Leili Anvar-Chenderoff's essay in this volume. Ed./trans.]

78 [On the mystical theology of 'true idolatry', see Lewisohn, *Beyond Faith and Infidelity*, chap. 8. Ed./trans.]

79 *Mā dar piyāla ʿaks-i rukh-i yār dīda-īm. Ay bīkhabar zi ladhat-i shurb-i mudām-i mā.* In *Dīvān-i Ḥāfiẓ*, ed. Khānlarī, *ghazal* 11: 2.

80 *Qur'ān* VII: 172. [For further discussion of the role played by this key Qur'ānic motif in Ḥāfiẓ's poems, see Leili Anvar's essay in this volume. Ed./trans.]

81 *Dīvān-i Ḥāfiẓ*, ed. Khānlarī, *ghazal* 273: 1 [Reading *talkh* for *mast*. Ed./trans.]

82 *Kulliyāt-i Saʿdī*, p. 509. [This is similar to Alexander Pope's thesis at the conclusion of his Essay on Man (IV: 315–20) that 'Virtue alone is Happiness here below', describing Virtue as: 'The joy unequal'd, if its end it gain, / And if it lose, attended with no pain: / Without satiety, tho' ever so blest, / And but more relish'd as the most distressed. / The broadest mirth unfeeling Folly wears, / Less pleasing far than Virtue's very tears'. Ed./trans.]

83 *Dīvān-i Ḥāfiẓ*, ed. Khānlarī, *ghazal* 426: 9. Trans. Bly and Lewisohn, *Angels*, p. 48.

84 *Dīvān-i Ḥāfiẓ*, ed. Khānlarī, *ghazal* 21: 1.

85 *Ibid.*, *ghazal* 22: 5.

86 *Ibid.*, *ghazal* 144: 5.

87 From his *Sharaf-nāma*, in Dastgirdī (ed.), *Kulliyāt-i Ḥakīm Niẓāmī Ganjavī*, pp. 602 (7: 1–2); 615 (11: 1–2).

88 Trans. Homerin, *'Umar Ibn al-Fāriḍ: Sufi Verse*, p. 50.<AQ26>

89 *Mathnawī*, ed. Nicholson, I: 133.

90 *Ibid.*, III: 1433.

91 *Kitāb-i Fihi mā fihi*, ed. Furūzānfar, p. 105; trans. Arberry, *The Discourses of Rumi*, p. 116.

92 *Dīvān-i Khwāja Ḥāfiẓ-i Shīrāzī*, ed. Anjawī-Shīrāzī, p. 205. *Man ki imrūzam bihisht-i naqd ḥāṣil mishavad, Vaʿda-yi fardā-yi zāhid ra chirā bavar kunam?*

93 *Kulliyāt-i Saʿdī*, p. 443. *Bakht-i javān dārad ānki bā tu qarīn ast / Pīr nagardad ki dar bihisht-i barīn ast.*

94 *Mathnawī*, ed. Nicholson, IV: 3262.

95 Qur'ān, XXI: 68–9; XXIX: 24. [See Khurramshāhī (ed.), *Dānishnāma-yi Qur'ān*, s.v. 'Nimrūd', II, pp. 2273–4. Ed./trans.]

96 [See Humā'ī, *Funūn-i balāghat*, pp. 328–31; Browne, *Literary History of Persia*, II, pp. 77–80. Ed./trans.]

97 *Dīvān-i Ḥāfiẓ*, ed. Khānlarī, *ghazal* 27: 2.

98 *Kulliyāt-i Saʿdī*, p. 551.

99 *Ibid.*, p. 568.

100 [See Moayyad, 'Farhād', *EIr*, IX, pp. 257–8. Ed./trans.]

101 Chigil is a city near the Kazakhstan border, not far from Kashgar in Xinjiang, renowned for its beautiful women.

102 *Dīvān-i Ḥāfiẓ*, ed. Khānlarī, *ghazal* 461: 5.

103 [See Khaleghi-Motlagh, 'Bīžān', *EIr*, IV, pp. 309–10. Ed./trans.]

104 [See Yarshater, ''Afrāsīāb', *EIr*, I, pp. 570–6. Ed./trans.]

105 *Dīvān-i Ḥāfiẓ*, ed. Khānlarī, *ghazal* 182: 4.

106 *Ibid.*, *ghazal* 59: 6.

107 *Ibid.*, *ghazal* 19: 7. [This is a reference to Qur'ān, XXVI: 119–20: 'And we saved him [Noah] and those with him in the laden ship. Then afterwards drowned the others.' Ed./trans.]

108 From his *Khusraw va Shīrīn*, in Dastgirdī (ed.), *Kulliyāt-i Ḥakīm Niẓāmī Ganjavī*, p. 81.

The Erotic Spirit: Love, Man and Satan in Ḥāfiẓ's Poetry

Ali Asghar Seyed-Gohrab

Yikīst turkī-u tāzī dar īn mu'āmala Ḥāfiẓ
Ḥadith-i 'ishq bayān kun bi-dān zabān ki tu dānī [1]

Ḥāfiẓ! Turkish and Arabic are the same in this business.
Describe the story of love in the language that you know.

Introduction

The characteristic strength of the poetry of Ḥāfiẓ (d. 791/1389) lies in his virtuoso use of a rich complex of themes and motifs in a single poem and even in a single couplet. The way he combines themes and motifs deriving from wine, love and nature poetry, from the ascetic, mystic and antinomian traditions, mesmerizes any Persian reader. Through this integration of themes, motifs and metaphors, Ḥāfiẓ allows a range of interpretations suiting the needs of each reader. He is the master of combining 'different modes of discourse' in a short poetic unit.[2] Although the couplets are written as part of a longer composition, they take on a life of their own, as independent units, in the reception history.

One of Ḥāfiẓ's primary themes is love. Although there is usually a profane and sometimes a purely romantic–erotic layer of interpretation in his poems on love, the theme of mystic love, which he knits to ascetic (*zuhdiyyāt*), bacchic (*khamriyyāt*) and antinomian (*qalandariyyāt*) themes, makes this poetry prismatic or polyfunctional. A reader unfamiliar with mystical lore will miss some of the dimensions of love being described, or find the work unclear. This chapter presents a close reading and commentary to show how a knowledge of this background can enrich our experience of reading Ḥāfiẓ's poetry. It will indicate how a theory of love can be reconstructed from the *Dīvān*, and show how heavily Ḥāfiẓ relied on the creation myth as it had been developed by the Persian Sufi mystics over the preceding centuries.[3]

The Islamic and Persian Background

Love has been treated by various authors and poets in the Islamic world, who give definitions, describe love's workings and impact, and discuss its purpose in human life. Most of the definitions one encounters in Persian poetry treat love as an ethico-mystical concept, an elusive but omnipresent force that ennobles man's character and unites man with his Creator. The 'love' described by the Sufi mystics, as R.A. Nicholson observed, 'is the emotional element in religion, the rapture of the seer, the courage of the martyr, the faith of the saint, the only basis of moral perfection and spiritual knowledge. Practically, it is self-renunciation and self-sacrifice, the giving up of all possessions – wealth, honour, will, life, and whatever else men value – for the Beloved's sake without any thought of reward.'[4]

Ḥāfiẓ, an eclectic poet, uses a wide range of the ideas on love propounded by mystics, physicians and philosophers over the previous centuries. Ḥāfiẓ's use of the term love corresponds entirely with his predecessors such as Sanā'ī (d. 525/1131), 'Aṭṭār (d. 618/1221) and Niẓāmī (d. 606/1209), who were all influenced by Aḥmad Ghazālī's (d. 520/1126) seminal treatise *Sawāniḥ*. While Sanā'ī produces a theory of love in his *Ḥadīqa*, and Niẓāmī shows the workings and impact of this force on human beings in his romances, Ḥāfiẓ, in his love lyrics, alludes primarily to the creation myth as it was used by the Persian Sufi mystics.

Islamic mystics recount their own version of the creation myth based on Love. In this story, God is portrayed as both Love and the Absolute Beloved, who has created the universe out of love. God's motivation to create mankind was His ardent desire to be loved by God's lover: mankind. Before man was created, the universe was in an absolute state of Oneness. Poets emphasize the solitude of absolute Oneness, saying that there was no name of existence in the world of Non-existence before God wished to reveal himself.[5] Despite the simplicity of the Muslim mystical theogony, poets often describe this Absolute Oneness at length.[6]

Mystics believe that the references to love in the Qur'ān indicate the special loving relationship between man and his creator, in which God functions as the Lover. Love occurs in several places of the Qur'ān. Words such as *ḥubb* and *wudd*, and derivations from these roots such as *maḥabba* and *mawadda*, are commonly used to refer to human and spiritual love. The Qur'ān refers to God by the appellation 'loving' (*Wadūd*, 11:90; 85:14). Addressing Moses in 20:39, God states: 'I lavish My love on you.' In verse 3:29, man is promised: 'God will love you and forgive you your sins.' In the verse 2:160, it is stated: '...the love of God is stronger in the faithful.' A favourite verse, to which I will shortly return, is 5:59, which underscores the reciprocal love between man and God: 'He loves them and they love Him.'

Although Ḥāfiẓ knew the Qur'ān by heart and often used the Qur'ānic vocabulary of love in his *Dīvān*, the term he usually uses for love is *'ishq* or 'passionate love', a non-Qur'ānic term depicting man's relationship with the divine in erotic terms. Ḥāfiẓ apparently follows a tradition of love founded by the twelfth-century Persian mystics such as Aḥmad Ghazālī.

It is unclear which mystic first used the term *'ishq* systematically to refer to the passionate love relationship between man and God.[7] Before the twelfth century, mystics commonly used *maḥabbat*, but from the twelfth century onwards this term was replaced by *'ishq*, or the two were used in parallel, as synonyms. Before the second half of the eleventh century, mystics generally avoided the term *'ishq* when referring to the love between man and God[8] because of the term's erotic import. Even in the twelfth century, during the time of Aḥmad Ghazālī, the term carried an erotic connotation, and mystics who used the term to explain the love relationship between man and God were criticized by theologians. To defend themselves, several twelfth-century Persian mystics pointed to traditions using the non-Qur'ānic term *'ishq*. In many treatises, even when the author talks about profane love, spiritual love is implicit and a metaphysical interpretation is usually possible. Earthly love is regarded as a preparation for spiritual love. For example, although at the beginning of the *Sawāniḥ*, the author promises the reader to speak about a love which does not belong to any direction, neither to the Creator nor to the creatures. However, he proves unable to keep his promise and, from the opening chapter, depicts spiritual love:[9]

> Distinction is incidental in the directions that love turns its face. The essence of love is free from dimensions; it must indeed have its face at no direction in order to be love. And yet, when the hand clutches the timeless moment-of-inspiration, I do not know unto which land the water will be conveyed. When a groom mounts the Sultan's steed, it is not his horse, yet it does no harm.[10]

Mystics such as Aḥmad-i Jām Nāmiqī (d. 536/1141) used several traditions in favour of *'ishq*, quoting, 'My servant does not stop approaching me till he becomes my lover and I his lover.'[11] Ibn 'Abbādī (d. 549/1154) devotes a whole chapter to *'ishq* in his *Ṣūfī-nāma*,[12] distinguishing several stages of love. In his opinion, there are five stages which bring man to the highest level of love (*'ishq*): 'When some trouble appears in the heart for an absentee, this is called longing [*shawq*]; when an understanding with someone is established, it is called love [*mawaddat*]; when the person chooses someone as a friend, it is called friendship [*khullat*]; when the friendship becomes free from any calamity, and honesty is employed to attain the friend's contentment, it is called love [*maḥabbat*]; when the person is melted in the melting-pot of *maḥabbat* and he turns his face towards annihilation, it is called passionate love [*'ishq*].'[13] Ibn 'Abbādī emphasizes that *'ishq* is the loftiest stage of passionate love in which ethical and mystical perfection can be accomplished. He underlines that not everyone is able to reach this elevated stage, and the mystic should follow a particular itinerary: 'Longing is for the novice; friendship is for he who is in the middle; love [*maḥabba*] is for he who has reached the end. And if someone reaches the perfection of passionate love [*'ishq*] he sees that the reality of love cannot be expressed by words.'[14]

Another important aspect of love is the relationship between the lover and the beloved. To explain this relationship, mystics usually rely on the verse (5:59): 'He loves them and they love Him.' Aḥmad Ghazālī has placed this verse at the very beginning of his treatise *Sawāniḥ* to draw the reader's attention to its significance. The entire treatise can be regarded as a commentary on this pregnant verse, describing the relationship between man and God as a loving union, and at the same time underscoring that God was first the lover and man the beloved.[15] The Qur'ān also informs us that God created man in His own image, in the fairest of forms (95:5). In commentaries on this verse, mankind is depicted as a limpid mirror displaying God's 'names and attributes' (*asmā wa ṣifāt*). Mystics cite the following tradition in which God states: 'The reason of My creating you is to see My vision in the mirror of your spirit, and My love in your heart.'[16] In short, God created the phenomenal world from Nothingness (*nīstī*) for the sake of man.[17]

Unlike other theoretical works on love, Ghazālī does not omit a mention of the primordial origin of love. In his view, love was created first, and then the Spirit (*rūḥ*). Although Ghazālī does not mention how God created love, it is clear from his treatise that love is identical with God and is eternal. Love exists first in an unadulterated form which flows to existence from God. Lingering on the border of existence, love waits for the human Spirit so that it can come down to the world. In Ghazālī's metaphor, the Spirit is depicted as the steed of love, which transports love to the earth. Here on earth, love assumes many faces – sometimes it is a sensual love, sometimes love between parent and child, and so on – but ultimately love seeks to return back to its place of origin. In its return journey, love is the steed and spirit is the rider, bringing love to its original abode.

Love's journey throughout the phenomenal world is often described by Persian mystics as an arc of descent. Love's primordial home in the world is the heart where man is enabled to develop his potential to realize perfection, so that his spirit can return to its original abode.

Man's relationship with God starts in pre-eternity (*azal*), when God, the essential source of love, created Adam and breathed into him the spirit from His own breath. Afterwards, He spoke to the loins of Adam on the day of *alast*, or 'Am I not your Lord?' Adam's progeny answer: 'Yes, we witness you are' (7:171).[18] Mystic poets interpret this verse as the 'Covenant' (*mīthāq*) between man and God, and the relationship between man and his creator is depicted in the most erotic images and metaphors.

Ḥāfiẓ: Love and Creation

Ḥāfiẓ's poetry is steeped in the theosophy of this school of Love and features almost all its mystical references. He refers several times to love and the creation of man and the world. Most of these references derive from the mystical interpretations of the creation myth. Time and again, Ḥāfiẓ emphasizes that the existence of love predates the creation of mankind and the world. Like the Persian Sufi mystics and poets before him, Ḥāfiẓ equates love with God, who is also the Absolute Beloved longing fervently to reveal His beauty. In His absolute solitude, God was self-sufficient and rich in every imaginable respect and did not need any lover or beloved. Theorists of love elaborate on this infinite richness when they discuss the term *istighnā* – divine independence, wealth or self-sufficiency – affirming that God as Beloved was not in need of man or the creation. Several times in his poetry, Ḥāfiẓ refers to the concept of *istighnā*, which belongs to the higher spiritual realm of love and the Beloved. In this famous couplet, Ḥāfiẓ refers to the shortcomings of man's love in respect to the Beloved's beauty:

> *Zi 'ishq-i nā-tamām-i mā jamāl-i yār mustaghnī-st*
> *ba āb-u rang-u khāl-u khaṭṭ cha ḥājat rū-yi zībā rā.*[19]
>
> The beauty of the beloved is rich in itself, it has no need of our incomplete love. What should a beautiful face do with lustre, hue, mole and down on the cheek?

What Ḥāfiẓ is stating here is that the Beloved never needed man, whom He created 'in the most beautiful of forms'[20] to love him. His love was a grace bestowed on mankind and was not merely for the physical beauty, which the Beloved Himself possessed. The term *istighnā* is also used to underscore the incomparable richness and self-sufficiency of love:

> *Giryi-yi Ḥāfiz cha sanjad pīsh-i istighnā-yi 'ishq*
> *k-andarīn ṭūfān namāyad haft daryā shabnamī.* [21]
>
> Of what weight are Ḥāfiẓ's tears before the wealth of love
> For in this storm, all seven seas appear to be a drop of dew.

Man's dependence on the Beloved is usually contrasted to the Beloved's longing for mankind:

> *Sāyih-i ma'shūq agar uftād bar 'āshiq chih shud?*
> *Mā bih ū muḥtāj būdīm ū bih mā mushtāq būd.*[22]
>
> Should the shadow of the Loved One fall upon the lovers, why is that?
> We were in need of Him, and He yearned for us.

This passionate longing of the Beloved for mankind is commonly regarded as the reason for God creating the world. One of the most important traditions concerning creation says: 'I [God] was a Hidden Treasure and I desired to be known, so I created the creation in order that I might be known.'[23] God created the world, leaving His infinitely rich solitude, so that man might know His essence and attributes.[24]

Based on this tradition, the world became viewed as an epiphany and revelation of love. Love functions as a *primum mobile*, setting everything in motion and binding everything together. Ḥāfiẓ refers to this epiphany of love, which is depicted as a ray of God's beauty, in the following famous couplet:

Dar azal partaw-yi ḥusnat zi tajallī dam zad
'Ishq paydā shud u ātash bih hama 'ālam zad.[25]

In the beginning, a ray of your Beauty shone out, sparked fire:
Love was seen, and the whole world burned.

Here, Ḥāfiẓ is referring to the beauty of the Beloved and how this beauty generates love. Mystics believe that the Beloved is the source of beauty and loves beauty. In chapter 51 of his *Sawāniḥ*, Aḥmad Ghazālī cites the famous tradition 'God is beautiful and loves beauty', emphasizing that everyone should either be in love with beauty, or with the lover of beauty. Ghazālī links this tradition to the doctrine of *shāhid-bāzī*, 'love-play through the contemplation' of mortal beauties, by which mystics try to attain direct communion with the Beloved, and to experience the primordial encounter with God. Ḥāfiẓ is dramatically expressing how the whole world is connected to the divine beauty. This idea of God's manifestation as an essentially beautiful being is repeated elsewhere in the *Dīvān*, for example:

'Ālam az shūr-u shar-i 'ishq khabar hīch nadāsht
fitna-angīz-i jahān ghamza-yi jādū-yi tu būd.[26]

The world knew naught of love's tumult and commotion:
The chaos-causer of the world was the witchery of a wink from you.

The allusion here is again to the dawn of creation, when there was no knowledge of anything, and the Beloved's flirtatious behaviour initiates disorder or rebellion, through which the world becomes aware of love. The Creator thus appears as the supreme Enchanter, captivating everything He creates through His matchless beauty.

Descent and Ascent

After revealing love, God creates Adam and his progeny, and strengthens his bond with human beings by a pact. This pact is usually known as the *'ahd-i alast*, or 'the pact of "Am I not your Lord [*alastu be-rabbikum*]?"' – alluding to the verse: 'And when thy Lord took from the Children of Adam, from their loins, their seed, and made them testify against themselves [saying], "Am I not your Lord?" They said,

"Yes, we testify"' (7:172). Mystics interpret their affirmative answer to God by saying that they were so captivated by the beauty of God that they involuntarily said *balā*, or 'Yes. We witness thou art.' Ḥāfiẓ too interprets this Qur'ān verse in this same mystical sense. Like Farīd al-Dīn 'Aṭṭār, who interprets man's answer as being a trial in which he is subjected to affliction (*balā'*), Ḥāfiẓ believes that the attainment of the highest stage of love is only possible by exertion and by accepting the affliction inflicted upon the lover by separation:

Maqām-i 'aysh muyasar nimīshavad bī-ranj
balī ba ḥukm-i balā' basta-and 'aḥd-i alast.[27]

The station of delight cannot be attained without exertion
The covenant of 'Am I not' linked 'yes' to trials' decree.

In their new translation of Ḥāfiẓ, Robert Bly and Leonard Lewisohn choose the following translation to illustrate this relationship between the covenant of Pre-eternity and man's affliction:

The waiting station of pleasure and delight
Always includes suffering. In Pre-eternity
The souls bound themselves to that tragedy.[28]

Commenting on the same Qur'ān verse (7:172), Annemarie Schimmel explains: 'the theme of Affliction, *balā'* is ingeniously combined with the word *balā*, "Yes", that the souls spoke at the Day of the Covenant, thus accepting in advance every tribulation that might be showered upon them until Doomsday.'[29] For this reason, the Persian Sufi mystics considered affliction to be the essence of love. In his theoretical treatise, Aḥmad Ghazālī defines love as affliction, insofar as the suffering that the separated lover experiences from love, results only in pain and anguish.[30] But this suffering is a purgative, purifying the lover from all attachments so that only love can exist. Accepting suffering and deprivation is another way of describing the mystical stages of *fanā* (annihilation) and *baqā* (indwelling with the Beloved), during which the mystic lover divests himself of everything that impedes his union with the Beloved. In Niẓāmī's romance *Laylī and Majnūn*, Majnūn suffers so much hardship voluntarily that he becomes, at a certain stage, identified with love and suffering. The description of his physical and moral traits converges with the definition of love. Ascetics use stringent discipline to divest themselves of all worldly interests by keeping vigil, eating little and avoiding involvement in the world: lovers do the same things as a result of love, and the mystic lover welcomes all hardship in order to attain to the Loved One.[31]

The separated lover can climb the ladder of love through exertion and voluntary suffering, the suffering having been accepted on his behalf with the 'Yes' uttered at the pact of *alast*. Ḥāfiẓ expands on this idea in the following verse:

'Ahd-i alast-i man hama bā 'ishq -i shāh būd
v-az shāhrāh-i 'umr bi-dīn 'aḥd bugzaram.[32]

My covenant of 'Am I not' was [a pact] with the love of the King,
This covenant is my pass on the King's highway of life.

The world of fate is seen as *shāh-rāh*, a 'highway', which the lover has to journey, keeping in mind the primordial pact. Only then will man be able to attain union with the King (*Shāh*) at the end of this arduous journey.

Part of the difficulty of this journey is that man must bear the 'burden of trust' (*bār-i amānat*). Perhaps the most famous line in this respect – in which Ḥāfiẓ summarizes the Qur'ān, *Surah* 33:72 that relates how this burden 'was offered to the heavens, to the earth, and to the mountains, but they refused the burden and were afraid to receive it, but man undertook to bear it' – is the following:

Āsimān bār-i amānat natavānist kishid
qur'a-yi kār ba nām-i man-i divāna zadand.[33]

The heavens could not bear the Trust's burden
When they cast the lot, it fell to me, the madman.

This trust has been interpreted variously as responsibility, or free will, but Sufi mystics commonly agree that the Trust refers to God's Love entrusted to mankind in eternity. In the opening *ghazal* of the *Dīvān*, in which a lover asks a cup-bearer to fill his cup to lessen the pain of love, Ḥāfiẓ again refers to this same divine burden (*bār*):

Shab-i tārīk u bīm-i mawj u girdābī chinīn hāyil
kujā dānand ḥāl-i mā sabukbārān-i sāḥilhā? [34]

A dark night, the fear of the waves and such a dreadful whirlpool:
What can the lightly burdened ones on the shore know of our situation?

Here, Ḥāfiẓ is emphasizing hardship on the path of love. To foreground the lover's agonizing state, the poet subtly uses asymmetry: in the first hemistich, the lover is complaining of his gloomy state as if he is trapped in a dark night, fearing the high dashing waves and the horrible whirlpools. The phrase *sabukbārān-i sāḥilhā* ('the lightly burdened of the shore') refers to angels who are lightly burdened because, unlike mankind, they have never been graced with Love or the burden of Trust. The phrase might also refer to those people who have renounced all worldly possessions and interests, and are, therefore, light of burden, but this is less likely since such people would have been through the seas and would have experienced the tribulations of the 'dark night'. Note that the long vowel *ī* in the first half verse is contrasted to the long vowel *ā* in the next hemistich, forming a perfect asymmetry, with the vowel *ī* being entirely avoided in the second hemistich.

Ḥāfiẓ coins variants on the theme of the burden of divine Trust when he uses 'the burden of love' (*bār-i 'ishq*). In the couplet below, we read:

Shāhidān dar jilva u man sharmsār-i kīsiham
Bār-i 'ishq u muflisī sa'b ast u mībāyad kishīd.[35]

The beauties are dressed to be seen, while I am embarrassed for my purse;
The burden of love and poverty weighs hard, but it must be borne.

In addition to this reference to the burden, Ḥāfiẓ also contrasts the position of man and angels. The word *shāhidān* means not only things that are gazed upon, such as beautiful youths, but also 'witnesses'.[36] In the latter sense, the term 'witnesses' alludes to the angels whom God invited to come to view the spectacle of the dawn of creation, so as to admire the creation of mankind. Angels are pure spiritual beings, whereas man is made of water and clay. Man was ashamed of himself when compared to the splendour of the angels, but despite his shortcomings he accepted to bear the burden of love.

Iblīs and the Angels

In the creation myth recounted by the Sufi mystics, the angels play an important role. Ḥāfiẓ refers several times to the angels' inability to understand love and the relationship between man and God. God invites the angels to the spectacle of creation to admire mankind, but when they hear that God is planning to appoint man as a vicegerent on earth (2:30), the angels wonder whether man is going to misuse his power and cause damage. Iblīs, or Satan, started an argument with God, disobeying His command to prostrate himself before mankind.[37] Although ultimately Iblīs was the only angel who disobeyed God's command, Ḥāfiẓ states that angels generally do not know love:

Firishta 'ishq nadānad ki chīst ay sāqī!
Bikhāh jām u gulābī ba khāk-i Ādam rīz.[38]

O cup-bearer, angels do not know what love is.
Ask for a beaker and pour rosewater on Adam's clay.

In another couplet, Ḥāfiẓ sings:

Jilva-ī kard rukhat dīd malak 'ishq nadāsht
'ayn-i ātash shud a-zīn ghayrat-u bar ādam zad.[39]

When Your countenance was revealed, it saw that angels had no love,
Its honour offended, it became all fire, and struck Adam's soul.

In addition to the fact that angels do not know love, Ḥāfiẓ is here referring to the concept of jealousy and offended honour (*ghayrat*): the lover desires to cut all connections with any other entity and reality than love. In his theoretical treatises on love, Aḥmad Ghazālī explains that at times jealousy in love goes so far as to effect the severance of ties between lover and Beloved, compelling the lover to focus his attention on love alone as his sole focus of worship.[40]

In other references, Ḥāfiẓ uses bacchanalian imagery to describe the loving relationship between man and his Creator at the moment of creation. The locality in which man is created is compared to a tavern, God's spirit breathed into man's body (15:29) is described as wine, and man's body made of water and clay symbolized by the beaker. In several couplets, angels are shown outside this tavern, denied access to this private moment of creation, but in this example *they* join in the creation:

Dūsh dīdam ki malā'ik dar-i maykhāna zadand
Gil-i Ādam bisirishtand u bih paymāna zadand.[41]

Last night, I saw that angels were knocking on the door of the wine-house
Kneading the clay of man and drinking wine.

According to Ḥafiẓ's commentator Bahā al-Dīn Khurramshāhī, this particular couplet, together with the next two lines of this *ghazal*, summarizes chapter 4 of the *Mirṣād al-'ibād* by Najm al-Dīn Rāzī (d. 654/1256), in which he depicts the workshop of creation as a tavern where the angels have brought the clay of Adam to the divine Vintner who will knead it into the shape of man, which God then 'perfected into a beautiful form' (Qur'ān 40:64).[42] In this chapter, Rāzī recounts how God orders Gabriel to bring dust from Earth to make the form of man. Rāzī refers to the fact that since man should be able to carry the Trust (*amāna*), he should have the power over both the worlds, insofar as his soul is from the spiritual world, 'the supreme height' (*'alā 'illī'īn*) and his body from the earth, the lowest of the low (*asfal al-sāfilīn*). God gives the angels, who precede man in the order of being and who have entered the tavern/workshop of being, the task of pouring his clay into the mould of the 'human form divine'.

Ḥāfiẓ refers several times to God kneading man's clay before He actually created him (38:72–5). According to mystics, God kneaded man's clay for 40 continuous days, adding love regularly into the compound so that love became an ineradicable part of man's nature. In the *Dīvān*, we find several references to this event. In the next couplet, addressing angels, Ḥāfiẓ emphasizes that God mixed man's clay with wine in the wine-house of love:

Bar dar-i maykhāna-yi 'ishq ay malak tasbīḥ-gūy
k-andar ānjā ṭīnat-i ādam mukhammar mīkunand.[43]

O angel, give praise at the door of love's wine-house
For inside, they are leavening the clay of mankind.

Using the imperative 'praise' in addressing the angels, Ḥāfiẓ highlights the special loving relationship between man and his Creator. Man's nature is prepared in the wine-house of love to which angels have no access; they should stay outside the door, simply praising God. Several concepts in this couplet are ambiguous. Love (*'ishq*) may be a synonym for God, and the wine-house would then be God's home. The word *ṭīnat* means literally 'a bit of clay', but it also means 'nature' or 'natural disposition', and *mukhammar*, literally meaning 'leavened' or 'fermented', is derived from the root *khamr* (wine). What Ḥāfiẓ is saying here is that man was created in a secluded place by God's very hand.

We have already seen how Iblīs refused to prostrate himself before Adam. As a lover of God, who had devotedly worshipped Him, Iblīs became jealous when he witnessed the loving relationship between God and mankind. The story of his disobedience as told by the mystics is complicated by the element that, when the angels bowed before Adam, they saw the image of God in him, thus avoiding the idolatry which Iblīs had said would occur. In one of his couplets, Ḥāfiẓ states:

Malak dar sujda-yi Ādam zamīn-būs-i tu niyyat kard
ki dar ḥusn-i tu chīzī yāft bīsh az ṭawr-i insānī.[44]

When the angels bowed before Adam, their intention was to kiss the ground before you,
because they saw in your beauty something transcending the human.

One of the reasons God allotted a special position to man was that He Himself instructed the Father of humankind, Adam, in the names and attributes (*asmā' va ṣifāt*). All the angels thus accepted man's special position and prostrated themselves before him. But Iblīs, who was an archangel (*malak al-muqarrab*), reproached God and proudly considered himself better than man. It would be beyond the scope of this short chapter to explain how, in Persian literature, this proud rebel became viewed as a model of the mystic lover by some, and considered an 'impostor' or 'pretender' (*mudda'ī*) by others.[45] Like the Sufi mystics, Ḥāfiẓ sees Iblīs as man's rival and characterizes him with such terms as 'quarrel-seeker' (*nizā'-jū*), 'egotist' or 'self-worshipper' (*khʷud-parast*), and 'non-adept' or 'non-initiate' (*nā-mahram*). Whether because he considered God as the only legitimate Beloved and focus of worship, or because he was jealous of man as a potential 'rival' (*raqīb*), Iblīs quarrelled with God and as a consequence was cursed with eternal separation from Him.[46] This is why poets such as Ḥāfiẓ depict Iblīs as an 'egotist' or 'self-worshipper' (*khʷud-parast*);

that is, one unable to understand subtle points of love. Iblīs' strict monotheism, his boasting of being the only true worshipper of God, led Ḥāfiẓ to consider him as a pretender or impostor:

> *Mudda'ī khʷāst ki āyad ba tamāshāgah-i rāz*
> *dast-i ghayb āmad-u bar sina-i nāmaḥram zad.*[47]
>
> The pretender wanted to come to see the secret spectacle:
> an invisible hand appeared and struck the chest of the outsider.[48]

In the next couplet, the poet underlines again the lofty position of mankind, contrasting it to the loveless nature of angels, personified by Iblīs. The poet advises man not to reveal the secret of love to the pretender, but to leave him to die of the pain of self-worship:

> *Bā mudda'ī magū'īd asrār-i 'ishq u mastī*
> *tā bīkhabar bimīrad dar dard-i khʷud-parastī.*[49]
>
> Do not tell the pretender the secrets of love and drunkenness,
> that he may die not knowing, in the torture of self-worship.

The 'secrets of love and drunkenness' refer to the exclusive loving experience of God and mankind, which is commonly described in Persian poetry through wine imagery. What is interesting here is that Iblīs is depicted as a worshipper of himself, whereas man is regarded as the one who is God's Beloved and bears the secret of love and of drunkenness. It is worth mentioning here that Ḥāfiẓ often uses wine imagery to illustrate this loving encounter between man and God. In such scenes, which have become clichés in Persian love poetry, God is the cup-bearer, His breath is wine, while man's body is the wine cup.[50]

Another aspect of the uneasy relationship between man and Iblīs is the latter's complaint about his treatment at the dawn of creation. Iblīs' complaint is one of the topoi of Persian mystical literature and many anecdotes recount how Iblīs mourns his condition. Drawing on this rich literature, Ḥāfiẓ refers in the following couplet to Iblīs' complaint:

> *Man malak būdam u firdaws-i barīn jāyam būd*
> *Ādam āvard darīn dayr-i kharāb-ābādam.*[51]
>
> I was an angel and lofty Paradise was my place
> Adam brought me to this worldly monastery.

In this verse, the former archangel Iblīs refers to his lofty position in the Paradise, describing how he was expelled and fell to the material world because of Adam.

To conclude, as we have seen there definitely does exist a full theory of mystical love which can be reconstructed from the above-mentioned couplets from the *Dīvān*, and which shows that Ḥāfiẓ had relied heavily on the creation myth elaborated by the Sufi mystics of the preceding centuries. Ḥāfiẓ's repeated allusions to verses and terms from the Qur'ān demonstrates his poetic achievement in creating this added mystical – but perhaps the principle and essential – dimension to the doctrine of love in Persian poetry. Combining bacchanalian imagery of wine and erotic love poetry with familiar Qur'ānic traditions and Persian Sufi doctrines, he thus succeeds in interweaving the mystical version of the creation myth with a philosophy of earthly love.

Notes

1 *Dīvān-i Ḥāfiẓ*, ed. Khānlarī, p. 950, *ghazal* 467: 7. All further quotations are from this edition. I would like to thank the editor of this volume for his invaluable comments. I am also grateful to S. McGlinn for his editorial assistance.

2 Analysing the development of *ghazal* poetry, J.T.P. de Bruijn ('Anvari and the *Ghazal*: an Exploration', p. 31) concludes that poets such as Anvari used 'different modes of discourse with the *ghazal*', highlighting how this development reached its zenith in the hands of Ḥāfiẓ.

3 For the background to the integration of mystical ideas and doctrines in Ḥāfiẓ's poetry, see Manūchihr Murtaḍawī's classic study on Ḥāfiẓ, *Maktab-i Ḥāfiẓ, ya Muqaddama bar Ḥāfiẓ-shināsī*, pp. 327–99. See also Dāryūsh Āshūrī's comparisons of the themes treated by Ḥāfiẓ with Maybudī's *Kashf al-asrār* and Najm al-Dīn Rāzī's *Mirṣād al-'ibād*, in his *Hastī-shināsi-yi Ḥāfiẓ: kāvushī dar bunyādhā-yi andīsha-yi* ū: on the development of the concept of love in Ḥāfiẓ's poetry, see pp. 399–422. Also see J.T.P. de Bruijn, *Persian Sufi Poetry*, III, esp. pp. 76–81, where one of the *ghazals* of Ḥāfiẓ is analysed.

4 *The Mystics of Islam*, p. 107.

5 Niẓāmī, *Makhzan al-asrār*, ed. Dastgirdī, p. 69, l. 16.

6 To give only one example, in the romance *Yūsuf va Zulaykhā*, 'Abd al-Rahmān Jāmī gives a splendid description of God's *istighnā* in a separate chapter, showing God's self-sufficiency before the creation of the world. See 'Abd al-Raḥmān Jāmī, *Yūsuf va Zulaykhā*, in *Mathnavī-yi haft awrang*, ed. Mudarris Gīlānī, pp. 591–3. Also see chapter 4 (*vādī-yi istighnā*) of Farīd ad-Dīn 'Aṭṭār, *Manṭiq al-ṭayr*, ed. Gawharīn, in which several aspects of the concept *istighnā* is illustrated. For an excellent analysis of the structure and function of this poem, see Davis, 'The Journey as Paradigm: Literal and Metaphorical Travel in 'Aṭṭār's *Manṭiq aṭ-ṭayr*', pp. 173–83.

7 For an elaborate analysis of the development of the theme of love and the use of the term *'ishq*, see Seyed-Gohrab, *Layli and Majnun: Love, Madness and Mystic Longing in Nizāmi's Epic Romance*, chapter 1.

8 See Pourjavady, *Ru'yat-i māh dar āsmān*, pp. 153ff.; for the use of various terms for love, see Pourjavady's series of articles in *Nashr-i Dānish* that appeared under the title 'Bāda-yi 'ishq 1–5', vol. 11, no. 6, 1370, pp. 4–13; vol. 12, no. 1, 1370, pp. 4–18; vol. 12, no. 2, 1370, pp. 6–15; vol. 12, no. 3, 1371, pp. 26–32; vol. 12, no. 4, 1371, pp. 22–30. See Pourjavady, 'Risāla'ī dar bāra-yi 'ishq', pp. 105ff.

9 *Sawāniḥ*, p. 3, *faṣl* 1 (3), ll. 18–19.

10 *Ibid.*, p. 5, *faṣl* 1 (3), ll. 13–16.

11 Aḥmad-i Jām Nāmiqī, *Uns at-tā'ibīn*, p. 210.

12 See *Sūfī-nāma*, ed. Yūsufī, pp. 170–3; 208–9.

13 *Ibid.*, pp. 170–1, ll. 18, 1–4.

14 *Ibid.*, p. 173, ll. 3–5.

15 Najm al-Dīn Dāya cites Kharaqānī (d. 450/1034) in his *Mirṣād al-'ibād*, ed. Riyāhī, p. 49; English translation by Algar, *The Path of God's Bondsmen*, p. 74; all further English references are to this edition and translation. A. Ghazālī quotes Bāyazīd Bistāmī in the *Sawāniḥ*, ed. Ritter, p. 41, *faṣl* 21 (4), ll. 18–20; cf. Rūzbihān Baqlī, *Sharḥ-i shaṭhiyyāt*, p. 60, l. 22.

16 A. Schimmel, *Mystical Dimensions of Islam*, p. 295.

17 See A. Ghazālī, *Sawāniḥ*, p. 4, *faṣl* 1 (1), l. 6, where the author expresses this thought.

18 For an elaborate discussion on this verse, see N. Pourjavady, "Ahd-i alast: 'aqīda-yi Abū Ḥāmid Ghazālī va jāygāh-i tārīkhī-yi ān', pp. 3–48.

19 *Dīvān-i Ḥāfiẓ*, ed. Khānlarī, p. 22, *ghazal* 3: 4.

20 Qur'ān 95:4.

21 *Dīvān-i Ḥāfiẓ*, ed. Khānlarī, p. 938, *ghazal* 461: 9.

22 *Ibid.*, p. 420, *ghazal* 202: 7.

23 Najm al-Dīn Dāya, *Mirṣād al-'ibād*, p. 49; English trans., p. 75.

24 *Ibid.*, p. 2; English trans., p. 26.

25 *Dīvān-i Ḥāfiẓ*, ed. Khānlarī, p. 312, *ghazal* 148: 1.

26 *Ibid.*, p. 424, *ghazal* 204: 4.

27 *Ibid.*, p. 56, *ghazal* 20: 5. A variant reading is *maqām-i 'ishq* (the station of love).

28 See Bly and Lewisohn, trans., *The Angels Knocking on the Tavern Door*, p. 59.

29 Schimmel, *Mystical Dimensions of Islam*, pp. 136–7.

30 *Sawāniḥ*, pp. 32–3, *faṣl* 16, ll. 2–7.

31 See Seyed-Gohrab, *Layli and Majnun*, chapter 5.

32 *Dīvān-i Ḥāfiẓ*, ed. Khānlarī, II, p. 1040, l. 1. Although this couplet is taken from a *qaṣīda* in a worldly context, the mystical import is so strong that it cannot be overlooked.

33 *Ibid.*, p. 374, *ghazal* 179: 3.

34 *Ibid.*, p. 18, *ghazal* 1: 5.

35 *Ibid.*, p. 466, *ghazal* 225: 2. On the term *shāhid*, see Abū'l-Ḥasan 'Abd al-Raḥmān Khatmī Lāhūrī, *Sharḥ-i 'irfānī-yi ghazalhā-yi-i Ḥāfiẓ*, ed. Khurramshāhī et al., II, p. 1352, on *ghazal* 192: 1 or vol. II, p. 1386 on *ghazal* 102: 2; Rajā'ī Bukhārā'ī, *Farhang-i ash'ār-i Ḥāfiẓ*, pp. 361ff. Isti'lāmī, in his *Dars-i Ḥāfiẓ: Naqd u sharḥ-i ghazalhā-yi Khwāja Shams al-Dīn Muḥammad Ḥāfiẓ*, commenting on *ghazals* no. 101: 2 (vol. I, pp. 326–7) and no. 346: 1 (vol. II, p. 889), rejects the opinion of some critics that the term *shāhid* here or anywhere else in the *Dīvān* – where it occurs some 15 times – refers to a young boy, asserting that 'in most of the instances it clearly refers to a beautiful woman, and in some other instances it absolutely *cannot* be interpreted as referring to a young boy with an unshaven face' (vol. I, p. 54).

36 In Ḥāfiẓ's poetry, the word *shāhid* also refers to the Prophet Muḥammad, who existed in eternity in the form of Light and witnessed the creation of the world.

37 Awn, *Satan's Tragedy and Redemption: Iblis in Sufi Psychology*, pp. 169ff.; see also Pourjavady, *Sulṭān-i ṭarīqat*, pp. 45–9; Āshūrī, *Hastī-shināsī*, pp. 171–80.

38 *Dīvān-i Ḥāfiẓ*, ed. Khānlarī, p. 536, *ghazal* 260: 3.

39 *Ibid.*, p. 312, *ghazal* 148: 2.

40 For a discussion of the concept of jealousy in combination with *malāmat* (blame), see *Sawāniḥ*, *faṣl* 4.

41 *Dīvān-i Ḥāfiẓ*, ed. Khānlarī, p. 374, *ghazal* 179: 1.

42 Rāzī, *Mirṣād al-'ibād*, ed. Riyāḥī, *bab* II, *faṣl* 4, pp. 65–82. See Khurramshāhī, *Ḥāfiẓ-nāma*, II, pp. 766–7.

43 *Dīvān-i Ḥāfiẓ*, ed. Khānlarī, p. 404, *ghazal* 194: 6.

44 *Ibid.*, p. 946, *ghazal* 465: 5.

45 *Ibid.*, p. 312, *ghazal* 148: 4. Ḥāfiẓ makes numerous allusions to this aspect of Iblīs in his *Dīvān*. See Siddīqīyān and Mīr'ābidīnī, *Farhang-i vāzhih-namā-yi Ḥāfiẓ* s.v. *Mudda'ī*. Being in the mystical tradition of the Sufi martyr Hallāj, Aḥmad Ghazālī deals briefly with this aspect of Iblīs in chapter 64 of the *Sawāniḥ*, in which he discusses the aspiration of love (*himmat-i 'ishq*). No reference is, however, made here to Iblīs as a pretender, rather his acceptance of God's curse as a blessing is underscored.

46 See also *Lavāyiḥ*, ed. Farmanish, pp. 4, 128, a commentary on Aḥmad Ghazālī's *Sawāniḥ*, which is wrongly attributed to Nāgawrī.

[47] *Dīvān-i Ḥāfiẓ*, ed. Khānlarī, p. 312, *ghazal* 148: 4.

[48] Also compare Zangī, *Munāẓara-yi chashm u dil*, p. 110; Iblīs is repeatedly criticized in 'Aṭṭār's works. See, for instance, *Manṭiq al-ṭayr*, pp. 161–2; see also P. Awn, *Satan's Tragedy*, pp. 45–9.

[49] *Dīvān-i Ḥāfiẓ*, ed. Khānlarī, p. 868, *ghazal* 426, l. 1.

[50] This is the purport, for instance, of the following couplet: *Dar azal dādast mā rā sāqī-yi la'l-i labat / jur'a-i jāmī ki man madhūsh-i ān jāmam hanūz*. 'In pre-eternity, the cup-bearer of the ruby of your lips has given us / A draught from a beaker, such that I am drunk with that wine today.' *Ibid*., p. 534, *ghazal* 259: 7.

[51] *Ibid*., p. 636, *ghazal* 310: 3.

The Radiance of Epiphany: The Vision of Beauty and Love in Ḥāfiẓ's Poem of Pre-Eternity

Leili Anvar

'The poet is occupied with frontiers of consciousness beyond which words fail though meaning still exists.' (T.S. Eliot[1])

In his *Dīvān*, which for more than six centuries has been a never-ending source of inspiration for scholars and illiterate people alike, Ḥāfiẓ constantly explores those 'frontiers of consciousness beyond which words fail though meaning still exists', as is confirmed by his poetic title 'Mouthpiece of the Invisible' (*Lisān al-ghayb*). Where words fail – and they constantly do so when what is at stake is the 'Invisible' or the realm of inner realities (*'ālam-i bātin*) – poetry produces mirror images that reflect what usually cannot be imagined, vocalized or remembered. In the same way that the shimmering mirrorlike surface of the mirror/cup reflects the face of the beauteous Cup-bearer (*Sāqī*), each *ghazal* and each image, and line in it, reflects, as successive mirrors/monads,[2] a whole world standing beyond the frontiers of consciousness. It could be argued that each line of the *Dīvān-i Ḥāfiẓ* is transfused with a beauty cast by this reflection of the Beloved in the same way as, in mystical terms,[3] the microcosm reflects the macrocosm.[4] Thus, his poetic images reflect both in their form and meaning an echo of the primordial beauty experienced by the human soul in pre-Eternity, when it emerged from nothingness by the command of the Creator.[5] The very intricacy of Ḥāfiẓ's poetry reflects the complexity of the experience of love,[6] which in turn is derived from the visual experience of beauty in all its ineffability and the resultant dilemma of integrating the variegated multiplicity of beauty's reality into a single discourse. Witness the profusion of both literary and mystical commentaries on Ḥāfiẓ's verse that cross-reference themselves so intricately, such that it is almost impossible to be simple when you speak of Ḥāfiẓ, precisely because what he has to say (or rather bear witness to) – that is, the complex reality of love – is impossible to recount in plain, simple words. That is also why attempts to paraphrase his verse utterly not only destroy the pervasive ambience of beauty and polysemic haze surrounding it, but also ultimately truncate the meaning of his poems. Maybe that is also why it is so difficult (some would say impossible) to translate Ḥāfiẓ into another language. The choice of poetry as the language of love is the result of the impossibility of expressing such experiences prosaically, a phenomenon that had already been, long before Ḥāfiẓ, chronicled in the writings of Aḥmad Ghazālī (d. 520/1126).[7] In his treatise on love entitled *Savāniḥ*, which is justly considered as the founding text of the School of Love in Sufism and the tradition of love poetry in Persian,[8] Ghazālī opens his treatise by emphasizing the impossibility of ever finding words capable of expressing the realities of love:

> The following words comprise some chapters dealing with the significations of love (*ma'ānī-yi 'ishq*), although the tales of love can never be fit into words nor contained within the confines of language. For those significations are virgins and the hand of verbal expression can never lift the veil behind which they are becurtained. Nonetheless, all our business is to bring those virginal significations together with the virile males of words in the private chamber of linguistic expression.[9]

Interestingly enough, as we can see, Ghazālī makes use of erotic images to characterize the strange operation of putting the experience of love into words, as if, by so doing, the author was so to speak raping the inner reality of love. At the same time, his image suggests that a full rendition of the reality of love in words is impossible in the same way as complete fusion is impossible in sexual intercourse. But the image also suggests that looking for words to define love is a process of love-making to meanings in the same way as the human lover desperately tries to make love to the Beloved. That effort itself constitutes the path of love. The goal cannot be attained except through silence, just as the realization of love cannot be attained but in annihilation. Time and again, when Ghazālī feels that his prose cannot encompass the vast field of love, he has recourse to poetry, citing a quatrain, either of his own composition or by way of quotation, without offering any further explanation. In a deeper sense, Ghazālī thus remedies the narrowness of language by transmuting verbal expression into visionary experience. Rather than letting us merely hear about what love is, he makes us to behold its various aspects through visual imagery, providing descriptions that resemble what came to be known in later works by Persian poets as 'divine flashes' (*Lama'āt*). Ghazālī's insistence on this visionary aspect of love, in which the radiance of the Beloved's beauty is the source of inspiration, soon became the founding principle of the tradition of the Persian mystical *ghazal*,[10] which reached the absolute perfection of its lyrical art with Ḥāfiẓ.[11]

In the Persian mystical *ghazal* in general and in Ḥāfiẓ's *ghazals* in particular, Beauty appears as a kind of disturbance, the creator of a commotion that stirs up Love. Beauty's commotion in turn is depicted as a luminous epiphany, which means that any discourse about love must necessarily recreate those radiant but tumultuous conditions. This lovely mêlée of Beauty's epiphany also participates in the universal Beauty of Being itself, thus bearing witness both to God's presence in all His creation and to His supreme Beauty, for 'Verily, God is beautiful and He loves beauty', as the Prophet's saying (*ḥadīth*) attests.[12] The function of the mystical *ghazal* is thus to reflect, in an aesthetically harmonious manner, this intimate connection between Beauty and Love.

In what follows, while analysing some of these mystical themes, I will discuss some of the key concepts (Beauty, Love, Grief and others) in the symbolic lexicon of Ḥāfiẓ's erotic philosophy, focusing on the following poem that I would call the *ghazal* of Pre-Eternity:

1 One day in pre-Eternity a ray of your beauty
Shot forth in a blaze of epiphany.
Then love revealed itself and cast down
A fire that razed the earth from toe to crown.
2 Your face revealed itself, but saw the Angels had
No love, then turned like fire consumed
With jealous rage, and struck the soul of man.
3 From love's flame reason wished to light
Its lamp. A lightning bolt of jealous wrath
Shot out and made all havoc of the world.
4 The impostor tried to scrutinize the scene
Of Mystery but from the Arcanum
A hand lashed out and smashed the stranger's chest.
5 For all the rest, from Fate's games of chance
Joy was ordained. My heart alone, that's racked
With woe, got grief by the lots of fate.
6 The higher soul which always longed to gain
Access to the well within your sunken chin,
Reached out its hand and grabbed those tangled locks.
7 Ḥāfiẓ, that day your book of *The Joy of Love*
Was composed for you, the pen crossed out
All means your heart could ever know delight.[13]

In Pre-Eternity...

The major theme of the *ghazal*, expressed in its very first word, is a vision of an event that took place 'in pre-Eternity' (*dar azal*), at a time when there was no time, referred to by Ḥāfiẓ in other poems in various terms as the 'Day of Pre-Eternity' (*rūz-i azal*),[14] the 'First Day' (*rūz-i avval*),[15] the 'Ancient Pledge' (*'ahd-i qadim*),[16] or the 'Day of the Covenant' (*rūz-i i alast*),[17] time functioning here as the setting for the founding event of Islam's metahistory. In fact, *dar* ('in') is a preposition of space and time, expressing the idea of an 'inner' space that is, at once, a time. As specialists know, and as simple readers of Ḥāfiẓ intuitively feel, each word chosen by the poet is important: each term has been honed and chiselled to convey a whole constellation of meanings and emotions in a nutshell. Pre-Eternity – *azal* – is one such technical term that brings to mind a whole range of religious and mystical traditions, and emotions related to those traditions that touch the heart, summoning up to the soul, as it were, echoes of a lost memory.

This whole gamut of psycho-spiritual experience that every sensitive and attuned Persian-speaking reader immediately apprehends from the term *azal* is better grasped when we examine the metahistory of the term. It is generally accepted that some major events took place on the 'Day of the Covenant' (*rūz-i i alast*) in pre-Eternity. According to the Qur'ān,[18] there was once a primordial 'day before time', before the actual creation (*khalq*), where, in a 'space without space', no distance between Creator and creature existed. In that prelapserian aeon, God taught Adam the names of all things,[19] and made a covenant with Adam. God then asked the yet unborn children of Adam – humanity-to-be – to testify whether He was not their Lord (the famous interrogation: *Alast bi-rabbikum?*). They all testified that He was their Lord. By their ecstatic rejoinder of 'Yes' to this divine query, they sealed the primordial pact of love between the Creator and His creatures. But accepting God as their Lord, Adam/humankind accepted the momentous Burden of the Trust (*bār-i amānat*)[20] that sealed man's fate. Muslim mystics have alternatively interpreted this 'burden' as being either love or knowledge.[21] But, for our poet, there is no opposition: naming things means both knowing words and the objects they denote, as well as loving them, insofar as words stand for the reality of things. The very root of the word for poetry – *shi'r* – in Arabic is derived from the verb *sha'ara* (to know, understand intuitively) and, due to its connection with knowledge and understanding, poetry is perceived as having an anagogic function.[22] In this particular *ghazal*, when discussing those events in pre-Eternity, Ḥāfiẓ clearly connects love to a superior knowledge bestowed upon man in the form of 'radiant beauty' on that pre-Eternal day.

'In pre-Eternity a ray of your beauty shot forth ...' (*Dar azal partaw-i ḥusnat zi tajallī dam zad*), Ḥāfiẓ writes. The verb *dam zadan* (translated here as 'shot forth') literally means to 'breathe forth', 'to expire' – the verb evoking the idea of a whispered secret breathed into the ear. It is important to note that the subject of the verb *partaw-i ḥusnat* ('a ray of your beauty') – and hence my title, the 'Radiance of Beauty' – is a visual reality that speaks to the ear and reveals something essential about the nature of the divine manifestation or epiphany (*tajallī*) that evoked that beauty. Here, again, these connotations of the word are essential because they are related to the idea of a luminous revelation. So, on that one day in pre-Eternity, a secret was both *seen* and *heard*: Beauty, an Attribute of the Creator's Face, was revealed and the secret of its manifestation, in a visible form, suggested. Told in terms of a dazzling fiery blaze (*ātash*) of light, that radiant 'ray' (*partaw*) flashed forth by divine 'epiphany' (*tajallī*), and it is this primordial event that triggered love in the human soul. The whole universe (*'ālam*)[23] is a result of this first manifestation, yet only man received its impact: was directly 'struck' by it. God himself wanted to reveal His beauty in order to be seen and loved; the Islamic tradition, 'I was a hidden treasure and I wanted to be known, so I created the world', is a very famous *ḥadīth*[24] that has inspired many mystics' vertiginous meditations on the nature of man and, indeed, on the meaning of created beings as mirrors reflecting the beauty of the Creator. Another idea related to the theme of primordial covenant (*alast*) and alluded to in the next verse by Ḥāfiẓ is that the angels could not understand this 'hidden treasure', since their natures did not allow them to bear the heavy burden of the weighty Trust bestowed by God upon mankind.[25] And, of course, this necessitates the superiority of mankind over the angels, although Ḥāfiẓ says elsewhere that:

> Both human beings and angels take their sustenance
> From the existence of love. The practice of devotion
> Is a good way to arrive at happiness in both worlds.[26]

All creatures are in fact produced out of the existence of love, but this does not necessarily mean that they can understand the nature of love or achieve union with the Beloved. For mankind, the problem is that by undertaking the 'voyage of descent' (*sayr-i nuzūlī*) from the upper celestial realm down to this lower material world, both mind and heart seem to have lost all memory of the pre-Eternal epiphany of beauty and the apparition of love. Therefore, the whole purpose of the mystics' returning 'voyage of ascent' (*sayr-i su'ūdī*) is to regain the state of the soul that allowed the contemplation of beauty. In other words, when the human soul enters the material body, it loses the memory of its real nature, origin and purpose. This may be a better way of understanding the passage of the Qur'ān referred to above (33:72), where it was stated that by accepting the Trust, man proved himself enigmatically to be 'an unjust tyrant and a fool' (*ẓalūman jahūlan*).[27] This folly may be read as humanity's forgetfulness and disposition to be heedless, because man is, in essence, a forgetful creature. 'A scholar', Al-Ma'arī reports, 'has argued that you are in fact named "man" (*insān*) on account of your forgetfulness (*nisyān*)'.[28] The adjective *ẓalūman* may thus be read to mean that not only is man unjust and cruel, to himself as well as tyrannous towards others, but as indicative of the state of anyone over whom darkness (*ẓulmat*) has fallen, having forgotten the memory of his pre-Eternal condition and so forfeited the divine Trust.

Only those privileged souls who have been singled out by destiny[29] have kept in their memory the recollection of that Day, the vision of which they can only narrate in a language that cannot be the language of common reality which has been built on the illusionary truth of logical thinking.[30] Ḥāfiẓ is one such privileged soul and this may account for his choice of 'Ḥāfiẓ' as his *nom de plume* (*takhalluṣ*) – that is, 'the one who remembers, who has preserved the memory' of what happened in pre-Eternity. 'Remembering' here implies not only keeping in mind the dazzling experience of epiphany – but also bearing consciously, with all its weight, the momentous Trust of love, along with its knowledge and the heavy responsibility which being a trustee entails. In another *ghazal*, in which Ḥāfiẓ describes the events that took place on the day of *alast* (referred to as *dūsh* or 'last night'), he states:

Last night it happened just before the break
Of dawn: the weight upon my spirit was
Then lifted off, and in that dreary murk
Of night, they gave me the water of
Eternal life. The beam that flashed out from
The Essence made me selfless, and the brew
They gave me from the Cup of Radiant
Theophany revealed to me the Attributes...
From here on in, my face will turn to face
The mirror of that all-reflective charm
And beauty, where these portents were made known
To me about the Essence's revelation.

... For all this honey and this sugar which
Flows from my speech is but the dividend
Of patience they bequeathed me from that pen:
My reed that's filled with sugary honey-dew.[31]

Here, in an allusion to the Water of Life, the poet clearly states that he was given a radiant vision that illuminated his soul and made him immortal and forever intoxicated. The fact that he narrates the Qur'ānic event as having happened personally to him, saving him from darkness, indicates that he has kept alive the memory of that pre-Eternal day and thus become himself, as a poet, a mirror reflecting that beauty. Recollecting the taste of that primordial event, one finds the allusion to his 'sugary' verse in the final line, the sugar-cane from which sugar originates, a stock metaphor in classical Persian poetry for the Beloved. So the poem becomes the place and time (note once again here: time and space are confused) where that pre-Eternal epiphany is evoked, arousing the memory of the listener or reader and favouring him with a poetic glimpse of the intoxicating beauty of the divine Essence. The many boasts that Ḥāfiẓ makes about his verse being redolent with the fragrance of Beloved's tresses[32] or indued with the scent of the Garden of Paradise during the time of Adam,[33] or his claim that the fruits of his pen are sweeter than sugar,[34] bear witness to this same idea, indicating that his poetry aims at reanimating the memory of the soul's pre-Eternal life through medium of stimuli drawn from the realm of the senses.[35]

But let us come back to our poem of pre-Eternity. In order to understand the vision of love and beauty in Ḥāfiẓ, it is necessary here to ponder the notion of the amorous melancholic passion known as *gham* (love's grief) that is so central to Persian love poetry and so closely associated to the experience of love. *Gham* is the grief generated by pining in love, conveying the sense of desolation experienced by the longing lover racked with lover's woes and cares. In this poem, it is juxtaposed (in v. 5) to delight and joy (the Perso-Arabic term *'aysh* used here denotes the unfeeling delight one gleans from superficial pleasures and careless amusements) and (in v. 7) to the light-heartedness (*dil-i khurram*) that comprises the sad privileges and graceless follies of the oblivious. This polarity between the care-stricken true lover graced with love's grief and the light-hearted dilettante alien to love's woes is often alluded to by Ḥāfiẓ, and, indeed, is featured in a very famous line from the opening *ghazal* in the *Dīvān*:

A pitchblack night
  Billows fearful foaming
    the whirlpool's dreadful
      swirling...
Those disenburdened men who stand so careless on the strand,
How can they ever comprehend our state of mind?[36]

The 'disenburdened' (in Persian: *sabukbārān-i sāhilhā*) are those who stand on the shore careless and unfeeling, unaware of love's pains and passion, and unaffected by any pangs of yearning. The 'ocean' here recalls the 'ocean of love' – the Sea of Divine Attributes in which the soul of the *Fedeli d'amore* dissolves like a drop and is annihilated, but in the deep passions and strong currents of which the 'disenburdened' dilettante, safe and dry on the seastrand, has no experience. The word 'burden' (*bār*) reappears here in the term *sabukbārān* ('disenburdened', literally: 'lightly burdened') that brings us back to the 'Burden of the Trust' (*bār-i amānat*), which in turn recalls the idea that those who do not partake of love can neither know its pains nor bear its burdens. Both by the medium of knowledge and through the experience of love, the 'Burden of the Trust' obliges man to endure pain, grief and longing. To remember is to regain consciousness of that weighty Trust, to become newly aware of what was lost of old and consequently to long to return, to desire to regain the day of union. These are some, but by no means all, the connotations of *gham* (love's grief) in the religion of love in classical Persian poetry.

Longing or yearning (*shawq*) is also an essential and central theme of the whole tradition of love literature in Islam, whether sacred or profane,[37] because union without separation is impossible, just as desire without loss and deprivation is meaningless. Love and longing are concomitants of each other. That is one reason why anyone who has beheld – and fallen in love with – the primordial beauty is also 'grief-stricken' (*ghamdīdih*): his heart has 'beheld' the grief – that is to say, has suffered it personally. Being racked by the memory of loss, he suffers the pangs of yearning which absence entails, which his longing betokens and which his status as a lover demands. There are innumerable lines throughout Ḥāfiẓ's *Dīvān* in particular,[38] and in Persian poetry in general, that allude to the centrality of longing in love and the paradox of joy in pain.

That memory Ḥāfiẓ keeps in mind – or rather preserves 'in heart' – is not only the remembrance of the radiant beauty witnessed by mankind on that fateful day of pre-Eternity (*Alast*), not only the mystery of the Beloved's epiphany and the retention of the covenant sealed then, it is the ready acceptance on the part of the lover to suffer for the sake of that primordial covenant the pain of alienation and exile in this lower realm, acquiescing to the sorrows and woes that will polish his heart and transform him into a perfect mirror reflecting the countenance of Beauty. Pain is the instrument of annihilation that burns up the ego of the lover and renders him selfless, and it is his selflessness that makes him susceptible to the ravishment of love. Hence pain and love are inseparable companions.[39] Where Ḥāfiẓ quips that 'At first Love appeared so simple but then hardships came up' (*ki 'ishq āsūn namūd avval, valī āftād mushkilhā*) in the very first opening line of the *Dīvān*, Taqī Purnāmdāriān wisely reminds us that:

> The word 'at first' [*avval*], transports us back to a beginningless beginning into a meta-history and to the event of the covenant of pre-Eternity [*mīthāq-i alast*] that is at once the *fons et origo* of mankind's love for God and the commencement of man's never-ending exile from the beloved through separation and his bootless entanglement in all the gruelling pains and hardships borne of love.[40]

This, indeed, is exactly the gist of Ḥāfiẓ's verse:

> Though Ḥāfiẓ be lost and gone, he has
> as yet an intimate tie of oneness
> With grief and sufferance in love – soulmate,
> By grace of that ancient covenant.[41]

Not incidentally, in the *Savāniḥ* this same dialectic of grief and love appears as an all-pervasive theme, where Ghazālī employs violent images to depict and justify the Beloved's cruelty. In one place, Ghazālī remarks: 'Love is a devourer of men; it consumes men, such that nothing else remains.'[42] The function of love's grief (*gham*) in the religion of love in Persian literature needs to be understood in exactly this sense, for *gham* serves not only to keep desire alive but also to burn away the selfhood of the lover, to ravish and deprive him of all that is not the Beloved.[43] It is for this reason that the missive of love's joy and delight can only be composed and dispatched to the poet when all the wherewithal of delight (all means by which the heart is delighted: *asbāb-i dil-i khurram*) had been crossed out and dissolved by the ravages of love's grief (*ghazal* 148, v. 7). At that point, viewed from the higher standpoint of the Reality of love's grief – 'the Mt Rubwa of Love' as Rūmī calls it[44] – can he again reflect in his heart the lost image: the icon of beauty.

Beloved and Lover, Beauty and Love

Apparently, the addressee of Ḥāfiẓ's Poem of Pre-Eternity is a 'you' that never appears as such, except in two possessive enclitics[45] and in two pronouns used as possessives.[46] 'You' is never the subject of any verb. But some aspects of this 'you' become active in a rather intensive way: to 'you' belongs 'a ray of your beauty', 'love', 'face', 'the lightning bolt of jealous wrath', and the invisible hand which from the Arcanum that lashes out. The end-rhyme phrase *zad*, repeated at the end of each couplet of this *ghazal*, is the third-person past tense singular of the verb *zadan* (to strike, to hit), and each time the verb is repeated, one senses from the rhyme word an element of violence either visual or physical. The anonymous 'you' of the poem manifests her- or himself in two different modes of action: either through dazzling radiance and light or through violence and rejection. The jealousy, exclusivity and cruelty of the Beloved are cast into relief by all the poem's verbs. Of course, Ḥāfiẓ is here consciously playing on the classical theme of the cruelly aloof and exclusive Beloved, who rejects her lover and hides herself behind veils of fiery splendour or shadowy darkness. In the context of the theme of the psycho-spiritual polarity of Love and Reason (*'ishq va 'aql*) in the Sufi tradition, it may be argued that reason (*'aql*) in v. 3a and the impostor (*mudda'ī*) in v. 4a are actually interior aspects of the lover's personality. Deep within the soul lies the remembrance of a radiant beauty beheld on the day of pre-Eternity, but which, if beheld by the eyes of reason or with the pretension of a swollen ego, cannot be seen. That epiphany is simply too radiant to be grasped by the crude faculties of ratiocination, too sublime to be approached with a merely notional understanding typical of the empty humbug and vain claims made by the spiritually immature and undeveloped personality of the poseur – *mudda'ī*.

In this context, Khurramshāhī explains in his commentary on this *ghazal* that the word epiphany (*tajallī*) appears twice in the Qur'ān. In one, there is a reference to 'Day of the Covenant' (*rūz-i i alast*) in pre-Eternity (7:172), and in the other to the story about Moses and his quest for the beautific vision. Moses entreated God to show Himself to him. 'Thou shalt not behold me', came the reply, 'but gaze upon the mountain and if it remain still, thou wilt see Me'. At which, God 'manifested Himself' in a blaze of epiphany (*tajallī*) to the mountain, which immediately 'came crashing down'. Unable even through this indirect epiphany to tolerate the divine radiance – *tajallī* – 'Moses fell down senseless' (7:143).[47] The key Qur'ānic term, which lends the poem its aesthetic tonality here, is *tajallī*. The term connotes a blinding light, a splendour and beauty that appears as pure omnipresent light. Just as the fiery nature of the experience of love dazzles the eye, so this light ravishes away the sight through its dazzling rays. The epiphany's violence is a direct consequence of its intensity of being. The awe produced by this overwhelming, burning presence is perhaps one reason why Ḥāfiẓ does not address the 'you' directly in the poem – for other than the human soul who has attained to the higher degrees of love, direct access to Beauty and Love means annihilation for all mortal beings.

Nonetheless, so long as the soul inhabits the material realm, it senses the need to regain that lost vision of beauty, although this vision can only be absorbed and understood by stages, step by step. The role of poetry is to make possible such a gradual visionary ascension. Here we may recall the Allegory of the Cave in Plato's

Republic, with its theory of intermediary luminosities and reflections intervening between the soul and vision of the Good. The soul's eyes, which heretofore had been accustomed to sombre tenebrous shadows of the cave, can only behold the sunlight directly once they gradually divest and raise their benighted vision out from the surrounding murky chiaroscuro. Similarly, the beauty and the intricacies of love, as well as the beauty and subtleties of the poem itself,[48] work as an introduction to the vision of beauty and the reality of love. The importance of vision is very often insisted upon by Ḥāfiẓ, who considers that beauty and love must be approached with the 'right vision' and 'insight' if their reality is to be contemplated, as he says:

> Since you aren't worthy of the side-glance
> Of the Darling, don't try for union. Looking directly
> Into Jamshid's cup doesn't work for the blind.[49]

Jamshid's cup (*Jām-i Jam*), a fabulous goblet which belonged to Jamshīd, a mythological king of the Pishdadian dynasty, was said to reflect the whole world, and in Persian poetry this cup symbolized the heart: a microcosm that reflects the macrocosm and the face of the Beloved. As such, it becomes the focus of contemplation. In another poem, the lover/poet relates an encounter with the 'wise mage' who 'holds up a cup' where, 'full of joy and delight', he contemplates 'in that mirror, a hundred different kind of scenes'.[50] In verses such as these, we apprehend that interior vision of the heart is the fundamental sense for the apprehension of truth and the acquisition of knowledge. Because the manifestation of truth is through beauty, the object of contemplation has to be the quintessence of beauty – that is, the Face of the Beloved, another microcosm which mirrors the macrocosm:

> In Persian poetry, the Face is seen rightly only in the eye and spoken truly on the tongue of the poet through whom the lover discourses. The poet/lover seeks the Face, convinced that within him lies that 'simple divine substance'. The search for the Face is then a penetration within the innermost self, through an outburst of 'pure love': the kind of love that witnesses the sign of the beauty of the Face outside the self.[51]

Juxtaposed to the lover/poet who possesses 'inner vision' and is thus capable of contemplation, as Aḥmad Ghazālī tells us,[52] we have the 'impostor' (*mudda'ī*, v. 4), who pretends to knowledge of things erotic, and though a stranger to love yet still wishes to witness the mystery of love and beauty. The term 'scene of Mystery' (*tamāshāgah-i rāz*) is literally the perspective from which the occult can be contemplated. Of course, not everybody is allowed access to that arcane locus of contemplation: neither the angels who are devoid of love, nor the false lover with his empty claims (*mudda'ī*), who, according to Sufi tradition,[53] is Satan himself, disregarding in his jealousy the apparition of the divine *tajallī* in Adam,[54] yet still trying to gaze upon what is forbidden to him.

'The stranger' (*nāmaḥram*) in popular parlance is one who is not allowed to see a woman 'unveiled',[55] who, if he does gaze upon her, deserves to be punished and spurned by society. The forbidden, veiled secret (*rāz*) referred to here is the beauty of the Beloved as it was once revealed to the human soul – before it was veiled and concealed from non-initiates.[56] Beheld from this perspective, Ḥāfiẓ is not only merely he who remembers the secret of pre-Eternity, but also the custodian of that secret.[57] As a faithful custodian, he knows that the secret cannot be divulged directly, but should be revealed only when suitably decked out in the veridical symbols and intricate subtleties of beautiful poetry. And, indeed, the reading of any of his *ghazals* is necessarily a mysterious process that brings up a myriad question. Who is speaking? To whom? Where? When? Which concepts do the images symbolize? Utter perplexity is part of the pleasure when reading a Persian *ghazal* in general, and a *ghazal* by Ḥāfiẓ in particular.[58] The apparent disparity of the distiches enhances this feeling of a kind of nuclear aesthetics that lacks unity, giving the deceptive impression that these lines are but 'orient pearls at random strung'.[59] And yet there is unity, but in a very oblique way. In the same way as the primordial vision of beauty and the all-encompassing experience of love constitute the founding metaphysical principles of creation and the secret of the unity of being, aesthetically the same structure presides over the design of the *ghazal*: it seems complicated to the extreme, upside down, discombobulated, even chaotic like the visible world of multiplicity, but the underlying unifying thread to the paradoxical reality of love and beauty is always there. If, in the beginning, beauty was one, when it descended into this world it appeared in multiple forms:

> On the day of Pre-Eternity, your Face in its glory
> Broke through from behind the veil. All of these forms
> Fell into the vast mirroring sea of imagination.[60]

Because of its multiple worldly forms, beauty cannot be contemplated as a unified whole, but has to be evoked in details: each detail of beauty in turn becomes an icon, a partial emblem indicative of its transcendent whole. The Beloved can actually never be described in totality (but can He/She be represented?), but only through classical and emblematic clichés such as the eye, the mole, the hair, the face, the lips... In the first chapter of his treatise on love, Aḥmad Ghazālī warns his reader that 'the difference between objects of love is accidental and fortuitous',[61] and later he gives an essential clue to the understanding of the representation of beauty in the mystic *ghazal*:

> In the realm of Imagination, sometimes Love manifests and reveals a sign of itself in some determined form, sometimes not. Sometimes it appears through the curl, sometimes through the down on the cheek, sometimes through the mole, sometimes through the stature, sometimes through the eye or through the eyebrow or through the coquettish glance, sometimes through the

> Beloved's laugh and sometimes through His/Her rebuke. And each of these significations is a sign indicative of a different kind of quest within the lover's soul.[62]

In our *ghazal*, though, Beauty is evoked mainly as a burning fire that is associated with pure light. The only physical details borrowed from the classical Persian poetic canon of beauty are the dimple (*chāh-i zanakhdān-i tu:* 'the well within your sunken chin') and the 'tangled locks', which suggest certain complications. Both these physical details stand in radical opposition to the theme of light, since the dimple-well and the tangled locks as images convey the idea of darkness and impenetrable gloom. In addition, the classical image is here reversed: usually the hair is used by the lover to pull himself out of the well,[63] whereas here (uniquely in the whole *Dīvān*) it is used to descend into it, because 'the higher celestial soul', the very soul that had witnessed the apparition of beauty in the form of light, desires the sunken well, the dimple in the chin. Symbolically the soul then desires to descend so as to experience the dark side of beauty. Indeed, the beauty of the beloved can be classified into two major categories: luminescent and dark, corresponding to the polarity of divine attributes of Grace (*luṭf*) and Wrath (*qahr*).[64] The opposition between these two is integral to the manifestation of human beauty, as in the poetic image juxtaposing the beloved's 'dark hair' to her 'shining face', for example. The dark side of beauty in Persian poetry is associated with the night, and is represented by the hair, the mole (in certain cases) and the well-dimple, alluding to worldly complications and the material entanglements, the experience of which, nonetheless, causes the maturation of the lover's personality on the path of love.[65] In this verse (148, v. 6), the descent down to earth is presented as the higher soul's hankering after contemplation of forms of beauty in the existential multiplicity of the world. One may also add that the image of the well in this verse immediately brings to mind the figure of Joseph of Egypt, exemplar *par excellence* of human beauty in Islam, whose imprisonment in the well at the hand of his jealous brothers symbolizes the terrestrial exile of the soul 'too good and fair for the world'. Just as Joseph eventually emerges from the well and meets his brilliant destiny, so the higher soul, itself an expiration of the Creator's breath of grace which has preserved something of its original divine beauty, after undergoing the long and painful journey of love, may come out of the well of the world and recover its memory. And, of course, this verse directly echoes the first line: for all started in time before time, in pre-Eternity (*azal*), at the time of the Covenant. Something happened then that caused the soul 'to fall' in love, that made it irrevocably decide to descend and acquiesce to its exile on earth and a life of pain and separation. So it came into the world, where it hankers after the forms of beauty that remind it of the formless beauty contemplated in *azal* and reflected in the forms of the *ghazal*.

The Book of The Joy of Love

Notwithstanding appearances, one of the major themes of the poem is the status of poetry in the process of remembrance. As we have already hinted, as is usually the case in *ghazal* poetry, the evocation of beauty is essentially visual. Beauty's 'ray' and love's 'fire' cannot by definition be directly grasped by reason or expressed in a discourse constructed according to the rules of logic. Any such attempt is doomed to be deconstructed by the powerful force of emotion. In matters of love, not only are reason and logic not teachers, but as 'Aṭṭār says,[66] following them leads to chaos. In order to contain the emotional tumult evoked by this experience and reflect the radiance of epiphany, another language must be found. If the purpose of the *ghazal* is to reflect and recreate the tumult raised by the experience of love,[67] it is but natural that its expression should be highly visual because the source of the emotion of love is, from the beginning, a dazzling vision. It is then not surprising that one of the underlying principles of any lyric poetry is the visualization of reality, however abstract. According to Frye:

> All poetic imagery seems to be founded on metaphor, but in the lyric, where the associative process is strongest and the ready-made descriptive phrases of ordinary prose furthest away, the unexpected or violent metaphor that is called catachresis has peculiar importance. Much more frequently than any other genre does the lyric depend for its main effect on the fresh or surprising image, a fact which often gives rise to the illusion that such imagery is radically new or unconventional.[68]

The importance of catachresis in the *ghazals* of Ḥāfiẓ in general, and in this *ghazal* in particular, seems to be related to the violence of the experience of love. Actually, it is not just a way of putting things: the catachresis is here supposed to produce a vision and arouse a commotion that should provide a glimpse of what really happened on the day of *alast* and, thus, to liberate the memory of the soul. And yet, for all the vividness of the image, it always remains but an allusion.[69] Each detail of beauty contributes to lift a veil, but, at the same time, the veil is never really lifted because the secret it conceals must not be told except by allusion.[70] Images, visions and the words that relate them are used here with a specific sense as inner images mirrored in the poem, in the heart, in the soul. They are imaginal representations of a reality which can only be configured within the form and music of language. This is why the status of poetry is so paradoxical: it reveals and conceals, shows and hides at the same time:

> This world and the next one too, are both
> A single blaze of light from his Face.
> I've told you both what's manifest and what is hid.[71]

As with Beauty's variegated manifestations, poetry is also both manifold and one, both dark and luminous, an expression of not only joy and delight, but also pain and grief. By crossing out all means of worldly delight and self-fulfilment (148, v. 7), the poet at last discovers that 'the source of all joy lies in pining in grief for the beloved [*gham-i nigār*]', as he says in one verse.[72] Yet the melancholic grief of love (*gham*) is by no means the end of the story. Such grief is in fact only a means to attain a higher form of joy. For composing the book or tale of Love's Joy harbours a secret that cannot be disclosed, a paradox impossible to grasp, whose vision is beyond articulation, yet which is allusively encapsulated in this verse here.

The 'book of *The Joy of Love*' is both Ḥāfiẓ's *ghazal* and his *Dīvān*, which constantly mirror each other in the same way as the cup reflects the face of the Beloved, who reflects the light of epiphany. And if polished and attentive enough to the secret music of Ḥāfiẓ, every heart may read that book and behold the radiance of that epiphany of Beauty in his poetry here and now.

Notes

1 *On Poetry and Poets*, p. 57.

2 The word 'monad' is here used in the sense developed in Leibniz's *Monadologie*: an independent entity, closed on itself but reflecting in its perfect sphere the whole universe. See Leibniz, *La Monadologie*, ed. Boutroux, pp. 141–4 (n. 167), 173–7.

3 This essay will not address the controversial question of whether Ḥāfiẓ is a mystical poet or not. The *ghazal* that is analysed here, definitely having a spiritual tone and content, will be analysed from a mystical perspective. On the problematic nature of Ḥāfiẓ's poetry, see the interesting remarks of Carl Ernst in his *Shambhala Guide to Sufism*, pp. 158–66.

4 On the importance of this conception in the symbolic expression of Sufi poets, see Pūrnāmdāriyān, *Ramz va dāstānhā-yi ramzī dar adab-i fārsi*, pp. 12–14.

5 On the mirror quality of lyric poetry, see Naṣru'llāh Purjavādī, 'Bāda-yi 'ishq (2): paydāyish-i ma'nā-yi majāzī-yi bada dar shi'r-i fārsī', *Nashr-i dānish*, XII/1 (1370/1991), pp. 4–18.

6 The opening verse of the *Dīvān* testifies to this key theme: 'Come, *Sāqī*, pass the cup round and present it / For love seemed so simple at first, but so many difficulties have arisen!' The difficulties (*mushkilhā*) here of course are the unforeseen complications that await every wanderer on the Path of Love. See the illuminating commentary on this and other themes in this *ghazal* by Pūrnāmdāriyān, *Gumshuda-yi lab-i daryā: ta'ammulī dar shi'r-i Ḥāfiẓ*, where a whole chapter (4, pp. 344–71) is dedicated to commenting on the erotic theology of this first *ghazal*.

7 For a biography and presentation of the life, thought, works and basic concepts of Aḥmad Ghazāli, see Lewisohn, 'Sawanih', in Greenberg (ed.), *Encyclopaedia of Love in World Religions*, II, pp. 535–8; idem., 'Al-Ghazali, Ahmad', in *The Encyclopedia of Philosophy*, 2nd edn, I, pp. 117–18.

8 See N. Purjavādī's introduction to his edition of Ghazālī's *Savāniḥ*; also see his 'Bāda-yi 'ishq', p. 16.

9 *Savāniḥ*, p. 1.

10 Actually, the importance of visionary experience is common to all lyric poetry, as Northrop Frye states: 'Understanding a poem literally means understanding the whole of it, as a poem, and as it stands. Such understanding begins in a complete surrender of the mind and senses to the impact of the work as a whole, and proceeds through the effort to unit the symbols toward a simultaneous perception of the unity of the structure.' *Anatomy of Criticism: Four Essays*, p. 77.

11 See, for example, the illuminating remarks of Annemarie Schimmel in her analysis of the characteristics of the Persian *ghazal*: 'The rhetorical devices which are an integral part of that poem, are very carefully observed: *murā'āt an-nazīr* requires that the images in a verse stand in a well-defined relation to each other. When the rose is mentioned, we can definitely expect a nightingale, and probably one or two more images from the garden. If a Qur'ānic prophet appears, his specific qualities or those of some other prophet are likely to appear. It is the art of the great masters to maintain a perfect equilibrium of images in such a way that they seem perfectly natural, as exemplified in the work of Ḥāfiẓ. This technique gives the verse a certain symmetry and, as in a perfect classical Persian miniature, everything has its place so that, as in miniature painting, one may speak of a two-dimensional system of signs that have equal, or near-equal value.' *As Through a Veil: Mystical Poetry in Islam*, pp. 58–9.

12 See Furūzānfar, *Aḥādīth-i Mathnawī*, no. 106.

13 See *Dīvān-i Shams al-Dīn Muḥammad Ḥāfiẓ*, ed. Sāyeh, *ghazal* 146; *Dīwān-i Ḥāfiẓ*, ed. Khānlarī, *ghazal* 148. Translation by Leonard Lewisohn.

14 *Dīvān-i Ḥāfiẓ*, ed. Khānlarī, *ghazal* 298: 4.

15 *Ibid.*, *ghazal* 259: 2.

16 *Ibid.*, *ghazals* 38: 9; 131: 6.

17 *Ibid.*, *ghazals* 21: 1; 22: 5.

18 Qur'ān, 7:172. See also Purjavādī, "Ishq-i azalī va bāda-yi alast', pp. 26–31.

19 Qur'ān, 3:31.

20 Actually, this Trust was first proposed to the heavens and earth and the mountains, but when they shrank from bearing it, Adam/man accepted it (Qur'ān, 33:72), not only because he was not aware of its weight, but because he was promised, so say the Sufis, a vision of the Face of God and the experience of love. Thus, Ḥāfiẓ (*Dīvān-i Ḥāfiẓ*, ed. Khānlarī, *ghazal* 179: 3) writes: 'The heavens could not bear the weight of the Trust. / When the lots were thrown again, the Trust / Fell on man, on me, an idiot and a fool.' Trans. Bly and Lewisohn, *The Angels Knocking on the Tavern Door*, p. 39. See also Peter Avery (trans.), *The Collected Lyrics of Háfiz of Shíráz*, p. 238, n. 1.

21 Purjavadī ("Ishq-i azalī...', p. 26) explains that the covenant at an earlier stage in the Sufi tradition had been interpreted as being a 'pact of mutual love'. [See also A.A. Seyed-Gohrab's essay in this volume – Ed.]

22 Shams al-Dīn Muḥammad, b. Qays al-Rāzī, the dry thirteenth-century theoretician of the art of poetry who is by no means a mystical author, states: 'Know that etymologically, the word *shi'r* [poetry] signifies knowledge and comprehension of the meanings by exact conjecture and correct reasoning.' *Al-Mu'jam fī ma'āyir ash'ār al-'ajam*, p. 188.

23 Etymology is again quite interesting here since the word for world (*'ālam*) is related to the root *'alima*, meaning 'to know, to perceive', having also developed into 'sign' (*'alāmat*), as if the whole universe were a sign that points towards knowledge of God.

24 Furūzānfar, *Aḥādīth-i Mathnawī*, no. 70.

25 See note 20 above.

26 *Ṭufayl-i hastī-yi 'ishqand ādamī u parī.* Trans. Bly and Lewisohn, *Angels*, p. 53: *Dīvān-i Ḥāfiẓ*, ed. Khānlarī, *ghazal* 443; *Dīvān-i Ḥāfiẓ*, ed. Sāyih, *ghazal* 441.

27 See note 20.

28 Abū'l-'Alā al-Ma'arrī, *Risālat al-ghufrān*, pp. 361–2. Quoted by Heller-Roazen, *Echolalias: On the Forgetting of Language*, p. 215.

29 In this *ghazal*, v. 5, the poet refers to the lots of destiny (*qur'a-yi qismat*) having been tossed and drawn for those who are heedlessly preoccupied with life's sensual pleasures (*'aysh*), but in another *ghazal* (*Dīvān*, ed. Khānlarī, *ghazal* 179: 3), he says that 'the lots of the affair' (*qur'a-yi kār*) came up 'on me, an idiot and a fool'. See also note 20 above.

30 See Heller-Roazen's illuminating essay *Echolalias*, which ends up with the image of the tower of Babel as a metaphor of mankind's imprisonment in oblivion: 'And as long as they continued to move in the air transformed by divine decree, they would continue to forget, and, in this way, to allow the forgotten to remain about them; they, and their children after them, would still breath in the element

of oblivion imposed upon them. Might they be our true ancestors? (...) The surest sign of our residence in the tower could well be that we no longer know it: to dwell within the ruined edifice, after all, is nothing if not to subsist on its confusing air. Destroyed, Babel, in this case, would persist; and we, consigned without end to the confusion of tongues, would, in obstinate oblivion, persist in it' (pp. 230–1).

31 Translation by Leonard Lewisohn; *Dīvān*, ed. Khānlarī, *ghazal* 178: 1, 2, 4; the last verse/stanza is not in Khānlarī's edition, but is found in variant readings in three of his other manuscripts.

32 *Ibid.*, *ghazal* 58: 7, 9.

33 *Ibid.*, *ghazal* 202: 10.

34 *Ibid.*, *ghazal* 40: 11.

35 Strangely enough, we may compare this to the enterprise of the French author Marcel Proust, who built his great novel *A la recherche du temps perdu* upon the memories generated from physical sensations related to sight and taste. Though contrary to Ḥāfiẓ, Proust deals only with sensations and sentiments generated in this earthly realm; in this work, the whole process of memory and remembrance is triggered by his delight in tasting a little madeleine soaked in tea. Savouring the taste of the madeleine suddenly brings back to the mind of the author his childhood, and the intimation of its flavour saves him and allows him to rebuild his memory and construct the whole novel: 'When from an ancient past, nothing survives, after the death of people, the destruction of things, more vivid by their very frailty, more immaterial, more persisting, more faithful, perfumes and tastes keep being remembered, like souls, they keep waiting, hoping, despite the ruin of all the rest and bearing on their almost impalpable droplets the vast edifice of memory.' Marcel Proust, *Du côté de chez Swann*, p. 47.

36 Translation by Leonard Lewisohn; *Dīvān-i Ḥāfiẓ*, ed. Khānlarī, *ghazal* 1: 5.

37 See Lewisohn, 'Shawḳ', *EI*², IX, pp. 376–7.

38 *Dīvān-i Ḥāfiẓ*, ed. Khānlarī, *ghazals* 26: 10; 57: 9; 63: 5; 91: 9; 156: 5; 173: 6; 177: 9; 189: 4; 201: 6; 218: 9; 237: 8; 250: 7; 255: 6; 291: 7, 10–11; 315: 4; 317: 7; 334: 5; 342: 7; 372: 7; 393: 8; 408: 2; 409: 7; 452: 1; 254: 9; 482: 10.

39 On the close connection between love and annihilation, see Leili Anvar-Chenderoff, 'Without Us from Us We Are Safe: Self and Selflessness in the *Dīwān of 'Attār*', pp. 241–54.

40 Pūrnāmdāriyān, *Gumshuda-yi lab-i daryā*, p. 356.

41 Translation by Leonard Lewisohn; *Dīvān-i Ḥāfiẓ*, ed. Sāyeh, *ghazal* 36: 9; ed. Khānlarī, *ghazal* 38: 9.

42 Aḥmad Ghazālī, *Sawāniḥ*, ed. H. Ritter, chap. 35, p. 54. See also *Sawāniḥ*, ed. Purjavādī, chap. 37, p. 30, on the 'heavy' but necessary burden of *gham*, and *ibid.*, chap. 45, p. 38. On the necessity for separation, see *Sawāniḥ*, ed. Ritter, chap. 39, pp. 61–2.

43 This is particularly evident in the story of Majnūn and Laylī, celebrated in Niẓāmi's *mathnawī* by that name, a tale renowned throughout all the Islamic world. See the remarkable analysis of this work by Seyed-Gohrab: *Laylī and Majnûn, Love, Madness and Mystic Longing.*

44 Jalāl al-Dīn Rūmī, *The Mathnawí of Jalálu'ddín Rúmí*, trans. and ed. Nicholson, III: 3753.

45 That is, the *at* of *ḥusnat* (your beauty) and of *rukhat* (your face) in verses 1a and 2a.

46 The *-i* (*tu*) in verses 6a (*chāh-i zanakhdān-i tu*) and 7a (*'Ishq-i tu*).

47 Khurramshāhī, *Ḥāfiẓ-nāma*, I, p. 598.

48 See Skalmowski's interesting article: 'The Meaning of the Persian Ghazal', which explores the complicated nature of the *ghazal*.

49 Translation by Bly and Lewisohn, *Angels*, p. 53; *Dīvān-i Ḥāfiẓ*, ed. Sāyeh, *ghazal* 441; ed. Khānlarī, *ghazal* 443: 2.

50 *Dīvān-i Ḥāfiẓ*, ed. Sāyeh, *ghazal* 137; ed. Khānlarī, *ghazal* 136: 3–5.

51 Charles-Henri de Fouchécour, '*Naẓar-bāzi*, les jeux du regard selon un interprète de Ḥāfiẓ', *Kār Nāmeh*, II/III (1995), pp. 3–10; p. 10.

52 *Baṣīrat-i bāṭin*. See *Savāniḥ*, ed. H. Ritter, p. 1.

53 The association of the phony *mudda'ī* with Iblīs/Satan can be found in Najm al-Dīn Rāzi, *Mirṣād al-'ibād*, ed. Riyāḥī, p. 317. See also Algar's translations of Rāzī's work, *The Path of God's Bondsmen*, p. 310.

This identification is also found in mystical commentary on this verse in Ḥāfiẓ's *Dīvān* by Abū'l-Ḥasan Khatmī Lāhūrī, *Sharḥ-i 'irfānī-yi ghazalhā-yi-i Ḥāfiẓ*, ed. Khurramshāhī *et al.*, II, p. 1049.

54 According to the word of the Prophet, 'God created Adam and theophanised [*fatajallī*] Himself within him'. Rāzi, *Mirṣād*, p. 316; *The Path*, trans. Algar, p. 310.

55 It is considered a sin to gaze at a forbidden object. In itself, the existence of such a concept shows the importance of gazing as an act in Islamic culture.

56 Lāhūrī in his commentary (*Sharḥ-i 'irfānī*, II, p. 1049), citing the *Ḥadīth-i qudsī*, 'Man is a mystery and I [God] am that mystery [*Aḥādīth-i Mathnawī*, p. 62]', considers this 'secret' as being the heart of Adam/Man which encompasses both the temporal macrocosm and the spiritual microcosm.

57 Thus, the related verbal form *ḥafaẓa* also means 'to protect'.

58 Thus, Gilbert Lazard speaks of the 'pervading mystery' of the *ghazal* genre in his 'Le langage symbolique du *ghazal*', pp. 60–71.

59 Arberry, 'Orient Pearls at Random Strung', pp. 699–712.

60 Translation by Bly and Lewisohn, *Angels*, p. 57; *Dīvān-i Ḥāfiẓ*, ed. Khānlarī, *ghazal* 107: 2.

61 *Savāniḥ*, ed. Ritter, p. 5.

62 *Ibid.*, p. 58 (*faṣl* 37–8).

63 *Dīvān-i Ḥāfiẓ*, ed. Khānlarī, *ghazals* 2: 6; 30: 3; 107: 6; 115: 9; 237: 5; 337: 5; 414: 5; 485: 1.

64 Cf. Shabistarī's *Gulshan-i rāz*, vv. 717–19, in Muwaḥḥid (ed.), *Majmū'a-i āthār-i Shaykh Maḥmūd Shabistarī*, p. 97.

65 Cf. Lāhūrī, *Sharḥ-i 'irfānī*, II, p. 1053.

66 *Manṭiq al-ṭayr*, ed. Gawharīn, p. 187, v. 3347.

67 The term *ghazal* (the fifth form of the verb *taghazzala*) literally means both to 'express the sorrow of love', and in Arabic poetry denotes an amatory elegy or song of love composed for a woman. See Blachère, '*Ghazal*', *EI*², II, pp. 1028–33.

68 *Anatomy of Criticism*, p. 281.

69 See Wickens, 'The Frozen Periphery of Allusion in Classical Persian Literature', pp. 171–90.

70 'For the greatest sin of the lover is *ifshā' as-sirr*, divulgence of the secret. ... Persian poets have therefore woven a veil of symbols in order to point to and at the same time hide the secret of love, longing and union.' Schimmel, *As Through a Veil*, p. 73.

71 Translation by Leonard Lewisohn; Dīvān-*i Ḥāfiẓ*, ed. Sāyeh, *ghazal* 353; ed. Khānlarī, *ghazal* 355: 4.

72 *Dīvān-i Ḥāfiẓ*, ed. Khānlarī, *ghazal* 249: 4. The whole verse is 'If others get joy and cheer from pleasures and delights / The source of all joy for us lies in pining with grief for the beloved' (*Gar dīgarān bi 'aysh u ṭarab khurramand u shād / Mā rā gham-i nigār buvad māyih-yi surūr*). For a good discussion of Ḥāfiẓ's preference of love's grief (*gham*) over joy, see Khurramshāhī, *Ḥāfiẓ-nāma*, I, pp. 606–7.

Part III

Ḥāfiẓ and the Persian Sufi Tradition

Ḥāfiẓ and the Sufi

Charles-Henri de Fouchécour

translated by Shusha Guppy and Leonard Lewisohn

By my title, 'Ḥāfiẓ and the Sufi', I have no wish to announce that my chapter will be a kind of recitation of tales (*ḥikāyat*) about the poet's relationship with the Sufis. Ḥāfiẓ himself tells us that tales and stories (*qiṣṣa*) don't interest him, whether they be epic, moral or mystical.[1] Indeed, he wished nothing more but to be a lyric poet (*ghazal-sarā*).[2] Therefore, in order to sort through his actual reflections and thoughts on this subject in the rich treasury of his verse, we must need to selectively consider his thoughts and place them in their proper context.

While I am not a specialist in Sufism, I have had a special attachment to classical Persian literature for a long time, and, in truth, how can anyone avoid encountering Sufism in Persian literature? Furthermore, is it not the case that one encounters the *Dīvān* of Ḥāfiẓ at a supreme summit of literature, where the high spirituality of the Persians expressed itself in a lyric poetry that had attained its fullest maturity?

Accordingly, I translated and commented on the whole of Ḥāfiẓ's *Dīvān* in order to be better able to relish this masterpiece.[3] What presumption – alas (*gustakhī kardam*)! To better appreciate the text of the *Dīvān*, in the following chapter I have endeavoured to situate this monument of literature within its own century, which was the fourteenth century of the Christian era corresponding to the eighth century of Hegira. This was a grand century, between the rule of the Mongols and Timurids, an epoch of great circulation of thought, in a world with multiple centres.

The School of Sufism in Eighth-/Fourteenth-Century Shīrāz

This century saw the establishment of the great Sufi orders, with Sufism taking its place among the eminent sciences of the time. It was during this century that an immense canon of Persian literature developed, as Dhabīḥu'llāh Ṣafā has demonstrated in his survey.[4] Diversified within well-defined genres, this literature was often designed for instruction. At the same time, by the compilation of manuals, some of which continued to be taught until recently, the doctrines of the Ash'arite school imposed itself among the theologians and mystics of the period.

For their part, abundant commentaries on the works of Muḥyī al-Dīn Ibn 'Arabī (d. 638/1240) also exerted an important influence. Shi'ite thought, too, was affirmed in this century, with masters such as Sayyid Ḥaydar Āmulī (782/1380). This too was the century of the *Sarbedars*, of the occult speculations of *Ḥurūfism*, of the revival of the Ḥanbalite school of theology, and it was also the era during which the founder of the Sufi order, to which the later Safavids adhered, also flourished. Additionally, it should be underlined that the spiritual and literary traditions of the Persian world had continued to persist in full force long after its Sufi founders – in particular Aḥmad Ghazālī (d. 520/1126) and 'Ayn al-Quḍāt Hamadhānī (d. 525/1131) – had passed away.

Space does not permit me here to dwell with any detail on the dozen most brilliant poets of the eighth/fourteenth century. But I do need to mention a few. Khwājū Kirmānī was born in Kerman in 689/1290 at the same time that Sa'dī was dying in Shīrāz. Khwājū died in 753/1352, long before the death of the men who best illustrate Persian *belles lettres* in that century. These include the likes of Ibn Yamīn Fariyūmadī, who died in 769/1368, and 'Ubayd-i Zākānī, who passed away in 772/1371, which was just before the death of 'Imād al-Dīn Faqīh Kirmānī in 773/1372. Salmān Sāvajī died a few years later in 778/1376, followed by Kamāl Khujandī in 803/1400. Between the latter two, Ḥāfiẓ died around 792/1390. Maghribī passed away in 810/1408 and Shāh Ni'matu'llāh Valī died in 834/1431.

Here, it will be directly relevant to the concern of this study if we focus on one of these poets, 'Imād Faqīh Kirmānī. Despite the geographical distance between Kirmān and Yazd, and between Shīrāz and Tabrīz or Baghdād, it is hard to imagine that 'Imād was unknown to his contemporaries, or that he would have been ignorant of them. 'Imād Faqīh possessed the most stable social position amongst all these poets. In his native Kirmān, he was protected by the princes of his time and occupied the highest position in the local religious hierarchy. Grand Master of a Sufi *Khānaqāh* in Kirmān, a position he had inherited from his father, he was also a Doctor of Law (*faqīh*), well-versed in jurisprudence. Besides holding these ranks, he was also the chief *Qāḍī* (judge) of his city, which conferred to him special influence, and in his youth Shāh Shujā' Muẓaffarī (reg. 759/1358–786/1384) had him as a tutor. Shāh Shujā' venerated 'Imād thereafter, and visited him almost every year. Shujā''s father, Mubāriz al-Dīn Muḥammad Muẓaffarī (reg. 754/1353–759/1357), the founder of the Muẓaffarīd dynasty, also had great esteem for him and tried to foster his religious and charitable undertakings in every way. In return, 'Imād Faqīh reciprocated his gratitude and voiced his high esteem of him – and this was during the very years when Ḥāfiẓ was satirizing and parodying Mubāriz al-Dīn as a strict *Censor morum* and Officer of the Vice-squad (*muḥtasib*) in Shīrāz.

Unlike Ḥāfiẓ, 'Imād Faqīh Kirmānī spoke clearly about the events that had an impact on his personal life. He also dated his writings and has left accounts of people with whom he dealt. Hence, by examining the dates he has given, one can follow the progression of his work and trace the gradual development of his thought as a poet, religious judge (*Qāḍī*) and Sufi shaykh. His entire oeuvre consists of poetry composed in the pure Persian tradition, featuring all the literary genres current during his age. Apart from a rich *Dīvān* composed over the course of his life, five *mathnawī* poems from him are also extant. The first of these is a debate (*munāẓira*) between various lovers and beloveds. The second is a treatise on good manners and proper conduct (*adab*), addressed to ten people with well-defined characters. In 756/1355, he wrote a treatise in *mathnawī* verse on Sufism called the 'Book of the Way' (*Ṭarīqat-nāma*), with a preface dedicated affectionately to Prince Mubāriz al-Dīn, who had been ruler of Shīrāz since 754/1353. The poem constitutes a sort of manifesto of the sacred alliance between piety and political power. 'Imād's fourth *mathnawī* is a bit of a mixture, compounded of seven poems of desolation, some lengthy counsel addressed to the prince, the story of the foundation of a Sufi meeting house (*khānaqāh*) in Kirmān, ranged alongside the poet's own dreams and visions. A fifth poem contains ten letters, modelled on the epistolary genre. In such works one can admire once again 'Imād Faqīh's poetic finesse, his sensitivity, his strength of soul, as well as his attention to the realities of life in Kirmān and the very personal way in which he incarnated the continuity of the grand tradition of classical Persian poetry.

As stated above, 'Imād's Book of the Way (*Ṭarīqat-nāma*) was a treatise on Sufism in the form of a poem. Written to instruct disciples, chapter by chapter it summarizes in a beautiful manner the *Miṣbāḥ al-hidāyat*, or 'The Lamp of the Guidance', which 'Izz al-Dīn Maḥmūd Kāshānī (d. 735/1334) had composed in Natanz. This great book of Persian prose was the fruit of immense knowledge in which Kāshānī aspired to encompass and express all the Islamic lore on Sufism of his time to the highest degree of perfection. It was also influenced by the famous ode (*Qaṣīda*) on the ecstasy of love by Ibn al-Fāriḍ (d. 633/1235), and modelled after the *'Awārif al-ma'ārif*, the most celebrated and exhaustive manual of Sufi discipline, doctrine and practice ever composed. The latter work, completed some time before 612/1215, was penned by the supreme founder of the Suhrawardī Sufi Order – Shihāb al-Dīn Abū Ḥafṣ 'Umar Suhrawardī (d. 632/1234).

Underlying this transmission of Sufi knowledge by books and teaching, we can also see the transmission of the living practice of the Sufis from master to disciple. One may clearly discern a direct line that connects the supreme master 'Umar Suhrawardī to one of his disciples, Najīb al-Dīn 'Alī (son of Najīb al-Dīn Buzghūsh, d. 678/1279, an eminent Shīrāzi Sufi master), who founded a Sufi order, and transmitted his knowledge down to his son and disciple Ẓāhir al-Dīn, as well as on to another disciple, Nūr al-Dīn Iṣfahānī. The latter in turn had important disciples, such as the above-mentioned Maḥmūd Kāshānī, as well as the celebrated 'Abd al-Razzāq Kāshānī (d. 730/1329). Our 'Imād Faqīh Kirmānī traced his initiatic affiliation to 'Umar Suhrawardī through his father, himself a disciple of a certain Zayn al-Dīn Kāmū'ī, who was a disciple of Suhrawardī, but who had also founded his own Sufi order (*ṭarīqa*). It is interesting to note that 'Imād advised his own disciples to read several pages from 'Umar Suhrawardī's *'Awārif al-ma'ārif* 'every morning',[5] and also recommended they regularly study Muḥammad Ghazālī's monumental *Revivification of the Sciences of Religion* (*Iḥyā' 'ulūm al-dīn*).

Herẹ, then, is a rough sketch of the Sufi world in which Ḥāfiẓ had to situate himself – a real world, where the influence of Sufism was the dominant factor, in Shīrāz as well as in Kirmān, in which 'Imād Faqīh Kirmānī occupied a position that can hardly be underestimated. Already well-known as poet when Mubāriz al-Dīn was still only a governor in the service of the last Mongol emperor Abū Sa'īd (reg. 717/1317–736/1335), 'Imād was attached to the last of the princes of the Īnjūid dynasty and to the most celebrated of the Muẓaffarids. While he had a spiritual and moral influence on these princes and their aristocratic circles, he also acted as a protector of the poor and downtrodden against the interests of 'the powerful and the rich'.[6] Just as much as he was a panegyrist who composed much adulatory verse for those in power, he also acted as a Sufi shaykh to several generations of faithful disciples in his monastery (*khānaqāh*) in Kirmān. He was a profoundly religious personality whose faith is evident from numerous exquisite supplications (*munājāt*) and lovely prayers imbued with sincerity. In summary, the person and the life of 'Imād Faqīh Kirmānī bring to mind the great model of collegial Sufism, Shaykh Shihāb al-Dīn Abū Ḥafṣ 'Umar Suhrawardī (539/1144–632/1234), who inhabited the highest echelon of Baghdad society, where he was politically attached to the Abbasid Caliph Al-Nāṣir Bi'llāh (575/1180–622/1225), as is well-known.

Before dealing with Ḥāfiẓ's views on Sufism, one must ask how the masters of intellectual thought in that age classified human beings. From studying their works, we are led to understand that they did so in proportion to their respective degrees of perfection. Thus, in his *Ṭarīqat-nāma*,[7] condensing for his disciples what 'Izz al-Dīn Kāshānī had elaborated in his *Miṣbāḥ al-hidāyat*,[8] which in turn had been extracted from the *'Awārif* of 'Umar Suhrawardī, 'Imād Faqīh Kirmānī explained that human beings (*mardum*) can be subdivided into three levels. On the first level are those perfect human beings, who have already arrived at the divine goal ordained by God. On the second level are those who walk on the road to perfection. The lowest level is called 'the terrain of insufficiency', which is inhabited by inferior types of human beings. The perfect human beings who are favoured by God are recipients of primordial divine grace: 'Such wayfarers are the just, companions of the Right. Those who tarry on the way are rebels, companions of the Left Hand.'[9]

Those who have arrived at the end of the Way (*wāṣilān*) are of three groups. First and foremost of them are the Prophets, who God sends back amongst humankind after they attain perfection so as to guide those who are still imperfect. Next come the Sufi masters (*mashāyikh-i ṣūfiyya*), who 'have attained the station of divine union [*wuṣūl*] by means of their perfect obedience and following of the Prophet. Afterwards, they have been authorized and commissioned to come back amongst men in order to bid them to follow the Path of the Prophet.' This second group, states Kāshānī,

> are perfect men who are capable of bringing others to perfection [*kāmilān-i mukammal*]. This is because by eternal Providence's overflowing grace, after having been immersed in the source of union [*'ayn al-jam'*] and drowned in the

abyss of divine Unity, they have been brought forth from the belly of the whale of Annihilation and cast upon the shores of Separation [*tafriqa*] where they are granted godly subsistence and vouchsafed salvation in order to guide men to salvation and to higher degrees [of perfection].[10]

Finally come those who, having reached the stage of perfection, have immersed themselves in the ocean of Union and have refused the task of perfecting other human beings.

Those that fare the Sufi way (*ahl-i sulūk*), however, are of two kinds. The first are those who exclusively long to contemplate the divine visage and pursue the highest degree, which is the Face of God (*wajh Allāh*). The second are seekers of paradise who are desirous of rewards in the realm hereafter.

The former in turn are divided into two categories: Sufic mystics (*mutaṣawwifa*) and those who incur blame (*malāmatiyya*). The *mutaṣawwifa* have acquired certain qualities of the Sufis, yet they 'still remain enmeshed in certain attributes of their carnal souls'.[11] The *malāmatiyya*, for their part, form a completely different category from the Sufis. Lengthy expositions have been consecrated by doctrinarians of Sufism over the centuries in an effort to categorize these blame-seekers, as can be seen from the *'Awārif* of Suhrawardī and the works of his descendants – indeed, as is visible in Sufi texts composed long before him. Space does not permit us to dwell on this august company here. Admired for their virtues of total devotion (*ikhlāṣ*) and perfect sincerity (*ṣidq*), they are nonetheless placed in a lower rank than the Sufis, for they still look at themselves, making an effort to hide their virtue, while the Sufi has freed himself definitely from any attention to and concern for himself. Whereas 'the partisans of self-blame' (*malāmatiyya*) are characterized as being 'totally devoted' (*mukhliṣān*), the Sufis 'are pure and emancipated from all taint and alloy' (*mukhlaṣān*).[12] We know that Ibn al-'Arabī 'places the Sufis in an intermediary category, above the ascetics [*zuhhād*] to be sure, but below the Blameworthy [*malāmiyya*], who are also called the Realizers [*muḥakkikūn*]'.[13] According to 'Izz al-Dīn, human beings who naught but seek the life of the next world are divided up, with regard to their respective pursuit of perfection, between the ascetics (*zuhhād*), the spiritually poor (*fuqarā'*), the servants (*khuddām*) and the devotees (*'ubbād*), categories that he endeavours to define.[14] But this is not the place to elaborate further on this spiritual typology.

These few remarks, however, do serve to underline the fact that the intelligentsia in the society of Shīrāz, Kirmān and other provincial capitals had a good overall grasp of the doctrinal framework of Sufism. This framework, with its particular mode of thinking, espoused the existence of a definite hierarchy of human beings, along with the notion of their respective degrees of religious perfection and, therefore, of various ranks of moral perfection, and, finally, of their life within society.

Ḥāfiẓ and the Sufi

suḥbat-i 'āfiyatat gar chih khwūs uftād ay dil
jānib-i 'ishq 'azīz ast, furū magdhārash.

Although consorting with what's safe and sound
Seems, dear heart, to be a joy and a delight,
Love too has much grace and chic and charm,
And her side too must not be forsworn.[15]

Ḥāfiẓ treats the figure of the Sufi harshly. In order for this to be understood, the force of the expressions which he uses against him must be shown. His impatience was the result of his exacting and rigorous demands, for it offended him to the core that a Sufi should use craftiness and deception whilst pursuing the way to perfection. On the contrary, Ḥāfiẓ knew all too well how to expound to a sincere Sufi exactly what this exacting spiritual ideal of perfection entailed. Amongst the Sufis with whom he was acquainted, the very notion of perfection seemed to have become utterly devalued, and hence his lament:

It's quite fit if waves of blood froth forth
From the ruby's heart by this fraud
And deceit – through which a broken shard
Had made the ruby's market crash.[16]

There are 12 different instances in his *Dīvān* where Ḥāfiẓ cites the technical term Perfection (*kamāl*). In ten of these, Perfection is attributed to the person he loves – that is, to her justice, the games she plays with her eyes and, above all, her beauty. In the other two instances, he employs the notion of Perfection vis-à-vis himself. In one verse, he describes himself as being in a state of 'perfect' bewilderment (*ḥayrat*) in which he is in union with his Beloved.[17] In another, he states that 'despite my perfect love for you, I live in utter deficiency just like a candle [*bā kamāl-i 'ishq-i tu dar 'ayn-i nuqṣānam chū sham'*]',[18] referring here to the idea that his own love, however complete, is still like a candle – snuffed out before the radiance of the Beloved's sun. Elsewhere, he expresses the same idea slightly differently, declaring that 'nothingness is the final end of every perfect thing that is' (*kay nīstī'st sar-anjām har kamāl kay hast*).[19]

The portrait that Ḥāfiẓ paints of the Sufis is quite a sombre one. He admits that he would have had far more tales to tell of them had not his master bid him to hold his tongue.[20] In outer appearance they seem to be simple spiritual mendicants, but in reality their grasping hands betray what they have up their sleeves.[21] They remind one, he says, of the piety of the cat: once its prayers and orisons are over, it is always ready to devour the partridge within its grasp.[22] Even the greatest among them, 'the royal falcons of the Spiritual Path', as he calls them, lack all stature and dignity, having contented themselves to assume the rank of flies.[23] Standing at their head is a man who surpasses them all as a votary of the Antichrist and a kind of atheist – a cipher for Tamerlane.[24]

The false piety of the Sufi is his first and foremost defect. On the one hand, one may find him suddenly transported in the throes of mystic rapture, uttering paradoxes and giving voice to words beyond the scope of ordinary reason – but these turn out to be nothing but nonsensical drivel.[25] If ecstasy moves him to dance, it is only a sleight of hand; it would seem as if by his trickery he aspires to outwit the conjuring heavens themselves.[26]

The second defect of the Sufi concerns his penchant for wine. Indeed, while he does drink 'wine' and imbibe from a 'cup', he is utterly ignorant of the spiritual purport of such terms. While at dawn he may receive some rapture and intoxication from the recitation of his litanies – just look at the way he ends up drunk in the evening![27] While the Sufi sips from the beaker, Ḥāfiẓ guards himself from the carboy.[28]

The third defect of the Sufi – and the most subtly hidden – is his failure to comprehend the suffering of love (*dard*).[29] Suffering love-passion is the sure mark of spiritual authenticity. A century before Ḥāfiẓ, Sa'dī had opened his chapter on love, in his *Būstān*, by treating this same subject.[30] Ḥāfiẓ, for his part, never refrained from designating the suffering of such love-passion as a sign indicative of true love. But the Sufi does not show any sign of love at all. In fact, he knows nothing more of love than does the angel. Under the Sufi's cassock (*khirqa*) lies hidden many a stain and fault, and so he advises that one should flee from those who sport such robes.[31] Indeed, such a Sufi is nothing but an 'animal well provided with fodder'.[32]

And yet, despite these strictures, Ḥāfiẓ declares the path of Sufism to be a good one, on one condition, however – that it lead beyond itself. As a way composed of rules, the Sufi Path should lead to where no rule exists save the Rule of Love. And there, the entire hierarchy of perfection is abolished.

Ḥāfiẓ indeed claimed for himself the title of Sufi. He belonged to the Sufis, he sighs, but 'has become infamous among them'.[33] And since he recognized that his Sufi cloak merely served to conceal his blemishes and faults, acting as a girdle for his hidden heresy (*zunnār*), to strip himself of it alone shall not do.[34] He decides therefore to take the further step of changing his status, setting aside 'the years of honour and repute enjoyed by illustrious ancestors', exchanging these for 'a cup of wine and the cup-bearer with a moonlike face'.[35] And yet, is this really a matter of his own free choice? On the contrary, he admits that 'it was the Sufi who took me to the Tavern [*maykada*] by means of the Way of Love [*ṭarīq-i 'ishq*]'.[36] So it was, in fact, *Sufism* that enabled Ḥāfiẓ to go beyond and to enter that higher Path of inspired libertinism (*rindī*):

> From the hierocosmic heaven I've come – a Sufi who's doomed
> To dwell down here in the temple with the Magians.[37]

In this lower realm where the Master of the Tavern also dwells, Ḥāfiẓ has become Love's 'libertine', liberated from all laws and solely driven by the force of love, thus realizing a spiritual state beyond even that of the high-ranking Sufi. At this juncture, he turns to the Sufi, and remarks:

> The cup's a mirror, in which, crystal-clear
> you may gaze, oh Sufi, and see therein
> The glow and sheen of the ruby wine.[38]

As he gazes at the glow glimmering off the sparkling surface of the wine, a hidden mystery is revealed to the Sufi, which is the jewel buried deep within each man.[39] Formerly, the Sufi used to shatter and smash his cup and wine-glass. Now, having imbibed the first draught of this wine, he has become initiated into the sapiential lore of *Eros* – Love's knowledge.[40]

Up until that point, a kind of fake virtue – phony sobriety and smug self-consciousness (*hushyārī*) – had prevented the Sufi from progressing. The Sufi was concerned about purity, but in fact, only love, which is 'the secret of his inebriation',[41] found when the lover has lost all care for and sense of self, is pure. Thus the poet invites his reader to 'Come see the purity of the ruby wine!'[42] Just as Sufi sets forth for his pious oratory of prayer (*ṣūma'a*) in pursuit of purity of self (*ṣafā*), Ḥāfiẓ makes his way to the Tavern in utter sincerity (*ṣidq*).[43]

If the ascetics can't understand anything about the secrets of inebriation, there are Sufis who are prepared to enter into this mystery. Though decked out in tattered robes and multi-coloured cloaks, they seek to relish the taste of the divine presence, yet crave knowledge of esoteric mysteries from those who are themselves benighted.[44] The Sufi who discovers the door of the Tavern at once renounces his backward asceticism,[45] and once having burned up his Sufi frock (*khirqa*) becomes converted into a sage mystic wayfarer (*'ārif-i sālik*).[46]

A Language of Mystery

Ḥāfiẓ, like so many poets before him, found an incomparably rich gamut of expressions in the metaphors of the cup, wine and drunkenness. In lyric poetry, wine offers a simple register whereby the bare outer purport of the metaphor relating to the meaning of prohibition and transgression can be transcended, and ecstasy and erotic union entered into. In terms of spirituality, however, this metaphor alludes to something experienced as a reality that is not only impossible to name and define, but also, paradoxically, something unthinkable rationally.

In the particular literary milieu in which Ḥāfiẓ lived, it had been well understood – ever since a generation earlier, when in 717/1317 Maḥmūd Shabistarī had composed his famous *Garden of Mystery* (*Gulshan-i rāz*) – how profane poetic imagery could be used to vividly convey ideas of a spiritual order. In this manner, court poetry and mystical poetry were united together. This is precisely what one finds in Ḥāfiẓ's *Dīvān*. In the fifteenth century AD, the grand commentator on Shabistarī's poem, Shams al-Dīn Muḥammad Lāhījī, in his *Mafātīḥ al-i'jāz fī sharḥ-i Gulshan-i rāz* (written c. 877/1472), showed just what was at stake. Thus, commenting on two couplets of the *Gulshan-i rāz*, he appealed to the important notion – of Akbarian inspiration – of the innermost mystery of theophany (*sirr al-tajalliyyāt*).[47] According to masters such as Shabistarī and Lāhījī, the mystical seer and knower (*'ārif*) could comprehend the totality of spiritual realities manifested within each particular reality of creation. Seen from this perspective, the entire world in its totality was viewed as a mirror in which God had reflected various facets of His divine Names in their totality. Each atom of creation was thus understood to be but another form and facet of the infinite number of the divine Names. Put another way, each Name refers to the totality of divine Names, all of which are collected and combined within God's Unicity. And that is what is meant by 'the innermost mystery of theophany'. In this fashion, a beautiful human face, along with each of its component features (eye, eyebrow, lip, etc.), as well as the cup, wine and drunkenness – each refers, in its own different way, to transcendent spiritual realities of which it is merely the outward form. The Cup is thus a mirror wherein the reflection of the Cup-bearer shines when He pours the pure Wine that inebriates the drinker and fills him with love if he be a true lover. The condition of this transfiguration had been expressed in Persian verse for a long time, and was well described by Sa'dī, for instance, in his *Būstān*, where he states: 'You shall never enter into yourself as long as you are with yourself, and yet no one knows this except by being outside oneself.'[48]

Such is the 'mystery of theophany', wherein the ineffable and paradoxical realities of the world of love are revealed to the intoxicated, who have been transported outside their personal 'selves'. Everything began at that primordial moment of the Eternal Covenant (see Qur'ān, 7:172), to which both Shabistarī[49] and Ḥāfiẓ[50] in their poetry refer. To express what can be understood of this mystery or secret, Ḥāfiẓ employs no other word but the Arabic *sirr*, or its Persian equivalent *rāz*. This term refers to the knowledge of a reality that can be communicated only by the 'keeper' of this secret, who is then at liberty to reveal it – or not – to one or another of its confidants. This 'mystery' relates to a reality beyond the bounds of normal sensory perception that is then 'translated' by the perceiving subject into what can only be an approximate language expressible in paradoxical terms, or voiced poetically through a language of analogy. Such a 'mystery' can be a 'secret' for the one who perceives it. At any rate it is kept a secret, revealed only to the initiates of the world of experience to which it belongs, or to one who has prepared himself for such an initiation.

In a study which is in every sense remarkable, 'Alī Sharī'at Kāshānī has recently demonstrated that in Persian mystical literature 'the term "secret" designates the heart or the soul's interior foundation. It is considered to be an infinitely subtle entity [*laṭīfa*], situated in the heart of the mystic as a kind of divine "deposit" [*vadī'a*].'[51] Such a heart is 'contemplative', and its 'secret' comprises the innermost chamber of the heart, which is a mystery, the reality of which can be directly *experienced*, but not *comprehended.*[52] Within his heart, then, lies the supreme secret – 'the secret of the secret' – which the gnostic himself cannot perceive, being known only to the 'Unique One'.[53] In Ḥāfiẓ, one comes across a different term which no doubt indicates the same reality – he speaks, for instance, of the existence of the 'gem [*gawhar*] of the secrets of beauty and love' in his heart,[54] or elsewhere describes the 'jewel' in his possession, stating he is in search of someone worthy of viewing and understanding it.[55] His very first interpreter, Shujā-yi Shīrāzī, was by no means mistaken: the chapter of his book entitled 'The Convivial Comrade',[56] written in 1426/830, which he devoted to 'eye-games' (*naẓar-bāzī*), was composed with Ḥāfiẓ's monument still in mind. In this work he explains that 'there exists in man a simple divine substance [*jawharī basīṭ ilāhī*]' integral to his being, and which constitutes 'a kind of power which other creatures do not possess'.[57] Ḥāfiẓ once confessed that:

> I don't know who the troubled being is who stamps
> About in my overworked heart. I am quiet and silent,
> And that person is always complaining and crying out.[58]

'That person', the 'he' (ū) referred to above, is so often the Nameless One, somebody (*fulānī*) in his verse. It seems to me that Ḥāfiẓ's use of the words *sirr* and *rāz* (secret and mystery) is different from what was transmitted by the tradition before him. This is what I will try to demonstrate.

Ḥāfiẓ was both a lyric poet and a man of high spirituality. As we know, he rejected all resort to expressions of paradox and nonsensical mystic transport (*shaṭḥ va ṭāmāt*),[59] which seemed to him to be only bombastic, grandiose and senseless utterances.[60] On the other hand, 'there is no pen with a tongue capable of expressing the mystery of love', he says.[61] Powerful inner and ineffable states of consciousness can solely be conveyed by means of musical instruments. Such states can only be expressed inwardly by instruments such as the harp or *rebab*, while the tambourine and the flute furnish them with an appropriate outward public expression.[62] As for the poet himself, just as one should 'Go to the garden to learn from the nightingale the secrets of love', so one must 'come to the banquet to gain from Ḥāfiẓ the art of the *ghazal*'.[63] Indeed, the flame of the candle speaks eloquently about the 'secret' of this subject, whereas the butterfly or moth – a symbol for the poet himself – 'is incapable of speaking about it'.[64] Holding in his deep heart the secret mystery of love, Ḥāfiẓ understood the paradox of wishing to hide it from everyone and yet seeking a confidant to whom he might reveal it. His poetry thus lies somewhere between verbal concealment and revelation. As he says: 'Last night with my own ears I heard from his lips such words as one should not ask.'[65]

The Cup, Wine and Drunkenness

Since the Cup of Wine (i.e., terms such as *jām* and its synonyms) symbolize the inverted dome of Heaven or the overturned celestial bowl of the firmament, it also ultimately alludes to the world of mystery concealed beneath the veil of heaven. The Cup is thus the mirror of heaven and what is inscribed thereupon. Yet it is something even more – for the world of heavenly mystery has left its trace in the mirror of the Cup.[66] For one who gazes within the Cup, it is thus possible to contemplate this mystery as well, to decipher the lines traced therein like it were a sort of spiritual astrolabe. Jamshīd, the Initiator of Kings, was the first to contemplate the mysteries of the heavenly world reflected in the Cup, or, to put it more precisely, he was the first to see the Cup itself divulging the mystery of the *mundus invisibilis* to him.[67] This is the condition of being intimate with, or a 'confidant' of the Cup. The Cup of wine thus initiates one into the mystery of 'both the worlds' (this world and the hereafter, earth and heaven) by grace of that ray of light, whose reflection it catches and which it then reflects back again.[68] Through the intoxication bestowed by its wine, the Cup also grants one access to the secret of the world marked out in the stars.[69] In fact, the mystery of each and every thing constitutes its very *raison d'être.*[70] The underlying cause behind creation of the world had been articulated at the very origin of all humanity, but to give voice to it again one must 'drink two cups'[71] – that is to say, redouble the intoxication to perform an act of anamnesis. The Cup also initiates one into the secret of Time, which may be disagreeable to man,[72] and yet the initiation into this secret is by grace of that pure wine that one quaffs from the Cup.[73]

Gnostic Cognition

By providing an initiation into the mysteries of heaven and earth, the Cup also initiates one into their primordial *raison d'être.* That primordial cause had been revealed in its entirety for the first time at the origin of the world, when the Beloved's beauty flashed forth in a ray of theophany, which in turn provoked the apparition of love.[74] In this primordial pact of fidelity, humanity's love for the Beloved had been signed and sealed.[75] Insofar as one apprehends it as it actually is, the Cup therefore simply serves to perpetuate what had always existed from the very beginning. We find ourselves here in another order of reality, for which the common Cup, Wine and Intoxication are but poor representations or figures of speech. Books cannot provide access to this kind of knowledge; reason here is but a pretentious impostor.[76] In truth, 'no one knows the mysteries of the invisible world'.[77] But the motes of dust dancing in the dazzling light of the Beloved's beauty reflected in the mirror of the real Cup may give access to this knowledge. That very Cup–mirror is the heart of man. The sorrows of love have the task of purifying the heart – which is the Cup and the mirror – for only through experiencing that grief and sorrow can the heart be cleansed of all regard and concern for the self. That purification causes the wine within the heart's Cup-mirror – the wine that is also the 'love' that the heart is enamoured of – to become pure and strained clear.[78] It is this wine that intoxicates the heart, which puts it in a state commensurate to its real nature. The nature of the heart is to be a mirror, to contemplate the mysteries which it reflects and which, in turn, it reflects back to their original author – its Beloved. For Beloved wished to contemplate Himself within an infinite variety of mirrors.

But who is really an initiate? 'Where', he asks – since it is impossible to discourse about these mysteries – 'is an adept in the mysteries?'[79] The 'secret of solitude' (*rāz-i khalwat*) experienced by one who is intimate with the Beloved, fire alone reveals. The candle here is the model: silent, it illuminates by its flame the assembly.[80] Similarly, the fiery conflagration caused by the poet–lover's words reveals well enough 'the burning condition of his heart'.[81] Besides, his visage itself bears testimony to the mark of love and is sufficient to betray him.[82] Above all, his tears reveal his experience of love's grief.[83] By concealing his secret he knows that he is working towards salvation,[84] and yet, already having lost his heart, the secret shall in the end come out![85] What is ultimately revealed by the 'secret' on which the poet stakes his life becomes exposed through his own conduct; that is to say, Ḥāfiẓ's combat with the hypocrisy of the fake Sufi. When his adversary, a meddling busybody, reproaches him for being a libertine lover, Ḥāfiẓ in turn accuses him of 'acting in opposition to the mysteries of the *mundus invisibilis*'.[86]

And yet it is well known that there is nothing more conducive to speech than conversing about secrets, so Ḥāfiẓ entreats God to give him a confidant with whom he may share his thoughts.[87] However, since that confidant after whom he hankers is always one who is supremely absent – the Beloved[88] – he ends up becoming his own personal confidant.[89] In fact, Ḥāfiẓ acknowledges himself to possess no true confidant save the wind,[90] for a human confidant for his secret does not actually exist.[91] In love's sanctuary, one cannot express oneself through conversation[92] since '*There* all the organs of one's body must be transformed into eyes and ears',[93] which is what he refers to as the 'ear of the heart' (*gūsh-i dil*).[94] Nonetheless, a kind of community in which spiritual exchanges and conversation (*ṣuḥbat*) could take place did exist for Ḥāfiẓ. This community consisted of those intimately familiar with the realities of the heart, who were the heart's adepts (*ahl-i dil*) and 'votaries of wine'.[95] Among this community of lovers a Cup was passed round, each handing it to his fellow in the turn of their circle, their bouts forming an endless round of drinks.[96] These lovers are the wise mystical wayfarers, and it is they alone, along with the Vintner or Wineseller, who have cognizance of the secret.[97]

Amongst this community, at a certain point in his life, Ḥāfiẓ testified to his own experience that he was 'a guardian of my own secret and cognizant of my own moment of mystical consciousness [*Ḥāfiẓ-i rāz-i khʷud u 'ārif-i vaqt-i khʷīsham*]'.[98] We must therefore assess the importance that he himself attached to his own literary monument: this short *Dīvān* of some 500 poems that took him some 50 years to compose:

Each verse that Ḥāfiẓ pens is a masterpiece
of gnostic lore and sapience.
Let's praise his fetching turn of phrase
and his stunning power of speech.[99]

Aware that evidence existed that there was within himself a certain 'substance' (*gawharī*) - a 'somebody' (*fulānī*) who was in reality more 'himself' than he was himself - Ḥāfiẓ experienced his 'self' as a wandering pilgrim. Standing outside the centre that he sought to attain, he spins upon himself in a circle like a compass.[100] Passion for the Beloved causes him to twirl in a dance like a mote of dust as he strives to reach the verge of the fountain-head of the dazzlingly bright sun.[101] At this point the swirling revolution of Time comes along, lays hold of and pulls him within that centre, which, as was explained above, is the 'Cup'.[102] Henceforth, talking to us 'from beyond the grave' - within his tomb - Ḥāfiẓ envisages himself as a lover awaiting the Beloved's visitation, and bids us farewell, leaving us with this verse to meditate on:

Should you pass by my shrine when I am gone
Ask for soul-power, spirit-force and *esprit*,
For all the world's pious rakes and holy reprobates
Will be pilgrims to my tomb.[103]

Notes

1 *Dīvān-i Ḥāfiẓ*, ed. Khānlarī, *ghazal* 264: 7.
2 *Ibid.*, *ghazal* 190: 6.
3 *Hafiz de Chiraz: Le Divān: Œuvre lyrique d'un spirituel en Perse au XIVe siècle*, introduction, commentary and translation by Charles-Henri de Fouchécour.
4 Ṣafā, *Tārīkh-i Adabiyāt-i Īrān*, III/1–2, pp. 623–1320.
5 'Imād Faqīh, *Mathnawī-yi Ṣafā-nāma*, 66,16, in 'Imād Faqīh, *Panj ganj*, ed./intro. Humāyūn-Farrukh, CIV–431; see *Ganj-i duvvum, Ṣafā-nāma*, pp. 17–91.
6 See, e.g., his *Suḥbat-nāma* (in *Panj ganj*, pp. 93–148), 124, 7.
7 'Imād Faqīh, *Ṭarīqat-nāma*, ed. Humāyūn-Farrukh, 241pp., section 2, h. 10, pp. 95–100.
8 See Kāshānī, *Miṣbāḥ al-hidāyat*, ed. Humā'ī, 10, section 3, pp. 114–16.
9 *Miṣbāḥ al-ḥidāyat*, p. 114.
10 *Ibid.*, p. 114.
11 *Ibid.*, p. 115.
12 *Ibid.*, p. 116.
13 Chittick, 'Taṣawwuf. 2. Ibn al-'Arabī and after in the Arabic and Persian lands, and beyond', *EI*², X, p. 317.
14 *Miṣbāḥ al-ḥidāyat*, pp. 116ff.
15 *Dīvān-i Ḥāfiẓ*, ed. Khānlarī, *ghazal* 272: 7.
16 *Ibid.*, *ghazal* 272: 3.
17 *Ibid.*, *ghazal* 168: 1.
18 *Ibid.*, *ghazal* 289: 6.
19 *Ibid.*, *ghazal* 20: 6.

20 *Ibid.*, *ghazal* 199: 8.
21 *Ibid.*, *ghazal* 426: 10.
22 *Ibid.*, *ghazal* 129: 8.
23 *Ibid.*, *ghazal* 446: 2.
24 *Ibid.*, *ghazal* 237: 6.
25 *Ibid.*, *ghazal* 366: 1.
26 *Ibid.*, *ghazal* 129: 1–2.
27 *Ibid.*, *ghazal* 155: 2.
28 *Ibid.*, *ghazal* 426: 10. [The English term 'carboy' is taken from the Persian-Arabic word *qarrabā* used by the poet here, referring to a large big-bellied bottle used to store wine or medicinal liquids. Ed./trans.]
29 *Dīvān-i Ḥāfiẓ*, ed. Khānlarī, *ghazal* 379: 6.
30 *Būstān-i Sa'dī*, ed. Yūsufī, III, v. 1904.
31 *Dīvān-i Ḥāfiẓ*, ed. Khānlarī, *ghazal* 379: 1–2.
32 *Ibid.*, *ghazal* 290: 8.
33 *Ibid.*, *ghazal* 107: 11.
34 *Ibid.*, *ghazal* 175: 5.
35 *Ibid.*, *ghazal* 358: 2.
36 *Ibid.*, *ghazal* 405: 4.
37 *Ibid.*, *ghazal* 353: 5.
38 *Ibid.*, *ghazal* 7: 2.
39 *Ibid.*, *ghazal* 49: 1.
40 *Ibid.*, *ghazal* 165: 3.
41 *Ibid.*, *ghazal* 186: 5.
42 *Ibid.*, *ghazal* 7: 1.
43 *Ibid.*, *ghazal* 215: 7.
44 *Ibid.*, *ghazal* 441: 5.
45 *Ibid.*, *ghazal* 255: 8.
46 *Ibid.*, *ghazal* 267: 3.
47 *Mafātīḥ al-i'jāz fī sharḥ-i Gulshan-i rāz*, ed. Khāliqī and Karbāsī, pp. 478–9, vv. 788–9.
48 *Kay tā bā kh^{w}udī dar kh^{w}udat rāh nīst/ vazīn nukta juz bīkh^{w}ud āgāh nīst. Būstān*, ed. Yūsufī, chap. 3, v. 1904, p. 111.
49 *Gulshan-i rāz*, vv. 417–24, in Shabistarī, *Majmū'a-i āthār-i Shaykh Maḥmūd Shabistarī*, ed. Muwaḥḥid, p. 84.
50 *Dīvān-i Ḥāfiẓ*, ed. Khānlarī, *ghazal* 20: 5.
51 'Le Secret et le Paradoxal en literature mystique persan: réflexion sur deux aspects fondamentaux de la mystique irano-islamique', p. 5.
52 *Ibid.*, p. 5.
53 *Ibid.*, p. 13.
54 *Dīvān-i Ḥāfiẓ*, *ghazal* 437: 2.
55 *Ibid.*, *ghazal* 373: 4.
56 Shujā, *Anīs al-nās*, ed. Īraj Afshar, XVI–424pp., facsim.
57 *Ibid.*, p. 151.
58 *Dīvān-i Ḥāfiẓ*, ed. Khānlarī, *ghazal* 26: 3 (trans. Robert Bly and Leonard Lewisohn).
59 *Ibid.*, *ghazal* 366: 1.
60 *Ibid.*, *ghazal* 270: 2.
61 *Ibid.*, *ghazal* 431: 3.
62 *Ibid.*, *ghazals* 239: 3; 247: 6; 270: 2.
63 *Ibid.*, *ghazal* 445: 8.
64 *Ibid.*, *ghazal* 481: 6.
65 *Ibid.*, *ghazal* 265: 4.

[66] *Ibid.*, *ghazal* 468: 5.
[67] *Ibid.*, *ghazal* 269: 4.
[68] *Ibid.*, *ghazal* 479: 2.
[69] *Ibid.*, *ghazal* 348: 6.
[70] An allusion to *ghazal* 264: 3.
[71] *Dīvān-i Ḥāfiẓ*, ed. Khānlarī, *ghazal* 329: 7.
[72] *Ibid.*, *ghazal* 318: 4.
[73] *Ibid.*, *ghazal* 273: 6.
[74] *Ibid.*, *ghazal* 148: 1–2.
[75] *Ibid.*, *ghazal* 20: 5.
[76] *Ibid.*, *ghazal* 148: 4.
[77] *Ibid.*, *ghazal* 114: 8.
[78] *Ibid.*, *ghazal* 7: 1–2.
[79] *Ibid.*, *ghazal* 27: 4.
[80] *Ibid.*, *ghazals* 87: 2; 481: 6.
[81] *Ibid.*, *ghazal* 156: 5.
[82] *Ibid.*, *ghazals* 189: 3; 200: 1.
[83] *Ibid.*, *ghazals* 190: 2; 221: 1; 392: 3.
[84] *Ibid.*, *ghazal* 385: 4.
[85] *Ibid.*, *ghazal* 5: 1.
[86] *Ibid.*, *ghazal* 183: 1.
[87] *Ibid.*, *ghazal* 461: 1.
[88] *Ibid.*, *ghazal* 267: 1.
[89] *Ibid.*, *ghazal* 330: 5.
[90] *Ibid.*, *ghazal* 325: 6.
[91] *Ibid.*, *ghazal* 483: 3.
[92] *Ibid.*, *ghazals* 238: 3; 327: 7.
[93] *Ibid.*, *ghazal* 281: 7.
[94] *Ibid.*, *ghazal* 170: 6.
[95] *Ibid.*, *ghazal* 256: 2.
[96] *Ibid.*, *ghazal* 271: 7.
[97] *Ibid.*, *ghazal* 238: 5.
[98] *Ibid.*, *ghazal* 333: 7.
[99] *Ibid.*, *ghazal* 275: 9.
[100] *Ibid.*, *ghazal* 223: 5.
[101] *Ibid.*, *ghazal* 351: 7.
[102] *Ibid.*, *ghazal* 87: 5–6.
[103] *Ibid.*, *ghazal* 201: 3.

The Religion of Love and the Puritans of Islam: Sufi Sources of Ḥāfiẓ's Anti-clericalism

Leonard Lewisohn

Mise-en-scène

There exists a strong tradition of parody and satire of religious dignitaries among the Persian poets that can be traced back to the early Seljuk period,[1] which makes it possible to speak of *anti-clericalism* in Islam as simultaneously a social phenomenon, literary topos and spiritual attitude. Although caricature and castigation of figures belonging to both the esoteric Sufi and exoteric clerical hierarchy appear among nearly all classical Persian poets – Sanā'ī, 'Aṭṭār, Nizārī Quhistānī and 'Ubayd Zakānī in particular – Ḥāfiẓ's *Dīvān* is unique in being almost entirely anti-clerical in composition.[2] In fact, one may say that his poems are as virulently anti-clerical as the communist poetry of Vladimir Mayakowsky and Nazim Hikmat in early twentieth-century Russia and Turkey are rabidly anti-capitalist. Yet Ḥāfiẓ's anti-clericalism comprises not simply socio-political criticism with a religious veneer. It represents his own original, hypersophisticated psychological re-evaluation of religious ideas and values, the literary and religious sources of which are directly derived from Sufi ethical and metaphysical doctrines, as well as teachings taken from the Qur'ān and *ḥadīth*, not to mention several other sources. Below, my focus of concern will be on the Sufi and other spiritual sources of his anti-clerical poetics, and in particular two characters in his lexicon: the sanctimonious Muslim pharisee or puritan ascetic (*zāhid*); and his nemesis: the Inspired Libertine (*rind*).[3]

The Graceless Zealot and the Creed of Love

> For Modes of Faith, let graceless zealots fight;
> His can't be wrong whose life is in the right.
>
> Alexander Pope[4]

Without exception, all members of the Muslim 'clergy'[5] of Ḥāfiẓ's day evoke his scorn and satire. The stock characters in the poet's anti-clerical lexicon include the

Preacher (*wā'iẓ*), Sufi Shaykh (*shaykh*), Judge (*qāḍī*) and the Lawyer or Jurist (*faqīh*). But the most reviled and villainous personality, the nightmare obsession of the whole of Ḥāfiẓ's *Dīvān*, is the Ascetic (*zāhid*), who exemplifies the Muslim Pharisee *par excellence*. The *zāhid* in England and New England from the sixteenth century down to the early eighteenth century was called a 'Puritan', 'Precisian' or 'Formalist', and in popular parlance today the newspapers normally dub him an 'extremist' or 'religious fundamentalist'.[6] Ḥāfiẓ refers altogether 36 times in his *Dīvān* to this Puritan *zāhid*. In each instance his tone of one of parody or sarcasm, voicing reproach, contempt, disdain or scorn.[7] At the same time, his strictures against asceticism and the ascetic philistine mentality are not waves lapping at the shores of hedonism. On the contrary, an ascetic eschewing of worldly materialism permeates Ḥāfiẓ's poetry. Ascetic renunciation (*zuhd*) as a spiritual ideal still held its place in his thought, as it did among Sufi poets whom he often emulated.[8]

Ḥāfiẓ's criticism of asceticism is directed at the lifeless formalism and the desiccated loveless piety of its heartless 'Muslim' practitioners. Exactly like the ideologically committed clerics of Saudi Arabia or the hardline ayatollahs devoted to the mint, anise and cummin (Matthew 23:23) of the *sharī'a*-oriented religion of the Islamic Republic of Iran, Ḥāfiẓ's Pharisee-ascetic, being insensible to *Eros*, professes a philistine ignorance of the paradoxes of erotic spirituality and the passions of apophatic theology. The ascetics' loveless nature had been a proverbial theme in Persian poetry from the time of Sanā'ī (d. 525/1131) at least,[9] but Ḥāfiẓ's antinomian verse seems single-mindedly dedicated to exposing the lack of practice of these puritans (whether they be the *shaykh*, *zāhid*, *faqīh*, *qāḍī* or *wā'iẓ*); indeed, their lack of knowledge of *Amor*. In one place, Ḥāfiẓ taunts the ascetic:

> Puritan! If once our witness of divine beauty in earthly
> Form[10] display herself to you, you'd never yearn again
> For anything else but for wine and women.[11]

Elsewhere, he stigmatizes his prudishness:

> The sign of the man of God is being a lover.
> Keep this secret to yourself – since I see no such sign
> In any of these shaykhs in this town![12]

Benighted in matters erotic, in his gravity the ascetic takes pride. The narrow-minded and vain nature of Ḥāfiẓ's pretentious puritan bears comparison with Angelo, the over-strict deputy of the state in Shakespeare's *Measure for Measure*, the character of which is described as being 'like a good thing being often read, grown sere and tedious'.[13] A century later in English literature we again encounter this same archetypal *zāhid*, in the characters of Formalist and Hypocrisy in *Pilgrim's Progress* by John Bunyan (1628–88). These two 'gentlemen', who were 'born in the land of Vain-glory', are reproached by Christian (hero of Bunyan's allegory) for proceeding without God's grace and mercy on the spiritual path, and berated for following 'the rude workings of your fancies'. Formalist and Hypocrisy, who cannot grasp that by obedience to 'laws and ordinances you will not be saved', finally arrive at the foot of Mt Difficulty. But instead of taking the narrow way that lay up that hill – 'the steep and high path' that leads to Mt Sion – they took byways to the left and right of the hill, ways that culminated in Danger and Destruction, where both perished.[14] Alluding to the Ascetic–Puritan's benighted understanding of the realm of the Spirit, in the following verse Ḥāfiẓ delivers a sort of Persian Sufiesque reprise to Christian's reproach to Formalist and Hypocrisy:

> If the zealous puritan never found the way
> To penetrate into Romance's universe, it's well –
> He's forgiven – since Love's a business that hinges
> On inculcation and tutelage.[15]

Exactly like those two other stock characters in Ḥāfiẓ's repertoire, the Counsellor and the Shaykh,[16] the *zāhid*, while extroverted in his formalist rites of piety, is full of censorious zeal, dogmatically railing at and cursing his fellow Muslims because they differ from him in ceremonies and phrases. Ḥāfiẓ pours scorn and ridicule on both of these formalist figures:

> The counsellor spoke contemptuously to me;
> He said: 'Wine is forbidden, period.' 'I agree
> With you,' I said. 'Also I don't listen to every jackass.'
>
> The angry shaykh said, 'Go, don't stay here.
> And give up love.' 'There's no need, brother
> For a fight here; I simply won't do that.'[17]

To mock the ascetic, Ḥāfiẓ backhandedly compliments him as being a 'reasonable' man in one verse,[18] but one must remember that in the poet's religion, obedience to 'lunatics' constitutes the sole sign of religious faith:

> Above homage and obeisance to lunatics
> Do not seek for more from us, for our sect's master
> Professed all intellectualism to be wickedness.[19]

By way of poetic allusion (*talmīḥ*), the 'master' of Ḥāfiẓ's 'sect', who thought intellectualism was wickedness and sin, here refers historically to Luqmān Sarkhasī, one of the greatest *wise fools* in the history of Persian Sufism and the master of the ascetic–libertine Sufi sage Abū Sa'īd ibn Abī'l-Khayr (357/967–440/1048).[20] Since in Ḥāfiẓ's faith, 'mad love alone comprises the way to union with the Beloved, traversing the Path *by means of reason* is necessarily sinful'.[21] The puritan ascetic is, on the other hand, a *sophomoric fool*, the archetypal idiot who believes himself wise, whose character is again depicted by another of Shakespeare's puritans: the sanctimonious steward Malvolio in *Twelfth Night*, described as 'a pedant that keeps a school i'th' church'.[22] All such pretension is despised in Ḥāfiẓ's creed of love, whence the poet advises:

> Don't kiss anything except the sweetheart's lip
> And the cup of wine, Ḥāfiẓ; friends, it's a grave mistake
> To kiss the hand held out to you by a Puritan.[23]

Alluding to some of the central doctrines of his theology of love, he contrasts his own passionate *engagement* in the Faith of Love (*madhhab-i 'ishq*) to the desiccated Muslim piety of 'the reasonable ascetic' (*zāhid-i 'āqil*):

> The hot brand which we have pressed onto
> Our lunatic hearts is so intense it would set fire
> To the straw piles of a hundred reasonable ascetics.[24]

Here, he has in mind a type of religious pedant, whose pedantry consists not merely in a narrow-minded interpretation of Islamic jurisprudence, but in intolerance for, and ignorance of, the higher religion of *Eros*.[25] This verse expresses the classic distinction in Sufi religious phenomenology between love and reason 'the contrast', as Annemarie Schimmel points out, 'between *nomos*-oriented religion and *eros*-oriented religion. On the one hand, we find a religion which is bound by the law and where the law, the *sharī'a* - and ... the *'aql*, intellect - leads human beings on a strictly prescribed way in which salvation is guaranteed, God-willing of course; and, on the other hand, the Sufi way of feeling, of experiencing the immediate presence of God already here and now.'[26] Ḥāfiẓian aesthetics dictates the sacrality of human love and beauty. In his religion of love all mortal beauty reflects and exemplifies divine loveliness, since only in the mirror of the former can the latter be contemplated. But the loveless ascetic, who doesn't understand how and why it is that the wine of divine beauty must be served up in the cup of human love and loveliness, always rejects love's creed, and so only evokes Ḥāfiẓ's derision:

> Oh ascetics, go away. Stop arguing with those
> Who drink the bitter stuff, because it was precisely
> This gift the divine ones gave us in pre-Eternity.[27]

Fault-finding and the Ascetic's Blinkered Religious Zeal

In Ḥāfiẓ's lexicon the ascetic (*zāhid*) is also synonymous with a kind of undeveloped or degenerate religious piety.[28] A puritan with a rigidly literal exoteric religious persuasion, he is the polar opposite of the unconventional, inspired libertine or pious rake (*rind*). Caricatures of his unpleasant nature - ill-natured, censorious and supercilious towards any others whom he considers to be of less devout nature - abound in Persian literature, alongside depictions of his self-aggrandizing display of piety and manipulation of faith for social advancement. Writing in Shīrāz a century before Ḥāfiẓ, Sa'dī relates the story of an ascetic who was invited to be the guest of a prince. At the royal banqueting table he ate less than was his custom, and after the meal he recited public prayers longer than was his habit at home. Upon returning home, the 'ascetic' asked his son to bring him something to eat.

'I had supposed you had eaten to satiety already at the King's table', the boy wondered aloud.

'Well, it seemed more to my benefit to curb my appetite there', his father prevaricated.

Discerning that his father's hypocritical pretence to abstention had eradicated all his claim to ascetic virtue, the lad quipped: 'Then recite your prayers over again as well for your good works up to now have also reaped no benefit for you.'[29]

As one can see from this vignette, as a stock character in Persian folklore the ascetic signifies spurious sanctity and specious piety,[30] which is why Ḥāfiẓ sarcastically counsels the puritan ascetic:

> Don't worry so much about the rogues and rakes,
> You high-minded Puritans. You know the sins of others
> Will not appear written on your own foreheads anyway.[31]

The poet's ironic caricature of the ascetic as 'high-minded'[32] has a double edge, for one who is 'high-minded' should always be forgiving, overlooking others' peccadilloes - never by definition intentionally censorious. But the ascetic suffers from what the great Anglican contemplative poet Isaac Watts (1674–1748), in his superb analysis of 'the abuse of religious emotions', diagnosed as 'unrighteous indignation'. Watts describes certain evangelical zealots of his day, 'who when convinced that such and such a practice is culpable or unlawful ... condemn it as inconsistent with true salvation ... as if it were blasphemy or idolatry ... and are ready to break into stern speeches and railing accusations against all who practice it, and pronounce them apostates and sinners of the first rank.'[33]

This misplaced zeal to rectify his neighbours' faults on the part of the ascetic, like Watts' Christian zealots and like the Scribes and Pharisees of the Gospels, prevents him from casting the beam out of his own eye for beholding the mote in his brother's.[34] In a brilliant parody on mountebank clerics in Cromwell's Reformation England, Samuel Butler (1612–80), in his satirical poem *Hudibras*, likewise furnishes us with the perfect cultural analogy to the conduct of the hypercritical *zāhid* in Ḥāfiẓ's *Dīvān*. Butler criticizes these Pharisetical clerics as being 'A sect whose chief devotion / lies In odd perverse antipathies, / In falling out with that or this / And finding somewhat still amiss.' Their obsession in always 'finding something still amiss'[35] finds an exact reprise in Ḥāfiẓ's scorn for his ascetic's penchant for fault-finding. May the sanctimonious ascetic be repaid in kind for his fault-finding, Ḥāfiẓ prays, supplicating that the 'hot air' of his religious pronouncements - literally 'the pall of his sighs' (*dūd-i āhash*) - befuddle his hyper-critical vision:

> Oh Lord, this egotistical ascetic, whose sights are always fixed on other's flaws
> And faults - Cloud the mirror of his mind with the vapour of his sighs![36]

Coleridge's paraphrase of 1 Corinthians 13:6–7 in this context springs to mind:

> A wrong done to thee think a cat's eye spark
> Thou wouldst not see, were not thine own heart dark.
> Thine own keen sense of wrong that thirsts for sin,
> Fear that - the spark self-kindled from within.[37]

Ḥāfiẓ's condemnation of fault-finding is not his own personal idiosyncrasy, but is exactly in line with the teachings of the Persian *futuwwat* tradition, where this vice is consistently condemned by most of its foremost thinkers,[38] and also echoes a number of verses in Rūmī's *Mathnawī* reviling the evils of exposing the flaws of one's neighbour (*'ayb-jū'ī*).[39] The key verse that best encapsulates Ḥāfiẓ's teaching on the vice of fault-finding is:

> I said to the master of the tavern: 'Which road is
> The road of salvation?' He lifted his wine and said,
> 'Not revealing the faults of other people.'[40]

Here, Ḥāfiẓ's master of the tavern, symbol of the supreme spiritual guide, expounds the doctrine that salvation lies in finding no fault and seeing no evil, a soteriological message traceable back to a homily told by the Prophet on the evils of fault-finding.[41] The above verse was directly inspired by the Sufi teachings of Shaykh Amīn al-Dīn Muḥammad Balyānī (668/1269–745/1344), the Master of the Kāzarūnī Order - praised by Ḥāfiẓ as being one of the 'five chief ornaments' who flourished during the reign of Shaykh Abū Isḥāq Īnjū (743/1342–753/1353).[42] In the *Miftāḥ al-hidāya wa miṣbāḥ al-'ināya*, Muḥammad, b. 'Uthmān's hagiography of Shaykh Balyānī, we find the following epigram ascribed to Aḥmad Ḥanbal, which provides the gist of the entire spiritual message of the verse: 'Salvation has ten parts: all ten of these consist in overlooking the faults of others.'[43]

Ḥāfiẓ's teachings about fault-finding in such verses were also influenced by the homiletic ethics of 'Aṭṭār. Because of its relevance to understanding the Persian Sufi background of Ḥāfiẓ's anti-clericalism, the following lengthy passage from Taqī Pūrnāmdāriyān's foundational study of Ḥāfiẓ here bears quotation:

If we compare the lengths that ʻAṭṭār goes to in denunciation of fault-finding with the constant allusions made by Ḥāfiẓ to refraining from cavilling and carping about other people's faults, coupled with his indictment of the Shaykh, the Ascetic, the Sufi, and the other sanctimonious, pseudo-religious formalists as being uninformed of the world of love and drunkenness due to their censorious nature, it is impossible to deny the influence of ʻAṭṭār on Ḥāfiẓ. ʻAṭṭār relates a tale about a dear spiritual adept who would continually say: 'For seventy years now all I feel is delight and rapture in knowing that a God exists of such stunning beauty, willing to allow a poor devotee such as myself intimacy and closeness to Him.' In the moral that ʻAṭṭār draws from this tale, he rhetorically asks: 'How will anyone preoccupied with criticizing others' faults ever find delight in divine love?'

You seek for faults to censure and suppress
And have no time for inward happiness –
How can you know God's secret majesty
If you look out for sin incessantly?
To share His hidden glory you must learn
That others' errors are not your concern –
When someone else's failings are defined
What hairs you split – but to your own you're blind![44]

In another story told by ʻAṭṭār, a drunkard finds fault with the conduct of another drunk, counselling him to drink fewer glasses of wine, so that 'you will be able to walk in a straight line like me without following anyone else'. The first drunkard, meanwhile, is unaware that he himself is blind drunk and being carried in a sack on the back of his mate. From the tale, ʻAṭṭār draws the moral that this type of cavilling arises from not being a lover, for the lover always sees all the Beloved's blemishes as indicative of her beauty and virtue:[45]

You cannot love, and this is why you seek
To find men vicious, or depraved, or weak –
If you could search for love and persevere
The sins of other men would disappear.[46]

Such fault-finding, castigation and harassment of others, done in order to secretly demonstrate one's own virtue and godliness, was a common practice among the false dissemblers of the *sharīʻa*-oriented piety in Ḥāfiẓ's day and age. But in the Canon Law (*sharīʻa*) of Ḥāfiẓ and his Magian Master, the only real sin consists in the upbraiding others for faults, harassing or causing them annoyance.[47] As Ḥāfiẓ says:

Cause no distress and grief to another;
Then go and do as you wish - for in
Our Holy Law no other sin than this exists.[48]

It should also be pointed out that the entire injunction to 'cause no distress and grief to another' (*mabāsh dar pay-i āzār*), propounded in his verse as the sole saving virtue in the entire Muslim Canon Law (*sharī'a*), was directly adopted by Ḥāfiẓ, not from 'Aṭṭār, but - once again - from Balyānī's Sufi teachings. (Indeed, there is probably much truth in the oral tradition kept by recent masters of the Persian Sufi Dhahabī Order that Balyānī was Ḥāfiẓ's Sufi master.[49]) In the *Miftāḥ al-hidāya wa miṣbāḥ al-'ināya*, there exists an entire separate chapter devoted to this very subject - 'On Avoiding Causing Distress to Others [*tark-i āzārī*]'[50] - where (in its very first paragraph) the theological genesis of Ḥāfiẓ's doctrine in this verse appears:

> The Master [Shaykh Balyānī] said: 'Whoever causes distress and annoyance [*āzār*: NB exactly the same word used by Ḥāfiẓ's verse] to people [lit. 'to God's servants'], proves himself devoid of faith in God. There is no greater sin [*gunāh*: NB again exactly the same word used by Ḥāfiẓ] than distressing someone's heart, nor is there any more meritorious act of devotion than bringing joy to someone's heart.' Thus, 'Abdu'llāh Anṣārī (d. 481/1089) declared: 'Whatever does not bring any comfort to someone else does not comprise devotional obedience; whatever does not aggrieve and distress a person is not a sin.'[51]

Interestingly (and not incidentally), Balyānī here also provides the entire text (in Arabic of course) of the Sermon on the Mount of Jesus.[52] For such pacifist sentiments, Ḥāfiẓ also had a definite penchant:

With all my strength of hand and fist and arm
What most I give thanks for is this:
That I cannot deploy my might and brawn
Despitefully on anyone to cause distress.[53]

The Sanctified Sinner and the Castaway Saint

Men with pomp of office clad,
In robes pontifical arrayed,
  But stained with avarice and pride:
They love to be preferred, adored
Affect the state and style of lord,
  And shine magnificently great:
They for precedency contend,

And on ambition's scale ascend
 Hard-labouring for the highest seat.
...O what a change they soon shall know,
When torn away by death, they go
 Reluctant from their splendid feasts,
Condemned in hottest flames to dwell,
And find the spacious courts of hell
 Paved with the skulls of Christian Priests!

Charles Wesley (1707–88)

In light of the foregoing discussion of the comparative religious psychology of the ascetic's degenerate religious zeal, and his tendency, like many archetypal spiritual prostitutes in other of the world's religions, to cast opprobrious stones at women taken in adultery, let us now reconsider the theosophical meaning underlying Ḥāfiẓ's verse cited above:

> Oh Lord, this egotistical ascetic, whose sights are always fixed on other's flaws
> And faults - Cloud the mirror of his mind with the vapor of his sighs![54]

Here, Ḥāfiẓ castigates the ascetic puritan's *metaphysically darkened vision*, which causes him to scoff at others' faults. Benighted, the ascetic's pride and conceit do not allow him to recognize the ubiquity of divine Providence nor realize that God's pre-eternal grace embraces the knave as well as the good. Paraphrasing in verse the Qur'ān's teaching on this subject - 'And whatever wrong a person commits rests upon himself alone; and no soul laden down with a burden [i.e. afflicted with a sin] shall be made to carry another's burden [i.e shall be responsible for someone else's wrong]'[55] - the poet asserts that cavilling at the vices of one's neighbour cannot serve to further one's own salvation, since 'the sins of another shall not appear written on your forehead'.[56] This same lesson is delivered by the poet to the ascetic in some other key verses:

> Whether I am good or bad is not exactly to the point.
> Go ahead and be who you are. This world we live in
> Is a farm, and each of us reaps our own wheat.[57]
>
> Whether we are drunk or sober, each of us is making
> For the street of the Friend. The temple, synagogue,
> The church and the mosque are all houses of love.[58]

What the ascetic in his *hubris* misses is precisely the virtue of spiritual poverty (*faqr*), one of the principle cornerstones of Ḥāfiẓ's Sufi teachings (see p. 169).[59] Hence, Ḥāfiẓ extols and exalts the humble entreaty and desperate neediness (*niyāz*) of the rake, the rogue, the sinner, the miscreant and the down-and-out homeless beggar over the Qur'ān-thumping puritan and sanctimonious fundamentalist *zāhid*:

> Some people say that good deeds will earn them
> A gated house in heaven. Being rakes and natural beggars,
> A room in the Magian tavern will be enough for us.[60]

The puritan ascetic, whose experience embraces only initial degrees of the spiritual path,[61] worships God for the sake of heaven and its delights (heavenly maidens, fruits and wines all promised in the Qur'ān). However, for those advanced on the path - that is, the inspired libertine (*rind*) and the lover (*'āshiq*) - the pursuit of paradise purely through the exercise of pious deeds and works of self-mortification is disdained and disparaged. The lover and enlightened libertine have already entered the realm of Paradise by virtue of following their higher *secta amoris*, expressed in the above verse by the symbol of the Magian Tavern,[62] whence Ḥāfiẓ says:

> When Paradise is mine today as cash in hand,
> Why then should I be taken in and count upon
> The Puritan's pledge of tomorrow's kingdom?[63]

The ascetic relies on his own efforts in the material realm to reach what he imagines to be paradise, whereas the lover and inspired libertine have long ago abandoned the longing for aught but the divine, the Beloved.[64]

Another problem concerns the differing spiritual *attitudes* of *rind* and *zāhid*. The difference between the inspired libertine and ascetic is one of *spiritual perspective* with regard to both action and contemplation. For the latter, the bare motion of formal rituals and pious observances (prayer, renunciation, etc.) takes precedence; for the former, it is the contemplative 'intention' (*niyyat*) of the heart and the fervour of spiritual neediness and poverty (*faqr*) which are of primary importance.[65]

This difference of spiritual attitudes between *rind* and *zāhid* harks back to the classical definition of 'ascetic renunciation' (*zuhd*) given by Abū'l-Qāsim Junayd (d. 297/910), cited in the earliest major work on Persian Sufism by Abū Ibrāmīm Mustamlī Bukhārī (d. 434/1042–3) - his monumental multi-volume commentary entitled *Sharḥ al-ta'arruf* on al-Kalābadhī's (d. 380/990) *Kitāb al-ta'arruf li-madhhab ahl al-taṣawwuf*. Junayd remarked: 'Ascetic renunciation [*al-zuhd*] is to empty one's hands of all possessions and divest the heart of pursuit of them.' Bukhārī then explains Junayd's saying with the comment that the first degree (of the hands) belongs to the common masses of devotees, whereas the second degree (of the heart) pertains to the spiritual Elect.[66] Ḥāfiẓ, referring precisely to this distinction, evokes in one verse the contrast in *spiritual perspectives* between the conceited ascetic on the one hand and humble *faqīr* on the other:

Since none of your affairs by prayer succeeds,
O Puritan, I prefer my drunken midnight cries,
My desperate beggary and hapless penury.[67]

The ascetic's vaunted *quantity* of *works* and practices (ritual devotions, public alms-giving and prayers) ultimately lead nowhere, as this verse attests, whence the emphasis Ḥāfiẓ places on the inspired libertine's interior *quality* and ardour of *faith* as the correct basis for all spiritual practice. The spiritual context of Ḥāfiẓ's emphasis in this verse on the higher virtue of the spiritual poverty of the 'rakes [*rind*] and natural beggars [*gidā*]', in whose company he delights, as the verse cited a page earlier also attests ('Some people say...'), is immediately illuminated once we consider this saying of Bāyazīd Basṭāmī (d. 261/875): 'I repent once from my sins, but must repent a thousand times over for my obedient devotion to God.' 'Aṭṭār comments on Bāyazīd's statement that taking pride in one's good deeds and being conceited about one's acts of worship is a moral failing much worse than any 'sin'.[68] In a similar vein, 'Abdu'llāh Anṣārī takes a critical snipe at both the Puritan ascetic's conceit and the learned intellectual's pride, and, castigating both, objects that 'The ascetic vaunts his self-discipline and the intellectual boasts of his learning'.[69]

In this respect, it should be underlined that in Ḥāfiẓian social ethics, dervish contentment (*qanā'at*) and spiritual poverty (*faqr*) are venerated as the supreme virtues, as numerous verses attest:

Do not disparage the weak and the skinny. Remember that,
You men of wealth. We know the one given the chief seat
In the Gathering is the *saddhu* sleeping in the street.[70]

Or:

You men of power and ways and means, such haughty
Pride is out of place. Don't let disdain swell your heads,
Since all your vaunted wealth and rank
Depends in the end upon the will of dervishes.[71]

Or:

If there's profit in this bazaar it lies
In the joyous contented dervish.
Grant me God the bliss of contentment
And the grace of being a happy dervish.[72]

The ascetic pays far more dearly for indulging in unctuous hubris about his specious piety, Ḥāfiẓ thus warns, than the libertine ever will for his 'licence':

You Puritans on the cold stone floor, you are not safe
From the tricks of God's zeal: the distance between the cloister
And the Zoroastrian tavern is not all that great.[73]

Hence, Ḥāfiẓ's antinomian refusal to rank the ascetic's vaunted austerity and acts of self-mortification (*zuhd*) above the sybarite rake's licentiousness (*fisq*), for both await God's final will - ever suspended till Judgement Day.[74] The distinction between sinner and saint is ever far from self-evident; who dares discern who's sinner and who's saint?

> Come, come! The glory of this universal factory
> Will not be made one whit more or less through austerity
> Of men like you or by debauchery of folk like me.[75]

Since happiness and bliss in this life and salvation and felicity in the hereafter can only be gained through abasement, humility and self-negation,[76] ultimately, says Ḥāfiẓ, the inspired libertine (*rind*) is destined to partake far more of God's grace than the proud ascetic:

> The ascetic had too much pride so could never soundly
> Traverse the Path. But the rake by way of humble entreaty
> And beggary at last went down to the House of Peace.[77]

The very anti-clerical - ostensibly amoral - doctrine expressed in this verse, which ranks the inspired libertine and sinful debauchee higher than the graceless zealot and self-satisfied puritan, is based on the parable of the Pharisee and the Publican in the Gospel of Luke (18:10–14).[78] This lovely gospel tale was then recast by the Sufis as the 'Story of the Sinner and Ascetic in the Company of Jesus' - the ascetic who rejected by God due to his pride and the sinner redeemed because of his humility. In the medieval Persian Sufi tradition, Luke's parable was first retold by Abū'l-Qāsim Qushayrī in his famous treatise on Sufism, later recounted by Abū Ḥāmid Ghazālī in the *Iḥyā' 'ulūm al-dīn*, and finally and lastly immortalized in verse by Sa'dī in his chapter on 'Humility' in the *Būstān* - all of which Ḥāfiẓ, the 'Memorizer' and redoubtable scholar of Islam's sacred scripture, certainly had read. Describing God's revelation to Jesus that the sinner's humble entreaty had reaped the fruit of salvation and the pride of the fair-seeming but hypocritical zealot, who thanked God he was not as other men are, earned him a place in the Fire, Ḥāfiẓ's doctrine in the above verse quite precisely encapsulates the gist of these verses from Sa'dī's *Būstān*:

> The signs of Glory struck his being, yet Jesus only heard an angelic epiphany amidst the ascetic's ignorant curses: 'Both the fool and the wiseman I accept', the Divine Call came. 'Both petitions I endorse, but the poseur of piety gets sent straight to hell, and the other, blackguard and profligate, I elevate to heaven in My Grace; for he turned to Me repentant, wept, was chastened and sobered by his darkened days, the opportunities cast away. I cannot cast out from the chancel of My Mercy anyone who seeks Me with such self-avowed wretchedness. But if the puritan dogmatist thinks he's defiled by the sinner in

> heaven's synod ... Very well, tell him not to worry. Let the self-proclaimed saint go to hell and the debauchee he despises go to paradise. For one rent his soul in remorse, seared in conscience, scalded himself with tears, while the other relied on his personal ascetic devotion.' If only he knew: in the court of the Opulent, helplessness excels pride, contrition outshines egoism. The clothes of pride are pretty, but its underwear is filthy. On this threshold poverty and contrition serve you better than self-adoration or devotion. ... Godliness and egoism are opposites ... It simply doesn't matter whether you're a profligate, fortune wasted away, or painstaking ascetic full of vain mortification. ... The wise all have their adages, pronounced for posterity. From Sa'dī learn by heart one maxim alone: The soul-mortified sinner, brooding on God is better than the canting ascetic [*zāhid*] affecting piety.[79]

As Sa'dī explains in this passage, it is egotism and self-righteousness which are the chief flaws of the Muslim ascetic's religious personality. These two vices act as a veil between his soul and God. This veil the Sufis refer to as 'the veil of the infidel selfhood'.

The Veil of the Infidel Selfhood

If it were not for his vain conceit and hypocrisy (*kh^{w}ud-bīnī, riyā*) - which in Ḥāfiẓ's view are considered to be the Mother of Evil[80] - the puritan might even be forgiven. But there is no possibility of spiritual knowledge or gnosis (*ma'rifat*), as long as conceit in one's own learning exists. Ḥāfiẓ views the true poet-savant as always 'selfless',[81] spiritual liberation lying in the negation of egocentric consciousness. This is the supreme Sufi art of *unselfconsciousness*, existence through nonbeing - literally *not seeing oneself*:

> As long as you see yourself learned and intellectual
> You'll lodge with idiots; moveover, if you
> Can stop seeing yourself at all, you will be free.[82]

The above verse provides an exact versification of a saying by the Sufi saint Shāh Shujā' Kirmānī (d. after 270/884) concerning the true meaning of 'learning' (*faḍl*): 'Learned and intellectual folk [*ahl-i faḍl*] may be said to be more virtuous than other people as long as they do not see their own learning, but once they perceive themselves to be learned or virtuous, they cease to have any virtue at all.'[83]

The notion of 'not seeing oneself' as the key to spiritual freedom, as Abū'l-Ḥasan 'Abd al-Raḥmān Khatmī Lāhūrī, commenting on this verse, points out, is best illustrated in a story told in the beautiful medieval Sufi work on the Divine Names: the *Rawḥ al-arwāḥ fī sharḥ asmā' al-malik al-fattāḥ* by Aḥmad Sam'ānī (d. 534/1140) about Bishr ibn Ḥārith Ḥāfī (d. 227/842), a Persian Sufi from Merv in Khurāsān. In his wanderings, Bishr Ḥāfī came across the immortal prophet Khiḍr (sometimes identified with the Biblical Elias and Ahasuerus by Muslim authors[84]) and appealed for his blessings. In reply, Khiḍr prayed, 'May God conceal your works of obedience from you'. 'The inner significance of Khiḍr's statement', Lāhūrī explains, 'in this adage may be epitomized: "How many acts of obedience are iniquity and how many sins are blessed!"', concluding:

> From this tale it may be understood that perceiving one's own learning and artistic talent and beholding one's intellectual learning and legal lore inhibits realization of direct visionary gnosis [*ma'rifat-i shuhūdī*]. This is because direct visionary gnosis only occurs in a state of the wayfarer's annihilation from his own self, character traits, and individual personality.[85]

As we have seen from the foregoing discussion, much of Ḥāfiẓ's genius is devoted to dissecting the psychopathology of religious hypocrisy, to composing lampoons in verse on spiritual materialism, and deriding the literalistic religious perspective based on rote learning and devotion by the book. In the following verse, Ḥāfiẓ derides the ascetic's vain egocentricity (*kh^{w}ud-bīnī*) and complains that the town preacher, who hypocritically lays claim to religious conviction and makes a show of faith he doesn't have, will never become a true Muslim:

> I know this sort of talk won't
>   be easy for the city preacher to take –
> But so long as he plays the hypocrite
>   and plies the craft of mummery
> A 'Muslim' is what he'll never be.[86]

Here, he has in mind both the *moral* and the *metaphysical* shortcomings of the pharisaical Islamic faith of such an impostor. On the *moral* level, the ascetic's vanity, fury and misplaced zeal is generated by *hubris*, insofar as practitioners of ascetic exercises tend to make a display of piety – turning private worship into public exhibitionism, thus leading to the malaise of hypocrisy (*riyā*). A danger of another sort is that the ascetic's excesses may lead to the development of psychic powers, causing him to fall into the delusion of imagining himself as a member of the elect and the company of the saints. Both are spiritual maladies of the worst sort.

Islam's greatest mystical theologian Abū Ḥāmid al-Ghazālī (d. 505/1111), in the course of his analysis of the psychology of the abuse of such religious emotions, thus observed that 'the second cause of pride arises from asceticism [*zuhd*] and religious devotion [*'ibādat*]. Ascetics, Sufis and pious devotees [*pārsā*] are often not without arrogance [*takabbur*], and their affliction with this vice may even reach the point that they imagine that others are actually obligated to serve them and appeal to them, assuming that their own pious devotion obliges everyone else to venerate them!'[87]

Furthermore, on the *metaphysical* level, the ascetic who suffers from *amour propre*, prepossessed of an infantile, inflated sense of self-importance, cannot transcend the artificial duality of percept and object, seer and seen, nor see beyond the illusory distinction between 'me' and 'thee', 'I' and 'thou'. Since he cannot apprehend the transcendental immersion of the part in the Whole, Lover in Beloved, or servant in the Lord, the ascetic doesn't understand that he *him-self* in his 'infidel Selfhood' constitutes the ultimate metaphysical sacrilege.[88] Ḥāfiẓ describes the struggle that rending the veil of Self/*him-self* entails him in the following famous verse:

> Between lover and beloved there exists
> No veil at all. You, you yourself are
> Your own veil: Ḥāfiẓ, get out of the way![89]

This line represents a gloss in verse on the Prophet's statement: 'Your greatest foe is your own soul between your ribs',[90] a *ḥadīth* which the Sufis traditionally interpreted to mean that 'your very self [*nafs-i kh^{w}ud*] is the greatest veil'.[91] Thus, when Bāyazīd was asked how he would describe the way to God, he replied: 'Once you remove yourself from blocking the way to God, you will have arrived at Him.'[92]

Excoriating his nescience, Ḥāfiẓ scoffs at the arrogance of the ascetic on both the moral and metaphysical level in many verses, of which the following is typical:

> Go away, you egoist ascetic! This mystery
> Behind the veil is concealed to the eye
> Of *you and me* - and hidden it shall remain.[93]

To sum up the discussion so far concerning the 'veil of the infidel selfhood': there are two main obstacles - respectively moral and metaphysical - impeding the ascetic's efforts at spiritual realization.

The first, the *moral* impediment that prevents the ascetic from rending the 'veil', is simply - to use the apt phrase descriptive of the condition of a fictional English Puritan, the steward Malvolio in Shakespeare's *Twelfth Night* - that he is 'sick of self-love'.[94] That is to say, that the ascetic is preoccupied with the delusion of his own virtue and moral excellence. This is the main reason why Ḥāfiẓ, from the spiritual station of inspired libertinism (*rindī*), deprecates the puritan ascetic (*zāhid*) for his conceit, arrogance and self-centredness, and extols instead the inspired libertine (*rind*), who has transcended these vices.[95]

Secondly, the *metaphysical* stumbling block to the ascetic's egocentric vision is his false distinction and discrimination of separative personal 'identities' ('you' vs. 'me'), so that, not having yet experienced immersion in the sea of the Unity of Being (again quoting Shakespeare's description of Malvolio), he tastes 'with a distempered appetite'.[96] Not having stepped outside the small courtyard of natural existence and thus unable to enter the *temenos* of the spiritual path, the ascetic has yet to learn that:

The beauty of the Friend has no veil
Nor mask her charm can conçeal;
Just let the pathway's dust first settle
And then you'll catch a glimpse of her.
But you who won't desert the court
Of human nature, how hope you'll ever take
A step upon the Sufi Path?[97]

For these reasons, being veiled from these mysteries of creation and the spiritual life, the ascetic is a moral, psycho-spiritual and metaphysical polytheist.[98]

Bacchanalian Piety: Ḥāfiẓ's Counter-Ethic and Riposte to Hidden Polytheism

To be Good only, is to be
A Devil or else a Pharisee.
William Blake[99]

Ḥāfiẓ's anti-clerical invectives to a large part assail the insidious invisible vice of hypocrisy. In the phenomenology of religious experience, hypocrisy is always portrayed as the most deeply hidden of the vices. In these lines from *Paradise Lost*, depicting Satan decked out in an angel's habit, accosting the archangel Uriel who guards the gate of Paradise, Milton gives an excellent description of the hiddenness of the vice of hypocrisy:

So spake the false dissembler unperceived;
For neither man nor angel can discern
Hypocrisy, the only evil that walks
Invisible, except to God alone...[100]

Ḥāfiẓ's considered hypocrisy in the form of the ostentatious display of religious piety to be the worst moral evil. He understood, as Khurramshāhī stresses, 'hypocrisy [*riyā*] to be the Mother of all Evil [*umm al-fasād*]. All throughout his life he thought it his personal duty to struggle against it in all its varieties and shapes, whether cloaked in the robes of members of exoteric legalistic Islam [*ahl-i sharīʿat*] or concealed beneath the garments of Sufi piety [*ahl-i ṭarīqat*]. Ḥāfiẓ's entire *Dīvān* is one long manifesto of opposition to religious hypocrisy.'[101] In Ḥāfiẓ's moral theology, Khurramshāhī continues:

> The sin most destructive of Islamic piety and most dangerous to humanity is hypocrisy [*riyā*]. The moral range of the sin of 'hypocrisy' in this respect Ḥāfiẓ extended broadly to include such vices as self-righteousness, smugness,

> conceited self-satisfaction [*khwūd-rā'ī*], putting on airs, ostentatious displays of ascetic piety [*zuhd-furūshī*], vaunting one's learning [*faḍl-furūshī*], considering oneself to be holy and sacrosanct, bragging of and setting stock in one's own acts of pious devotion, superciliousness, mendacity, imposture, deceit, duplicity in one's relation to God and man, cruel lack of feeling [*bīdardī*], being without love and wisdom, and so on. It can be definitively affirmed that no one anywhere or any time throughout the history of Islamic civilization has ever gone to battle against hypocrisy [*riyā'*] with such pugnacity or laboured with such zealous determination to uproot this vice as has Ḥāfiẓ.[102]

His obsessive hatred of hypocrisy (*riyā*) is the chief theme of his anti-clerical poetics and remains the principle political reason why he is still, six centuries on, the most popular bard in his homeland - the 'Islamic' Republic of Iran, where religious quacks and sanctimonious swindlers still call all the shots and only duplicitous con-men adept in the black arts of pious dissimulation can eke out a decent living.

Ḥāfiẓ's predominant social attitude is *anti-hypocritical.* In his eyes, vice itself often becomes preferable to the pious masquerade of virtue,[103] which is why one finds him in certain verses petulantly indulging in a kind of Rimbaudesque celebration of perversion:

> Lift up the tulip-cup: its eyes' drunken narcissus gaze,
> And set on me the label 'pervert'. With so many judges
> That are set over me, O Lord, who should I take to be my judge?[104]

Ḥāfiẓ's condemnation of hypocrisy as the 'supreme sin'[105] has many antecedents in classical Sufi texts, where it is repeatedly condemned as a vice. In his *The Hundred Fields*, the first treatise written in Persian on the classification of the spiritual stations of the Sufi Path, 'Abdu'llāh Anṣārī (d. 482/1089) of Herat, the eminent Ḥanbalite theologian and leading stylist of Persian rhyming prose, characterizes hypocrisy as *shirk* or 'polytheism' - that is, association of other gods with God.[106] *Shirk* is the worst heresy in Islamic thought. Abū Ḥāmid Muḥammad al-Ghazālī (d. 505/1111) explains that hypocrisy is 'an act of devotion performed publicly so that people think that one is especially pious'.[107] Since hypocrisy involves the perpetuation of an emotional pretence - the heart's vocation devotion to the One God, but the mind's avocation being a neurotic obsession with society and people - the Sufis discerned how such dissimulation easily becomes transmuted into an 'interior polytheism'. 'Know that the slightest ostentatiousness [*riyā'*] constitutes polytheism',[108] Imām 'Alī famously pronounced.

'Polytheism' in this context is psychological, not doxological, relating to the subtle notion of 'hidden polytheism' (*shirk-i khafī*), to which the Prophet alluded in his saying: 'The creeping of *shirk* in my community is more hidden [*akhfā*] than the creeping of a black ant over a hard rock on a dark night.'[109] Shakespeare excellently sums up the horror of the hiddenness of the schizophrenic polytheistic perspective, in which the rigidity of moral virtue is secretly transformed into the rigidity of evil, when he remarked that:

> 'Tis too much prov'd, that with devotion's visage
> And pious action we do sugar o'er
> The devil himself.[110]

Ḥāfiẓ criticizes the spiritual fakes and showmen of his day in exactly this psychological sense, mocking those who he referred to as 'the cabal of hypocrites' (*ahl-i riyā*), which is translated in the verse below as 'people whose words and deeds don't match':

> I want to be far away from people whose words
> And deeds don't match. Among the morose and heavy-
> Hearted, a heavy glass of wine is enough for us.[111]

To redress counterfeit religiosity and hypocritical displays of religious fervour in which outward colours of devotion and piety but serve to camouflage a lack of inward ardour, he advocated a *counter-ethic of bacchanalian piety* in his poetry.[112] The following verse is a typical expression of this *malāmatī* ethic:

> I am so disgusted in my heart by the hypocrisy
> Of the Muslim abbey that if you were
> To wash me in wine, that would be a just thing.[113]

Since, on the *moral* plane, any sort of self-abnegation, whether psychical or physical, helps the devotee avoid falling prey on the *psychospiritual* plane to hidden polytheism, *malāmatīs* such as Ḥāfiẓ deliberately attracted blame to themselves. In brief, this is the gist - a *malāmatī* practice used as a spiritual device - underlying most of the poet's bacchanalia. Through this counter-ethic the poet detached himself from the sin of conceit and self-satisfaction - even if occasion demanded he be condemned for 'impiety' or 'infidelity':

> Go into town where all the taverns are
>   and give the winesellers this news:
> Say: Ḥāfiẓ is 'born again', that he forswears
>   the cozenage of abstinence and sham austerity.[114]

As a high principle of *malāmatī* practice, the drinking of wine in Ḥāfiẓ's lexicon is the benchmark of authentic bacchanalian piety. This explains why in his verse he always spits out the sobriquet 'ascetic' (*zāhid*) as a term of abuse and why it carries exclusively negative connotations. More than the ill apparent in wine or drunkenness, the real evil lies in believing the heresy of the holier-than-thou selfhood of the devotee himself. The chicanery of religious pretence and hypocritical ostentation consequently came to be viewed as a far graver sin than consumption of intoxicating beverages – which is precisely the ethical message inculcated by such bacchanalian pronouncements as:

> Drink wine. To sin a hundred times alone
> Where no one knows is better than these orisons
> They offer up for public pious dissimulation.[115]

Going on the offensive with this radical anti-clerical rhetoric, as an act of defiance to religious fraudsters, Ḥāfiẓ declares that *there may even be a kind of religious piety in wine drinking*:

> The drinking of wine in which there's no chicanery
> Or putting on an act is better than the cant of phoney
> Ascetical piety and its counterfeit devotions set on display.[116]

Just as today defenders of women's rights, in order to defy the brutal and repressive mullahocracy in Iran, predicate their activities as being a *Lipstick Jihad* – the title of Azadeh Moaveni's delightful memoir of reporting for *Time* magazine in the Ayatollahs' Republic – for poets resisting the tyranny of religious despots, such petulantly defiant bacchanalian language indeed proved very effective. Since there is certainly far more virtue in being a notorious drunkard in public than grace in being a good hypocrite in private, Ḥāfiẓ argues:

> They say hypocrisy is kosher but the wineglass is prohibited?
> Which Sufi Path is this? How great a government, what
> Pure Holy Canon Law, what fine Faith this all shows us![117]

Such anti-clerical bacchanalian expressions (a dozen others just as brazen might be cited) allowed Ḥāfiẓ to clarify his position in regard to the sanctimony of Muslim clerics, with their hypocritical masquerade of enforcing abstention from wine. He stresses that open and public consumption of wine is ethically preferable and even morally superior to Muslim prohibitionists, who would give a false impression of abstinence:

> Godfearing piety and holy duty: leave those to ascetics.
> To us leave wine, and let time decree between
> The two which one the Friend shall choose.[118]

* * *

> I beg your pardon, ascetics, I'll never abandon
> The lip of the friend nor the bottle of wine.
> To me it's these that comprise 'religion'![119]

* * *

Don't kiss anything except the sweetheart's lip
And the cup of wine, Ḥāfiẓ; friends, it's a grave mistake
To kiss the hand held out to you by a Puritan.[120]

Even if drinking does itself constitute a fault of character, what real harm does it wreak? In any case, who's really faultless? The poet challenges the Pharisee:

So what if now and then I drink a cup or two of wine?
From blood of grapes the wine comes – not from your veins!
What kind of 'vice' is this from which these 'faults and flaws' arise?
And if wine has its flaws, well, tell me, where's one faultless man?[121]

Elsewhere, elaborating the metaphor of the incendiary nature of nomocentric Muslim religiosity when stripped of *Eros*, he describes the Muslim pharisees and ascetics as letting the wildfire of their passions spread among their congregations, while allowing religious raptures degenerate into unrighteous rage, by their zeal thus destroying the very foundation of faith:

The fire of ascetic renunciation and hypocrisy
Will eventually consume the harvest of religion.
Ḥāfiẓ, throw off your Sufi robe and go on your way.[122]

As we have seen, Ḥāfiẓ is quite vocal about the spiritual shortcomings of the fundamentalist *zāhids*. He assails the empty formalism of their faith in nearly every *ghazal*, fulminating against their preoccupation with their neighbour's faults and refusal to acknowledge their own, satirizing their half-baked religious zeal insensitive to erotic spirituality, upbraiding their hypocrisy and sanctimony, conceit and egotism.

In what follows, I will explore another aspect of Ḥāfiẓ's counter-ethic: his positive theology of sin, which constitutes the poet's wicked, anti-clerical riposte to the puritan's religiose pietism.

'Some Rise by Sin and Some by Virtue Fall': Ḥāfiẓ's Positive Theology of Sin

The literary and spiritual doctrines that sustain the poet's positive theology of sin can be traced back to the diverse Islamic spiritual traditions.[123] To show this, let us first revisit the verse cited several pages back which introduced the sybarite rake as sound of faith, though leading an unconventional life construed to be 'sinful' by narrow-minded puritans:

> The ascetic had too much pride so he could never soundly
> Traverse the Path. But the rake by way of humble entreaty
> And beggary at last went down to the House of Peace.[124]

Addressed to the self-righteous ascetic, this verse on first glance sounds like a simple 'salvation through sin' doctrine typical of the 'school of decadence' view of Ḥāfiẓ, advocated by his nineteenth-century *fin-de-siècle* translators such as John Payne and Richard Le Gallienne.[125] But the crassness and naivety of their interpretation becomes evident once we examine Ḥāfiẓ's theology of sin in the light of early Islamic ethical teachings. At the finale of his lengthy interpretation of this verse, 'Abd al-Raḥmān Khatmī Lāhūrī relates an interesting moral conundrum with which the sixth Shī'ite Imām, Ja'far al-Ṣādiq (d. 148/765) was once presented: 'What kind of sin causes the devotee to gain closeness to God, and what sort of act of pious obedience causes the devotee to be estranged from God?'

'Any act of devotional obedience that leads to pride causes the devotee's estrangement from God [*bu'd*], but any sin that culminates in remorse, regret and shame will result in the devotee's intimacy and proximity to God [*qurbat*]',[126] the Imām retorted. Elsewhere, he remarked in a similar vein:

> Any sin that begins with fear and culminates in begging forgiveness in fact brings a devotee to God, whereas any work of religious obedience which begins with smug self-satisfaction and culminates in swollen-headedness [*'ujb*] will cause him to become a castaway. Therefore the "righteous" devotee who is conceited is a sinner, whereas the sinner who begs forgiveness can be said to be devoutly righteous.[127]

Here, it may be noted that such theological pronouncements on the value of the 'blessed sin' by Imām al-Ṣādiq merely elaborate an idea that had already been broached in a seminal saying ascribed to his illustrious ancestor (the first Shī'ite), Imām 'Alī (d. 21/661): 'The sin that grieves you is better in the sight of God than the virtue that makes you proud.'[128] Furthermore, it is hardly incidental that Imām Ṣādiq was one of the main founders of Sufi love mysticism.[129] Further research into the spiritual teachings and Sufi mystics of his period immediately following him reveals that Ḥāfiẓ's unconventional views about sin not only have many antecedents in early Shī'ite thought and parallels among *ḥadīth* of the Prophet, but are directly modelled on certain sayings by the classical masters of the Persian Sufi tradition as well.

In their strict differentiation between the jurisprudence of the heart (*fiqh al-bāṭin*) and the exoteric demands of the Islamic canonical legal code,[130] the sayings of both Imāms convey to us the important spiritual message broached briefly above, namely that vanity and pride are vices far more detrimental to the pursuit of virtue than any of the common peccadilloes defined by literalist *Sharī'a*-centric piety. From the ninth century onwards, numerous sayings by Persian Sufi teachers began to reiterate this (a)moral message. A review of some of these sayings here will be very useful:

- Yaḥyā ibn Mu'ādh Rāzī (d. 258/871) declared: 'The contrition of sinners is far better than the pompous pretensions and display of piety put on by sanctimonious worshippers.'[131]

- One of the followers of Abū Sa'īd ibn Abī'l-Khayr (d. 440/1048) asked him: 'Does the devoted worshipper of God cease to being a devotee if he sins?' 'If he is a devotee, not at all,' argued the master, 'for the sinning of our father Adam, peace be upon him, did not cause him to lose his rank as God's devotee or make him cease to be God's devotee. Be a devotee of Him, then go do wherever you like. For sin accompanied by contrition is certainly better than devotional worship with pride [as can be seen from the fact that] Adam exhibited contrition [and so was saved], whereas Iblīs acted with pride [and so was damned].'[132]

- Anṣārī even famously versified in his *Munājāt* Imām 'Alī's dictum cited above: 'O Lord, I despair of such obedient devotion of mine as makes me proud, but blessed be that sin which makes me beg forgiveness!'[133]

In a myriad verses, Ḥāfiẓ elaborates this same liberated and liberal Persian Sufi attitude towards sin, drawing on such sayings.

In the following verse, his ironical contrast of the conceited self-esteem of the ascetic engaged in ritual 'prayers' (*namāz*) to his own drunkenness (*mastī*) and poverty of spirit (*niyāz*) - the vainglorious attitude of the former by implication incurring his damnation - inculcates exactly the same moral message found in the sayings cited above:

> The starchy ascetic puffed up with prayers and me
> With meagre means, drunken ways and poverty -
> Betwixt and between, let's see who God will favour.[134]

In fact, this verse recasts a Gospel saying very popular among Sufis that was cited by Ḥāfiẓ's favourite Sufi master, Amīn al-Dīn Balyānī, mentioned above. Jesus warned his disciples: 'O disciples, how many lamps are blown out by a little breeze, and how many devotees have been ruined by conceit.' Taking a cue from this saying, Balyānī moralizes:

> If swollen-headedness [*'ujb*: NB the same term used by Ḥāfiẓ in this verse] and pride [*kibr*] can vitiate all the good deeds of devotees [*'ābidān*] who are *close to God*, then the case of those who are *far from God* is made all the more impalpable. So make the sum and substance of your character to be indigence, humility, lowliness and poverty of spirit, that you may be saved.[135]

In addition to the sayings narrated by the above authors, the main sources of Ḥāfiẓ's enlightened theology of sin were the multi-volume Koran commentary in Persian - *Kashf al-asrār* - by Rashīd al-Dīn Maybudī (d. 520/1126), Anṣārī's chief spiritual heir, and the Najm al-Dīn Rāzī's (d. 654/1256) *Mirṣād al-'ibād*, the latter being the most important medieval manual of Sufism in Persian. In his chapter on the creation of man, Rāzī explains as follows how God justified the superiority of Adam's sin over the Angels' virtue:

> Divine munificence and lordly wisdom whispered into the innermost core of the angels' hearts: 'How can you ever grasp of what we have intended from all eternity to the end of time with this handful of dust? ... But you have never had anything to do with this affair of Love, so you can be excused. You are but dry ascetics dwelling in cloisters of holy retirement [*zāhidān-i ṣūma'a-nīshīn ḥaẓā'ir-i quds*]. What knowledge can you ever have of the wayfarers who inhabit the Taverns of Ruin of Love [*kharābāt-i 'ishq*]? How can those with a 'safe and sound' character [*salāmatiyān*] savour the delights sensed, ever relish the sweet taste enjoyed by those who incur public blame and censure [*malāmatiyān*]?'[136]

As Dāryūsh Āshūrī explains in his intertextual study of the *Dīvān* and these two seminal Sufi classics,[137] Ḥāfiẓ inserted much of the same vocabulary, imagery and ideas from many of Rāzī's passages directly into his poetry. For example, just as Rāzī described God's rebuke to the angel-ascetics dwelling in Paradise for their loveless temperament, so Ḥāfiẓ in similar terms criticizes the ascetics (*zāhidān*) of this world:

> You puritans on the cold stone floor, you are not safe
> From the tricks of God's zeal: the distance between the cloister
> And the Zoroastrian tavern is not, after all, that great.[138]

In the following verse, like Rāzī, Ḥāfiẓ rebukes the dry 'ascetic' (*zāhid*) for residing in the safety of the 'cloister' (*ṣūma'a*), identifying himself with Adam destined to inhabit the tavern (*kharābat*):

> *Maqām-i aṣlī-yi mā gūsha-yi kharābāt-ast*
> *khudāyash khayr dahād har-ki īn 'imārat kard*

> Before all time, our primordial
> Degree was in the tavern corner:
> God grace with goodness he
> Who raised high this edifice.[139]

Ḥāfiẓ emulates Rāzī's imagery and ideas in numerous other verses.[140] Like Rāzī, he celebrates the sinful, suffering, tavern-haunting Adam who courts reproach (*malāmat*), and contrasts him unfavourably to the insensitive ascetic, homologous on the earthly plane to the 'holy' angels in heaven endowed with a 'safe and sound character' (*salāmat*).[141] Juxtaposed to these smug egotistical angel-ascetics, Adam is identified both by Rāzī and Maybudī[142] as the prototypical 'holy sinner'. Adam's spiritual degree is nonetheless exalted, insofar as he is destined by his lowly, earthly and sinful nature to reveal God's qualities of Mercy and Beauty during his journey (*safar*) 'down under' through the realm of mortality, where he is divinely destined to be ensnared in human love. Ḥāfiẓ's entire mythopoetic theogony is permeated by Adam's tragic journey from metahistory into time, where the theme of his Fall is reiterated verse after verse:

Man Ādam-i bihishtī-am ammā darīn safar
ḥālī asīr-i 'ishq-i javānān-i mahvasham

I am Adam come down from heaven
Yet, here and now, in this journey, remain
Bewitched - ensnared in love
With youths with faces like the moon.[143]

Adam, Father of Mankind, is the archetypal inspired libertine (*rind*). Insofar as all men in being 'blessed sinners'[144] resemble Adam, recreants to God in this realm *ici-bas*, Ḥāfiẓ taunts the ascetic:

I'm not the only one who has fallen away
From the holy cell; my father Adam himself
Let the eternal heaven slip out of his hands![145]

In conclusion, Ḥāfiẓ's oxymora of the 'blessed sin' (the idea of 'vice' as leading through the vale of humility and self-abasement up to redemption and felicity) contrasted to 'accursed virtue' directing one up the hill of self-righteous sanctimony, only to be cast down into perdition - 'Some rise by sin, and some by virtue fall'[146] - should be seen as representing a natural elaboration of Sufi theosophical doctrine within the common esoteric tradition of early Islamic spirituality and not any radical innovation. It is clear that the quotations adduced above from the early Shī'ite tradition and the later Persian Sufi authors such as Maybudī and Rāzī provide us with the right spiritual perspective to understand the exalted stature accorded to the inspired libertine (*rind*) in Ḥāfiẓ's poetry. Counterbalancing the vice of pride, sin functions as an adjunct of humility.[147]

Ḥāfiẓ's positive attitude towards sin had definite antecedents in the tenets of the *Malāmatiyya* of Khurāsān several centuries before him, as well as being staunchly underpinned by a combination of Qur'ānic verses and *ḥadīths* of the Prophet. In the Qur'ān, God's essential character is described as compassionate, merciful and forgiving.[148] One verse praises 'the godfearing who expend in prosperity and adversity in almsgiving, and restrain their rage, and pardon the offences of their fellowmen; and God loves the good-doers; who, when they commit an indecency or wrong themselves, remember God, and pray forgiveness for their sins, and who shall forgive sins but God?'[149] Divine mercy is so all-encompassing that it 'embraces all things',[150] and men and women together are thus enjoined not to 'despair of God's mercy! Surely, God forgives all sins'.[151] Furthermore, the celebrated Sacred Tradition, 'My mercy precedes My wrath',[152] informs us that the divine Nature is not vengeful, but predominantly merciful.

Given these precedents in Muslim scripture, *ḥadīth* and Sufi doctrine, it is hardly surprising to find that the fundamental keynote of Ḥāfiẓ's moral theology is an emphasis on God's mercy and forgiveness (*'afw*) of sin.[153] To this theme he even devoted an entire *ghazal*, the first three verses of which are particularly relevant to this discussion:

> Last night I heard a singer from
>   A tavern nook strike up this tune:
> 'Drink wine, for God forgives all sin:
>   Divine indulgence has again
> Reprieved you – all's now pardoned.
>   – A bulletin from Mercy's seraphim.'
> The singer paused, then cried out once more:
>   'God's grace and favour is supreme,
> His grace is there although we err;
>   God's benison is greater than our sin.
> But hold your tongue; it's best you're mute:
>   This secret point keep clandestine.'[154]

A literary precedent – perhaps original archetype? – for these verses appears in the *Manāqib al-'ārifīn*, the sensational hagiographical account of Rūmī's life and times by Aflākī. Following the successful completion of a period of 40 days' seclusion (*chilla*), Aflākī relates how Rūmī asked his son Bahā' al-Dīn Sulṭān Walad to relate the greatest divine mystery divulged to him during his retreat. According to Aflākī, Sulṭān Walad said:

> When thirty days had elapsed in withdrawal I saw various lights like lofty mountains pass before my gaze and they went by uninterruptedly one troop after another. From the midst of these lights I clearly heard a voice, saying: '*Verily, God forgives sins altogether* (39/53).' This voice reached the ear of my consciousness in unbroken succession, and from the pleasure of the voice I lost my senses. And again I saw red-, green-, and white-coloured tablets held up before my sight, and written on them were the words: *'Every sin is forgiven you except turning away from me.'*

Straightaway Mowlānā let out a shout and began to spin about, and a tumult broke out due to the excitement of the companions. Mowlānā said: 'Bahā' al-Dīn, it is just as you have seen and heard, and a hundred times more! But for the sake of the honor of the religious law and obedience to the Bearer of the Law, keep the secrets concealed and do not tell them to anyone.'[155]

According to Sufi theosophical teachings about the Divine Names, God's forgiveness is thus manifested through a 'theophany' (*tajallī*) of certain divine Names and Attributes that reveal His Mercy. For instance, God manifests Himself as the 'Veiler of Faults' and 'Concealer of Vices' (*Sattār al-'uyūb*) under the aegis of His divine Name: 'The All-forgiving' (*Al-Ghaffār*). Ḥāfiẓ devoted an entire *ghazal* to describing his own experience of theophanic illumination with the divine Attributes, describing how:

> ... The beam that flashed out from
> The Essence made me selfless, and the brew
> They gave me from the Cup of Radiant
> Theophany revealed to me the Attributes...[156]

When bathed in the radiant glory of this theophany of divine Mercy, all human sin appears negligible and insignificant, sings Ḥāfiẓ, echoing Sulṭān Walad's vision of God's forgiveness of all sins. The Shīrāzī poet takes recourse to the same Sufi theological doctrine of God's 'all-forgiving' Nature in two other verses – both of which, though cited above, merit repetition here:

> Don't look with contempt at a drunk like me,
> For all the vaunted glory of the *Sharī'a*
> Cannot trashed by such small minutiae.[157]

* * *

> Come, come! The glory of this cosmic factory
> Shall not be made one whit less or more through austerity
> Of men like you or by debauchery of folk like me.[158]

The Metaphysical Justification of Sin

> Virtue itself turns vice, being misapplied,
> And vice sometime's by action dignified.
>
> Shakespeare[159]

One of the most paradoxical ideas in Ḥāfiẓ's theology of sin by which he justifies the inspired libertine's salvation is what might be called the *metaphysical justification of sin*.[160] The inspired libertine, enthralled in the chains of *Eros*, has realized the exalted degree of spiritual poverty, and paradoxically becomes a free spirit who neither sighs for Heaven nor quakes in fear of Hell, which is why:

The beggar on your back street does not have need
Of any of Heaven's eightfold Mansions; the captive
In your chains is free of both this world and the Next.[161]

His metaphysical justification of sin leads him to advocate the antinomian view that paradise is the final fate of *sinners* rather than the reward for those who are especially pious and good, and hence his boast:

Heaven is ordained for us. Paradise our destiny.
  Oh theologian, go away!
It's erring sinners who deserve God's generosity.[162]

The poet here definitely *does not mean* that any foolish sinner deserves heaven more than the inspired seer. The epithet 'theologian' (*khudā-shināś*: 'knower of God') given to the pretentious and sanctimonious ascetic is meant sarcastically, not seriously.[163] Although Ḥāfiẓ's poetic theology is here couched in a language subversive to orthodox Islamic soteriology, the theological doctrine underpinning the apparent blasphemy of the verse is based on a number of venerable sources in classical Islamic thought. Here only one of these need be mentioned. Ghazālī relates that once the Prophet said: 'There are certain devotees who will enter paradise *because* of committing a sin.' 'How can that be?' he was asked. Muḥammad responded: 'The devotee may commit a sin, and then feel remorseful about it and so repent of it, thus keeping it before his mind until the day he enters Paradise.'[164]

Complementing Ḥāfiẓ's doctrine of the *metaphysical justification of sin* appears the sister concept of the *metaphysical necessity of sin*. In *The Sinners' Paradise*, a major work consecrated to the spiritual necessity of sin in Islam, Shaykh Aḥmad Jām (Zhanda Pīl, d. 520/1126)[165] explains this doctrine as follows:

Gnosis is a 'burning light' and the lamp from which it shines is a 'burning light',[166] – the gnostic's chest the receptacle for its light – so the light of gnosis [*nūr-i maʿrifat*] keeps the gnostic 'warm' in the same way that the lamp warms up the glass. Just as whatever you put in that lamp will be burnt up by it, so every sin which the light of gnosis shines upon is obliterated and annulled. Just as firewood cannot withstand fire, so sin cannot resist gnosis. Just as a candle cannot be used as a lamp in the sunshine, nor even be used during daylight, so the gnostic, when illumined by the shining rays of gnosis, does not need to have recourse to any rational mode of demonstration or guidance in order to know God. Likewise, just as a lamp is of benefit in the darkness of the night, the lamp of gnosis also performs its proper service when confronted by the turbidity of sin and the darkness of heretical innovation [*bidʿat*].

... God Almighty has compared gnosis to a fire so that we will know that just as nothing can withstand fire, which burns up everything that is combustible,

> no sin can resist being consumed by the existence of gnosis: in fact, the more firewood [i.e. sin] there is, the higher, hotter and brighter becomes the fire. Now I would have to write an entire book in order to expound this topic fully, but this much is enough for one who is intelligent, wise and spiritually informed.
>
> God Almighty has created the gnostic [*'ārif*] for the sake of sinning [*gunāh kardan*], as the Tradition (that expresses this idea best) states 'If you did not sin, God would have to create another company of sinners to sin, that He might forgive them.'[167] In another tradition it is related that one of the prophets of the early tribes of Israel entreated God: 'O God, this people of mine sin excessively. Rectify them!' God sent him this revelation: 'If they did not sin, I would have to create another community to sin, so that I could show them mercy. These seas of Mercy are all for the sake of sinners. I have created the sinners, and did they not exist, sin would not exist, so all would be in vain.'
>
> Therefore, the sin of the gnostic believer [*mu'min-i 'ārif*] can be likened to firewood and gnosis compared to fire. As long as fire is there, what danger can firewood present? For when the fire is lit, the firewood is made naught. How should fire burn fire? The fire requires wood to give off light, needing it as fuel, so that people may derive benefit from it. Whether there is a whole bushel of firewood or a hundred or a hundred thousand bushels, it matters not: the quality of fire is the same – although the more firewood there is, the higher and brighter dances its flame, and the more combustible the fire is.[168]

The same phenomenon of gnosis produced through the fire of sin is expounded in the *Kashf al-asrār* by Maybudī, who depicts Adam, prototype of all human beings, as having been 'first scorched by the fire of divine guidance [in Paradise], then [cast out of Paradise] cooked in the oven of the punishment of *Adam sinned and disobeyed his Lord* (Qur'ān XX: 121), from which the sustenance of love generated by the fire [of his sin] was vouchsafed him'.[169] The fires of sin only generate wisdom and gnosis for Adam-the-lover, archetype of the enlightened libertine. In a poem modelled after (and written in the same rhyme and metre as) the work of the greatest Persian bacchanalian poet Nizārī Quhistānī (d. 721/1321),[170] Ḥāfiẓ expresses this classical Sufi doctrine as follows:

> My life is a black book. But don't rebuke a drunk
> Like me too much. No human being can ever read
> The words written on his own forehead.
>
> When Ḥāfiẓ's coffin comes by, it'll be all right
> To follow behind. Although he is
> A captive of sin, he is on his way to the Garden.[171]

Guided by his higher consciousness that bestows upon him a perception of the unity of opposites through Love, the sinner–sage thus understands like Ḥāfiẓ:

> Howeversomuch I am steeped in sin in a hundred different ways
> Since I've become acquainted with Love, I number myself
> Among the company of those who enjoy God's mercy.[172]

Since love transcends all religious commandments, overrules all sentient, illusory and temporal phenomena, resolves all conflicts raging between the various scholastic schools of theology and jurisprudence, Ḥāfiẓ issues this ecumenical call for the unity of religions from the station of Love which still resounds today:

> Let's forgive the seventy-two sects for their ridiculous
> Wars and misbehaviours. Because they couldn't accept
> The path of truth, they took the road of moonshine.[173]

Conclusion

As the above discussion has shown, in order to understand Ḥāfiẓ's views on the vice and virtue of sinners or saints, we need to comprehend *the interior, spiritual sense* in which he approached the Qur'ān and the *ḥadīth*. We must also study the *nuances* of his usage of the symbols of the mystical Sufi tradition in which his verse is steeped.[174] If Ḥāfiẓ in his verse inveighs against the fundamentalist Islam of the puritan *zāhid*, his antinomianism is not simply 'blasphemy for the blasphemy's sake'; rather it is part of his counter-ethic of bacchanalian piety put at the service of *Eros*. What is 'profane' in his verse is not opposed to the Sacred as such; rather the stock figures of the 'drunkard' (*mast*), 'pervert' (*fāsiq*) and 'inspired libertine' (*rind*) are deliberately employed as part of the *malāmatī* and *qalandarī* lexicon of the profane to scoff at religious cant and sanctimony. Part of Ḥāfiẓ's anti-clerical repertoire, these terms belong to the armoury of his bacchanalian counter-ethic that he wielded as poetic weapons in his perpetual battle with Islam's own hypocrites and Pharisees.

The same may be said of Ḥāfiẓ's vaunting of sin and exaltation of the sinner, his claim that God is the blessed sinner's, not the self-righteous pietist's friend - all his views on these matters have precise *religious* references with *ethical* connotations,[175] and are squarely based on well-known early Persian Sufi *theoerotic* and *metaphysical* doctrines.[176] Underlying his passionate contempt for the Muslim pharisees and puritans of his day, if one can detect the presence of a higher *moral* message in his philosophical doctrine of 'inspired libertinism', it is perhaps best encapsulated in this verse:

> Heart-friend, I guide you well along Salvation's way:
> Neither vaunt perversity nor hawk austerity.[177]

Notes

1 See Javādī, *Tārīkh-i ṭanz dar adabiyāt-i fārsī*, pp. 93–124. I would like to thank Terry Graham and Jason Elliot for their many helpful comments on earlier versions of this essay.

2 M.R. Shafīʿī-Kadkanī, *Zamīna-i ijtamāʿī-yi shiʿr-i fārsī*, pp. 311–12, stresses anti-clerical content of Ḥāfiẓ's verse, underlining how all the parody and invective in his poetry and all his social criticism and satire is aimed at figures of religious authority who personify sanctimony and cant.

3 For an overview of the inspired libertine's role in his poetry, see my Prolegomenon 2, pp. 31–55 above.

4 Pope, *Essay on Man*, IV: 305–6.

5 Cf. the many useful citation of verses from Ḥāfiẓ on this subject in Khurramshāhī, *Ḥāfiẓ-nāma*, I, pp. 365ff., and the excellent assembly of 'Descriptive Adjectives, Names and the Qualities of Worldliness in Ḥāfiẓ' in Bihishtī's *Sharḥ-i junūn*, pp. 680–735.

6 The Puritan movement was the 'militant tendency' within English Protestantism, and lasted down to the late seventeenth century in England and into the early eighteenth century in the USA. The actual word 'Puritan' was coined in the middle of the sixteenth century by the English as a handy term of abuse and insult directed at non-conformist Protestant clergy (Collinson, 'Antipuritanism', pp. 19–23), being one of several pejorative nicknames applied to the hotter sort of hyper-zealot who wished to 'reform the Reformation'. The 'fraudulent piety' of many Puritans in English society, who often incarnated 'the very sins which Puritans attribute to the ungodly: unprincipled greed, deception and dishonesty; and especially, sexual depravity' (*ibid.*, p. 29), led the Puritan to become the stereotype of a religious hypocrite in Elizabethean drama, since 'hypocrisy was the kind of key signature for everything else attributed to Puritans' (*ibid.*, p. 27). Originally a word with a positive connotation denoting a person of upright and public godliness, the term 'Puritan' soon became an antithetical stigma hurled at religious hypocrites who were the real puritans' less-than-ideal representatives. This stereotypical connotation of 'Puritan' as a religious hypocrite renders it a near-perfect translation, or at least a handy English idiomatic equivalent, for Ḥāfiẓ's *zāhid*, a character with almost identical traits in Persian literature. The term 'puritan' in the Islamic context has recently been successfully employed to great effect as a convenient label for the most notorious of modern *zāhids*: the Wahhabi fundamentalists of contemporary Saudi Arabia. See Khaled Abou El Fadl, *The Great Theft: Wrestling Islam from the Extremists*, the chapters on 'The Rise of the Early Puritans' and 'The Story of Contemporary Puritans'. My usage of terms such as 'puritan', 'pharisee' and 'fundamentalist' here is not meant to reflect any particular historical denomination in any religion, past or present, nor do I wish to efface the full splay and delicate nuances of centuries of Muslim religious and literary historical usage of terms such as *zāhid*, *faqīh*, and so on, by means of these terminological generalizations. Needless to say, the lives and writings of many members of the historical 'Puritan' movement, such as John Milton (1608–74) and John Bunyan (1628–88), do exemplify a certain type of esotericism and often even give voice to their staunch opposition to the fulminations of religious zealots, occasionally after the manner of Ḥāfiẓ.

7 The references to the Khānlarī edition, given by Daniela Meneghini Correale in her *The Ghazals of Hafez: Concordance and Vocabulary*, are, for *zāhid*: 22: 5; 66: 8; 70: 3; 70: 11; 72: 1; 75: 8; 78: 1; 84: 7; 135: 6; 146: 6; 154: 3; 154: 6; 177: 5; 188: 11; 197: 2; 201: 4; 249: 5; 258: 8; 266: 4; 324: 7; 354: 2; 364: 2; 366: 7; 392: 9; 409: 4; 411: 5; 457: 4; 458: 5; 464: 4; 464: 12; 471: 6; and, for *zāhidān*: 30: 6; 115: 4; 192: 1; 290: 7.

8 One example of this must here suffice: 'Sleep and feed have driven you far away from the degree of your Self. You will reach the degree of your Self when you become without sleep and feed.' *Dīvān-i Ḥāfiẓ*, ed. Khānlarī, *ghazal* 478: 45. Cf. an identical sentiment in Shakespeare's *Hamlet* (IV.4.33–35): 'What is man / If the chief good and market of his time / Is but to sleep and feed?' Lāhūrī (*Sharḥ-i ʿirfānī-yi Dīvān-i Ḥāfiẓ*, IV, p. 2845) explains this line as follows: 'In the *Ādāb al-murīdīn* [by Abū'l-Najīb Suhrawardī, d. 563/1168], treating the subject of renouncing gluttony and satiety, it is written, "One who sleeps without cognizance of God is spiritually negligent [*al-ghāfil*]", and Yaḥyā bin al-Muʿādh [d. 258/872] remarked, "If hunger were bought and sold in the bazaars, the seeker of the life hereafter would not be allowed to purchase any other ware". So the poet is saying, "O philosopher,

your sleeping without cognizance of God, on a full stomach satiated on food which is of doubtful provenance, has made you fall far away from the degree of passionate love ... but when you arrive and attain union with the Friend and become eternally subsistent through Him by means of love, then you will become without sleep and feed, for as long as you abide on the level of sleep and feed, you are but the cohort of brutes and beasts".'

9 Unlike Sanā'ī, however, Ḥāfiẓ never composed poetry solely devoted to ascetic themes (called *zuhdiyyāt*).

10 On the 'witness of divine beauty in the flesh', *shāhid*, mentioned some 15 times in the *Dīvān*, see my Prolegomenon 2, pp. 43–55. Ḥāfiẓ's rebuke to the ascetic here has Khayyāmesque overtones, and the entire *ghazal* may be usefully read as a political satire on the oppressive ruler Amīr Mubāriz al-Dīn Muẓaffar (1353–8) as well; cf. Isti'lāmī, *Dars-i Ḥāfiẓ*, II, p. 1210.

11 *Dīvān-i Ḥāfiẓ*, ed. Khānlarī, *ghazal* 471: 6.

12 *Ibid.*, *ghazal* 350: 5.

13 *Measure for Measure*, IV.ii.8–9.

14 *The Pilgrim's Progress*, pp. 83–6.

15 *Dīvān-i Ḥāfiẓ*, ed. Khānlarī, *ghazal* 154: 3.

16 I take a cue from Lāhūrī's grand commentary: *Sharḥ-i 'irfānī-yi ghazalhā-yi-i Ḥāfiẓ*, IV, p. 2365, where he identifies the counsellor and shaykh mentioned in this *ghazal* (345: 5–6 here – and also elsewhere in Ḥāfiẓ's *Dīvān*) with the ascetic Puritan (*zāhid*).

17 *Dīvān-i Ḥāfiẓ*, ed. Khānlarī, *ghazal* 345: 5–6. Translation by Bly and Lewisohn, *The Angels Knocking on the Tavern Door*, p. 51.

18 Referring to *Zāhid-i 'āqil*, see *ibid.*, *ghazal* 364: 2, discussed on the next page.

19 *Ibid.*, *ghazal* 48: 4. *Varā-yi ṭā'at-i dīvānagān zi mā maṭlab. Ki shaykh-i madhhab-i mā 'āqilī guna dānist.*

20 Lāhūrī, *Sharḥ-i 'irfānī*, I, pp. 207–8 correctly identifies *Shaykh-i madhhab-i mā* with Luqmān, mentioned in 'Aṭṭār's *Manṭiq al-ṭayr*, ed. Gawharīn, vv. 3741–52. On 'Aṭṭār's holy fools, see Ritter, *The Ocean of the Soul*, pp. 165–87.

21 Haravī, *Sharḥ-i ghazalhā-yi Ḥāfiẓ*, I, p. 251; Lāhūrī, *Sharḥ-i 'irfānī*, I, p. 207.

22 *Twelfth Night*, III.ii.72–3.

23 *Dīvān-i Ḥāfiẓ*, ed. Khānlarī, *ghazal* 385: 9. Trans. by Bly and Lewisohn, *Angels*, p. 22.

24 *Ibid.*, *ghazal* 364: 2.

25 See the extended discussion by Murtaḍawī, *Maktab-i Ḥāfiẓ*, pp. 399–422 of Ḥāfiẓ's erotic doctrine; see especially the sections on the superiority of the path of love over all other paths (pp. 406–7); the superiority of love over reason (pp. 414–15); and the topos of the 'religion of love' (p. 418).

26 Schimmel, 'Reason and Mystical Experience in Islam', pp. 142–3.

27 *Dīvān-i Ḥāfiẓ*, ed. Khānlarī, *ghazal* 22: 5. Trans. by Bly and Lewisohn, *Angels*, p. 7. Lāhūrī (*Sharḥ-i 'irfānī-yi Dīvān-i Ḥāfiẓ*, I, p. 428), thus commenting on this verse, explains that 'it is through the forms of mortal beauty [*suwar-i husniyya*] that God-as-Absolute in reality attracts the hearts of lovers to Himself'. See the discussion of *shāhid-bāzī* and *naẓarbāzī* in my Prolegomenon 2.

28 Cf. Lāhūrī, *Sharḥ-i 'irfānī-yi Dīvān-i Ḥāfiẓ*, I, p. 546.

29 *Gulistān-i Sa'dī*, ed. Khaṭīb Rahbar, II: 6, pp. 152–3.

30 Such religious mountebanks and dissembling puritan ascetics are a phenomenon of daily life in the modern-day Persianate culture of Iran and Afghanistan. Following the clerical *coup d'état* of 1979, there is hardly a major Iranian writer who has not depicted in detail the *zāhid*'s humbug and counterfeit piety. Sa'īdī Sīrjānī's *O Short-cuffed Men!* (*Ay kūta-āstīnān*; for Sīrjānī's analysis of Ḥāfiẓ's radical anti-clericalism, see pp. 261–88; esp. 282–8) – the title being taken from a verse by Ḥāfiẓ referring to greedy mountebank dervishes (*Dīvān-i Ḥāfiẓ*, ed. Khānlarī, *ghazal* 426: 10b) – is one of the most famous works in this regard (with thanks to Kamran Talattof for this reference). Likewise, see the many descriptions provided by the father of modern Tajik literature, Sadriddin Aini (1878–1954), of his experience of the chicanery of seminary school teachers and their students in Bukhara, and the hypocritical *zāhids* and sanctimonious mullahs throughout Tajikistan in his monumental autobiography (with thanks to Ibrahim Gamard and Ravan Farhadi for this reference) – see Aini, *Bukhara*

Reminiscences, pp. 137–47; Perry and Lehr (trans.), *The Sands of Oxus: Boyhood Reminiscences of Sadriddin Aini*, pp. 145–7; 151–61; 249ff. A typical picture of a modern sanctimonious Afghan *zāhid* is provided by Rory Stewart in *The Places in Between*, pp. 217–19.

31 *Dīvān-i Ḥāfiẓ*, ed. Khānlarī, *ghazal* 78: 1.

32 A more literal translation of the Persian phrase *zāhid-i pākīza-sirisht* is '*pure-natured* ascetic'. It should be underlined that this descriptive adjective was borrowed by Ḥāfiẓ from the *maqṭa'* of a *ghazal*, written in the same rhyme by Khwājū Kirmānī (d. 742/1342): see *Dīwān-i Khwājū Kirmānī*, ed. Qāni'ī, pp. 385–6, *ghazal* 57: v. 9, to which Ḥāfiẓ responded here.

33 Isaac Watts, *Abuse of the Emotions in Spiritual Life* (1746), in Jeffery (ed.), *English Spirituality in the Age of Wesley*, p. 73.

34 Matthew, 7:3.

35 *Hudibras*, ed. Henry G. Bohn (London: Henry G. Bohn, 1859), Canto I, Part 1, 207–10, p. 13.

36 *Dīvān-i Ḥāfiẓ*, ed. Khānlarī, *ghazal* 258: 8.

37 From his poem 'Forebearance'.

38 See my 'The Metaphysics of Justice and the Ethics of Mercy in the Thought of 'Ali ibn Abi Talib', pp. 108–46, where the origins of this attitude are traced back to the Persian Sufi chivalric tradition.

39 See *Mathnawī*, ed. Nicholson, I: 1394–402; II: 3027–45; II: 881–5; IV: 367–8. Ḥāfiẓ's moral advice to the ascetic in the first three verses of *ghazal* 78 may be, I think, modelled on Rūmī, *Mathnawī*, II: 881–3, Nicholson's comment on which is relevant here: 'Any one who regards the faults of his neighbours instead of his own resembles the idolater who worships an idol instead of devoting himself to God.'

40 *Dīvān-i Ḥāfiẓ*, ed. Khānlarī, *ghazal* 385: 4. Trans. by Bly and Lewisohn, *Angels*, p. 21. Although Khānlarī's *lectio* is *rāz* (secret), three of his manuscripts read *'ayb* (fault), which is the reading we follow here (this is also Qazwīnī and Ghanī's *lectio*).

41 As Lāhūrī relates, the Prophet taught that only Imām 'Alī (not 'Umar, Uthmān or Abū Bakr) had grasped that the main condition for salvation lay in 'revealing the upright virtues [*rāst*] of God's devotees and concealing their faults'. Lāhūrī moralizes that 'indeed, being a dervish totally consists in concealing the faults of people' (*Sharḥ-i 'irfānī-yi Dīvān-i Ḥāfiẓ*, IV, p. 2563). For the full story, see Bly and Lewisohn, *Angels*, p. 90, n. 81. The emphasis of Ḥāfiẓ's master on the virtue of abstaining from censure of one's neighbours is akin to Blake's view that 'Mutual forgiveness of each vice / Such are the Gates of Paradise'. Blake's verse echoes a line in the *Dīvān*, ed. Khanlari, *ghazal* 476: 7.

42 Ghanī, *Baḥth dar āthār*, p. 124; Browne, *A Literary History of Persia*, III, p. 275.

43 Maḥmūd ibn 'Uthmān, *Miftāḥ al-hidāya wa miṣbāḥ al-'ināya: Sīrat-nāma-i Shaykh Amīn al-Dīn Muḥammad Balyānī*, p. 110.

44 *Manṭiq al-ṭayr*, vv. 3013–16; trans. Darbandi and Davis, *The Conference of the Birds*, p. 155.

45 This is the theme of *ghazal* 183: 2: 'View my love as the perfection of the mystery of *Eros*, not as the taint of sin. / You know that everyone without artistic talent ends up as a critic.'

46 *Manṭiq al-tayr*, vv. 3026–7; trans. Darbandi and Davis, *The Conference of the Birds*, p. 155.

47 Pūrnāmdāriyān, *Gumshuda-yi lab-i daryā: Tā'ammulī dar ma'nā va ṣūrat-i sh'ir-i Ḥāfiẓ*, pp. 18–19.

48 *Dīvān-i Ḥāfiẓ*, ed. Khānlarī, *ghazal* 76: 6. Ḥāfiẓ repeats exactly the same moral message elsewhere (*ghazal* 67: 10), stating even more bluntly that, 'eternal salvation lies in causing no soul distress' (*Dilash bi-nāla miyāzār va khatm kun Ḥāfiẓ/ ki rastigārī jāvīd dar kam āzārī-ast*).

49 For a good discussion of which see Murtaḍawī, *Maktab-i Ḥāfiẓ*, pp. 271–5. Mu'īn (*Ḥāfiẓ-i shīrīn-sukhan*, I, p. 289) also underlines the 'deep influence' of Balyānī on Ḥāfiẓ.

50 'Uthmān, *Miftāḥ al-hidāya*, pp. 112–16.

51 *Ibid*., p. 112. Note the near identity of terminology here between Balyānī's dictum, Anṣārī's epigram (*Harchi nay rāḥat, nay ṭā'at, va harchi nay āzār, nay gunāh*) and Ḥāfiẓ's verse: *mabāsh dar pay-i āzār va harchih khwāhī kun / kay dar sharī'at-i mā ghayr az īn gunāhī nīst!* Ḥāfiẓ's acquaintance with Balyānī's own *Dīvān* (unfortunately still unpublished!) is demonstrated by the number of verses where Ḥāfiẓ imitates him, on which see Muḥammad Amīn Riyāḥī in his *Gulgasht dar shi'r va andīsha-yi Ḥāfiẓ*, pp. 217–18. 'Abd al-Ḥusayn Zarrīnkūb's dogmatic opinion (*Az kūcha-i rindān*, p. 168) that Ḥāfiẓ actually had no real 'devotional commitment' (*irādat*) to Balyānī is now dated, since he does not mention nor

take into account any of these quite demonstrable poetic and pedagogic influences of the Kāzarūnī Shaykh on Ḥāfiẓ. For further discussion of Ḥāfiẓ's relation to this Sufi master, also see Mu'īn, *Ḥāfiẓ-i shīrīn-sukhan*, I, pp. 288–90. The best overview of Ḥāfiẓ's close relationship to the Sufi tradition of his day (and excellently annotated critical refutation of Zarrīnkūb's views on the same) is given by the seminal article penned by the Markaz-i Taḥqīqāt-i fārsī-yi Īrān va Pākistān, 'Gāmī-yi chand *Bā Kāravān-i Ḥulla*'.

52 'Uthmān, *Miftāḥ*, p. 111. The passage is from Matthew (5:44): 'Do not resist the one who is evil. But if one strikes you on the right cheek, turn to him the other also; and if any one would sue you and take your coat, let him have your cloak as well.'

53 *Dīvān-i Ḥāfiẓ*, ed. Khānlarī, *ghazal* 318: 5.

54 *Ibid.*, *ghazal* 258: 8.

55 Qur'ān, 6:164. This theme is repeated frequently in the Qur'ān; see: 17:15; 35:18, 39:7.

56 *Dīvān-i Ḥāfiẓ*, ed. Khānlarī, *ghazal* 78: 1.

57 Muḥammad Dārābī (in his mystical commentary on Ḥāfiẓ, *Laṭīfa-yi ghaybī*, p. 85) asserts that this couplet alludes to the *ḥadīth*: 'This world is farmland of the Next.' Both Haravī (*Sharḥ-i Ghazalhā-yi Ḥāfiẓ*, I, p. 364) and Khurramshāhī (*Ḥāfiẓ-nāma*, I, p. 395) view these two couplets as paraphrasing Qur'ān 5:105 – 'O you who believe! You have charge of your own souls. He who errs cannot injure you if you are rightly guided. To God you will all return and He will then inform you of what ye used to do.' Both verses comprise versified paraphrases of the Sufi teachings of Amīn al-Dīn Balyānī to the same effect – see 'Uthmān, *Miftāḥ al-hidāya*, p. 139.

58 *Dīvān-i Ḥāfiẓ*, ed. Khānlarī, *ghazal* 78: 2–3. Ḥāfiẓ's ideas and imagery in this *ghazal* closely imitate *ghazals* by Nizārī Quhistānī and Khwājū Kirmānī, written in the same metre and rhyme. See *Dīwān-i Khwājū Kirmānī*, ed. Qāni'ī, p. 385; and *Dīvān-i Ḥakīm Nizārī Quhistānī*, pp. 920–1; *ghazal* 343. See my 'Sufism and Ismā'īlī Doctrine in the Persian Poetry of Nizārī Quhistānī', p. 251, n. 107.

59 See the chapter on *faqr* in Bukhārā'ī, *Farhang-i ash'ār-i Ḥāfiẓ*, pp. 509–23; also cf. Khurramshāhī, *Ḥāfiẓ-nāma*, I, pp. 264–6.

60 *Dīvān-i Ḥāfiẓ*, ed. Khānlarī, *ghazal* 262: 3.

61 'Know that ascetic renunciation [*zuhd*] is the first station of disciples [*murīdān*].' Bukhārī, *Sharḥ al-ta'arruf li-madhhab ahl al-taṣawwuf*, p. 1219.

62 According to 'Abdu'llāh Anṣārī, there are three degrees of devotion: to the world, to the hereafter, and to God. The *zāhid* longs for the second degree (of the hereafter), but the lover / inspired libertine (*'āshiq / rind*) is devoted only to God (the third degree), and thus is freed of the world, the hereafter, from mankind, and his own personal self-finitude. See Field 5 (*irādat*) in *Sad maydān*, in *Majmū'a-yi Rasā'il Farsī-yi Khʷāja 'Abdu'llāh Anṣārī*, ed. Sarvar Mullā'ī, pp. 262–3.

63 *Dīwān-i Khʷāja Ḥāfiẓ-i Shīrāzī*, ed. Anjawī-Shīrāzī, p. 205.

64 In the early Muslim mystical tradition, four degrees of yearning or longing (*shawq*) for God are mentioned, beginning with renunciation (*zuhd*), then fear (*khawf*), yearning for Paradise (*al-shawq ilā'l-janna*) and, lastly, Love for God (*maḥabba li-Lāh*), but from Anṣārī's (d. 481/1089) time onwards, the Sufi tradition in Persia jettisoned and largely rejected this early ascetic ideal of 'yearning for paradise' in favour of the pure love of God in the heart (*shawq al-qalb*). I have outlined this development in my article on yearning: 'Shawḳ', *EI*², IX, pp. 376–7. See as well Pūrjavādī, 'Rindī-yi Ḥāfiẓ', in his *Bū-yi jān*, p. 271.

65 Pūrjavādī, 'Rindī-yi Ḥāfiẓ', in *Bū-yi jān*, p. 255.

66 *Sharḥ al-ta'arruf*, p. 1220.

67 *Dīvān-i Ḥāfiẓ*, ed. Khānlarī, *ghazal* 392: 9.

68 'Aṭṭār, *Tadhkirat al-awliyā'*, ed. Isti'lamī, p. 190. This same emphasis on humility is reflected in Nietzche's saying, 'Many a one hath cast away his final worth when he hath cast away his servitude'. Nietzsche, *Thus Spake Zarathustra*, I, 17, in *The Philosophy of Nietzsche*, p. 65. Cited by Edinger, *Ego and Archetype: Individuation and the Religious Function of the Psyche*, p. 27. See my discussion of Ḥāfiẓ's view of sin below. As Pūrjavādī points out: 'The inspired libertine is endowed with "works" but his works are completely different from those of the ascetic. The "works" of the inspired libertine estrange him

from his egocentric "self" and bring him near to the beloved, whereas the "works" of the ascetic only estrange him, creating distance between him and his beloved. It is for this reason that Ḥāfiẓ assigns a negative value to all the ascetic's pious works and practices.' 'Rindī-yi Ḥāfiẓ', in *Bū-yi jān*, pp. 271–2.

69 'Ayn al-Quḍāt Hamadhānī, *Tamhīdāt*, no. 393, p. 300: 3.

70 *Dīvān-i Ḥāfiẓ*, ed. Khānlarī, *ghazal* 117: 6.

71 *Ibid.*, *ghazal* 50: 9.

72 *Ibid.*, *ghazal* 431: 7. As Qāsim Ghanī, and following him, Khurramshāhī and Haravī note, this verse paraphrases a saying of the Prophet Muḥammad: 'In God's eyes the most beloved of God's devotees is the poor dervish contented with what he has and satisfied with the daily bread given by God to him.' Ḥāfiẓ's line is actually a verse-epigram on Abū Ḥāmid al-Ghazālī's ethical teachings, summarizing one of the chapter headings – 'The Virtue of Being a Dervish and Contentment', *Faḍilat-i darvīshī va khursandī* – of his *Kīmiyā-yi sa'ādat*, II, pp. 424–5. See Haravī, *Sharḥ-i ghazalhā-yi Ḥāfiẓ*, III, p. 1791; Khurramshāhī, *Ḥāfiẓ-nāma*, II, p. 1163. Ḥāfiẓ's Sufi teachings on contentment (*riḍā, qanā'at, khursandī*) are summarized by Khurramshāhī, *Ḥāfiẓ-nāma*, I, p. 490. Cf. Shakespeare's verses: 'Poor and content is rich, and rich enough, / But riches fineless is as poor as winter / To him that ever fears he shall be poor' (*Othello*, III.iii), which provide a perfect Christian homologue to Ḥāfiẓ's verse.

73 *Dīvān-i Ḥāfiẓ*, ed. Khānlarī, *ghazal* 75: 8.

74 See *Ibid.*, *ghazal* 241: 8.

75 *Ibid.*, *ghazal* 468: 4. In lieu of Khānlarī's *fasḥat*, I am following the variant reading of *rawnaq* found in the commentaries of Haravī and Khurramshāhī, and in the editions of Qazvīnī, Anjavī Shīrāzī and several others. Alternatively, one may translate the verse as: 'Come, for the productivity of this workshop won't grow less / Through austerities like yours or indulgences like mine.' I understand Hāfiẓ as expressing the same message that Alexander Pope (*Essay on Man*, IV: 135–6) intended to pose in his rhetorical question: 'The good must merit God's special care, / But who, but God, can tell us who they are?'

76 Cf. *Dīvān-i Ḥāfiẓ*, ed. Khānlarī, *ghazal* 81: 4. The doctrine that there is no virtue higher than lowliness of spirit and humility is too well known among mystics to merit comment here; nonetheless, it seems very relevant here to cite the observation of the English mystic William Law (1686–1761) that 'a humble state of soul is the very state of religion, because humility is the life and soul of piety... For this reason, no people have more occasion to be afraid of the approaches of pride than those who have made some advances in a pious life. For pride can grow as well upon our virtues as our vices, and steals upon us on all occasions. *Every good thought that we have, every good action that we do, lays us open to pride and exposes us to the assaults of vanity and self-satisfaction...' A Serious Call to a Devout and Holy Life*, pp. 228–9. Italics mine.

77 *Dīvān-i Ḥāfiẓ*, ed. Khānlarī, *ghazal* 84: 7.

78 'Two men went up into the temple to pray; the one a Pharisee, and the other a publican. The Pharisee stood and prayed thus with himself, God, I thank thee, that I am not as other men *are*, extortioners, unjust, adulterers, or even as this publican. I fast twice a week, I give tithes of all that I possess. And the publican, standing afar off, would not lift up so much as *his* eyes unto heaven, but smote upon his breast, saying, God be merciful to me a sinner. I tell you, this man went down to his house justified *rather* than the other: for every one that exalteth himself shall be abased; and he that humbleth himself shall be exalted' (Luke, 18:10–14).

79 *Būstān-i Sa'dī*, ed. Īzadparast, pp. 184–8. The translation has been revised from my own translation of these verses in Nurbakhsh, *Jesus in the Eyes of the Sufis*, pp. 101–6.

80 Khurramshāhī, 'Mayl-i Ḥāfiẓ bih gunāh', in his *Dhihn u zabān-i Ḥāfiẓ*, pp. 77.

81 The two key verses on this theme in Ḥāfiẓ's *Dīvān* are: 'Between lover and beloved there exists / No veil at all. You, you yourself are / Your own veil: Ḥāfiẓ, get out of the way!' (*Dīvān-i Ḥāfiẓ*, ed. Khānlarī, *ghazal* 260: 9, discussed below) and: 'In the realm of inspired libertinism, no thought of "self" or "self-opinion" exists. In this religion all thought of self and all egocentric opinions are infidelity' (*ghazal* 484: 10). On the notion of selflessness in Persian Sufi poetry, see the beautiful article by Leili Anvar-Chenderoff, '"Without us, from us we are safe": Self and Selflessness in the *Dīvān* of 'Aṭṭār'. See also Bukhārā'ī, *Farhang-i ash'ār-i Ḥāfiẓ*, pp. 157–60.

82 *Dīvān-i Ḥāfiẓ*, ed. Khānlarī, *ghazal* 426: 3.

83 ʻAṭṭār, *Tadhkirat*, ed. Istiʻlami, p. 379.

84 Wensinck, 'al-Khaḍir', *EI*², IV, p. 904.

85 *Sharḥ-i 'irfānī-yi Dīvān-i Ḥāfiẓ*, IV, p. 2862. The doctrine is versified in another line by Ḥāfiẓ: 'Wash your hands clean of the base copper of existence, like men of the Path / till you find the Alchemy of Love and become gold' (*Dīvān-i Ḥāfiẓ*, ed. Khānlarī, *ghazal* 478: 3).

86 *Ibid.*, *ghazal* 220: 1.

87 Ghazālī, *Kīmiyā-yi sa'ādat*, II, p. 260; cited by Khurramshāhī, *Ḥāfiẓ-nāma*, II, p. 851.

88 For a detailed discussion of the 'veil of the infidel selfhood' in Sufism, see my *Beyond Faith and Infidelity*, pp. 296–9.

89 *Dīvān-i Ḥāfiẓ*, ed. Khānlarī, *ghazal* 260: 9. This verse, in which the poet apparently addresses himself, is, as Pūrjavādī notes ('Rindī-yi Ḥāfiẓ', in his *Bū-yi jān*, p. 279), penned as a rebuke of the inspired libertine (*rind*) to himself.

90 See Furūzānfar, *Aḥādīth-i Mathnawī*, p. 9 for this and other similar *aḥadīth*.

91 Maybudī, *Kashf al-asrār*, VI, p. 440.

92 Cited by Bukhārā'ī, *Farhang-i ash'ār-i Ḥāfiẓ*, p. 160.

93 *Dīvān-i Ḥāfiẓ*, ed. Khānlarī, *ghazal* 201: 4. I disagree with Haravī (*Sharḥ-i ghazalhā-yi Ḥāfiẓ*, II, p. 866), who simply interprets the expression *you and me* (*man u tū*, also translatable as 'I and thou', 'me and thee', or 'mine and thine') in this verse to mean both the poet and the ascetic together. Such an interpretation ignores the whole literary and technical history of this particular phrase in earlier Sufi texts, where it signifies the false pride of the egocentric selfhood (*maniyat*) that veils the mystic. ʻAṭṭār thus writes: 'Whoever retains a dualistic self-identity [*dū'ī*] is like a polytheist: the catastrophe we face all comes from I-ness [*manī*] and you-ness [*tū'ī*]' (*Ilāhī-nāma*, ed. Fu'ād Rūḥānī, v. 2015). Elsewhere, he writes: 'A myriad indications of hypocrisy still remain within you as long as there is one atom of selfhood left / If you think yourself secure from selfhood [*manī*], both worlds will act as foes to you' (*Manṭiq al-ṭayr*, ed. Shafī'ī-Kadkanī, vv. 2948–9).

94 *Twelfth Night*, I.v.89.

95 Cf. Pūrjavādī, 'Rindī-yi Ḥāfiẓ', pp. 221f.

96 *Twelfth Night*, I.v.90. Olivia to Malvolio again.

97 *Dīvān-i Ḥāfiẓ*, ed. Khānlarī, *ghazal* 137: 6–7.

98 When in one *ghazal* (385: 3), Ḥāfiẓ maintains that 'in our Path [*ṭarīqat*] it's pure infidelity [*kāfarī*] to take offence', Lāhūrī (*Sharḥ-i 'irfānī*, IV, p. 2562) paraphrases the subtle Sufi metaphysical doctrine underlying Ḥāfiẓ's unitary mystical vision as follows: 'Our theosophical persuasion [*mashrab*] consists in keeping faith with and preserving any true bonds of relationship that we have formed with everyone, cheerfully bearing the burdens of blame of all and sundry, and not ever becoming distressed. The reason for this is that in our mystical way [*ṭarīqat*], according to the tenets of our theosophical persuasion, getting offended by attention to the illusion of what's other [*ghayr*; i.e. than God] constitutes infidelity [*kāfarī*] and "hidden polytheism" or "associationism" [*shirk-i khafī*]. Those who have realized the spiritual station of pure divine Unity [*maqām-i tawḥīd-i ṣarf*] perceive through direct vision that save God Almighty, there is no other really existing Being and active Agent in existence, and that all other entities, qualities and actions are annihilated, null and void. They comprehend that all the delights that they experience are but radiant reflections cast by the light of absolute divine Beauty [*jamāl-i muṭlaq*] and consider that every pain and grief that afflicts them to be another ray cast by the light of absolute divine Majesty [*jalāl-i muṭlaq*]. If they were to become offended by some irritation whilst endowed with such traits of personality, they would thus be allowing someone else to participate and share in the divine Activity – and that would constitute heresy on the Sufi way [*kufr-i ṭarīqat*] and a "hidden polytheism".' Hidden polytheism is discussed below, p. 175.

99 *Blake: Complete Writings*, p. 754, vv. 27–8.

100 Milton, *Paradise Lost*, III: 681–4.

101 Khurramshāhī, 'Mayl-i Ḥāfiẓ bih gunāh', in his *Dhihn u zabān-i Ḥāfiẓ*, p. 77.

102 *Ibid.*, p. 68. Elsewhere he observes: 'Ḥāfiẓ's had only one sole motivation in haranguing and assailing the Preacher, Ascetic, Sufi and Policeman throughout his *Dīvān*. That was his struggle against hypocrisy, for these figures were high representatives of the Pharisaical sanctimony and cant which typified his age' (*Ḥāfiẓ-nāma*, II, p. 819).

103 For other studies on hypocrisy in Ḥāfiẓ's thought, see Muḥammad Shafī'ī, 'Mubāriza-i Ḥāfiẓ bā riyā", in Manṣūr Rastigār (ed.), *Maqālātī dar-bāra-i zindagī va shi'r-i Ḥāfiẓ*, pp. 330–41; Fattī, *Ḥāfiẓ rā chinīn pindāshta-and*, pp. 105–12; Yathribī, *Āb-i ṭarabnāk: taḥlīl-i mawḍū'ī-yi Dīvān-i Ḥāfiẓ*, pp. 483–5, who devotes an entire sub-section in his chapter on Ḥāfiẓ's verses about hypocrisy to those written on the theme of the 'preference of vice [*fasād*] over hypocrisy and ostentation'.

104 *Dīvān-i Ḥāfiẓ*, ed. Khānlarī, *ghazal* 335: 4.

105 Khurramshāhī, *Ḥāfiẓ-nāma*, II, p. 818.

106 Anṣārī, *Sad maydān*, in *Majmū'a-i Rasā'il-i fārsī-yi ... Anṣārī*, pp. 318–19.

107 Khurramshāhī, *Ḥāfiẓ-nāma*, II, p. 818. Also cf. Lāhūrī's definitions of hypocrisy: *Sharḥ-i 'irfānī*, II, p. 1460.

108 *Nahj*, p. 83; *Peak*, p. 216. I am indebted to Dr Reza Shah-Kazemi, here and elsewhere throughout this chapter, for all references to *Nahj al-Balāgha*.

109 Cited by Sayyid Ḥaydar Āmulī in his commentary on Sūra Yūsuf, XII: 106; 'And most of them believe not in God, except that they are polytheists [*illū wa hum mushrikūn*]', *Al-Muḥīṭ al-a'ẓam*, I, p. 284. The *ḥadīth* is found in slightly differing versions in *Masnad* Ibn Ḥanbal, vol. 4, p. 403; *al-Mustadrak*, vol. 1, p. 113; and Tabarsī in his comment on verse VI: 108. I am indebted to Dr Reza Shah-Kazemi for these references, which are given by the editor of *Al-Muḥīṭ*, Muḥsin al-Mūsawī al-Tabrīzī, vol. I, p. 284, n. 54.

110 *Hamlet* III.i.47–9. Polonius to Ophelia.

111 *Dīvān-i Ḥāfiẓ*, ed. Khanlari, *ghazal* 262: 2. Trans. by Bly and Lewisohn, *Angels*, p. 31. See also *ghazal* 347: 4.

112 On Ḥāfiẓ's bacchanalia (a topic frequently discussed and studied by scholars), the best sources relevant to my analysis here are: Bukhārā'ī, *Farhang-i ash'ār-i Ḥāfiẓ*, pp. 197–8; Khurramshāhī, *Ḥāfiẓ-nāma*, I, pp. 153–4.

113 *Dīvān-i Ḥāfiẓ*, ed. Khanlari, *ghazal* 26: 7. Trans. by Bly and Lewisohn, *Angels*, p. 31.

114 *Ibid.*, *ghazal* 126: 10.

115 *Ibid.*, *ghazal* 191: 6. Ḥāfiẓ's doctrine in this verse follows Niẓārī Quhistānī's bacchanalian tenets exactly, as I have shown in my 'Sufism and Ismā'īlī Doctrine in ... Nizārī Quhistānī', pp. 233–5.

116 *Ibid.*, *ghazal* 25: 4.

117 *Dīwān-i Khwāja Ḥāfiẓ-i Shīrāzī*, ed. Anjawī-Shīrāzī, p. 145.

118 *Dīvān-i Ḥāfiẓ*, ed. Khānlarī, *ghazal* 115: 4.

119 *Ibid.*, *ghazal* 30: 6.

120 *Ibid.*, *ghazal* 385: 9.

121 *Ibid.*, *ghazal* 25: 7–8. Cf. Khurramshāhī, 'Mayl-i Ḥāfiẓ bih gunāh', p. 74; Mazār'ī, *Mafhūm-i rindī dar shi'r-i Ḥāfiẓ*, pp. 107–8.

122 *Dīvān-i Ḥāfiẓ*, ed. Khānlarī, *ghazal* 399: 8.

123 See also Khurramshāhī's remarkable essay on 'Ḥāfiẓ's Penchant for Sin' ('Mayl-i Ḥāfiẓ bih gunāh'), in his *Dhihn u zabān-i Ḥāfiẓ*, pp. 61–92; also his *Ḥāfiẓ-nāma*, I, pp. iii–viii, where the same subject is broached.

124 *Dīvān-i Ḥāfiẓ*, ed. Khānlarī, *ghazal* 84: 7.

125 Cf. Yohannan, 'The Persian Poet Ḥāfiẓ in England and America', pp. 107–19.

126 Lāhūrī, *Sharḥ-i 'irfānī-yi ghazalhā-yi-i Ḥāfiẓ*, I, p. 490. See also Losensky (trans.), *Farid ad-Din 'Attār's Memorial of God's Friends*, p. 51.

127 *Tadhkirat al-awliyā'*, ed. Isti'lāmī, p. 17.

128 *Nahj al-Balāgha*, 43, p. 414; trans. Sayed Ali Reza, *Peak of Eloquence*, no. 46, p. 581.

129 John Taylor, 'Ja'far al-Ṣādiq: Spiritual Forebear of the Ṣūfīs', pp. 112ff.; Carl Ernst, 'The Stages of Love in Early Persian Sufism', pp. 436–7.

130 See my 'Overview: Iranian Islam and Persianate Sufism', in Lewisohn (ed.), *The Heritage of Sufism*, I, pp. 19–24, where this distinction is discussed in detail.

[131] Anṣārī, *Ṭabaqāt al-ṣūfiyya*, pp. 7, 321; cited by Khurramshāhī, *Ḥāfiẓ-nāma*, I, p. v.

[132] Ibn Munawwar, *Asrār al-tawḥīd*, ed. Shafī'ī-Kadkanī, pp. 302–3; cited by Khurramshāhī, *Ḥāfiẓ-nāma*, I, p. v. These sayings were also cited in my footnote to Bly and Lewisohn, *Angels*, pp. 87–9, n. 3.

[133] *'Ilāhīl Bīzāram az ṭā'atī kay marā bi-'ujb andāzad; mubārak ma'ṣīatī kay marā bi-'udhr āwarad!'*

[134] *Dīvān-i Ḥāfiẓ*, ed. Khānlarī, *ghazal* 154: 6.

[135] 'Uthmān, *Miftāḥ al-hidāya*, p. 103.

[136] *Mirṣād al-'ibād*, ed. Riyāḥī, p. 71.

[137] Dāryūsh Āshūrī, *'Irfān u rindī dar shi'r-i Ḥāfiẓ*, pp. 122–3.

[138] *Dīvān-i Ḥāfiẓ*, ed. Khānlarī, *ghazal* 75: 8. Trans. by Bly and Lewisohn, *Angels*, p. 10.

[139] *Diwan-i Ḥāfiẓ*, ed. Khānlarī, *ghazal* 127: 3.

[140] Āshūrī, *'Irfān u rindī*, pp. 128f.

[141] Cf. this verse: *Man-i sar-gashta ham az ahl-i salāmat būdam / Dām-i rāham shikān-i turra-yi hindū-yi tu būd* (I once belonged among the sound and fit / though now I am a wanderer adrift. / Your pleated Hindu ringlet was set as ruse / there on my way: I tripped the noose and took the bait), in *Dīwān-i Khʷāja Ḥāfiẓ-i Shīrāzī*, ed. Anjawī-Shīrāzī, p. 77. Cf. the term *salāmat* ('sound and fit') employed by Rāzī in the above passage in exactly the same sense; for further comparisons of similar terms, see Āshūrī, *'Irfān u rindī*, pp. 68–139.

[142] *Kashf al-asrār*, III, p. 297.

[143] *Dīvān-i Ḥāfiẓ*, ed. Khānlarī, *ghazal* 329: 3. Cf. Lāhūrī, *Sharḥ- 'irfānī*, IV, p. 2393.

[144] *Dīvān-i Ḥāfiẓ*, ed. Khānlarī, *ghazal* 332: 6.

[145] *Ibid.*, *ghazal* 78: 6. Translation by Bly and Lewisohn, *Angels*, p. 33.

[146] *Measure for Measure* II.i.38, Escalus to Angelo.

[147] This idea is best expressed by the Qājār Persian poet Mu'tamid Nishāṭ-i Iṣfahānī (d. 1244/1828) in this verse: 'If one cannot behave with pious obedience then commit a sin one must: by hook or crook a way must be found to gain the heart of the Friend!' (*Ṭā'at az dast niyāyad guna'ī bayād kard/ dar dil-i dūst bi-har ḥīla rahī bayād kard.*), *Dīvān-i Nishāṭ-i Iṣfahānī*, p. 96, *ghazal* 117: 1.

[148] See Daud Rahbar's *God of Justice: A Study in the Ethical Doctrine of the Qur'an*, which analyses 90 different concepts of divine Forgiveness in the Qur'an.

[149] A.J. Arberry's translation of the Qur'ān (3:134–5), slightly modified.

[150] Qur'ān 3:156; 40:7.

[151] Qur'ān 39:53.

[152] Furūzānfar, *Aḥādīth-i Mathnawī*, p. 26, n. 64.

[153] Four *ghazals* at least (58: 1–3; 306: 3; 314: 10; 332: 5) in his *Dīvān* testify to Ḥāfiẓ's faith in God's ultimate redemption and forgiveness of all sins. In many other *ghazals*, he begs God to forgive his faults, conceal his vices and overlook his sins, since 'the good name of the *Sharī'a* will not be tarnished by something so trite' (219: 7). Basing himself on Qur'ān: 'Do not despair of God's mercy, Who forgives all sins' (39:53), in *ghazal* 397 (v. 4), he reiterates the doctrine of this angelic messenger (*surūsh*): 'Bring wine, for the seraphim of the Unseen realm gives glad tidings that the grace of God's mercy prevails over all.' Lāhūrī explains the doctrine: 'The ascetic recluse as well as the drunken libertine, the pious philanthropist as well as the miscreant sinner all should have hope in God's grace and mercy.' *Sharḥ-i 'irfānī-yi ghazalhā-yi-i Ḥāfiẓ*, IV, p. 2611.

[154] *Dīvān-i Ḥāfiẓ*, ed. Khānlarī, *ghazal* 279: 1–3.

[155] Aflākī, *The Feats of the Knowers of God (Manāqeb al-'ārefīn)*, trans. John O'Kane, p. 554.

[156] *Dīvān-i Ḥāfiẓ*, ed. Khānlarī, *ghazal* 178: 2. The entire *ghazal* is discussed *in extenso* by Leili Anvar above, pp. 123–39.

[157] *Ibid.*, *ghazal* 219: 6. The reading of first hemistich cited here appears in five of Khānlarī's variant manuscripts, although Khānlarī's own *lectio* ('Cover the faults of a drunk like me under the skirt of your forgiveness...') demonstrates this point with equal effectiveness.

[158] *Ibid.*, *ghazal* 468: 4, following here the variant reading of *rawnaq* [for Khānlarī's *fasḥat*], found in the editions of Haravī, Khurramshāhī, Anjavī Shīrāzī and several other editions.

[159] *Romeo and Juliet*, II.iii.17–18.

160 Ḥāfiẓ's most famous verse (from a *ghazal* absent from many scholarly editions of the *Dīvān*), often cited in this context, is: 'Infidelity is unavoidable in the Workshop of Love. If Abū Lahab did not exist, then who would be burnt in Hellfire?' Cf. Dārābī, *Laṭīfa-yi ghaybī*, p. 122; Lāhūrī, *Sharḥ-i 'irfānī*, I, p. 1091.

161 *Dīvān-i Ḥāfiẓ*, ed. Khānlarī, *ghazal* 36: 4.

162 *Ibid.*, *ghazal* 190: 5.

163 See the analyses of this verse by Isti'lāmī, *Dars-i Ḥāfiẓ*, I, p. 535; Khurramshāhī, *Ḥāfiẓ-nāma*, I, p. 713; Lāhūrī, *Sharḥ-i 'irfānī-yi ghazalhā-yi-i Ḥāfiẓ*, II, p. 1439.

164 Ghazālī, *Kīmiyā-yi sa'ādat*, II, p. 326; cited by Khurramshāhī, *Ḥāfiẓ-nāma*, I, pp. 713–14.

165 On whom, see Heshmat Moayyad and Franklin Lewis, *The Colossal Elephant and His Spiritual Feats, Shaykh Ahmad-e Jām: The Life and Legend of a Popular Sufi Saint of 12th Century Iran.*

166 The reference here to the burning light is taken from the following famous Qur'ānic verse (24:35): 'God is the light of the heavens and the earth. The similitude of His light is as a niche wherein is a lamp. The lamp is in a glass. The glass is as it were a shining star. This lamp is kindled from a blessed tree, an olive neither of the East nor of the West, whose oil would almost glow forth (of itself) though no fire touched it. Light upon light. God guides unto His light whom He will. And God speaks to mankind in parables, for God is the Knower of all things.'

167 See the long footnote with detailed discussion of the provenance of this *ḥadīth*, given by the text's editor 'Alī Fāḍil, *Rawḍat al-Mudhbibīn*, pp. 259–61.

168 Aḥmad Jām, *Rawḍat al-Mudhbibīn va jannat al-mushtāqīn*, chapter on 'Wisdom and Guidance of People', pp. 34–7.

169 *Kashf al-asrār*, VI, p. 190.

170 I have detailed many of the influences of Nizārī's antinomianism and imagery on Ḥāfiẓ in a paper on 'The Influence of Nizārī on Ḥāfiẓ', delivered at the International Society for Iranian Studies 6th Biannual Conference, London, as part of a panel on 'Classical Persian Poetry and Ismaili Thought' (3 August 2006).

171 *Dīvān*, ed. Khānlarī, *ghazal* 77: 7. Trans. by Bly and Lewisohn, *Angels*, p. 66. See *Dīvān-i Ḥakīm Nizārī Quhistānī*, I, pp. 920–1, vv. 3429–37. Both *ghazals* are written in the same *Baḥr-i mujtath-i muthamman-i makhbūn-i makhzūf* metre. Khwājū Kirmānī (*Dīvān-i Khwājū Kirmānī*, ed. Qāni'ī, pp. 385–6, *ghazal* 57: 1–10) also later imitated Nizārī's rhyme and meaning (although Khwājū's metre is different), attesting to influence of both poets on Ḥāfiẓ. Haravī (*Sharḥ-i ghazalhā-yi Ḥāfiẓ*, I, p. 361) points out that verse 3 of this *ghazal* (77) is also modelled on a quatrain by Khayyām.

172 *Dīvān-i Ḥāfiẓ*, ed. Khānlarī, *ghazal* 306: 3.

173 *Ibid.*, *ghazal* 179: 4. Trans. by Bly and Lewisohn, *Angels*, p. 39. Lāhūrī explains that the poet means that one cannot recognize the truth of religion until one first perceives the Reality (*ḥaqīqat*) of faith and attains inward certainty. As a consequence of that inward certainty, 'one looks with compassion and mercy on the followers of all other faiths and creeds, and does not deny them however benighted and misguided they may be. This is one of the ideas especially recognized by the Sufis ... As long as the Reality (*ḥaqīqat*) of faith is not unveiled to one, the aspirant will rely on his powers of deduction and personal striving (*qiyās va ijtihād*), which only generate religious differences (*ikhtilāf*).' Lāhūrī, *Sharḥ-i 'irfānī-yi ghazalhā-yi-i Ḥāfiẓ*, III, pp. 1183–4.

174 On Ḥāfiẓ's immersion in Sufi writings, see Zarrīnkūb, *Az kūcha-i rindān*, p. 168.

175 On Ḥāfiẓ's ethics, see Khurramshāhī, 'Ḥāfiẓ dar farhang-i mā', pp. 151–2.

176 In this respect, I fully endorse Khurramshāhī's ('Mayl-i Ḥāfiẓ bih gunāh', p. 92) conclusion that 'Ḥāfiẓ's understanding of the true sense and inner meaning of sin did not lead him "astray" into "error", but rather conveyed him from the error of Appearance along the royal road to Reality and Truth. By understanding the interior truth of sin, he freed himself from the narrow straits of pride and egotism, to be raised into the wide open expanse of heart-consciousness, where he experienced some of the sublimest degrees the human soul may know. In this fashion, when he partook of the Fruit of Knowledge from the Tree of Sin, the secrets of the philosophy of "inspired libertinism" (*rindī*) were revealed to him.'

177 *Dīvān-i Ḥāfiẓ*, ed. Khānlarī, *ghazal* 278: 6.

Jalāl al-Dīn Davānī's Interpretation of Ḥāfiẓ

Carl W. Ernst

One of the perennial debates about the poetry of Ḥāfiẓ has revolved around the interpretation of his poetry, whether it should properly be considered part of the secular tradition of Persian court poetry, or whether it should be interpreted in some kind of mystical or allegorical sense in relation to Sufism. This question has been discussed since the very dawn of European Orientalist scholarship, having formed a significant part of the labours of Sir William Jones and his successors. Without attempting to summarize the details of this extensive debate, we can take a recent example as an indication of how hotly this question can be argued; I have in mind the overview to the multi-authored article on Ḥāfiẓ in the *Encyclopaedia Iranica*, penned by the distinguished scholar and editor of the *Encyclopaedia*, Dr Ehsan Yarshater. He writes:

> It was only natural that a Sufistic interpretation should be applied to the poems of Hafez, ignoring in the process many indications to the contrary. Some commentators and even some Western translators of Hafez, notably Wilberforce Clarke, a translator of the *Divān* (London, 1974), satisfied themselves, to the point of utter absurdity, that every single word written by Hafez had a mystical meaning and no line of Hafez actually meant what it said. The reading of Hafez as codified poetry implying an esoteric meaning for each line or word propounded the view that his ghazals can be read at two levels, one apparent, the other hidden – the latter representing the intended meaning. Deciphering Hafez's underlying meaning grew into an esoteric art, not dissimilar to the explanations offered by the addicts of 'conspiracy theories' (q.v.) in political affairs....

Then, acknowledging some ambiguity in the application of the term *'ārif* (gnostic) to Ḥāfiẓ, Dr Yarshater makes it quite clear that he rejects any significant association of the poet with institutional Sufism:

> On the other hand, if by *'āref* is meant a 'mystic,' that is, a person who believes in the theory and practice of Sufism, is attached to a certain Order or the circle of a Sufi mentor (*pīr*) or a *khānaqāh*, or allows the clarity of his mind to be clouded by the irrational and obfuscated by the woolly thinking of some Sufis

> and their belief in miraculous deeds ascribed to their saints, then the epithet is a misnomer.[1]

The *Encyclopaedia* is not of one mind on this matter; the section by Franklin Lewis on the image of the rogue (*rind*) in Ḥāfiẓ is considerably more nuanced in balancing the denunciation of religious hypocrisy with the symbolism of spiritual authenticity.[2]

Be that as it may, in this article I will not attempt to decide whether Ḥāfiẓ is by intention a secular or mystical poet, since the question as posed may in fact be badly framed. Instead, I would like to examine the case of one of the very earliest formal commentators on the poetry of Ḥāfiẓ, Jalāl al-Dīn Davānī (d. 908/1502), the eminent philosopher and scholar of Shīrāz.[3] Davānī is credited with half a dozen short untitled texts commenting on various verses by Ḥāfiẓ. Although these are generally undated, in one of these writings the author refers to the near completion of another of his works (the *Shawākil al-ḥūr*, dated 872/1468); thus we can conclude that Davānī is certainly one of the earliest, if not the very first, to write a separate commentary on Ḥāfiẓ. The fact that Davānī lived in Shīrāz not long after the death of Ḥāfiẓ gives his interpretations a special significance for the likely reader reception of his poetry by at least some contemporary audiences.[4] Three of these commentaries by Davānī have been collected together in a convenient edition by Ḥusayn Muʿallim, entitled *Naqd-i niyāzī*, and as representative samples, these will constitute the basis for the following observations.[5]

The first of Davānī's commentaries on Ḥāfiẓ focuses on the well-known verse, *dūsh dīdam ki malāyik dar-i maykhāna zadand / gil-i Ādam bi-sirishtand u bi-paymānah zadanḍ*: 'Last night I saw the angels knocking on the tavern door; / they mixed the clay of Adam and threw it as a cup.' In the opening pages, he describes his aim as follows:

> The purpose of this introduction is that certain of the sincere lovers, in the times of conversation and the hours of closeness, asked about the commentary on a verse by 'the tongue of the moment', Master Shams al-Millat wal-Dīn Muḥammad Ḥāfiẓ ... After that request was fulfilled, two or three words were speedily written down to the taste of the unitarians and the path of the Sufis. On completion, that document was lost. Once more they began to ask, and with the help of time it was formed in our way with correct composition and written with a verified description. Its basis was established in the path of the unitarians, the Sufis, and the sages, since to each of these groups on this subject there is a perspective and a reflection, and in accordance with the grasp of every soul there is a condition of recollection. Beware not to get lost in 'every tribe knew its drinking place [*mashrab*]' (Q 2:60). Every person in this knowledge is associated with a path. One may have achieved eternal happiness, while another is stuck at the beginning of the alphabet. One person takes pleasure in ecstasy and listening to music, while another finds peace in dancing. Most sought textual confirmation [for their path] from the verses of the poet referred to, so that their objectives would also become illuminated [by

> his poetry], and the sorrowful soul would find fresh fragrances from the breeze of that garden.[6]

It is important to underline the extent to which multiple interpretations of the verse of Ḥāfiẓ are assumed to be normal. Davānī's procedure in this particular text is, on the surface at least, systematic. He undertakes to explore the verse from three different perspectives: first, the unitarians; second, the Sufis; and third, the Peripatetic and Illuminationist sages (*ḥukamā*). Davānī does not precisely indicate who these groups are or how they differ from one another – there is certainly at this time a fair amount of overlap between the concerns of philosophers and Sufis, for example. His category of unitarians is similar to the use of that term by 'Azīz al-Dīn Nasafī, to describe a kind of philosophical mystic.[7] In any case, for Davānī it seems to be an important methodological principle to acknowledge these different perspectives, which he likens to the different 'drinking places' found by each of the 12 Israelite tribes in the Qur'ānic text, playing upon the alternate meaning of this word (*mashrab*) as a school or teaching. It is also noteworthy that Davānī applies an oracular epithet to Ḥāfiẓ, calling him 'the tongue of the moment' (*lisān al-waqt*). His approach is not literary in the ordinary sense, but exegetical, even as it acknowledges that all readers are likely to find their own perspectives confirmed by the poetry of Ḥāfiẓ.

The discussion of the unitarians is the longest, and it is divided into six separate sections or 'observations' (entitled *mashhad*), each devoted to the interpretation of a particular symbol or aspect of the verse: 1) last night; 2) the speaker of the verse; 3) the angels; 4) the tavern; 5) the clay of Adam; 6) the meaning of throwing the clay of Adam in the form of a cup. Davānī defends this focus on individual images with the following justification:

> The subtle *qalandars* and realized great ones are of the view that, in order that the brides of meaning should remain hidden from the unworthy and should not be pawed by the worldly, the realities of gnosis have been displayed in the cloak of similitudes, and spiritual meanings in the forms of perceptible things. They have taken their inspiration from this verse: 'These are the similitudes that We coin for the people, and none understands except the wise' (Q 29:43). Verse: 'When you hear the name spoken, run towards the thing that is named; / otherwise the speech of ecstatics remains a riddle.' Necessarily, whenever the people of the heart tell a secret, they reveal their aims by the method of metonymy [*kināyat*], so that the people of interpretation [*ta'wīl*] may understand the goals of those melodies through experiential proofs.[8]

So Davānī's method depends upon reading individual words and coded symbols that metaphorically represent unstated realities.[9] This is a robust hermeneutic that he applies without hesitation, while still locating the exercise aesthetically in the realm of poetry framed in performance with musical melody (*tarāna*).

When Davānī implements his interpretation of the symbols employed by Ḥāfiẓ, he does so in this section with a highly technical philosophical vocabulary that is presumed to furnish a categorical explanation. It is, moreover, framed in a very ornate style, drawing on arcane vocabulary and expressed with the artifices of rhyming prose. There are frequent citations of anonymous lines of Persian poetry (which I will skip for reasons of brevity), as well as Arabic verses from the Qur'ān, and the occasional deployment of *ḥadīth*. This may be seen in his exploration of the meaning of 'last night' according to the unitarians:

> Know that existence has a substance and a determination. From the perspective of substance, this demands that in a purely absolute fashion it should be freed from every limitation and denuded of all relationships. Pure being, which does not set foot in manifestation, and transcendence, which is no companion to relationship, they call the absolutely hidden presence and the reality in truth ... Necessarily, from this degree, by a path that is absolutely required and by necessary volition, the nightingales of that garden [i.e., the unitarians] express the absolute substance with the phrase 'clear day'. ... Likewise, the determination of existence, which is the source of the emanation of providence, from the perspective of the understanding of those who are near perceptible things, is expressed by the phrase 'dark day', because the degrees of determination have hidden the beauty of reality. The people of spiritual meaning have called that the veil of the two worlds. And the tress is the allusion, and the lock of hair and the mole are the expression, for the same thing ... Thus according to those who are perfumed by this fresh breeze, the metonyms for the divine reality and the degree of determination are morning and night ... The first they call the hidden divine identity, and the second they say is the degree of unity; this is an example of the melody of the unitarians.

Then, observing that, in reality, there is no night and day for God, Davānī reverses the symbolism:

> Yes, but the times of pre-Eternity and post-Eternity are joined in the point of now, even if the intellect says that that situation is impossible. In short, the Muḥammadan faqirs call the period of the extension of reality 'perpetual time' [*waqt-i sarmadī*] and by way of deceiving the unworthy and clouding the sight of those lost in the desert of ignorance, they call that 'last night'. ... And the period of the extension of determination and existence, which requires manifestation and disclosure, in their parlance is called duration [*dahr*]. By metonymy, they call that 'today'.[10]

The method employed in this interpretation is notable both for its assumption of the Neoplatonic–Avicennan cosmology and metaphysics typical of Davānī's age, and for the characteristic equivalency that he posits between philosophical concepts and poetic images. A notable expression of this way of reading symbols in Persian literature from a Sufi perspective was the *Gulshan-i rāz* of Maḥmūd Shabistarī (d. after 740/1340), a work doubtless known to Ḥāfiẓ as well as Davānī.[11] Moreover, the concept of an esoteric methodology is deeply rooted in Davānī's approach to symbolism, both as an obstacle for the unworthy and a key for the initiate.

Skipping over the remainder of the section on the unitarians (which is the longest section in his treatise), we can contrast Davānī's treatment of the way that the Sufis understand the symbolism of 'last night':

> Know that the chivalrous Sufi youths have an eternity from annihilation in God, and a progression from the ascensions of sanctity. From the contents of this verse, they understand a different secret, by reason of the fact that they are the world-revealing cup ... First, one should know what 'last night' is in their parlance, and why the tress and mole are its likeness, since they are an expression for the grain and the trap. Yes, realizing that requires an introduction.[12]

Here too, Davānī provides a cosmology, but this time it is much more psychological and dramatic, as Sufi dervishes enact the cosmic unfoldment from divine latency to phenomenal reality in their response to the call of divine love. Sufi authorities, such as 'Ayn al-Quḍāt, Ḥallāj, Ibn Khafīf and Rūzbihān, are invoked and quoted. On the symbolism of 'last night', Davānī explains, 'altogether, the group of Sufis expresses the period of this travel from the realm of nonexistence [to] essential and compulsory possibility, with the help of spiritual love and the overpowering of spiritual longing, as "last night". In that situation, sobriety was produced from intoxication and attainment [from] the root of existence.'[13] Summarizing the sense of the first half of the verse, he writes: 'In the period of the travel of existing things, I turned around the folds and orbits, and I saw the degrees of each attainment. In their midst, however much the angels were praising the sea of divine isolation, and had no impurity within the veil of chastity, they still did not have the adornment of being wounded by love.'[14] In conclusion, he observes, 'this was a sample of commentary on the verse by the experience of the Sufis, who annihilate multiplicity in unity, and at the time of intoxication speak in the manner of the people of sobriety.'[15] So while there is some parallel between the views of the unitarians and the Sufis on this verse, insofar as both groups see it as symbolizing the cosmogonic process of God's creation of the world, they nevertheless express it in very different terms.

Davānī begins the section on the sages by commenting sarcastically that, while the philosophical sage is close to the Sufi, his sight has been darkened by the overturning of intellect mixed with imagination. Intellect and logic, as Rūmī points out, are poor supports. Davānī continues: 'Altogether, "last night" in the technical language of the philosophical sages is the time of the release of the rational soul from the control of the body by contemplation of its superior origins, for the intellect, because of being veiled with the coverings of the body, has no portion either of the wine or of the cask, and it is excluded by the proximity of nature from witnessing the sources of emanation.'[16] Davānī then goes into an explanation of the union of the rational soul with the Active Intellect according to the theories of the Illuminationist and Peripatetic schools of philosophy. He explains that Ḥāfiẓ wishes to portray the ascending soul as saying something like the following:

> With the eye of realization I gazed upon the forms of existence from above and below, I saw the separate intellects, which transcend acceptance and rejection, who by contemplating their own perfection in the fields of possibility were knocking on the door of the tavern of universal creation and their own luminous perfection. This is an expression for the comprehensive Adamic presence.[17]

While the tone of this explanation has a mocking character, it is quite technical and thoroughly immersed in one of the chief academic discourses of premodern Islamic thought.

Finally, it may come as no surprise that some of the companions of Davānī had requested that he provide a very brief commentary on this verse; evidently, some of them had simply gotten lost in the intricate gyrations of the preceding three sections. Here is how he responded:

> Know that the gist of the verse is that when burning love – may it be ever fortunate and victorious – with the aid of the momentary inspiration [*waqt*] went forth in the form of its own display and became the mirror of the pure condition of every beauty in the clear moment during that journey of a victorious king, it brought the degrees of its own perfection into view in the forms that are present. It witnessed its own essential and potential spiritual faculties, which went in search of the tavern and the wine-selling master with shouts and cries. If they were joined in presence with some of the active degrees which they call 'immutable entities' [*a'yān-i thābita*] and were free from a general measure of spiritual suffering, yet since their power of longing was still in action, they searched for the most perfect of the lights of manifestation and the limit of adornment. Then with complete effort they knocked on the door of the tavern of love, for they had the remainder of creation on their heads. If they had a crown of stability on the head of ambition and sought that universal existence, these degrees have a limit: it is the master of the merciful breath [*nafas-i raḥmānī*], Isrāfīl[18] and his trumpet. Necessarily from his mixed clay, which the dervishes say is the elemental human power and the upright body, they expressed it as a cup, and they trained him to the limits of all ways. Thus here they call the 'immutable entities' persons. There, the first love sees itself as the last, and it finds its own beauty to be exceedingly glorious in the completeness of its perfection. This is on the principle that for anything to see itself in itself is like seeing itself in a mirror, but the latter form of seeing is superior and more

> perfect; therefore the first seeing [gazing at oneself] is [only] a likeness, and the second seeing [in a mirror] is [true] reflections of beauty.[19]

Whether Davānī's associates found any additional clarity in this concluding passage, with its dense language drawing upon the vocabulary of Ibn 'Arabī, can best be imagined.

The second treatise on Ḥāfiẓ by Davānī has a much more literary bent than the first, focusing as it does upon an entire poem, the *ghazal* beginning *dar hama dayr-i mughān nīst chū man shaydā'ī*: 'In all this temple of the Magi no one is as wild as me.' The ostensibly literary character of this commentary is further enhanced by the quotation of numerous other verses by Ḥāfiẓ, cited to substantiate a consistent point of view ascribed to the author. Nevertheless, Davānī maintains here a consistent hermeneutic that assumes a deep structure of concealing and revealing the divine mysteries as the operative principle behind all serious literature. Once again, he confers oracular titles upon Ḥāfiẓ, calling him this time 'the tongue of the moment and the interpreter of time' (*lisān al-waqt, tarjumān al-zamān*). As before, Davānī is responding to the importunities of his friends who sought a solution to the mysteries of Ḥāfiẓ, and he apologizes for the delay in hopes that his work will be appreciated by connoisseurs. He begins the treatise with an introduction,[20] in which he lays out his strategy of interpretation, drawing explicitly on images and figures associated with martyrdom for having revealed the secret, such as Ḥallāj and 'Ayn al-Quḍāt Hamadānī:

> The jealousy of love's power demands that the subtle secrets of its effects should be hidden in the privacy of inner sanctums and the retreats of the hidden essence. The loveliness of that holy beauty should not have its veil polluted by the gaze of impure worldlings, who are by no means cleansed of the abandonment of poverty and the impurities of connections to existing things.
>
> > (Arabic verse): We, the men of the tribe, say the charms of Laylā should be seen when the stars arise, / for how should Laylā be seen with an eye that sees others and is not cleansed with tears?
> > (Persian verse): I performed ablutions with tears, as the men of the path say; / first be pure yourself, and then cast your eyes on the pure one. [Ḥāfiẓ][21]
>
> It is for this reason that the illustrious divine way [*sunnat*] has been ordered in this fashion, the fundamentals of the explanation of which are based upon the categorical principles of the sign that 'you shall not find any change in the way [*sunnah*] of God' (Qur'ān 33:62). This is because some of the people of realities are hidden from the eyes of ignorant formalists by the clothing of conventional forms, and they lose themselves in the midst of the generality of people by sharing their remaining customs. This is the path of the people of soundness.

(Persian verse): I am a rogue, and the people call me a Sufi; / see this nice name that I have discovered!

And some, having fled from the affairs of the ignorant mob to the cave of the abiding darkness of nonexistence, have wagered the cash of the two worlds in the dice house of isolation and asceticism with a single throw, and have cast themselves beyond the sight of men, on account of being uprooted from the forms of customary conventions. This is the style of the audacious ones of the corner of blame.

(Persian verse): My heart's upset with the monastery and the stained cloak. / Where is the temple of the Magi, and where's the pure wine? [Ḥāfiẓ][22]

Even though in the path there may be a group between these two positions, the aim of both factions is the concealment of realities, for in the law of love, for the intoxicated lover revealing secrets is a crime. Even though gradually the wine-bearer of ecstasy gives them another swallow of the wine of realities in the goblet of time, and every moment from the arrival of the cups of satisfaction with the manifestations of majesty and glory they have another increase, continually the voice of divine power gives the cry that:

(Persian verse): It is the Sultan's feast, so don't get drunk; / have a cup of wine, and then shut up!

And if occasionally the hopeless lover gives off some smoke from the overwhelming flames of the fires of love, and like an incense-burner releases sighs from within, he keeps them concealed and imprisoned at the bottom of his skirt of infamy, for [as the *ḥadīth* states] 'My friends are underneath my domes; no one knows them except me.' And if from the overwhelming force of intoxication he utters a word of the secrets of love, they take him to the gallows of blame.

(Arabic verse): By the secret, if they are effaced, their blood is shed; / thus it is that the blood of lovers may be shed. ['Ayn al-Quḍāt]
(Persian verse): For the helpless one who spills the secret of love, / tell him to scratch his face with the fingers of blame.
That friend by whom the gallows was ennobled – / his crime was this: he made the secrets public. [Ḥāfiẓ][23]

It is for this reason that if any of the children of the path of longing has an appropriately delicate relationship with this group from his original nature, he may be worthy of the inheritance of those great ones by reason of that spiritual proximity, by reason of 'We joined to them their seed' (Qur'ān 52:21).

Or they may fall under the suspicion of belonging to the group of the mob who are 'like beasts' (Qur'ān 7:179). This is because the lustful ones of delicate temperament, whose intended prayer direction is the acceptance of the masses, are rebuffed by those ferocious attacks from concentrating on the sacred target of love.

> (Persian verse): Sufi, pass us by in safety, for this red wine / steals heart and religion from you in a manner that – don't ask! [Ḥāfiẓ][24]
> My friends, haul back your reins from the tavern road; / because Ḥāfiẓ travelled by this path, and now he's poor.[25]

And despite the fact that deceptive and fickle love demands the concealing of secrets from the perspective of God's essential power, from the perspective of the perfection of the beloved it demands manifestation and revealing. Every moment in a visual and visionary location she is displayed in a different way to the heart and eye of the astonished lover. With glances mixed with elegance and looks most exciting, she places the words describing her own beauty on the tongue of that silent one, and then with the tongue of the assault of divine wrath, she begins to reproach and interrogate that unfortunate wretch. It is here that the cry arises from the lovers' disposition.

> (Persian verse): She showed her face, and herself described her face; / since things are so, why does it hurt my heart?

Throughout this introduction, Davānī assumes that these two perspectives – the concealment of the secret of love, and its revelation – frame the character of poetry around the interaction of the lover and the beloved. He adduces additional proof from the *ḥadīth* of the Prophet, particularly the well-known saying, 'I was a hidden treasure, and I longed to be known', which makes the manifestation of the universe the result of the divine self-disclosure.

Davānī then inserts another digression which he calls a reminder (*tadhkira*), devoted to the concept of love as that which joins together extremes and unites opposites. Love achieves these goals both by concealing secrets and by giving indications that remove veils. He explains these ambiguities as usual with illustrative verses:

> (Persian verse): His eyebrow says no, but his eyes say yes!
> (Persian verse): That longing is worth a hundred souls when the lover / says 'I don't want to', but wants to with a hundred souls.

Davānī goes on, in a passage dense with allusions to Sufi doctrines, to describe how this cosmic role of love encompasses the unfolding emanation of the different levels of existence, and their perfection which is attained through the Seal of the

Prophets, that is, Muḥammad. This passage links the cosmic role of the Prophet Muḥammad with his experience of heavenly ascension, described in the Qur'ān (53:9) as approaching 'two bows' lengths or nearer' to the divine presence. Davānī qualifies the two arcs (*qaws*) of the 'bows' lengths' as comprising the prophetic role in cosmic manifestation (*ẓuhūr*) and the saintly degree of consciousness (*shu'ūr*). This permits him to connect the notion of gradual manifestation and unveiling with 'the Seal of the Saints', the esoteric figure whose advent had been proclaimed by al-Ḥakīm al-Tirmidhī and whose role was claimed by Ibn 'Arabī. Davānī is fully aware of the messianic implications of this linkage, citing in support the well-known prophetic *ḥadīth* on the coming of one who shall 'fill the earth with justice and equity as it is now filled with oppression and injustice'. The approach of the apocalypse means that overflowing revelation is available everywhere, including in poetry:

> Since the time of the manifestation of that holy one draws near, the annunciation of those lights increase daily in display and manifestation, and the proofs of the truth of this claim are established on the page of time's conditions, if anyone with an insightful glance looks closely. For the grace of flowing geniuses and the close capacity of most of the children of the time is advanced in relation to their fathers, and their ambitions likewise by the same relation, again by the benefits of the approaching time of the revered inheritor and master of time [i.e., the expected messiah], as the saying goes (Arabic verse): 'the Earth has a portion of the cup of generosity.' The secrets of gnosis are pronounced on every tongue, and the shout is raised of the original aim of reality, in accordance with the voices of differing capabilities.
>
> > The secret of God, which the gnostic traveller tells to no one – / I am amazed where the wine sellers heard it from. [Ḥāfiẓ][26]
>
> And since the perfection of consciousness [*ish'ār*, a pun on *ash'ār*, 'verses'] is from the special characteristics of the creation of the Seal [of the Saints], those who resort to the deserts of annihilation in explanation of the realities of joy, having taken the path of poetic similitudes, express sublime intentions with the customary images of rogues with shameless cheeks.[27]

To demonstrate his point that poetry is the expression of mystical truths, Davānī then quotes in support two verses from the famous wine ode (*al-Khamriyya*) of the master of Arabic mystical poetry, Ibn al-Fāriḍ (d. 1235). As with his other quotations, Davānī does not bother to provide the author's name, assuming that the reader will be familiar with it.

At this point, Davānī shifts into a quick allegorical exposition of the frequently appearing images of non-Muslim religious groups ('infidels') that appear so often in Persian poetry:[28]

> The wayfarer at the beginning of the path, who is concerned with the perfection of the soul, has both himself and God in view. From this perspective, whoever wants to bring himself to God in this way has a relationship with the Magi [*majūs*], who believe in light and darkness. Both himself and the light of God are his contemplation, and by the very same expression, they call the seeker a Zoroastrian [*gabr*], as is the case in the poetry of Mawlana Jalāl al-Dīn Rūmī. Like this expression, sometimes they call him a Christian, since he affirms the reality of himself, God, and his own seeking and concentration, just as the Christians believe in the Trinity. And they call the station of love the tavern, considering that in this degree the constraint of dividing into self and the other is removed from the character of the gnostic...[29]

Having established this principle of poetic symbolism, Davānī goes on to comment on the image of the cup that represents the heart, adding several other Persian verses by Ḥāfiẓ in support, and referring explicitly to the poetry of Fakhr al-Dīn 'Irāqī as an example of the same symbolic principle. This remark concludes the 'reminder' passage, after which the commentary proper can begin.

It is apparent that this second treatise by Davānī is based on a more thoroughgoing hermeneutical framework than the first treatise, in which he had simply outlined the possibilities of three complementary perspectives on a particular verse by Ḥāfiẓ. To be sure, the first treatise is also firm in insisting on the principle of metonymy, in which a term used in a poem is considered to be a symbol for an underlying spiritual reality. The metaphysical assumptions underlying the second text are more technical and, indeed, esoteric, relying upon long traditions of philosophical and mystical reflection, and intertextual reference. It is noteworthy that Davānī here asserts that poetry must be read not only in terms of the dialectic of secrecy and disclosure, but also in relation to mystical teachings about the consciousness of the Prophet Muḥammad, the esoteric figure of the Seal of the Saints, and the universal impact of the coming advent of the expected messiah. This is of course the very same hermeneutic that Davānī would bring to bear on any other text, including the Qur'ān.

Enough has been said so far to make it clear how Davānī approaches the poetry of Ḥāfiẓ, and for reasons of space I will not attempt to go through his exposition of the details of the lyric that is explored in the second treatise, fascinating though these interpretations are. Nor will I linger on the third treatise in the anthology of Davānī's writings on Ḥāfiẓ, which is extremely short and basically uses a single verse as a springboard for arguing the doctrine of predestination.[30] Instead, I would like to turn briefly to an issue of historical or narrative interpretation that is also offered by Davānī, who clearly assumes that the verses of Ḥāfiẓ were written 'in the form of describing his own state [*bi-ṣūrat-i vaṣf al-ḥāl-i kh^{w}ud*]'.

While commenting on a variation of the saying attributed to Jesus, that one should not present wisdom before the unworthy, Davānī recalls the story that he heard from a dervish, who maintained that Ḥāfiẓ was a disciple of a Sufi master. The name of the master is given as Shaykh Maḥmūd ʻAṭṭār, who is described as an outstanding Sufi of his time. The same source maintained that, during a visit to the shrine of Shaykh Ibn Khafīf in Shīrāz, he encountered a master there who was deeply immersed in the teachings of Shaykh Rūzbihān Baqlī. When the narrator described Shaykh Maḥmūd ʻAṭṭār, his interlocutor replied that that was his own master. Davānī concludes that this is the justification for commentators to explain the poetry of Ḥāfiẓ in terms of his spiritual states. Most modern scholars have focused on this account as a piece of historical evidence to be considered in deciding upon the facticity of Ḥāfiẓ's connection to Sufism, or else its refutation.[31] Frequent attempts have been made to link the poetry of Ḥāfiẓ with the Sufi teachings of Rūzbihān.[32]

Yet it is interesting to see the accompanying hermeneutical argument that Davānī adds alongside this ostensibly historical account:

> Secondly, there is that which most of the literati say about some of the states of the author [Ḥāfiẓ], which are on the lips of the people. 'And God has insight into the conditions of his servants.' They have understood his words in the same external meanings that no intellectual would consider it legitimate to restrict to those suppositions. They have placed the finger of astonishment on the teeth of thought from the interpretation of [his verses] by the likes of these spiritual realities. They are completely ignorant of the contents of 'Don't look at who speaks, look at what is spoken', and the meaning of 'Know the man by the truth, not the truth by the man'.[33] And if it is assumed that the intelligent person has in no way even a glimmering of truth in relation to this meaning, the derivation of these meanings from him is the ultimate manifestation and distinction, and the source of insight. The possessor of a spiritual state has spiritual states as a result of that. If someone charges himself, he knows without a hint of doubt or imagination that from [the vendor's cry of] 'Country thyme!' [*saʻtar barrī*] he hears, 'Open up and see my piety' [*asʻa tara birrī*].[34] For that reason, he is overwhelmed with ecstasy, by the latter path, for which parallel meanings may be discovered for the likes of these sayings.[35]

While the argument is a trifle convoluted, I take this to mean that, first of all, ordinary people have understood the verses of Ḥāfiẓ in the most external and literal sense. Yet if someone knows nothing of the spiritual meanings of such expressions, and yet nevertheless discovers them through accidental similarity, this is in reality a genuine source of insight and, indeed, ecstasy. There are numerous examples of such 'accidental' discoveries in Sufi lore. Yet the implication is that the legitimacy of the mystical interpretation of Ḥāfiẓ does not in fact rest upon the argument from authority, which asserts the historical connection of Ḥāfiẓ with the Sufi tradition through actual initiation. It rather rests upon the adventitious and even serendipitous discovery of inner meanings, which by their very nature point to the insight of the listener rather than being dependent upon the intention of the writer.

I have suggested elsewhere that Sufi poetry is not defined by the author so much as by the audience.[36] For a reader such as Davānī, the poetry of Ḥāfiẓ exists on a continuum that ranges from Sufis such as Ḥallāj and 'Ayn al-Quḍāt to the philosopher Ibn Sīnā,[37] and the profane Abbasid court poet Abū Nuwās.[38] For him, it was just as natural and inevitable to employ a Sufi hermeneutic for the poetry of Ḥāfiẓ as it was for Sa'īd al-Dīn Farghānī (d. 701/1301), Ṣadr al-Dīn Qunawī (d. 752/1351), or 'Abd al-Ghanī al-Nābulusī (d. 1143/1731) to write detailed mystical commentaries on the Arabic poems of Ibn Fāriḍ.[39] Davānī is clearly an advocate of the systematic interpretation of poetry by a metaphysical system of correspondences based on writers such as Ibn 'Arabī and Suhrawardī, and for this he has been criticized for not respecting the clear sense of the text of Ḥāfiẓ.[40] Whether or not Ḥāfiẓ would have appreciated or approved of the philosophical and mystical interpretations which have been brought to his verses, the testimony of Davānī makes it abundantly clear that such interpretations have been present among the readers of Ḥāfiẓ from a very early date.

Notes

1 Ehsan Yarshater, 'Hafez I. An Overview', *EIr*, XI, pp. 464–5.

2 Franklin Lewis, 'Hafez, VIII. Hafez and *Rendi*', *EIr*, XI, pp. 483–91.

3 A useful overview of the metaphysical views of Davānī was provided in an early article by Mehmed Ali Ayni, 'Note sur l'idéalisme de Djelaleddin Davānī', pp. 236–40.

4 Reza Pourjavady, 'Kitāb-shināsi-i āthār-i Jalāl al-Dīn Davānī', pp. 81–139; see especially items numbered 8–14, pp. 90–4, and the author's remarks on p. 91. One of these commentaries (Pourjavady, no. 8) has also been discussed by Terry Graham, 'Hafiz and His Master', pp. 35–40.

5 Jalāl al-Dīn Davānī Kāzarūnī, *Naqd-i niyāzī, dar sharḥ-i do bayt u yik ghazal az Khwājah Ḥāfiẓ*.

6 *Ibid.*, p. 44.

7 See the comments on the *ahl-e waḥdat* ('monists') in Herman Landolt, 'Nasafī, 'Azīz b. Moḥammad', *Encyclopaedia Iranica* www.iranica.com/newsite/articles/unicode/sup/Nasafi_Aziz.html.

8 Davānī, *Naqd*, pp. 44–5.

9 See Ch. Pellat, 'Kināya', *EI*², V, pp. 116–18.

10 Davānī, *Naqd*, pp. 45–7.

11 See Hâfez de Chiraz, *Le Divân*, trans. Fouchécour, pp. 19–20, 113–14, 160.

12 Davānī, *Naqd*, p. 64.

13 *Ibid.*, p. 67.

14 *Ibid.*, p. 68.

15 *Ibid.*, p. 71.

16 *Ibid.*, p. 72.

17 *Ibid.*, p. 74.

18 In the Islamic tradition, Isrāfīl figures as an angel of death, and in particular the angel who blows the trumpet on the Day of Resurrection.

19 Davānī, *Naqd*, p. 76. The last sentence paraphrases the famous opening lines of the first chapter of Ibn 'Arabī's *Fuṣūṣ al-ḥikam*: 'The Reality wanted to see the essence of His Most Beautiful Names or, to put it in another way, to see His own Essence, in an all-inclusive object encompassing the whole [divine] Command, which, qualified by existence, would reveal to Him His own mystery. For the seeing of a thing, itself by itself, is not the same as it seeing itself in another, as it were in a mirror; for it appears

to itself in a form that is invested by the location of the vision by that which would only appear to it given the existence of the location and its [the location's] self-disclosure to it' (Ibn al-'Arabī, *The Bezels of Wisdom*, trans. Austin, p. 50).

20 Davānī, *Naqd*, pp. 172–5.

21 This verse can be found in *Dīvān-i Ḥāfiẓ*, ed. Khānlarī, *ghazal* 258: 7.

22 *Ibid.*, *ghazal* 2: 3.

23 *Ibid.*, *ghazal* 136: 6.

24 *Ibid.*, *ghazal* 266: 4 (reading *zāhid* instead of *ṣūfī*).

25 *Ibid.*, *ghazal* 163: 8.

26 *Ibid.*, *ghazal* 238: 8.

27 Davānī, *Naqd*, p. 178.

28 On which, see Alessandro Bausani, *Storia della letteratura persiana*, pp. 247, 263–9; Lewisohn, 'Sufi Symbolism and the Persian Hermeneutic Tradition: Reconstructing the Pagoda of Attar's Esoteric Poetics', pp. 255–308.

29 Davānī, *Naqd*, p. 179.

30 *Ibid.*, pp. 266–74.

31 Akbar Sobūt, 'Pīr-i Gol-rang', *Encyclopedia of the World of Islam*, 5: 381.

32 For a recent attempt to link Ḥāfiẓ to Rūzbihān, see the useful article by 'Alī Sharīat Kāshānī, 'La pré-éternité et la pérennité de l'amour et de la beauté en literature mystique persane de Rūzbehān à Ḥāfeẓ', pp. 25–54.

33 Two sayings commonly attributed to 'Alī ibn Abī Ṭālib.

34 For this celebrated example of the Sufi doctrine of listening (*samā'*), which befell Abū Ḥulmān in Baghdad, see al-Sarrāj al-Ṭūsī, *Kitāb al-luma' fi'l-taṣawwuf*, p. 289, line 9; Abū Ḥāmid al-Ghazālī, *Iḥyā' 'ulūm al-dīn*, Book 18.3, p. 1145 (in this edition, the second expression erroneously repeats the first); Duncan Black MacDonald, 'Emotional Religion in Islam', *JRAS* (1901–2, part 1), pp. 195–252, citing p. 238. Ghazālī states the underlying principle as follows: 'meanings that predominate in the heart precede in the understanding, despite the words.' For further on this theme, see Lewisohn, 'The Sacred Music of Islam: *Samā'* in the Persian Sufi Tradition', pp. 1–33, esp. pp. 18–19.

35 Davānī, *Naqd*, p. 193.

36 Ernst, *The Shambhala Guide to Sufism*, chap. 6.

37 Davānī, *Naqd*, pp. 216–17.

38 *Ibid.*, p. 81.

39 Dāwūd ibn Maḥmūd Qayṣarī, *Sharḥ Ṭā'iyyat Ibn al-Fāriḍ al-kubrá*; and *Ṭā'iyyah-i 'Abd al-Raḥmān Jāmī: tarjumah-i Ṭā'iyyah-i Ibn Fāriḍ, bi-indimām-i sharḥ-i Maḥmūd Qayṣārī bar Ṭā'iyyah-i Ibn Fāriḍ*; Farghānī, *Mashāriq al-ḍararī*; Dermenghem, trans., *L'Eloge du vin (Al khamriya): poème mystique de 'Omar ibn al Faridh, et son commentaire par 'Abd al Ghani an Nabolosi*. Davānī quotes Ibn al-Fāriḍ in *Naqd*, p. 71 (see note, p. 93), p. 178 (see note, p. 216).

40 Fouchécour, *Le Divân*, p. 20.

Part IV

Ḥāfiẓ's Romantic Imagery and Language of Love

Heavenly and Earthly Drunkenness. By Sulṭān-Muḥammad, probably painted in Herāt, AD 1526 or 1527. Page from a *Dīvān* of *Ḥāfiẓ*. Harvard Art Museum, Arthur M. Sackler Museum, Promised Gift of Mr. and Mrs. Stuart Cary Welch, Jr. Partially owned by the Metropolitan Museum of Art and the Arthur M. Sackler Museum, Harvard University, 1988. In honour of the students of Harvard University and Radcliffe College, 1988.460.3. Photo: Allan Macintyre © President and Fellows of Harvard College.

Incident in a Mosque. By Shaykh-Zāda, probably painted in Herāt, AD 1526 or 1527. Painting (recto, text; verso, folio 77r) from a *Dīvān* of *Ḥāfiẓ*, left-hand side of a bifolio. Harvard Art Museum, Arthur M. Sackler Museum, Gift of Stuart Cary Welch, Jr., 1999.300.2. Photo: Allan Macintyre © President and Fellows of Harvard College.

Lady Belovéd within the Prayer-Niche, Holding A Sprig of Narcissi. By Muḥammadī of Herāt, ca. AD 1565. Detached album leaf. Soudavar collection, on loan to the Sackler Gallery of Art, Washington, D.C.

Majnūn First Sees Laylī in the Mosque-School within the Prayer-Niche. By Bihzād or his fellow-painter Qāsim ʻAlī. Herāt, AD 1494. Illustration to a *Khamsa* of Niẓāmī; British Library, Or. 68100, folio 106 verso.

The Allegory of Drunkenness and the Theophany of the Beloved in Sixteenth-Century Illustrations of Ḥāfiẓ

Michael Barry

An intensely 'Ḥāfiẓian' ambience permeated the entire tradition of miniature painting in greater Persia during the fourteenth through seventeenth centuries, but few studies yet exist of the erotic theology and mystical symbolism that sustained the aesthetic premises of this tradition and underpinned later Persian coded conventions of manuscript illustration under the Jalayirid, Timurid, Turcoman and Safavid dynasties.[1] This is especially true of the four illustrations discussed below, two of which directly illustrate a *ghazal*[2] from the most beautiful known manuscript of the *Dīvān*, probably produced for Prince Sām Mīrzā, brother to Shāh Ṭahmāsb, in Safavid-ruled Herāt (in present-day Afghanistan) in 1526/7 AD.[3]

The first painting, which was explicitly created by way of illustration–homage to Ḥāfiẓ, was the work of the renowned miniaturist Shaykh-Zāda, probably painted in Herāt circa 1526 or 1527 AD. Scholars have entitled this miniature, quite appropriately adorning the cover of the present volume devoted to the theme of the 'Religion of Love' in Ḥāfiẓ's poetry, as *Incident in a Mosque*. Here we see a preacher addressing the faithful in conventional words, while a member of the congregation intuitively grasps the inner truth of the sermon's words, and falls into mystical ecstasy. However, Shaykh-Zāda's painting is not an 'illustration', but rather an evocation of the contrast between orthodox preachers, who defend the outward practices of religion, and ecstatic Sufis who perceive its inner truth, which Ḥāfiẓ draws throughout the *Dīvān*. The painter intends to convey the general mood, and symbolic thrust, of the *Dīvān* as a whole.

As the outstanding connoisseur of Persian art who once owned and published this picture, the late Stuart Cary Welch considered it the crowning achievement of Shaykh-Zāda, a disciple of the great Timurid and early Safavid master Bihzād (ca. 1465–1535 AD). A resident of Herāt, Shaykh-Zāda continued to work faithfully in Bihzād's manner some years after Bihzād himself had, in effect, retired from active painting. Bihzād, in 1526–7, was officially still grand-master of the Safavid realm's craftsmen of the book (ever since his appointment to this prestigious post by Shāh

Ismāʿīl in 1522 AD), but the jeweller's precision demanded by such miniature labour strained the eyesight and shortened the practical working life of these meticulously painstaking artists of the sixteenth century. Shaykh-Zāda perpetuated Bihzād's classical Herātī style with the vivid, gemlike tints of his little figures' robes that leap to the eye, and almost dance against the flat-patterned but intricate geometry of the mosque's deep blue arch and carpeting – geometry brought to life through sheer vigorous colour.

Only scale, as often remarked, distinguishes the painter's miniature gateway from its model, one of the soaring tiled arches of Herāt's Friday Mosque. Classical Persian painting's bold juxtapositions of primary, unshadowed, highly costly hues – derived from cinnabar (red), orpiment (yellow), malachite (green) and powdered lapis lazuli rinsed in linseed oil (ultramarine) – within a bold geometric framework that powerfully ignores foreshortening provoked the admiration of Matisse.

Closer inspection reveals Shaykh-Zāda's expressively drawn faces, reflections again of Bihzād's probing lessons in psychological rendition, and also four inscriptions charged with symbolic meaning. The upper left-hand corner frames the verses of the *ghazal* which this painting specifically 'illustrates' or rather visually comments upon. But the 'tilework' inscription over the main arch, and a second inscription running across the lintel above the window to the left, quote from two other of Ḥāfiẓ's *ghazals*: indications that the painter was deeply versed in all Ḥāfiẓ's poetry and wished to address several themes at once, themes recurrent throughout the *Dīvān* and regarded as important in sixteenth-century tradition.

The allegorical key unlocking the intent of many fifteenth- and sixteenth-century Persian and then Indo-Islamic manuscript illuminations lies in such deliberate resort, by the painters, to direct visual allusions to the matter of *another poem*, or, indeed, to outright *verbal quotations from another poem*, often discreetly inserted as calligraphic bands within the architectural 'tilework' (as is the case here), *in order to throw further spiritual light upon the poem or episode ostensibly illustrated.*

Carefully deciphered Persian and Indian manuscript illuminations of this period thus offer us pointed commentaries – not only visually through drawing and paint, but even in a strictly literary sense with further added verses – of the major poets of the Iranian canon. These artistic clues should prove no less precious to us than the written glosses of the age's most learned scribes. Ḥāfiẓ's deeper meanings, as understood by painters far more steeped than ourselves in their own cultural tradition, appear further revealed in the wrinkled brows and quizzical glances of Shaykh-Zāda's tiny but moving human characters.

Martin Dickson identified the painting's inscription, in his personal communication to S. C. Welch's cited work on Safavid painting,[4] where the upper left-hand corner contains a couplet from Ḥāfiẓ which reads:

Vāʿiẓān k-īn jalva dar miḥrāb u minbar mīkunand,
Chūn bi khalvat mīravand, ān kār-i dīgar mīkunand!

Preachers who preen in prayer-niche and pulpit,
When in private, quite another matter do they practise –
than they preach![5]

The main arch's inscription, featuring another verse from a different *ghazal* by Ḥāfiẓ, reads:

Burū bi kār-i khʷud, ay vā'iẓ, īn chi faryādast?
Ma-rā futād dil az rāh. Turā, chi uftādast?

Go about your business, preacher! What is this outcry for?
My heart, for me, fell off the path. So what fell off, for you?[6]

The window lintel's inscription is capped with another of Ḥāfiẓ's lines, reading:

Ravāq-i manẓar-i chashm-i man, āshiyāna-yi tust!
[Karam numāy u furūd ā, ki khāna, khāna-yi tust!]

The arch of my eye's orbit is your very nest!
[Show mercy and come down! For this eye's house – is yours!][7]

And over the closed door, within the mosque's arch, runs a further inscription, not exactly from the *ghazals*, but an invocation commonly seen in Bihzād's and other Timurid master-painters' architectural settings:

Yā Mufattiḥ al-Abwāb!

Oh Opener of Gates!

The overt theme of Shaykh-Zāda's painting is the contrast so often stressed by Ḥāfiẓ himself – as the artist implies by quoting from the second *ghazal* over the arch – between the superficial or hypocritical preacher, perched upon his pulpit and draped in correct ritual observance, and the honest Sufi ecstatic with true inner spiritual love.

But Shaykh-Zāda plays a further visual game with his citation from a third *ghazal*, fraught with even profounder meaning. A cluster of the painter's astonished spectators (one bites his finger in awe), those framed by the mosque's arched window on the left, are shown here to behold a spiritual mystery disclosed by the artist through the very shape of the arched window, itself reflected by the quoted hemistich immediately above: clearly alluding to the *ravāq-i manẓar-i chashm-i man*, literally 'the arch of the window of the eye of me'; that is, to the eye's orbit, and more sharply, to just what that eye sees and to what vision lodges within that same eye's orbit: Thou, the *Tajallī* or Divine Manifestation, here the Divine made visible through the heart and mind and countenance of the ecstatic Sufi writhing in union with the Divine upon the carpeted floor.

The mosque's faithful understand this mystery, and turn their eyes away from the preacher, towards the ecstatic devotee. In the composition's centre, the kneeling prince, most probably Shāh Ṭahmāsb himself, with his turban wrapped around the typical towering pointed skullcap or *tāj-i Ḥaydarī* ("Alī's crown') favoured by the early Safavids, bends his glance in the correct direction. Most members of the congregation with similar Shi'ite turbans cup their hands in prayer, respectfully hide them in the long sleeves of their caftans, or wipe tears with a kerchief or shawl, moved to the depths of their being by the mystical experience. Those who cannot contemplate the Mystery directly turn to question their companions, who gesticulate in explanation. One bearded and yellow-coated character in the lower left who does thus look away, gripping his wand of office, is almost certainly the 'guardian' or *raqīb*, a stock figure in classical Persian poems and paintings alike (as in another Ḥāfiẓ *ghazal*, where the accepted soul describes itself as able to 'pass beyond the warden's force in every case' – *tavān guzasht zi jūr-i raqīb dar hama hāl*),[8] whose charge is to prevent those unworthy from approaching royalty or the Beloved or, allegorically, the Divine Presence, despite, here, a youth's explanatory gestures. Then again, this same guardsman, who himself does not merit to look directly upon the Divine Mystery, contemplates the refraction of this Divine Mystery upon the youth's handsome countenance: for the youth further wears an archer's ring upon his thumb, a tiny detail which implies that this youth's glance can pierce like an arrow straight through the guardian's heart. As the painter states over the main arch, God alone chooses unto whom He shall open the Mystery's Doors.

The white-bearded painter himself, in astrakhan cap, kneels with folded hands at the bottom of the picture in a posture of reverent humility, just over his diminutive signature scrawled upon a floor-tile as if for the faithful to step on: *amala Shaykh-Zāda* (Shaykh-Zāda wrought [this]). The painter listens intently as a learned master – his own teacher Bihzād?, or Ḥāfiẓ himself? – expounds to him the meaning of the scene. Shortly after completing this painting, Shaykh-Zāda quit Safavid service, perhaps not feeling properly appreciated, as S.C. Welch suggests,[9] to take up residence at the Sunnī Uzbek court of Bukhārā.

The illustration of the romantic imagery of Ḥāfiẓ's poetry in *Incident in a Mosque* provides an excellent introduction to the Sufi symbolism underlying another equally famous miniature painting that also belongs to the same manuscript of the *Dīvān*, copied for the Safavid prince Sām Mīrzā. To this illustration of Ḥāfiẓ's *Dīvān*, featured on the back cover of this volume, art historians generally give the title of 'Allegory of Otherworldly Drunkenness' or 'Heavenly and Earthly Drunkenness'. It was painted by Sulṭān-Muḥammad, being a page from the same manuscript from 1526 or 1527 AD.[10] Like Shaykh-Zāda, but an even more powerful and visionary artist, the master from Tabrīz, Sulṭān-Muḥammad (who should now recognizably rank in the public eye with his exact contemporaries Bosch, Dürer, Leonardo and Giorgione in the

West, Cheou Ch'en and Shūkei Sesson in the East, as one of the very greatest painters of the early sixteenth-century world) intends to evoke the mood of the entire *Dīvān*, not one particular episode.

Sulṭān-Muḥammad's chosen scene is a *samā'*, the spiritual 'audition' of the dervishes with their music and dance, waving the long sleeves of their caftans as they spiral in 'drunken' state. More extant fifteenth- and sixteenth-century paintings of the *samā'* grace the *Dīvān* of Ḥāfiẓ than the works of any other Persian poet, including even manuscripts of Mawlānā Jalāl al-Dīn Rūmī himself (which are rarely illustrated). Such paintings underscore how much traditional readers in the Iranian and Indo-Muslim worlds perceived Ḥāfiẓ's *Dīvān* to be a pre-eminent allegory of Sufi love and mystical frenzy. Sulṭān-Muḥammad, mindful of the poet's playfully paradoxical praise throughout the *Dīvān* of the *rind* or spiritual 'rogue', that is, the dervish who, out of humility, deliberately seeks to shock and court the 'blame' (*malāmat*) of the conventionally pious through apparently outrageous behaviour, here portrays every type of mystic: from laymen enthusiastically throwing themselves into the dance, to three wildly caricatured, clownlike *qalandar* dervishes with shaven eyebrows, moustaches and beards, to the lower left.

Under powerful magnification, the vivid details of this prodigious painting retain all their sharpness and loom into bold relief, especially under raking light – like the kind that might have been cast by a flickering candle held by the prince who owned this volume and gazed on its particulars with vision heightened by wine laced with cannabis (Shāh Ṭahmāsb, as we know, was most partial to the 'ruby' and 'emerald' until repentance in middle age): from the tiny pearly rows of teeth of the singer with the tambourine, to the individually painted strands of every beard and the thickly applied whipped-cream folds of the turbans, the raised swirls upon the clay wine jars (almost invisible to the naked eye, but amazingly clear under a glass), the encrusted gems of the angels' crowns, and the almost undetectable gold spots sprinkled upon the walls to make the entire illumination glow. To the lower right, a tipsy prince with turban-egret (Prince Sām Mīrzā?) extends his foot to be kissed by another participant in a drunken stupor; in fact, Sulṭān-Muḥammad slyly amuses himself by drawing *three* legs to this strange prince: one extended, the two others folded beneath him; the artist signed this picture in minute characters within the 'tilework' over the lintel of the palace's door: 'the work of Sulṭān Muḥammad' (*'amala Sulṭān-Muḥammad*).

This illumination accompanies another of Ḥāfiẓ's *ghazals*, which it directly faces in the original manuscript. One of this *ghazal*'s verses (though not included in Khānlarī's critical edition) appears encapsulated above the picture:

Girifta sāghar-i 'ishrat firishta-yi Raḥmat,
Zi jur'a bar rukh-i ḥūr u parī gulāb zada.

Mercy's angel gripped communion's cup
And poured a draft that pinked a huri's
And a fairy's cheek.[11]

But this painting could just as easily have 'illustrated', say, *ghazal* number 192:

Yār-i mā chūn gīrad āghāz-i samā',
Qudsiyān bar 'arsh dast-afshān kunand.

When our Beloved takes it to start on the *Samā'*,
The very angels would shake forth their sleeves
Unto the Throne![12]

Ḥāfiẓ himself, as the *Lisān al-ghayb* or 'Tongue of the Unseen World', and with the bulging eyes of a visionary, reads in the magic palace's window from his own *Dīvān*. The poet reclines beneath the rooftop of the angels in their heavenly sphere, but is yet himself raised high above most human dwellers in this lower world.

The poet, as privileged intermediary, interprets the mysteries of the upper world, which only privileged seers like himself may behold, and then relays them through his poetry to the receptive souls of the faithful below. Wine, one of Sufism's favoured (and ultimately Zoroastrian-derived) metaphors for divine light (red at dawn, golden at noon) and for the illuminating and creative divine wisdom or Intellect, descends from its celestial heights, where it is first only quaffed by angels (their cheeks flushed by its warmth), down into this world's receiving vessels: through clay jars formed of this earth from which we ourselves are moulded, then through decanters of mystical instruction poured by this 'tavern's' spiritual teachers, and finally to the cups that symbolize our hearts. As the wine inflames us, its warmth dissolves the veils of our earthly illusions and senses and allows our mystical intuition to transcend our arrogant everyday rationalizations, so that, as alert readers of Ḥāfiẓ's lessons and visions, we may clearly behold the heavenly mysteries in turn, and dance for joy. The mystical ecstasy imparted by Ḥāfiẓ's verses is a 'drunkenness' that is a higher form of perception.

By a deliberate trick of paint, Sulṭān-Muḥammad causes a scarlet peony, part of the 'tilework' décor within the alcove wherein the poet reads, to burst flamelike directly atop (or actually from) the poet's own decanter, whence the poet pours unto us his verses: a metaphor for the flaming wine of divine inspiration further relayed below through the clay jar, wherein a handsome page or 'young Magus' dips a ladle to fill our flagons and so quench our spiritual thirst. He is the *sāqī* or cup-bearer of the holy brew, and himself offers his comely countenance unto our neo-Platonic contemplation of the mirrored beautiful ideas in his soul as a *shāhid* or 'witness' to them. Another line in the poem 'illustrated' tells (upon the painting's facing leaf) how the rays of the dawning wine-flame not only blank out the moon, but, by mirrored reddening upon the flushed countenances of the 'young Magi', overwhelm the very light of the sun:

Shu'ā'-i jām u qadaḥ, nūr-i māh pūshīda!
'Idhār-i mugh-bachigān, rāh-i āfitāb zada!

Rays from the cup and goblet overcloaked the moon's own light!
The Magi children's reddened cheeks waylaid the very sun![13]

The painter captures the difficult quintuple imagery, solar, winelike, kisslike, archangelic, hence 'intellectual' (in the medieval 'dawnlike' or 'illuminating' sense of successive emanating archangelic Intellects from the footstep or threshold of God's Throne, that shine down and so 'kiss' with their quickening light the successive planes of created being), of another of the text's extremely demanding verses:

Khirad kih mulham-i Ghayb ast, bahr-i kasb-i sharaf
Zi bām-i 'arsh, sadash būsa bar janāb zada.

Intellect, the Unseen World's inspirer,
to catch its every nobleness
on high
From the rooftop of the Throne,
Bestowed a hundred kisses
On its edge.[14]

The picture's pavilion is, indeed, the famous 'Tavern of the Magi', or rather, here, the 'Enclosure' or 'Palace of the Magi', *Sarāy-i Mughān* – as the poem's first line states, but a pavilion that is also planted like a 'tent' (*khayma*) in the midst of the 'ruinous' (*kharāb*) domain of this lower illusory world, with the expected deliberate wordplay on the Persianized Arabic term for 'ruins' (*kharābāt*) that came to mean 'tavern' in Persian usage, one of the most recurrent of all the *Dīvān*'s images and puns. Here the 'Chief Magus' or Sufi master – with his venerable snowy beard, seated towards the lower right, pours spiritual wine from true wisdom's decanter, into the cup from which avidly drinks a disciple:

Dar-i Sarāy-i Mughān rufta būd u āb zada,
Nishasta Pīr u ṣalā'ī bi shaykh u shāb zada.

The door to the Magi's Palace was swept and watered clean
And there sat the Elder Master, pouring out his Fire
To old and young alike.[15]

Sulṭān-Muḥammad's careful composition, which the spirited movement of his mordantly observed individual characters stirs to life, shows the Divine Light's descent (*nuzūl*) from the higher planes of Being to the lower: in the careful hierarchy of Islamicized neo-Platonic thought and imagery upon which Ḥāfiẓ so much plays in verse. It is the descent of the 'wine'-like Light, lowered from on high like a decanter at the end of a *tār* or 'string' (or 'rope', on the left), a metaphor for the all-connecting and all-pervading emanation of the divine creative clarity, from its most rarefied and immaterial heavenly configurations, to its densest and most visible embodiments on earth.

Pertinent here also is a verse from another of Ḥāfiẓ's *ghazals* – with its reference to the 'thread' or 'string', like a strand of the Beloved's hair, that links the entire chain of Being from the highest to lowest planes:

Zulfat hazār dil ba-yakī tār-i mū bi-bast,
Rāh-i hazār chāragar az chār-sū bi-bast.

Your tress has bound a thousand hearts within one single strand
And blocked on every side the path of a thousand
remedy-makers [who would untie such knots].[16]

The same *ghazal* invokes the intoxicated *samā'*:

Muṭrib chi parda sākht, ki dar parda-yi samā'
Bar ahl-i wajd u ḥāl dar-i hāy i hū! bibast.

What curtain-tune struck up this minstrel?
Who played and drew a *samā'* curtain
Clear across the Howling Gate
Before these folk of ecstasy
And rapture.[17]

We thus get, from top to bottom, through the 'string of Being' which lowers the 'wine':

a) The angelic plane of immaterial celestial images where the 'wine' is pure light.

b) The intermediary plane where visionary mystics and poets perceive these celestial images, invisible to ordinary humans, and transmute them into visible form – as if 'pouring wine' – for the benefit of receptive souls (privileged painters such as Sulṭān-Muḥammad serve this spiritual purpose too, a dignity accorded to figurative artists that was foreshadowed under the Timurids, and fully recognized in the Safavid and then Mughal and finally Ottoman domains, ever since the official endorsement of figurative art, by the highest clerical and royal authorities in Tabrīz and Herāt, with Bihzād's royal edict of appointment in 1522 AD as the *maẓhar-i nawādir-i ṣuwar*, or 'manifestation of the rarities of the image-configurations').

c) The intoxicating effect of the thickening, visible 'wine'.

d) The tipsy singers and musicians responding to the 'wine'.

e) The dancers to the music and song inspired by the 'wine'.

f) The exhausted dancers sinking into the spiritual 'annihilation' or *fanā'* of the mystical ecstasy induced by the 'wine'.

Stuart Cary Welch liked to emphasize the contrast in artistic temperament between painters of the late fifteenth-century School of Herāt, classical and restrained, but as fire under ice, and the more openly flamboyant and expressionist masters of the late fifteenth-century Tabrīz School. Shāh Ismā'īl's conquests by 1510 AD united both princely cities under Safavid rule. Manuscripts such as this great 1526–7 *Dīvān* of Ḥāfiẓ brought together one of the most gifted living Herātī masters of the age, Shaykh-Zāda, and a supreme Tabrīzī master, Sulṭān-Muḥammad, in a magnificent combination of pictorial art not unworthy of the poet they 'illustrate'.

Any discussion of the erotic theology and mystical symbolism underlying the illustrations of Ḥāfiẓ during this period would be incomplete without addressing the theme of the Sophianic feminine in Persian miniature painting. In respect to both metaphysics and aesthetics, the notion of the divine feminine underpins the entire Sufi doctrine of the theophany of the beloved in Ḥāfiẓ's poetry. The most extraordinary depiction of this favourite theme of Persian neo-Platonic Sufi writers[18] is found in the two pictures to which we shall now turn:

a) 'Majnūn First Sees Laylī in the Mosque-School within the Prayer-Niche', by Bihzād or his fellow-painter Qāsim 'Alī, Herāt, 1494 AD; illustration to a *Khamseh* of Niẓāmī; British Library, Or. 68100, folio 106 verso.

b) 'Lady Beloved within the Prayer-Niche, Holding A Sprig of Narcissi', by Muḥammadī of Herāt, ca. 1565 D; detached album leaf; Soudavar collection, on loan to the Sackler Gallery of Art, Washington, DC.

Although neither of these thematically related pictures directly 'illustrates' the *Dīvān* of Ḥāfiẓ, both of them reflect indirectly – and very pertinently – the central doctrines of Ḥāfiẓian love mysticism. Sixteenth-century court artists of the Persianate world (including Turkey and India) took into their ken the entire accepted Persian literary canon, as this had fully crystallized in the expected curriculum of educated élites by the close of the fifteenth century. This canon included both Ḥāfiẓ and the earlier poet whose narrative imagery arguably most profoundly inspired him, Niẓāmī. As Alessandro Bausani has famously observed, Niẓāmī's literary characters – the Lady of the Red Pavilion, the lovers Laylī and Majnūn, the partners in the love triangle Shīrīn, Farhād and Khusraw Parvīz – turned into quasi-Platonic Archetypes in the perceptions of later Persian, Indo-Persian and Turkish poets and their illustrators. To Niẓāmī's archetypes should be added the poet 'Attār's configuration of the Beloved as a Byzantine princess adored by the Shaykh Ṣan'ān. Ḥāfiẓ openly compares himself in one *ghazal* to Shaykh San'ān,[19] and repeatedly refers to himself as a 'Farhād'[20] and especially as a 'Majnūn'.[21] It logically follows that where Ḥāfiẓ calls himself 'Ṣan'ān', 'Farhād' or

'Majnūn', then the poet's implied Beloved is the Lady Beloved, more properly, the Divine perceived by the faithful under the aspect of the Sophianic feminine – as in this verse:

Dawr-i Majnūn guzasht u nawbat-i mā-st,
Har kasī panj rūza nawbat-i ū-st.

Majnūn's turn has passed, and now it's mine,
And every five-day character's own turn
Upon this earth.[22]

The focus of Majnūn's mystical meditation is the female manifestation of the Divinity. Niẓāmī's famous narrative poem makes it as limpidly clear as medieval Persian allegory can bear that the Lady Laylī mirrors the Godhead. When Majnūn throws himself upon Laylī's tomb at the end of the romance, the distraught lover explicitly addresses his departed Beloved as the *Dizh-Bānū*, 'my Lady of the Castle'; that is, Niẓāmī deliberately assimilates the Arabian Beloved to another of his own literary creations, the Lady of the Red Pavilion (in the *Haft Paykar* and the ultimate source of Puccini's *Turandot*): an allegory of the Divine who hides within the fastness of Her fortress as the Queen of the Other World, and who chooses through an icon suspended over Her gate to manifest Herself unto human lovers, posing through the icon the riddle of Her combined invisible Transcendance and visible Immanence, and so drives Her lovers mad to the point of courting death.

The mystical imagery of classical Persian Sufi epic – and lyrical – poetry thus can most definitely configure the Divine Beloved as a female. That this is so lies beyond all denial in the case of Niẓāmī's celebrated heroines and their literary derivatives, although, in other poets, ambiguity lurks, as Shabistarī in his *Garden of Mystery* (*Gulshan-i rāz*) so well puts it:

Hadīth-i zulf-i jānān bas darāz ast,
Chi shāyad guft az ān? K-ān jāy-i rāz ast.

Long is the story of the loved one's curls
And what should we say thereof? There lurks the secret.[23]

In turn, relentlessly to translate Ḥāfiẓ's 'Friend' (*yār*) as a *masculine* Beloved finds justifications in equivocal Persian neuters, Platonic precedent, the grammar of much Arabic and Urdu poetry, and of course on historical grounds in awareness of the traditional civilization's segregation between the sexes, and social acceptance of boy-love (as with the celebrated fondness of Sultan Maḥmūd for his page Ayāz[24]). But to resort everywhere to *exclusively* male pronouns flies in the face of clear references to the Lady Laylī, to Queen Shīrīn, or even to the *Sīmurgh* (a legendary fowl not only feminine in Avestic, but in numerous medieval Islamic miniatures that unmistakeably depict Her as a mother-bird carrying the hero Zāl to Her nest, to Her chicks, and to Her unhatched eggs).

Conversely, one might argue that it was the sheer difficulty of access to female society, for adult males in this poet's culture, that enhanced the very mystery and poetic power of the symbolism of the Veil.[25] Servile page-boys might availably pour wine at male lords' dinner parties, but countless classical Persian verses stress the remoteness of the hidden and desired Lady as the Hidden One, dwelling with mystical rapture on the idea of the sudden revelation of the Beloved's features emerging from Her Veil. In such a cultural context, that is really feminine imagery.

The Veil (*ḥijāb, niqāb, parda*) need not refer only to the Lady's outdoor garment, but may also mean Her night-dark tresses that frame her countenance sparkling like unto moonlight (mirroring the sunlike Divine). Although the pronoun's gender remains a matter of choice, Charles-Henri de Fouchécour's already (and deservedly) classic translation of Ḥāfiẓ could, I think, feminize the Beloved of *ghazal* 216, where She intermittently, teasingly and cruelly snatches Her Veiling Tresses from Her Lover's grasp and hides Her countenance behind them, in verbal play upon the mystical notion of *iltibās* or 'veiling' – as if She were, indeed, the Lady of the Red Pavilion:

Chū dast bar sar-i zulfash zanam, bi tāb ravad!
Var āshtī ṭalabam, bā sar-i 'itāb ravad!
Chū māh-i naw, rah-yi nazzārigān-i bīchāra
Zanad bi gūsha-yi abrū u dar niqāb ravad!

When I carry my hand to the tip of Her curl,
She angrily seethes!
If peace I implore, then She utterly blames me!
Like a new moon, she waylays Her gazers wretchéd
With a cut from Her eyebrow's corner –
Then hides again within Her Veil![26]

When the Veil lifts, a further arresting image struck in Ḥāfiẓ's verse is the *miḥrāb*-like shape that the lover perceives in the twin-arched eyebrows of the Beloved's countenance. The metaphor signifies unmistakeably the mystery of *tajallī*, the Divine 'epiphany': the Beloved's face is the direction towards which the true devotee must turn, like the Koranic angels once commanded by the Lord to worship the human form as the supreme locus of God's chosen visible manifestation. Ḥāfiẓ writes in another *ghazal*:

Dar ṣawma'a-yi zāhid u khalvat-i Ṣūfī,
Juz' gūsha-yi abrū-yi Tu, miḥrāb-i du'ā nīst.

In the hermit's retreat and Sufi's lone abode,
Save in your Eyebrow's corner, no prayer's *miḥrāb* exists![27]

Or again in a different verse from this *ghazal*:

Namāz dar kham-i ān abrūān-i miḥrābī
Kasī kunad ki bi khūn-i jigar ṭahārat kard.

Prays to those eyebrows' *mihrāb*-like curve
One who washes for worship in heart's blood.[28]

Fouchécour here aptly comments: 'La voûte est faite des sourcils de l'Aimé. Les sourcils sont le mihrab de l'amant.'[29] Now, this poetic tradition of the Beloved's brows and countenance explicitly assimilated to a *miḥrāb* is no mere literary conceit but a driving Sufi spiritual symbol,[30] and found its chief visual expression in fifteenth- and sixteenth-century Persianate pictorial art, in the convention of representing Laylī Herself, an outstanding female focus of *tajallī* if ever there was one, seated within the very arch of the prayer-niche of the mosque wherein Qays, the future Majnūn, first beholds Her. When called upon in 1494 AD at the court of Herāt to illustrate in Niẓāmī's romance the very moment (encapsulated in the page's calligraphy) when a gust of wind 'blows the Veil from Her own Beauty' (*Burqa' zi jamāl-i khwīsh bar-dāsht*), the artist (probably Bihzād) depicted his Laylī ensconced within the very heart of the *miḥrāb*, with a Koranic quotation (3:39) inscribed in 'tilework' calligraphy directly above Her:

Wa huwa qā'im-un yuṣallī fi-l-miḥrāb

Upright he standeth who prayeth towards [literally 'in'] the *miḥrāb.*

The upright devotee in the painting is young Qays himself, who beholds and recognizes the female *tajallī* in the *miḥrāb* and dips his stylus into his inkwell to write his very first mystical love poem in Her praise: as the 'Majnūn', he will of course be the archetypal dervish poet, a rôle and rank to which Ḥāfiẓ, in turn, explicitly claims succession.[31] Majnūn's Beloved is, of course, the Lady.

The Laylī-in-the-*miḥrāb* motif recurs in a number of extant fifteenth- and sixteenth-century paintings, not only as direct illustrations to Niẓāmī or his imitators, but as individual album leaves. The version in the Soudavar collection by Muḥammadī of Herāt, painted in about 1565 AD, is an interesting variant of an earlier image (now in the Harvard Fogg Museum) drawn in Tabrīz in about 1540 AD, and attributed by S.C. Welch[32] to Sulṭān-Muḥammad's son Mīrzā 'Alī. In Muḥammadī's slightly later version, all the tradition's pictorial and ultimately poetic and mystical conventions come together.

Muḥammadī's Lady is a heavenly Queen, as made clear by Her crown and also even by the kerchief dangling from Her sleeve (Islamic art almost certainly borrowed this attribute of the royal kerchief, grasped in the fist or tucked into the belt, from the *mappa* brandished by the consul and later even by emperors in Roman and

Byzantine tradition). The twin arches of the Lady's eyebrows are mirrored by the arch of the *miḥrāb* within which she sits, Muḥammadī's significant addition to Mīrzā 'Alī's prototype, drawn from so many Persianate artists' representations of Laylī. With equal mystical significance, the Lady contemplates a sprig of narcissi, symbols of human eyes, indeed of Her own eyes, as Ḥāfiẓ so often writes – as in this opening of one *ghazal*:

Ghulām-i nargis-i mast-i Tu tājdārān-and,
Kharāb-i bāda-yi la'l-i Tu hūshyārān-and.

Even crownéd kings are slaves to your tipsy narcissi,
The wisest turn tavern-wrecked in your lips' ruby-red wine.[33]

In conclusion, painters, poets and mystics in the Persianate tradition, whether in Iran or India, as we have seen closely, mirror each others' meanings and deserve, indeed demand, to be studied together. Muḥammadī's Lady contemplates Herself in the Narcissi, like the Godhead of Sufi thought contemplates the Divine Self through the very eyes of human devotees. Islamic tradition, in thought, paint and verse, in actual and utterly attestable fact (for the paintings bear irrefutable witness) ascribed the highest conceivable dignity – Divine manifestation – to the female principle. Ḥāfiẓ, as a self-proclaimed 'Majnūn', does so too. Such dignity should not be obscured in either studies or translations today. To quote an earlier contemporary of Ḥāfiẓ to whom the poet of Shīrāz owed a considable literary debt, Khwājū Kirmānī:

Zi ṣūrat bibar tā bi ma'nī rasī, / Chū Majnūn shavī, kh^{w}ud bi Laylī rasī!

Now through the icon pass! until you reach the MEANING:
Be like to a Majnūn! Hie yourself now and reach
Unto the Lady Laylī.[34]

Notes

1 The mainly connoisseurly and stylistic approach to Persian art of twentieth-century European and American scholars (Stchoukine, Pope, Gray, Robinson, Welch and his school, etc.) has helped classify materials and identify individual artists, indispensable tasks to be sure, but the three eminent modern Iranian scholars pointing the way to profounder decipherment of their own artistic tradition – in light of its literary, royal and religious symbolism – have been Chahryar Adle (inter alia, *Art et société dans le monde iranien*, Paris 1982); Assadullah Souren Melikian-Chirvani (inter alia, *Le chant du monde: L'Art de l'Iran safavide*, Paris 2007); and Abolala Soudavar (inter alia, *Art of the Persian Courts*, New York 1992). This writer cannot overstate his debt to such masters and also to many conversations with Dr Reza Feyz in my own *Figurative Art in Medieval Islam and the Riddle of Bihzād of Herāt (AD 1465–535)*, New York and Paris 2004.

2 *Dīvān-i Ḥāfiẓ*, ed. Khānlarī, *ghazal* 194: 404.

3 It formerly belonged in the Stuart Cary Welch collection in Cambridge (Massachussetts), but is now dispersed between the Fogg Art Museum, Harvard University; the Metropolitan Musem of Art in New York City; and the new Museum of Islamic Art in Qatar. See Stuart Cary Welch, *Persian Painting: Five Royal Safavid Manuscripts of the Sixteenth Century*, New York 1976, and S.C. Welch (with Sheila Canby and Norah Titley), *Wonders of the Age*.

4 Welch, *Wonders of the Age*, no. 42, p. 123.

5 *Dīvān-i Ḥāfiẓ*, ed. Khānlarī, *ghazal* 194: 404. This and other translations from the Persian are mine. See also Fouchécour, *Hafiz de Chiraz*, pp. 545–7. Dickson's no. 199 is after the Ghanī and Qazvīnī 1941 edition.

6 *Dīvān-i Ḥāfiẓ*, ed. Khānlarī, *ghazal* 36: 88 (no. 35 in the Ghanī and Qazvīnī edition).

7 *Ibid.*, *ghazal* 35: 86 (no. 34 in the Ghanī and Qazvīnī edition). In Khānlarī's edition, instead of *āshiyāna-yi tust*, the variant reading *āstāna-yi tust* is printed, although six of his manuscripts feature the former *lectio* that appears in the painting.

8 *Ibid.*, *ghazal* 297: 4b, p. 610.

9 *Wonders of the Age*, p. 125, no. 42.

10 Gift of S.C. Welch, now co-owned by the Fogg Art Museum, Harvard University, and the Metropolitan Museum of Art, New York.

11 *Dīvān-i Ḥāfiẓ*, ed. Khānlarī, *ghazal* 413: 842 (no. 422 in the Ghanī and Qazvīnī edition). See also Fouchécour, *Hafiz de Chiraz*, no. 413, pp. 1020–2.

12 *Dīvān-i Ḥāfiẓ*, ed. Khānlarī, *ghazal* 192: 3, p. 400.

13 *Ibid.*, *ghazal* 413: 3, p. 842.

14 *Ibid.*, *ghazal* 413: 10, p. 842.

15 *Ibid.*, *ghazal* 413: 1, p. 842.

16 *Ibid.*, *ghazal* 32: 1, p. 80.

17 *Ibid.*, *ghazal* 32: 6, p. 80.

18 [See Austin, 'The Sophianic Feminine in the Work of Ibn 'Arabī and Rumi' – Ed.]

19 *Dīvān-i Ḥāfiẓ*, ed. Khānlarī, *ghazal* 79: 6.

20 *Ibid.*, *ghazals* 97, 108, 185.

21 E.g. *ibid.*, *ghazal* nos. 41, 55, 60, 111, 341, 449.

22 *Ibid.*, *ghazal* 60: 6.

23 *Gulshan-i rāz* in Ṣamad Muwaḥḥid (ed.), *Majmū'a-i āthār-i Shaykh Maḥmūd Shabistarī*, p. 98, v. 760.

24 Cf. *Dīvān-i Ḥāfiẓ*, ed. Khānlarī, *ghazal* 254: 5, p. 524.

25 [Cf. Chittick, 'The Paradox of the Veil in Sufism', – Ed.]

26 *Dīvān-i Ḥāfiẓ*, ed. Khānlarī, *ghazal* 216: 1–2, p. 448.

27 *Ibid.*, *ghazal* 70: 11, p. 156.

28 *Ibid.*, *ghazal* 127: 4, p. 270.

29 Fouchécour, *Hâfez de Chiraz*, p. 482.

30 [See Nurbakhsh, *Sufi Symbolism*, vol. 1: *The Esoteric Symbolism of the Parts of the Beloved's Body*, pp. 7–8, s.v. 'The Prayer-Niche of the Eyebrow (*meḥrāb-e ābrū*), with the verses of Ḥāfiẓ cited there', – Ed.]

31 *Dīvān-i Ḥāfiẓ*, ed. Khānlarī, *ghazal* 60: 6.

32 Welch, *Wonders of the Age*, p. 185, no. 70.

33 *Dīvān-i Ḥāfiẓ*, ed. Khānlarī, *ghazal* 190, p. 396.

34 *Humāy u Humāyūn*, ed. K. 'Aynī, p. 32, bottom line.

Transfiguring Love: Perspective Shifts and the Contextualization of Experience in the *Ghazals* of Ḥāfiẓ

James Morris

The following observations grow out of several decades of experience teaching the *ghazals* of Ḥāfiẓ to students lacking any direct access to the original Persian – and out of an even longer period of immersion in the multilingual complex of now largely unfamiliar spiritual, philosophic, scientific and theological disciplines which provided the original cultural context and network of symbolic allusions that were once intimately familiar to this poet and his original learned courtly audiences, together with his connoisseurs and imitators throughout subsequent centuries. Not surprisingly, the greatest challenge and frustration of that contemporary pedagogical situation is how to communicate clearly and adequately those implicit structures and assumptions which must be understood, in order to begin to appreciate the full poetic richness and spiritual depths of Ḥāfiẓ's lyrics.

The focus of this chapter is on only one key dimension of that wider hermeneutical and pedagogical problem: the characteristic progression of metaphysical and existential shifts in perspective – first revealing, and then potentially transforming each reader's love, desire, will and self-understanding – that typically structures and unifies each of Ḥāfiẓ's *ghazals*. As we shall see, that distinctive underlying structural feature of Ḥāfiẓ's writing (which is normally invisible in English translation) also helps to explain some of the mysterious spiritual efficacy of his poetry in the therapeutic process of spiritual divination and illumination, the longstanding ritual of *fa'l*, paralleling the familiar uses of the *I Ching*.

One way to begin explaining that distinctive process of transformation is to start with the fundamental existential challenge with which this poet actually concludes each of his lyrics, with all that is actually evoked and intended by the far-reaching implications of his poetic penname 'Ḥāfiẓ', a deeply problematic expression which is too often taken simply in its familiar social usage referring to someone who has memorized the Qur'ān. With a heightened appreciation of the potential aims and demands highlighted by that repeated concluding reminder, we then move on to introduce the intended effects and forms of participation suggested by this poet's distinctive unifying rhetoric of carefully orchestrated, progressively shifting perspectives, voices and audiences, before briefly illustrating concretely how those unifying poetic features are developed in two typical shorter *ghazals*.

Background and Contexts

Becoming 'Ḥāfiẓ': The Ḥ-F-Ẓ Root and its Wider Qur'ānic Resonances

The spiritual world view assumed by Ḥāfiẓ and his original audiences – a perspective at once metaphysical, religious, aesthetic and ethical – can be summed up as an infinite play of unique, ever-renewed theophanies, in which all of our experience is understood as the constantly shifting Self-manifestation of the One divine Source, the ever-renewed 'Signs' of the creative Breath, as they are reflected in the mirror of each divine-human spirit. Yet Ḥāfiẓ's lyrics, of course, are not intended to teach or explain that familiar metaphysical perspective or the richly complex, constantly intersecting registers of its symbolic expression – both of which were already intimately familiar to his original learned and courtly audiences. Instead, they are designed *to awaken the actual realization of that reality* within the uniquely personal and shifting situations of his individual readers. That guiding intention, and its far-reaching demands and implications, are beautifully summarized in the multivalent meanings and associations of his concluding pen-name.

To begin with, the familiar Qur'ānic divine attribute or distinctive quality of Being, that is suggested by the Arabic active present participle *ḥāfiẓ* immediately evokes in each informed reader a complex semantic family of divine Qualities and corresponding human responses and responsibilities, while it simultaneously heightens our awareness of our relative realization of that particular divine Name, including our deeply rooted failures to do justice to its demands. The resulting ironic complicity of the poet and his readers is of course one of the most familiar features of the concluding verses of Ḥāfiẓ's *ghazals*. At a second, deeper stage of reflection and attention, which necessarily resonates with the reader's active assimilation of each preceding line of Ḥāfiẓ's *ghazal*, we are reminded that this same familiar concluding expression can often also be read (in its original Arabic) as an even more compelling *singular imperative*, demanding that we realize and put into action – 'assiduously, constantly, and perseveringly', as the intensive third-form imperative implies[1] – all the implications and responsibilities of our true human spiritual reality and ultimate destiny, as someone who is indeed '*Ḥāfiẓ*'.

So let us start with the multiple meanings of that key Arabic root (*ḥ-f-ẓ*), which occurs a total of 44 times in the Qur'ān: 15 times in relation to God (and 3 more regarding His angels or spiritual intermediaries); 6 times in relation to the Prophet; with the remaining 20 verses referring to corresponding human qualities and responsibilities, or the lack thereof. As with each of the other divine Names and attributes in the Qur'ān, the dramatic interplay of these two equally essential metaphysical perspectives – the divine Reality and its ongoing human manifestations and discoveries – lies at the heart of all the love-imagery of Ḥāfiẓ and the wider poetic tradition culminating in his work; that is, in its pervasive symbolic framework of the ongoing mutual courtship of the human soul and divine Beloved. The complex range of meanings of this *ḥ-f-ẓ* root in the Qur'ān are very wide indeed, including: (a) to maintain, sustain, uphold; (b) to protect, guard, preserve. These first two meanings are most obviously involved in the verses referring to *God*'s creative and sustaining activities. But other related aspects of this Arabic root more obviously relating to our corresponding human demands and responsibilities include: (c) to watch out, take care, bear in mind; (d) to be heedful, mindful, attentive; and finally (e) to follow, observe, comply with (an oath, covenant, divine command, etc.). Thus, by the time we have reached the end of each of Ḥāfiẓ's poems, he suggests, reminds us, and then often insists – in the immediate, insistently personal singular imperative – that we reflect on our actual realization of each of these fundamentally human spiritual responsibilities. In other words, the 'Ḥāfiẓ' penname and its corresponding imperative sense provide a constantly reinforced reminder of those fundamental human–divine covenants which, in the Qur'ānic perspectives familiar to the poet's original readership, constitute our very being and ultimate purpose.

Equally importantly, the Arabic root *ḥ-f-ẓ* does not stand alone in the Qur'ān, so that at each concluding repetition Ḥāfiẓ's readers (or at least those familiar with its underlying scriptural background) are also immediately reminded of an equally important set of closely associated symbols, realities and obligations. To begin with those 15 verses where this Arabic root explicitly describes God's actions, this expression is directly connected to the most fundamental divine functions – that is, to God's constant creation, sustaining and protecting of the heavens and the earth; of the divine Archetype of all creation and revelation, the heavenly 'Book' and cosmic 'Reminder' (*al-dhikr*); of the angels (6:61); of the 'Pedestal' (*kursī*) of the divine Throne (2:255), that encompasses all manifest being; and of that 'Tablet' recording the cosmic Qur'ān (85:22). Indeed, God is repeatedly described, using an intensive form of this same root and divine Name, as '*Ḥāfiẓ* of every thing' (11:57; 34:21; 42:6) – a quality inseparably associated with His infinite creative Love and Compassion: God is the Best Sustainer/Protector (*Ḥāfiẓ*) and the Most Loving/Compassionate of the Loving Ones (12:64).

When we turn to consider those 20 verses where this same Arabic root (*ḥ-f-ẓ*) is used to describe specifically human spiritual virtues, the fields of semantic association are equally fundamental and far-reaching. Most simply, that verb is often applied to our human responsibility for upholding and carrying out our oaths and agreements (5:89), an emphasis immediately recalling the central Qur'ānic theme of God's primordial Covenant with all human souls, the famous *rūz-i alast* (at 7:174) that is alluded to throughout Ḥāfiẓ's poetry and the traditions of which it was a part. Thus this same root is applied to our responsibility to follow God's commandments (9:112); to preserve modesty and self-restraint (24:30–1 and four other verses); to properly uphold and bear witness to 'the Book of God' (5:44); or – in ironic contrast to the behaviour of Joseph's siblings (12:12, 81) – to properly care for all our human brothers. Moreover, in a number of other key Qur'ānic passages (at 4:34; 50:31–5; and especially 33:35), this distinctive human attribute of being *ḥāfiẓ* is closely tied to a long catalogue of closely related, near-synonymous central spiritual virtues characterizing the very highest rank of prophets, saints and realized human beings, those granted 'the Day of Eternity' (50:34). These spiritual qualities and obligations include remembering God greatly/repeatedly (33:35); being contrite and penitent (50:32); and most pointedly and mysteriously, safeguarding and preserving the Unseen (*ghayb*) which God has preserved (4:34; 12:81). Finally, the essential dependence of all these active human qualities, expressed by this *ḥ-f-ẓ* root upon the foundation of divinely inspired awareness or direct spiritual knowing (*'ilm*), is explicitly highlighted in the prophet Joseph's emphatic self-description (12:55), using Arabic expressions ordinarily reserved in the Qur'ān for divine Names: 'Verily I am *ḥāfiẓ* and truly knowing (*'alīm*)'!

Given the range and spiritual depth of all these pre-eminently human responsibilities and spiritual imperatives associated by the Qur'ān with the qualities of being truly *ḥāfiẓ*, it is not surprising that the concluding lines of Ḥāfiẓ's poems often convey a profoundly ironic and realistically self-deprecating, sometimes openly humorous note, even as they necessarily evoke the full range of qualities and ideals evoked by this far-reaching divine – and potentially human – Name.

Finally, it is particularly important to note how insistently and repeatedly the Qur'ān stresses that the Prophet Muḥammad (6:104 and five other verses) – and more generally, all those with true faith (at 83:33) – are *not* themselves responsible for (*ḥāfiẓ/ḥafiẓ*) the spiritual decisions and ultimate fate of other human beings who may fail to follow and put into right practice the divine guidance. Being *ḥāfiẓ*, as the Qur'ān pointedly insists in all these verses, is necessarily a *uniquely individual* spiritual responsibility, and the emphasis on that uncompromising spiritual individuality is surely one of the most familiar distinguishing hallmarks of all of Ḥāfiẓ's poetry. Thus these particular Qur'ānic verses, in so pointedly stressing the necessarily *individual* nature of each human being's spiritual responsibilities, directly point to some of the most recurrent themes and dramatic contrasts throughout his *ghazals*. They are directly mirrored in Ḥāfiẓ's paradoxical glorification of the inner freedom and true responsibility of the inspired 'free spirit' (*rind*) and one who intentionally incurs blame (*malāmatī*), whose conscious spiritual integrity poignantly exposes the recurrent human tendency – epitomized in his *ghazals* by the hypocritical pretensions of the judgemental 'critic' and the 'prosecutor/pretender' (the *muḥtasib* and *mudda'ī*), in all their familiar inner and outer masks – to replace each soul's unique experience and inalienable individual responsibility by careful outward conformity to a safely limited set of shared social conventions.

From Assumption to Awareness: Dialogical Perspective Shifts in the Poetic Journey

Thus from the perspective evoked and suggested by this multi-faceted and revealing pen-name, each *ghazal* of Ḥāfiẓ constitutes a very particular kind of inner journey, whose goal is to become – at least momentarily and relative to each reader's unique existential starting point – *ḥāfiẓ*, in all the senses of that term we have just briefly outlined. While the aim of this chapter is to highlight that characteristic pattern of progressive shifts in perspective that are meant to be elicited within the reader in the course of that poetic journey, it may be helpful to recall a few of the more visible beginnings and conclusions of that overall process of spiritual transformation, since each poem understandably highlights only a few recurrent phases, stages and manifestations of that wider process. Thus, to mention only a small sample of those unifying and guiding parameters familiar to any reader of Ḥāfiẓ, we can speak of the perspective shifts from the mortal human-animal (*bashar*) to the theomorphic, spiritual and fully human being (*insān*); from duality and lonely separation (from the divine Beloved) to realized presence and reunion; from random likes and aversions to reasoned choice and intentional union with the One Will; from unconscious ignorance or delusion to spiritual awareness and inspired knowing; from self-centred impulses and desires to true mutual love and compassion; from a painful sense of cosmic determinism to the realization of true freedom; from inevitable conflict to providential harmony; or from the prison of earthly time to the timeless realm of the Spirit.

Now while the list of those contrasting metaphysical perspectives typically opening and closing each *ghazal* could be expanded indefinitely, what is most crucial for understanding the inner working and distinctive progression of these lyrics is something much simpler and more directly experienced. That is to say, each individual normally begins this particular spiritual and poetic journey, not with a conscious set of determinant metaphysical or theological ideas, but instead with a particular, immediate and undeniable *emotional state* (often anxious, fragile or uncomfortable), which itself has apparently been 'caused' or occasioned by the particular outward circumstances and constraints of our momentary mundane condition. At a deeper level, of course, that specific initial existential state reflects and is ultimately generated by an underlying, normally unconscious interpretive framework, by an apparently given set of determining psychological assumptions. But normally we all quickly learn how practically ineffective it is to attempt to change or remove such particular states and feelings simply through the purely abstract discussion and manipulation of such deeply embedded concepts and belief-patterns – all the more so as that kind of metaphysical reflection often tends to arrive only at still further intellectual paradoxes and antinomies. As with any effective therapy, actual spiritual transformation requires the mysterious awakening and engagement of unsuspected spiritual resources of desire, intention and understanding – whether those openings subjectively appear to us as either inner or external – that at first seem invisible or impossibly remote.

Hence what is practically needed in this recurrent initial predicament posed by each *ghazal* – and what is so richly provided already in the unique rhetorical structures of the Qur'ān and their creative reflections in the immense earlier Sufi literature familiar to Ḥāfiẓ (both poetry and prose) – is an operative repertoire of literary tools that are particularly effective in first eliciting and then ultimately transforming our unconsciously governing inner metaphysical assumptions. And this requisite transformation of perspective cannot be primarily abstract and conceptual, but rather must bring into play all the intimately associated personal memories, choices, emotions and earlier experiences that together give our largely unconscious assumptions their existentially dominant influence on our outlook and experience at this particular point in time. This is where the unique artistry and extraordinary guiding wisdom of Ḥāfiẓ are so powerfully evident, as attested by centuries of repeated efforts, in many subsequent Islamicate languages and poetic traditions, to somehow re-create his poetry's distinctive spiritually transforming effects. Thus it is essential to keep in mind, as we continue to identify, analyse and illustrate some of the key formal elements contributing to this particular dialogical pattern of perspective shifts in Ḥāfiẓ, that the outlining of these literary techniques is not an end in itself. What we are seeking to understand is rather their unifying goal and final cause; that is, how and why these different constituent rhetorical features actually work – as they certainly so often do – in gradually moving each actively engaged reader towards a more effective and memorable realization of genuinely becoming 'ḥāfiẓ', including the particularly urgent individual obligations which that rediscovered divine attribute (and human imperative) reveals and entails each time.

Within the *ghazals* of Ḥāfiẓ, these typical progressive shifts in metaphysical perspective are expressed through the masterly use of a familiar set of rhetorical devices, each of which have their own operative and literary equivalents in Rūmī and other earlier classics of this spiritual and poetic tradition.[2] Most fundamental in Ḥāfiẓ, of course, is the richly evocative *dramatic dialogical embedding* of these shifting perspectives, whose mysterious and intentionally provocative development is best illustrated through the actual analysis of the short poems later in this chapter. In other words, just as throughout the Qur'ān, each line of Ḥāfiẓ normally suggests and requires the most careful attention to the dynamic, often highly unstable, inner connection or implicit 'conversation' between four equally essential elements. These elements of metaphysical dialogue include the particular momentary existential situation (at once spiritual, psychological, material) of the external reader/listener; the corresponding apparent, imagined state of the internal speaker(s) of each line; the potential audience(s) for the internal speaker(s); and, finally, the spectrum of possible tones, purposes and (mis-)understandings connecting the first three essential participants (reader, internal speaker and that speaker's audiences).

As indicated by the complexities of this already simplified schematic summary, Ḥāfiẓ notoriously revels in creating – often already *within* each line of his *ghazals* – a richly contrasting set of intensely dramatic, intentionally mysterious, open-ended and multi-faceted potential constellations of understanding. In consequence, the awakening and effective application of those potential alternative understandings, at each moment, entirely depends on the particular range of imagined meanings which each reader is able to supply for each of these indispensable dialogical components, embedded in the intensely condensed internal dramatic speech of each line of the *ghazal*. Perhaps the most immediate way for modern, non-expert readers of Ḥāfiẓ in translation to begin to appreciate all that is potentially going on within these short *ghazals* – indeed, often within a single line – is to encounter some of the extraordinarily dramatic, richly evocative miniature paintings, which were later inspired by and devoted to mirroring and elucidating these unique poetic masterpieces.[3]

The particular demands of this uniquely polyvalent, multi-dimensional dramatic dialogical structure of each line of the *ghazal* on the properly prepared and seriously engaged reader can perhaps best be appreciated by students approaching Ḥāfiẓ's *ghazals* with little or no prior cultural preparation, by analogy to the similar degree of active intellectual and affective participation (and preparation) required by Plato's dramatic dialogues, or by the hexagrams of the *I Ching*, which itself so closely mirrors the traditional divinatory rituals and expectations surrounding the *Dīvān* of Ḥāfiẓ. Perhaps an even closer analogy, for some readers, may be suggested by the familiar features of complex role-playing computer games; or by recent cinematic thinkers fascinated with depicting the complex interplay between each human actor's outward destiny, character and inner history, fateful decisions, and the revealing consequences of our inner and outward acts of free will.[4] For within each distinctively multi-faceted line of Ḥāfiẓ, the actively engaged reader is unavoidably challenged to 'write out' – and simultaneously to *act* out, since it is our own self and inner personal history and imagination that is so pointedly mirrored in our particular hypothetical understandings of the possible speakers, audiences and speech-situations at issue – several plausible, but necessarily contrasting, mini-dramas, along with the further consideration of their eventual outcomes.

Next, in the following line or two, Ḥāfiẓ typically moves on to evoke a radically different perspective (both metaphysical and practical) that – just as with the interplay of different characters and personalities in Plato's dialogues or other great dramas – immediately tends to cast a very different light on the issues and alternatives raised by the immediately preceding lines. Thus each reader's simultaneous active inner creation and subsequent reflective re-consideration of each of these alternating mini-dramas – only further enriched by their interactions with the further dramas and perspectives of each succeeding line – precisely mirrors the familiar existential processes by which participants in therapy gradually become more aware of – and eventually responsible for and relatively detached from – the largely unconscious, non-reflective, and painfully one-dimensional dramas and dilemmas that originally brought them into the therapeutic quest. This is also why, just as with the study of Plato and other great dramatists, teachers quickly discover that the best practical initiation into these typically individualized and unavoidably interactive psychospiritual complexities of Ḥāfiẓ's poetry is through carefully attentive *group* reading and study. For such shared discussion quickly reveals and highlights the dramatic alternative perspectives and resulting dialogues (together with their manifold individual implications and outcomes) so carefully embedded in each successive line and half-line of his *ghazals*.

In short, these progressive dialogical perspective shifts are part of a carefully crafted process designed to elicit from Ḥāfiẓ's readers both new relevant experiences and contrasting interpretive alternatives, through such familiar devices as evocative but initially puzzling symbols (paralleling a key feature of the earliest Qur'ānic *surahs*); contrasting schemas of interpretation, including the elaborate metaphysical and philosophical traditions well known to Ḥāfiẓ and his original audiences; and the familiar Qur'ānic principles of explicit metaphysical paradox and incongruity. Second, these dramatic shifts help to heighten each reader's awareness of key unconscious elements (i.e., our inwardly operative assumptions, blinders, prejudices, and so on) and previously unexamined possibilities, through the carefully suggestive mirroring of those inadequate assumptions or their destructive consequences, emotionally heightened by Ḥāfiẓ's frequent (and often disarmingly self-deprecating) use of humour and irony. Third, Ḥāfiẓ often uses these sudden perspective shifts to elicit each reader's habitual forms of projection (i.e., the emotionally charged mirroring of our own inner impulses in others), through more openly voicing our inner conflicts and assumptions in the guise of those familiar, recurrent conflicts and dramas that run through all his poems. Finally, each *ghazal* as a whole integrates those preceding elements in the reader's gradual movement from an opening state of one-sided egoistic desire and associated emotions (needfulness, anxiety, longing, nostalgia, despair; or transient sensual distraction from that deeper suffering) to the potential transfiguration of that desire in the active reciprocity of true mutual love and spiritual awareness; that is, in all the states and actions of the divine *Ḥāfiẓ* – and His or Her human mirrors – which are so pointedly and insistently recalled in each *ghazal*'s concluding line.

For the poet's concluding pen-name is at once divine Name, human description and obligation, and *singular* active imperative. As such, however we may encounter it at the end of each *ghazal*, it constitutes an unavoidably revealing litmus test of where this challenging poetic voyage has left us, especially in contrast to the uniquely personal situation and dilemmas with which each of us necessarily begins this journey. Like the 'Book' of all our actions, thoughts and influences that each soul, according to the Qur'ān, is given to contemplate at its judgement, each *ghazal* brings us face to face with our own humanity, and with the immediate imperatives we discover there.

Two Illustrative Ghazals

Due to practical pedagogical concerns relevant to English-language students of Ḥāfiẓ who are unable to read the Persian (including the ready availability, range and variety of translated *ghazals*, their relative literalness, and the helpful provision of a facing Persian text), I have based the following two illustrations on my own slightly revised versions of the translations by Elizabeth T. Gray in *The Green Sea of Heaven: Fifty Ghazals from the Dīwān of Ḥāfiz*, pp. 49 and 69. The original translations have been supplemented here only as necessary to indicate particular important original textual key words or clues (usually more literal or in some cases underlying Arabic meanings) that are referred to in the following discussion of each *ghazal*. The particular numbers identifying each *ghazal* here (6, 13) refer to their original order in that published volume of English translations.

Perspective Shifts in Ghazal 6*: The 'Absence' of the Friend*

This short and relatively straightforward *ghazal*[5] offers a richly illustrative introduction to Ḥāfiẓ's typical use of subtle and rapidly shifting, typically ambivalent shifts in perspective and voice. To begin with, almost every phrase in the opening line – as we shall see in more detail below – offers a complexly evocative set of inescapable existential alternatives (engaging and awakening each reader's will, love, understanding and intention), which are then articulated and given voice in an ongoing, gradually ascending internal dialogue throughout the rest of the poem. For the sake of simplicity, we could call these two parallel starting points the 'two faces of the intellect' (*'aql*), already so familiar from the Qur'ān and centuries of earlier Islamic spiritual poetry; that is, the intrinsically limited, ego-mind of the human-animal (*bashar*), in contrast with the all-inclusive, inspired and penetrating spiritual Intelligence. Initially, each pair of verses retains a single similar formal perspective, while at the same time subtly preparing the way for the more comprehensive points of view articulated in the following set of lines. The final verse, as is usually the case with Ḥāfiẓ, stands alone as the definitive – hence almost always knowingly ironic and multi-faceted – response to all the preceding interrogations, inherently recapitulating and integrating all those possible multiple perspectives within the whole of each reader's experience.

Ghazal 6

[1] O dawn wind, where is the Friend's resting-place/shrine/tomb?
Where is that moon's stopping-place, that rogue, killer/enticer of lovers?

[2] The night is dark, the way to the valley of (the burning bush) is up ahead.
Where is the fire of Sinai? Where is the promised time of seeing (the Friend)?

[3] Whoever comes into this world bears the mark of ruin/transience:
In this tavern/ruins, say: Where is the sober/wise one?

[4] He who understands spiritual signs lives with glad tidings.
There are so many subtleties: Where is the intimate of secrets?

[5] Every tip of my hair has thousands of works with You:
We, where are we? And the work-less blamer, where is he?

[6] Reason has gone mad. Where are those dark/musk-scented chains?
The Heart of/from Us went into retreat. Where is the eyebrow of the Heart-Holder (Friend)?

[7] Wine, musician and rose are all ready, but
Life without the Friend is not ready! Where is the Friend?

[8] Ḥāfiẓ, don't be pained by the wind of autumn across the plain of Eternity/time:
Have a wise thought: say, where is the rose without thorns?

Lines 1-2: Lost and Indeterminate Subject and Object – but Richly Evocative Audience

In the first two opening lines here, both the speaker and the identity of the beloved Friend,[6] the object of the speaker's deepest longing, are all kept carefully and rigorously indeterminate – an indeterminacy which readily draws in and encourages each reader to read these lines as a strictly personal soliloquy, immediately substituting the peculiar situation of their own unique experience of love, loss and nostalgic longing. However, the audience and time of this recurrent plaint also suggest immediately concrete and undeniable signs of hope and *presence*: the first dawn light, and the wind-messenger of the divine Beloved, with its fresh spring reminders of the reality and proximity of the Garden. The second line – indeed, like each of the phrases in the opening verse – continues that opening question, but filled with the poignant reminder of the still abstract possibility of reunion: of those transforming theophanic encounters that tauntingly remain, at this moment, either in the mythical past (the burning bush and Mt. Sinai) or in the still distant eschatological future (each soul's 'promised *seeing* [*ru'yā*]', and ultimate meeting with God). Yet that abstract reminder is itself enough to suggest and constitute that inner way and lifelong path which will be revealed and discovered in the rest of the poem. Hence the constant concluding 'Where?' refrain already begins to move away from the opening hopeless, helpless complaint to a nascent, more focused and hopeful inner quest.

Lines 3–4: The Voice of Abstract, Generalized Reason

In these lines, Ḥāfiẓ suddenly switches to the distant, all too annoying voice of abstract, detached and universal wisdom – to the familiar most outward (and equally abstract) 'narrative' voice of the Qur'ān, that voice which pointedly speaks to the indeterminate 'you-all' ('say' here is unusually in the second-person *plural*). In the familiar modern imagery of animated cartoons, this reminder of the transient nature and dualistic conditions of 'this lower life' (*dunyā/jahān*) is the remonstrative voice of the white angel on the protagonist's shoulder, accurate and pertinent, but also painfully soft and distant. And in line 3, Ḥāfiẓ gives full ironic voice to the bitterly hopeless, despairing anger that such sober, abstract reasonableness tends to evoke among those (and each part of our self) still helplessly attached to these passing tavern-ruins. Surprisingly, then, line 4 unexpectedly provides the beginning of a real, effective - and necessarily individual - answer to that ironic query, pointing towards the radical transformation of perspective articulated in the first person in verses 5–6. Appropriately enough for the turning-point of the entire poem, the first half-line of verse 4 (together with the beginning of the second half) offers what is still a poignantly abstract reminder of those dozens of Qur'ānic verses emphasizing the omnipresence of the divine Signs, in every domain and instant of our inner and outer experience, and of the 'glad tidings' (*bishārat/bushrā*) necessarily flowing from their proper appreciation and understanding.

Hence the conclusion of this line, marking the climactic transition of the whole *ghazal*, is a poignantly personal question, perhaps even the voice of an entirely different speaker (already the 'I' of lines 5–6?). For each of us, there is only one possible and indispensable 'intimate of spiritual secrets', and no real choice (or way out of this dilemma) but to turn in the direction of that Friend.

Lines 5-6: The Heart's Essential 'Work' of I and Thou

In line 5, Ḥāfiẓ, at least, openly takes that inevitable turn inward, from the abstract, critical intellect to the necessarily personal and uniquely individual - powerfully marked here by the very first mention of 'I' and the divine, Buberian 'Thou' - to the *Heart* (*dil/qalb*), the dynamic, mutual meeting place of the divine Spirit and all its individual manifestations, and the unique locus of the defining human *Work* of creation, spiritual transformation and awakening. As the second half of line 5 indicates, those who are consciously busy with that infinite sacred Work of the divine-individual 'We' are indeed in a radically different place from that complaining, critical, fault-finding 'ego-self' whose many inner voices (already richly amplified in lines 1–4) are all too familiar to each of us. The forcefully emphasized 'We' opening the second half of line 5 is not a polite rhetorical substitute for Ḥāfiẓ's or our own ego-self (much less a vague bunch of people), but rather a radical and far-reaching, truly transforming insight into this poet's own distinctive reading and understanding of that peculiarly mysterious divine 'We'-voice which so intimately speaks so much of the Qur'ān. The essential identity of this profoundly personal divine/human 'We' with the transforming presence of the *Walī*/Friend is highlighted here by its explicit opposition to the censorious 'blamer' (*malāmatgar*, the inner ego-'blamer'). That opposition here is meant to openly echo the famous Qur'ānic verse 5:54 on the saving, restorative divine function of all the saintly Friends of God, '... who do not fear the blame of any blamer'.

Line 6 then moves on to describe more completely the decisive inner transformation - and the constantly available spiritual choice - between the real 'We' of the

Friend/Spirit and the self-separating, illusory ego, which was so sharply evoked in line 5. This inner union of the heart-self and its divine Creator-Beloved Friend always remains bewildering and 'crazy' (*dīvāna/hayrān*) to our limited ego-intellect. For our individual intellect alone – in Ḥāfiẓ's already classic poetic imagery for conveying the foundational *ḥadīth* of the blinding Face of the divine Beloved and its '70,000 veils' of all created manifestation[7] – by its very nature cannot see beyond the endless veils of created phenomena, which for it are always psychic 'chains' of distraction and temptation. Only the Heart, when it is properly focused or 'withdrawn' into itself (*khalwa/gūsha-girift*), can follow the subtle fragrances of divine attraction – here echoing that perfumed dawn-breeze (*nasīm*) which so evocatively opens this *ghazal* – back to the very Eye/Essence (*'ayn/ābrū*) of the One 'Heart-holder' and always present Friend.

Thus line 6 leaves each reader faced directly with one essential question: with the apparent choice between seeing – and living – in perspective, in that loving awareness of Heart and Spirit which is both real and always connected with the divine Friend (every hair linked 'by thousands of works'). Or else of disintegrating and returning to the lonely separation of the ego-intellect and all the familiar sufferings (the 'thorns' of the concluding line) inherent in its 'nearer-world' (*dunyā*) of transient material entities, space and time – all quite literally destined to the pervasive ruins (*kharābāt*) of line 3. Or between the divine Friend, the Beloved Herself, and her dark and endlessly veiling – but also fragrantly alluring! (*mushkīn/mishkīn*) – chain of tresses. More honestly, of course, we rarely seem to have much effective choice between these two alternatives, finding our conscious selves, from moment to moment, apparently entranced in one of these states or the other.

But Ḥāfiẓ's final poignant 'Where?' here obviously does not mean that we have simply returned to the initial helplessness and despair that marked the beginning of the poem. For the poet has actually brought his readers a very long way at this point, and his final two lines in fact are devoted to clarifying the realization and deeper insight into the universal nature of each Heart's individual *path* and *work*, which has only now become possible. In short, we are simply asked to begin to recognize that the 'Path' of this quintessentially human Work is not the apparent, dramatic motion from one lower spiritual point to another apparently higher one, as in the progression from line 1 here to line 5. Rather, that uniquely individual work, and resulting path, always lies in the *ongoing dynamic process* of spiritual learning and growth that constantly takes our heart back and forth from one state and momentary spiritual stopping-place (*manzil*, in line 1) to another. So that what we first took as separation, loss and failure is in reality the essential precondition for the ongoing human task of loving, of the striving and discovery of the Friend.

Lines 7–8: Recognizing the Friend's Work: Recapitulation and Conclusion

Line 7 here, like the end of line 6, might at first appear like another simple and poignant repetition of the spiritual dilemmas first raised in the opening verse;

indeed, its opening (and pointedly eschatological) banquet-imagery, at first glance, is as close to familiar and banal as one will ever find in this poet.[8] And Ḥāfiẓ clearly intends for that confusion to arise, since he leaves it quite ambiguous whether we are to read line 7 simply as a continuation of the very personal and intimate voice of lines 5–6, or as a return to the more inclusive, objective, wiser voice that his readers often expect from his conclusion – the kind of all-knowing, reproaching wisdom-voice we clearly do find in the last line here. The transforming answer to that dilemma, as we might expect, comes in the second half of line 7, where we are reminded that Life itself (*'aysh*, which is far more than just enjoyment) is impossible without the Friend. So this time, what is pointedly absent from this scene is the opening pretence of the lost and lonely ego. Since we have been reminded that that Friend *is* 'with you all wherever you may be' (57:4), there can be no question now of who is asking, and who is really being asked.

The concluding line 8 of this *ghazal* is a particularly striking illustration of the essential double function and meaning of Ḥāfiẓ's pen-name: both as *vocative* – addressed to *every* human being and to all the far-reaching responsibilities of our cosmic role and potential as *ḥāfiẓ*; and in this case also as *imperative*, demanding (in the intensive third Arabic verbal form) that we actively, assiduously, constantly 'be mindful, watch out, observe, uphold and be heedful'. And both functions, of course, are unavoidably in the necessarily individual *singular* form.

Beyond that telling form of address, the rest of the first half-line here appears at first as a beautiful poetic reworking of the famous *ḥadīth*: 'Don't curse *al-dahr* [the apparent cyclical eternity, suffering and fatality of the material world's order, often blamed in pre-Islamic poetry], because it is among God's Names!'[9] But Ḥāfiẓ's concluding, typically ironic formulation here – together with the rest of this *ghazal* – goes much deeper in offering a deeply insightful explanation of the reasons underlying that Prophetic prohibition. For as the preceding lines have made clear, it is in fact *only* through the transforming human Work of our own necessarily unique and individual experience of suffering, loss, distance and separation – through constantly discovering the cyclical polarities and oppositions inherent in all those divine Names that are mirrored in the fully human being (*insān*) – that we can ever begin to discover, appreciate, know and love that Friend whose apparent painful, arbitrary 'absence' (and constant guiding Presence) makes the whole drama of loss and redemption possible.

Voice and Perspective Shifts in Ghazal *13: Surrender or Separation?*

This short, apparently simple *ghazal*[10] well illustrates the particular challenges of interpretation that so often arise when Ḥāfiẓ leaves out some of the familiar grammatical and syntactical markers that normally signal important shifts in perspective and tone or voice. In the face of such intentional indeterminacy, each reader's particular understanding of the shifts in question, both in voice and perspective, tends to be built – as we shall see below – on the basis of apparent allusions to connected problems, meanings and frameworks of interpretation familiar from other *ghazals* and from the poet's wider cultural and literary background. In this case, for example, we are obliged to assume from the start that the pointedly contrasting perspectives, quite clearly articulated in verses 5–7, must be read back into the first half of the poem, and particularly into the two halves of the opening verse.

Ghazal 13

> [1] What is more happy than life/pleasure, spiritual conversation, the garden, and spring?
> Where is the *Sāqī*? Say, what is the cause of waiting/expectation?
>
> [2] Take as a blessing each instant of happiness that is given to you:
> No one knows (for sure) what the outcome of the Work is.
>
> [3] The connection of life is tied with a single hair: Be aware/wise!
> Focus on (the cause of) your own pain – what is the pain of fate/time/the world?
>
> [4] The real meaning of the Water of Life and the garden of Iram:
> What is it but the edge of this flowing stream and wholesome/delicious wine?
>
> [5] Since the sober ['veiled ones'] and the intoxicated are both from one tribe,
> We, to whom should we give the Heart? What is (arbitrary) choosing?
>
> [6] What does the heavenly sphere know of the Secret behind the veil? Silence!
> O critic/pretender/complainer, what is your quarrel with the Veil-Keeper?!
>
> [7] The ascetic wants the drink of Kawthar, and Ḥāfiẓ wants the Cup (of the heart):
> So between the two, which does the Creater/Doer choose!?

Line 1: 'What is the Cause *of this Waiting?'*

The opening verse of this *ghazal* sets out the two opposing metaphysical perspectives that are contrasted throughout this poem. The first half-line, a purely rhetorical question – and in reality an ecstatic exclamation of pure delight – straightforwardly articulates Ḥāfiẓ's (and each accomplished spiritual Knower's) immediate perception of the inherent good of the Spirit and the realized divine Presence, of the 'Garden' of divine proximity as already present in the purified and receptive human Heart, and in the active 'spiritual conversation' (*suḥbat*) or interaction with the Beloved that fills it. In poignant contrast – both emotionally and spiritually – the twin questions forming the second half of this opening verse raise the recurrent problem of that unconscious spiritual blindness and profound 'veiling' of the heart (line 5), which leave the critic/plaintiff/pretender (*mudda'ī* of line 6) and piously hopeful ascetic (*zāhid* of line 7) feeling painfully separated from God, unhappily waiting for the imagined future coming of the divine Wine-bearer (*sāqī*), and desperately searching for the presumably external cause (*sabab*) of this difficult separation and interminable state of expectation.

If the first half-line represents a kind of immediate, uncomplicated spiritual communication (*suḥbat*) between Ḥāfiẓ and each of his receptive readers, the perspective of estrangement and longing assumed in the second half-line is much more problematic, in that the relationship of the questioner and his or her intended audience assumed there can be understood on at least three distinct levels, each with very different meanings. To begin with, from the perspective of the speaker of the first half-line (whether we conceive of that voice as Ḥāfiẓ himself, or his persona of the idealized spiritual Knower familiar to his readers from many other *ghazals*), the two parallel questions in the second half-line are entirely ironic, perhaps even openly mocking, since that opening speaker is well aware that he or she is *not* waiting or expectant, and always knows (as we are told again and again in the Qur'ān and *ḥadīth*) that the divine *Sāqī* and promised Gardens are *already* with us and at hand. Instead, if we do assume that same opening speaker is also raising these two questions, then most charitably he can only be doing so as an initially pointed, well-intentioned challenge to that host of deeply 'veiled' (lines 5–6) critics, ascetics and hypocritically pious 'pretenders' – familiar characters in each of Ḥāfiẓ's spiritual dramas – inquiring inwardly as to why they still find themselves waiting for that same God whose Face, as they must paradoxically admit, we all must see 'wherever we turn' (2:115). Finally, we can understand these two questions as reflecting the inner state of all those 'veiled' individuals, plaintively wondering why God still keeps them personally 'waiting' (until death or some other future time) to reappear and fulfil all those repeated metaphysical assurances and scriptural promises – assertions which the Qur'ān itself tellingly places in the *present continuous* tense, though they paradoxically insist on reading them into their own imagined or wished-for future.

The particular word for 'cause' (*sabab*) in the second opening question here also suggests the underlying metaphysical issue or controversy shaping the entire poem, since in the longstanding language of Islamic philosophy and spirituality this technical term referred specifically to our mind's grasp of the complex chains of relative, secondary, spatio-temporal 'occasions' for the manifest appearances in this world: or in other words, to the conception of our destiny as depicted according to the deterministic material world view of the philosopher-scientists of that time. For Ḥāfiẓ, of course, that opening analytical perspective of the ego-intellect here is dramatically contrasted to the spiritual Knower's immediate perception of God as the One and Unique Cause, the ever-renewed *Creator* (*kardagār*) at every instant, whose Presence in the Heart is so emphatically recalled and celebrated at the very end of this *ghazal* (line 7).

Lines 2–3: The 'Instant' and its Demands

In these following verses, it is not immediately clear whether the speaker and intended audience (apparently an undetermined singular 'you', effectively identified with each engaged reader) is the same as the opening voice (= Ḥāfiẓ's own persona?) at the very beginning of the poem. Certainly the tone of confidence and particular emphasis of its spiritual teachings in these two lines closely echo the advice of the wise *pīr*, Magus, and related spiritual guide-figures familiar from so many other *ghazals*. What more particularly distinguishes this mature voice of wisdom here is its immediate, careful correction – first theoretical, and then intensely practical – of the recurrent human illusions underlying those two initial pained questions offered by the critic/ascetic/pretender at the end of the opening line. The Sufi, according to a famous traditional phrase, is the 'child of the present instant' (of the Heart's *waqt* or 'eternal now' that tellingly opens line 2 here), and his spiritual Work is to remain attentive in the Heart with God, filled with the awareness of each new instant of the ever-renewed creation – the essential point with which Ḥāfiẓ concludes this poem. For the 'veiled' ones (in lines 5–7), of course, all the meanings and realities described in scripture are envisaged as 'elsewhere' and in an imagined 'another time' than this real now – an illusion (and self-delusion) so profound that the sad ascetic of this *ghazal*'s final line would happily trade wilful suffering and self-imposed separation for his imagined future reward.

The next line 3 then moves on to the more practical spiritual consequences of this initial metaphysical reminder: 'Be conscious!' and closely attentive to that subtle life-connection ('a single hair') of the Spirit-breath always connecting the human Heart and its Creator at every instant. (Essentially, this command suggests the same meaning and central human responsibility conveyed by the Arabic verbal imperative form *ḥāfiẓ*, as explained earlier in this chapter.) Above all, the second half of line 3 reminds us that this inner spiritual attentiveness, that quintessential human 'Work'[11] and duty just highlighted in line 2, quickly reveals the ways that the real hidden cause of our apparent separation from the Beloved – answering the poignant initial query at the end of line 1 – lies nowhere but in our own distractions, expectations and deeper veils of self-delusion.

Line 4: Here and Now

Whatever its speaker and audience, line 4 provides perfectly balanced and centrally situated aesthetic continuation of this *ghazal*'s beatific opening half-line, which is recalled and reaffirmed yet again in the contrasting terms of the poem's closing comparison (line 7). It is certainly possible to read this central verse as a direct continuation of the same voice in lines 2–3, poignantly – and no doubt somewhat provocatively – expressing the natural consequence of those preceding lines' emphasis on the immediacy of the Heart's direct Knowing of the divine theophanies. For the divine Presence is certainly to be found exclusively in each human soul's unique 'here', just as it can be found solely in the Heart's unique present instant (lines 2–3). But the apparent coincidence between the poet's opening self-described idyll and these particular ostensible scriptural–symbolic correlates – only valid if we assume that the speaker is indeed still the same here and in the *ghazal*'s opening half-line – also suggests a naive and highly problematic attitude. It is almost as though Ḥāfiẓ were instead ironically reminding his less perceptive readers of the recurrent dangers and classic misunderstandings that flow from such symbolic attempts to communicate the most essential spiritual realities to unprepared audiences. For such naively literalist (if not forthrightly stupid) readers might well read this middle line, like the opening verse, as though the poet were actually speaking only of this particular outward wine and stream of Shīrāz – rather than of that Wine and Stream and spiritual Conversation of ever-renewed creation, which fills each human heart at every moment. In that case, one might imagine this line being spoken instead, with heavy implicit irony, by a rather gullible and uncritical, easily tempted and already intoxicated adolescent listener, who is excitedly responding to his own fantasy image of this poem's three opening lines.

Line 5: Divine 'Veiling', Wisdom and Surrender

Line 5 marks the essential turning-point in this *ghazal*, in that the speaker (who may still be the same sage in these concluding lines as in lines 2–3) now reminds his readers – and simultaneously includes them all, in the sudden emphatically repeated 'We' at the very beginning of the second half-line – that our common humanity means that we *all* find ourselves, from time to time, in the contrasting states of sober uprightness and befuddled intoxication, of painful 'veiling' (the underlying Qur'anic meaning of *mastūr*), and of spiritual illumination and union. We have already noted Ḥāfiẓ's repeated allusions in so many other poems (including the preceding *ghazal* just discussed here) to the spiritual necessity, in the divine school of each soul's earthly life, of experiencing and passing through the constant cyclical phases and oppositions of the different divine Names, before we can reach the realized state of *insān*, of the fully human being's theomorphic perfection. Likewise here, the radically opposed perspectives, expressed in the preceding and concluding lines by the fully enlightened sage (the inspired spiritual Knower) and the self-centred, egoistic complaints and hypocritical manipulations of the critic/pretender/ascetic, are brought together in such a way that Ḥāfiẓ's readers – as an integral part of this 'one tribe' of Adam – are obliged to recognize those dimensions and polarities within themselves.

Even more pointedly and controversially – since the remaining lines continue to elaborate this point – Ḥāfiẓ forcefully reminds us here (following strict and repeated Qur'ānic precedents) that all the transformations and states of our Heart, at each stage of our path, are inevitably and ultimately in God's hands, not solely the result of our own illusion of 'arbitrary choosing' (*ikhtiyār*). For in reality they are always guided and determined by the ineluctable and all-Wise divine Will (*kh*ʷ*āsta/irādat*), highlighted in the final words of this *ghazal*. From that perspective, once again, the 'We' significantly beginning the second half-line here refers not simply to our common humanity, but to the two dramatically contrasting possibilities which that human state always offers us. For to the extent that the 'We' in question is the loving dyad of I and Thou, of our true self in surrendered harmony with the Spirit and the Beloved's Intention (the 'amorous glance', *'ishva*, in all its infinite and constantly changing forms), then there is no illusion of arbitrary or random willing (*ikhtiyār*), where our choice and God's are already the same. This is the familiar 'spiritually intoxicated' state of inner trusting surrender (*taslīm/islām*) and proximity already beautifully conveyed by so many of the earlier lines here – and a state which even Ḥāfiẓ's most recalcitrant readers may have experienced from time to time.

The other way of understanding and experiencing this 'We' is, of course, at least as familiar to every reader. Instead of the human soul and Spirit in union and surrender, we can also focus on the constantly struggling and competing tendencies, tropisms and aversions of our ego-self (*nafs*), whose complexities and deep-rooted contrariness readily give rise to our common illusion of arbitrary wilfulness (*ikhtiyār*), and to the endless oppositions, complaints and fruitless hidden scheming (*makar*) of the critic/plaintiff/pretender (*mudda'ī*) and pious ascetic (*zāhid*) alike. That illusion – and the pathways to its eventual dissolution – are the subjects of the following line.

Since the theme of God's 'veiling' of the normally 'sober' human soul (*mastūr*, in the first half of line 5) – understood here and throughout Ḥāfiẓ not as some sort of deserved punishment or arbitrary destiny, but as the most essential metaphysical *precondition* for our spiritual growth and perfection – is what most essentially connects lines 5 and 6 here (and, indeed, ultimately unifies *all* the verses of this *ghazal*), it is absolutely essential to refer back at this point to the underlying Qur'ānic description of this situation at verses 17:45–53. Not only is the inner state of those who are momentarily veiled beautifully described at this point (see the partial translation immediately below), but, more significantly, the Qur'ān here goes on to describe their railing and carping, blindness and illusions, and constant bitter questioning of God and the Prophet, in such vivid and dramatic terms that it is immediately clear that this whole *ghazal* can be seen as a beautiful poetic, orchestral transposition of that long scriptural passage. Here are the first two verses of that decisive Qur'ānic section, which also pointedly highlights the ultimate divine responsibility for all the states of the human Heart, the ongoing reality that Ḥāfiẓ so forcefully emphasizes in this line and throughout this *ghazal*:

> And whenever you recite the Qur'ān, We place between you and between those who do not have faith [=spiritual certainty] in the spiritual world a veiled barrier (*hijāb mastūr*). And We place over their hearts shrouds, lest they

should understand It, and deafness upon their ears. So whenever you mention your Lord, the One Himself, in the Qur'ān, they turn their backs in loathing ... (17:45–6).

Ḥāfiẓ's intelligent readers – in his own time, as today – would immediately recognize here the dramatic (and, one suspects, quite intentional) parallels to the almost identical forms of spiritual incomprehension and misunderstanding that his own inspired verses have so frequently encountered throughout history.

Line 6: Discovering the Divine Secret

In this penultimate line, Ḥāfiẓ – or the enlightened persona who has spoken throughout most of the preceding lines – directly addresses the strident, previously unnamed 'pretentious critic' (*mudda'ī*) whose voice we first encountered in the second half of the opening verse, who was looking there for the (humanly manipulable or knowable) this-worldly 'cause' (*sabab*) for all those reprehensible features of this world and creation, which such characters (within each of us!) unavoidably see as the signs of an inexplicable divine tardiness, absence or general failure to perfect the world according to the fantasies of their own imagination. The Mystery that lies beyond the veil of the celestial spheres (*falak*), of course, is the infinite divine domain of the spiritual and imaginal worlds of the Heart – a reality too often invisible and silent for such veiled and deafened characters, as the underlying Qur'ānic verse just cited so pointedly emphasizes.

But Ḥāfiẓ's essential point here has nothing to do with the relative merits of particular philosophical or theological schemas of causality. Instead, the poet's bold exhortation of 'Silence!' here – explicitly echoing one of Rumi's favourite closing injunctions in so many of his celebrated *ghazals* – is not so much an expression of impatience, as it is the indispensable first *practical* step towards the Heart's eventual spiritual opening and transformation. Even the slightest effort of attempted meditation and silence, as we can all only too easily verify, quickly reveals both the radical contrast between the inspirations and illuminations of the heart, on the one hand, and the endless chattering and quarrelling and plotting of the ego (*nafs*), of our recalcitrant 'monkey-mind' that is, indeed, so rarely truly silenced. Ḥāfiẓ's final question, at the end of the second half-line here, pushes the 'pretender-critic' to pursue that process of meditation and introspection – of the constant Qur'ānic injunction of *dhikr* or spiritual recollection, in all its senses – even more deeply, until we begin to discover all the depths of pride, impulse, manipulation and grandiose self-divination lurking beneath this only too familiar hidden quarrel with God.

Now precisely to the extent that Ḥāfiẓ's reader takes this injunction and question to heart, this penultimate verse will quickly begin to reveal another very different, entirely transformed meaning. For the complex cosmological associations of the key terms *sabab* and *falak*,[12] as we have explained, inevitably suggest at first glance that the 'Veil' and 'Veil-Keeper' mentioned here must refer to God and to the apparently impenetrable metaphysical barrier – or so the thickly veiled critic imagines it! – between this visible world of matter, space and time, and that vast spiritual realm whose infinite realities he can only imagine (as does the pious ascetic/*zāhid* of the final line) in terms of more familiar fantasies and parallels drawn from his experience of this lower world. But once the attentive reader begins to realize that the truly problematic veils and their 'keeper' in question are none other than the barriers of his own ego-self (*nafs*), of its profound 'compound ignorance', confusions and chattering distractions, then every word of this line takes on a radically ironic meaning – and above all, profoundly different *practical* implications and consequences.

The source and nature of the critic/pretender's perennial illusions is further defined and highlighted at this point by the key term *nizā'* ('quarrelling'), whose many telling Qur'ānic usages repeatedly focus on the multiplicity of conflicting perspectives and futile stratagems and plotting that characterize those who rely on their own limited means and worldly understanding, without true spiritual insight and inspired guidance. The description of the panicked reaction of Pharaoh and his counsellors to the challenges of Moses (at 20:62), for example, also emphasizes the intrinsic secrecy and hiddenness of these murky psychic depths of the *nafs*: 'So they quarrelled among themselves about this matter, and they kept secret their plotting.' That inner psychic realm is indeed a 'secret behind a veil', unknown to the heavenly spheres – but potentially very familiar to those who undertake the Work-path of silence and spiritual purification.

Line 7: Balance, Surrender and the Divine Perspective

The true *ḥāfiẓ* – in each of those transforming and far-reaching senses that we explored at the beginning of this chapter – already knows that the theophanic, mirroring Heart is indeed always filled with the wine of *Kawthar* and the Spirit at every instant – as is, of course, the deeper heart of the critic and ascetic as well, 'if they only knew'. And in the course of life each reader, each human being, has passed back and forth between those polar states of 'veiling' (with its concomitant resistance, dissipation and empty imagining) and of ecstatic union and surrender (*mastī*) enough to appreciate both perspectives, to at least recognize each of the contrasting voices and possibilities that are so beautifully articulated throughout the course of this *ghazal*. The *apparent* human choice, then, is as simple here at the end as it was in the first half-line of this verse: between wanting what *is*, the ever-renewed plenitude of created Being; and desiring an imagined illusion, while ignoring or even deprecating what actually is (and its Creator).

But to state the issue that bluntly in fact serves only to highlight our apparent existential helplessness and inability to influence or carry out that choice at all: neither the true *ḥāfiẓ* nor the veiled critic and ascetic seem to 'choose' what is actually gifted to each of them in every instant. Hence the paradox – and deeper existential challenge – of the poem's final half-line, whose question likewise seems to be equally rhetorical: 'So between them, what is the Wish of the Creator/Worker?' – of the One Whose Will, as the Qur'ān insists countless times, is truly absolute and unimpeded. Again, the question itself seems at first a near truism: God's creation always Wills exactly what is. But that Willing of what is means not only these two nearly caricatured extremes of human surrender and desire, or of veiling and understanding, that unfold and intertwine in the course of this enchanting *ghazal*. That Willing also includes the more familiar inner movement back and forth between those extremes that constitutes the constant actual turnings and unveilings of our Heart (*inqilāb al-qalb*).

So the simple recognition of these dramatic alternatives immediately provides its own ineluctable answer: Ḥāfiẓ the poet leaves us with the next, imperative stage of the divine Wish – with the appropriate action and intention of the true *ḥāfiẓ* (already so perfectly exemplified in each of these *ghazals*), whose silent, joyful surrender to that Wish means recognizing and upholding each of these covenants so deeply embedded in our being and creation.

Conclusion: Engagement, Participation and Communicating Ḥāfiẓ

Since the purpose of this chapter is simply to introduce certain basic rhetorical structures and presuppositions of Ḥāfiẓ's poetry for students limited to working with translations, the best possible conclusion is to move on to explore how those distinguishing features are developed in other, often more complex poems throughout his *Dīvān*. At the same time, it may be helpful to point out that comparable spiritual intentions and correspondingly inventive literary structures (or their visual and aural equivalents) can be found in many other fields of the later Islamic humanities, including other visual and musical arts, in ways I have suggested in a number of related studies. In each of those fields, much work is still needed in order to reveal and elaborate the still unappreciated role of such characteristic artistic devices – whether we are exploring them elsewhere in Ḥāfiẓ, in the Qur'ān, Rūmī's *Mathnawī*, the unique language of Ibn 'Arabī, or many other masterworks of the Islamic humanities – in ensuring the effective participation and engagement of each reader (or listener/viewer), a participation which is almost always at once spiritual, intellectual, aesthetic and certainly (in the comprehensive Platonic sense) erotic.

Engagement and Participation

My original discovery of the existence of these distinctive dialogical perspective shifts and their deeper functions in the *ghazals* of Ḥāfiẓ grew out of many years of experiencing and then reflecting on the extraordinary power and efficaciousness of his poems when consulted for spiritual guidance (the familiar process of divination known as *fa'l* or *fa'lgīrī, tafa'ul*) – a mysterious but demonstrable quality and influence of his writing which I had repeatedly witnessed in the experience of friends and colleagues from very different cultures, backgrounds and walks of life, and which I had only seen roughly paralleled in very similar uses of the Qur'ān and the *I Ching*. It was first in that long practical and therapeutic context of frequenting Ḥāfiẓ that I began to appreciate and explore the ways that the peculiar intense combination of this poet's very different voices and perspectives perfectly mirrored – and so deeply engaged and revealed – different, often initially unconscious or inchoate dimensions of our soul (intellect, mind, desire, inner and outer conditioning, personality), which together shape and determine each individual's unique perception of the world, of the depths and possibilities of each unique situation in which we find ourselves. Compared with the *I Ching*, however, with its relative emphasis on the archetypal regularities and patterns of the more visible human social and political worlds, the particular mastery (and mystery) of Ḥāfiẓ clearly lies in his extraordinary revelation of inner spiritual worlds and insights – in his long-acknowledged, but always mysterious, unique efficacy as the 'voice of the Unseen' (*lisān al-ghayb*). There is nothing like watching Ḥāfiẓ so fully and richly mirrored in the varying reactions of a classroom of committed students to realize how comprehensive and inclusive his cast of characters and archetypal dramas really are – and how powerfully even translations of his *ghazal*s can continue to engage such new audiences today.

Communicating Ḥāfiẓ

Given the distinctive structural features of the two *ghazal*s highlighted in this chapter, it should be obvious that students of Ḥāfiẓ interested in translations designed to more faithfully convey the forms and meanings of the original poetic text – a project which will always remain indispensable for any student or lover of poetry who is actually interested in learning to read and explore Ḥāfiẓ in something approaching the original Persian – must pay special attention to each of the key rhetorical and structural features illustrated above. Thus translators or teachers having that particular pedagogical aim in mind need to preserve, note or make visible in some way to their non-Persian readers at least the following basic information:

- The essential perspectival clues and signs – key pronouns, number (singular or plural), verb tenses, imperatives, questions, and so forth – embedded in each line and half-line of this poetry.
- The essential thematically unifying terms or themes, which are almost always deeply embedded in a bilingual, widely related semantic field drawn from the Qur'ān and subsequent literary and practical spiritual traditions (Sufism, philosophy, theology, and so on), which must be clearly and fully explained to modern, non-specialist audiences.
- Those intended key alternative meanings or potential levels of understanding (whether of whole lines or of key terms), which shift and transform kaleidoscopically as each reader's own understanding and perspective is awakened.

Because of the shrinking number of contemporary readers and interpreters who are sufficiently familiar with even a few of the most essential fields of traditional Islamicate learning and artistic forms assumed by Ḥāfiẓ and his original audiences (Qur'ān, *ḥadīth*, Islamic philosophy, Kalām theology, a particularly immense and rich Sufi intellectual tradition, and so many earlier Persian and Arabic poets), the challenges of elucidating these complex rhetorical unities and their intellectual presuppositions are becoming increasingly demanding and difficult, both for scholarly specialists and especially for their wider potential audiences. Against that backdrop, one can only hope that scholars aware of these growing pedagogical needs will eventually take up the challenge of providing students and lovers of Ḥāfiẓ – especially those limited to English and languages other than Persian – with something like the spectrum of more literal, carefully annotated translations and essential interpretive tools and studies that are now so readily available at every level for students of Dante, Plato or the *I Ching*.

Finally, a more widespread appreciation of these distinctive structural features in Ḥāfiẓ should also help future editors, translators and other critics in their necessary editorial judgements regarding the often difficult and recurrent questions of alternative verse orders, choices of alternative readings and manuscript evidence, authenticity and the like. The usefulness of this awareness is particularly obvious with regard to the much-debated question of the unity of the *ghazal* form, as well as in encouraging a more adequate appreciation of the different structures and forms of the *ghazal* favoured by those later poets in various Islamicate languages, who were so widely influenced by the prestigious model of Ḥāfiẓ's poetic work.

Notes

1. Lane, *An Arabic-English Lexicon*, part 2, p. 602.
2. In particular, the underlying Qur'ānic roots and inspiration of these characteristic perspective shifts and other related rhetorical features are discussed in much greater detail in my forthcoming volume, *Openings: From the Qur'ān to the Islamic Humanities*.
3. See my study of a remarkable later Safavid illustration of Ḥāfiẓ and the *ghazal* in question in 'Imaging Islam: Intellect and Imagination in Islamic Philosophy, Poetry and Painting', *Religion and the Arts*, XII/1–3 (February 2008), special volume on 'The Inter-Religious Imagination', ed. R. Kearney, pp. 294–318 and 466.
4. For instance, in *Sliding Doors* (directed by P. Howitt, 1998) and K. Kieslowski's *Blind Chance* (*Przypadek*, 1987); or the similar depiction of alternative destinies in *Run, Lola, Run* (*Lola Rennt*, directed by T. Tykwer, 1988).
5. *Dīvān-i Ḥāfiẓ*, ed. Khānlarī, *ghazal* 27.
6. As throughout these *ghazals*, the *yār* ('Friend') evokes at once God as *al-Walī* (the Close, Protecting One), and also each of the protecting and guiding 'Friends of God' (*walī Allāh*) described in several key passages of the Qur'ān. This keynote term (*yār*) is repeated twice here in the last half-line of verse 7, and indicated as well in Ḥāfiẓ's direct allusion at the end of line 5 to the famous verse 5:54 from the Qur'ān on the divine renewing/salvific function of these Friends of God as the *malāmiyya*: '... those who do not fear the blame of any blamer.'

[7] According to the version in Ibn Māja's *Sunan* (I, 44): 'God has 70 [or 700/70,000] veils of light and darkness: if He were to remove them, the radiant splendours of His Face would burn up whoever was reached by His Gaze.' Wensinck, *Concordance* (I, 464), also cites related versions of this same *ḥadīth* from the collections of both Muslim and Ibn Ḥanbal.

[8] Or at least on the surface, at first reading, since in fact the simple, curiously dangling 'but' (*valī*) at the end of the first half-line here is itself also the Qur'ānic Arabic term for the divine 'Friend' (*yār*), whose presence (and apparent absences) are the subject of the entire *ghazal*.

[9] Bukhārī's *Sahīh*, chapter on *tafsīr* (of *Sura* 45); also found in the *ḥadīth* collections of Muslim and Ibn Hanbal.

[10] *Dīvān-i Ḥāfiẓ*, ed. Khānlarī, *ghazal* 66.

[11] *Kār*: intentionally echoing the eternally 'Working-Creator', *Kardagār*, who appears at and as the conclusion of this journey, at the very end of line 7. See also line 5 of the preceding *ghazal*.

[12] The heavenly 'spheres' whose motions together were assumed, in the accepted Ptolemaic-Aristotelean cosmology of Ḥāfiẓ's time, to be the ultimate (visible) instruments of the chains of divine causality, or the ultimate ground of those apparent secondary causes (*sabab*) that are inquired about at the end of the opening verse.

The Semiotic Horizons of Dawn in the Poetry of Ḥāfiẓ

Franklin Lewis

For His anger is but for a moment,
His favor is for life;
Weeping may endure for a night,
But joy comes in the morning.

– Psalm 30:5 (New King James Version)

Es tagt, es wirft auf's Meer den Streif die Sonne;
Aufflatternd sucht der junge Greif die Sonne;
Auch du lick' auf und singe Morgenhymnen,
Als aller Wesen Bild begreif' die Sonne...

– August von Platen, from 'Ghaselen X'[1]

Au réveil, si douce la lumière - et ce bleu - Le mot 'Pur' ouvre mes lèvres.

Le jour qui jamais encore ne fut, les pensées, le tout en germe considéré sans obstacles - le Tout qui s'ébauche dans l'or et que nulle chose particulière ne corrompt encore.

Le Tout est commencement. En germe le plus haut degré universel...

– Paul Valéry (1913)[2]

The present study considers a question of comparative literature, that of a particular literary topos of dawn, the 'Alba', and, beyond that, the wider horizons of the mythopoesis of dawn and its associated *locus amoenus* in the *ghazal* tradition, with particular reference to its development in the poems of Ḥāfiẓ of Shīrāz. Speaking of mythic time, the kernel of this essay was actually written more than two decades ago, in 1986, and then buried away in a drawer.[3] A few years later, my elder daughter, Sahar, was born. Since she is now at the dawn of her own college career, and the hour of parting from her childhood home approaches, it seemed an opportune moment to resurrect this chapter as a memento of all the happy days she has brightened our household.

The Alba

Dawn is a symbolically charged time in many literary traditions, perhaps most famously in the medieval Provençal lyric – or, in the terminology now preferred, Occitan lyric, since the *langue d'oc* was not delimited to the county of Provence, but flourished in Poitou and Aquitaine, and eastward beyond this, throughout much of southern France and into northern Italy, in a region now dubbed Occitania. A small but important corpus of Troubadour poems sharing particular features has been classified generically as 'dawn' poetry. This genre is named *Alba*, which word appears as a refrain in many of these poems, though the French word 'aube' or 'aubade' is sometimes applied to thematically related poems in the *langue d'oïl*, and an even larger corpus of medieval German poetry in this genre goes under the name *Tagelied*.[4] By the twelfth or thirteenth century, the Occitan tradition already recognized these 'Alba' poems, which were probably sung to musical accompaniment (and perhaps even danced or acted, in at least three voices), as belonging to a distinct thematic convention, or genre, of their own.[5] Although these dawn songs are well known, and have been considered by some to be, along with the *sirventes*,[6] 'perhaps the most famous, peculiar and representative of Provençal forms',[7] they are actually a rather minor genre, not much practised by the major Troubadour poets, and generally composed in a popular tone with comparatively unsophisticated versification. However widespread the genre must have been, only a small number of *Alba* survive: Alfred Jeanroy counted 16 Occitan *Alba* poems,[8] though at least one additional Occitan or Provençal *Alba* was discovered after his 1934 study of the matter. In 1944, Martín de Riquer tallied 18 poems as belonging to this canon,[9] while in 1965, B. Woledge, using more restrictive criteria, accepted just nine troubadour *Albas*, with four further poems in the penumbra of the *Alba*, possibly 'derivatives of the main genre', insofar as they are all concerned in some way with 'the parting of lovers at dawn'.[10] The five common characteristics of the nine poems, which Woledge felt were central to and representative of the *Alba* genre, include the following features:

1) They describe the feelings of lovers who, after a night spent together, must separate at dawn because it would be dangerous for them to be found together.
2) In addition to the two lovers, they have a third character, a watchman who announces the coming of dawn.
3) All except one [of these nine] have a refrain containing the word *Alba* ('dawn').
4) Most of them contain a certain amount of dialogue, or a combination of narrative with direct speech.
5) All seem to have been written either in the late twelfth century to middle thirteenth century, with few if any being from the late thirteenth.

In a footnote, Woledge adds that in five of the nine poems a further characteristic is that the lovers are in danger from 'the jealous one' or 'the husband'.[11] He also points out that poets made both secular and religious use of the *Alba* theme. Frank Chambers succinctly describes the *Alba* – which he apparently assimilates to the French *aubade* and the German *Tagelied* – as follows: 'a dawn song, ordinarily expressing the regret of two lovers that day has come so soon to separate them.' He furthermore suggests that the *Alba* 'probably grew out of the medieval watchman's cry, announcing from his tower the passing of the night hours and the return of the day'. This watchman will sometimes stand guard to protect the lovers' privacy.[12] Indeed, it has been argued that the watchman of the *Alba* can be identified with the muezzin on his minaret at dawn. However, Arthur Hatto rejects this theory, because in the existing examples of lovers awakened by either the muezzin or the Balkan *Hodzha*, the lovers are non-Muslims. On these grounds, Hatto argues that any Andalusian connections to the *Alba* should be through Mozarabic models, and not Muslim ones, though he does not find much evidence for this in existing Mozarabic dawn songs.[13]

Whatever its origins, the *Alba* topos became well ingrained into European literary traditions,[14] with the topos of dawn as the time of parting of two lovers suffusing medieval European and renaissance literature. An excellent example of the survival of the contours of the *Alba* can be seen in Shakespeare's *Romeo and Juliet*, Act 3, Scene V, set in Capulet's orchard, with Juliet standing at the window, conversing with Romeo, about whether the bird they hear is the nightingale ('nightly she sings on yon pomegranate tree'), or the lark, 'herald of the morn'. Romeo points out that even if he disagrees with Juliet, he is happy to submit to her command, though the Duke's order of banishment means death for him if discovered still in town in the daylight. Juliet's nurse comes to warn her that her mother is coming to her chamber, in which she has enjoyed her tryst with Romeo. Beware, the day is broke! Exit Romeo.

Woledge's study enumerating the characteristic features of the *Alba* appeared in Arthur Hatto's marvellously wide-ranging survey of dawn poetry in world literature, *Eos*.[15] The chapters therein on the Arabic and Persian traditions were written by Bernard Lewis with S.M. Stern (pp. 215–43), and G.M. Wickens (pp. 243–7), respectively. Concerning Arabic, Lewis and Stern claim that it 'has no dawn-poetry as a special genre' like the *Alba*, because 'there are in Arabic no independent poems of a fixed structure having as their sole theme the separation of lovers at dawn'. They do, however, recognize it as a 'fairly frequent' motif, if not an indispensable one, in Arabic love poetry (specifically the erotic poetry of the Umayyad period, though they include numerous examples from the Abbasid era and from Andalusia). Of course, the dawn already figured in pre-Islamic poetry as the hour of parting of migrating tribes (the verb *ibtakara*, indeed, means to part at dawn), and also of the disappearance of the *ṭayf al-khayāl*, the phantom image of the beloved which torments the lover during his sleepless night.[16] Dawn also interrupts the nocturnal wassail, marking the end of the drinking soirée, which lasts throughout the night. But there is a second kind of drinking occasion, the morning draught (and also the morning hunt), which may instead make the poet impatient for the signs of dawn to arrive. But as far as lovers are concerned, in a poetic context dawn is the enemy, because the night of union is never long enough.

Lewis and Stern's negative assessment of the existence of dawn poetry, per se, in the Arabic tradition would seem to be greatly undermined by the 33 excellent examples they do produce of just such poetry, including, for example, the following poem by the Umayyad caliph, al-Walīd II (reg. 125–6/743–4)[17]:

Qāmat ilayya bi-taqbīl^{in} *tu'āniqu-nī*
rayya'l-'iẓāmi ka-anna'l-miska fī fī-hā
Udkhul fadaytu-ka lā yash'ur bi-nā aḥad^{un}
nafsī li-nafsika min dā'in tufaddī-hā
Bitnā kadhālika lā nawm^{un} *'alā surur*^{in}
min shiddati'l-wajdi tudnī-nī wa-udnī-hā
Ḥattā idhā mā bada'l-khayṭāni, qultu la-hā:
ḥāna'l-firāq^{u} *fa-kāda'l-ḥuzn*^{u} *yushjī-hā*
Thumma'nṣaraftu wa-lam yash'ur bi-nā aḥad^{un}
wa'llāhu 'annī bi-ḥusni'l-fi'li yajzī-hā.

She rose to greet me with kisses, embracing me
Full-limbed, fragrant as if musk was in her mouth
'Enter, my dear one, so that none knows of us
I am your ransom against suffering.'
Thus we lay the night, without sleep, on our couches [pillows]
From the force of passion, she clasped me, and I clasped her
Until the two threads appeared,[18] I said to her:
'The time for parting has come,' and grief almost overcame her
Then I left her, and none knew of us [was aware of us]
May God reward her for her good deed.

Beyond the several examples Lewis and Stern do reproduce, many other examples of an *Alba* topos in Andalusian poetry are found in Ibn Qūzmān of Cordoba (d. 555/1160), including his *Zajal* 141, which parodies the theme – always an indication that something has become canonical in a tradition. This and several other examples led Dionisia Empaytaz de Croome to argue that 'numerous dawn poems in the Hispano-Arabic tradition ... show links with Iberian dawn poetry ... dawn partings, which some scholars would prefer to keep out of the Iberian Peninsula altogether, appear in the Muslim literature of Spain as frequently as the *Alba* in Old Provençal Poetry.'[19]

As for the Persian tradition, Wickens argues that 'the *Alba* form is not of common occurrence in Persian' and is 'in no sense a recognized poetical convention'. However, he held out hope that one day a 'considerable yield of dawn poems' might be found among Persian poetry manuscripts, especially of the mystical tradition, insofar as the *majālis* of the Sufi lodges commonly lasted throughout the night.[20]

Though this assumption that dawn and the *Alba* was a naturalistic, rather than a mythopoeic, setting is far wide of the mark, Wickens does offer us two Persian examples of the *Alba* theme, one a passage from Firdawsī describing Zāl's tryst with Rūdāba, which led to the birth of Rustam, which we will pass over here, and the other from a *ghazal* of Sa'dī, as follows:

Imshab sabuktar mīzanand in ṭabl-i bī-hangām rā
yā vaqt-i bīdārī ghalaṭ būd-ast murgh-i bām rā
Yik lahẓa būd īn, yā shabī, k-az 'umr-i mā tārāj shud
mā ham-chunān lab bar labī nā-bar-girifta kām rā
Ham tāza-ruyam, ham khajil, ham shādmān, ham tang-dil
k-az 'uhda bīrūn āmadan natvānam īn payghām rā [21]
Gar pāy bar farqam nahī tashrīf-i qurbat mīdahī
juz sar nimīdānam nihād az 'udhr-i īn iqdām rā.[22]
Chūn bakht-i nīk-anjām rā bā mā bi-kullī ṣulḥ shud
bugdhār tā jān mīdahad bad-gū-yi bad-farjām rā
Sa'dī 'alam shud dar jahān, ṣūfīy u 'āmī gū bidān
Mā but-parastī mīkunīm āngāh chunīn aṣnām rā.

Wickens renders the poem in prose as follows:

> Tonight they must be beating more swiftly the unwelcome watchdrum, or else the rooftop-bird has mistaken the hour of waking. Was this a moment or a whole night thus plundered from our lives, and we still lip to lip with our desire unsatisfied? Now smiling am I, now in constraining, now rejoicing and now sad at heart – still I fail to convey this message. If you but deign to place your foot upon my neck, you honour me by your proximity: verily but for my low-laid head I know no welcome to offer your approaching footsteps. Since good fortune has at last become reconciled to us, let the malignant slanderers go hang! Sa'dī has become a marked man in the eyes of the world: bid them know, then, mystics and mob alike – we may be idolators, but then what idols![23]

I would here like to offer in fulfilment of Wickens' prescient hope two further Persian examples of *Alba* poems, both of which turn up in Mudarris-i Raḍavī's edition of the *Dīvān* of Sanā'ī. The first (*ghazal* 215) echoes strongly with the Arabic *Alba* example of Walīd II, which was cited above:

Man naṣīb-i khʷīsh dūsh az 'umr-i khʷud bar dāshtam
k-az saman bālīn u az shamshād bastar dāshtam
Dāshtam dar bar nigārī rā ki az dīdār-i ū
pāya-yi takht-i khʷud az khʷurshīd bartar dāshtam
Nargis u shamshād u sūsan, mushk u sīm u māh u gul
tā bi hangām-i saḥar har haft dar bar dāshtam

Bar nihāda bar bar-i chūn sīm u sūsan dāshtam
lab nihāda bar labī chūn shīr u shikar dāshtam
Dast-i ū bar gardan-i man hamchū chanbar būd o man
dast-i khʷud dar gardan-i ū hamchū chanbar dāshtam
Bāmdādān chūn nigah kardam basī farqī nabūd
chanbar az zar dāsht ū, sūsan zi 'anbar dāshtam
Chūn mu'adhdhin guft yik 'Allāhu akbar' kāfar-am
gar umīd-i ān digar Allāhu akbar dāshtam.

Last night
my life's fantasies
were all fulfilled:

I bedded down
on a pillow of jasmine,
on a slender trunk, (1)
held in my embrace
a beauty who
as I looked on her
made me feel
the bed stood
high above
the sun. (2)

Narcissus,
slender trunk,
lilies,
musk and silver,
moon and rose,
clear through till dawn,
I hugged all seven in my arms (3)
My breast
pressed
to a breast
like silver and lilies,
my lips
pressed
upon lips
like milk and sugar; (4)
Her arms and my arms
encircled circled
my neck her neck
like a band, like a band (5)

When I looked
in the morning's light,
that's almost how it was:
she had a necklace of gold
and I a lily of ambergris (6)
As the Muezzin
pronounced his first 'Allāhu akbar' –
I'm a heathen
if I wished him
to complete the pair. (7)

And here is the second short *Alba ghazal* (no. 236) from Sanā'ī, in which the muezzin again heralds the morning and disrupts the lovers' congress:

Āmad bar-i man jahān u jānam / uns-i dil u rāḥat-i ravānam
Bar khʷāstam-ash bi-bar giriftam / bifzūd hizār jān u ravānam
Az qadd-i buland u zulf-i pushtash / guftam ki magar bi āsimān-am
Chūn sar bi-nihād dar kināram / raft az bar-i man jahān u jānam
Faryād marā zi bāng-i mu'adhdhin
Man banda-yi bāng-i pāsibān-am.

My world and my soul
came to my side,
companion to my heart,
comfort of my psyche.
I called her over
pressed her in embrace;
my spirit multiplied
a thousand fold
within
me.
Gazing the length of that tall body
and the twines of tress down her back,
I thought:
I must be in the heavens
No sooner had she laid her head upon my breast,
than my world and my soul
left my side.
Save me from the call of the Muezzin!
I'm a slave to the cry of the night watchman!

Given the small corpus of less than a score of poems, according to Woledge, that has allowed us to identify the *Alba* as a thematic genre of Occitan poetry, the existence of the four above-mentioned poems of al-Walīd II, Sa'dī and Sanā'ī surely requires that we reconsider and reject the thesis that Persian and Arabic lack the *Alba* genre. Except for the fact that the word 'Alba' does not of course reprise in these poems (though, in the first of the two Sanā'ī poems quoted here, two different Persian equivalents for 'dawn' do in fact appear: *hangām-i saḥar* and *bāmdādān*) – most of the defining characteristics of Woledge's canon are manifestly evident here, and thus qualify the poems as belonging thematically to this international genre.

A few further examples from the final lines of other *ghazals* by Sanā'ī will be offered here as further evidence that this type of ending is indeed part of a conventional topos of which Sanā'ī was consciously aware, and which remained present in the poet's mind, even where the poem is not entirely structured like the Persian *Albas* above. From *ghazal* 173, line 7, in a poem which lacks a *takhalluṣ*, we find the poet, in the absence of the Beloved, enjoying the presence of his or her phantom image, and not wanting the day to dispel this pleasant reverie:

Bā hijr-i tu har shab zi pay-i vaṣl-i tu gūyam:
'Yā rab tu shab-i 'āshiq u ma'shūq makun rūz'.

In your absence every night,
in search of union
I proclaim:
O Lord,
do not turn
the night of
the lover and beloved
to
day.

The following complaint of the all-too-swift arrival of the morning that concludes the lovers' meeting comes from Sanā'ī's *Qaṣīda* 77 (which is, however, in fact, a *ghazal*):

V-ān shab ki marā būd bi khalvat bar-i ū bār
pīsh az shab-i man ṣubḥ zi kuhsār bar āmad.

And that night,
when I had my visit with him
all alone,
before my night was through
the morning rose
above the mountains.

And, finally, from the last three lines of a nine-line *ghazal* (Mudarris-i Raḍavī, *Qaṣīda* 153), we find the *takhalluṣ* introducing a monologue delivered to the Beloved at dawn, summarizing the poem and the sufferings of the previous night. Though it approaches the *Alba* topos from a different angle – that of a tryst unmet at all, rather than one that must come to an end at sunrise – it nevertheless confirms the existence of the *Alba* genre. In fact, Martín de Riquier notes the existence of a class of Provençal poems which complain at dawn about the previous night's separation, and has dubbed this twist on the dawn-theme, *Contra-Alba* poems[24]:

Gīram ki Sanāʾī az ghamat murd / bārī sukhanash bi-ṭabʿ bi-nyūsh
Ay rū-yi tu būd dūsh tā ṣubḥ / az nāla-yi ū jahān pur az jūsh
Yā rabb shab-i kas mabād hargiz / z-īn gūna ki ū gudhāsht shab dūsh.

I guess that Sanāʾi
died pining for thee;
now drink
his words into your mind. (7)
Last night,
without your face,
dusk to daylight
the world was
in turmoil
filled with his lamentations: (8)
O Lord,
let no one ever
pass the night
the way he spent
last night. (9)

To my knowledge, this genre of Persian *Alba* and contra-*Alba* poems has not been previously noticed or studied, or even recognized as such, with the exception of Wickens' article.

What's Hecuba to Ḥāfiẓ, you may be asking at this point. Ḥāfiẓ, unfortunately, did not compose any poems like the two of Sanāʾī above. In fact, the word muezzin (*muʾadhdhin*) does not even occur in the poetic lexicon of Ḥāfiẓ, so we cannot expect to see the same scenes we found in the Sanāʾī *Albas*. But Saʿdī's *Alba ghazal* beginning, 'Tonight they must be beating more swiftly the unwelcome watchdrum' (*Imshab sabuktar mīzanand in ṭabl-i bī-hangām rā*), did not feature the muezzin character either, so perhaps we should begin by looking for poems similar to this one in the corpus of Ḥāfiẓ. While the *Dīvān* of Ḥāfiẓ does preserve two poems rhyming in *-ām* with the radīf *rā*, neither uses rhymes similar to this poem of Saʿdī, nor do the two *ghazals* without *radīf* and rhyming in *-ām* give any hint that Ḥāfiẓ had his eye on this poem of Saʿdī to offer a poetic riposte (*javāb*).

But the first line of Saʿdī's *ghazal* pairs the dawn and the bird on the roof (*bām*), and we do indeed find such a collocation in Ḥāfiẓ (324: 9):

Man ān murgham ki har shām u saḥargāh / zi bām-i 'arsh mīāyad ṣafīram.

I am a bird whose shrill cry rises each dusk and dawntide from the roof of God's throne.

But neither this line nor this poem will have much to do with Sa'dī's motif, other than the lexical overlap. Worse yet, we find no topical correspondences in the corpus of Ḥāfiẓ to vocabulary like *bī-hangām*, which never occurs (the word *hangām* occurs only rarely – four times – and not in particular connection with the dawn). The word *ṭabl* is a *hapax legomenon* for Ḥāfiẓ, and its single occurrence is irrelevant to our comparison. Even *imshab* occurs relatively infrequently, only six times in the *ghazals* of Ḥāfiẓ, despite this word having become a standard *radīf* in the works of other poets by this time, to such an extent that it almost constitutes a sub-genre of the *ghazal* all by itself. Although the word *imshab* does naturally – here, in more than one sense of the word 'naturally' – collocate with the idea of dawn and its associated motifs for Ḥāfiẓ, the occurrences do not seem particularly relevant to the *Alba* notion of the lover's parting, as it occurs in Sa'dī's example. The following line can be seen as typical of Ḥāfiẓ's usage of 'tonight':

Ay ṣabā imshabam madad farmāy / ki saḥargāh shikuftanam havas ast. (43: 5)

Morning breeze, come to my aid tonight / for I crave blossoming at dawn.

However, at least one of the *imshab* lines does indeed allude to the contra-*Alba* theme, but, as I hope to show below, the release from suffering that comes at dawn does not necessarily have to be associated with the *Alba*, the contra-*Alba* or even with love:

Bas-am ḥikāyat-i dil hast bā nasīm-i saḥar
valī bi bakht-i man imshab saḥar nimīāyad.

It's enough for me to tell my heart's tale to the breeze at dawn
But with my ill fortune, no dawn will come tonight.

If Ḥāfiẓ was not mindful of this poem by Sa'dī, what of those two *Alba* poems of Sanā'ī? The first began 'Last night my life's fantasies were all fulfilled' (*Man naṣīb-i khwīsh dūsh az 'umr-i khwud bar dāshtam*), which *radīf* Ḥāfiẓ does not employ, nor any of its conjugant variants in the past tense (*dāshtīm, dāshtī, dāsht*), and which rhyme he does not use in its simple form without a refrain. I have not looked to see everywhere the rhyme *-ar* may occur in combination with another *radīf*, but one key word from this poem, *bastar*, does not appear in the lexicon of Ḥāfiẓ at all. The word *chanbar* occurs only twice in Ḥāfiẓ, and that not quite in the motif of the lovers' tryst. However, recalling Sanā'ī's example 'Her arms and my arms encircled circled my neck her neck like a band, like a band' (*Dast-i ū bar gardan-i man hamchū chanbar būd u man / dast-i khʷud dar gardan-i ū hamchū chanbar dāshtam*), we may see some residual association with the word *gardan* and the notion of parting in the following token of *chanbar* (from Ḥāfiẓ 291: 9):

Falak magar chu saram dīd asīr-i chanbar-i 'ishq
bi-bast gardan-i ṣabram bi rīsmān-i firāq.

When the celestial sphere saw my head caught in the noose of love
It bound separation's tether fast around my patient neck.

The word *kāfar*, which was crucial to the last line of Sanā'ī's poem in its pairing with *Allāhu akbar*, occurs only thrice in Ḥāfiẓ, twice in the phrase *kāfar-i 'ishq*, though not as a rhyme, and not as part of an *Alba* topos. *Allāhu akbar* does occur once in Ḥāfiẓ (*ghazal* 40: 9), but not in association with the muezzin's call; rather, with a comparison based on Khiḍr and the Spring of Life, whose waters originate in darkness (*ẓulumāt*), to the waters of the Allāhu Akbar spring in Shīrāz.

The only other potentially distinctive word from this poem which might possibly collocate with the motif of the lovers' tryst is the word 'lot' (*naṣīb*), which Ḥāfiẓ uses only four times, and only once in this amorous context (156: 3):

Ravā madār khudāyā ki dar ḥarīm-i viṣāl
raqīb maḥram u ḥirmān naṣīb-i man bāshad.

O God, in the sanctuary of union do not permit
Intimacy to the rival and have deprivation be my lot.

Though this involves a lover's tryst, it is neither bounded in time by the evening or the dawn, nor is this theme developed in the rest of the *ghazal*. So here, again, there is no fateful semiosis with *naṣib*.

What, then, of the second poem of Sanā'ī? 'My world and my soul came to my side, / companion to my heart, comfort of my psyche' (*Āmad bar-i man jahān u jānam/ uns-i dil u rāḥat-i ravānam*). Unfortunately, Ḥāfiẓ took no conscious notice of this poem, either; he has no poems in this rhyme and *radīf*, and the only truly distinctive word in this short poem, besides *mu'adhdhin* (which as we have already noted, Ḥāfiẓ does not use), is the nightwatchman (*pāsibān*). Perhaps the nightwatchman will stumble onto an early morning lover's tryst in Ḥāfiẓ, and uncover an arresting *Alba* scene for us?

Pāsibān appears only twice in Ḥāfiẓ, and its synonym *'asas* but once (261:5). Of these three occurrences, the nightly tryst of love is twice implicated, as follows:

'Ishrat-i shabgīr kun bī-tars k-andar shahr-i 'ishq
shabruvān rā āshnā'ī-hā-st bā mīr-i 'asas.

Make love at night without fear, for in the metropolis of love
Those who go by night in stealth are well known to the chief of police.

The meaning of this line may be that the lovers are themselves like thieves (*shabraw*) who sneak around at night, and the police already know who they are, but do not prosecute them in the city of love. Alternatively, it may be that the *shabruvān* are real criminals, who might pose a potential threat to the lovers – a category of people who also go about at night in pursuit of illicit love. Rather than prosecuting them, the nightwatchmen are protecting them from the real criminals.

It may not be inappropriate to ask why the watchman appears here, since the watchman is significant not only to Sanā'ī's *Alba* poem, but also to the *Alba* poems of the Troubadours. As mentioned, the word 'policeman' (*'asas*) occurs as a *hapax legomenon* in the Ḥāfiẓian corpus, and 'nightwatchman' (*pāsibān*) occurs but twice. There are, however, two other patrolling dangers to be avoided: the 'royal political police' (*shaḥna*) and the vice officer (*muḥtasib*). The *muḥtasib* enforces fair business practices and ensures that public morality is not violated by drinkers or lovers. To Ḥāfiẓ, the *muḥtasib* is a sharp-eyed (42: 1) spoiler of the pleasures of wine (144: 4) and a smasher of the chalice (146: 7), greatly to be feared (278: 4, 290: 7), perhaps because of his role in enforcing the criminalization of wine in Shīrāz (354: 4). Like some other officials, notably preachers, the *muḥtasib* is guilty of posing (195: 9), he is drunk with hypocrisy (*riyā*), and should be defied wherever possible (290: 7, 280: 2b). In Ḥāfiẓ's Shīrāz, the *muḥtasib* sometimes patrolled with the royal political police (*shaḥna*, 48: 9) against wine, though the poet dismisses the latter as ineffectual (73: 4), even beseeching the 'constable of the convivium' (*shaḥna-yi majlis*) to prevent Ḥāfiẓ's beloved from drinking with any rival (116: 11). Our chief watchman, the *mīr-i 'asas*, is here (261: 5) associated with the possible interruption of lovers' trysts, though depending on how we read this line (as suggested above), he may in actuality be facilitating them. Likewise, the metaphorical *pāsibān*, in the following line of Ḥāfiẓ, protects the phantom tryst that takes place in the seclusion of the lover's heart (319: 8):

Pāsibān-i ḥaram-i dil shuda-am shab hama shab
tā dar īn parda juz andīsha-yi ū nagudhāram.

I've become watchman of the precincts of the heart at night all night
Forbidding entry behind the curtain to all but thought of him.

By contrast, the *muḥtasib* is an adversary, whom Ḥāfiẓ boldly confronts with the fact of his status as lover (338: 1a; see also 355: 8):

Man nay ān rind-am ki tark-i shāhid u sāghar kunam
muḥtasib dānad ki man īn kār-hā kamtar kunam.

I am not one to give up chalice and cherub;
The vice officer knows not to expect it often of me.

We might recall here that the watchman of many *Alba* poems, like Juliet's nurse, is actually an authority figure in league with the lovers, protecting their tryst, though he or she is supposed to be preventing such mischief and vice. Sanā'ī's example contrasts the *pāsibān*, as the friendly voice of the night, with the muezzin's terminal announcement of the dawn.

The line of Ḥāfiẓ which evokes the chief watchman does so with the Arabic term for watchman (*'asas*). It is needed here for the rhyme, of course, but as it happens this *ghazal* repeatedly evokes the Arabic traditions of the *nasīb* and *ẓa'n*, the camel litter departing with the Beloved, who is here explicitly named 'Salmā', a common beloved's name in the Arabic poetic tradition. All of this Arabizing does not quite dovetail, however, so neatly with the poem's specific geographical coordinates in Azerbayjan, at the Araxes River. The opening apostrophe to the easterly morning breeze (*ṣabā*) suggests that the poem should begin at dawn, with a message bearing kisses to that fragrant spot (261:1):

Ay ṣabā gar bugdharī bar sāḥil-i rūd-i aras
būsa zan bar khāk-i ān vādī u mushkīn kun nafas.

Eastern Breeze! If you pass by the banks of the Aras River
Kiss the earth of that valley and perfume your breath with musk.

Other conventions of the Arabic *nasīb* on display in this poem include the advice-givers (*nāsiḥān*, line 4), whose earnest counsel the lover ignores, actually turning their sayings (*qawl*) into Arabic songs (*qawl*), set to the lovely music of the Rebec (*rabāb*). We might here recall that in the European *Alba*, the watchman who stands guard over the lovers is often a musician.[25]

In the line after we meet the chief watchman, the poet reminds us that the business of lovemaking is quite serious: *'ishqbāzī kār-i bāzī nīst* (line 6). 'Lovemaking is no game' – it requires self-sacrifice. But though this poem plays with conventions related to the *Alba* theme, it does not lead to a parting at dawn and therefore cannot be classified as an *Alba*. Although we may discern some fragmentary elements of the *Alba* topos here, they do not necessarily allude directly to the tradition, since the nightly tryst can indeed occur outside of the framework of the dawn's early light, disrupting the night's late love.

There is at least one *ghazal* from Ḥāfiẓ that seems to have some of the tiles of the *Alba* scene, albeit in a somewhat re-arranged mosaic. This *ghazal* makes no allusion to the three poems of Sa'dī and Sanā'ī which we have been discussing, but it does have the following elements: an opening line that may be set at dawn, just after a message has come on the breeze from the beloved, who has invariably travelled far away, leaving the lover behind (98:1):

Dūsh āgah-ī zi yār-i safar karda dād bād
man nīz dil bi-bād daham har chi bād bād. (line 1)

Last night the wind brought a memento from that friend who journeyed away
I, too, will give my heart to the wind – *que sera sera!*

Today the poet realizes that those who are close to him, and had counselled him against giving his heart to the beloved, were giving good advice (line 4). The morning breeze gives hope of reunion and brings back to life the lover whose weak body had almost ceased to exist (line 6).

But we are still somewhat far from the *Alba* tradition. Perhaps the century of the *Alba* had passed by the time Ḥāfiẓ wrote his *ghazals*. If that is the case, it testifies to the dynamism of the tradition, which, though highly conventional in many ways, is discarding or re-arranging certain earlier motifs and generating new ones. If that is not the case and we can find evidence of *Alba* poems in the contemporaries of Ḥāfiẓ, then we may simply note that Ḥāfiẓ found the topos uninteresting or clichéd. If we have come up short in our search for *Alba* poems in Ḥāfiẓ, what then can we say about his mythopoeisis of the dawn?

Charles-Henri de Fouchécour's *La Description de la nature*, a seminal study of nature in the poetry of ʿUnṣurī, Farrukhī, Manūchihrī, Qaṭrān, Azraqī and Muʿizzī,[26] has shown us the utility, indeed the necessity, of looking diachronically and synchronically at catalogues of related images and topoi in Persian poetry. Not only does this process help us to understand the tradition's symbols better and more precisely, bringing the semiotic contours of various natural settings and topoi in Persian poetry into sharper relief, it also enables us to perceive more clearly the particularities with which individual poets invest certain conventional topoi, themes and, indeed, genres. Some of the items and features of the landscape Fouchécour describes obviously collocate with the larger scene and setting of dawn. Although the full range of auroral motifs are not typically invoked wholesale in any given *ghazal*, as soon as one such motif is invoked, the poet may potentially choose to amplify and develop this one motif by evoking another of the associated images, characters and ideas in the auroral catalogue. For the *ghazal*, this catalogue may include the morning breeze, or zephyr, that wafts from the east/north-east in the springtime (*ṣabā*);[27] the brightness of day; the appearance of the beloved or the arrival / dispatch of a message to him or her; the fragrance and freshness of the garden; the appearance of the rose; a call from the wine tavern; a morning draught of wine; prayer; and so on. Fouchécour's collection of data and summary description of the catalogue of images occurs mostly in the Persian *qaṣīda* poetry written about two centuries preceding Ḥāfiẓ, but will nevertheless provide us with a frame of reference by which we can anticipate a horizon of expectations for the various clusters of imagery in the corpus of Ḥāfiẓ, such as the times and seasons of the year and their associated festivals; the nightingale (*bulbul*, *ʿandalīb*) and birds more generally (*murgh*, 138ff.); the wind (95ff.); the stars and the heavenly bodies (218–20), and so forth. A portion of Fouchécour's study, 'Les heures du poète' (26–7), treats the vocabulary of the times of day that typically appears in eleventh-century Persian poetry, including the dawn. From this we learn that, in Farrukhī's *qaṣīdas*, sunset is the hour of fortune's arrival. For Manūchihrī, the day departs too quickly, because it means the poet must leave his Beloved. The sky is purified at night. In the nights of spring, we see the shining of the rose, the tulip and pomegranate blossom, and we hear the nightingale. For Farrukhī, the turtledove sings late at night, the dew falls and the perfume of spring arises in the middle of the spring night, which is shorter than the day, even though the night seems long for the unrequited lover – a theme which we have seen as part of the contra-*Alba* in the *ghazal*.

Fouchécour notes (pp. 26–7) that the various terms for dawn, daybreak and morning, such as *shabgīr*, *sapīda-dam*, *pagāh*, *saḥar*, *bāmdād* or *ṣubḥ*, do not seem to be poetically differentiated. These terms all evoke flowers, the singing of birds, dew and rain, breeze and wind, fragrance, fog, thunder, rainbows and snow. The moon shines at dawn, things become clear, and all the natural phenomena which Manūchihrī associates with the day – such as the sun climbing the eastern sky, and the cock crowing and calling out to the drinkers – are on display. For Manūchihrī, the morning libation is a moment out of time, neither hot nor cold, without cloud, sun, wind or dust. Dawn is also associated with Nawrūz and the vernal festivities of renewal.

Of course, the realm of the *qaṣīda* is not necessarily semiotically identical with he realm of the *ghazal*, but many of the associations apply equally to the world of the *ghazal* and to the world of the royal spring poem. This is understood intuitively enough when reading through the *nasīb* of the Ghaznavid *qaṣīda*, but we may also draw upon a number of secondary studies to buttress this impression. Julie Meisami has fleshed out the semiotic universe of the poetic garden, as a mirror of paradise,[28] and the Lirica Persica project in Venice has created a delimited poetic corpus (1,000 lines each from a good number of poets, in a meticulously scientific Romanized transliteration), which can facilitate frequency studies and comparisons of particular images and motifs between poets, all with a view towards creating, eventually, a very devoutly-to-be-wished historical dictionary of the *ghazal*. One example of the type of study this data allows can be seen in the work of Daniela Meneghini Correale,[29] whose complete inventory of the vocabulary of Ḥāfiẓ – including lemmatized frequency lists, a concordance, and a Romanized, grammatically parsed corpus of the *Dīvān* of Ḥāfiẓ – has been an indispensable tool for the current study, and in my previous work.[30] And yet the basic tabulations for the comments that follow were done in the dark days before 1988, when Meneghini Correale's *The Ghazals of Ḥāfiẓ: Concordance and Vocabulary*[31] appeared, some 600 years after the poet's death. Consequently, there may be some small discrepancies between the frequencies I have tabulated here, and those provided by Correale's concordance and vocabulary. These differences will mostly stem from my attempt to count the occurrences of words in the entire *Dīvān*, and not just in the *ghazal*s of Ḥāfiẓ.

Claude Lévi-Strauss has shown us how mythology encodes certain cultural values. Arnold Van Gennep and Victor Turner have demonstrated that various cultural rituals give meaning to and symbolically encode certain periods of social-cultural transition. These encoded rituals sometimes implicitly inform literary and other artistic works, and making them explicit may therefore yield critical insights into these works. In the case of the tripartite Arabic *qaṣīda*, for example, Suzanne and Jaroslav Stetkevych have uncovered a rite of passage, with the stage of separation articulated in the *nasīb*; the stage of liminality symbolized in the journey section of the *raḥīl*; and the stage of aggregation, or reintegration, symbolized in the *fakhr* section of the poem. The animals that the poet encounters in the *raḥīl*, a journey often undertaken at night, are all symbolic of the sojourner's outcast state.[32]

Similarly, an analysis of the specific time-frames of the Persian *ghazal*, the characters and events with which particular time periods and scenes are specifically and perhaps exclusively associated, the catalogue of motifs and images which radiate from it, and – in short – the semiotic horizons of the time-frame, may likewise prove useful in understanding the fixed-form of the Persian *ghazal*.

The Hour of Dawn in Ḥāfiẓ

Approximately 90, or nearly one-fifth, of the *ghazal*s of Ḥāfiẓ explicitly refer to dawn or early morning, which time must therefore constitute a significant semiotic horizon in his mythopoesis, particularly if these words come at a formative point in the poem, such as the first or the last line. In the rest of this chapter, I will attempt a lexical/semiotic inventory of dawn and the archetypal scenes, poetic situations and emotions attendant upon its evocation. Do the different words for dawn, daybreak and morning each have their own semiotic valency, or do they all evoke more or less an undifferentiated mythopoetic time? Consideration will be given to dawn in relation to other poetic time-frames (night, seasons, festivals) and its role as a sacred, or *in illo tempore* time, in which suffering is resolved and meaning is revealed. By isolating the semantic horizons of dawn as a topos, it is hoped that the relationship between certain themes and topoi, and therefore the architectonics of his *ghazal*s, may emerge in somewhat clearer relief.

I take it as a clear premise of this study that dawn is indeed the paramount mythopoetic hour of the day, and symbolically saturated for Ḥāfiẓ. Ḥāfiẓ announces to us that he composes poetry at night and weeps at dawn, for the laughing and crying of lovers come from two different places (373: 6):

Khanda vu girya-yi 'ushshāq zi jā'ī digar ast
mīsurāyam bi shab u vaqt-i saḥar mīmūyam.

The laughter and tears of the lovers comes from some other quarter
I compose at night and weep at dawntide.

This completely inverts the Psalmist's setting for joy and grief: 'Weeping may endure for a night, but joy comes in the morning.' Rather, our poet composes and carouses at night and weeps in the morning light. This significant line comes in the penultimate position of a seven-line *ghazal*, which contrasts the spiritual attraction Ḥāfiẓ finds in the fragrance of musk at the tavern, with the preacher's assumption that he is sniffing the door of the tavern. These can be seen as the two different sources from which joy and grief come to the lovers.

Forms of this verb *mū'īdan* (to weep) occur only twice in the *Dīvān*, and only this once in reference to Ḥāfiẓ himself, so the word may bear some special weight (though we may also note that a word of this form is required in this rhyming position in the poem). Dawn is the time for sorrow, or the articulation of suffering, in contrast to the night, which is the time for joy and poetry. One may note that the frequent comparison of the poet to a sweet-singing bird may influence this image; the nightingale sings his courtship songs, beating his breast with his wings, at night. It is worth remembering here, with Ḥusayn-'Alī Mallāḥ,[33] that *ḥāfiẓ* is often the stage-name or professional description of a singer, that is someone with a good voice, and not simply someone who knows the Qur'ān by heart. Confirmation for this comes in the *Iḥyā al-mulūk*, where the names of six singers (*mughannī*) are mentioned, all of whom share the title 'ḥāfiẓ'.[34] Indeed, this title is still used for certain kinds of singers in Tajikistan.[35] Sūdī of Bosnia, in his commentary on the *Dīvān* of *Ḥāfiẓ* (v.1, p. 31), mentions that the poet had a good voice. It is also clear from the pairing of *qawl u ghazal* with musicians in the poems of Ḥāfiẓ (e.g. 91: 9, 141: 2, 272: 4, 370: 8 and the *Mughannī-nāma*, p. 1058: 5b) that he alludes thereby to the first and second movements of the musical *nawba* performance, as explained a generation after his death by 'Abd al-Qādir Marāghī (d. 838/1435), in which first Arabic poems are sung (*qawl*) and then Persian songs (*ghazal*), then *tarāna* (a *rubā'ī* text which is sung in either language), and finally *furūdāsht* (Arabic lyrics again). So, it may well be that Ḥāfiẓ not only memorized the Qur'ān, but could also chant it, and his poems, in a pleasing manner.

Let's first inventory Ḥāfiẓ's lexicon of dawn.

Saḥar occurs 49 times in the *Dīvān*, including 47 times in the *ghazals*. It is the primary word for dawn, obviously, and when it occurs in the *ghazals*, roughly 25 per cent of the time, it is in the first line, thus creating the temporal setting. Furthermore, this sememe appears in other lexical forms in the *ghazals*, such as *saḥargah* (eight times, three in the first line), *saḥargahān* (once), *saḥargahī* (once), *saḥargāh* (twice), *saḥargāhān* (twice, once in the first line), *saḥarī* (eight times, never in the first line), *saḥar-khīz* and *saḥar-khīzān*, again never in the first line.

Ṣubḥ occurs 46 times in the *Dīvān*, 42 of them in *ghazals*, and in the first line in seven of those *ghazals*, or one-sixth of the time. This generic word for morning is often a symbol of hope, as in 162: 4: *ṣubḥ-i umīd ki shud mu'takif-i parda-yi ghayb / gū burūn āy ki kār-i shab-i tār ākhar shud* ('to the morning of hope, which sat in devout retreat behind the curtain of the unseen say, come out, for the long dark night is over'); or 323: 4: *bar āy ay āftāb-i ṣubḥ-i umīd / ki dar dast-i shab-i hijrān asīr-am* ('come out, o sun of the morning of hope / for I am captive in the grasp of the night of separation'). This contra-*Alba* theme, where the morning of hope scatters the darkness of the night, with its attendant sorrow and weeping over separation from the Beloved, would seem to dominate the topos of dawn in Ḥāfiẓ. Several compound nouns and adverbs of time are built upon this word, including *ṣubḥdam* (11 incidences, two in line 1), *ṣubḥ-furūgh* (once), *ṣubḥgah* (once, in the first line), *ṣubḥgāh* (five times, once in line one), *ṣubḥgāhī* (four times), *ṣubḥī* (once) and *ṣubḥ-khʷān* (once). The fact that *ṣubḥ* is often used in the sense of sunrise, rather than some later point of the morning, is attested by the fact that it often occurs with the verb *damīdan*, to break: *mī-damad ṣubḥ* (13: 1), *ṣubḥ-i dawlat mī-damad* (14: 1), and so on.

Bāmdād occurs three times, and once again in the form *bāmdādān*, the latter in a poem (288:1) which is mystically infused with the primordial sunrise, and a virtually – and quite unusually for the *ghazal* – enjambed first and second lines:

bāmdādān ki zi khalvatgah-i kākh-i ibdā'
sham'-i khāvar fikanad bar hama aṭrāf shu'ā '
bar kishad āyina az jayb-i ufuq charkh u dar ān
bi-namāyad rukh-i gītī bi hizārān anvā'.

In the morn as the candle of the east casts its rays
from the seclusion of the palace of creation over everything
the wheel of heaven draws out the mirror from the collar of the horizon
to show the face of the earth in its myriad forms.

Pagāh occurs only once, as an adjective for *bāmdād*, meaning early in the morning, and it occurs at the start of the one poem where we do find it, setting the time and tone for *ghazal* 408:

khunak nasīm-i mu'anbar, shamāma-yi dilkhʷāh
ki dar havā-yi tu bar khāst bāmdād-i pagāh.

Fresh the fragrant breeze, the heartsome perfume
which stirred up early in the morn, craving your ambience.

Sipīda-dam, likewise a *hapax legomenon* in the Ḥāfiẓ corpus, occurs later in this same poem where we find *pagāh*, but as part of a metaphorical conceit rather than a poetic time-frame.

Other locutions do occur, some based on verbs, some on less frequently appearing nouns, but in the preponderance of cases, these words do not bear symbolic weight in creating a mythopoesis for the poem. Often they are simple binary oppositions – as in sleep/wake or night/day – or metaphors and similes, not meant to necessarily establish the mythic time of the poem. For example, we find *damīdan* in the past tense for rising of the metaphorical sun:

Guftam ay bakht bi-khusbīdī u khʷurshīd damīd. (399: 2)

I said, fortune, you slept late and the sun arose.

I have not checked for the near synonym of *bar āmadan* or *nūr afkandan*, and so on, where the sun is subject; however, the words for sun (*āftāb* and *khʷurshid*; *shams* does not occur in the *ghazals*) do not necessarily seem to specify sunrise as the poetic time of the poem where these words occur in the first line of the *ghazal*.

However, the word ***Ṭulū'***, meaning sunrise, occurs four times, though sometimes also said of the moonrise (110: 3), sometimes of the solar wine in the dawning-place of the drinking cup (288: 3), and sometimes employed in a virtuosically playful manner, as in this line (55: 3):

Zi mashriq-i sar-i kū-y āftāb-i ṭal'at-i tu
agar ṭulū' kunad ṭāli'am humāyun ast.

If the sun of your radiant countenance, from the east of the quarter
dawns, my astrological chart will augur royal, auspicious.

The word ***Ṣabāḥ*** occurs twice, once in the phrase *har ṣabāḥ u masā* (443: 8), every morning and evening, meaning simply 'all the time'. In the other incidence, however, *ṣabāḥ* does actually have a ritual, or even transcendent, semiotic charge, and determines the time-frame of the poem, situating the actions in a mythopoetic realm (128: 1):

Bi āb-i rawshan-i may 'ārifī ṭahārat kard
'ala 'ṣ-ṣabāh ki maykhāna rā ziyārat kard.

With the bright water of wine, a Gnostic made ablutions
When at dawn he made pilgrimage to the wine tavern.

This wine poem continues with celestial imagery, as follows:

Hamān ki sāghar-i zarrīn-i khʷur nahān gardīd
hilāl-i 'ayd bi-dawr-i qadaḥ ishārat kard
Khʷushā namāz u niyāz-i kasī ki az sar-i dard
bi āb-i dīda va khūn-i jigar ṭahārat kard
Bi rū-yi yār naẓar kun zi dīda minnat dār
ki kār-i dīda hama az sar-i baṣārat kard

Dilam bi ḥalqa-yi zulfash bi jān kharīd āshūb
chi sūd dīd nadānam ki īn tijārat kard
Agar imām-i jamā'at ṭalab kunad imrūz
khabar dahīd ki Ḥāfiẓ bi may ṭahārat kard.

As soon as the golden goblet of the sun disappeared
The festive crescent signalled to send the chalice around
How blessed the prayers and supplications of him whose pain
has washed him pure with teardrops and heart's blood
Look on the face of the friend and count your blessings for your eye –
That it conducted the business of the eye with insight
My heart in the ringlets of his hair bought disturbance, heart and soul
I cannot imagine what profit it saw in this transaction
If the Chief Prayer Leader summons me today
Give him this excuse: Ḥāfiẓ has purified himself with wine.

Of course, dawn can be conjured up without actually mentioning it, by summoning related elements of the topos, which we partially inventory as follows.

The appearance of the nightingale occurs 49 times in the *ghazals* in the form of the ***Bulbul***, and a further seven in the form of ***'Andalīb***. Various other terms for bird, some of which may also signify the nightingale, occur in the *ghazals*, such as *murgh-i shab-khʷān* (twice), *hazār* (twice), and the generic *murgh* (57 times). Obviously, not all these occurrences are at dawn, and the birds are not always sweetly twittering, but there is often an association, implicit or explicit, with the dawn and with the rose (e.g. 'At dawn the bird of the meadow said to the newly blossomed rose'. *Ṣubḥdam murgh-i chaman bā gul-i naw-khāsta guft*, 81: 1a). Khurramshāhī identifies the following characteristics with the nightingale: he is not colourful, but he has a melodically pleasing song, is extremely eloquent and often sings *ghazals*, and he is utterly in love.[36]

We may add that he suffers in his love (209: 7):

bar ṭarf-i gulshanam gudhar uftād vaqt-i ṣubḥ
ān dam ki kār-i murgh-i chaman āh u nāla būd.

I passed by the border of the garden at the hour of morning
at the moment when the efforts of the meadow-bird were sighing and lamenting.

In the following *ghazal* of seven lines (456), the *bulbul* is on nearly every branch:

Raftam bi bāgh ṣubḥdamī tā chinam gulī
āmad bi gūsh nāgaham āvāz-i bulbulī
Miskīn chu man bi 'ishq-i gulī gashta mubtalā
v-andar chaman fikanda zi faryād ghulghulī

Mīgashtam andar ān chaman u bāgh dam bi-dam
mīkardam andar ān gul u bulbul ta'ammulī
Gul yār-i ḥusn gashta va bulbul qarīn-i 'ishq
īn rā taghayyurī nih va ān rā tabaddulī
Chūn kard dar dilam athar āvāz-i 'andalīb
gashtam chunān ki hīch namāndam taḥammulī
Bas gul shikufta mīshavad īn bāgh rā valī
kas bī-balā-yi khār nachīda-ast az ū gulī
Ḥāfiẓ madār umīd-i faraj az madār-i carkh
Dārad hizār 'ayb u nadārad tafaḍḍulī.

I went to the garden in the morning to pick a rose
Suddenly the song of a nightingale came to my ears
The poor thing, like me, was destroyed by his love for a rose
And in the meadow he raised up a hue and cry
As I strolled in the meadow and garden for a spate
I was reflecting on that rose and the nightingale
The rose became the beloved beauty and the nightingale, mate of love
This was changed to that, and that transformed to this
When the song of the Philomel worked upon my heart
It made me such that I could not stand it anymore
Many a rose is blossoming in this garden, yet
No one picks a rose from it without the prick of the thorn
Ḥāfiẓ, do not hope for release from the turning heavens
It has endless faults and not a single mercy.

In this poem, then, the poet's persona reflects upon the morning/dawn symbol of the nightingale and its hopes as lover, and rejects all hope, in that love of roses comes with the prick of the thorn, and that is the unchanging fate of the world.[37]

As for the morning libation of wine, ***Ṣabūḥ***, which occurs six times, always paired with another word for morning or late night (it appears a further nine times in other tokens of the lexeme *ṣabūḥī, ṣabūḥī-zadagān*) – we will come to this topos in the discussion below, on the sacrality of dawn.

We also find the easterly morning breeze, ***Ṣabā***, which is invoked 105 times in Ḥāfiẓ's *ghazals* (most probably more than that in his entire oeuvre, if we also count his other forms) – that is to say, almost one of every five *ghazal*s. Another word for the breeze, ***Nasīm***, occurs 65 times and may sometimes, but not always, waft at dawn. This breeze is associated with sunrise and spring time, coolness and fragrance, which make the flowers blossom. It is also the breeze to which lovers tell their secrets. Khurramshāhī is of the opinion that Ḥāfiẓ may use the symbol of the pleasant fragrant breeze of morning (*nasīm*, with which he more or less seems to pair *ṣabā*) more than any other Persian poet. Furthermore, he ventures that the *bād-i ṣabā*, or simple *ṣabā*, is one of the active entities and heroes of the poetics of Ḥāfiẓ's *Dīvān*.[38]

Always associated with the morning, and usually in tandem with the breeze, is the messenger, ***Barīd***, which occurs three times, as in *barīd-i ṣubḥ* (276: 3), or *barīd-i ṣabā* (88: 3b), and *barīd-i bād-i ṣabā*. Another word for messenger, ***Payk***, occurs more frequently (13 times), and may be associated with the dawn breeze, when modified by a word like *ṣabā* or governed by *nasīm*, but it may also occur, like ***Payām*** (message), in other contexts. In this particular meaning then, we do see some variation in the semiotic charge of the vocabulary.

When the speaking persona of the *ghazal* relates something that happened 'last night' (***Dūsh***), especially towards the opening of the poem, we can assume that the locutionary act depicted in the poem is situated temporally at dawn or early morning. As we have already seen some examples of this above, there is no need for further examples here. The appearance of angels or a call from on high (*malā'ik*, *ṣidā-yi ghayb*, *lisān al-ghayb*, etc.), the hour of prayer or recitation of scripture (*du'ā*, *vird/awrād*, *dars*) may also be mentioned in this context.

Ghazal 235 provides a good example of a poem that by secondary and tertiary images evokes a setting at dawn. Though no word for dawn or morning appears in the poem, four lines conspire to clearly place the poem in an auroral ambience, with the sweet and holy fragrance of the beloved, or perhaps even an angel, brought by the breeze; the mention of last night and an augury or horoscope; the caravan bells that rouse the sleeping travellers to depart; and the nightingale, whose cry is normally heard at night or just prior to dawn:

Line 1: *muzhda ay dil ki masīḥā nafasī mīāyad*
ki zi anfās-i khʷushash bū-yi kasī mīāyad.

Glad-tidings, heart, for here comes a living, breathing Messiah
Whose sweet breaths are redolent with someone's arrival.

Line 2: *az gham-i hijr makun nāla u faryād ki dūsh*
zada-am fāl-ī u faryād-rasī mīāyad.

Do not wail and cry over the sorrow of separation
For last night, I took an augury, and someone's coming to our aid.

Line 5: *kas na-dānist ki manzilgah-i ma'shūq kujāst*
īn-qadar hast ki bāng-i jarasī mīāyad.

No one knows where the abode of the beloved is
Only this much – that the sound of caravan bells are coming.

Line 7: *khabar-i bulbul-i īn bāgh bi-pursīd ki man*
nāla'ī mīshinavam k-az qafasī mīāyad.

Ask what happened to this garden's nightingale, for
I hear a wailing coming from a cage.

Perhaps the contra-*Alba* view of dawn as release, which we have surmised to be dominant in the dawn topos of Ḥāfiẓ, is reinforced by the religious hours, with dawn the time of prayers and litanies. As the Qur'ān instructs, dawn is the time when a white thread can be discerned from a black thread, the point at which fasting from food and sex begin in Ramadan (*Sura* 2: 187). Dawn is, then, a sacral and ritual moment, one of the fixed times of prayer, perhaps the most significant of them (*Sura* 17: 78–9): 'Perform prayers when the sun declines unto the dark of the night, and recitation at dawn (*al-fajr*); verily the dawn recitation is attested.' Morning is seen as breathing away the darkness and dispelling it (*wa-ṣ-ṣubḥu idhā tanaffasa*, 81: 17–18), and dawn is the hour when salvation came to Lot's household (minus his wife): *najaynā-hum bi saḥar*^{in} *ni'mat*^{an} *min 'indi-nā. Kadhālika najzī*[39] *man shakara* (54: 33–5). Most important, perhaps, because Ḥāfiẓ quotes it directly (*shab-i qadr ast u tay shud nāma-yi hijr / salām*^{un} *fīhi ḥatā maṭla'u l-fajr*: 246: 1), is the *Surat al-Qadr* (97), a night better than a thousand months, a night in which the angels and the Spirit descend, a silent night that is peace until the break of dawn.

This religious and spiritual dimension of dawn and the morning is stipulated more than once in the *Dīvān*, as for example in the opening line of *ghazal* 24:

Bi jān-i kh^{w}*āja va ḥaqq-i qadīm u 'ahd-i durust*
ki mawnis-i dam-i ṣubḥam du'ā-yi dawlat-i tu-st.

By your life, good sir, and the bonds of old, and faithful troth
My companion at the break of morn is my prayers for your good fortune.

This poem has a political dimension – prayer said for the patron and his reign. But Ḥāfiẓ's prayers may also take him to the beloved (237: 9):

Maraw bi kh^{w}*āb ki Ḥāfiẓ bi bārgāh-i qabūl*
zi vird-i nīm-i shab u dars-i ṣubḥgāh rasīd.

Do not sleep, for Ḥāfiẓ has attained this court of acceptance
Through late-night prayer and morning study (of scripture).

The poet may here intend a mundane Beloved, but the language used has some sacral overtones. Fortune seems to smile upon the poet after he prays all night long and the true dawn begins to break (225: 4):

Gū'iyā kh^{w}*āhad gushūd az dawlatam kāri ki dūsh*
man hamī kardam du'ā va ṣubḥ-i ṣādiq mīdamīd.

It seems that my fortune will open a way for my affairs, for last night
I was continually praying, and the true morn was breaking.

Recall now that our poet has said (373: 6: *Khanda vu girya-yi 'ushshāq zi jā'ī digar ast / mīsurāyam bi shab u vaqt-i saḥar mīmūyam* [The laughter and tears of the lovers comes from some other quarter / I compose at night and weep at dawntide]) that night is the time to compose poetry, and dawn is the time to weep. Here, the temporal sites seem to be reversed; fervent supplications at night, and release at dawn. Or perhaps this is not a total reversal, and the act of composing sincere poems is an earnest form of supplication and prayer. Indeed, the poet sometimes plays with this notion of prayer, deliberately undermining its pious implications, as here, in the last line (line 7) of *ghazal* 409:

Shawq-i lab-at burd az yād Ḥāfiẓ
dars-i shabāna vird-i saḥargāh.

Yearning for your lips made Ḥāfiẓ forget
his nightly lessons, his morning litanies.

It is not only the Beloved's lips that bring the oblivion of forgetfulness. Wine may drive away the fear of the dawn of Resurrection Day (260: 8):

Piyāla bar kafanam band tā saḥargah-i ḥashr
bi may zi dil bi-baram hawl-i rūz-i rastākhīz.

Bind a wine chalice to my shroud, so that at the dawntide of Resurrection
I may wash from my heart with wine the fear of the Day of Judgement.

Of course, the morning libation may be an antidote to the hypocrisy of various small-minded and prosecutorial officials, and as such it may bring sincerity and therefore authenticity and purity, if not always clear answers (280: 3):

Aḥvāl-i shaykh u qāḍi u shurbu'l-yahūdishān
kardam su'āl ṣubḥdam az pīr-i may-furūsh.

I asked the Sage wine-seller at dawn about
the Shaykh and the Judge and their Jewish-drinking.

Thus the wine tavern becomes the locus – the ruins on the outskirts of town, where the non-Muslims drink clandestinely so as not to offend public morality, the liminal space outside society – while the dawn becomes the poetic moment when divine intervention arrives, allowing wine and relief, or mystical intoxication (479: 1):

Saḥaram hātif-i maykhāna bi dawlat-kh^{w}āhī
guft bāz āy ki dīrīna-yi īn dargāhī.

At dawn a call from the wine tavern, wishing good fortune
It said, come back, for you are an old haunter of this court.

The wise wine-seller; the disembodied, angelic call; and also the cup-bearer, all minister the morning offering, and impart wisdom, tidings of good fortune and promises of release from suffering (388: 1):

Ṣubḥ ast sāqiyā qadaḥī pur sharāb kun
dawr-i falak darang nadārad shitāb kun.

It's morning, cup-bearer, fill a goblet up with wine
The turning heavens do not hesitate: be quick!

But ultimately in the topography of Ḥāfiẓ, there is but little distinction to be made between tavern and true temple: both are sanctified spots of authenticity, untainted by hypocrisy. Real angels descend on the night of Power, and Ḥāfiẓian dawn is the time when angels and voices make their visitations. An enigmatic and ultimately spiritual wayfarer recounts the tale of his mysteries at dawn[40] and the call from heaven is also heard at dawn, as in this opening line (431: 1):

Saḥar bā bād mīguftam hadīth-i ārizūmandī
khaṭāb āmad ki vāthiq shaw bi alṭāf-i khudāvandī.

At dawn I was telling my tale of yearning desire
A call came, saying 'be assured of the divine blessings'.

Or this one (279: 1–2):

Hātifī az gūsha-yi maykhāna dūsh
Guft bibakhshand gunah may binūsh
'Afv-i ilāhī bukunad kār-i kh^{w}īsh
Muzhda-yi raḥmat birisānad surūsh.

A call came from the corner of the tavern last night
It said, they'll forgive sin, drink wine!
Divine forgiveness will do its work
Tidings of mercy will be brought by an angel.

Prayers at dawn and sighs at night, tearful morning supplications and plaintive night-time utterance; these are the keys that lead us to the treasured object of desire, the path and procedure that will join us to the beloved.[41] This then is the sacred value of the dawn, the moment of divine grace, in response to supplication and the suffering of the night of separation and liminality. The poet is rejoined to his waking society and to the world as it is, not having bettered things much, but having been consoled by God for the sufferings he has endured. *Ghazal* 189, in one verse (5), tells us what we should do about this discovery:

Sirishk-i gūsha-gīrān rā chu dar yāband, durr yāband
rukh-i mihr az saḥar-khīzān nagardānand agar dānand

The tears of those who retreat to solitude:
When [you][42] find those, you'll find pearls
if you know anything, you won't turn the sunny face of affection
from those who rise at dawn

Notes

1 August von Platen, from 'Ghaselen, X', as quoted in el-Shabrawy, 'German Ghazals: An Experiment in Cross Cultural Literary Synthesis', p. 62.

2 Paul Valéry, *Cahiers*, II: 1261, as quoted in Franklin, *The Rhetoric of Valéry's Prose Aubades*, p. 3.

3 The idea for this essay came from my student days, in classes I took with Professors Heshmat Moayyad and Jaroslav Stetkevych. I am grateful to Professors Leonard Lewisohn and James Morris for organizing, with the Iran Heritage Foundation, the conference on 'Ḥāfiẓ and the School of Love in Classical Persian Poetry' at Exeter University in the spring of 2007, which provided the opportunity to flesh out these ideas more fully.

4 See Heinen, 'Thwarted Expectations: Medieval and Modern Views of Genre in Germany', pp. 334–46. On the question of the *Alba* genre, as well as other genres of this and somewhat later periods, see Dronke, *The Medieval Lyric*, esp., for the *Alba*, pp. 167–85.

5 Woledge, 'Old Provençal and Old French', pp. 343 and 346–8 for the performance context.

6 A topical, often political, poem with precise contemporary references, perhaps most akin in the Persian tradition to the *qiṭ'a*. The most prosodically complex and dignified genre of the Troubadours is probably the canso, typically a love poem. These circulated with the poets' *vida*, or with a *razo*, similar to the *aṣbāb al-nuzūl* of Qur'anic exegesis, or the circumstances of composition often provided in medieval Persian literary anthologies, or hagiographies (e.g. Shams al-Dīn Aflākī's *Manāqib al-'ārifīn*, about the life and poetry of Rūmī). Poems of the *Alba* genre, because they contain dialogue, are seen by Woledge as dramatic poems, in contrast to most Provençal lyrics, which are monologues of the poet speaking about his love.

7 Saintsbury, *The Flourishing of Romance and the Rise of Chivalry*, p. 366.

8 Jeanroy, *La Poésie lyrique des Troubadours*, p. 339.

9 Kay, 'Alba' in *The Oxford Companion to Literature in French*, p. 17.

10 Woledge, 'Old Provençal and Old French', p. 346.

11 *Ibid.*, pp. 345–6 and p. 346, n. 7.

12 Chambers, 'Alba', in *The Princeton Encyclopedia of Poetry and Poetics*, p. 8.

13 Hatto, *Eos: An Inquiry*, pp. 76–7.

14 According to Hatto, *Eos: An Inquiry*, p. 87, who gives instances of the *Alba* topos interfering in European translations of the Biblical Song of Songs (*Shir ha-shirim*). There is a particular crux at verse

2:17, where the Authorized Version (KJV) of the English Bible reads as follows: 'Until the day break and the shadows flee away, turn, my beloved, and be thou like a roe or a young hart upon the mountains of Bether.' The Hebrew passage does not suggest an *Alba* scene, according to Hatto, who draws upon J.B. Segal's chapter on Hebrew in the *Eos* volume, arguing that the Hebrew passage concerns the falling of night (the time when the shadows flee) because the word *shel* represents shadows that protect from sunlight, not shadows of the dark (pp. 206–7 and n. 37). See, however, the contrary view of Ariel and Chana Bloch, in *The Song of Songs: A New Translation*, p. 157, who do argue that the Hebrew reads as a dawn scene. This would mean that the *Alba* scene could have roots in Mediterranean mythopoetics, possibly spread through the influence of Hellenism.

15 Hatto, ed. *Eos: An Inquiry*, where Woledge's contribution, 'Old Provençal and Old French', appears on pp. 344–89.

16 Lewis and Stern, 'Arabic', in *Eos*, ed. Hatto, pp. 216–17.

17 *Ibid.*, p. 230. I have followed their translation, only introducing suggestions in brackets.

18 The dawn has come when there is enough light to distinguish a white from a black thread.

19 Empaytaz de Croome, *Albor: Mediaeval and Renaissance Dawn-Songs in the Iberian Peninsula*, pp. 6–7.

20 Wickens, 'Persian', in *Eos*, ed. Hatto, p. 244.

21 A variant reading has *in'ām rā*, which seems preferable.

22 A variant reading has *nihādan 'udhr-i...*

23 Wickens, 'Persian', in *Eos*, ed. Hatto, pp. 246–7.

24 Quoted in Empaytaz de Croome, *Albor*, p. 6, without specific attribution to the particular work of de Riquier in which the notion is elaborated. However, it comes from Martín de Riquer, *Las Albas provenzales, Introduccíon, textos y version castellana*, p. 12, where he argues that the religious *Alba* poems developed out of the contra-*Alba*, where the dawn is desired.

25 Shapiro, 'The Figure of the Watchman in the Medieval Alba', pp. 607–39, citing pp. 619–19.

26 C.-H. de Fouchécour, *La Description de la nature dans la poésie lyrique persane du XIeme siècle.*

27 On which, see Rasūlī, 'Ṣabā', pp. 915–16.

28 Julie Scott Meisami, 'The World's Pleasance: Ḥāfiẓ's Allegorical Gardens' and also her 'Allegorical Gardens in the Persian Poetic Tradition: Nezami, Rumi, Hafez'.

29 For example, her *The Handling of Ab/water in Farrukhi, Hafiz and Talib.*

30 Lewis, 'Hafez. viii. Hafez and Rendi', and 'Hafez. ix. Hafez and Music', *EIr*, XI, pp. 483–91 and 491–8.

31 *The Ghazals of Ḥāfiẓ: Concordance and Vocabulary.*

32 Of their many relevant works, see, for example, Suzanne P. Stetkevych, 'Structuralist Interpretations of Pre-Islamic Poetry: Critique and New Directions', pp. 98–9; and Jaroslav Stetkevych, *The Zephyrs of Najd: The Poetics of Nostalgia in the Classical Arabic Nasīb.*

33 Ḥusayn-'Alī Mallāḥ, *Ḥāfiẓ va mūsīqī*, p. 8, n. 3.

34 Ḥusyan ibn Muḥammad ibn Maḥmūd-i Sīstānī, *Iḥyā al-mulūk: shāmil-i tārīkh-i Sīstān az advār-i bāstānī tā sāl-i hizār va bīst va hasht-i hijrī qamarī*, p. 10 and n. 2. See also Bāstānī Pārīzī, 'Ḥāfiẓ-i chandīn hunar', pp. 10–11.

35 See van den Berg, *Minstrel Poetry from the Pamir Mountains*, p. 32.

36 Khurramshāhī, *Ḥāfiẓ-nāma*, I, p. 149.

37 The same idea is reiterated in *ghazal* 209.

38 Khurramshāhī, *Ḥāfiẓ-nāma*, pp. 118–20.

39 Recall the poem of al-Walīd II, cited in the beginning, which ends with this verb: *wa'llāhu 'anni biḥusni l-fi'li yajzī-hā.*

40 *Saḥargah rahruvī dar sar-zamīnī / hamī guft īn mu'ammā bā qarīnī* (474: 1).

41 *Du'ā-yi ṣubḥ u āh-i shab kilīd-i ganj-i maqṣūd-ast / bi-dīn rāh u ravish mīraw ki dar dildār payvandī* (431: 2).

42 In fulfilment of its own homiletic journey, this essay here substitutes 'you' for what the poet has written as 'they'.

Ḥāfiẓ and the Language of Love in Nineteenth-Century English and American Poetry

Parvin Loloi

Some of the Persian poets have been known in the West since the middle of the seventeenth century, through the accounts of such travellers as Sir Thomas Herbert.[1] Translations of Ḥāfiẓ first appeared in the West (in Latin), produced by such pioneers of Orientalism as Meninski, in his *Linguarium Orientalium* (Vienna 1680), and Thomas Hyde (1636–1703), the Laudian Professor of Arabic at Oxford, who in his *Syntagma Dissertationum* (published posthumously in 1768) translated a poem by Ḥāfiẓ, and was also the first to translate from Khayyām. The first English translation of a *ghazal* by Ḥāfiẓ, under the title of 'A Persian Song', was published by Sir William Jones in his *Grammar of the Persian Language* (1771, pp. 135–40). Jones presented both literal and verse translations of the 'Turk-i Shīrāz' *ghazal*, which was to become very popular amongst the Romantics over the following century. Jones' 'Persian Song', indeed, became a model for later translators of Ḥāfiẓ in English. In the remainder of the eighteenth century, only one more selection from Ḥāfiẓ appeared in English.

The nineteenth century, however, was much more productive. Numerous (and very varied) versions of Ḥāfiẓ appeared in both English and German. The English translators approached the poetry of Ḥāfiẓ from many different angles and in terms of many different conceptions of his work. Many translations were made in India and served primarily as cribs for the use of students of Persian in the Indian Civil Service. The first complete translation of *The Dīvān...* (1891) of Ḥāfiẓ, by Lieut. Col. H. Clarke, treats Ḥāfiẓ as a Sufi mystic, but unfortunately the language is particularly graceless. The literal translation is heavily interpolated with notes, which makes his text hard to read and incapable of giving any hint of the quality of Ḥāfiẓ's lyricism. A number of translators chose to present Ḥāfiẓ in prose. The most notable of these was E.B. Cowell,[2] who argued that to translate Ḥāfiẓ in verse would be to impose formal concepts on his work which were alien to Persian poetical forms, an idea forcefully repeated by Peter Avery and John Heath-Stubbs[3] in the following century. Amongst the nineteenth-century translators who preferred to employ (in the words of Jones) 'modulated but unaffected prose',[4] seeking to unite readability and euphony, Samuel Robinson and Justin Huntly McCarthy[5] deserve mention. The majority of translators, however, preferred to use English poetical forms to present

Ḥāfiẓ to the English reader. Unfortunately, they often tried to judge and understand Ḥāfiẓ according to their own classical training and ideas. As a result, they found disunity in Ḥāfiẓ's poetry and felt obliged to improve the original by taking excessive liberties in their treatment of Ḥāfiẓ's imagery and language. Such are the translations made by Herman Bicknell and Alexander Rogers,[6] but the most vociferous voice in this respect is that of Richard Le Gallienne. Since he did not know any Persian himself, Le Gallienne relied on the translations by Clarke and Payne. He confidently explained that 'the difficulty of inconsequence I have endeavoured to overcome, partly by choosing those poems that were least inconsequent, partly supplying links of my own, and partly by selecting and developing the most important motives which one frequently finds in the same ode'.[7] Le Gallienne's versions are in stanzaic form in imitation of Jones' 'A Persian Song', where each *bayt* (verse-unit) is translated into a six-line stanza. Jones drastically changed the imagery of the original, thus not only trivializing but also muddying the clarity of Ḥāfiẓ's language. Most translators who have chosen to present Ḥāfiẓ in English verse forms have unfortunately chosen this path, with the exception of Gertrude Lowthian Margaret Bell, whose *Poems from the Divan of Hafiz* (London 1897) still remains the best both in accuracy and eloquence.

Another group of translators, such as A.J. Arberry and Colonel Frank Montague Randall,[8] have chosen successfully to use the quatrain form, which gives an idea of the Persian *bayt*. Rundall imitates the mono-rhyme of the original. Among the free verse translations, that of Peter Avery and John Heath-Stubbs' *Hafiz of Shiraz* (London 1952) is probably the best. Earlier versions in free verse fail to give any notion of Ḥāfiẓ's greatness. The versions by Walter Leaf, John Payne and Paul Smith, on the other hand, imitate the strict metre and rhyme scheme of the original. Such translations have (very reasonably) been described as 'literary acrobatics' by Massud Farzaad.[9] Only Walter Leaf can be said to have just managed to escape falling and breaking his neck.[10]

Notable among the English versions of Ḥāfiẓ are the very good 'imitations' or 'creative translations' made by such outstanding poets as Elisabeth Bridges and Basil Bunting, who succeed in communicating much more of the spirit of Ḥāfiẓ than the more literal translations generally do.[11] The twentieth century has seen a reemergence of interest in the Persian Sufi tradition, and as part of this tradition Ḥāfiẓ's poetry has undergone a revival in English translation, particularly in America. The results, unfortunately, have not always been satisfactory. Such poets as Thomas Crow, Michael Boylan and Daniel Landinsky,[12] who have heavily relied on earlier translations, have produced versions which are more reminiscent of twentieth-century American spiritual idioms than the ecstatic language of the great fourteenth-century Persian poet. Landinsky stands at the extreme of this spectrum. The excessive liberties taken with the language and imagery are such that it is often hard to recognize (or imagine) any Persian original in Ḥāfiẓ. There are, however, exceptions amongst these translators; the translations of Elisabeth Gray Jr, for example, a Persianist who worked with Robert Lowell at Harvard, contain accurate versions in simple, readable language which give some sense of Ḥāfiẓ's mystical sensibility, if not his poetic achievement.[13] And, more recently, the collaboration between a Sufi scholar, Leonard Lewisohn, and an American poet, Robert Bly, has given us 30 of the more esoteric poems of Ḥāfiẓ in contemporary American poetic idiom, with a particularly informative chapter as well as notes on the complicated Sufi symbols and traditions employed in Persian poetry, and particularly in the poetry of Ḥāfiẓ.[14]

Whether to interpret Ḥāfiẓ's poems as profane love lyrics, or as the expressions of mystical longing for the Divine Beloved, has been a perennial question underlying the interpretation and translation of Ḥāfiẓ. Some modern critics, such as Bashiri,[15] interpret Ḥāfiẓ as a poet heavily imbedded in Sufi philosophy; others such as Rehder[16] (like Gertrude Bell) think Ḥāfiẓ is only a secular love poet. To register the multi-facetedness of Ḥāfiẓ has proved beyond the scope of almost all translators of Ḥāfiẓ, so that most versions are seriously flawed. With a few exceptions, the English translations of Ḥāfiẓ have rarely managed to convey any of the vigour of his language or convincingly re-inscribe the true merits of a great poet.[17]

Translations, however poor, have always played an important role in revitalizing and renewing the literature and poetry of other nations and languages. The Romantic period, both in Europe and America, saw a literary revolution in which Orientalism played a significant role, but 'it is important to recognize that interest in the oriental did not necessarily conflict with admiration for western classical literature. Most often, it went along with that; which ... reveals something of the complexity of taste in the Romantic period.'[18] When von Hammer-Purgstall published his translation of Ḥāfiẓ in German,[19] it immediately attracted the attention of Goethe, who recognized an affinity in the mysticism of Ḥāfiẓ. As a result, he composed his *West-östlicher Divan* (1819), based on Ḥāfiẓ's poetical works. The German translations of von Hammer-Purgstall and Goethe's book were, in their turn, very influential across the Atlantic on such Transcendentalist poets as Emerson, as well as on later English poets such as Alfred Lord Tennyson, the Poet Laureate. Ḥāfiẓ's poetry was received and understood in many different ways. Sir William Jones initially introduced him as a profane love poet and compared him to Anacreon. In fact, Jones' 'Persian Song' became so well known that Byron, writing in 1811 to Charles Dallas, alludes to it casually to emphasize and clarify his point:

> My dear sir – As Gifford has been ever my 'Magnus Apollo', any approbation such as you mention, would, of course, be more welcome than 'all Bokhara's vaunted gold, than all the Gems of Samarkand'.[20]

Byron also wrote a parody of Jones' 'A Persian Song', which I have discussed elsewhere.[21] Here, however, with particular reference to the subject of the present book, I shall concentrate on the sublime rather than the exotic.

Sir William Jones' writings were read by many of the Romantics; both Byron and Shelley possessed his complete *Works*. Jones, in his numerous essays on Persian literature, repeatedly refers to the poems of Ḥāfiẓ for illustration. Jones opens his essay *On The Mystical Poetry of The Persians And Hindus* with the statement:

> A FIGURATIVE mode of expressing the fervour of devotion, or the ardent love of created spirits towards their beneficent Creator, has prevailed from time immemorial in *Asia*; particularly among the Persian theists, both ancient ... and modern *Súfis*, ... and their doctrines are also believed to be the source of that sublime, but poetical, theology, which glows and sparkles in the writings of old *Academicks.*[22]

A page later, Jones quotes two passages from two renowned Western scholars: one from Isaac Barrow (1630–77), the mathematician, Greek and classical scholar at Cambridge and a significant theologian; the other from M. Jacques Necker (1732–1804), Swiss financier and educationalist whose works were greatly admired during the French Revolution. Referring to Barrow, Jones writes that he

> describes Love as 'an affection or inclination of the soul toward an object, proceeding from an apprehension and esteem of some excellence or convenience in it, as its *beauty*, worth, or utility, and producing, if it be absent, a proportionable desire, and consequently an endeavour, to obtain such an *approximation to it, or union with it, ...*'.[23]

Jones further explains that Barrow's description

> was designed to comprise the tender love of the Creator towards created spirits. The great philosopher bursts forth in another place ... The following panegyric on the pious love of human souls toward the Author of their happiness: 'Love is the sweetest and most delectable of all passions; and, when by the conduct of wisdom it is directed in a rational way toward a worthy, congruous, and attainable object, it cannot otherwise than fill the heart with ravishing delight: such, in all respects superlatively such, is God ... *our souls, from its original instinct, vergeth toward him as its centre, and can have no rest, till it be fixed on him:* he alone can satisfy the vast capacity of our minds, and fill our boundless desires.'[24]

Jones further explains that 'this passage ... differs only from the mystical theology of the *Súfis* and *Yógis*, as the flowers and fruits of Europe differ in scent and flavour from those of *Asia*, or as European differs from *Asiatick* eloquence: the same strain, in poetical measure, would rise up to the odes of SPENCER on *Divine Love* and *Beauty*, and in a higher key with richer embellishments, to songs of HAFIZ and JAYADÉVA, the raptures of *Masnavì*, and the mysteries of *Bhágavat.*' To emphasize the affinity between the Eastern and Western ideals of mysticism Jones further quotes a long passage from Necker. For the sake of brevity, only a short extract is given. Writing about 'men', Necker, as quoted by Jones, writes of how they may consider '*themselves as an emanation from that infinite Being*, the source and cause of all things ... who pervades all nature with his divine spirit, as a universal soul'. Necker further illustrates that

> when we presume to seek his motive in bestowing existence: benevolence is that virtue, or, to speak more emphatically, that *primordial beauty*, which preceded all times and all worlds ... It may even be imagined, that love, the brightest ornament of our nature, love, enchanting and sublime, is mysterious pledge for assurance of those hopes; since love, by disengaging us from ourselves, by transporting us beyond the limits of our own being, is the first step in our progress to a joyful immortality.[25]

Jones then compares these two passages with some of the main doctrines of Eastern mysticism:

> If these two passages are translated into *Sanscrit* and *Persian*, I am confident, that the *Védántis* and *Súfis* would consider them as an epitome of their common system; for they concur in believing, that the souls of men differ infinitely in *degree*, but not at all in kind, from the divine spirit ... that the spirit of God pervades the universe ... that he alone is perfect benevolence, perfect truth, perfect beauty; that the love of him alone is *real* and genuine love ... that from eternity without beginning to eternity without end, the supreme benevolence is bestowing happiness or the means of attaining it; that men can only attain it by performing their part of *primal covenant* between them and the Creator; that nothing has pure absolute existence but *mind* or *spirit* ... that we ... must attach ourselves exclusively to God, who truly exists in us, as we in him; that we retain even in this forlorn state of separation from our beloved, the idea of *heavenly beauty*, and the *remembrance* of our *primeval vows*; that the sweet musick, gentle breezes, fragrant flowers, perpetually renew the primary *idea*, refresh our fading memory ... From these principles flow a thousand metaphors and poetical figures, which abound in the sacred poems of the Persians...[26]

Jones' elaboration on the central ideas of Sufism is particularly significant when he writes about the Qur'ānic Primordial Covenant between God and created man. Jones then introduces Ḥāfiẓ as a mystical poet and writes: '[a]fter his juvenile passions had subsided, we may suppose that his mind took that religious bent, which appears in most of his compositions; for there can be no doubt that the following distichs, collected from different odes, relate to the mystical theology of the *Sufis*.'[27] In the following pages, Jones translates 22 couplets from Ḥāfiẓ.

A number of the Romantic poets read very extensively and eagerly in the literature of the East; apart from Jones' translations, they had access to other early translations, either in books devoted to Ḥāfiẓ or (as was the case with Jones) scattered amongst essays and travel books.[28] Lord Byron is the only poet of this period who had first-hand experience of the Sufis in his travels in the Levant.[29] He is perhaps the only Romantic poet to make extensive use of these 'thousand metaphors and poetical figures'. A couple of examples will have to suffice here. The most prominent Ḥāfiẓian allusions employed by Byron are those of that inimitable pair of allegorical lovers: the rose (*gul*) and the nightingale (*bulbul*). In *The Bride of Abydos*, Byron actually uses the Persian name for 'rose':

> Know ye the land of the cedar and vine,
> Where the flowers ever blossom, the beams ever shine;
> Where the light wings of Zehyr, oppress'd with perfume,
> Wax faint o'er the garden of Gul in her bloom;
> Where the citron and olive are fairest of fruit,
> And the voice of the nightingale is never mute.[30]

There are other relevant lines in *The Bride of Abydos*, and the Ḥāfiẓian garden of love, rose and nightingale and breeze are invoked in many other of Byron's poems, such as *Don Juan* and *The Giaour*.[31] This last poem also includes a passage which is indicative of Byron's understanding of the mysticism that is present in Ḥāfiẓ's poetry:

> Her eye's dark charm 'twere vain to tell,
> But gaze on that Gazelle,
> It will assist thy fancy well;
> As large, as languishingly dark,
> But Soul beam'd forth in every spark
> That darted from beneath the lid,
> Bright as the jewel of Giamschid ...
> On her might Muftis gaze, and own
> That through her eye the immortal shone;
> On her fair cheek's unfading hue
> The young pomegranate's blossoms strew
> Their bloom in blushes ever new;
> Her hair in hyacinthine flow,
> When left to roll its folds below.[32]

Byron could have easily found sources for these passages in Jones' translations. We might, for example, compare the following passages in Jones:

> Zéphyr, dis tenrement a ce chvreuil delicat,
> c'est toi qui nous fais desirer les collines et les deserts. [...]

Est-ce l'arrogance de ta beauté, O rose, qui ne
te permet pas de demander des nouvelles du rossignol amoureux? [...]

Les belle qualites de l'ame sont les pièges d'un vin
coeur instruit: on ne prend pa un oiseau prudent avec des filets et des lacs.

and again:

J'aime une beauté, comme la rose, est sous
l'ombrage d'un couvert d'hyacinthes; ses joues sont
aussi claires qu'un ruisseau; ses lèvres de rubis
respirent la plus douce haleine.

Quand elle etend sur ces joues le piège de ses beaux cheveux, elle dit au zephyr: Garde notre secret.

Ses joues sont unies & agréables. O ciel!
Donne-lui une vie éternelle, car ses charmes sont éternelles![33]

In Byron's poem we have the comparison of the Beloved's eyes to a gazelle's dark eyes. In Persian mystical poetry the gazelle is 'shy and fugitive'; it 'escapes every attempt at capture and yet can easily catch the heart of ... the lover'.[34] *Jām-i Jam* (Byron's 'jewel of Giamschid') is commonly known in Persian mystical poetry as 'a symbol of esoteric knowledge ... and it came to represent the glass of enlightenment'.[35] Byron's employment of Ḥāfiẓ's allegorical imagery is numerous and varied – all part of his extensive knowledge of Oriental literature. Shelley, on the other hand, was a Platonist like his American counterpart Emerson.

We know that Shelley read Jones' *Works*. He ordered them when he was residing in Italy.[36] Almost all Shelley critics acknowledge his debt to Sir William Jones.[37] John Holloway has suggested that there was Persian influence on the early poems such as 'The Indian Serenade' and 'From the Arabic'.[38] Sataya S. Pachori argues that 'The Indian Serenade' is an imitation of one of Ḥāfiẓ's poems which Shelley was familiar with, and that in the poem 'Shelley ... may have borrowed the idea of the mystical unity in lovers from Ḥāfiẓ and Jones. In order to achieve the divine unity, the Shelleyan serenader has to renounce his phenomenal self and retain the noumenal one.'[39] Shelley, like many other Romantic poets, was a Platonist. He translated Plato's *Symposium* (and several other dialogues), and was also influenced by the German neo-Platonists and transcendentalists. In his short essay *On Love*, Shelley writes:

[Love] is the bond and the sanction which connects not only man with man, but with everything which exists. We are born into the world, and there is something within us which, from the instant that we live, more and more

> thirsts after its likeness ... We dimly see within our intellectual nature a miniature as it were of our entire self, yet deprived of all that we condemn or despise, the ideal prototype of everything excellent or lovely that we are capable of conceiving as belonging to the nature of man ... the portrait of our external being ... [is] a mirror whose surface reflects only the forms of purity and brightness; a soul within our soul that describes a circle around its proper paradise ... the invisible and unattainable point to which Love tends; and to attain which, it urges forth the powers of man to arrest the faintest shadow of that, without which there is no rest and respite to the heart over which it rules. Hence in solitude ... we love the flowers, the grass, and the waters, and the sky. The motion of the very leaves of spring, in the blue air, there is then found a secret correspondence with our heart. There is eloquence in the tongueless wind, and a melody in the flowing brooks and the rustling of the reeds beside the soul, awaken the spirits to a dance of breathless rapture ... like the voice of the beloved singing to you alone.[40]

Shelley's philosophy of Love is of course strongly influenced by neo-Platonism, and is essentially an explanation of the doctrine of emanation which is shared between Sufism and Platonic ideals. Shelley, like Emerson, sought Ideal Beauty and the Universal Soul, and many of his poems reflect and record such a search. This is central to poems such as *Alastor*, *Prometheus Unbound*, *Adonis* and the *locus classicus* of his poetry of Divine Love, *Epipyschidion* (and to many other poems too). 'I always seek', he says, 'in what I see the manifestation of something beyond the present and tangible object'.[41] Shelley's doctrines have much in common with Sufism, in part because both have their roots in Greek philosophy. As we have seen, Jones compares Ḥāfiẓ's poetry to Spenser's neo-Platonic poem *An Hymn in Honour of Love*; likewise, Shelley's *Hymn to Intellectual Beauty* has been compared to Spenser's *Hymn:*

> If Shelley had not read Plato at all, he could have got the quintessence of Platonism from Spenser's Hymns [*Four Hymns*]. An Hymn in Honour of Love contains many direct references to doctrines of the *Symposium*: that Eros was 'begot of Plentie and Penurie,' that Love tempers the elements of the universe, that mortals 'multipy the likeness of their Kynd,' that man
>
> Breathes a more immortal mynd,
> Not for lusts sake, but for eternitie,
> Seekes to enlarge his lasting progenie.[42]

In order to compare further the closeness of imagery employed both by Shelley and Ḥāfiẓ, it is useful to look briefly at the image of 'the veil' in the two poets. In *Prometheus Unbound*, the image of the fallen veil is used in order to reveal 'pristine purity'[43]:

How thou art changed! I dare not look on thee;
I feel but see thee not. I scarce endure
The radiance of thy beauty. Some good change
Is working in the elements, which suffer
Thy presence thus unveiled. [...]

... love, like the atmosphere
Of the sun's fire filling the living world,
Burst from thee, and illumined earth and heaven
And the deep ocean and the sunless caves
And all that dwells within them; [...]

Such art thou now: nor is it I alone, [...]

But the whole world which seeks thy sympathy.
Hearest thou not sounds i' the air which speak the love
Of all articulate beings?[44]

If we compare Shelley's lines with these lines by Ḥāfiẓ, as translated by Jones, the similarities become apparent:

In eternity without beginning, a ray of thy beauty began to gleam;
When Love sprang into being, and cast flames over all nature;

On that day thy cheek sparkled even under the veil,
and all this beautiful imagery appeared on the mirror of our fancies.[45]

The image of the veil is, of course, as much a Platonic image as it is of Persian Sufi poetry. It is this shared idealism and philosophy which first attracted one of the fathers of American poetry to read the Persian poets.

Emerson, like Shelley, was opposed to the orthodox church, and sought in his transcendental views, which, again like the ideas of Shelley, were nurtured by the German philosophers, to establish a Universal Soul. In fact, echoes of what Shelley writes on Love are also discernible in Emerson's essay on 'Love'. Strikingly, Emerson places as an epigraph to his essay a quotation from the Qur'ān, 'I was as a gem concealed; / Me my burning ray Revealed',[46] which is the central doctrine of Sufism. Emerson had read Ḥāfiẓ in Sir William Jones' works when he was still a young boy. He later came across von Hammer's *Diwan* and tried his hand at translating Ḥāfiẓ into English from German. His notebooks contain many finished and unfinished translations from Ḥāfiẓ.[47] His Essay on 'Persian Poetry' also contains many translations from Ḥāfiẓ.[48] According to Emerson: 'Ḥāfiẓ is the prince of Persian poets, and in his extraordinary gifts adds to some of the attributes of Pindar, Anacreon, Horace and Burns, the insight of a mystic, so that his work sometimes affords a deeper glance at Nature than belongs to any of these other poets.'[49] In one of his journals, Emerson writes that Ḥāfiẓ is

> characterised by a perfect intellectual emancipation which he also provokes in the reader; Nothing stops him. He makes the daregod & daredevil experiment. He is not to be scared by a name, or a religion. He fears nothing. He sees too far; he sees ... throughout; such is the only man I wish to see and to be.[50]

Ḥāfiẓ, it appears, is his touchstone; his is that poetry which is most capable of 'inoculating the reader with poetic madness'.[51] It was this 'poetic madness' which stimulated Emerson to the translation of Ḥāfiẓ and to the employment of the Persian poet's allegorical imagery in his own poetry. Emerson's first full translation of a poem of Ḥāfiẓ was the *Sāqī-nāma*. In the process of translating, he became fascinated with the imagery of wine and the *Sāqī* (Wine-bearer), which in the Sufi tradition are respectively symbols for ecstatic spiritual intoxication and for the Primordial Cup-bearer or spiritual master. These images and their implications were later reflected in two poems, both called 'Bacchus'. One is complete, the other fragmentary. In both, the influence of Ḥāfiẓ's poem is obvious. Yohannan has offered an elucidation of the fragmentary 'Bacchus'.[52] Here the complete 'Bacchus' is discussed briefly (though quoted in abridged form):

> Bring me wine, but wine which never grew
> In the belly of the grape,
> Or grew on vine whose tap-roots, reaching through
> Under the Andes to the Cape,
> Suffer no saver of the earth to scape. [...]
>
> We buy ashes for bread;
> We buy diluted wine;
> Give me of the true, –
> Whose ample leaves and tendrils curled
> Among the silver hills of heaven
> Draw everlasting dew;
> Blood of the world,
> Form of forms, and mould of statures,
> That I intoxicated,
> And by the draught assimilated,
> May float at pleasure through all natures;
> The bird-language rightly spell,
> And that which roses say so well. [...]
>
> Pour, Bacchus! The remembering wine;
> Retrieve the loss of me and mine!

Vine for vine be antidote,
And the grape requite the lote!
Haste to cure the old despair, –
Reason in Nature's lotus drenched,
The memory of ages quenched;
Give them again to shine;
Let wine repair what this undid;
And where infection slid,
A dazzling memory revive;
Refresh the faded tints,
Recut the aged prints,
And write my old adventures with the pen
Which on the first day drew,
Upon the tablets blue,
The dancing Pleaides and eternal man.[53]

Emerson is obviously aware of the mystical symbolism of 'wine', though we have the Greek god of wine replacing Ḥāfiẓ's *Sāqī*. Here the wine does not grow on a tree, but is a 'true' wine '[w]hose ample leaves and tendrils curled / Among the silver hills of heaven', and, like the wine of Ḥāfiẓ, it refreshes and rejuvenates the spirit – it is a 'Universal Wine'. In this poem, as in many of his other poems, Emerson also succeeds in incorporating his theory of Nature – essentially that of the Romantics on both sides of the Atlantic.[54]

Ḥāfiẓ's popularity did not diminish later on in the nineteenth century. His influence can be seen in Tennyson's poetry most forcefully. Tennyson, who tried to learn Persian in order to read Ḥāfiẓ, had two very well-known teachers – Edward Fitzgerald and Professor E.B. Cowell. The three were firm friends, and I have elsewhere established the literary relations between them.[55] Unfortunately the limits of this chapter will not allow any extensive discussion of Ḥāfiẓ's influence on the most notable poet of the Victorian era, but some aspects of the way in which Ḥāfiẓ is reflected in his poetry must be discussed briefly. From an early age, Tennyson was interested in Eastern mysticism. Hallam Tennyson writes:

> The philosophers of the East had a great fascination for my father, and he felt that the Western religion might learn from them much of spirituality. He was sure too that Western civilization had even in his time developed Eastern thought and morality...[56]

It was, once again, through Sir William Jones' works that Tennyson first became familiar with Ḥāfiẓ, and he learned some Persian under the tutelage of Fitzgerald. Tennyson was almost certainly aware of Tholuck's *Ssufismus, sive theosophia persarum pantheistica* (Berlin 1821), and more than likely read it as well, since Fitzgerald had acquired a copy when preparing to translate Jāmī's *Salaman and Absal*. Tennyson was also interested in the works of Goethe and read *West-östlicher Divan*. By that time there were also many translations of Ḥāfiẓ available to the public, as well as, of course, E.B. Cowell's own essays and translations. So an eager soul such as Tennyson would have had ample resources to make use of in getting to know Ḥāfiẓ intimately. His knowledge of the esoteric and erotic language of Ḥāfiẓ is reflected abundantly in his poetry. Here we can only elaborate on a few examples. The mystical imagery of Ḥāfiẓ occurs repeatedly in such poems as *The Princess*, 'The Gardener's Daughter', 'The Day Dream', 'Vision of Sin', 'Akbar's Dream' and *In Memoriam*; but the *locus classicus* is found in 'The Lover's Tale':

> She was dark-haired, dark-eyed:
> Oh, such dark eyes! A single glance of them
> Will govern a whole life from birth to death,
> Careless of all things else, led on with light
> In trances and in visions: look at them,
> You lose yourself in utter ignorance;
>
> Methought a light
> Burst from the garland I had woven, and stood
> A solid glory on her bright black hair;
> A light methought broke from her dark, dark eyes.[57]

Direct echoes of Ḥāfiẓ are discernible in this poem if we compare these lines with some lines in Ḥāfiẓ:

> The curves of thy hair is the snare of infidelity and of faith [...]
> Thy comeliness is the miracle of beauty, but the story of thy glance is visible magic.
> [...] let there be a hundred shouts of praise to that dark eye, which has magical powers in the killing of lovers [...]
> How can anyone on whom thy capricious glance has fallen, that glance which always waits in ambush with the bow of thy eyebrow.[58]
>
> One night my heart was dark that I sought to find it in the darkness of thy hair, I saw thy face and drank a cup of wine from thy lips.
> At once I embraced thee, and the waves of thy hair embraced my heart, I placed my lips, and made sacrifice of my heart and soul.[59]

Another passage from 'The Lover's Tale' will clarify further to what extent Tennyson's poem is permeated by images of Sufi Unity:

> ... we woke
> To gaze upon each other. If this be true,

At thought of which my whole soul languishes
And faints, and hath no pulse, no breath – as though
A man in some still garden should infuse
Rich atar of the rose,
Till drunk with its own wine, and overfull
Of sweetness, and in smelling of itself,
It fall on its own thorns – if this be true –
And that way my wish leads me evermore
Still to believe it – 'tis so sweet a thought,
Why in the utter stillness of the soul
Doth questioned memory answer not, nor tell
Of this our earliest, our closest-dawn,
Most loveliest, earthly-heavenliest harmony?[60]

It is relevant to consider another pattern of Sufi imagery frequent in Ḥāfiẓ, as manifested in Tennyson. The image of 'the veil' employed by Shelley is also prominent in Tennyson:

'Not for thee,' she said,
'O Bulbul, any rose of Gulistan
Shall burst her veil.'[61]

Ḥāfiẓ contains many lines which provide parallels for this passage; for example:

> The song of the bird rises up, where is the flagon of wine? The bulbul makes its clamour, saying 'who has torn the rose's veil?'[62]

In both 'De Profundis' (II, ll. 39–56) and the last stanza of *In Memoriam* (LVI, ll. 25–8), the image of the veil is employed in a very Sufistic manner (as seen in Ḥāfiẓ). In the first poem it is the symbol of what divides the known from the unknown, whereas in the second it operates very much in the sense of both Sufi and Platonic doctrines of the body understood as a veil which hides the soul, a veil which the soul yearns to tear away in order to reveal itself, as Ḥāfiẓ says:

> Ḥāfiẓ! thou thyself art thy own veil. From its midst rise up, and attain the beloved.[63]

This short survey has, I hope, shown something of how widespread the employment of the Ḥāfiẓian language of love was in the work of both British and American poets. As we have seen, anything like a full understanding of the implications of Ḥāfiẓ's poetry has arisen only gradually. Early Orientalists such as Jones and later scholars such as E.B. Cowell were important in this process; but as far as the poets were concerned, perhaps the greatest influence (especially on the poetry of Tennyson and

Emerson) was Goethe's *West-östlicher Divan*. Goethe called Ḥāfiẓ his spiritual master, and his authority was crucial in advancing the understanding of the Persian poet in the West. Ḥāfiẓ's work has left distinct and important traces on the imagery, on some of the poetic forms, and on important areas of thought, amongst British and American poets of the nineteenth century. This chapter has been able only to treat superficially the rich materials relevant to the widespread influence of Ḥāfiẓian imagery, poetical language and thought on the poetry of this period. Yet, unfortunately, it has to be recognized that, with the exception of Tennyson and Emerson, none of the other major English-language poets of the nineteenth century made really extensive use of the poetry of Ḥāfiẓ in their own work. In this regard none can compare with Goethe, who stands alone as a re-creator of Ḥāfiẓ in another poetic tradition.

Notes

1 See my 'Historical Background to English Translations of Hafiz'.

2 Cowell's translations were published in various periodicals. For a complete list, see my book, *Hafiz, Master of Persian Poetry: A Critical Bibliography*, pp. 332–3.

3 See the introduction to Avery and Heath-Stubbs, *Hafiz of Shiraz* (1952 edition).

4 Quoted in Clarke, *The Dīvān ... Hāfiz-i-Shīrāzī* (Calcutta 1891), p. viii.

5 Samuel Robinson, *A Century of Ghazals, or a Hundred Odes, Selected and Translated from the Diwan of Hafiz* (1875). Justin Huntly McCarthy, *Ghazals from the Divan of Hafiz...* (1893).

6 Herman Bicknell, *Hafiz of Shīrāz: Selections from his Poems...* (1875). Alexander Rogers, *Persian Anthology; being translations from the Gulistan of Sadi, the Rubaiyyat of Hafiz and the Anwar-i-Suheili...* (1889).

7 Richard Le Gallienne, *Odes from the Divan of Hafiz* (1905), p. xviii. Also John Payne, *The Poems of ... Hafiz of Shīrāz* (1901).

8 Arberry, 'Orient Pearls at Random Strung'; 'Hafiz and his English Translators', pp. 111–28 and 229–49; *Fifty Poems of Hafiz, Text and Translations*; and his *Immortal Rose, an Anthology of Persian Lyrics* (1948). The translations by Rundall, *Selections from the Rubaiyât & Odes of Hafiz...* were originally published anonymously, but when they were well received he acknowledged his authorship.

9 Farzaad, *To Translate Hafez*, p. 15.

10 Walter Leaf, *Versions from Hafiz, An Essay on Persian Metre*; John Payne, *The Poems of ... Hafiz of Shiraz* (1901); Paul Smith, *Divan of Hafiz*, 2 vols (1983).

11 Elizabeth Bridges, *Sonnets from Hafiz and Other Verses* (1921); Basil Bunting, *Uncollected Poems* (1991). For further information on Bunting's translations, see Loloi and Pursglove, 'Basil Bunting's Persian Overdrafts: A Commentary', pp. 343–53.

12 Crow, *Wineseller's Street: Renderings of Hafiz* and *Drunk on the Wine of the Beloved*; Boylan, *Hafez: Dance of Life*; Landinsky, *I Heard God Laughing*, *The Subject Tonight is Love*, *The Gift: Poems by Hafiz, the Sufi Master*, and *Love Poems from God*.

13 Gray, *The Green Sea of Heaven*.

14 Bly and Lewisohn, *Angels*.

15 Bashiri, 'Hafiz's Shirazi "Turk": A Structuralist Point of View', pp. 178–97 and 248–68.

16 Rehder, 'The Unity of the Ghazals of Hafiz', pp. 55–96; and the translations in Kritzeck (ed.), *Anthology of Islamic Literature*.

17 For a comprehensive study of English translations of Ḥāfiẓ, see my book, *Hafiz, Master of Persian...* and my 'Translations of Hafiz in English', in *EIr*, XI, pp. 498–500.

18 Holloway, *Widening Horizons in English Verse*, p. 33.

19 Joseph von Hammer-Purgstall, *Mohammed Schemsed-din Hafis. Der Diwan* (1812–13), 2 vols.

20 *The Works of Lord Byron, Letters and Journals*, ed. Prothero, vol. II, p. 27.

21 For further information on the literary influences of Persian on Byron, see my 'Byron in Persian Costume'.

22 Sir William Jones, *The Works* (1789), I, p. 445.

23 *Ibid.*, p. 446.

24 *Ibid.*, pp. 446–7.

25 *Ibid*, pp. 448–50.

26 *Ibid.*, pp. 450–1.

27 *Ibid*, p. 453.

28 For a complete list of these, see my *Hafiz, The Master of Persian Poetry*.

29 See Blackstone, 'Byron and Islam: the Triple Eros', pp. 325–6.

30 *The Bride of Abydos*, I: 5–10, in *The Poetical Works of Lord Byron* (1961), p. 264.

31 For further discussion of this allegorical imagery, see my 'Byron in Persian Costume', pp. 23–6.

32 *The Giaour*, lines 943–9 and 491–7, in *The Poetical Works of Lord Byron*, pp. 252–64.

33 Jones, *The Works*, V, pp. 513–14 and p. 469.

34 Schimmel, *A Two-Colored Brocade: The Imagery of Persian Poetry*, p. 193.

35 *Ibid.*, p. 109.

36 See Shelley, *The Letters*, ed. Jones, vol. 1, pp. 343–5.

37 See, for example, Schwab, *The Oriental Renaissance: Europe's Discovery of India and The East*, p. 195; and V. De Sola Pinto, 'Sir William Jones and English Literature', pp. 686–97.

38 Holloway, *Widening Horizons in English Verse*, p. 48.

39 Pachori, 'Shelley's "Indian Serenade": Hafiz and Sir William Jones', pp. 10–26. The quotation is taken from p. 19. The Ḥāfiẓian poem in question (*Ay muṭrib-i khūshnavā...*) is thought to be an apocryphal, but was very popular in India. It has been translated into English many times, even by recent translators. See my book *Hafiz, Master of Persian Poetry*, p. 241.

40 Shelley, *The Complete Works*, ed. Peck, vol VI: *Prose*, pp. 201–2.

41 Quoted in Notopoulos, *The Platonism of Shelley: A Study of Platonism and the Poetic Mind*, p. 19. Also see Holmes (ed.), *Shelley on Love: Selected Writings.*

42 Notopoulos, *op. cit.*, p. 105. Spenser's lines are from *An Hymn in Honour of Love*, II, lines 103–5.

43 Evans, 'Masks of the Poet: A Study of Self-Confrontation in Shelley's Poetry', pp. 70–107; the quotation is taken from p. 77.

44 Shelley, *Prometheus Unbound*, verses 16–20, 26–9, 32, 34–6, in *The Complete Poetical Works*, ed. Hutchinson, p. 240.

45 Jones, *The Works*, vol. I, p 453. [For the Persian original of these verses, see *Dīvān-i Ḥāfiẓ*, ed. Khānlarī, *ghazal* 148: 1–2. For a detailed study of this whole *ghazal*, see the chapter by Leili Anvar-Chenderoff in this volume, pp. 123–39. Ed.]

46 Emerson, *Emerson: Complete Works: His Essays, Lectures, Poems, and Orations*, I, pp. 71–80. Emerson here mistakenly assumed this to be a Qur'ānic verse. It is, in fact, the paraphrase of the famous *Ḥadīth* (prophetic tradition): 'I was a Hidden Treasure, I desired to be known; therefore I created the creation in order that I might be known.' (Quoted in Arberry, *Sufism*, p. 28.)

47 For a list of Emerson's translations from Persian, see Yohannan, *Persian Poetry in England and America*, pp. 299–302. All his translations of Ḥāfiẓ have since been published in Bloom and Kane (eds), *Ralph Waldo Emerson: Collected Poems and Translations*, pp. 465–90.

48 For his Ḥāfiẓ translations, see my *Hafiz, Master of Persian Poetry*, p. 337.

49 Emerson, 'Persian Poetry', in *The Atlantic Monthly*, pp. 724–34. The quotation is on p. 724.

50 See *Journals and Miscellaneous Notebooks of Ralph Waldo Emerson*, X, p. 165.

51 *Ibid.*, XVI, p. 138.

52 Yohannan, *Persian Poetry in England and America*, p. 133.

53 Emerson, *Complete Works* (1883–94), vol. IX, *Poems*, pp. 111–13.

54 For Emerson's view of Nature, see his essay *Nature*, in his *Works* (Riverside edn 1883–94), vol. 3, p. 161; and my 'Aspects of Sa'di's Reception in Nineteenth Century America'.

55 See my 'Tennyson, FitzGerald, and Cowell: A Private Relationship', pp. 5–17.

56 Hallam Tennyson, *Alfred Lord Tennyson, a Memoir*, II, p. 388.

57 'The Lover's Tale', II, 71–6; II, 357–60, in *The Poems of Tennyson*, ed. Ricks, pp. 299–348.

58 *Dīvān-i Ḥāfiẓ*, ed. Khānlarī, *ghazal* 56: 1–4. All the quotations are taken from this edition. (My translations unless otherwise mentioned.)

59 *Ibid.*, *ghazal* 311: 6–7.

60 'The Lover's Tale', I, 259–73, in *The Poems of Tennyson*, ed. Ricks.

61 *The Princess*, II, 103–5, in *The Poems of Tennyson*, ed. Ricks.

62 *Dīvān-i Ḥāfiẓ*, ed. Khānlarī, *ghazal* 224: 2.

63 *Ibid.*, *ghazal* 260: 9.

Bibliography

Quṭb al-Dīn al-'Abbādī, *Al-taṣfiya fī aḥwāl al-mutaṣawwifa*, ed. Gh. Yūsufī (Tehran: Bunyād-i Farhang-i Īrān 1347/1968; reprinted Tehran: Intishārāt-i 'Ilmī 1368/1989)

——, *Ṣūfī-nāma*, ed. Gh. Yūsufī (Tehran: Intishārāt-i 'Ilmī 1368/1989)

Khaled Abou El Fadl, *The Great Theft: Wrestling Islam from the Extremists* (New York: HarperCollins 2005)

Kamal Abu Deeb, *Al-Jurjani's Theory of Poetic Imagery* (Warminster: Ans & Phillips 1979)

Adonis, *Sufism and Surrealism*, trans. J. Cumberbatch (London: Saqi Books 2005)

Shams al-Dīn Aḥmad-e Aflākī, *The Feats of the Knowers of God (Manāqeb al-'ārefīn)*, trans. John O'Kane (Leiden: E.J. Brill 2002)

Mahnaz Ahmad, *Persian Poetry and the English Reader from the Eighteenth to the Twentieth Century*. MLitt dissertation, University of Newcastle upon Tyne, UK, 1971

Nazir Aḥmed, 'Credibility of the *Dīwān* of Ḥāfiẓ Published by the Late Mr. Qazwini and by Dr. Khānlarī', *Indo-Iranica* (Ḥāfiẓ-Shīrāzī Number), LX/1–4 (1987), pp. 63–82.

——, 'Naẓarī bar '*Dīwān-i Ḥāfiẓ*' Chāp-i Duktur Qāsim-i Ghanī u Qazwīnī u Chāp-i Duktur Khānlarī', *Taḥqīqāt-i islāmī*, VI/1–2 (1991)

Sadriddin Aini, *Bukhara Reminiscences*, trans. Holly Smith (Moscow: Raduga Publications 1986)

——, *The Sands of Oxus: Boyhood Reminiscences of Sadriddin Aini*, trans. John Perry and Rachel Lehr (Costa Mesa, CA: Mazda 1998)

Partaw 'Alavī, *Bāng-i jaras: rāhnamā-yi mushkilāt-i* Dīwān-i Ḥāfiẓ (Tehran: Intishārāt-i Khwārazmī 1365/1986, 3rd edn)

Sayyid Ḥaydar Āmulī, *Al-Muḥīṭ al-a'ẓam fī ta'wīl kitāb Allāh al-'azīz al-muḥkamūm* (Qom: Mu'assassa Farhangī wa Nashr-i Nūr 'Alā Nūr 1380/2001), 2 vols

Anqaravī, *Sharḥ-i kabīr-i Anqaravī bar Mathnawī-yi Mawlawī*, trans. into Persian by 'Iṣmat Satārzāda (Tehran: Intishārāt-i Zarrīn 1374/1995)

'Abdu'llāh Ansāri, *Ṭabaqāt al-ṣūfiyya*, ed. Muḥammad Sarvar-Mūllā'ī (Tehran: Ṭūs [Sahāmī 'ām] 1362/1983)

——, *Majmu'a-yi Rasā'il-i fārsī-yi Khwāja 'Abdu'llāh Ansāri*, ed. Muḥammad Sarvar Mawlā'ī (Tehran: Intishārāt-i Tus 1377/1998), 2 vols

Leili Anvar-Chenderoff, '"Without us, from us we are safe": Self and Selflessness in the *Dīvān* of 'Aṭṭār', in L. Lewisohn and C. Shackle (eds), *'Attar and the Persian Sufi Tradition: The Art of Spiritual Flight* (London: I.B.Tauris & The Institute of Ismaili Studies 2006), pp. 241–54

A.J. Arberry, 'Hafiz and his English Translators', *Islamic Culture*, 20 (1946), pp. 111–28 and 229–49

——, 'Orient Pearls At Random Strung', *Bulletin of the School of Oriental and African Studies*, 11 (1946), pp. 699–712

——, *Fifty Poems of Ḥāfiẓ, Text and Translations* (Cambridge: Cambridge University Press 1947)

——, *Immortal Rose, an Anthology of Persian Lyrics* (London: Luzac & Co. 1948)

——, *Shīrāz: Persian City of Saints and Poets* (Norman: University of Oklahoma Press 1960)

——, *Aspects of Islamic Civilization* (Ann Arbor: University of Michigan Press 1967)

——, *Sufism* (London: Allen & Unwin 1972)

——, *Classical Persian Literature* (Richmond: Curzon Press 1994 [reprint of the 1954 edn])

Qamar Āriyān, *Chihrah-yi Masīḥ dar adabiyāt-i fārsī* (Tehran: Intishārāt-i Mu'īn 1369/1990)

Dāryūsh Āshūrī, *Hastī-shināsi-yi Ḥāfiẓ: kāvushī dar bunyādhā-yi andīsha-yi ū* (Tehran: Nashr-i Markaz, 1377/1998)

——, *'Irfān u rindī dar shi'r-i Ḥāfiẓ* (Tehran: Nashr-i Markaz 1381/2003)

——, *Rindī va naẓar-bāzī.* Typescript of unpublished article

Muḥammad 'Alī Ātashisawdā, 'Zabān-i 'āmmiyāna dar ghazal-i Ḥāfiẓ', *Nāma-yi Farhangistān*, VIII/3 (1385/2007), pp. 85–112

Farīd al-Dīn 'Aṭṭār, *Ilāhī-nāma-yi Shaykh Farīd al-Dīn 'Aṭṭār-i Nayshābūrī*, ed. Fu'ād Rūḥānī (Tehran: Intishārāt-i Zawwār, 1339/1960)

——, *Manṭiq al-ṭayr*, ed. Ṣādiq Gawharīn (Tehran: Intishārāt-i 'Ilmī va farhangī 1342/1963)

——, *Ilāhī-nāma*, ed. H. Ritter (Tehran: Tūs 1359/1980)

——, *Dīvān-i 'Aṭṭār*, ed. T. Tafaḍḍulī (Tehran: Markaz-i Intishārāt-i 'Ilmī va farhangī 1362/1983, 3rd edn)

——, *The Conference of the Birds*, trans. Afkham Darbandi and Dick Davis (Harmondsworth and New York: Penguin Books 1984)

——, *Tadhkirat al-awliyā'*, ed. M. Isti'lāmī (Tehran: Intishārāt-i Zawwār, 1370/1991, 6th edn)

——, *Guzīda-yi Manṭiq al-ṭayr*, ed. Ḥusayn Ilāhī Ghomshei (Tehran: Intishārāt-i 'Ilmī va farhangī 1373/1994)

——, *Manṭiq al-ṭayr*, ed. Muḥammad Riḍā Shafī'ī-Kadkanī (Tehran: Intishārāt-i Sukhan 1383/2004)

——, *Farid ad-Din 'Attār's Memorial of God's Friends*, trans. Paul Losensky (New York: Paulist Press 2009)

R.J.W. Austin, 'The Sophianic Feminine in the Work of Ibn 'Arabī and Rumi', in L. Lewisohn (ed.), *The Heritage of Sufism: I: The Legacy of Mediaeval Persian Sufism* (Oxford: Oneworld 1999), pp. 233–46

Peter Avery (trans.), *The Collected Lyrics of Háfiz of Shíráz* (London: Archetype 2007)

—— and John Heath-Stubbs, *Hafiz of Shīrāz: Thirty Poems*, Wisdom of the East Series (London: John Murray 1952); reissued: New York: Handsel Books 2003 and London: Archetype 2006

P.J. Awn, *Satan's Tragedy and Redemption: Iblis in Sufi Psychology* (Leiden: E.J. Brill 1983)

Mehmed Ali Ayni, 'Note sur l'idéalisme de Djelaleddin Davani', *Revue neo-scholastique de philosophie*, new series 8 (1931), pp. 236–40

Abū'l-Mafākhir Yaḥyā Bākharzī, *Awrād al-aḥbāb wa Fuṣūṣ al-ādāb*, vol. 2: *Fuṣūṣ al-ādāb*, ed. Īrāj Afshār (Tehran 1979)

Rūzbihān Baqlī, *Le Jasmin des fidèles d'amour (Kitāb abhār al-'āshiqīn)*, ed. H. Corbin and M. Mu'īn (Tehran: Anjuman-i Īrān-shināsī-yi Farānsa dar Tihrān 1981)

G. William Barnard and Jeffery J. Kripal (eds), *Crossing Boundaries: Essays on the Ethical Status of Mysticism* (New York: Seven Bridges Press 2002)

Michael Barry, *Figurative Art in Medieval Islam and the Riddle of Bihzād of Herāt (AD 1465-1535)* (Paris and New York: Flammarion 2004)

Muḥammad Riḍā Barzigar-Khāliqī, *Shākh-i nabāt-i Ḥāfiẓ: sharḥ-i ghazalhā, hamrāh bā muqaddama, talaffaẓ-i vāshigān-i dushvār, durust-khʷānī-yi abyāt va farhang-i iṣṭilāḥāt-i 'irfānī* (Tehran: Zawwār 1382/2004)

Iraj Bashiri, 'Hafiz's Shīrāzi "Turk": A Structuralist Point of View', *The Muslim World*, LXIX (1979), pp. 178–97 and 248–68

Bāstānī Pārīzī, 'Ḥāfiẓ-i chandīn hunar', *Majalla-yi haft hunar*, 4 (Tehran, 1349/1970), pp. 10–11.

Alessandro Bausani, *Storia della letteratura persiana* (Milano: Nuova Accademia 1960)

——, *Religion in Iran: from Zoroaster to Baha'ullah*, trans. J.M. Marchesi (New York: Bibliotheca Persica 2000)

J.E. Bencheikh, 'Ma'nā', *EI²*, VI, pp. 346–9

Gabrielle R. van den Berg, *Minstrel Poetry from the Pamir Mountains* (Wiesbaden: Reichert 2004)

Anne H. Betteridge, '*Ziārat:* Pilgrimmage to the Shrines of Shīrāz', PhD dissertation, University of Chicago, 1985

Herman Bicknell, *Hafiz of Shīrāz: Selections from his Poems* (London: Trubner & Co. 1875)

Sayyid Aḥmad Bihishtī, *Sharḥ-i junūn: tafsīr-i mawḍū'ī-yi Dīvān-i Khʷāja Shams al-Dīn Muḥammad Ḥāfiẓ Shīrāzī* (Tehran: Rūzāna 1371/1992)

R. Blachère, 'Ghazal', *EI²*, II, pp. 1028–33

Bernard Blackstone, 'Byron and Islam: the triple Eros', *Journal of European Studies*, IV (1970), pp. 325–63

William Blake, *Blake: Complete Writings*, ed. G. Keynes (London: Oxford University Press 1972)

Ariel and Chana Bloch, *The Song of Songs: A New Translation*, with an Introduction and Commentary (Berkeley: University of California Press 1995)

Francois de Blois, *Persian Literature: A Bio-Bibliographical Survey, Poetry to ca. A.D. 1100*, vol. V/2 (London: Royal Asiatic Society 1992)

Yury Boboev, *Muqaddama-yi adabiyāt-shināsī* (Dushanbe: Nashriyyāt-i 'Irfān 1974)

James Boswell, *The Life of Samuel Johnson* (Oxford: Birkbeck-Hill Edition 1917)

C.E. Bosworth, *The New Islamic Dynasties: A Chronological and Genealogical Manual* (Edinburgh: Edinburgh University Press 1996)

Mary Boyce, 'A Novel Interpretation of Hafiz', *Bulletin of the School of Oriental and African Studies*, XV (1953), pp. 279–88

Michael Boylan, *Hafez: Dance of Life* (Washington, DC: Mage Publishers 1988)

Elizabeth Bridges, *Sonnets from Hafiz and Other Verses* (Oxford: Oxford University Press 1921)

Dominic Brookshaw, 'Odes of a poet-princess: the *ghazals* of Jahān-Malik Khātūn', *Iran: Journal of the British Institute of Persian Studies*, XLIII (2005), pp. 173–95

E.G. Browne, *A Literary History of Persia* (Cambridge: Cambridge University Press 1906–30), 4 vols

J.T.P. de Bruijn, 'Hafez, III. Hafez's Poetic Art', *Encyclopaedia Iranica*, XI, pp. 469–74

——, 'Rind', *EI*[2], VIII, p. 531

——, *Of Poetry and Piety: The Interaction of Religion and Literature in the Life and Works of Hakim Sana'i of Ghazna* (Leiden: E.J. Brill 1983)

——, *Persian Sufi Poetry: An Introduction to the Mystical Use of Classical Persian Poems* (Surrey: Curzon 1997)

——, 'Comparative Notes on Sana'i and 'Attar', in L. Lewisohn (ed.), *The Heritage of Sufism*, I: *The Legacy of Mediaeval Persian Sufism* (Oxford: Oneworld 1999), pp. 361–79

——, 'The *Qalandariyyat* in Persian Mystical Poetry, from Sana'i Onwards', in L. Lewisohn (ed.), *The Heritage of Sufism*, II: *Classical Persian Sufism from its Origins to Rumi* (Oxford: Oneworld 1999), pp. 75–86

——, 'Anvari and the ghazal: an exploration', in Daniela Meneghini (ed.), *Studies on the Poetry of Anvari* (Venice: Università Ca' Foscari di Venezia, 2006), pp. 7–36

Aḥmad 'Alī Rajā'ī Bukhārā'ī, *Farhang-i ash'ār-i Ḥāfiẓ* (*Glossary of Ḥāfiẓ's Verse*) (Tehran: Intishārāt-i 'Ilmī 1364/1985, 2nd edn)

Abū Ibrāmīm Mustamlī Bukhārī, *Sharḥ al-ta'arruf li-madhhab ahl al-taṣawwuf*, ed. M. Rawshan (Tehran: Intishārāt-i Asāṭīr 1373/1994), 5 vols

Basil Bunting, *Uncollected Poems*, ed. Richard Caddell (Oxford: OUP 1991)

John Bunyan, *The Pilgrim's Progress* (London: Penguin Books 1987)

J. Christoph Bürgel, *The Feather of Simurgh: The 'Licit Magic' of the Arts in Medieval Islam* (New York: New York University Press 1988)

——, 'Ambiguity: A Study in the Use of Religious Terminology in the Poems of Hafiz', in Michael Glünz and J.C. Bürgel (eds), *Intoxication, Earthly and Heavenly: Seven Studies on the Poet Hafiz of Shīrāz* (Bern: Peter Lang 1991)

Mihdī Burhānī, 'Mājarā-yi hamsar-i Ḥāfiẓ', *Ḥāfiẓ-shināsī*, IX (1367/1988), pp. 123–37

——, 'Kīmiyā-garī-yi Ḥaḍrat-i Shāh va Ḥāfiẓ', *Ṣūfī*, 39 (1374/1995), pp. 16–20

Bushāq Aṭ'amah-i Shīrāzī, *Kulliyāt-i Bushāq Aṭ'amah-i Shīrāzī*, ed. Manṣūr Rastigār-Fasā'ī (Tehran: Mīrāth-i maktūb 1382/2003)

Lord Byron, *The Works of Lord Byron, Letters and Journals*, ed. Rowlande E. Prothero (London: John Murray 1903), 4 vols

——, *The Poetical Works of Lord Byron*, Oxford Standard Authors (London and New York: Oxford University Press 1961)

Claude Cahen, 'Futuwwa', *EI*², II, pp. 961–9

Margaret L. Caton, *Hāfez: 'Erfān and Music as Interpreted by Ostād Mortezā Varzi* (Costa Mesa, CA: Mazda 2008)

Frank M. Chambers, 'Alba', in *The Princeton Encyclopedia of Poetry and Poetics*, ed. Alex Preminger. Enlarged edition (Princeton: Princeton University Press 1974), pp. 26–7

Malek Chebel, *Encyclopédie de l'amour en Islam: érotisme, beauté et sexualité dans le monde arabe, en Perse et en Turquie* (Paris: Payot 1995), 2 vols

D. Chenu, *Nature, Man, and Society in the 12th Century*, trans. J. Taylor and L.K. Little (Chicago: University of Chicago Press 1968)

William Chittick, 'Taṣawwuf. 2. Ibn al-'Arabī and after in the Arabic and Persian lands, and beyond', *EI*², X, pp. 317–24

——, *The Vision of Islam* (St Paul, MN: Paragon 1994)

——, 'The Paradox of the Veil in Sufism', in Elliot Wolfson (ed.), *Rending the Veil: Concealment and Secrecy in the History of Religions* (New York: Seven Bridges Press 1999), pp. 59–86

Patrick Collinson, 'Antipuritanism', in John Coffery and Paul Lim (eds), *The Cambridge Companion to Puritanism* (Cambridge: Cambridge University Press 2008), pp. 19–33

Michael Cook, *Commanding Right and Forbidding Wrong in Islamic Thought* (Cambridge: Cambridge University Press 2000)

Henry Corbin, *En Islam iranien: Aspects spirituals et philosophiques* (Paris: Éditions Gallimard 1971), 4 vols

——, *The Man of Light in Iranian Sufism*, trans. Nancy Pearson (Boulder and London: Shambhala 1971)

——, *Histoire de la philosophie islamique* (Paris: Gallimard 1986)

Daniela Meneghini Correale, *The Ghazals of Hafez: Concordance and Vocabulary* (Rome: Cultural Institute of the Islamic Republic in Iran in Italy 1988)

——, *The Handling of Ab/water in Farrukhi, Hafiz and Talib* (Venice: Quaderni del Dipartimento di Studi Eurasiatici, 1993)

D. Empaytaz de Croome, *Albor: Mediaeval and Renaissance Dawn-Songs in the Iberian Peninsula* (Department of Spanish and Spanish American Studies, University of London, King's College: UMI Monographs' Sponsor Series 1980)

Thomas Crow, *Wineseller's Street: Renderings of Hafiz* (Bethesda, Maryland: Iran Books 1998)

——, *Drunk on the Wine of the Beloved: 100 Poems of Hafiz* (Boulder: Shambhala 2001)

Muḥammad Dārābī, *Laṭīfa-yi ghaybī* (Shīrāz: Intishārāt-i Kitābkhāna-yi Aḥmadī Shīrāzī 1357/1978)

Valī'ullāh Darūdiyān (ed.), *Īn Kimiyā-yi hastī: Majmū'a-i maqālahā va yād-dāshthā-yi Ustād Duktar Muḥammad Riḍā Shafī'ī-Kadkanī* (Tehran: Intishārāt-i Āyidīn 1385/2006)

Jalāl al-Dīn Davānī (Kāzarūnī), *Sharḥ-i baytī az Ḥāfiẓ*, manuscript in the Punjab University library, Lahore, quoted in *Faṣl-nāma-yi rāyzanī-yi farhangī-yi Jumhūrī-yi Islāmī-yi Īrān*, vol. I, no. 3. (Islāmābād: Markaz-i Taḥqīqāt-i Fārsī-yi Īrān u Pākistān 1985)

——, *Naqd-i niyāzī, dar sharḥ-i du bayt u yik ghazal az Khwāja Ḥāfiẓ*, ed. Ḥusayn Mu'allim (Tehran: Amīr Kabīr, 1373/1995)

Dick Davis, 'Sa'dī', *EI*², VIII, pp. 719–23

——, 'The Journey as Paradigm: Literal and Metaphorical Travel in 'Aṭṭār's Manṭiq aṭ-Ṭayr', *Edebiyât: The Journal of Middle Eastern Literatures*, 4/2 (1993), pp. 173–83

——, 'On Not Translating Hafiz', *New England Review*, 25/1&2 (2004), pp. 310–18

'Azīz Dawlatabādī, 'Kamāl Khujandī va Ḥāfiz Shīrāzī', in *Tuḥfa-yi darvīsh: guzīda-yi ash'ār va majmū'a-i maqālāt* (Tehran: Intishārāt-i Satūda 1379/2000), pp. 529–35

Dawlatshāh Samarqandī, *Tadhkirat al-shu'arā'*, ed. E.G. Browne (London: 1901)

——, *Tadhkirat al-shu'arā'*, edited by Muḥammad 'Abbāsī (Tehran: Kitābfurūshī Bārānī 1958)

Abū'l-Ḥasan al-Daylamī, *Kitāb 'aṭf al-alif al-ma'lūf 'alā'l-lām al-ma'ṭūf*, trans. Jean-Claude Vadet, *Le Traité d'Amour Mystique d'al-Daylami* (Paris: Librairie Champion 1980)

Emile Dermenghem, trans., *L'Éloge du vin (Al khamriya): poème mystique de 'Omar ibn al Faridh, et son commentaire par 'Abd al Ghani an Nabolosi* (Paris, Les Éditions Véga 1980)

Muḥammad Dhū'l-Riyāsitayn, *Farhang-i vāzhahā-yi īhāmī dar ash'ār-i Ḥāfiẓ* (*Dictionary of Ambivalent Terms in Ḥāfiẓ's Verse*) (Tehran: Farzān 1379/2000)

'Alī Akbar Dihkhudā, *Lughat-nāma*, eds M. Mu'īn and M. Ja'far Shahīdī (Tehran: Mu'assasa-yi *Lughat-nāma Dihkhudā*; Tehran University Press 1373/1994). 15 vols including introduction. Article on 'Ḥāfiẓ Shīrāzī', vol. 5, pp. 7486–501

G.H.B. Dihqāni-Taftī, *Masīḥ va masīḥiyyat nazd-i Īrāniyān*, I: *Sayr-i ijmālī dar tārīkh*; II: *Dar shi'r-i fārsī dawrān-i sabk-i kuhan*; III: *Dar naẓm u nathr u hunar-i mu'āṣir* (London: Suhrāb 1992–4), 3 vols

Peter Dronke, *The Medieval Lyric* (Cambridge: D.S. Brewer 1996, 3rd edn)

John Dryden, *Essays of John Dryden*, ed. W.P. Ker (Oxford 1926)

Edward Edinger, *Ego and Archetype: Individuation and the Religious Function of the Psyche* (Baltimore, MD: Penguin Books 1973)

T.S. Eliot, *On Poetry and Poets* (London: Faber & Faber 1957)

Jason Elliot, *Mirrors of the Unseen: Journeys in Iran* (London: Picador 2006)

R.W. Emerson, 'Persian Poetry', *The Atlantic Monthly*, I (April 1858), pp. 724–34

——, *Complete Works: His Essays, Lectures, Poems, and Orations* (London: Bell & Daddly 1866), 2 vols

——, *Complete Works* (Riverside Edition: London: Waverly Book Company 1883–94), 12 vols

——, *The Journals* (Boston: Houghton Mifflin Co. 1912), 10 vols

——, *Journals and Miscellaneous Notebooks of Ralph Waldo Emerson*, various eds (Cambridge, MA: Harvard University Press 1960), 16 vols

——, *Ralph Waldo Emerson: Essays and Lectures* (New York: Library of America 1983)
——, *Collected Poems and Translations*, eds Harold Bloom and Paul Kane (New York: Library of America 1994)
Encyclopedia of Persian Language and Literature (*Dāneshnāme-ye Zabān-o Adab-e Fārsī*), ed. Esmā'īl Sa'ādat (Tehran: Iranian Academy of Persian Language & Literature 1386/2007), vol. 2: entry on 'Ḥāfiẓ', by multiple authors, pp. 637–68
Carl Ernst, *Words of Ecstasy in Sufism* (Albany: SUNY 1985)
——, 'The Stages of Love in Early Persian Sufism from Rābi'a to Rūzbihān', in Leonard Lewisohn (ed.), *The Heritage of Sufism: Classical Persian Sufism from its Origins to Rumi* (Oxford: Oneworld 1999), pp. 435–56
——, 'Rūzbihān Baqlī on Love as "Essential Desire"', in A. Geise and J.C. Bürgel, *God is Beautiful and He Loves Beauty: Festschrift in honour of Annemarie Schimmel* (Berlin: Peter Lang 1994), pp. 181–9
——, *The Shambhala Guide to Sufism* (Boston: Shambhala 1997)
James C. Evans, 'Masks of the Poet: A Study of Self-Confrontation in Shelley's Poetry', in *Keats-Shelley Journal*, XXIV (1975), pp. 70–107
Sa'īd al-Dīn ibn Aḥmad Farghānī, *Mashāriq al-ḍararī: sharḥ-i* Ṭā'iyyah-i *Ibn Fāriḍ*, ed. Jalāl al-Dīn Āshtiyānī ([Mashhad: s.n.] 1978)
M. Farzaad, *To Translate Hafez* (Tehran: n.p. 1935)
Ḥamid Farzām, *Taḥqīq dar aḥwāl va naqd-i āthār va afkār-i Shāh Ni'matu'llāh Walī* (Tehran: Surūsh 1374/1995)
Manṣūr Rastigār-Fasā'ī, *Ḥāfiẓ: paydā'ī va pinhān-i zindigī, murūrī dar shi'r, zindigī va indīshahā'ī Ḥāfiẓ* (Tehran: Sukhan 1385/2006)
Hūshang Fattī, *Ḥāfiẓ rā chinīn pindāshta-and* (Shīrāz: Intishārāt-i Navīd 1385/2006)
Ève Feuillebois-Pierunek, *A La Croisée des voies célestes: Faxr al-Din 'Erāqi, poésie mystique et expression poétique en Perse médiévale* (Tehran: Institut Français de Recherche en Iran 2002)
C.-H. de Fouchécour, *La Description de la nature dans la poésie lyrique persane du XIeme siècle: Inventiare et analyse des themes* (Paris: Librairie C. Klincksieck 1969)
——, '*Naẓar-bāzī*: le jeux du regard selon un interprète de Hāfez', *Kār-Nāmeh*, 2–3 (1996), pp. 3–10
——, *Hafiz de Chiraz: Le Divān: Oeuvre lyrique d'un spirituel en Perse au XIVe siècle*, introduction, commentary and translation by Charles-Henri de Fouchécour (Paris: Verdier 2006)
Ursula Franklin, *The Rhetoric of Valéry's Prose Aubades* (Toronto, Buffalo and London: Toronto University Press 1979)
Northrop Frye, *Anatomy of Criticism: Four Essays* (New York: Penguin Books 1990)
Badī' al-Zamān Furūzānfar, *Aḥādīth-i Mathnawī* (Tehran: Amīr Kabīr 1361/1982)
Qāsim Ghanī, *Baḥth dar āthār u afkār u aḥwāl-i Ḥāfiẓ*, vol. 2: *Tārīkh-i 'aṣr-i Ḥāfiẓ yā tārīkh-i fārs va maḍāfāt va iyālāt-i mujāvarih dar qarn-i hashtum* (Tehran: Intishārāt-i Zawwār 1383/2004), 2 vols

Ahmad Ghazālī, *(Sawāniḥ) Aphorismen über die Liebe*, ed. H. Ritter (Istanbul: Ma'ārif 1942)

——, *Sawāniḥ*, ed. N. Purjavādī (Tehran: Bunyād-i Farhang-i Irān 1359/1981)

——, *Sawānih: Inspirations from the World of Pure Spirits*, trans N. Pourjavady (London: KPI 1986)

——, *Sawāniḥ al-'ushshāq*, ed. H. Ritter (Tehran: Tehran University Press / Markaz-i Intishārāt-i Dānishgāhī 1368/1989)

Abū Ḥāmid al-Ghazālī, *Kīmiyā-yi sa'ādat*, ed. Ḥusayn Khadīvjam (Tehran: Intishārāt-i 'Ilmī u Farhangī 1361/1982, 2nd edn)

——, *Iḥyā' 'ulūm al-dīn* (Cairo: Dār al-Shu'ab, n.d.), 4 vols

Ḥusayn Ilāhī Ghomshei, 'Of Scent and Sweetness: 'Aṭṭār and his Legacy in Rūmī, Shabistarī and Ḥāfeẓ', in Leonard Lewisohn and Christopher Shackle (eds), *'Aṭṭār and the Persian Sufi Tradition* (London: I.B.Tauris 2006), pp. 27–56

—— (ed.), *Dīwān-i Ḥāfiẓ* (Tehran: Intishārāt-i Payk-i 'Ulūm 1382/2003)

Gīsū Darāz and Sayyid Muḥammad Ḥusaynī, *Sharḥ-i Risāla-yi Qushayrī* (Haydarābād: lithograph edition 1361/1942)

Michael Glünz (ed.), *Intoxication Earthly and Heavenly: Seven Studies on the Poet Hafiz of Shīrāz* (Berne: Peter Lang 1991)

Terry Graham, 'Hafiz and His Master', *Sufi*, 42 (summer 1999), pp. 35–40

Elizabeth T. Gray, *The Green Sea of Heaven: Fifty Ghazals from the Dīwān of Hāfiz* (Ashland, OR: White Cloud Press 1995)

Lois Anita Griffen, *The Theory of Profane Love Among the Arabs: the Development of the Genre* (New York: NYU Press 1971)

G.E. von Grunebaum, 'Bayān', *EI*[2], I, pp. 1114–16

Ḥāfiẓ Shīrāzī, *Dīwān-i Khwāja Shams al-Dīn Muḥammad Ḥāfiẓ Shīrāzī*, ed. Muḥammad Qazvīnī and Qasīm Ghanī (Tehran: Kitābkhāna Zawwār 1320/1941)

——, *Dīwān-i Khwāja Ḥāfiẓ-i Shīrāzī*, ed. S.'Abū'l-Qāsim Anjawī-Shīrāzī (Tehran: Sāzmān-i Intikhābāt-i Jāwidān 1358/1979)

——, *Dīwān-i Khwāja Shams al-Dīn Muḥammad Ḥāfiẓ*, ed. Parvīz Nātil Khānlarī (Tehran: Intishārāt-i Khawārazmī 1359/1980), 2 vols

——, Vincent Mansour Monteil and Akbar Tajvidi (trans.), *L'Amour, l'amant, l'aimé: cente ballades du Divān* (Paris: Sindbad 1989)

——, *Dīvān-i Shams al-Dīn Muḥammad Ḥāfiẓ*, ed. Sāyeh (Tehran: Nashr-i Kārnāma 1371/1992)

Ḥusayn Ma'ṣūmī Hamadānī, 'Chirā Ḥāfiẓ? Ta'ammulī dar ma'nā-yi tārīkhī-yi Ḥāfiẓ-shināsī-yi mā', *Nashr-i dānish*, VIII/6 (1367/1988)

'Ayn al-Quḍāt Hamadhānī, *Tamhīdāt*, ed. Afif Osseiran (Tehran: Intishārāt-i Manūchihrī 1341/1962)

Joseph von Hammer-Purgstall, *Mohammed Schemsed-din Hafis. Der Diwan* (Stuttgart and Tübingen: Thle 1812–13), 2 vols

'Alī Muḥammad Ḥaqq-shinās, 'Ma'nā va āzādī dar shi'r-i Ḥāfiẓ', *Yādnāma-i Doctor Aḥmad Tafaḍḍulī*, ed. 'Alī Ashraf Ṣādiqī (Tehran: Intishārāt-i Sukhan, 1379/2000), pp. 143–60

Ḥusayn ʻAlī Haravī, ʻSukhanī az taṣḥīḥ-i jadīdī az *Dīvān-i Ḥāfiẓ*', in Naṣru'llāh Purjavādī (ed.), *Darbāra-i Ḥāfiẓ: bar-guzīda-i maqālahā-yi Nashr-i Dānish (2)* (Tehran: Nashr-i Markaz-i Dānishgāhī 1365/1986), pp. 141–55

——, 'Nuktahā dar taṣḥīḥ-i *Dīvān-i Ḥāfiẓ*', in Naṣru'llāh Purjavādī (ed.), *Darbāra-i Ḥāfiẓ: bar-guzīda-i maqālahā-yi Nashr-i Dānish (2)* (Tehran: Nashr-i Markaz-i Dānishgāhī 1365/1986), pp. 177–202

——, *Sharḥ-i ghazalhā-yi Ḥāfiẓ* (Tehran: Nashr-i Nū 1367/1988), 4 vols

Kāvūs Ḥasanlī, *Chishma-i khūrshīd: bāz-khwānī-yi zindagī, andīsha va sukhan-i Ḥāfiẓ-i Shīrāzī* (Shīrāz: Intishārāt-i Navīd 1385/2006)

A. Hatto (ed.), *Eos: An Inquiry into the Theme of Lovers' Meetings and Partings at Dawn in Poetry* (London, The Hague and Paris: Mouton 1965)

ʻAbd al-Ḥusayn Hazhīr, *Ḥāfiẓ tashrīḥ*, ed. Mihdī Suhaylī (Tehran: Intishārāt-i Ashrafī 1345/1966)

Hubert Heinen, 'Thwarted Expectations: Medieval and Modern Views of Genre in Germany', in William D. Paden (ed.), *Medieval Lyric: Genres in Historical Context* (Urbana and Chicago: University of Illinois Press 2000), pp. 334–46

Daniel Heller-Roazen, *Echolalias: On the Forgetting of Language* (New York: Zone Books 2005)

Michael Hillmann, *Unity in the Ghazals of Ḥāfiẓ* (Chicago: Bibliotheca Islamica 1976)

M. Hodgson, *The Venture of Islam* (Chicago and London: University of Chicago, 1974–7), 3 vols

John Holloway, *Widening Horizons in English Verse* (London: Routledge & Kegan Paul 1966)

Richard Holmes (ed.), *Shelley on Love: Selected Writings* (London: Flamingo 1996)

Ted Hughes, *Shakespeare and the Goddess of Complete Being* (London: Faber & Faber 1992)

ʻAlī al-Hujwīrī, *Kashf al-maḥjūb*, ed. V.A. Zhukovskii (St Petersburg 1899; reprinted, Leningrad 1926)

——, *The 'Kashf al-maḥjūb:' The Oldest Persian Treatise on Sufism*, trans. R.A. Nicholson (Gibb Memorial Series, no. 17. 1911; reprinted London 1976)

Jalāl al-Dīn Humā'ī, *Funūn-i balāghat va ṣanāʻāt-i adabī* (Tehran: Chāpkhāna-yi Ittiḥād 1382/2003, 21st edn)

Kamāl al-Dīn Ḥusayn, b. ʻAlī Wāʻiẓ-i Kashifī, *Futuwwat-nāma-yi Sulṭānī*, ed. Jaʻfar Maḥjūb (Tehran: Bunyād-i farhang-i Īrān 1350/1971)

Lewis Hyde, *Trickster Makes the World: Mischief, Myth and Art* (New York: North Point Press 1998)

Ibn ʻArabī, *Fuṣūṣ al-ḥikam*, ed. A. Affīfī (Beirut: Dār al-Kitāb al-Arabī 1946)

——, *The* Tarjumán al-Ashwáq*: A Collection of Mystical Odes*, ed. and trans. R.A. Nicholson (London: Theosophical Publishing House 1978)

——, *Ibn al-ʻArabī: The Bezels of Wisdom*, trans. R.J.W. Austin (New York: Paulist Press 1980)

——, *Stations of Desire: Love Elegies from Ibn ʻArabi*, trans. Michael Sells (Jerusalem: IBIS 2000)

'Umar Ibn al-Fāriḍ, *'Umar Ibn al-Fāriḍ: Sufi Verse, Saintly Life*, trans. Th. Emil Homerin (New York: Paulist Press 2001)

Aḥmad-i Jām Nāmiqī, *Uns at-tā'ibīn*, ed. 'A. Fāḍil (Tehran: Intishārāt-i Ṭūs 1368/1989)

Ḥāfiẓ Ḥusayn Ibn Karbalā'ī Tabrīzī, *Rawḍāt al-jinān va jannāt al-janān*, ed. Ja'far Sulṭān al-Qurrā'ī (Persian Texts Series No. 20. Tehran: BTNK 1344/1965), 2 vols

Fakhr al-Dīn 'Irāqī, *Fakhruddin 'Iraqi: Divine Flashes*, trans. by W.C. Chittick and P.L. Wilson (London: SPCK 1982)

——, *Lama'āt*, in his *Dīvān*, ed. Nasrīn Muḥtasham (Tehran: Zawwār 1372/1994)

Muḥammad 'Alī Islāmī-Nadūshan, 'Tarjuma-nāpadhīrī-yi Ḥāfiẓ', *Ḥāfiẓ-pazūhishī*, IX (1384/2006), pp. 19–26

Muḥammad Isti'lāmī, *Dars-i Ḥāfiẓ: Naqd u sharḥ-i ghazalhā-yi Kh^{w}āja Shams al-Dīn Muḥammad Ḥāfiẓ* (Tehran: Intishārāt-i Sukhan 1382/2003), 2 vols

Sergey Ivanov, *Holy Fools in Byzantium and Beyond*, trans. Simon Franklin (Oxford: OUP 2008)

Toshiko Izutsu, *A Comparative Study of the Key Philosophical Concepts in Sufism and Taoism - Ibn 'Arabī and Lao-Tzu* (Tokyo: Keio Institute 1966)

Peter Jackson et al. (eds), *The Cambridge History of Iran*, VI: *The Timurid and Safavid Periods* (Cambridge: Cambridge University Press 1986)

Muḥammad Ghufrānī Jahramī, 'Mākhaz-i andīshahā-yi Sa'dī: Rūzbihān Baqlī Shīrāzī', in *Dhikr-i jamīl-i Sa'dī: Buzurgdāsht-i Hashtṣadumīn sālgard-i tawallud-i Shaykh-i ajal Sa'dī* (Shīrāz: n.d.), vol. 3, pp. 95–112

Shaykh Aḥmad Jām, *Rawḍat al-Mudhbibīn va jannat al-mushtāqīn*, ed. 'Alī Fāḍil (Tehran: Mu'assisa-yi Muṭāla'āt u taḥqīqāt-i farhangī 1372/1993)

'Abd al-Raḥmān Jāmī, *Yūsuf u Zulaykhā*, in *Mathnavī-yi haft uwrang-i Jāmī*, ed. A.M. Mudarris Gīlānī (Tehran: Intishārāt-i Sa'dī, 1337/1958)

——, *Nafaḥāt al-uns min ḥaḍarāt al-quds*, ed. Maḥmūd 'Ābidī (Tehran: Intishārāt-i Iṭalā'āt 1370/1991)

——, *Ṭā'iyyah-i 'Abd al-Raḥmān Jāmī: tarjumah-i Ṭā'iyyah-i Ibn Fāriḍ, bi-inḍimām-i sharḥ-i Maḥmūd Qayṣarī bar Ṭā'iyyah-i Ibn Fāriḍ* (Tehran: Intishārāt-i Nuqta, 1997)

Ḥasan Javādī (trans.), *'Obeyd-e Zakani: The Ethics of Aristocrats and Other Satirical Works* (Piedmont, CA: Jahan Book Co. 1985)

——, *Tārīkh-i ṭanz dar adabiyāt-i fārsī* (Tehran: Intishārāt-i Kāravān 1382/2003)

Alfred Jeanroy, *La Poésie lyrique des Troubadours* (Toulouse: E. Privat and Paris: H. Didier 1934), 2 vols

David L. Jeffery (ed.), *English Spirituality in the Age of Wesley* (Grand Rapids, MI: Eerdmans Publishing Co 1981)

Sir William Jones, *The Works* (London: G.G. & J. Robinson 1789), 6 vols

——, *A Grammar of the Persian Language* (London 1823, 8th edn)

Ahmet Karamustafa, *God's Unruly Friends: Dervish Groups in the Islamic Later Middle Period, 1200–1550* (Salt Lake City: University of Utah Press 1994)

'Izz al-Dīn Maḥmūd Kāshānī, *Miṣbāḥ al-ḥidāya*, ed. Jalāl al-Dīn Humā'ī (Tehran: Kitābkhāna Sanā'ī, 1946, 2nd edn)

'Abd al-Razzāq Kāshānī, *Tuḥfat al-ikhwān fi khasā'is al-fityān*, ed. Sayyid Muḥammad Dāmādī (Tehran: Intishārāt-i 'Ilmī u farhangī 1369/1990)

'Alī Sharī'at Kāshānī, 'La Prééternité et la pérennité de l'amour et de la beauté en literature mystique persane de Rūzbehān à Ḥāfeẓ', *Luqmān*, 17/2 (2001), pp. 25–54

——, 'Le Secret et le Paradoxal en literature mystique persan: réflexion sur deux aspects fondamentaux de la mystique irano-islamique', *Revue Eurorient*, 21 (2006), pp. 3–10

Homa Katouzian, 'Sufism in Sa'di, and Sa'di on Sufism', in L. Lewisohn (ed.), *The Heritage of Sufism*, II: *Classical Persian Sufism from its Origins to Rumi* (Oxford: Oneworld 1999), pp. 191–201

Sarah Kay, 'Alba', in Peter France (ed.), *The Oxford Companion to Literature in French* (Oxford: Clarendon Press 1995), p. 17

John Keats, *Complete Poems and Selected Essays of John Keats* (New York: Modern Library paperback 2001)

Annabel Keeler, *Sufi Hermeneutics: the Qur'an Commentary of Rashīd al-Dīn Maybudī* (Oxford: Oxford University Press 2006)

Jalāl Khāliqī-Muṭlaq, 'Tan-kāma-sarayī dar adab-i fārsī', in *Irānshināsī*, VIII/1 (spring, 1375/1996), pp. 15–54

——, 'Zībā'ī-yi kamāl-i maṭlūb dar zan dar farhang-i Īrān', in *Irānshināsī*, VIII/4 (1376/1997), pp. 703–16

Khāqānī, *Dīwān-i Khāqānī*, ed. Mīr Jalāl al-Dīn Kuzārī (Tehran; Nashr-i Markaz 1378/1999)

'Umar Khayyām, *Rubáiyát of Omar Khayyam*, trans. Edward Fitzgerald, ed. R.A. Nicholson (London: Adam & Charles Black 1909), reprinted Tehran (Siphir 1384/2005), with facing Persian texts, edited with an introduction by Huṣayn Ghomshei

Kamāl al-Dīn Khujandī, *Dīwān-i Kamāl al-Dīn Mas'ūd Khujandī*, ed. 'Azīz Dawlatābādī (Tehran: 1337/1958)

——, *Dīwān-i Kamāl al-Dīn Mas'ūd Khujandī*, ed. K. Shidfar (Moscow: Intishārāt-i Dānish 1975)

Baha' al-Din Khorramshahi [= Khurramshāhī], 'Hafez, II. Hafez's Life and Times', *Encyclopaedia Iranica*, XI, pp. 465–9

Bahā' al-Dīn Khurramshāhī, 'Uslūb-i hunarī-yi Ḥāfiẓ va Qur'ān', in Naṣru'llāh Purjavādī (ed.), *Darbāra-i Ḥāfiẓ: bar-guzīda-i maqālahā-yi Nashr-i Dānish (2)* (Tehran: Nashr-i Markaz-i Dānishgāhī 1365/1986), pp. 3–20

——, *Chārdah ravāyat: majmū'a-yi maqāla darbārah-i shi'r u shakhṣiyyat-i Ḥāfiẓ* (Tehran: Nashr-i Parvāz 1367/1988)

——, *Ḥāfiẓ-nāma: sharḥ-i alfāẓ, i'lām, mafāhīm-i kilīdī va abyāt-i dushvār-i Ḥāfiẓ* (Tehran: Intishārāt-i Surūsh 1372/1993)

——, 'Mayl-i Ḥāfiẓ bih gunāh', in his *Dhihn u zabān-i Ḥāfiẓ* (Tehran: Intishārāt-i Nāhīd 1379/2000), pp. 61–92

——, *Dhihn va zabān-i Ḥāfiẓ* (Tehran: Intishārāt-i Nāhīd 1379/2000, 1st edn)

—— (ed.), *Dānishnāma-yi Qur'ān* (Tehran: Gulshan 1381/2002), 2 vols

——, *Dhihn va zabān-i Ḥāfiẓ* (Tehran: Intishārāt-i Nāhīd 1384/2005, 3rd edn)
——, 'Ḥāfiẓ dar farhang-i mā u farhang-i mā dar Ḥāfiẓ', in *Ḥāfiẓ Hāfiẓa-yi mā'st* (Tehran: Intishārāt-i nashr-i Qaṭra 1385/2006)
——, *Az sabza tā sitāra: maqālatī va mabāḥathī dar zamīna-yi Qur'ān-pazhūhī, Ḥāfiẓ-pazhūhī...* (Tehran: Nashr-i Qaṭra 1386/2007)
Akbar Khudāparast (ed.), *Majmū'a-i maqālāt dar-bāra-i Ḥāfiẓ* (Tehran: Intishārāt-i Hunar va Farhang 1363/1984)
Khwāndamīr, *Habīb al-siyar*, ed. Jalāl al-Dīn Humā'ī (Tehran: Kitāb-khāna-i Khayyām 1333/1954), 4 vols
L. Kinberg, 'What is meant by *Zuhd*', *Studia Islamica*, LXI (1985), p. 27–44
'Alī Aṣghar Maẓharī Kirmānī, 'Shāh Ni'matu'llāh Walī Kirmānī va Khwāja Ḥāfiẓ Shīrāzī', *Ṣūfī*, 26 (1374/1995), pp. 12–21
Awḥad al-Dīn Kirmānī, *Dīvān-i rubā'iyyāt-i Awḥad al-Dīn Kirmānī*, ed. Aḥmad Abū Maḥbūb, introduction by M.I. Bastānī-Pārīzī (Tehran: Surūsh 1380/2001)
Faqīh Kirmānī, *Dīwān-i qaṣā'id va ghazaliyyāt-i Khwāja 'Imād al-Dīn 'Alī Faqīh Kirmānī*, ed. Rukn al-Dīn Humāyūn-Farrakh (Tehran: Ibn Sīnā 1348/1969)
——, *Mathnawī-yi Ṣafā-nāma*, in 'Imād Faqīh, *Panj ganj*, ed. and intro. Rukn al-Dīn Humāyūn-Farrukh (Tehran: Intishārāt-i Dānishgāh-i Millī-yi Irān, no. 126, 1357/1978)
——, *Ṭarīqat-nāma*, ed. Rukn al-Dīn Humāyūn-Farrukh (Tehran: Intishārāt-i Asāṭīr 1374/1995)
Khwājū Kirmānī, *Humāy u Humāyūn*, ed. K. 'Aynī (Tehran 1992)
——, *Dīwān-i Khwājū Kirmānī*, ed. Sa'īd Qāni'ī (Tehran: Intishārāt-i Āftāb 1374/1995)
Sa'īd Niyāz Kirmānī (ed.), *Dawlat-i pīr-i mughān bād kay bāqī sahl-ast: Majmū'a-yi maqālāt-i Ḥāfiẓ-shināsī* (Tehran: Intishārāt-i Pāzhang 1374/1995)
Muḥsin Kiyānī, *Tārīkh-i khānaqāh dar Īrān* (Tehran: Ṭahūrī 1369/1991)
Koran, *The Koran Interpreted*, trans. A.J. Arberry (Oxford: Oxford University Press 1983)
James Kritzeck (ed.), *Anthology of Islamic Literature* (Harmondsworth: Penguin Books 1964)
Melissa Kwasny (ed.), *Toward the Open Field: Poets on the Art of Poetry, 1800–1950* (Middletown, CN: Wesleyan University Press 2004)
Muḥammad ('Asīrī') Lāhījī, *Mafātīḥ al-i'jāz fī sharḥ-i Gulshan-i rāz*, ed. Muḥammad Riḍā Barzgār Khāliqī and 'Iffat Karbāsī (Tehran: Zawwār 1371/1992)
Abū'l-Ḥasan 'Abd al-Raḥmān Khatmī Lāhūrī, *Sharḥ-i 'irfānī-yi ghazalhā-yi-i Ḥāfiẓ*, ed. Bahā' al-Dīn Khurramshāhī, Kūrush Manṣūrī and Ḥusayn Muṭī'ī-Amīn (Tehran: Nashr-i Qaṭra 1374/1995), 4 vols
Herman Landolt, 'Nasafī, 'Azīz b. Moḥammad', *Encyclopaedia Iranica*, www.iranica.com/newsite/articles/unicode/sup/Nasafi_Aziz.html
E.W. Lane, *An Arabic-English Lexicon* (London: Williams & Norgate, 1865)
William Law, *A Serious Call to a Devout and Holy Life*, ed. Paul Stanwood (London: SPCK 1978)
Gilbert Lazard, 'Le Langage symbolique du ghazal', *Convegno internazionale sulla poesia di Ḥāfiẓ* (Rome: Accademia nazionale dei Lincei 1978), pp. 60–71

Walter Leaf, *Versions from Hafiz, An Essay on Persian Metre* (London: G.R. Richards 1898)
Oliver Leaman, 'Ma'nā. 2. In Philosophy', *EI*², VI, p. 347
Richard Le Gallienne, *Odes from the Divan of Hafiz, Freely Rendered from Literal Translations* (London: Duckworth & Co. 1905)
G.W. Leibniz, *La Monadologie*, ed. annotée et précédée d'une exposition du système de Leibniz par Emile Boutroux (Paris: Librairie Delagrave 1983)
R. Lescot, 'Chronologie de l'oeuvre de Hafiz', *Bulletin d'Études Orientales de l'Institut Français de Damas*, X (1944), pp. 57–100
Franklin Lewis, 'Hafez, VIII. Hafez and *Rendi*', *Encyclopaedia Iranica*, XI, pp. 483–91
——, 'Hafez, IX. Hafez and Music', *Encyclopaedia Iranica*, XI, pp. 491–8
——, *Rumi: Past and Present, East and West: The Life, Teachings and Poetry of Jalāl al-Din Rumi* (Oxford: Oneworld 2000)
Leonard Lewisohn, 'Homam-i Tabrizi', in *Encyclopaedia Iranica*, XII/4, pp. 434–5
——, 'Shawḳ', *EI*², IX: 376–7
——, 'Muḥammad Shīrīn Maghribī Tabrīzī', *Sufi: A Journal of Sufism*, 1 (1988–9), pp. 30–5
——, 'The Life and Poetry of Mashriqī Tabrīzī (d. 1454)', *Iranian Studies*, XXII/2–3 (1989), pp. 99–127
—— (ed.), *Dīvān-i Muḥammad Shīrīn Maghribī*, Persian text edited with notes, introduction and index; Wisdom of Persia Series XLIII (Tehran: McGill Institute of Islamic Studies, Tehran Branch; London: SOAS 1994)
——, 'The Life and Times of Kamāl Khujandī', in Maria Subtelny (ed.), *Annemarie Schimmel Festschrift* (*Journal of Turkish Studies*, vol. 18, Harvard University 1994), pp. 163–76
——, *Beyond Faith and Infidelity: the Sufi Poetry and Teachings of Mahmud Shabistari* (Richmond: Curzon 1995)
——, 'The Sacred Music of Islam: *Samā'* in the Persian Sufi Tradition', *British Journal of Ethnomusicology* 6 (1997), pp. 1–33
—— (ed.), *The Heritage of Sufism:* I: *The Legacy of Mediaeval Persian Sufism* (Oxford: Oneworld 1999)
——, 'In Quest of Annihilation: Imaginalization and Mystical Death in the *Tamhīdāt* of 'Ayn al-Quḍāt Hamadhānī', in Lewisohn (ed.), *The Heritage of Sufism*, I: *Classical Persian Sufism: from its Origins to Rūmī* (Oxford: Oneworld 1999), pp. 285–336
——, 'Overview: Iranian Islam and Persianate Sufism', in Lewisohn (ed.), *The Heritage of Sufism:* II: *The Legacy of Mediaeval Persian Sufism* (Oxford: Oneworld 1999), pp. 75–86
——, 'The Transcendental Unity of Polytheism & Monotheism in the Sufism of Shabistarī', in Lewisohn (ed.), *The Heritage of Sufism:* II: *The Legacy of Mediaeval Persian Sufism* (Oxford: Oneworld 1999), pp. 379–406
—— (ed.) (with David Morgan), *The Heritage of Sufism:* III, *Late Classical Persianate Sufism: the Safavid and Mughal Period* (Oxford: Oneworld 1999)

——, 'The Esoteric Christianity of Islam: Interiorisation of Christian Imagery in Medieval Persian Sufi Poetry', in Lloyd Ridgeon (ed.), *Muslim Interpretations of Christianity* (London: Curzon Press 2001), pp. 127–56

——, 'Sufism and Ismā'īlī Doctrine in the Persian Poetry of Nizārī Quhistānī (645–721/1247–1321)', in *Iran: Journal of the British Institute of Persian Studies*, XLI (2003), pp. 1–23

——, 'Ta'ammulati dar usul-i naẓarī u ravish-i tarjuma-yi āsh'ār-i ṣūfiyānih-i fārsī', translated by Majd al-Dīn Kayvānī, in Ḥusayn Ilāhī Qumshihī and Sayyid Aḥmad Bihishtī (eds), *Kīmiyā: Daftarī dar adabiyāt u hunar u 'irfān* (Tehran: Intishārāt-i Rawzana 1382/2003), pp. 354–86

——, 'Farid al-Din 'Attar', in Lindsay Jones (ed.), *The Encyclopaedia of Religion* (New York: Macmillan Reference & Thomson Gale 2005, 2nd edn), I, pp. 600–3

——, 'Al-Ghazali, Ahmad', in Donald Borchert (ed.), *The Encyclopedia of Philosophy* (New York: Macmillan Reference & Thomson Gale 2006, 2nd edn), I, pp. 117–18

—— (ed.), with Christopher Shackle, *'Attar and the Persian Sufi Tradition: The Art of Spiritual Flight* (London: I.B.Tauris & The Institute of Ismaili Studies 2006)

——, 'Sufi Symbolism and the Persian Hermeneutic Tradition: Reconstructing the Pagoda of Attar's Esoteric Poetics', in Leonard Lewisohn (ed.) with Christopher Shackle, *'Attar and the Persian Sufi Tradition: The Art of Spiritual Flight* (London: I.B.Tauris & The Institute of Ismaili Studies 2006), pp. 255–308

——, 'The Metaphysics of Justice and the Ethics of Mercy in the Thought of 'Ali ibn Abi Talib', in A. Lakhani (ed.), *The Sacred Foundations of Justice in Islam*, Introduction by S.H. Nasr (Vancouver: Sacred Web 2006), pp. 108–46

——, 'Divine Love in Islam', in Yudit Greenberg (ed.), *Encyclopaedia of Love in World Religions* (New York: Macmillan Reference & Thomson Gale 2007), I, pp. 163–5

——, 'Sawanih', in Yudit Greenberg (ed.), *Encyclopaedia of Love in World Religions* (New York: Macmillan Reference & Thomson Gale 2007), II, pp. 535–8

—— (trans.) with Robert Bly, *The Angels Knocking on the Tavern Door: 30 Poems of Hafez* (New York: HarperCollins 2008)

John Limbert, *Shīrāz in the Age of Hafez* (Seattle: University of Washington Press 2004)

Jill Line, *Shakespeare and the Fire of Love* (London: Shepheard-Walwyn 2004)

Parvin Loloi, 'Translations of Hafiz in English', in *EIr*, XI, pp. 498–500

—— (with Glyn Pursglove), 'Basil Bunting's Persian Overdrafts: A Commentary', *Poetry Information*, 19 (1978), pp. 51–8; reprinted in C.F. Terrell (ed.) *Basil Bunting: Man and Poet* (Maine, CT: National Poetry Foundation 1980), pp. 343–53

——, 'Byron in Persian Costume', in *Swansea Review: a Journal of Criticism* (Byron's Bicentenary Issue), 5 (November 1988), pp. 19–40

——, 'Tennyson, FitzGerald, and Cowell: A Private Relationship with Public Consequences', in Sabine Coelsch-Foisner and Holger Klein (eds), *Private and Public Voices in Victorian Poetry* (Tübingen: Stauffenburg Verlag 2000)

——, *Hafiz, Master of Persian Poetry: A Critical Bibliography – English Translations Since the Eighteenth Century* (London: I.B.Tauris 2004)

——, 'Historical Background to English Translations of Hafiz', in *The Study of Persian Culture in the West (from the Seventeenth to Twentieth Century)*, collected papers of a conference held at the Hermitage Museum, St Petersburg, June 2004 (London: I.B.Tauris, forthcoming)

——, 'Aspects of Sa'di's Reception in Nineteenth Century America', in Mehdi Aminrazavi (ed.), *Sufism and American Literature* (Albany: SUNY 2010)

Paul Losensky, *Welcoming Fighani: Imitation and Poetic Individuality in the Safavid-Mughal Ghazal* (Costa Mesa, CA: Mazda 1998)

——, 'Kamāl of Khojand', in *Encyclopedia Iranica*, forthcoming

Abū'l-'Alā al-Ma'arrī, *Risālat al-ghufrān*, ed. 'Āsha 'Abd al-Raḥmān (Cairo: Dār al-ma'ārif 1963)

Duncan Black MacDonald, 'Emotional Religion in Islam as affected by Music and Singing, being a translation of the *Ihya 'Ulum ad-Din* of al-Ghazzali with Analysis, Annotation, and Appendices', *Journal of the Royal Asiatic Society of Great Britain and Ireland* (1901–2, part 1), pp. 195–252

——, 'Emotional Religion in Islam', *Journal of the Royal Asiatic Society of Great Britain and Ireland* (1901–2, part 2), pp. 705–48

——, 'Emotional Religion in Islam', *Journal of the Royal Asiatic Society of Great Britain and Ireland* (1903, part 3), pp. 1–28

Muḥammad Shīrīn Maghribī, *Dīwān-i Muḥammad Shīrīn Maghribī*, Persian text edited by Leonard Lewisohn with notes, introduction and index; Wisdom of Persia Series XLIII (Tehran: McGill Institute of Islamic Studies, Tehran Branch; London: SOAS 1993)

Ḥusayn-'Alī Mallāḥ, *Ḥāfiẓ va mūsīqī* (Tehran: Intishārāt-i Vizārat-i farhang va hunar 1351/1972)

B.F. Manz, *The Rise and Rule of Tamerlane* (Cambridge: Cambridge University Press 1989)

Markaz-i Taḥqīqāt-i fārsī Īrān va Pākistān, 'Gāmī-yi chand *Bā Kāravān-i Ḥulla*', *Dānish: Faṣl-nāma-yi rāyizanī-yi farhangī-yi jumhūrī-yi islāmī-yi Īrān. Islāmābād*, I/3 (Fall 1364/1985), pp. 71–144

Steven Marx, *Shakespeare and the Bible* (Oxford: Oxford University Press 2000)

Louis Massignon, *The Passion of al-Ḥallāj: Mystic and Martyr of Islam*, trans. Herbert Mason (Princeton: Princeton University Press 1982), 4 vols

—— *Essai sur les origines du lexique technique de la mystique musulmane* (Paris: J. Vrin 1954); English trans. by Benjamin Clark as *Essay on the Origins of the Technical Language of Islamic Mysticism* (Notre Dame, IN: University of Notre Dame Press 1997)

Rashīd al-Dīn Maybudī, *Kashf al-asrār wa 'uddat al-abrār*, ed. 'Alī Aṣghar Ḥikmat (Tehran: Intishārāt-i Dānishgāhī 1952–60), 10 vols

Fakhr al-Dīn Mazār'ī, *Mafhūm-i rindī dar shi'r-i Ḥāfiẓ*, trans. K. Maḥmūdzāda (Tehran: Intishārāt-i Kavīr 1373/1994)

Justin Huntly McCarthy, *Ghazals from the Divan of Hafiz* (London: David Nutt 1893)

Julie Meisami, 'Allegorical Techniques in the *Ghazals* of Hafez', *Edebiyat*, IV/1 (1979), pp. 1–41

——, 'The world's pleasance: Ḥāfiẓ's allegorical gardens', *Comparative Criticism*, V (1983), pp. 153–85
——, 'Allegorical Gardens in the Persian Poetic Traditions', *International Journal of Middle Eastern Studies*, XVII/2 (1985), pp. 229–60
——, *Medieval Persian Court Poetry* (Princeton, NJ: Princeton University Press 1987)
——, 'The Ghazal as Fiction: Implied Speakers and Implied Audience in Ḥāfiẓ's Ghazals', in Michael Glünz and C.C. Bürgel (eds), *Intoxication Earthly and Heavenly: Seven Studies on the Poet Hafiz of Shīrāz* (Bern: Peter Lang 1991), pp. 89–103
——, 'Ḥāfiẓ in English: Translation and Authority', *Edebiyāt*, VI (N.S. 1995), pp. 55–79
S. Meskoob, *Iranian Nationality and the Persian Language 900–1900: The Roles of Court, Religion and Sufism in Persian Prose Writing*, translated from Persian by Michael Hillmann (Washington, DC: Mage 1992)
John Milton, *Complete Shorter Poems*, ed. John Carey (London: Longman 1981)
Mīrkhwand (Muḥammad b. Khāvandshāh Balkhī), *Rawḍat al-ṣafā*, ed. 'Abbās Zaryāb (Tehran: Intishārāt-i 'Ilmī 1375//1996), 2 vols
Heshmat Moayyad and Franklin Lewis, *The Colossal Elephant and His Spiritual Feats, Shaykh Ahmad-e Jām: The Life and Legend of a Popular Sufi Saint of 12th Century Iran* (Costa Mesa, CA: Mazda 2004)
Muḥammad Mu'īn, *Ḥāfiẓ-i shīrīn-sukhan* (Tehran: Intishārāt-i Mu'īn 1370/1991), 2 vols
Ḥusayn 'Alī Mumtaḥan, 'Sukhanī chand dar mājarā-yi zindigī-yi Shāh Manṣūr Muẓaffarī: mamdūḥ-i Khwāja Ḥāfiẓ Shīrāzī', in Manṣūr Rastigār (ed.), *Maqālātī dar-bāra-i zindagī va shi'r-i Ḥāfiẓ* (Shīrāz: Intishārāt-i Dānishgāh-i Pahlavī 1350/1971), pp. 431–64
Muḥammad Ibn Munawwar, *Asrār at-tawḥīd fī maqāmāt Shaykh Abū Sa'īd*, ed. M.R. Shafī'ī-Kadkanī (Tehran: Āgāh 1366/1987), 2 vols
Manūchihr Murtaḍawī, *Maktab-i Ḥāfiẓ: Muqaddama bar Ḥāfiẓ-shināsī* (Tehran: Intishārāt-i Sitūda 1384/2005, 4th edn)
Nāgawrī [wrongly attributed], *Lavā'iḥ*, ed. R. Farmanish (Tehran: Manūchihrī, n.d.)
S.H. Nasr, 'Spiritual Chivalry', in S.H. Nasr (ed.), *Islamic Spirituality*, II: *Manifestations* (New York: Crossroad 1991), pp. 304–15
R.A. Nicholson, *The Mystics of Islam* (London: Arkana 1989)
F. Nietzsche, *The Philosophy of Nietzsche* (New York: Modern Library, Random House 1942)
Mihrdād Nīknām, *Kitāb-shināsī-yi Ḥāfiẓ* (Shīrāz: Markaz-i Ḥāfiẓ-shināsī 1381/2002)
Mu'tamid Nishāṭ-i Iṣfahānī, *Dīvān-i Nishāṭ-i Iṣfahānī*, ed. Ḥusayn Nakh'ī (Tehran: Intishārāt-i Sharq 1362/1983)
Niẓāmī Ganjavī, *Makhzan al-asrār*, ed. W. Dastgirdī (Tehran: Intishārāt-i Armaghān, 1313/1934; 2nd edn, Intishārāt-i 'Ilmī, 1363/1984)
——, *Kulliyāt-i Ḥakīm Niẓāmī Ganjavī*, ed. Waḥīd Dastgirdī (Tehran: Intishārāt-i Bihzād 1378/1999)
Nizārī Quhistānī, *Dīvān-i Ḥakīm Nizārī Quhistānī*, ed. 'Alī Riḍā Mujtahidzāda, Introduction by Maẓāhir Muṣaffā (Tehran: Intishārāt-i 'Ilmī 1371/1992)

James A. Notopoulos, *The Platonism of Shelley: A Study of Platonism and the Poetic Mind* (Durham, NC: Duke University Press 1949)
Javad Nurbakhsh, *Traditions of the Prophet.* vol. I, trans. Leonard Lewisohn (New York: KNP 1981)
——, *Jesus in the Eyes of the Sufis*, trans. Leonard Lewisohn and Terry Graham (London: KNP 1983)
——, *Spiritual Poverty in Sufism*, trans. Leonard Lewisohn (London: KNP 1984)
——, *Sufi Symbolism*, vol. 1: *The Esoteric Symbolism of the Parts of the Beloved's Body*, trans. Leonard Lewisohn et al. (London: KNP 1984)
——, *Sufi Symbolism*, vols. 2–15, trans. T. Graham et al. (London and New York: KNP 1984–2004)
Paul Nywia, *Exégèse coranique et langage mystique* (Beirut: Dar El-Machreq 1970)
Richard Onians, *The Origins of European Thought* (Cambridge: Cambridge University Press 1951)
Azize Özgüven, 'Two Mystic Poets: Yunus Emre and William Blake', in A. Turgut Kut and Günay Kut (eds), *In Memoriam Abdülbakı Gölpinarli, Journal of Turkish Studies*, 20 (1996), pp. 234–47
Sataya S. Pachori, 'Shelley's "Indian Serenade": Hafiz and Sir William Jones', in *Osmania Journal of English Studies*, XI/1 (1974–5), pp. 10–26
A. Papadopoulo, *Islam and Muslim Art* (New York: Harry N. Abrams 1979)
Firoozeh Papan-Matin, 'Love: Nima's Dialogue with Hafez', in Ahmad Karimi-Hakkak and Kamran Talattof (eds), *Essays on Nima Yushij* (Leiden: E.J. Brill 2004), pp. 173–92
John Payne, *Poems of Hafiz of Shīrāz* (London: Printed for the Villon Society 1901)
Octavio Paz, *The Double Flame: Love and Eroticism* (Orlando, FL: Harcourt 1995)
Ch. Pellat, 'Kināya', *EI*[2], V, pp. 116–18
V. De Sola Pinto, 'Sir William Jones and English Literature', *Bulletin of the School of Oriental and African Studies*, XI, 1946, pp. 686–97
Reza Pourjavady, 'Kitāb-shināsī-yi āthār-i Jalāl al-Dīn Davānī', *Ma'ārif*, XV/1–2 (1377/1998), pp. 81–139
Marcel Proust, *Du côté de chez Swann* (Paris: Gallimard; Bibliothètheque de la Pléiade 1954)
Naṣru'llāh Purjavādī, *Sulṭān-i ṭarīqat: Sawāniḥ-i zindigī u sharḥ-i athār-i Khʷāja Aḥmad Ghazālī* (Tehran; Instishārāt-i Āgāh, 1358/1979)
——, 'Ḥusn va malāḥat: baḥthī dar zībā'ī-shināsī-yi Ḥāfiẓ', in Naṣru'llāh Purjavādī (ed.), *Darbāra-i Ḥāfiẓ: bar-guzīda-i maqālahā-yi Nashr-i Dānish (2)* (Tehran: Nashr-i Markaz-i Dānishgāhī 1365/1986), pp. 21–38
——, 'Risāla'ī dar bāra-yi 'ishq', in *Ma'ārif*, VI/3 (March 1990), pp. 105–28
——, "Aḥd-i alast: 'aqīda-yi Abū Ḥāmid Ghazālī va jāygāh-i tārīkhī-yi ān', *Ma'ārif*, VII/2 (November 1990), pp. 3–48
——, "Ishq-i azalī va bāda-yi alast', *Nashr-i dānish*, XII/3 (1370/1991), pp. 26–31
——, 'Bāda-yi 'ishq' *1-5*, *Nashr-i dānish*, XI/6 (1370/1991), pp. 4–13; XII/1 (1370/1991), pp. 4–18; XII/2 (1370/1991), pp. 6–15; XII/3 (1371/1991), pp. 26–32; XII/4 (1371/1992), pp. 22–30

——, *Bū-yi jān: maqālahā-yi darbāra-yi sh'ir-i 'irfānī-yi fārsī* (Tehran: Intishārāt-i Markaz-i Dānishgāhī 1372/1993)

——, *Ru'yat-i māh dar āsimān: barrasī-yi tārīkhī-yi mas'alih-i liqā'Allāh dar kalām va taṣawwuf* (Tehran: Nashr-i Dānishgāhī 1375/1996)

——, 'Pīr-i gulrang', *Nashr-i dānish*, XVI/4 (1378/1999), pp. 43–54

Taqī Pūrnāmdāriyān, *Ramz va dāstānhā-yi ramzī dar adab-i fārsi* (Tehran: Shirkat-i Intishārāt-i 'Ilmi va Farhangi 1363/1984)

——, *Gumshuda-yi lab-i daryā: Tā'ammulī dar ma'nā va ṣūrat-i sh'ir-i Ḥāfiẓ* (Tehran: Intishārāt-i Sukhan 1382/2003)

'Alī-Riḍā Dhakāvatī Qarāguzlū, 'Ḥāfiẓ dar miyān-i haftād u dū millat', *Taḥqīqāt-i Islāmī*, 3/1&2 (1367/1988), pp. 61–74

Shāh Qāsim-i Anvār, *Kulliyāt-i Qāsim-i Anvār*, ed. Sa'īd Nafīsī (Tehran: Kitābkhāna-yi Sanā'ī 1337/1958)

Dāwūd ibn Maḥmūd Qayṣarī, *Sharḥ Ṭā'iyyat Ibn al-Fāriḍ al-kubrā*, ed. Aḥmad Ibn Fāriḍ Ibn Aḥmad Mazīdī (Beirut: Dār al-Kutub al-'Ilmiyyah, 2004)

'Abū'l-Qāsim al-Qushayrī, *Al-risāla fī 'ilm al-taṣawwuf* (Cairo: 1912)

——, *al-Risāla al-Qushayriyya* (Cairo: 1966), 2 vols

——, *Tarjama-i Risāla-yi Qushayrī*, ed. Badī' al-Zamān Furūzānfār (Tehran: Intishārāt-i 'Ilmī u farhangī 1379/2000, 7th edn), Persian translation of the *Risāla* by Abū 'Alī Ḥasan ibn Aḥmad al-'Uthmānī

——, *The Principles of Sufism by al-Qushayri*, trans. B.R. Von Schlegell (Berkeley, CA: Mizan Press 1990)

Abū'l-Qāsim Rādfar, *Ḥāfiẓ-pazhūhān va Ḥāfiẓ-pazhūhī* (Tehran: Nashr-i Gustarda 1368/1989)

Paul Radin, *The Trickster: A Study in American Indian Mythology* (New York: Schocken Books 1972)

Daud Rahbar, *God of Justice: A Study in the Ethical Doctrine of the Qur'an* (Leiden: E.J. Brill 1960)

Manṣūr Rastigār (ed.), *Maqālātī dar-bāra-i zindagī va shi'r-i Ḥāfiẓ* (Shīrāz: Intishārāt-i Dānishgāh-i Pahlavī 1350/1971)

Akhtar Rasūlī, 'Ṣabā', in Ḥasan Anūsha (ed.), *Dānish-nāma-yi adab-i Fārsī. 2: Farhang-nāma-yi adabī-yi fārsī* (Tehran, 1376/1997), pp. 915–16

Najm al-Dīn Rāzī, *Mirṣād al-'ibād*, trans. Hamid Algar as *The Path of God's Bondsmen from Origin to Return* (Delmar, NY: Caravan Books 1982)

——, *Mirṣād al-'ibād*, ed. Muḥammad Amīn Riyāḥī (Tehran: Intishārāt-i 'Ilmī u farhangī 1374/1995)

Shams al-Dīn Muḥammad, b. Qays al-Rāzī, *Al-Mu'jam fī ma'āyir ash'ār al-'ajam*, ed. Sīrūs Shamīsā (Tehran: Intishārāt-i Firdaws 1373/1994)

R.M. Rehder, 'The Unity of the Ghazals of Hafiz', *Der Islam*, 51 (1974), pp. 55–96

John Renard, *Seven Doors to Islam: Spirituality and the Religious Life of Muslims* (Berkeley: University of California Press 1996)

Lloyd Ridgeon, *Sufi Castigator: Ahmad Kasravi and the Iranian Mystical Tradition* (London: Routledge 2006)

Martín de Riquer, 'Las Albas provenzales. Introducción, textos y versión castellana', Anexo al número XII de *Entregas de poesía* (Barcelona 1944)

Hellmut Ritter, *The Ocean of the Soul: Men, the World and God in the Stories of Farīd al-Dīn 'Aṭṭār*, trans. John O'Kane (Leiden: E.J. Brill 2003)

Muḥammad Amīn Riyāḥī, *Gulgasht dar shi'r va andīsha-yi Ḥāfiẓ* (Tehran: Intishārāt-i 'Ilmī 1374/1995)

Neal Robinson, *The Sayings of Muḥammad* (Hopewell, NJ: Ecco Press 1991)

Samuel Robinson, *A Century of Ghazals, or a Hundred Odes, Selected and Translated from the Diwan of Hafiz* (London: Williams & Worgate 1875)

H. Roemer, 'The Jalayirids, Muzaffarids and Sarbadārs', in P. Jackson and L. Lockhart (eds), *The Cambridge History of Iran*, VI: *The Timurid and Safavid Periods* (Cambridge: Cambridge University Press 1986), pp. 1–41

Alexander Rogers, *Persian Anthology; being translations from the Gulistan of Sadi, the Rubaiyyat of Hafiz and the Anwar-i-Suheili* (London: Bevington & Co. 1889)

Abū 'Abdu'llāh Ja'far Rūdakī, *Muḥīt-i zindigī va aḥwāl u ash'ār-i Rūdakī*, ed. Sa'īd Nafīsī (Tehran: Amīr Kabīr 1381/2002)

Jalāl al-Dīn Rūmī, *The Mathnawí of Jalálu'ddín Rúmí*, trans. and ed. R.A. Nicholson (London: E.J.W. Gibb Memorial Trust 1924–40; Gibb Memorial Series N.S.), 8 vols

——, *Kitāb-i Fihi mā fihi*, ed. Badī' al-Zamān Furūzānfar (Tehran: Amīr Kabīr 1348/1969)

——, *Kulliyyāt-i Shams ya Dīvān-i kabīr*, ed. B. Furūzānfar (Tehran: Amīr Kabīr 1355/1976), 9 vols

——, *Mathnawī-yi ma'nawī*, ed. R.A. Nicholson (reprint: Tehran: Amir Kabir 1984, bi-sa'-yi Nasru'llāh Pūrjavādī), 4 vols (with index)

——, *The Discourses of Rumi*, trans. A.J. Arberry (Richmond: Curzon Press 1993)

——, Alan Williams, *Rumi, Spiritual Verses: the First Book of the Masnavi-ye Ma'navi* (London: Penguin Books 2006)

Colonel F.M. Rundall, *Selections from the Rubaiyât & Odes of Hafiz* (London: J.M. Watkins 1920)

Rūzbihān al-Baqlī al-Shīrāzī, *Le Jasmin des fidèles d'amour ('Abhar al-'āshiqīn)*, ed. H. Corbin and M. Mu'īn (Tehran: Institut Français d'Iranologie de Téhéran; Bibliothéque Iranienne, 8: 1958)

——, *Sharḥ-i shaṭḥīyyāt*, ed. H. Corbin (Tehran: Departement d'iranologie de l'Institut Franco-iranien; Bibliothéque Iranienne 12: 1966)

——, *Kitāb mashrab al-arwāḥ*, edited by N.M. Hoca (Istanbul: Maṭba'at Kulliyyāt al-Ādāb, 1973)

——, *Tafsīr 'arā'is al-bayān* (Lucknow: Nawal Kishör, 1898)

Jan Rypka, 'Poets & Prose Writers of the Late Saljuq and Mongol Periods', in J.A. Boyle (ed.), *The Cambridge History of Iran*, V: *The Saljuq and Mongol Periods* (Cambridge: Cambridge University Press 1968), pp. 550–625

——, *A History of Iranian Literature* (Dordrecht: D. Reidel Publishing Co. 1968)

Sa'dī, *Gulistān-i Sa'dī*, ed. Khalīl Khaṭīb Rahbar (Tehran: Intishārāt-i Ṣafī 'Alī Shāh 1347/1968)

——, *Kulliyyāt-i Sa'dī*, ed. Muḥammad 'Alī Furūghī (Tehran: Amīr Kabīr 1363/1984)

——, *Būstān-i Sa'dī*, ed. Nūru'llāh Īzadparast (Tehran: Dānish 1368/1989)

——, *Būstān-i Sa'dī*, ed. Ghulām-Ḥusayn Yūsufī (Tehran: Intishārāt-i Khwārazmī 1369/1990)

Dhabīḥu'llāh Ṣafā, *Tārīkh-i Adabiyāt-i Īrān* (Tehran: Intishārāt-i Firdaws 1373/1994, 13th edn), 8 vols

Javād Majdzāda Ṣahbā, 'Sukhanī chand dar bāb-i aḥwāl va ash'ār-i Ḥāfiẓ', *Ḥāfiẓ-shināsī*, VIII (1367/1988), pp. 163–240; part 2 continued in *Ḥāfiẓ-shināsī*, IX (1367/1988), pp. 178–238

'Abd al-'Aẓīm Ṣā'idī, *Bā Ḥāfiẓ tā kahkishān-i 'irfān va akhlāq* (Shīrāz: Intishārāt-i Navīd 1369/1990, 3rd edn)

George Saintsbury, *The Flourishing of Romance and the Rise of Chivalry*, Periods of European Literature, II (New York: C. Scribners Sons 1897)

Ja'far Sajjādī, *Farhang-i lughāt wa iṣṭilāḥāt wa ta'bīrāt-i 'irfānī* (Tehran: Kitābkhāna-yi Ṭāhūrī 1362/1983)

——, *Farhang-i 'ulūm-i 'aqlī* (Tehran: Intishārāt-i Anjuman-i Ḥikmatu Falsafi-yi Īrān 1361/1982)

Salmān Sāvajī, *Dīvān-i Salmān Sāvajī*, ed. Manṣūr Mushfiq (Tehran: Intishārāt-i Ṣafī 'Alī Shāh 1367/1988)

Kamāl al-Dīn 'Abd al-Razzāq Samarqandī, *Maṭla'-i sa'dayn va majma'-i baḥrayn*, ed. 'Abd al-Ḥusayn Navā'ī (Tehran: Kitābkhāna-yi Ṭāhūrī 1353/1974)

Nizāmī-i 'Arūḍī Samarqandī, *Chahār Maqāla*, trans. E.G. Browne, *Chahār Maqāla* (E.J.W. Gibb Memorial Series, London: Luzac & Co. 1921; reprinted Cambridge University Press 1978)

Sanā'ī Ghaznavī, *Dīvān-i Ḥakīm Abū'l-Majd Majdūd b. Ādam Sanā'ī Ghaznavī*, ed. Mudarris Raḍavī (Tehran: Intishārāt-i Kitābkhāna Sanā'ī 1362/1983)

Suhaylā Sārimī, *Muṣṭalahāt-i 'irfānī wa mafāhīm-i bar-jasta dar zabān-i 'Aṭṭār* (Tehran: Institute for Humanities and Cultural Research 1373/1994)

M. Sarraf (ed.), *Rasa'il-i javamardan*, French introduction and synopsis by H. Corbin (Tehran: French–Iran Institute 1973)

Jalāl Sattārī, *'Ishq-i ṣūfiyāna* (Tehran: Nashr-i Markaz 1374/1995)

Elaine Scarry, *On Beauty and Being Just* (Princeton, NJ: Princeton University Press 1999)

J. Schimdt, 'Ḥāfiẓ and Other Persian Authors in Ottoman Bibliomancy: The Extraordinary Case of Kefevī Hüseyn Efendi's *Rāznāme* (Late Sixteenth Century)', *Persica*, 21 (2006–7), pp. 63–74

Annemarie Schimmel, 'The Ornament of the Saints: The Religious Situation in Iran in Pre-Safavid Times', *Iranian Studies*, VII, nos 1–2 (1974), pp. 88–111

——, *Mystical Dimensions of Islam* (Chapel Hill: University of North Carolina Press 1975)

——, *As Through A Veil: Mystical Poetry in Islam* (New York: Columbia University Press 1982)

——, 'Ḥāfiẓ and His Contemporaries', in Peter Jackson and L. Lockhart (eds), *The Cambridge History of Iran*, vol. 6: *The Timurid and Safavid Periods* (Cambridge: Cambridge University Press 1986), VI, pp. 929–47

——, 'The Genius of Shīrāz: Sa'di and Hafez', in E. Yarshater (ed.), *Persian Literature* (New York: Persian Heritage Foundation, 1988) pp. 214–48

——, *A Two-Colored Brocade: The Imagery of Persian Poetry* (Chapel Hill and London: University of North Carolina Press 1992)

——, 'Reason and Mystical Experience in Islam', in Farhad Daftary (ed.), *Intellectual Traditions in Islam* (London: I.B.Tauris & the Institute of Ismaili Studies 2000), pp. 130–45

——, *The Poet's Geography* (London: Al-Furqān Islamic Heritage Foundation 2000)

Eric Schroeder, 'Verse Translation and Hafiz', *Journal of Near Eastern Studies*, VII/4 (1948), pp. 209–21

Raymond Schwab, *The Oriental Renaissance: Europe's Discovery of India and The East*, trans. Gene Patterson-Black and Victor Reinking (New York: Columbia University Press 1984)

Ali Asghar Seyed-Gohrab, *Layli and Majnun: Love, Madness and Mystic Longing in Nizami's Epic Romance* (Leiden: E.J. Brill 2003)

Muḥammad Riḍā Shafī'ī-Kadkanī, 'Ḥāfiẓ va Bīdil dar Muḥīt-i adabī-yi Māvarā'nahr dar qarn-i nūzdahum', *Ḥāfiẓ-shināsī*, ed. Sa'īd Niyāz Kirmānī (Tehran: Intishārāt-i Pāzhang 1367/1988), no. 8, pp. 25–46

——, 'Dar tarjuma-nāpadhīrī-yi shi'r (On the Untranslatability of [Ḥāfiẓ's] Poetry)', in Valī'ullāh Darūdiyān (ed.), *Īn Kimiyā-yi hastī: Majmū'a-i maqālahā va yād-dāshthā-yi Ustād Duktar Muḥammad Riḍā Shafī'ī-Kadkanī* (Tehran: Intishārāt-i Āyidīn 1385/2006), pp. 125–33

——, *Zamīna-i ijtamā'ī-yi shi'r-i fārsī* (Tehran: Nashr-i Aktarān 1386/2007)

Muḥammad Shafī'ī, 'Mubāriza-i Ḥāfiẓ bā riyā'', in Manṣūr Rastigār (ed.), *Maqālātī dar-bāra-i zindagī va shi'r-i Ḥāfiẓ* (Shīrāz: Intishārāt-i Dānishgāh-i Pahlavī 1350/1971), pp. 330–41

Shāh Ni'matullāh Walī, *Risālahā-yi Ḥaḍrat-i Sayyid Nūr al-Dīn Shāh Ni'matu'llāh Valī*, ed. Javād Nūrbakhsh (Tehran: Intishārāt-i Khāniqāh-i Ni'matullāhī 2535 Shāhanshāhī/1976), 4 vols

——, *Kulliyyāt-i ash'ār-i Shāh Ni'matu'llāh Valī*, ed. Javad Nurbakhsh (Tehran: Intishārāt-i Khāniqāh-i Ni'matullāhī 1361/1982)

Maḥmūd Shabistarī, *Majmū'a-i āthār-i Shaykh Maḥmūd Shabistarī*, ed. Ṣamad Muwaḥḥid (Tehran: Kitābkhāna-i Ṭahūrī 1986)

——, *Gulshan-i rāz*, in Ṣamad Muwaḥḥid (ed.), *Majmū'a-i āthār-i Shaykh Maḥmūd Shabistarī* (Tehran: Kitābkhāna-i Ṭahūrī 1365/1986)

Charlotte el-Shabrawy, 'German Ghazals: An Experiment in Cross-Cultural Literary Synthesis', *Alif: Journal of Comparative Poetics*, The Self and the Other, 3 (spring 1983), pp. 56–79

Riḍāzāda Shafaq, *Tārīkh-i adabīyāt-i Īrān* (Tehran 1321/1942)

Sīrūs Shamīsā, *Shāhid-bāzī dar adabiyāt-i fārsī* (Tehran: Firdaws 1381/2002)
Marianne Shapiro, 'The Figure of the Watchman in the Medieval Alba', *Modern Language Notes* 91/4 (May 1976), pp. 607–39
Daryoush Shayegan, 'The Visionary Topography of Hafiz', trans. Peter Russell, *Temenos: A Review Devoted to the Arts of the Imagination*, VI (1985), pp. 207–32
Percy Bysshe Shelley, *The Complete Poetical Works*, ed. Thomas Hutchinson (London: Oxford University Press 1960)
——, *Complete Poems of Shelley* (London: Softback Preview 1993)
——, *The Letters*, ed. F.L. Jones (Oxford: Clarendon Press 1964), 2 vols
——, *The Complete Works*, ed. Walter E. Peck (New York: Gordon Press 1965), 10 vols
'Isā b. Junayd Shīrāzī, *Shadd al-izār 'an zawwār al-mazār*, ed. Muḥammad Qazwīnī, introduction by Abbās Iqbāl (Tehran, 1328/1949)
——, *Tadhkira-yi Hazār-mazār: tarjuma-yi Shadd al-izār*, ed. Nūrānī Viṣāl (Shīrāz: Intishārāt-i Kitābkhāna-yi Aḥmadī 1364/1985)
Ma'ṣūm 'Alī Shāh Shirāzī, *Ṭarā'iq al-ḥaqā'iq*, ed. M.J. Maḥjūb (Tehran: Kitābkhāna-yi Barānī 1345/1966), 3 vols
Shujā-yi Shīrāzī, *Anīs al-nās*, ed. Īraj Afshar (Tehran: BTNK 1350/1971)
M. Siddīqīyān and A. Mīr'ābidīnī, *Farhang-i vāzhih-namā-yi Ḥāfiẓ* (Tehran: Intishārāt-i Amīr Kabīr, 1366/1987)
Sa'īdī Sīrjānī, *Ay kūta-āstīnān* (Tehran: n.p. 1364/1985)
Ḥusayn ibn Muḥammad ibn Maḥmūd-i Sīstānī, *Iḥyā al-mulūk: shāmil-i tārīkh-i Sīstān az advār-i bāstānī tā sāl-i hizār va bīst va hasht-i hijrī qamarī*, ed. Manūchihr Sutūda (Tehran: Bungāh-i Tarjuma va Nashr-i Kitāb, 1966)
Al-Siyūtī, *Jāmi' al-ṣaghīr* (Cairo: Dār al-Kitub al-'Ilmiyya 1373/1953)
Wojciech Skalmowski, 'The Meaning of the Persian Ghazal', *Orientalia Lovaniensia Periodica*, XVIII (1987), pp. 141–62
——, 'Le *Qalandar* chez Ḥāfeẓ', in C. Balay, C. Kappler and Z. Vesel (eds), *Pand-o Sokhan: Mélanges offerts à Charles-Henri de Fouchécour* (Tehran: Institut Français de Recherche en Iran 1995), pp. 275–86
Margaret Smith, *Al-Ghazālī: The Mystic* (London: Luzac & Co. 1944)
Paul Smith, *Divan of Hafiz* (Melbourne: New Humanity Books 1983), 2 vols
Akbar Sobūt, 'Pīr-i Gol-rang', *Encyclopedia of the World of Islam*, V, p. 381
Paul Sprachman, *Suppressed Persian: An Anthology of Forbidden Literature* (Costa Mesa, CA: Mazda 1995)
Jaroslav Stetkevych, *The Zephyrs of Najd: The Poetics of Nostalgia in the Classical Arabic Nasīb* (Chicago: University of Chicago Press 1993)
Suzanne P. Stetkevych, 'Structuralist Interpretations of Pre-Islamic Poetry: Critique and New Directions', *Journal of Near Eastern Studies* 42/2 (1983), pp. 85–107
Rory Stewart, *The Places in Between* (London: Picador 2004)
Will Stockland, 'The *Kitab-i Samak 'Ayyar*', *Persica*, XV (1993–5), pp. 143–82
Muḥammad Sūdī Busnawī (of Bosnia), *Sharḥ-i Sūdī bar Dīvān-i Ḥāfiẓ*, trans. 'Iṣmat Satārzāda (Tehran: Intishārāt-i Anzalī, 1362/1983, 4th edn)

Sara Sviri, 'Ḥakīm Tirmidhī and the *Malāmatī* Movement in Early Sufism', in L. Lewisohn (ed.), *The Heritage of Sufism*, I: *Classical Persian Sufism: from Its Origins to Rumi* (Oxford: Oneworld 1999), pp. 583–613

Humān-i Tabrīzī, *Dīwān-i Humān Tabrīzī*, ed. R. Aywaḍī (Tabriz: 1970)

al-Tahānawī, *Kashshāf iṣṭilāḥāt al-funūn (A Dictionary of the Technical Terms Used in the Sciences of the Musalmans)*, eds M. Wajih, Abd al-Haqq, G. Kadir and Nassau Lees (Calcutta: Asiatic Society of Bengal 1862), 2 vols

'Alī ibn Abī Ṭalib, *Nahj al-Balāgha*, ed. 'Azīzullāh al-'Utārdī (Tehran: Nahj al-Balāgha Foundation, 1372/1993); trans. Sayed Ali Reza, *Peak of Eloquence* (New York: Tahrike Tarsile Qur'ān 1996)

Garcin de Tassy, *Rhetorique et prosodie des langues de l'Orient musulman* (Paris: Maisonneuve 1873)

John Taylor, 'Ja'far al-Ṣādiq: Spiritual Forebear of the Ṣūfīs', *Islamic Culture*, XL/1 (1966), pp. 97–113

Alfred Lord Tennyson, *The Poems of Tennyson*, ed. Christopher Ricks (London: Longmans 1969)

Hallam Tennyson, *Alfred Lord Tennyson, a Memoir* (London: Macmillan 1897), 2 vols

Finn Thiesen, *A Manual of Classical Persian Prosody* (Wiesbaden: Otto Harrassowitz 1982)

——, 'Pseudo-Ḥāfez: A Reading of Wilberforce Clarke's Rendering of *Divān-i Ḥāfeẓ*', *Orientalia Suecana*, LI–LII (2002–3), pp. 437–59

J.S. Trimingham, *The Sufi Orders in Islam* (Oxford: Oxford University Press 1973)

Adīb Ṭūsī, 'Muqāyisa bayn-i shi'r-i Sa'dī va Ḥāfiẓ', in Manṣūr Rastigār (ed.), *Maqālātī dar-bāra-i zindagī va shi'r-i Ḥāfiẓ* (Shīrāz: Intishārāt-i Dānishgāh-i Pahlavī 1350/1971), pp. 40–60

Abū Naṣr al-Sarrāj al-Ṭūsī, *Kitāb al-luma' fi'l-taṣawwuf*, ed. R.A. Nicholson. E.J.W. Gibb Memorial Series, 22 (London: Luzac & Company Ltd 1914; reprint edition: 1963)

Maḥmūd ibn 'Uthmān, *Miftāḥ al-hidāya wa miṣbāḥ al-'ināya: Sīrat-nāma-i Shaykh Amīn al-Dīn Muḥammad Balyānī*, ed. 'Imād al-Dīn Shaykh al-Ḥukamā'ī (Tehran: Intishārāt-i Rawzana 1376/1997)

Paul Valéry, *Cahiers*, ed. Judith Robinson (Paris: Gallimard 1973–4), 2 vols

Josef Van Ess, 'Skepticism in Islamic Religious Thought', *Al-Abḥāth*, 21/1 (1968), pp. 1–18

John Vyvyan, *Shakespeare and the Rose of Love: A Study of the Early Plays in Relation to the Medieval Philosophy of Love* (New York: Barnes & Noble 1960)

Muḥammad Isa Waley, 'Contemplative Disciplines in Early Persian Sufism', *The Heritage of Sufism*, II: *Classical Persian Sufism: from its Origins to Rūmī*, ed. Leonard Lewisohn (Oxford: Oneworld 1999), pp. 497–548

——, 'Didactic Style and Self-Criticism in 'Aṭṭār', in Leonard Lewisohn and Christopher Shackle (eds), *'Attār and the Persian Sufi Tradition: The Art of Spiritual Flight* (London and New York: I.B.Tauris and the Institute of Ismaili Studies 2006), pp. 215–40

S.C. Welch, *Wonders of the Age: Masterpieces of Early Safavid Painting* (Cambridge, MA: Fogg Art Museum, Harvard University 1979)

Richard White, *Love's Philosophy* (New York: Rowman & Littlefield 2001)

G.M Wickens, 'Ḥāfiẓ', *EI*[2], III, pp. 55–7

——, 'An Analysis of Primary and Secondary Significations in the Third *Ghazal* of Ḥāfiẓ', *Bulletin of the School of Oriental and African Studies*, XIV/3 (1952), pp. 627–38

——, 'The Frozen Periphery of Allusion in Classical Persian Literature', *Literature East and West*, XVIII/2–4 (1974), pp. 171–90

H. Wilberforce Clarke (trans.), *The Dīvān ... Hāfiz-i-Shīrāzī* (Calcutta: Government of India Central Printing Office 1891), 2 vols. Reprinted as *Dīvān-i-Hāfiz* (Bethesda, MD: Ibex Publishers 1998), 1 vol.

Peter Wilson, 'The Witness Game: Imaginal Yoga & Sacred Pedophilia in Persian Sufism', in *Scandal: Essays in Islamic Heresy* (New York: Autonomedia 1988), pp. 93–121

B. Woledge, 'Old Provençal and Old French', in A. Hatto (ed.), *Eos: An Inquiry into the Theme of Lovers' Meetings and Partings at Dawn in Poetry* (London, The Hague and Paris: Mouton 1965), pp. 344–89

Ehsan Yarshater, 'Hafez, I. An Overview', *EIr*, XI, pp. 461–5

Iḥsān Yārshāṭir [=Ehsan Yarshater], *Shi'r-i fārsī dar 'ahd-i Shāhrukh: āghāz-i inkhiṭāṭ dar shi'r-i fārsī* (Tehran: Intishārāt-i Dānishgāh 1334/1954)

Rashīd Yāsimī, 'Salmān va Ḥāfiẓ', in *Maqālahā va risālaha*, ed. Īrāj Afshār (Tehran: Bunyād-Maḥmūd Afshār 1373/1994), pp. 599–602

——, *Sharḥ-i aḥwāl-i Salmān Sāvajī* (Tehran: Kitābkhāna-yi Mashriq, n.d.)

Frances Yates, *The Occult Philosophy in the Elizabethan Age* (London: RKP 1979)

Sayyid Yaḥyā Yathribī, *Āb-i ṭarabnāk: taḥlīl-i mawḍū'ī-yi Dīvān-i Ḥāfiẓ* (Tehran: Intishārāt-i Āftāb 1381/2002)

John Yohannan, 'The Persian Poet Hafiz in England and America', PhD dissertation, Columbia University, 1939

——, *Persian Poetry in England and America: A 200 Year History* (New York: Caravan Books 1977)

Robert Zaehner, *Zurvan: a Zoroastrian Dilemma* (Oxford: Oxford University Press 1955)

'Ubayd Zākānī, *'Obeyd-e Zakani: The Ethics of Aristocrats and Other Satirical Works*, trans. Hasan Javadi (Piedmont, CA: Jahan Book Co. 1985)

——, *Kulliyāt-i 'Ubayd Zākānī*, ed. Muḥammad Ja'far Maḥjūb (New York: Bibliotheca Persica Press 1999)

Muḥammad Zangī, *Zangī-nāma*, ed. I. Afshār (Tehran: Khāja, 1372/1993)

'Abd al-Ḥusayn Zarrīnkūb, *Az kūcha-i rindān: dar-bāra-i zindagī va andīsha-i Ḥāfiẓ* (Tehran: Intishārāt-i Amīr Kabīr 2536/1977)

—— *Justujū'ī dar taṣawwuf-i Irān* (Tehran: Amīr Kabīr 1357/1978)

'Abbās Zaryāb-khū'ī, *Ā'yina-yi jām* (Tehran: Intishārāt-i 'Ilmī 1368/1989)

Index of Proper Names, Places, Works and Themes

'Abdu'llāh, Qiwām al-Dīn 16, 19, 20
'Abbādī, Quṭb al-Dīn al- 45
Abbasids 146, 209, 253
Abraham 100
Abū Bakr, Caliph 94, 190
Abū Ḥanīfa 77
Abū Isḥāq Īnjū 4–5, 10, 20–23, 27, 61–62, 164
Abū Sa'īd ibn Abī'l-Khayr 161, 180
Active Intellect 202
Adam xiii, 41, 51, 79, 97–98, 102, 110, 112, 115–118, 126, 128, 132, 137, 139, 180–182, 186, 198–199, 202, 243
affliction 8, 42, 72, 100, 113, 172
Aflākī 183, 195
Afrāsiyāb 63, 101
Alba 251, 252–266, 268, 273, 276, 278
Alexander the Great 30
'Alī ibn Abī Ṭālib 4, 72, 175, 179, 180, 190, 210
Al-Nāṣir Bi'llāh, Caliph 146
Al-Walīd II, Caliph 254, 258, 277
Amīrī Fīrūzkūhī 15
Amor 7, 9, 28, 40, 53, 54, 78, 79, 81, 91, 102, 160
see also *eros; 'ishq*
Āmulī, Ḥaydar 144, 194
Andalusia 80, 253, 254
angels 51, 79, 89, 114–118, 125, 127, 132, 149, 174, 181, 198, 199, 201, 209, 217, 218, 223, 228, 229, 237, 272, 273, 275
annihilation 45, 54, 55, 109, 113, 124, 130, 131, 138, 147, 172, 201, 206, 221
Anṣārī, 'Abdu'llāh xxvi, 44, 73, 166, 169, 175, 180, 190, 191, 194, 195
anti-clericalism 159, 164, 189
antinomianism 93, 94, 187, 196
apophatic theology 160
Araxes River 263
Arberry, A.J. 3, 55, 65, 139, 280, 292
ascetic 4, 22, 31, 32, 34, 42, 49, 52, 54, 95, 96, 98, 100, 107, 159–165, 167–182, 185, 189, 190–195, 240–244, 246
see also *zāhid*
ascetics 3, 4, 10, 23, 33, 34, 98, 113, 147, 150, 160, 162, 172, 177, 178, 181, 189, 241
see also *zuhhād*
Ash'arite school 143
Āshūrī, Dāryūsh 18, 119, 181, 195
'Aṭṭār, Farīd al-Dīn xxiv, 6, 11–12, 22, 32, 36–37, 42–43, 66, 68, 79–80, 95–96, 100, 103–104, 108, 113, 119, 121, 135, 159, 165–166, 169, 189, 191–193, 208, 295–296, 300, 302, 313–314, 317
'Aṭṭār, Maḥmūd 208
Attributes, divine 87, 129, 134, 184
Avery, Peter 14, 137, 279, 280, 292
'Awārif al-ma'ārif 145
Awḥadī Marāghī 6
Awn, Peter 120, 121
'Ayn al-Quḍāt Hamadhānī xxiii, xxvi, 44–46, 70, 72, 77, 103, 144, 146, 148, 192, 201, 202–203, 209, 302, 307
Azerbayjan 13, 263

bacchanalia / bacchanalian tendencies xxii, xxv, xxvi, 9, 22, 24, 41, 42, 85, 92, 96, 97, 99, 116, 119, 174, 176, 177, 186, 187, 194
Baghdādī, Abū Ṭāhir al- 67
Balyānī, Amīn al-Dīn 6, 164, 166, 180, 190, 191
Barrow, Isaac 282
Barry, Michael 213
Bausani, Alessandro 68, 210, 221
Bayḍāwī, al- 61
Bayqarā, Farīdun b. Ḥusayn 13
beauty 5, 6, 8, 13, 29, 41–53, 69, 70, 83, 84, 85, 87, 89, 92, 97, 98, 102, 105, 111, 112, 113, 117, 123–136, 138, 148, 152, 153, 160, 162, 165, 174, 182, 189, 193, 200, 202, 203, 205, 224, 256, 271, 282, 283, 286, 287, 290
Bell, Gertrude 281

beloved/beloved 5, 7, 21, 24, 27, 28, 29, 44, 46, 48, 49, 52, 53, 54, 63, 65, 70, 71, 78, 79, 81, 85, 89, 98, 108, 110, 111, 112, 113, 116, 117, 118, 123, 124, 127, 128, 130, 131, 132, 133, 134, 136, 139, 148, 153, 154, 155, 161, 168, 173, 192, 205, 213, 216, 218, 221, 222, 223, 224, 229, 231, 236, 238, 241, 242, 253, 258, 262, 263, 264, 265, 268, 271, 272, 273, 276, 277, 281, 283, 286, 291
bibliomancy 58
  see also *fa'l / fa'lgīrī*
Bicknell, Herman 280, 292
Bīdil 59
Bihzād 213, 214, 215, 216, 220, 221, 224
Bishr ibn Ḥārith Ḥāfī 171–172
Bīzhan 101
Blake, William 39, 68, 105, 174, 190
blame 7, 8, 36, 38, 40–42, 49, 52–54, 68, 69, 72, 73, 91, 120, 147, 176, 181, 193, 204, 217, 230
  see also *malāmat*
Bly, Robert 104, 113, 156, 281
Boylan, Michael 280
Bridges, Elisabeth 280, 292
Brookshaw, Dominic 57
Browne, E.G. 60, 61, 64
Buddhism 39
Bukhārā 27, 216
Bukhārī, Abū Ibrāmīm Mustamlī 168, 191, 250
Bunting, Basil 280, 292
Bunyan, John 160, 188
Bürgel, J-C. 298, 301
Burhānī, M. 61
Burning Bush 100, 235, 236
Bushāq Aṭ'amah-i Shīrāzī 11
Butler, Samuel 163
Buzghūsh, Najīb al-Dīn 145
Byron 281, 284, 285, 293

calamity 97, 109
Calcutta 14, 292
Calvin xv
catachresis 135
Central Asia 14, 16, 18, 101
Chaucer xv
Chittick, William 104, 155
Christianity xv, 36, 39, 53, 68, 90, 96
contentment 25, 28, 33, 109, 169, 192
contra-*Alba* 259, 260, 265, 268, 273, 277
Correale, Daniela 188, 265
Covenant, pre-eternal xiv, xx, 41, 97, 98, 110, 113, 114, 125, 126, 127, 129, 130–131, 134, 137, 151, 229, 247, 283
Cowell, E.B. 279, 289, 290, 291, 292, 294
Crow, Thomas 280, 292
cup, wine 25, 84, 118
cupbearer 25, 84, 92, 96, 98, 114, 115, 118, 121, 123, 149, 151, 218, 275, 288
Cup-mirror 153, 154

Damascus 4, 5
Dārābī, Muḥammad 51, 64, 72, 191
Darius 30
Davānī, Jalāl al-Dīn 198–209
Dawlatshāh Samarqandī 26, 58
Daylamī, Abūl-Ḥasan al- 70
De Bruijn, J.T.P. 57, 68, 119
detachment 33, 37, 38, 42, 66, 67
Dhahabī Sufi Order 166
Dhū'l-Nūn al-Miṣrī 44
Dickson, Martin 214, 226
Dīvān-i Shams 67, 137
divine Names 55, 70, 151, 171, 184, 228, 230, 239, 243
divine Qualities 228
divine Unity 52, 54, 68, 69, 147, 193, 285
drunkard 52, 96, 98, 165, 177, 187
drunkenness 37, 40, 92, 96, 98, 118, 150, 151, 153, 165, 176, 180, 213, 216, 218
Dryden, John 300

ecstasy 37, 48, 145, 149, 150, 198, 204, 208, 213, 218, 220, 222
Egypt 37, 80, 89, 134
Eliot, T.S. 123
Elliot, Jason 188
Emerson, R.W. xxvii, 28, 65, 281, 285–289, 292, 293, 294
England 4, 16, 160, 163, 188, 194
epiphany 24, 112, 123–129, 131, 135, 136, 170, 223
Ernst, Carl 58, 70, 136, 194, 197
eros 5, 6, 8, 17, 28, 30, 34, 48, 50, 78, 79, 81, 82, 91, 93, 94, 95, 102, 150, 160, 162, 178, 184, 187, 286
erotic contemplation 43, 45, 48, 49, 54
erotic gaze 49, 54
erotic philosophy 125
erotic spirituality xxiii, xxiv, xxvii, 7, 31, 36, 41, 47, 48, 50, 80, 81, 85, 89, 160

erotic theology 3, 26, 32, 44, 46, 47, 50, 51, 85, 86, 136, 213, 221
erotic union 150
eroticism xxiv, 6, 7
eyebrow 40, 68, 82, 86, 133, 151, 205, 217, 223, 224, 225, 236, 290

Fadl, Khaled Abou El 188
Farghānī, Sa'īd al-Dīn 209
Farhād 101, 221
Farrukhī 29, 264, 265
Farrukhzād, Furūkh 15
Fars 3, 4, 6, 23, 26
Farzaad, Massud 280, 292
fatalism 239
Fattī, Hūshang 194
fault-finding 162, 164, 165, 237
fedeli d'amore 43, 50, 91, 96–99, 129
female *shāhid* 48, 71, 222–225
Feuillebois-Pierunek, Eve 44, 69, 70
Ficino, Marsilio 3
Firdawsī 12, 63, 100, 101, 255
Fitzgerald, Edward 85, 104, 289, 294
Florence 3, 4
flute 152
forgiveness 179, 180, 182, 183, 184, 195, 275
Fouchécour, Charles Henri de 14, 56, 58, 61, 64, 65, 66, 72, 138, 143, 155, 210, 223, 224, 226, 264, 265, 277
France 252
Frye, Northrop 135, 136
fundamentalists 34, 38, 62, 160, 168, 178, 187, 188

gardens 3–5, 33, 47, 67, 80, 100, 128, 137, 150, 152, 186, 199, 200, 236, 240, 241, 264, 265, 270, 271, 273, 277, 284, 291
gazelle 80, 284, 285
Ghanī, Qāsim 14, 20, 21, 23, 28, 56–64, 66, 69, 190, 192, 226
Ghazālī, Abū Ḥāmid al- 120, 145, 170, 172, 175, 185, 192, 193, 196, 210
Ghazālī, Aḥmad al- xxiv, 44, 46, 47, 70, 108, 109, 110, 112, 113, 116, 120, 124, 130, 132, 133, 136, 138, 144
Ghomshei, Ḥusayn Ilahī 77
gnosis 54, 171, 172, 185, 186, 199, 206
gnostic 44, 49, 66, 85, 87, 93, 152, 153, 155, 185, 186, 197, 206, 207, 269
goblet 77, 96, 97, 132, 204, 219, 270, 275

Goethe, Johann Wolfgang von 4, 281, 290, 292
Graham, Terry 188, 209
Gray, Elizabeth T. 235, 280, 292
grief 25, 26, 69, 89, 93, 125, 128, 129, 130, 136, 139, 153, 154, 166, 193, 254, 267
Grunebaum, G.E. von 67
Gulandām, Muḥammad 13, 17, 19, 20, 60
Gulshan-i rāz 14, 59, 67, 73, 105, 139, 150, 151, 156, 201, 222, 226

Ḥāfiẓocentricism 16
Ḥallāj, Manṣūr 22, 77, 201, 203, 209
Hammer-Purgstall, Joseph von 281, 293
Ḥanbal, Aḥmad 164
Haravī, Huṣayn 'Alī 59, 61, 62, 63, 64, 69, 189, 191, 192, 193, 195, 196
Heath-Stubbs, John 280, 292
heaven 7, 22, 51, 68, 91, 100, 102, 149, 153, 168, 170, 181, 182, 184, 185, 192, 268, 275, 287, 288, 289
hell 39, 68, 167, 170, 171, 184
Herāt 213, 214, 220, 221, 224
Herbert, Thomas 68, 279
hidden polytheism 69, 174, 175, 176, 193
Ḥikmat, Alī 'Aṣghār 309
Ḥilālī 8
Hujwīrī, 'Alī 40, 41, 42, 53, 67, 73
humility 170, 180, 182, 191, 192, 216, 217
Ḥurūfism 144
Hyde, Thomas 279
hypocrisy 11, 23, 33, 38, 39, 55, 62, 66, 72, 154, 160, 161, 171, 172, 174–178, 188, 193, 194, 198, 262, 274, 275
see also *riyā*

I Ching 18, 227, 233, 248, 249
Iblīs 72, 115, 117, 118, 120, 121, 138, 180
Ibn 'Abbādī. See 'Abbādī, Quṭb al-Dīn al-
Ibn 'Arabī, Muḥyī al-Dīn 19, 60, 61, 70, 80, 85, 103, 143, 147, 203, 206, 209, 226
Ibn al-Fāriḍ 145, 206, 210
Ibn Baṭṭūṭa 3, 4
Ibn Karbalā'ī, Ḥāfiẓ Ḥusayn 44
Ibn Khafīf 4, 201, 208
Ibn Qūzmān of Cordoba 254
Ibn Yamīn 144
Ibrāhīm, Abū'l-Fatḥ 13
ill-fame 8, 9, 10, 42, 53, 90
Illuminationists 3, 199, 202
imagination 3, 5, 43, 46, 97, 133, 201, 208, 233, 245, 249

Imām ʻAlī. See ʻAlī ibn Abī Ṭālib
impostor 33, 34, 58, 62, 117, 118, 125, 131, 132, 153, 172
see also *muddaʻī*
India 13, 14, 16, 18, 37, 85, 221, 225, 279, 293
Indian Style 15
infidelity 7, 39, 41, 45, 53, 69, 78, 83, 176, 192, 193, 196, 290
see also *kufr*
insanity 92
inspired libertine 8, 23, 31–36, 38, 39, 42, 43, 48–54, 72, 73, 85, 90, 159, 163, 168, 169, 170, 173, 182, 184, 187, 188, 191, 193
see also *rind*
intoxication 28, 40, 80, 84, 92, 97, 98, 149, 153, 201, 204, 243, 274, 288
Iqbāl, Muḥammad 59
ʻIrāqī, Fakhr al-Dīn 6, 11, 19, 36, 44, 47, 61, 207
Iṣfahān 26, 27
Iṣfahānī, Nūr al-Dīn 145
Ishrāqīs. See Illuminationists
Isrāfīl 202, 209
Istanbul 14, 16
Istiʻlāmī, Muḥammad 62, 63, 64, 65, 66, 67, 71, 120, 189, 194, 196
Italy 46, 252, 285

Jahān-Malik Khātūn 11, 57, 298
Jām, Aḥmad-i 109, 119, 185, 196
Jāmī, ʻAbd al-Raḥmān al- 18, 47, 70, 119, 121, 210, 289
Jamshīd 132, 153
Javādī, Ḥasan 188
jealousy 41, 88, 116, 120, 131, 132, 203
Jesus 101, 102, 166, 170, 180, 207
Johnson, Samuel 298
Jones, William 197, 279, 280–287, 289, 291, 293
Joseph (the Prophet) 69, 89, 134
Junayd, Abū'l-Qāsim al- xxv, 168
Junayd-i Shīrāzī 4, 55

Kalābadhī, Abū Bakr al- 168
Kalām 249
Kamāl al-Dīn Ismāʻīl Iṣfahānī 6
Kamāl Khujandī 11, 44, 46, 48, 50, 56, 57, 58, 63, 72, 144
Kāshānī, ʻAbd al-Razzāq 145
Kāshānī, ʻAlī Sharīʻat 151, 210
Kāshānī, ʻIzz al-Dīn Maḥmūd 145, 146
Kashf al-maḥjūb 40, 41, 67, 69, 73
Kashshāf, al- 17, 20
Kasravī, Aḥmad 59
Kāzarūnī Sufi Order 164
Keats, John 4, 36, 67
Keeler, Annabel 305
Khāliqī-Muṭlaq, Jalāl 56
Khānlarī, Parvīz Nātil 14
Khāqānī 5, 6
Khayyām, ʻUmar 6, 85, 189, 196, 279
Khiḍr 172, 261
Khurāsān xii, 13, 171, 182
Khurramshāhī, Bahā al-Dīn 15, 32, 38, 42, 49, 56, 57, 59–62, 64–69, 72, 73, 104, 106, 116, 120, 131, 138, 139, 174, 188, 191, 192, 195, 270, 271
Khusraw Parvīz II 101
Khwājū Kirmānī 6–10, 21, 48, 56, 61, 71,144, 190–191, 196, 225
Khwāndamīr 306
Khwārazm 64
Kirmānī, ʻImād al-Dīn Faqīh xxv, 9, 57, 144, 145, 146
Kirmānī, Awḥad al-Dīn 46, 47, 48
Kulliyāt-i Shams 103, 104, 105
see also *Dīvān-i Shams*

Lāhījī, Muḥammad 14, 54, 59, 73, 151
Lāhūrī, Abū'l-Ḥasan ʻAbd al-Raḥmān Khatmī 14, 48, 49, 53, 54, 58, 63, 66, 67, 68, 69, 72, 85, 120, 139, 171, 172, 179, 188, 189, 190, 193, 194, 195, 196
Landinsky, Daniel 280
Lao Tzu 18
Laylī 13, 138, 221, 222, 224, 225
Lazard, Gilbert 139
Le Gallienne, Richard 280, 292
Leaf, Walter 280, 292
Leibniz 136
Lewis, Franklin 58, 196, 198, 209, 251
libertinage 34, 50
Limbert, John 33, 55, 61, 66
Loloi, Parvin 279, 292
longing xxiii, 93, 109, 111, 128, 129, 168, 191, 201, 202, 204, 205, 234, 236, 241, 281
love's grief 128, 129, 130, 139, 154
lovemaking 124, 263
love-passion 42, 79, 149

Maʻālī, Abū Naṣr Abū'l- 24

madness 92, 119, 138, 288
Maghribī, Muḥammad Shīrīn 144
Magians 149
Magus 218, 219, 242
Majnūn 113, 138, 221, 222, 224, 225
Malik al-Shu'arā Bahār 59
Mallāḥ, Ḥusayn-'Alī 267, 277
Manūchihrī 264, 265
Marāghī, 'Abd al-Qādir 267
Maṭla' al-sa'dayn 63, 64
Mayakowsky, Vladimir 159
Maybudī, Rashīd al-Dīn xv, 19, 52, 73, 119, 180, 182, 186, 193
McCarthy, Justin Huntly 279, 292
Mecca 95, 96
Meisami, Julie 265
Melikian-Chirvani, Assadullah Souren 225
mercy, divine 183, 184
metaphor 6, 28, 40, 58, 65, 72, 78, 84, 91, 92, 96, 101, 107, 110, 119, 128, 135, 137, 150, 178, 199, 218, 219, 223, 262, 268, 269, 283, 284
Middle East 300, 310
Miftāḥ al-hidāya 166, 190, 191, 195
Milton, John 39, 68, 174, 188, 193
Minorsky, V. xvii
Mīrkhwand 22, 24, 62
Moaveni, Azadeh 177
Moses 100, 108, 131, 246
Mt. Sana'i 68, 100
Mubariz al-Dīn Muḥammad Muẓaffarī 20
Mu'īn, Muḥammad 11, 18, 20, 55–61, 65, 68, 69, 70, 190, 191
multiplicity 54–55, 123, 133, 134, 201, 246
Murtaḍawī, Manūchihr 119, 189, 190
Murvārīd, Shihāb al-Dīn 'Abdu'llāh 13
Muẓaffarids / Muẓaffarīd dynasty 26, 61, 144, 146

Nābulusī, 'Abd al-Ghanī al- 209
Nasafī, 'Azīz al-Dīn 199
Nāṣir al-Dīn Shāh xii
Nāṣir-i Khusraw 61
neediness 167, 168
see also *niyāz*
Neoplatonism 200
Neoplatonists 200
Nicholson, R.A. 108
nightingale 5, 137, 152, 200, 253, 264, 265, 267, 270, 272, 273, 284
see also *bulbul*
Nishapur 37, 79
Nishāṭ-i Iṣfahānī, Mu'tamid 195
Nizāmī Ganjavī 103, 106
Nizārī Quhistānī 6, 159, 186, 191, 194, 196
nothingness 110, 123, 148
see also *nīstī*

Orientalism 279, 281
Ottoman Turkey 14, 16

panegryrics 20, 26
Papadopoulo, A. 47, 70
Papan-Matin, Firoozeh 59
paradise 5, 6, 48, 51, 100, 118, 128, 147, 168, 171, 174, 181, 185, 186, 190, 191, 265, 286
Pārīzī, Bāstānī 277
pārsā 172
pāsibān 261, 262, 263
passionate love 89, 108, 109, 189
see also *'ishq*
Payne, John 179, 280, 292
Paz, Octavio 69
Peripatetics 199, 202
Persian court poetry 197
Plato 233, 249, 286
Platonism 286
polytheism 69, 174, 175, 176, 193
see also *shirk*
poverty 16, 25, 26, 28, 115, 167, 168, 169, 171, 180, 184, 203
see also *faqr*
predestination 207
pre-Eternity 93, 97, 98, 110, 113, 121, 123, 125–130, 133, 134, 162, 200
see also *azal*
Prophet Muḥammad 63, 120, 192, 206, 207, 230
Provence/Provençal poetry 69, 252, 254, 259, 276
puritanism and puritans 34, 42, 52, 77, 159, 160, 162, 163, 169, 178, 181, 187, 188
see also *zāhid*
Pūrnāmdāriyān, Taqī 60, 66, 136, 138, 164, 190

Qarāguzlū 66
Qaṣīda 10, 12, 21, 22, 24, 120, 145, 258, 264, 265, 266
Qāsim Anvār, Shāh 10
Qazvīnī, Muḥammad 14, 55, 63, 64, 192, 226

Qiwām al-Dīn, Ḥajjī 16, 22
Qunawī, Ṣadr al-Dīn 209
Qushayrī, Abū'l-Qāsim al- 44, 70, 170

Randall, Colonel Frank Montague 280
Rastigār-Fasā'ī, Manṣūr 56, 57
rational soul 67, 201, 202
Rāzī, Najm ad-Dīn 116, 120, 181, 182, 195
Rehder, Robert 281, 292
Renard, John 47, 70
renunciation 36, 38, 92, 108, 160, 168, 178, 191
see also *zuhd*
repentance 94, 95, 96, 97, 102, 217
see also *tawba*
reproach 8, 24, 39, 41, 52, 53, 91, 160, 161, 181, 205
see also *malāmat*
resurrection 97, 99, 100, 209, 274
Ridgeon, Lloyd 59
Rimbaud, Arthur 36, 67
Ritter, Helmut 65, 68, 69, 70, 71, 120, 138, 139, 189
Robinson, Samuel 104, 225, 279, 292
Romantic period 281
Romantic poets 4, 46, 78, 283, 284, 285
Romantics 71, 279, 281, 289
rose 4, 23, 82, 98, 137, 236, 254, 256, 258, 264, 265, 270, 271, 284, 285, 288, 291
Rūdakī 78
Rūmī, Jalāl al-Dīn 5, 6, 8, 11, 12, 14, 29, 36, 57, 59, 67, 69, 70, 78, 81, 82, 83, 86, 87, 89, 92–95, 99, 100, 102–105, 130, 138, 164, 183, 184, 190, 201, 207, 217, 232, 247, 276
Rustam 101, 255
Rūzbihān al-Baqlī 44
Rypka, Jan 61

Sa'dī 255, 258
Ṣādiq, Ja'far al- 179, 194
Sadriddin Aini 59, 189
Ṣafā, Dhabīḥu'llāh 56, 143, 155
Safavids 16, 144, 213, 214, 216, 220, 221, 249
Saki 10, 93, 98
see also *saqī*
Salmān Sāvajī 8, 144
Sām Mīrzā, Prince 213, 216, 217
Sam'ānī, Aḥmad 171
Samarqand 13, 27
Samarqandī, 'Abd al-Razzāq 25, 26
Samarqandī, Niẓāmī-i 'Arūḍī 314
Sanā'ī, Abū'l-Majd Majdūd ibn Ādam xxiii–xxiv, xxvi, 6, 36, 37, 42, 43, 78, 92, 108, 159, 160, 189, 257, 258, 259, 260, 261, 262, 263
Sārimī 66
Satan 102, 107, 115, 132, 138, 174
Saudi Arabia 160, 188
Sawāniḥ 46, 108, 109, 110, 112, 119, 120, 138
Sāwī, Jamāl al-Dīn 37
Scarry, Elaine 70
Schimmel, Annemarie 55, 56, 58, 61, 62, 69, 113, 120, 137, 139, 162, 189, 293
Schroeder, Eric 48, 71
secta amoris 52, 82, 83, 168
selfhood 51, 54, 92, 94, 130, 171, 173, 176, 193
selflessness 7, 73, 84, 130, 138, 192
self-negation 170
Seneca 39, 68
service 97, 98, 146, 185, 187, 216, 279
sex and sexuality 4, 7, 10, 46, 47, 124, 188, 273
Shabistarī, Maḥmūd 14, 54, 67, 88, 104, 105, 150, 151, 156, 201, 222, 226
Shafī'ī, Muḥammad 194, 296
Shafī'ī-Kadkanī, Muḥammad 59, 188, 193, 195
Shāh Ismā'īl 221
Shāh Manṣūr 21, 26, 27, 29, 60, 64
Shāh-nāma 101
Shāh Ni'matu'llāh Walī 57, 301, 306
Shāh Shujā 10, 20, 21, 23, 24, 26, 27, 29, 63, 66, 144, 171
Shāh Ṭahmāsb 213, 216, 217
Shāh Yaḥyā 21, 26, 27, 64
Shahriyār 15
Shakespeare 16, 175
Sham'ī 14
shame 8, 9, 34, 42, 53, 57, 63, 179
shamelessness 38, 39
Shams-i Tabrīzī 93
Sharaf-nāma 98
Shayegan, Daryush xxii, 31, 33, 66
Shaykh Ṣan'ān 90, 100
Shaykh, Sufi 144, 146, 160
Shaykh-Zāda 213–216, 221
Shelley 4, 7, 27, 37, 46, 64, 65, 68, 73, 281, 286, 287, 291, 293
Shiblī Nu'mānī 61
Shīrāz 3–7, 10, 11, 13, 15, 16, 19, 20, 24–27, 30, 33–36, 47, 49, 54, 58–61, 71, 143–147, 163, 198, 208, 225, 243, 251, 261, 262

Shīrāzī, Quṭb al-Dīn 3
Shīrīn 78, 101, 221, 222
Simnānī, 'Alā' al-Dawla 8
Sīrjānī, Sa'īdī 189
Smith, Margaret 316
Sophianic Feminine 221, 222, 226, 296
Spenser 27, 286, 293
spirit 110
 see also *rūḥ*
St Augustine xv
Stetkevych, Jaroslav 266, 276, 277
Stetkevych, Suzanne 277
Stoicism 39
Sūdī 14, 58, 60, 267
Sufism 19, 40, 43, 46, 62, 65, 67, 69, 93, 124, 136, 143, 145, 146, 147, 149, 161, 168, 170, 181, 191, 193, 194, 197, 208, 218, 248, 283, 286, 287, 289
Suhrāb Sihpihrī 15
Suhrawardī, Abū'l-Najīb 188
Suhrawardī, Shihāb al-Dīn Abū Ḥafṣ 'Umar 145, 146
Sulṭān Walad, Bahā al-Dīn 183, 184
Sulṭān-Muḥammad 216, 217, 218, 219, 220, 221, 224
Surūrī 14
Symposium (Plato's) 44, 70, 285, 286

Tabriz 3, 8, 9
Tadhkirat al-shu'arā' 56, 58, 64
Tajikistan 18, 59, 189, 267
tambourine 152, 217
Tamerlane 26–27, 62, 64, 149
Ṭarīqat-nāma 145, 146, 155
Tassy, Garcin de 317
tavern 5, 10, 23, 37, 52, 54, 60, 62, 96, 97, 116, 149, 150, 164, 168, 169, 176, 181, 183, 189, 198, 199, 202, 205, 207, 218, 219, 225, 235, 237, 264, 267, 269, 274, 275
 see also *kharābāt*
Taylor, John 194, 299
Tennyson 4, 281, 289, 290, 291, 292, 294
theology of sin 178–184
theophanies 228, 243
theophany 43, 44, 84, 85, 128, 151, 153, 184, 213, 221
Tholuck 289
Tīmūr 20
 see also *'Tamerlane'*
Timurids 143, 220
Tirmidhī, al-Ḥakīm al- 206, 317
transcendentalists 94, 281, 285
Transoxiania 16, 26, 27
trobar clus poetry 46
troubadours 46, 262, 276
Turkey 14, 16, 37, 159, 221
two bows' lengths 206

United States 16
Universal Soul 283, 286, 287
'Unṣurī 29, 264
'Uthmān, Caliph 17, 164, 190, 191, 195
Uways al-Qaranī xv

Valéry, Paul 251, 276
veil of the infidel selfhood 171–174, 193
veil 10, 42, 50, 52, 62, 67, 85, 89, 124, 133, 135, 137, 139, 153, 171, 173, 174, 192, 193, 200, 201, 203, 223, 224, 226, 240, 245, 246, 286, 287, 291
veiling 28, 85, 223, 238, 241, 243, 244, 246, 247
Villon, Francois 36

Walīd II, Caliph 254, 255, 258, 277
watchman 252, 253, 257, 261, 262, 263, 277
Watts, Isaac 163, 190
Welch, Stuart Cary 213, 214, 216, 221, 224, 225, 226
West-östlicher Divan 281, 290, 292
Wickens, G.M. 253, 254, 255, 259, 277
Wilberforce Clarke, H. 197
Williams, Alan 104
wine 5, 7, 8, 23–25, 33, 41, 42, 48, 53, 62, 64, 66, 77, 80, 81, 84, 85, 90, 93, 96–99, 107, 116–119, 121, 149, 150, 151, 153, 154, 156, 160–162, 164, 165, 176, 177, 178, 183, 195, 202, 204–206, 217–221, 223, 225, 236, 241, 243, 246, 262, 264, 269–271, 274, 275, 288–291
wine-bearer 204, 241, 288
wineseller 154, 176, 292
witness 26, 43, 44, 45, 47, 48, 49, 51, 53, 69, 70, 92, 97, 110, 113, 123, 124, 128, 132, 160, 189, 218, 225, 229
 see also *shāhid*
Woledge, B. 252, 253, 257, 258, 276, 277

Yates, Frances 318
Yeats, W.B. 22, 52, 62
Yohannan, John 194, 288, 293

Zaehner, R.C. 318
Ẓahīr Faryābī 6
Zākānī, 'Ubayd 5, 10, 21, 33, 57, 61, 144
Zamakhsharī 61
Zarrīnkūb, A.H. 20, 23, 24, 55–66, 68, 190, 191, 196
Zayn al-'Ābidīn, Sulṭān 20, 24, 25, 26, 27
Zayn al-Dīn Kāmū'ī 145
Zoroastrians & Zoroastrianism xv, xx, 39, 87, 169, 181, 207, 218
Zulaykhā 89, 119

Index of Persian and Arabic Technical Terms

'ābidān 180
adab 145
'afw 183
'ahd-i alast 97, 112
ahl-i 'ilm 19
ahl-i dil 154
ahl-i sharī'at 174
ahl-i sulūk 147
ahl-i ṭarīqat 174
'ālam-i bātin 123
alast / alastu bi-rabbikum 97, 110, 113, 127, 129, 135
see also 'ahd-i alast
'andalīb 264, 271
'aql 131, 162, 235
'ārif 32, 70, 151, 186, 197
'asas 261, 262, 263
'āshiq 111
'āshiqī 50, 54
asmā wa ṣifāt 110
awliyā' 4, 53, 62, 191, 194
awrād 272
'ayn al-jam' 146
'ayyār 39
a'yān-i thābita 202
azal 110, 126, 134

badnāmī 10, 57, 105
balā 72, 97, 113
see also affliction
bāmdād 265, 268
baqā 113
bār-i amānat 114, 126, 129
barīd 272
bashar 105, 231, 235
bayān 67, 107
bīdardī 175
bulbul 264, 270–272, 284, 291
see also nightingale
but-parastī-yi ḥaqīqī 97

dahr 200, 239
dam-i masīḥ 101
dard 42, 79, 103, 118, 149, 269
dhawq-i mastī 98
dhikr 105, 229, 245
dīn al-ḥubb 80
dīvāna 90, 91, 238
du'ā 223, 272, 273, 277
dunyā 65, 236, 238
dūsh 116, 127, 198, 255, 259, 260, 264, 272, 273, 275

fa'l / fa'lgīrī 227, 247
falak 245, 261, 275
fanā' 54, 55, 113, 221
faqīh 144, 160, 188
faqīr 37, 168
faqr 64, 167, 168, 169, 191
fiqh al-bāṭin 179
fisq 105, 170
fiṭra 87, 104
fiṭrat Allāh 87
fuqarā' 147
futuwwat 164

ghaffār, al- 184
gham 105, 128, 129, 130, 136, 138, 139, 272
ghayb 13, 70, 118, 123, 218, 219, 230, 248, 267, 272
ghayrat 53, 115, 116

havas 92, 93, 105, 260
Ḥāfiẓ-shināsī 14, 15, 59, 119
ḥayrat 148
ḥijāb 223
ḥulūl 44
ḥusn-parast 85

ibāḥatī 93, 105
'ibādat 172
ibn al-waqt 99

īhām 48, 67, 91
ikhlāṣ 147
ikhtiyār 244
'ilm al-balāgha 67
'ilm al-bayān 67
'ilm 230
'ilm-i ḥudhūrī xxii, xxiii
'ilm-i ma'ānī va bayān 67
inqilāb al-qalb 247
insān-i kāmil 43
irādat 190, 191, 244
'ishq 50, 108, 109, 112, 119
'ishqbāzī 263
'ishva 244
islām 104, 244
istighnā 65, 111, 119
istiqbāl 12, 24, 57, 63
ittiḥād 44

jalāl-i muṭlaq 69, 193
jām 153
jamāl-i ḥaqīqī 49, 50
jamāl-i muṭlaq 69, 193
jamāl-parastī 47, 85
Jām-i Jam 132, 285
Jamīl, al- 50

kāfar 85, 261
kāfar-i 'ishq 84, 261
kāfarī 69, 193
kamāl 148
kāmilān-i mukammal 146
khalwa 238
khalwat 154
khamriyāt 107
khānaqāh 3, 4, 9, 37, 38, 144, 146
kharābāt 5, 23, 54, 96, 181, 219, 238
khawf 191
khirqa 52, 72, 104, 105, 149, 150
khiyāl 97
khubān 47, 71
khullat 109
kināyat 199
kufr-i ḥaqīqī 53
kufr-i ṭarīqat 69, 193
kursī 229

lāhūt 44
laṭīfa 151
lā-ubālī 36, 90, 91, 105
lisān al-ghayb 13, 123, 248, 272
lisān al-waqt 199, 203
luṭf 134

ma'ānī 46, 67
ma'nā 45, 67
ma'rifat 171, 172, 185
ma'shūq 28, 48, 53, 54, 65, 71, 272
ma'shūqa-i majāzī 53
ma'shūq-i ḥaqīqī 48
madhhab-i 'ishq 32, 43, 46, 53, 71, 77, 81, 85, 102, 104, 162
madhhab-i ahl-i ṭarīqat 85
madhhab-i muḥaqqiqān 45
madhhab-i pīr-i mughān 85, 104
madhhab-i ṭarīqat 104
maḥabbat 87, 109
maḥabbat-i ḥaqīqī 48
maḥabbat-i majāzī 48
malāmat 36, 40, 42, 52, 53, 72, 73, 120, 181, 217
malāmatī 7, 37, 38, 40, 41, 42, 49, 53, 67, 68, 69, 187, 230
malāmatī ethics 36, 39, 176
malāmatī spirituality 28
malāmatiyān 181
malāmatiyya 55, 147, 182
mamdūḥ 22, 24, 28, 65
mashhad 199
mashrab 69, 193, 198, 199
mast 96, 187
mastūr 243, 244
mawaddat 109
maykada 149
maykhāna 96, 198, 269, 275
miḥrāb 17, 214, 224, 225
mīthāq 110
  see also covenant
mu'adhdhin 259, 261
  see also muezzin
mubāḥī 90, 91, 93
mudda'ī 117, 118, 120, 131, 132, 138, 230, 241, 244, 245
muezzin 78, 253, 257, 259, 261, 263
mughannī 267
mugh-bachchih 84
muḥtasib 23, 35, 62, 144, 262
mukhlaṣān 147
mukhliṣān 147
munāẓira 145
mundus imaginalis 5
mutaṣawwifa 147

nafas-i raḥmānī 202
nafs 38, 244, 245, 246
nafs-i ammara 45
nafs-i nāṭiqa 67
nām u nang 42, 57
namāz 180, 224, 269
naqd-i ḥāl 100
naqd-i waqt 99
nasīb 263, 265, 266
nāsiḥān 263
nasīm 238, 271–272
nāsūt 44
Nawrūz 7, 265
naẓar-bāz/naẓar-bāzī 42, 43, 49, 51, 72, 138, 152
niqāb 223
nīstī 110
niyāz 168, 180
niyyat 117, 168

pīr 197, 242
pīr-i kharābāt 96
pīr-i mughān 64, 85, 104

qahr 72, 134
qalandarī 38, 42, 105, 187
qalandariyya 32, 36, 37, 42, 50, 55
qalandariyyāt 68
qalandars 36, 37, 38, 39, 42, 50, 52, 55, 65, 72, 90, 91, 105, 199, 217
qallāsh 90, 91
qawl u ghazal 267
qiṭa 63
qurbat 179, 255

rabāb 263
raḥīl 266
raḥmat 72, 87, 217, 275
raqīb 117, 216, 261
rāz 133, 151, 152, 190
rind xix, xxiii–xxv, 23, 31–37, 39, 42, 43, 49, 50, 54, 55, 65, 67, 68, 72, 90, 91, 159, 163, 168, 170, 173, 182, 187, 191, 193, 198, 217, 230
see also inspired libertine
rindān 32–33, 36, 66
rindān-i madrasa 35
rindān-i pākbāz 35
rindī xxiii, 11, 31, 32, 42, 43, 50, 51, 53, 54, 55, 65, 67, 73, 149, 173, 196
riyā 23, 171, 172, 174–175, 262
see also hypocrisy

ru'yā 236
rūḥ 110
rūz-i alast 97, 98, 229

ṣabā 260, 263, 264, 271, 272, 277
ṣabāḥ 269
sabk-i hindī 15
ṣabūḥī 271
saḥar 255, 258, 260, 265, 266, 274, 275
saḥargah 267, 277
salāmat 36, 40, 181, 195
sāqī 84, 92, 96, 115, 123, 136, 218, 240, 241, 288, 289
see also Saki
Sāqī-nāma 64, 98, 288
Sarāy-i mughān 219
sattār al-'uyūb 184
sayr-i nuzūlī 127
sayr-i su'ūdī 127
shāhid 43, 44, 45, 46, 49, 51, 53, 69, 70, 71, 120, 189, 218
shāhidān 115
shāhid-bāz 42, 47
shāhid-bāzī 43–44, 46–47, 49, 53, 69, 71, 112, 189
shāhid-i ghaybī 45
shaḥna 262
shahwat 72
Sharī'a 23, 42, 88, 90, 162, 165, 166, 179, 184, 195
Sharī'a-oriented Islam 85, 160
shaṭḥ va ṭāmāt 152
shaṭḥiyāt 31, 120
shawq al-qalb 191
shawq ilā'l-janna, al- 191
shawq 109, 129, 191, 274
see also longing
shirk 175
see also polytheism
ṣidq 147, 150
sipīda-dam 265, 268
ṣubḥ 265, 268, 270, 272, 275
suḥbat 241
ṣūma'a 150, 181
suwar-i husniyya 49, 85, 189

ta'wīl 199
tafa'ul 247
tafrīd 53
tafriqa 147
tafsīr 18, 250
tajallī 112, 126, 131, 132, 184, 215, 223, 224

tajrīd 53
takabbur 172
talmīḥ 100, 161
taqwā 31
tarāna 199, 267
ṭarīqa 145
tark-i āzārī 166
tarsā-bachchih 84
taslīm 244
tatabbu‘ 12
tawḥīd 54
ṭulū‘ 269

‘ubbād 147
‘ujb 42, 179, 180

vird 272

waḥidiyat 68
wajh Allāh 147
Walī, al- 249
waqt 45, 202, 242
waqt-i sarmadī 200
wara‘ 73
wāṣilān 146
waẓīfa 19
wuṣūl 146

zāhid 32, 50, 52, 55, 159, 160, 161, 162, 163, 168, 171, 173, 176, 181, 187, 188, 189, 190, 191, 210, 223, 241, 244, 246
  see also ascetic
zuhd 31, 160, 168, 170, 172, 191
zuhdiyyāt 107, 189
zuhhād 147
  see also ascetics
ẓuhūr 206
ẓulmat 127